American Urban Politics in a Global Age

The Reader

SEVENTH EDITION

Edited by

Paul Kantor
Fordham University

Dennis R. Judd
University of Illinois at Chicago

Routledge
Taylor & Francis Group

LONDON AND NEW YORK

First published 2013, 2010, 2008, 2006 by Pearson Education, Inc.

Published 2016 by Routledge
2 Park Square, Milton Park, Abingdon, Oxon OX14 4RN
711 Third Avenue, New York, NY 10017, USA

Routledge is an imprint of the Taylor & Francis Group, an informa business

ISBN: 9780205251759 (pbk)
Cover Photo: Stock photo © franckreporter

Library of Congress Cataloging-in-Publication Data

American urban politics in a global age / [edited by] Paul P. Kantor,
Dennis R. Judd.—7th ed.
    p. cm.
  ISBN-13: 978-0-205-25175-9
  ISBN-10: 0-205-25175-7
1.   Urban policy—United States. 2.   Municipal government—United States.
3.   Metropolitan government—United States.   I. Kantor, Paul, 1942–
II. Judd, Dennis R.
  HT123.A6664 2013
  320.8′50973—dc23

                                                                2012000857

To my grandchildren, Jennifer, Dylan, Miranda, Jake, Weston, Wyatt, Eliza, and Katie: you make the world go round!

Dennis R. Judd

To my wonderful daughter, Elizabeth, and her global generation.

Paul Kantor

Contents

PREFACE TO THE 7TH EDITION

In the three years since the 6th edition of this book was published an astonishing social and political transformation has begun to fundamentally reshape the politics of America's cities and urban regions. The changes have unfolded so rapidly that it we have been forced to thoroughly rethink *American Urban Politics in the Global* Age. The readers of our previous editions will notice that this is becoming a habit, but it is one we can correct only if the changes originally prompted by globalization begin to slow down. Instead, the opposite seems to be happening. The most immediately pressing issues arise from the Great Recession of 2008–2010 and its continuing effects, the increasingly bitter battles over immigration and the ethnic tensions these provoke, and the growing awareness of the extremes of inequality that characterize American society. These issues play out against a background that is itself constantly changing: the economic restructuring associated with the international economy continues to evolve, the political competition prompted by racial and ethnic differences take new forms; and the politics of the fragmented metropolis has, if anything, intensified. And, finally, natural disasters seem to have joined terrorism has a major challenge to the resilience of cities and urban regions. This 7th edition represents an attempt to treat all these topics in one volume.

Despite our desire to account for dramatic new developments we wish to emphasize that they are best understood when placed into historical context. The political and social structures undergirding American urban politics have endured over time remarkably unchanged, and they continue to powerfully shape today's politics and policy choices. For example, from the nation's founding to the present America's cities have engaged in a vigorous economic competition; this was true for cities on the frontier, and it is just as true today. All of the selections are placed in thematic context by means of editors' essays that provide a thematic context for understanding how the selections fit together. This book is a suitable companion for any good urban politics text, but its organization and themes fit particularly well with Dennis R. Judd and Todd Swanstrom's *City Politics,* a textbook also published by Pearson Longman Publishers.

We wish to thank Mr. Reid Hester, our Longman political science editor, for championing this book. His interest, ideas and encouragement were essential to this enterprise. Dennis Judd wishes to thank Anahit Gomptian for her assistance in copying materials and other tasks. Ms. Emily Saurhoff at Pearson Longman also provided invaluable help in preparation of the manuscript.

PAUL KANTOR
DENNIS R. JUDD

Editors' Introductory Essay
Governing the Metropolis in the Global Era

Urban governance in the global era is in some ways entirely different from any previous period. At the same time, the past continues to shape contemporary urban politics. Although apparently in contradiction, each of these statements is true. This is why it is important to explain the contours of American urban politics by taking both into account. For this reason, the selections selected for this book acknowledge and often make explicit reference to historical precedents as a way of bringing into focus today's political processes and policy problems.

American Urban Politics in a Global Era is organized into three parts. Part One contains selections examining the thesis that the economic imperative powerfully shapes contemporary urban politics. As these selections attest, urban governments place economic growth and prosperity high on the local political agenda; this priority powerfully shapes urban politics. Part Two is composed of selections dealing with a second imperative, governance: In the global era, and, for that matter, throughout American history, the representation of group and citizen interests have decisively shaped what local governments do. In particular, racial and ethnic diversity and the conflicts occasioned by successive waves of immigration have obliged American urban governments to pay close attention to the task of negotiating conflicting claims among the many contending interests that make up the urban polity. The selections in Part Three address the political factors that determine the competence and resilience of the American system of urban governance in the face of new social challenges. A fundamental feature of the nation's governance system is its extreme fragmentation. Power and authority are decentralized and dispersed in the American intergovernmental system. Further, within metropolitan areas, a multitude of highly autonomous governments operate with little or sometimes no coordination by higher governmental authorities. These realities have tremendous implications for the ability of local governments to cope with many of the challenges of our time. These come in various forms. The most vivid recent examples include the terrorist attacks of 9/11, the stresses of the lingering economic crisis, and a series of recent natural disasters. The responses to these challenges suggest that the ability of cities and urban regions to manage sudden or long term stresses is determined in considerable measure by America's political arrangements and governmental systems.

PART ONE: GLOBALIZATION AND THE ECONOMIC IMPERATIVE

If "all politics is local," as a congressman famously observed decades ago, the phrase can now be interpreted to mean that the processes of globalization can be understood best by the imprint they leave on local communities. The imperative of local economic growth has been a constant feature of urban politics for most of the nation's history. All through the nineteenth century, local elites were tireless promoters of local growth because they instinctively understood that some cities—but not all—would prosper in the international urban system that was emerging in the industrial age. Today the competition is fiercer than ever before because the economic restructuring associated with globalization has intensified competition among cities. In the twentieth century, the fragmentation of metropolitan regions gave new life to the competitive struggle for growth, but the battle tended to be fought out more at the regional than national level. The politics of local communities everywhere has been reshaped by the accelerating movement of people, capital, information, and goods around the globe. Cities have been thrown into intense interurban competition because investors send their money to wherever it yields the highest profits.

Cities of all sizes, including those in the suburbs, must compete for the sectors of the new economy not only within their own metropolitan areas, but also, in effect, in an international arena. The global economy has favored investments in postindustrial business sectors such as finance, real estate, insurance, and a variety of service activities. In global cities all over the world highly educated white-collar professionals—for example, corporate managers, management consultants, legal experts, accountants, computer specialists, financial analysts, media and public relations specialists—work in clusters of downtown skyscrapers or on high-tech office parks in the suburbs.[1] Even the smaller cities further down the urban hierarchy must try to find a unique niche that will secure their futures. Urban areas act as free-trade zones offering subsidies to attract malls, big-box stores, and affluent residents.

Economic competition among jurisdictions will remain a basic fact of the global era into the foreseeable future. By the early twentieth century, cities occupied well-defined places in the industrial urban hierarchy. Globalization has torn that system apart. In the global era, cities are dependent on the decisions made by highly mobile, transnational corporations. New technologies in computers, communications, materials, production, and business organization have enabled businesses to disperse many of their activities to far-flung locations in suburbia, the Sunbelt, and foreign production sites. Many traditional industrial activities that once were undertaken in cities, such as steelmaking and garment and appliance manufacturing, have migrated to lower-cost locations in foreign countries in the Asian rim, the Caribbean, Mexico, and South and Central America. The so-called global office has become commonplace: Large corporations have concentrated their headquarters activities in major cities while decentralizing all other business operations to a multitude of sites.

The competitive struggle for economic prosperity has enormous implications for local politics and public policy. This struggle keeps local officials fixated on economic matters for the simple reason that the rules of the game are constantly changing. Yesterday it was manufacturing; today it is a complex mix of services and the economic benefits flowing from tourism and culture. All cities try to get their share, but the options available to them are limited, and especially so for poorer and smaller places. This economic imperative can be read by observing the transformation of city skylines. In recent decades, restored waterfronts and historic buildings, gleaming office towers, luxury hotels, convention centers, sports stadiums—and the list goes on—have sprung up in central cities everywhere. Cities commonly try to attract investment by offering such lures as historic tax credits, tax subsidies, and public improvements. Surrounding suburbs try to outdo one another to influence the location of malls, big-box stores, retail clusters, and office parks. To attract the most affluent workers in the globalized service economy, all cities must offer a high level of urban amenities.[2]

The imperative of growth powerfully influences the way cities are governed. In the years after World War II, when the movement to the suburbs and the decline of inner-city economies threatened to plunge the cities into permanent decline, downtown business interests mobilized to preserve their investments. In city after city, coalitions lead by aggressive mayors and corporate CEOs led campaigns to revitalize the downtowns. The concept of the "urban regime" emerged in the late 1980s as an elegant metaphor for describing the concentration of power in the city hall-business alliances, and the regime concept quickly became the dominant paradigm in the scholarly literature on urban power (see the selections in Chapter 1).

It is difficult to know if stable urban regimes of this kind continue to govern in the global era. An emerging literature in urban politics shows that globalization has dispersed power more widely and reduced the influence of the CEO-lead organizations. Corporate buyouts, mergers, and the internationalization of corporate structures have reduced the ranks of business leaders interested in local politics. In their stead, a new leadership has emerged that reflects the shape of the new service economy: developers, the leaders of nonprofit organizations, and professionals working in cultural institutions have filled the gap left by the lagging interest of corporate CEOs. Since the 1990s, tourism and culture have led the revitalization of many central cities. The new political leadership often seeks to translate culture into policies that maybe are heavily weighted in favor of tourists and affluent downtown residents. High-end residential and tourist enclaves exist in virtually all cities whatever their racial and ethnic makeup, and the policies used to promote such developments have sometimes provoked political conflict. Even though the specific political actors may have changed over time, city politics continues to pivot around the economic imperative.

PART TWO: GOVERNING THE MULTIETHNIC METROPOLIS

As important as the economic imperative may be, a political logic also is a central feature of urban politics. The singular focus on local economic growth sometimes provokes opposition. Critical comments in the letters sections of local newspapers appear because it often seems that local governments do little else but support physical development and respond to the needs of affluent people. In most cities, however, public officials try to achieve—or appear to achieve—some kind of balance. At least to some degree, the ballot box acts as a counterweight. All but the most homogeneous and prosperous local communities must manage a complex politics marked by changing public opinion, interest-group competition and racial, ethnic, and class differences. An increasing volume of capital flows may be a defining feature of globalization, but so also is the movement of people across borders and from place to place. The logic of the marketplace treats cities purely as locations for private economic activity, but the political logic of democratic processes motivates public officials to build political support for what they seek to accomplish.[3]

This dynamic is not new to the global era. In the nineteenth century, a rapidly expanding urban electorate became an enduring fixture in the politics of cities. This development radically changed the complexion of local politics. By the 1840s, property qualifications to vote were abolished almost everywhere, a reform that enhanced the influence of immigrant voters. After the Civil War, city populations exploded when waves of immigrants from abroad and migrants from rural areas came in search of jobs in the factories. Wide-open political struggles began to replace oligarchic control by business elites. A new generation of politicians organized party machines as a way of mobilizing the urban electorate by buying loyalty and favors with cash, jobs, contracts, and other material inducements. Whatever their merits or shortcomings, the machines gave the immigrants a voice in local politics. This new-found influence became the lightning rod for many of the political conflicts of the late-nineteenth and early-twentieth centuries.

There are obvious parallels with today's urban politics. In the last few decades an immigrant floodtide has made cities and urban regions more racially and ethnically diverse than ever before. More immigrants came to the United States in the 1990s than in any previous decade of the nation's history, and the flow is continuing. The social and political effects of large-scale population movements are dramatically evident in big global cities such as Miami, New York, Chicago, and San Francisco. In these places—and in many smaller places too—the recent surge in immigration has changed the complexion of local politics.

The diverse ethnic makeup of the globalized metropolis constitutes a sharp break from the demographic changes that unfolded for much of the twentieth century. In the years after World War II, millions of blacks left the southern states and settled in northern cities, and in the same years whites fled the inner cities for the suburbs. The result was a metropolis with extraordinarily high levels of racial segregation and racial tension. The movements into and out of the cities created a nearly unbridgeable social chasm that threatened to rend the fabric of American society. As blacks moved into central-city neighborhoods, whites resisted, often violently. These tensions began to ease by the 1970s when blacks became incorporated into local politics systems. A black political leadership first emerged in the central cities, and over time blacks have been elected to political office throughout the federal system; indeed, in 2008 an African American was elected to the presidency.

Immigration has unleashed far-reaching changes. Immigrants from Asia, Latin America, the Caribbean, and Eastern and Central Europe now constitute a substantial and growing proportion of the residents of America's cities and of its suburbs. As the ethnic complexion of cities has become more diverse, urban politics has increasingly become defined by a process of interethnic bargaining. A power struggle is taking place between newly arrived immigrants, African Americans, and middle- and upper-class residents. It has become clear that there is no singular "minority" interest; instead, the new immigrants often compete with blacks in the electoral arena and beyond. Sometimes the tensions are difficult to manage. At the same time, it must be recognized that the presence of minorities in positions of political leadership has reduced the mutual suspicions and hostilities that characterized interracial and interethnic relations just a few decades ago.

Not long ago these observations would have applied mainly to the central cities. But immigrants of all ethnic backgrounds are now settling in the suburbs as much as in the central cities. The old urban pattern, with a troubled central city surrounded by rank on rank of suburbs, is breaking down. The new urban pattern is extremely complex. In central cities, rising levels of social inequality characteristic of United States society are written on the urban landscape.

Affluent downtown and gentrified neighborhoods are sharply separated from the neighborhoods inhabited by the urban poor. High-rise condominium and townhouse developments sometimes sit only a block or two from neighborhoods with extreme levels of poverty. Affluent empty-nesters and young professionals are moving back downtown. Central cities are once again becoming hotspots for culture, nightlife, and fun, but a few blocks away the scene may be very different. In cities facing the social problems that arise from immigration and social polarization, it should occasion no surprise that the debate over policies that seem weighted heavily in favor of affluent downtown residents should become a source of contention.

In the suburbs, a parallel process has been unfolding. In the 1990s a large number of Asians and Latinos began moving into the suburbs, and many of them ended up in ethnic enclaves that were sharply separated from more affluent neighborhoods.[4] At the same time, many suburbs were becoming multiethnic, and in those cases a politics of interethnic bargaining has evolved in which minorities have become, or are in the process of becoming, incorporated into electoral politics and institutions. In other suburbs, a politics of marginalization, distrust, and hostility carries the day. Metropolitan areas are typically fragmented into a multitude of separate jurisdictions. Probably more often, however, immigrants are sharply separated from the neighborhoods inhabited by affluent residents. For example, during the 1990s two streams moved to Orange County, California, just outside Los Angeles: highly educated professionals and foreign-born immigrants. The two streams could hardly have been more different: high-income families making more than $150,000 per year jumped by 184 percent in the county, but at the same time the number of foreign-born immigrants increased by 48 percent.[5] Commenting on these trends, a noted demographer said the county could go in two directions: either a "mostly gated-community-type mentality" or "Immigrants start integrating into middle-class areas, so you have a blended suburbia."[6]

The multiethnic metropolis has prompted a variety of political responses. Many affluent suburbanites have retreated into protected, privatized enclaves, a trend that is also occurring in the central cities. A large proportion of urban residents commute from subdivisions, gated communities, townhouse developments, and condominium complexes to high-rise downtown office buildings or suburban office parks, drive to enclosed malls and mall complexes for shopping, and commute to entertainment and tourist bubbles to enjoy themselves.[7] Escape from the public realm fragments the metropolis not only into separate suburban jurisdictions, but also into privatized and protected spaces that separate affluent from poorer residents as efficiently as ever before.

PART THREE: THE POLITICS OF URBAN RESILIENCE

For at least two centuries American cities have been forced to cope with a range of problems associated with economic and demographic change, poverty, and inequality. But recent events show that in the global era urban governments will need to respond to panoply of new and somewhat unfamiliar challenges. Terrorist attacks, prolonged economic crises, and natural disasters seem to have become all too familiar aspects of a globalized world. The governmental systems of local governments may or may not prove to be capable of adequately addressing these new problems.

It is important to consider whether the basic structure of governance in America's urban areas prepares cities and urban regions for the challenges of the global era. Critics have long decried the American system of urban governance. On the surface, the fracturing of urban regions into a multitude of governments seems obviously dysfunctional in a variety of ways. For decades, movements sprang forth seeking the regional consolidation of governments, but attempts to achieve this goal failed decade after decade. Although comprehensive reform proved to be elusive, more modest attempts have been tried to achieve some degree of regional governance or to reduce inequality among jurisdictions. One of the most notable of these took effect in Minnesota in 1967, when the state legislature approved the creation of a Metropolitan Council for the Minneapolis urban region. Four years later, in what advocates called the "Minnesota Miracle" because of the unlikely compromises that made it possible, the state legislature approved a plan to partially equalize local revenues by requiring cities and towns in some parts of the state to participate in tax-sharing plans.[8] The purpose of this tax-sharing scheme was to curb the use of tax abatements and direct subsidies designed to lure shopping centers and other businesses to particular municipalities.

As long as the reformers stuck to modest tax-sharing and some planning coordination among municipalities, the plan provoked little controversy. But in the 1990s, when a Democratic-controlled Minnesota legislature passed a bill that would have required cities to assume a "fair share" of low- and moderate-income housing, vigorous opposition emerged, and Republican gains in the state house soon ended any such initiative. However, in 1994 a coalition of struggling suburbs joined representatives from Minneapolis and St. Paul and managed to push a Metropolitan Reorganization Act through the legislature. The Metropolitan Council for the Twin Cities suddenly became a $600 million regional government that operated sewer and transit services and supervised the regional airport.[9] In the same year, the legislature also took a step toward regional land use planning when it passed the Metropolitan Land Use Reform Act. The legislation did little—it only protected farmers from public assessments and tax increases that often forced them to sell to developers—but it provided a framework for the future. That future has not been realized, however, in large part because of the passionate opposition ignited by proposals that would curb the autonomy of local governments. And, it should be kept in mind, Minnesota is considered a model; even less has been done in most other metropolitan regions. Simply put, Americans are not predisposed to change the governance of urban areas very much.

Do governmental structures of the American federal system and of local governments obstruct the ability of cities to effectively address the problems that confront them? It is clear that the fragmented system of government in the United States is not well equipped to respond to emergencies, a fact brought home by flooding on the Mississippi River near St. Louis in June 2008. Governments at all levels found it hard to respond to the imminent danger to dikes protecting small towns because the levees were "owned and maintained by all sorts of towns, agencies, even individual farmers."[10] The task of responding is at least equally difficult when it comes to smaller, incremental, less dramatic and more intractable problems, such as urban poverty, a shortage of affordable housing, gang violence, and inadequate education.

Since the withdrawal of federal urban programs in the 1980s, cities have been on their own. The Great Recession beginning in 2008 has seriously compromised the ability of local governments even to provide adequate levels of public services and build and maintain necessary infrastructure. This is part of the reason why aid to state and local governments was included in the $787 billion stimulus package passed by Congress on February 13, 2009. The American Recovery and Reinvestment Act sent $79 billion of fiscal assistance directly to the states. Of immediate relevance to the cities, it also authorized $144 billion for infrastructure projects undertaken by state and local governments and $41 billion for school districts. The stimulus package provided a greater influx of federal money than at any time since the 1930s, but it did not restructure the intergovernmental system, and it did not spare local governments from making deep cuts in their budgets. The federal dollars were designated for infrastructure projects; cities were not allowed to use them to solve current budgetary problems. As a result, in 2010 and 2011 cities slashed their budgets even deeper.

Any hope that the federal government would once again come to the aid of cities was dashed by the bitter opposition mounted against federal stimulus spending by the Republican-led Congress. Indeed, Republicans even made the extension of disaster relief a political issue in the wake of the two tropical storms that hit the East Coast in the fall of 2011, by demanding that any federal appropriations for devastated communities be offset by cuts in existing programs. In the American system of governance it is hard to acknowledge that local governments may not always have the capacity or resilience necessary for coping with unusually pressing public problems.

The governance of urban communities happens within contours defined by history as well as by the sweep of new political developments. The political choices and policy responses of the present era may sometimes seem subject to forces that beg explanation, but it helps to keep in mind that the past and the present—and, for that matter, the future—are linked by political structures and governmental processes that have proved to be enduring in the American context. The long view seems to indicate that the way we govern our cities and urban areas are likely to remain largely unchanged, and that the governance structures of urban America, however disorganized they may seem, will manage to rise to the task.

NOTES

1. Saskia Sassen, *The Global City: New York, London, Tokyo*, 2nd ed. (Princeton, NJ: Princeton University Press, 2001).
2. Richard Florida, *The Rise of the Creative Class* (New York: Basic Books, 2002).
3. Todd Swanstrom, "Semisovereign Cities: The Politics of Urban Development," *Polity* 21 (Fall 1988): 83–110.
4. John R. Logan, "The New Ethnic Enclaves in America's Suburbs," a report by the Lewis Mumford Center for Comparative Urban and Regional Research (Albany, NY: 2002), pp. 1–2.
5. Jim Hinch and Ronald Campbell, "Gated Enclaves One Future for Orange County," *Orange County Register*, May 15, 2002 (www.ocregister.com).
6. Ibid., quoting William Frey, a demographer in the Milken Institute of Los Angeles.
7. Dennis R. Judd, "Enclosure, Community, and Public Life," in Dan A. Chekki (ed.), *Research in Community Sociology: New Communities in a Changing World* (Greenwich, CT: JAI Press, 1996), pp. 217–238.
8. See the Minnesota Historical Society, "Public Education: The Minnesota Miracle," www.mnhs.org/library/tips/history_topics/18public.html.
9. Myron Orfield, *Metropolitics: A Regional Agenda for Community and Stability* (Washington, D.C.: Brookings Institution Press, and Cambridge, Mass.: Lincoln Institute of Land Policy, 1997), p. 13.
10. Monica Davey, "Call for Change Ignored, Levees Remain Patchy," *New York Times*, June 23, 2008 (http://www.nytimes.com/2008/06/22us/22midwest.html).

Studying Urban Governance in a Global Age

Local communities cannot be preserved without a measure of economic vitality, and this is why growth and prosperity have always been among the most important priorities of urban residents and their civic leaders. Local residents have a huge stake in the continued vitality of the place where they live; it is where they have invested their energy and capital; it is the source of incomes, jobs, and a sense of personal identity and community. For these reasons, although the policy priorities and public expenditures of local governments are always subject to bargaining and compromise, the imperative of growth will always remain high on the local political agenda no matter how pressing other matters may be.

As Paul E. Peterson points out in Selection 1, there are constant debates about the "public interest" that cities ought to pursue. Some people might demand that cities spend a substantial share of their public resources on "redistributive" policies designed to help those most in need. Others might promote a second, quite minimalist, view that city governments should do little more than provide the services necessary to make the city a healthy and functional environment. Peterson proposes a third alternative when he argues that cities have no choice but to place a high priority on policies that will stimulate economic growth. Such policies, he says, respond to a "unitary interest" that all urban residents hold in local economic vitality: "It is in the city's interest . . . to help sustain a high-quality local infrastructure generally attractive to all commerce and industry." This logic dictates that even the social health of a city depends on its economic prosperity: "When a city is able to export its products, service industries prosper, labor is in greater demand . . . tax revenues increase, city services can be improved, donations to charitable organizations become more generous, and the social and cultural life of the city is enhanced."

In Peterson's analysis, the leaders of cities cannot leave economic growth to chance because cities compete with one another. City governments are unable to control the movement of capital and labor across their borders. Unlike the national government, they lack the authority to regulate immigration, currency, prices, and wages, or the import or export of goods and services. City governments, therefore, are constrained to compete for capital investment or suffer decline in the economic well-being of the community. Cities occupy a particular space, but businesses can move; therefore, if the local business environment is not pleasing to them, investors and businesses will go elsewhere. If they heed Peterson's logic, politicians will take care to keep business firms or middle-class residents happy by avoiding expensive social programs; instead, they will try to minimize taxes, avoid expensive regulations, and offer a variety of subsidies to keep and attract people who can invest in the city and its economy.

City Limits, the book from which the Peterson selection is taken, ignited a controversy among urban scholars—a controversy that has not died down completely even after three decades (Peterson's book was published in 1981). Many scholars took Peterson to task for his assumption that growth benefits everyone. Others accused him of ignoring the complexities of local politics by pointing out that the mix of local policies differs substantially from city to city depending on population demographics, the political influence and the degree of political participation of various groups, and governmental powers and structures. The importance of local prosperity is likely to always be high on the agenda, but politicians must also mobilize sufficient political support to remain in office; in other words, they must win elections. Mayors must often perform a delicate balancing act that requires them to protect and enhance the economic base of a city while at the same time mobilizing sufficient political support to remain in office and implement their policies.

Partially in response to Peterson's book, a literature on "urban regimes" emerged that provided detailed descriptions of the process by which local policy priorities were decided. The book *Regime Politics* (1989), which quickly became a classic in the field of urban politics, was based on a detailed case study of postwar politics in Atlanta. As described by Clarence N. Stone in Selection 2, the two most powerful partners of what he called the *urban regime* in Atlanta included the mayor and the city's downtown business elite. In his study, Stone pointed out mayors were motivated to join the coalition because they lacked the resources to do much about Atlanta's economic problems on their own. Likewise, the business community required a local government capable of coordinating the massive resources necessary for saving the downtown from decline. By working together, all the participants could accomplish goals that none of them could achieve on their own. Stone noted, "What makes governance in Atlanta effective is not the formal machinery of government, but rather the informal partnership between city hall and the downtown business elite. This informal partnership and the way it operates constitute the city's regime; it is the same means through which major policy decisions are made."

At first glance it might seem that Stone has done little more than describe the political mechanism used by cities to support the kinds of growth policies advocated by Paul Peterson. A deeper look, however, reveals something very different. In the selection from *Regime Politics* (and in much greater detail in the book) Stone notes that although Atlanta's urban regime was dominated by City Hall and business, it offered "a combination of selective incentives and small opportunities" to groups able to press their political demands. Rather than governing in a top-down manner, it avoided popular resistance by offering material benefits to the black middle class of the city. The regime, in other words, was able to recognize that there were legitimate interests in addition to those tied directly to economic development.

Selection 3, by Dennis R. Judd and David Laslo, offers evidence that the City Hall-downtown business alliance described by Stone may have collapsed in most cities due to the economic restructuring associated with globalization. To test the continued viability of Clarence Stone's original concept, these authors attempted to replicate his study of Atlanta by tracing the governance coalitions in St. Louis from 1952 to 1996. They found that a regime like Atlanta's existed but only for little more than a decade, and that in the mid-1960s it was replaced by a governance structure dominated by a CEO-led organization. In this period, which lasted from 1965 to 1992, the downtown corporate community defined the local political agenda, and mayors were in a distinctly dependent role. In the 1990s, however, a wave of merges and buyouts, the growth of small business organizations, and the formation of special-purpose authorities fundamentally changed the local political system. The authors call the complex institutional structure that now governs the city the *new ecology of governance,* and suggest that this mode of governance may have replaced regimes in most cities sometime in the 1990s, if not before. If this is so, participation in urban politics now involves many more political interests than in the past, and this would make it likely that economic development would remain as only one of several policy priorities pursued by urban governments.

1

The Interests of the Limited City

PAUL E. PETERSON

Like all social structures, cities have interests. Just as we can speak of union interests, judicial interests, and the interests of politicians, so we can speak of the interests of that structured system of social interactions we call a city. Citizens, politicians, and academics are all quite correct in speaking freely of the interests of cities.[1]

DEFINING THE CITY INTEREST

By a city's interest, I do not mean the sum total of the interests of those individuals living in the city. For one thing, these are seldom, if ever, known. The wants, needs, and preferences of residents continually change, and few surveys of public opinion in particular cities have ever been taken. Moreover, the residents of a city often have discordant interests. Some want more parkland and better schools; others want better police protection and lower taxes. Some want an elaborated highway system; others wish to keep cars out of their neighborhood. Some want more inexpensive, publicly subsidized housing; others wish to remove the public housing that exists. Some citizens want improved welfare assistance for the unemployed and dependent; others wish to cut drastically all such programs of public aid. Some citizens want rough-tongued ethnic politicians in public office; others wish that municipal administration were a gentleman's calling. Especially in large cities, the cacophony of competing claims by diverse class, race, ethnic, and occupational groups makes impossible the determination of any overall city interest—any public interest, if you like—by compiling all the demands and desires of individual city residents.

Some political scientists have attempted to discover the overall urban public interest by summing up the wide variety of individual interests. The earlier work of Edward Banfield, still worth examination, is perhaps the most persuasive effort of this kind.[2] He argued that urban political processes—or at least those in Chicago—allowed for the expression of nearly all the particular interests within the city. Every significant interest was represented by some economic firm or voluntary association, which had a stake in trying to influence those public policies that touched its vested interests. After these various groups and firms had debated and contended, the political leader searched for a compromise that took into account the vital interests of each, and worked out a solution all could accept with some satisfaction. The leader's own interest in sustaining his political power dictated such a strategy.

Banfield's argument is intriguing, but few people would identify public policies as being in the interest of the city simply because they have been formulated according to certain procedures. The political leader might err in his judgment; the interests of important but politically impotent groups might never get expressed; or the consequences of a policy might in the long run be disastrous for the city. Moreover, most urban policies are not hammered out after great controversy, but are the quiet product of routine decision making. How does one evaluate which of these are in the public interest? Above all, this mechanism for determining the city's interest provides no standpoint for evaluating the substantive worth of urban policies. Within Banfield's framework, whatever urban governments do is said to be in the interest of their communities. But the concept of city interest is used most persuasively when there are calls for reform or innovation. It is a term used to evaluate existing programs and to discriminate between promising and undesirable new ones. To equate the interests of cities with what cities are doing is to so impoverish the term as to make it quite worthless.

The economist Charles Tiebout employs a second approach to the identification of city interests.[3] Unlike Banfield, he does not see the city's interests as a mere summation of individual interests but as something which can be ascribed to the entity, taken as a whole. As an economist, Tiebout is hardly embarrassed by such an enterprise, because in ascribing interests to cities his work parallels both those orthodox economists who state that firms have an interest in maximizing profits and those welfare economists who claim that politicians have an interest in maximizing votes. Of course, they state only that their model will assume that firms and politicians behave in such a way, but insofar as they believe their model has empirical validity, they in fact assert that those constrained by the businessman's or politician's role must pursue certain interests. And so does Tiebout when he says that communities seek to attain the optimum size for the efficient delivery of the bundle of services the local government produces. In his words, "Communities below the optimum size seek to attract new residents to lower average costs. Those above optimum size do just the opposite. Those at an optimum try to keep their populations constant."[4]

Tiebout's approach is in many ways very attractive. By asserting a strategic objective that the city is trying to maximize—optimum size—Tiebout identifies an overriding interest which can account for specific policies the city adopts. He provides a simple analytical tool that will account for the choices cities make, without requiring complex investigations into citizen preferences and political mechanisms for identifying and amalgamating the same. Moreover, he provides a criterion for determining whether a specific policy is in the interest of the city—does it help achieve optimum size? Will it help the too small city grow? Will it help the too big city contract? Will it keep the optimally sized city in equilibrium? Even though the exact determination of the optimum size cannot presently be scientifically determined in all cases, the criterion does provide a useful guide for prudential decision making.

The difficulty with Tiebout's assumption is that he does not give very good reasons for its having any plausibility. When most economists posit a certain form of maximizing behavior, there is usually a good commonsense reason for believing the person in that role will have an interest in pursuing this strategic objective. When orthodox economists say that businessmen maximize profits, it squares with our understanding in everyday life that people engage in commercial enterprises for monetary gain. The more they make, the better they like it. The same can be said of those welfare economists who say politicians maximize votes. The assumption, though cynical, is in accord with popular belief—and therefore once again has a certain plausibility.

By contrast, Tiebout's optimum size thesis diverges from what most people think cities are trying to do. Of course, smaller communities are often seeking to expand—boosterism may be the quintessential characteristic of small-town America. Yet Tiebout takes optimum size, not growth or maximum size, as the strategic objective. And when Tiebout discusses the big city that wishes to shrink to optimum size, his cryptic language is quite unconvincing. "The case of the city that is too large and tries to get rid of residents is more difficult to imagine," he confesses. Even more, he concedes that "no alderman in his right political mind would ever admit that the city is too big." "Nevertheless," he continues, "economic forces are at work to push people out of it. Every resident who moves to the suburbs to find better schools, more parks, and so forth, is reacting, in part, against the pattern the city has to offer."[5] In this crucial passage Tiebout speaks neither of local officials nor of local public policies. Instead, he refers to "economic forces" that may be beyond the control of the city and of "every resident," each of whom may be pursuing his own interests, not that of the community at large.

The one reason Tiebout gives for expecting cities to pursue optimum size is to lower the average cost of public goods. If public goods can be delivered most efficiently at some optimum size, then migration of residents will occur until that size has been reached. In one respect Tiebout is quite correct: local governments must concern themselves with operating local services as efficiently as possible in order to protect the city's economic interests. But there is little evidence that there is an optimum size at which services can be delivered with greatest efficiency. And even if such an optimum did exist, it could be realized only if migration occurred among residents who paid equal amounts in local taxes. In the more likely situation, residents pay variable prices for public services (for example, the amount paid in local property taxes varies by the value of the property). Under these circumstances, increasing size to the optimum does not reduce costs to residents unless newcomers pay at least as much in taxes as the marginal increase in costs their arrival imposes on city government.[6] Conversely, if a city needs to lose population to reach the optimum, costs to residents will not decline unless the exiting population paid less in taxes than was the marginal cost of providing them government services. In most big cities losing population, exactly the opposite is occurring. Those who pay more in taxes than they receive in services are the emigrants. Tiebout's identification of city interests with optimum size, while suggestive, fails to take into account the quality as well as the quantity of the local population.

The interests of cities are neither a summation of individual interests nor the pursuit of optimum size. Instead, policies and programs can be said to be in the interest of cities whenever the policies maintain or enhance the economic position, social prestige, or political power of the city, taken as a whole.[7]

Cities have these interests because cities consist of a set of social interactions structured by their location in a particular territorial space. Any time that social interactions come to be structured into recurring patterns, the structure thus formed develops an interest in its own maintenance and enhancement. It is in that sense that we speak of the interests of an organization, the interests of the system, and the like. To be sure, within cities, as within any other structure, one can find diverse social roles, each with its own set of interests. But these varying role interests, as divergent and competing as they may be, do not distract us from speaking of the overall interests of the larger structural entity.[8]

The point can be made less abstractly. A school system is a structured form of social action, and therefore it has an interest in maintaining and improving its material resources, its prestige, and its political power. Those policies or events which have such positive effects are said to be in the interest of the school system. An increase in state financial aid or the winning of the basketball tournament are events that, respectively, enhance the material well-being and the prestige of a school system and are therefore in its interest. In ordinary speech this is taken for granted, even when we also recognize that teachers, pupils, principals, and board members may have contrasting interests as members of differing role-groups within the school.

Although social roles performed within cities are numerous and conflicting, all are structured by the fact that they take place in a specific spatial location that falls within the jurisdiction of some local government. All members of the city thus come to share an interest in policies that affect the well-being of that territory. Policies which enhance the desirability or attractiveness of the territory are in the city's interest, because they benefit all residents—in their role as residents of the community. Of course, in any of their other social roles, residents of the city may be adversely affected by the policy. The Los Angeles dope peddler—in his role as peddler—hardly benefits from a successful drive to remove hard drugs from the city. On the other hand, as a resident of the city, he benefits from a policy that enhances the attractiveness of the city as a locale in which to live and work. In determining whether a policy is in the interest of a city, therefore, one does not consider whether it has a positive or negative effect on the total range of social interactions of each and every individual. That is an impossible task. To know whether a policy is in a city's interest, one has to consider only the impact on social relationships insofar as they are structured by their taking place within the city's boundaries.

An illustration from recent policy debates over the future of our cities reveals that it is exactly with this meaning that the notion of a city's interest is typically used. The tax deduction that homeowners take on their mortgage interest payments should be eliminated, some urbanists have argued. The deduction has not served the interests of central cities, because it has provided a public subsidy for families who purchase suburban homes. Quite clearly, elimination of this tax deduction is not in the interest of those central city residents who wish to purchase a home in the suburbs. It is not in the interest of those central city homeowners (which in some cities may even form a majority of the voting population), who would then be called upon to pay higher federal taxes. But the policy might very well improve the rental market in the central city, thereby stimulating its economy—and it is for this reason that the proposal has been defended as being in the interest of central cities.

To say that people understand what, generally, is in the interest of cities does not eliminate debate over policy alternatives in specific instances. The notion of city interest can be extremely useful, even though its precise application in specific contexts may be quite problematic. In any policy context one cannot easily assert that one "knows" what is in the interest of cities, whether or not the residents of the city agree. But city residents do know the kind of evidence that must be advanced and the kinds of reasons that must be adduced in order to build a persuasive case that a policy is in the interest of cities. And so do community leaders, mayors, and administrative elites.

ECONOMIC INTERESTS

Cities, like all structured social systems, seek to improve their position in all three of the systems of stratification—economic, social, and political—characteristic of industrial societies. In most cases, improved standing in any one of these systems helps enhance a city's position in the other two. In the short run, to be sure, cities may have to choose among economic gains, social prestige, and political weight. And because different cities may choose alternative objectives, one cannot state any one overarching objective—such as improved property values—that is always the paramount interest of the city. But in as much as improved economic or market standing seems to be an objective of great importance to most cities, I shall concentrate on this interest and only discuss in passing the significance of social status and political power.

Cities constantly seek to upgrade their economic standing. Following Weber, I mean by this that cities seek to improve their market position, their attractiveness as a locale for economic activity. In the market economy that characterizes Western society, an advantageous economic position means a competitive edge in the production and distribution of desired commodities relative to other localities. When this is present, cities can export goods and/or services to those outside the boundaries of the community.

Some regional economists have gone so far as to suggest that the welfare of a city is identical to the welfare of its export industry.[9] As exporters expand, the city grows. As they contract, the city declines and decays. The economic reasoning supporting such a conclusion is quite straightforward. When cities produce a good that can be sold in an external market, labor and capital flow into the city to help increase the production of that good. They continue to do so until the external market is saturated—that is, until the marginal cost of production within the city exceeds the marginal value of the good external to the city. Those engaged in the production of the exported good will themselves consume a variety of other goods and services, which other businesses will provide. In addition, subsidiary industries locate in the city either because they help supply the exporting industry, because they can utilize some of its by-products, or because they benefit by some economies of scale provided by its presence. Already, the familiar multiplier is at work. With every increase in the sale of exported commodities, there may be as much as a four- or fivefold increase in local economic activity.

The impact of Boeing Aircraft's market prospects on the economy of the Seattle metropolitan area illustrates the importance of export to regional economies. In the late sixties defense and commercial aircraft contracts declined. Boeing laid off thousands of workmen, the economy of the Pacific Northwest slumped, the unemployed moved elsewhere, and Seattle land values dropped sharply. More recently, Boeing has more than recovered its former position. With rapidly expanding production at Boeing, the metropolitan area is enjoying low unemployment, rapid growth, and dramatically increasing land values.

The same multiplier effect is not at work in the case of goods and services produced for domestic consumption within the territory. What is gained by a producer within the community is expended by other community residents. Residents, in effect, are simply taking in one another's laundry. Unless productivity increases, there is no capacity for expansion.

If this economic analysis is correct, it is only a modest oversimplification to equate the interests of cities with the interests of their export industries. Whatever helps them prosper redounds to the benefit of the community as a whole—perhaps four and five times over. And it is just such an economic analysis that has influenced many local government policies. Especially the smaller towns and cities may provide free land, tax concessions, and favorable utility rates to incoming industries.

The smaller the territory and the more primitive its level of economic development, the more persuasive is this simple export thesis. But other economists have elaborated an alternative growth thesis that is in many ways more persuasive, especially as it relates to larger urban areas. In their view a sophisticated local network of public and private services is the key to long-range economic growth. Since the world economy is constantly changing, the economic viability of any particular export industry is highly variable. As a result, a community dependent on any particular set of export industries will have only an episodic economic future. But with a well-developed infrastructure of services, the city becomes an attractive locale for a wide variety of export industries. As older exporters fade, new exporters take their place and the community continues to prosper. It is in the city's interest, therefore, to help sustain a high-quality local infrastructure generally attractive to all commerce and industry.

I have no way of evaluating the merits of these contrasting economic arguments. What is important in this context is that both see exports as being of great importance to the well-being of a city. One view suggests a need for direct support of the export industry; the other suggests a need only for maintaining a service infrastructure, allowing the market to determine which particular export industry locates in the community. Either one could be the more correct diagnosis for a particular community, at least in the short run. Yet both recognize that the future of the city depends upon exporting local products. When a city is able to export its products, service industries prosper, labor is in greater demand, wages increase, promotional opportunities widen, land values rise, tax revenues increase, city services can be improved, donations to charitable organizations become more generous, and the social and cultural life of the city is enhanced.

To export successfully, cities must make efficient use of the three main factors of production: land, labor, and capital.[10]

LAND

Land is the factor of production that cities control. Yet land is the factor to which cities are bound. It is the fact that cities are spatially defined units whose boundaries seldom change that gives permanence to their interests. City residents come and go, are born and die, and change their tastes and preferences. But the city remains wedded to the land area with which it is blessed (or cursed). And unless it can alter that land area, through annexation or consolidation, it is the long-range value of that land which the city must secure—and which gives a good approximation of how well it is achieving its interests.

Land is an economic resource. Production cannot occur except within some spatial location. And because land varies in its economic potential, so do the economic futures of cities. Historically, the most important variable affecting urban growth has been an area's relationship to land and water routes.

On the eastern coast of the United States, all the great cities had natural harbors that facilitated commercial relations with Europe and other coastal communities. Inland, the great industrial cities all were located on either the Great Lakes or the Ohio River–Mississippi River system. The cities of the West, as Elazar has shown, prospered according to their proximity to East-West trade flows.[11] Denver became the predominant city of the mountain states because it sat at the crossroads of land routes through the Rocky Mountains. Duluth, Minnesota, had only limited potential, even with its Great Lakes location, because it lay north of all major routes to the West.

Access to waterways and other trade routes is not the only way a city's life is structured by its location. Its climate determines the cost and desirability of habitation; its soil affects food production in the surrounding area; its terrain affects drainage, rates of air pollution, and scenic beauty. Of course, the qualities of landscape do not permanently fix a city's fate—it is the intersection of that land and location with the larger national and world economy that is critical. For example, cities controlling access to waterways by straddling natural harbors at one time monopolized the most valuable land in the region, and from that position they dominated their hinterland. But since land and air transport have begun to supplant, not just supplement, water transport, the dominance of these once favored cities has rapidly diminished.

Although the economic future of a city is very much influenced by external forces affecting the value of its land, the fact that a city has control over the use of its land gives it some capacity for influencing that future. Although there are constitutional limits to its authority, the discretion available to a local government in determining land use remains the greatest arena for the exercise of local autonomy. Cities can plan the use of local space; cities have the power of eminent domain; through zoning laws cities can restrict all sorts of land uses; and cities can regulate the size, content, and purpose of buildings constructed within their boundaries. Moreover, cities can provide public services in such a way as to encourage certain kinds of land use. Sewers, gas lines, roads, bridges, tunnels, playgrounds, schools, and parks all impinge on the use of land in the surrounding area. Urban politics is above all the politics of land use, and it is easy to see why. Land is the factor of production over which cities exercise the greatest control.

LABOR

To its land area the city must attract not only capital but productive labor. Yet local governments in the United States are very limited in their capacities to control the flow of these factors. Lacking the more direct controls of nation-states, they are all the more constrained to pursue their economic interests in those areas where they do exercise authority.

Labor is an obvious case in point. Since nation-states control migration across their boundaries, the industrially more advanced have formally legislated that only limited numbers of outsiders—for example, relatives of citizens or those with skills needed by the host country—can enter. In a world where it is economically feasible for great masses of the population to migrate long distances, this kind of restrictive legislation seems essential for keeping the nation's social and economic integrity intact. Certainly, the wage levels and welfare assistance programs characteristic of advanced industrial societies could not be sustained were transnational migration unencumbered.

Unlike nation-states, cities cannot control movement across their boundaries. They no longer have walls, guarded and defended by their inhabitants. And as Weber correctly noted, without walls cities no longer have the independence to make significant choices in the way medieval cities once did.[12] It is true that local governments often try to keep vagrants, bums, paupers, and racial minorities out of their territory. They are harassed, arrested, thrown out of town, and generally discriminated against. But in most of these cases local governments act unconstitutionally, and even this illegal use of the police power does not control migration very efficiently.

Although limited in its powers, the city seeks to obtain an appropriately skilled labor force at wages lower than its competitors so that it can profitably export commodities. In larger cities a diverse work force is desirable. The service industry, which provides the infrastructure for exporters, recruits large numbers of unskilled workers, and many manufacturing industries need only semiskilled workers. When shortages in these skill levels appear, cities may assist industry in advertising the work and living opportunities of the region. In the nineteenth century when unskilled labor was in short supply, frontier cities made extravagant claims to gain a competitive edge in the supply of ordinary labor.

Certain sparsely populated areas, such as Alaska, occasionally advertise for unskilled labor even today. However, competition among most cities is now for highly skilled workers and especially for professional and managerial talent. In a less than full-employment economy, most communities have a surplus of semiskilled and unskilled labor. Increases in the supply of unskilled workers increase the cost of the community's social services. Since national wage laws preclude a decline in wages below a certain minimum, the increases in the cost of social services are seldom offset by lower wages for unskilled labor in those areas where the unemployed concentrate. But even with high levels of unemployment, there remains a shortage of highly skilled technicians and various types of white collar workers. Where shortages develop, the prices these workers can command in the labor market may climb to a level where local exports are no longer competitive with goods produced elsewhere. The economic health of a community is therefore importantly affected by the availability of professional and managerial talent and of highly skilled technicians.

When successfully pursuing their economic interests, cities develop a set of policies that will attract the more skilled and white collar workers without at the same time attracting unemployables. Of course, there are limits on the number of things cities can do. In contrast to nation-states, they cannot simply forbid entry to all but the highly talented whose skills they desire. But through zoning laws, they can ensure that adequate land is available for middle-class residences. They can provide parks, recreation areas, and good-quality schools in areas where the economically most productive live. They can keep the cost of social services, little utilized by the middle class, to a minimum, thereby keeping local taxes relatively low. In general, they can try to ensure that the benefits of public service outweigh their costs to those highly skilled workers, managers, and professionals who are vital for sustaining the community's economic growth.

CAPITAL

Capital is the second factor of production that must be attracted to an economically productive territory. Accordingly, nation-states place powerful controls on the flow of capital across their boundaries. Many nations strictly regulate the amount of national currency that can be taken out of the country. They place quotas and tariffs on imported goods. They regulate the rate at which national currency can be exchanged with foreign currency. They regulate the money supply, increasing interest rates when growth is too rapid, lowering interest rates when growth slows down. Debt financing also allows a nation-state to undertake capital expenditures and to encourage growth in the private market. At present the powers of nation-states to control capital flow are being used more sparingly and new supranational institutions are developing in their place. Market forces now seem more powerful than official policies in establishing rates of currency exchange among major industrial societies. Tariffs and other restrictions on trade are subject to retaliation by other countries, and so they must be used sparingly. The economies of industrialized nations are becoming so interdependent that significant changes in the international political economy seem imminent, signaled by numerous international conferences to determine worldwide growth rates, rates of inflation, and levels of unemployment. If these trends continue, nation-states may come to look increasingly like local governments.

But these developments at the national level have only begun to emerge. At the local level in the United States, cities are much less able to control capital flows. In the first place, the Constitution has been interpreted to mean that states cannot hinder the free flow of goods and monies across their boundaries. And what is true of states is true of their subsidiary jurisdictions as well. In the second place, states and localities cannot regulate the money supply. If unemployment is low, they cannot stimulate the economy by increasing the monetary flow. If inflationary pressures adversely affect their competitive edge in the export market, localities can neither restrict the money supply nor directly control prices and wages. All of these powers are reserved for national governments. In the third place, local governments cannot spend more than they receive in tax revenues without damaging their credit or even running the risk of bankruptcy. Pump priming, sometimes a national disease, is certainly a national prerogative.

Local governments are left with a number of devices for enticing capital into the area. They can minimize their tax on capital and on profits from capital investment. They can reduce the costs of capital investment by providing low-cost public utilities, such as roads, sewers, lights, and police and fire protection. They can even offer public land free of charge or at greatly reduced prices to those investors they are particularly anxious to attract. They can provide a context for business operations free of undue harassment or regulation. For example, they can ignore various external costs of production, such as air pollution, water pollution, and the despoliation of trees, grass, and other features of the landscape. Finally, they can discourage labor from unionizing so as to keep industrial labor costs competitive.

This does not mean it behooves cities to allow any and all profit-maximizing action on the part of an industrial plant. Insofar as the city desires diversified economic growth, no single company can be allowed to pursue policies that seriously detract from the area's overall attractiveness to capital or productive labor. Taxes cannot be so low that government fails to supply residents with as attractive a package of services as can be found in competitive jurisdictions. Regulation of any particular industry cannot fall so far below nationwide standards that other industries must bear external costs not encountered in other places. The city's interest in attracting capital does not mean utter subservience to any particular corporation, but a sensitivity to the need for establishing an overall favorable climate.

In sum, cities, like private firms, compete with one another so as to maximize their economic position. To achieve this objective, the city must use the resources its land area provides by attracting as much capital and as high a quality labor force as is possible. Like a private firm, the city must entice labor and capital resources by offering appropriate inducements. Unlike the nation-state, the American city does not have regulatory powers to control labor and capital flows. The lack thereof sharply limits what cities can do to control their economic development, but at the same time the attempt by cities to maximize their interests within these limits shapes policy choice.

LOCAL GOVERNMENT AND THE INTERESTS OF CITIES

Local government leaders are likely to be sensitive to the economic interests of their communities. First, economic prosperity is necessary for protecting the fiscal base of a local government. In the United States, taxes on local sources and charges for local services remain important components of local government revenues. Although transfers of revenue to local units from the federal and state governments increased throughout the postwar period, as late as 1975–76 local governments still were raising almost 59 percent of their own revenue.[13] Raising revenue from one's own economic resources requires continuing local economic prosperity. Second, good government is good politics. By pursuing policies which contribute to the economic prosperity of the local community, the local politician selects policies that redound to his own political advantage. Local politicians, eager for relief from the cross-pressures of local politics, assiduously promote goals that have widespread benefits. And few policies are more popular than economic growth and prosperity. Third, and most important, local officials usually have a sense of community responsibility. They know that, unless the economic well-being of the community can be maintained, local business will suffer, workers will lose employment opportunities, cultural life will decline, and city land values will fall. To avoid such a dismal future, public officials try to develop policies that assist the prosperity of their community—or, at the very least, that do not seriously detract from it. Quite apart from any effects of economic prosperity on government revenues or local voting behavior, it is quite reasonable to posit that local governments are primarily interested in maintaining the economic vitality of the area for which they are responsible.

Accordingly, governments can be expected to attempt to maximize this particular goal—within the numerous environmental constraints with which they must contend. As policy alternatives are proposed, each is evaluated according to how well it will help to achieve this objective. Although information is imperfect and local governments cannot be expected to select the one best alternative on every occasion, policy choices over time will be limited to those few which can plausibly be shown to be conducive to the community's economic prosperity. Internal disputes and disagreements may affect policy on the margins, but the major contours of local revenue policy will be determined by this strategic objective.

NOTES

1. Flathman, R. E. 1966. *The public interest* (New York: John Wiley).
2. Banfield, E. C. 1961. *Political influence* (Glencoe, Illinois: Free Press). Ch. 12.
3. Tiebout, C. M. 1956. A pure theory of local expenditures. *Journal of Political Economy* 64: 416–424.
4. Ibid., p. 419.
5. Ibid., p. 420.
6. Bruce Hamilton, "Property Taxes and the Tiebout Hypothesis: Some Empirical Evidence," and Michelle J. White, "Fiscal Zoning in Fragmented Metropolitan Areas," in Mills, E. S., and Oates, W. E. 1975. *Fiscal zoning and land use controls* (Lexington, Massachusetts: Lexington Books). Chs. 2 and 3.
7. See Weber, "Class, Status, and Power," in Gerth, H. H., and Mills, C. W., trans. 1946. *From Max Weber* (New York: Oxford University Press).
8. For a more complete discussion of roles, structures, and interests, see Greenstone, J. D., and Peterson, P. E. 1976. *Race and authority in urban politics.* Phoenix edition (Chicago: University of Chicago Press). Ch. 2.
9. Cf. Thompson, W. R. 1965. *A preface to urban economics* (Baltimore, Maryland: Johns Hopkins University Press).
10. I treat entrepreneurial skill as simply another form of labor, even though it is a form in short supply.
11. Elazar, D. J. 1976. *Cities of the prairie* (New York: Basic Books).
12. Weber, M. 1921. *The city* (New York: Collier Books).
13. United States Department of Commerce, Bureau of the Census. 1977. *Local government finances in selected metropolitan areas and large counties: 1975–76.* Government finances: GF 76, no. 6.

2

Urban Regimes

CLARENCE N. STONE

What makes governance in Atlanta effective is not the formal machinery of government, but rather the informal partnership between city hall and the downtown business elite. This informal partnership and the way it operates constitute the city's regime; it is the means through which major policy decisions are made.

The word "regime" connotes different things to different people, but in this [selection] regime is specifically about the *informal arrangements* that surround and complement the formal workings of governmental authority. All governmental authority in the United States is greatly limited—limited by the Constitution, limited perhaps even more by the nation's political tradition, and limited structurally by the autonomy of privately owned business enterprise. The exercise of public authority is thus never a simple matter; it is almost always enhanced by extraformal considerations. Because local governmental authority is by law and tradition even more limited than authority at the state and national level, informal arrangements assume special importance in urban politics. But we should

From Clarence N. Stone, "Urban Regimes: A Research Perspective" and excerpt from "Conclusion" from *Regime Politics: Governing Atlanta, 1946–1988,* pp. 3–12, 238–245. © 1989 by the University Press of Kansas. Reprinted by permission of the University Press of Kansas.

begin our understanding of regimes by realizing that informal arrangements are by no means peculiar to cities or, for that matter, to government.

Even narrowly bounded organizations, those with highly specific functional responsibilities, develop informal governing coalitions.[1] As Chester Barnard argued many years ago, formal goals and formal lines of authority are insufficient by themselves to bring about coordinated action with sufficient energy to accomplish organizational purposes,[2] commitment and cooperation do not just spring up from the lines of an organization chart. Because every formal organization gives rise to an informal one, Barnard concluded, successful executives must master the skill of shaping and using informal organization for their purposes.

Attention to informal arrangements takes various forms. In the analysis of business firms, the school of thought labeled "transaction cost economics" has given systematic attention to how things actually get done in a world full of social friction—basically the same question that Chester Barnard considered. A leading proponent of this approach, Oliver Williamson,[3] finds that what he terms "private orderings" (as opposed to formal and legal agreements) are enormously important in the running of business affairs. For many transactions, mutual and tacit understanding is a more efficient way of conducting relations than are legal agreements and formal contracts. Williamson quotes a business executive as saying, "You can settle any dispute if you keep the lawyers and accountants out of it. They just do not understand the give-and-take needed in business."[4] Because informal understandings and arrangements provide needed flexibility to cope with nonroutine matters, they facilitate cooperation to a degree that formally defined relationships do not. People who know one another, who have worked together in the past, who have shared in the achievement of a task, and who perhaps have experienced the same crisis are especially likely to develop tacit understandings. If they interact on a continuing basis, they can learn to trust one another and to expect dependability from one another. It can be argued, then, that transactions flow more smoothly and business is conducted more efficiently when a core of insiders form and develop an ongoing relationship.

A regime thus involves not just any informal group that comes together to make a decision but an informal yet relatively stable group *with access to institutional resources* that enable it to have a sustained role in making governing decisions. What makes the group informal is not a lack of institutional connections, but the fact that the group, *as a group*, brings together institutional connections by an informal mode of cooperation. There is no all-encompassing structure of command that guides and synchronizes everyone's behavior. There is a purposive coordination of efforts, but it comes about informally, in ways that often depend heavily on tacit understandings.

If there is no overarching command structure, what gives a regime coherence? What makes it more than an "ecology of games"?[5] The answer is that the regime is purposive, created and maintained as a way of facilitating action. In a very important sense, *a regime is empowering*. Its supporters see it as a means for achieving coordinated efforts that might not otherwise be realized. A regime, however, is not created or redirected at will. Organizational analysis teaches us that cognition is limited, existing arrangements have staying power, and implementation is profoundly shaped by procedures in place.[6] Shrewd and determined leaders can effect purposive change, but only by being attentive to the ways in which existing forms of coordination can be altered or amplified.[7]

We can think of cities as organizations that lack a conjoining structure of command. There are institutional sectors within which the power of command may be much in evidence, but the sectors are independent of one another.[8] Because localities have only weak formal means through which coordination can be achieved, informal arrangements to promote cooperation are especially useful. *These informal modes of coordinating efforts across institutional boundaries are what I call "civic cooperation."* In a system of weak formal authority, it holds special importance. Integrated with the formal structure of authority into a suprainstitutional capacity to take action, any informal basis of cooperation is empowering. It enables community actors to achieve cooperation beyond what could be formally commanded.

Consider the case of local political machines. When ward politicians learned to coordinate informally what otherwise was mired in institutional fragmentation and personal opportunism, the urban political machine was created and proved to have enormous staying power.[9] "Loyalty" is the shorthand that machine politicians used to describe the code that bound them into a cohesive group.[10] The political machine is in many ways the exemplar of governance in which informal arrangements are vital complements to the formal organization of government. The classic urban machines brought together various elements of the community in an informal scheme of exchange and cooperation that was the real governing system of the community.

The urban machine, of course, represents only one form of regime. In considering Atlanta, I am examining the governing coalition in a nonmachine city. The term "governing coalition" is a way of making the notion of regime concrete. It makes us face the fact that informal arrangements are held together by a core group—typically a body of insiders—who come together repeatedly in making important decisions. Thus, when I refer to the governing coalition in Atlanta, I mean the core group at the center of the workings of the regime.

To talk about a core group is not to suggest that they are of one mind or that they all represent identical interests—far from it. "Coalition" is the word I use to emphasize that a regime involves bringing together various elements of the community and the different institutional capacities they control. "Governing," as used in "governing coalition," I must stress, does not mean rule in command-and-control fashion. Governance through informal arrangements is about how some forms of coordination of effort prevail over others. It is about mobilizing efforts to cope and to adapt; it is not about absolute control. Informal arrangements are a way of bolstering (and guiding) the formal capacity to act, but even this enhanced capacity remains quite limited.

Having argued that informal arrangements are important in a range of circumstances, not just in cities, let me return to the specifics of the city setting. After all, the important point is not simply that there are informal arrangements; it is the particular features of urban regimes that provide the lenses through which we see the Atlanta experience. For cities, two questions face us: (1) Who makes up the governing coalition—who has to come together to make governance possible? (2) How is the coming together accomplished? These two questions imply a third: What are the consequences of the *who* and *how*? Urban regimes are not neutral mechanisms through which policy is made; they shape policy. To be sure, they do not do so on terms solely of the governing coalition's own choosing. But regimes are the mediating agents between the ill-defined pressures of an urban environment and the making of community policy. The *who* and *how* of urban regimes matter, thus giving rise to the further question of *with what consequences*. These three questions will guide my analysis of Atlanta.

URBAN REGIMES

As indicated above, an urban regime refers to the set of arrangements by which a community is actually governed. Even though the institutions of local government bear most of the formal responsibility for governing, they lack the resources and the scope of authority to govern without the active support and cooperation of significant private interests. An urban regime may thus be defined as the *informal arrangements by which public bodies and private interests function together in order to be able to make and carry out governing decisions*. These governing decisions, I want to emphasize, are not a matter of running or controlling everything. They have to do with *managing conflict* and *making adaptive responses* to social change. The informal arrangements through which governing decisions are made differ from community to community, but everywhere they are driven by two needs: (1) institutional scope (that is, the need to encompass a wide enough scope of institutions to mobilize the resources required to make and implement governing decisions) and (2) cooperation (that is, the need to promote enough cooperation and coordination for the diverse participants to reach decisions and sustain action in support of those decisions).

The mix of participants varies by community, but that mix is itself constrained by the accommodation of two basic institutional principles of the American political economy: (1) popular control of the formal machinery of government and (2) private ownership of business enterprise.[11] Neither of these principles is pristine. Popular control is modified and compromised in various ways, but nevertheless remains as the basic principle of government. Private ownership is less than universal, as governments do own and operate various auxiliary enterprises from mass transit to convention centers. Even so, governmental conduct is constrained by the need to promote investment activity in an economic arena dominated by private ownership. This political-economy insight is the foundation for a theory of urban regimes.[12]

In defining an urban regime as the informal arrangements through which public bodies and private interests function together to make and carry out governing decisions, bear in mind that I did not specify that the private interests are business interests. Indeed, in practice, private interests are not confined to business figures. Labor-union officials, party functionaries, officers in nonprofit organizations or foundations, and church leaders may also be involved.[13]

Why, then, pay particular attention to business interests? One reason is the now well-understood need to encourage business investment in order to have an economically thriving community. A second reason is the sometimes overlooked factor that businesses control politically important resources and are rarely absent totally from the scene. They may work through intermediaries, or some businesses may even be passive because others represent their interests as property holders, but a business presence is always part of the urban political scene. Although the nature of business involvement extends from the direct and extensive to the indirect and limited, the economic role of businesses *and the resources they control* are too important for these enterprises to be left out completely.

With revived interest in political economy, the regime's need for an adequate institutional scope (including typically some degree of business involvement) has received significant attention. However, less has been said about the regime's need for cooperation—and the various ways to meet it.[14] Perhaps some take for granted that, when cooperation is called for, it will be forthcoming. But careful reflection reminds us that cooperation does not occur simply because it is useful.

Robert Wiebe analyzed machine politics in a way that illustrates an important point: "The ward politician . . . required wider connections in order to manage many of his clients' problems. . . . Therefore clusters of these men allied to increase their bargaining power in city affairs. But if logic led to an integrated city-wide organization, the instinct of self-preservation did not. The more elaborate the structure, the more independence the ward bosses and area chieftains lost."[15] Cooperation can thus never be taken as a given; it must be achieved and at significant costs. Some of the costs are visible resources expended in promoting cooperation—favors and benefits distributed to curry reciprocity, the effort required to establish and maintain channels of communication, and responsibilities borne to knit activities together are a few examples. But, as Wiebe's observation reminds us, there are less visible costs. Achieving cooperation entails commitment to a set of relationships, and these relationships limit independence of action. If relationships are to be ongoing, they cannot be neglected; they may even call for sacrifices to prevent alienating allies. Forming wider connections is thus not a cost-free step, and it is not a step that community actors are always eager to take.

Because centrifugal tendencies are always strong, achieving cooperation is a major accomplishment and requires constant effort. Cooperation can be brought about in various ways. It can be induced if there is an actor powerful enough to coerce others into it, but that is a rare occurrence, because power is not usually so concentrated. More often, cooperation is achieved by some degree of reciprocity.

The literature on collective action focuses on the problem of cooperation in the absence of a system of command. For example, the "prisoner's dilemma" game instructs us that noncooperation may be invited by a number of situations.[16] In the same vein, Mancur Olson's classic analysis highlights the free-rider problem and the importance of selective incentives in inducing cooperation.[17] Alternatively, repeated interactions permit people to see the shortcomings of mutual noncooperation and to learn norms of cooperation.[18] Moreover, although Robert Axelrod's experiments with tit for tat computer programs indicate that cooperation can be instrumentally rational under some conditions, the process is not purely mechanical.[19] Students of culture point to the importance of common identity and language in facilitating interaction and promoting trust.[20] Size of group is also a consideration, affecting the ease of communication and bargaining among members; Michael Taylor, for example, emphasizes the increased difficulty of conditional cooperation in larger groups.[21]

What we can surmise about the urban community is thus twofold: (1) cooperation across institutional lines is valuable but far from automatic; and (2) cooperation is more likely to grow under some circumstances than others. This conclusion has wide implications for the study of urban politics. For example, much of the literature on community power has centered on the question of control, its possibilities and limitations: to what extent is domination by a command center possible and how is the cost of social control worked out. The long-standing elitist–pluralist debate centers on such questions. However, my line of argument here points to another way of viewing urban communities; it points to the need to think about cooperation, its possibilities and limitations—not just any cooperation, but cooperation of the kind that can bring together people based in different sectors of a community's institutional life and that enables a coalition of actors to make and support a set of governing decisions.

If the conventional model of urban politics is one of social control (with both elitist and pluralist variants), then the one proposed here might be called "the social-production model." It is based on the question of how, in a world of limited and dispersed authority, actors work together across institutional lines to produce a capacity to govern and to bring about publicly significant results.

To be sure, the development of a system of cooperation for governing is something that arises, not from an unformed mass, but rather within a structured set of relationships. Following Stephen Elkin, I described above the basic configuration in political-economy terms: popular control of governmental authority and private ownership of business activity. However, both of these elements are subject to variation. Populations vary in characteristics and in type of political organization; hence, popular control comes in many forms. The economic sector itself varies by the types of businesses that compose it and by the way in which it is organized formally and informally. Hence there is no one formula for bringing institutional sectors into an arrangement for cooperation, and the whole process is imbued with uncertainty. Cooperation is always somewhat tenuous, and it is made more so as conditions change and new actors enter the scene.

The study of urban regimes is thus a study of who cooperates and how their cooperation is achieved across institutional sectors of community life. Further, it is an examination of how that cooperation is maintained when confronted with an ongoing process of social change, a continuing influx of new actors, and potential break-downs through conflict or indifference.

Regimes are dynamic, not static, and regime dynamics concern the ways in which forces for change and forces for continuity play against one another. For example, Atlanta's governing coalition has displayed remarkable continuity in the post-World War II period, and it has done so despite deep-seated forces of social change. Understanding Atlanta's urban regime involves understanding how cooperation can be maintained and continuity can prevail in the face of so many possibilities for conflict.

STRUCTURE, ACTION, AND STRUCTURING

Because of the interplay of change and continuity, urban regimes are perhaps best studied over time. Let us, then, take a closer look at historical analysis. Scholars make sense out of the particulars of political and social life by thinking mainly in terms of abstract structures such as democracy and capitalism. Although these are useful as shorthand, the danger in abstractions is that they never capture the full complexity and contingency of the world. Furthermore, "structure" suggests something solid and unchanging, yet political and social life is riddled with contradictions and uncertainties that give rise to an ongoing process of change and adjustment. Much of the change that occurs is at the margins of basic and enduring relationships, making it easy to think in terms of order and stability. Incrementalists remind us that the present is the best predictor of the near future. But students of history, especially those accustomed to looking at longer periods of time, offer a different perspective. They see a world undergoing change, in which various actors struggle over what the terms of that change will be. It is a world shaped and reshaped by human efforts, a world that never quite forms a unified whole.

In historical light, social structures are less solid and less fixed than social scientists have sometimes assumed. Charles Tilly has argued that there is no single social structure. Instead, he urges us to think in terms of multiple structures, which "consist of shifting, constructed social relations among limited numbers of actors."[22] Philip Abrams also sees structures as relationships, relationships that are socially fabricated and subject to purposive modification.[23]

Structures are real but not fixed. Action does not simply occur within the bounds set by structures but is sometimes aimed at the structures themselves, so that a process of reshaping is taking place at all times. Abrams thus argues that events have a two-sided character, involving both structure and action in such a way that action shapes structures and structures shape actions. Abrams calls for the study of a process he labels as "structuring," by which he means that events occur in a structured context and that events help reshape structure.[24]

Abrams therefore offers a perspective on the interplay of change and continuity. This continuity is not so much a matter of resisting change as coping with it. Because the potential for change is ever present, regime continuity is a remarkable outcome. Any event contains regime-altering potential—perhaps not in sudden realignment, but in opening up a new path along which subsequent events can cumulatively bring about fundamental change.[25] The absence of regime alteration is thus an outcome to be explained, and it must be explained in terms of a capacity to adapt and reinforce existing structures. Events are the arena in which the struggle between change and continuity is played out, but they are neither self-defining nor free-formed phenomena. They become events in our minds because they have some bearing on structures that help shape future occurrences. It is the interplay of event and structure that is especially worthy of study. To identify events, one therefore needs to have some conception of structure. In this way, the researcher can focus attention, relieved of the impossible task of studying everything.

There is no escaping the necessity of the scholar's imposing some form of analysis on research. The past becomes known through the concepts we apply. Abrams sees this as the heart of historical sociology: "The reality of the past is just not 'there' waiting to be observed by the resurrectionist historian. It is to be known if at all through strenuous theoretical alienation."[26] He also reminds us that many aspects of an event cannot be observed in a direct sense; too much is implicit at any given moment.[27] That is why the process, or the flow of events over time, is so important to examine. That is also why events are not necessarily most significant for their immediate impact; they may be more significant for their bearing on subsequent events, thus giving rise to modifications in structure.

PROLOGUE TO THE ATLANTA NARRATIVE

Structuring in Atlanta is a story in which race is central. If regimes are about who cooperates, how, and with what consequences, one of the remarkable features of Atlanta's urban regime is its biracial character. How has cooperation been achieved across racial lines, particularly since race is often a chasm rather than a bridge? Atlanta has been governed by a biracial coalition for so long that it is tempting to believe that nothing else was possible. Yet other cities followed a different pattern. At a time when Atlanta prided itself on being "the city too busy to hate," Little Rock, Birmingham, and New Orleans pursued die-hard segregation and were caught up in racial violence and turmoil. The experience of these cities reminds us that Atlanta's regime is not simply an informal arrangement through which popular elections and private ownership are reconciled, but is deeply intertwined with race relations, with some actors on the Atlanta scene able to overcome the divisive character of race sufficiently to achieve cooperation.

Atlanta's earlier history is itself a mixed experience, offering no clear indication that biracial cooperation would emerge and prevail in the years after World War II. In 1906, the city was the site of a violent race riot apparently precipitated by inflammatory antiblack newspaper rhetoric.[28] The incident hastened the city's move toward the economic exclusion and residential segregation of blacks, their disenfranchisement, and enforcement of social subordination; and the years after 1906 saw the Jim Crow system fastened into place. Still, the riot was followed by modest efforts to promote biracial understanding, culminating in the formation in 1919 of the Commission on Interracial Cooperation.

Atlanta, however, also became the headquarters city for a revived Ku Klux Klan. During the 1920s, the Klan enjoyed wide support and was a significant influence in city elections. At this time, it gained a strong foothold in city government and a lasting one in the police department.[29] In 1930, faced with rising unemployment, some white Atlantans also founded the Order of Black Shirts for the express purpose of driving blacks out of even menial jobs and replacing them with whites. Black Shirt protests had an impact, and opportunities for blacks once again were constricted. At the end of World War II, with Atlanta's black population expanding beyond a number that could be contained in the city's traditionally defined black neighborhoods, another klanlike organization, the Columbians, sought to use terror tactics to prevent black expansion into previously all-white areas. All of this occurred against a background of state and regional politics devoted to the subordination of blacks to whites—a setting that did not change much until the 1960s.

Nevertheless, other patterns surfaced briefly from time to time. In 1932, Angelo Herndon, a black Communist organizer, led a mass demonstration of white and black unemployed protesting a cutoff of work relief. Herndon was arrested, and the biracial following he led proved short-lived. Still, the event had occurred, and Atlanta's city council did in fact accede to the demand for continued relief.[30] In the immediate postwar period, a progressive biracial coalition formed around the successful candidacy of Helen Douglas Mankin for a congressional seat representing Georgia's fifth district. That, too, was short-lived, as ultra-conservative Talmadge forces maneuvered to reinstitute Georgia's county-unit system for the fifth district and defeat Mankin with a minority of the popular vote.[31]

It is tempting to see the flow of history as flux, and one could easily dwell on the mutable character of political alignments. The Atlanta experience suggests that coalitions often give expression to instability. Centrifugal forces are strong, and in some ways disorder is a natural state. What conflict does not tear asunder, indifference is fully capable of wearing away.

The political incorporation of blacks into Atlanta's urban regime in tight coalition with the city's white business elite is thus not a story of how popular control and private capital came inevitably to live together in peace and harmony. It is an account of struggle and conflict—bringing together a biracial governing coalition at the outset, and then allowing each of the coalition partners to secure for itself an advantageous position within the coalition. In the first instance, struggle involved efforts to see that the coalition between white business interests and the black middle class prevailed over other possible alignments. In the second instance, there was struggle over the terms of coalition between the partners; thus political conflict is not confined to "ins" versus "outs." Those on the inside engage in significant struggle with one another over the terms on which cooperation will be maintained, which is one reason governing arrangements should never be taken for granted.

Atlanta's urban regime therefore appears to be the creature of purposive struggle, and both its establishment and its maintenance call for a political explanation. The shape of the regime was far from inevitable, but rather came about through the actions of human agents making political choices. Without extra-economic efforts by the city's business leadership, Atlanta would have been governed in a much different manner, and Atlanta's urban regime and the policies furthered by that regime might well have diverged from the path taken. History, perhaps, is as much about alternatives not pursued as about those that were. . . .

THE POLITICAL RAMIFICATIONS OF UNEQUAL RESOURCES

From Aristotle to Tocqueville to the present, keen political observers have understood that politics evolves from and reflects the associational life of a community. How people are grouped is important—so much so that, as the authors of the *Federalist* essays understood, the formation and reformation of coalitions [are] at the heart of political activity. Democracy should be viewed within that context; i.e., realizing that people do not act together simply because they share preferences on some particular issue.

Overlooking that long-standing lesson, many public-choice economists regard democracy with suspicion. They fear that popular majorities will insist on an egalitarian redistribution of benefits and thereby interfere with economic productivity. As worded by one economist, "The majority (the poor) will always vote for taxing the minority (the rich), at least until the opportunities for benefiting from redistribution run out."[32] In other words, majority rule will overturn an unequal distribution of goods and resources. This reasoning, however, involves the simple-minded premise that formal governmental authority confers a capacity to redistribute at the will of those who hold office by virtue of popular election. The social-production model of politics employed here offers a contrasting view. Starting from an assumption about the costliness of civic cooperation, the social production model suggests that an unequal distribution of goods and resources substantially modifies majority rule.

In operation, democracy is a great deal more complicated than counting votes and sorting through the wants of rational egoists. In response to those who regard democracy as a process of aggregating preferences within a system characterized by formal equality, a good antidote is Stein Rokkan's aphorism, "Votes count but resources decide."[33] Voting power is certainly not insignificant, but policies are decided mainly by those who control important concentrations of resources. Hence, governing is never simply a matter of aggregating numbers, whether for redistribution or other purposes. . . .

Of course, the election of key public officials provides a channel of popular expression. Since democracy rests on the principle of equal voting power, it would seem that all groups do share in the capacity to become part of the governing regime. Certainly the vote played a major role in the turnaround of the position of blacks in Atlanta. Popular control, however, is not a simple and straightforward process. Much depends on how the populace is organized to participate in a community's civic life. Machine politics, for example, promotes a search for personal favors. With electoral mobilization dependent upon an organizational network oriented toward patronage and related considerations, other kinds of popular concerns may have difficulty gaining expression.[34] The political machine thus enjoys a type of preemptive power, though the party organization is only one aspect of the overall governing regime.

On the surface, Atlanta represents a situation quite different from machine politics. Nonpartisan elections and an absence of mass patronage have characterized the city throughout the post-World War II era. Yet it would hardly be accurate to describe civic life in Atlanta as open and fluid. Nonpartisanship has heightened the role of organizations connected to business, and the newspapers have held an important position in policy debate. At the same time, working-class organizations and nonprofit groups unsupported by business are not major players in city politics.

Within Atlanta's civic sector, activities serve to piece together concerns across the institutional lines of the community, connecting government with business and each with a variety of nonprofit entities. The downtown elite has been especially adept at building alliances in that sector and, in doing so, has extended its resource advantage well beyond the control of strictly economic functions. Responding to its own weakness in numbers, the business elite has crafted a network through which cooperation can be advanced and potential cleavages between haves and have-nots redirected.

Consider what Atlanta's postwar regime represents. In 1946, the central element in the governing coalition was a downtown business elite organized for and committed to an active program of redevelopment that would transform the character of the business district and, in the process, displace a largely black population to the south and east of the district. At the same time, with the end of the white primary that same year, a middle-class black population, long excluded from power, mobilized its electoral strength to begin an assault on a firmly entrenched Jim Crow system. Knowing only those facts, one might well have predicted in 1946 that these two groups would be political antagonists. They were not. Both committed to an agenda of change, they worked out an accommodation and became the city's governing coalition. The alliance has had its tensions and even temporary ruptures, but it has held and demonstrated remarkable strength in making and carrying out policy decisions.

To understand the process, the Atlanta experience indicates that one must appreciate institutional capacities and the resources that various groups control. That is why simple preference aggregation is no guide to how coalitions are built. The downtown elite and the black middle class had complementary needs that could be met by forming an alliance, and the business elite in particular had the kind and amount of resources to knit the alliance together.

Politics in Atlanta, then, is not organized around an overriding division between haves and have-nots. Instead, unequally distributed resources serve to destabilize opposition and encourage alliances around small opportunities. Without command of a capacity to govern, elected leaders have difficulty building support around popular discontent. That is why Rokkan's phrase, "Votes count but resources decide," is so apt.

UNEQUAL RESOURCES AND URBAN REGIMES

Regimes, I have suggested, are to be understood in terms of (1) who makes up the governing coalition and (2) how the coalition achieves cooperation. Both points illustrate how the unequal distribution of resources affects politics and what differences the formation of a regime makes. That the downtown elite is a central partner in the Atlanta regime shapes the priorities set and the trade-offs made. Hence, investor prerogative is protected practice in Atlanta, under the substantial influence of the business elite *within* the governing coalition. At the same time, the fact that the downtown elite is part of a governing coalition prevents business isolation from community affairs. Yet, although "corporate responsibility" promotes business involvement, it does so in a way that enhances business as patron and promoter of small opportunities.

Similarly, the incorporation of the black middle class into the mainstream civic and economic life of Atlanta is testimony to its ability to use electoral leverage to help set community priorities. The importance of the mode of cooperation is also evident. Although much of what the regime has done has generated popular resistance, the black middle class has been persuaded to go along by a combination of selective incentives and small opportunities. Alliance with the business elite enabled the black middle class to achieve particular objectives not readily available by other means. This kind of enabling capacity is what gives concentrated resources its gravitational force.

The pattern thus represents something more than individual cooptation. The black middle class as a group benefited from new housing areas in the early postwar years and from employment and business opportunities in recent years. Some of the beneficiaries have been institutional—colleges in the Atlanta University system and a financially troubled bank, for example. Because the term "selective incentives" implies individual benefits (and these have been important), the more inclusive term "small opportunities" provides a useful complement. In both cases, the business elite is a primary source; they can make things happen, provide needed assistance, and open up opportunities. At the same time, since the downtown elite needs the cooperation of local government and various community groups, the elite itself is drawn toward a broad community-leadership role. Although its bottom-line economic interests are narrow, its community role can involve it in wider concerns. Selective incentives, however, enable the elite to muffle some of the pressure that might otherwise come from the larger community.

Once we focus on the regime and the importance of informally achieved cooperation, we can appreciate better the complex way in which local politics actually functions. Public-choice economists, fearful that democracy will lead to redistribution, misunderstand the process and treat politics as a causal force operating in isolation from resources other than the vote. That clearly is unwarranted. Atlanta's business elite possesses substantial slack resources that can be and are devoted to policy. Some devotion of resources to political purposes is direct, in the form of campaign funds, but much is indirect; it takes on the character of facilitating civic cooperation of those efforts deemed worthy.

The business elite is small and homogeneous enough to use the norms of class unity and corporate responsibility to maintain its cohesion internally. In interacting with allies, the prevailing mode of operation is reciprocity, reinforced in many cases by years of trust built from past exchanges. The biracial insiders have also been at their tasks long enough to experience a sense of pride in the community role they play. Even so, the coalition is centered around a combination of explicit and tacit deals. Reciprocity is thus the hallmark of Atlanta's regime, and reciprocity hinges on what one actor can do for another. Instead of promoting redistribution toward equality, such a system perpetuates inequality.

Reciprocity, of course, occurs in a context, and in Atlanta, it is interwoven with a complex set of conditions. The slack resources controlled by business corporations give them an extraordinary opportunity to promote civic cooperation. Where there is a compelling mutual interest, as within Atlanta's downtown elite, businesses have the means to solve their own collective-action problem and unite behind a program of action. Their resources also enable them to create a network of cooperation that extends across lines of institutional division, which makes them attractive to public officials and other results-oriented community groups. In becoming an integral part of a system of civic cooperation, Atlanta's business elite has used its resource advantage to shape community policy and protect a privileged position. Because the elite is useful to others, it attracts and holds a variety of allies in its web of reciprocity. The concentration of resources it has gathered thus enables the elite to counter demands for greater equality.

SOCIAL LEARNING VERSUS PRIVILEGE

Instead of understanding democratic politics as an instance of the equality (redistribution)/efficiency (productivity) trade-off, I suggest an alternative. Policy actions (and inactions) have extensive repercussions and involve significant issues that do not fit neatly into an equality-versus-efficiency mold. There is a need, then, for members of the governing coalition to be widely informed about a community's problems, and not to be indifferent about the information. That is what representative democracy is about.

For their part, in order to be productive, business enterprises need a degree of autonomy and a supply of slack resources. It is also appropriate that they participate in politics. However, there are dangers involved in the ability of high-resource groups, like Atlanta's business elite, to secure for themselves a place in the governing coalition and then use that inside position along with their own ample resources to shape the regime on their terms. Elsewhere I have called this "preemptive power,"[35] and have suggested that it enables a group to protect a privileged position. The ability to parcel out selective incentives and other small opportunities permits Atlanta's business elite to enforce discipline on behalf of civic cooperation by vesting others with lesser privileges—privileges perhaps contingently held in return for "going along."

The flip side of discipline through selective incentives is a set of contingent privileges that restrict the questions asked and curtail social learning. Thus, one of the trade-offs in local politics can be phrased as social learning versus privilege. Some degree of privilege for business may be necessary to encourage investment, but the greater the privilege being protected, the less the incentive to understand and act on behalf of the community in its entirety.

The political challenge illustrated by the Atlanta case is how to reconstitute the regime so that both social learning and civic cooperation occur. The risk in the present situation is that those who govern have only a limited comprehension of the consequences of their actions. Steps taken to correct one problem may create or aggravate another while leaving still others unaddressed. Those who govern can discover that only, it seems, through wide representation of the affected groups. Otherwise, choices are limited by an inability to understand the city's full situation.

No governing coalition has an inclination to expand the difficulties of making and carrying out decisions. Still, coalitions can be induced to attempt the difficult. For example, Atlanta's regime has been centrally involved in race relations, perhaps the community's most difficult and volatile issue. Relationships within the governing coalition have been fraught with tension; friction was unavoidable. Yet the coalition achieved a cooperative working relationship between the black middle class and the white business elite. In a rare but telling incident, black leaders insisted successfully that a 1971 pledge to build a MARTA spur to a black public-housing area not be repudiated. The newspaper opined that trust within the coalition was too important to be sacrificed on the altar of economizing. Thus the task of the governing regime was expanded beyond the narrow issue of serving downtown in the least expensive manner possible; concerns *can* be broadened.

Although no regime is likely to be totally inclusive, most regimes can be made more inclusive. Just as Atlanta's regime was drawn into dealing with race relations, others can become sensitive to the situations of a larger set of groups. Greater inclusiveness will not come automatically nor from the vote alone. Pressures to narrow the governing coalition are strong and recurring. Yet, if civic cooperation is the key to the terms on which economic and electoral power are accommodated, then more inclusive urban regimes can be encouraged through an associational life at the community level that reflects a broad range of perspectives. The problem is not an absence of associational life at that level but how to lessen its dependence on business sponsorship, how to free participation in civic activity from an overriding concern with protecting insider privileges, and how to enrich associational life so that non-profit and other groups can function together as they express encompassing community concerns.

This step is one in which federal policy could make a fundamental difference. In the past, starting with the urban-redevelopment provision in the 1949 housing act and continuing through the Carter administration's UDAG program, cities have been strongly encouraged to devise partnerships with private, for-profit developers, thus intensifying already strong leanings in that direction. Since these were matters of legislative choice, it seems fully possible for the federal government to move in another direction and encourage nonprofit organizations. The federal government could, for example, establish a program of large-scale assistance to community development corporations and other nonprofit groups. Some foundations now support such programs, but their modest efforts could be augmented. Programs of community service required by high schools and colleges or spawned by a national-level service requirement could increase voluntary participation and alter the character of civic life in local communities. It is noteworthy that neighborhood mobilization in Atlanta was partly initiated by VISTA (Volunteers in Service to America) workers in the 1960s and continued by those who stayed in the city after completing service with VISTA. This, however, is not the place to prescribe a full set of remedies; my aim is only to indicate that change is possible but will probably require a stimulus external to the local community.

SUMMING UP

If the slack resources of business help to set the terms on which urban governance occurs, then we need to be aware of what this imbalance means. The Atlanta case suggests that the more uneven the distribution of resources, the greater the tendency of the regime to become concerned with protecting privilege. Concurrently, there is a narrowing of the regime's willingness to engage in "information seeking" (or social learning). Imbalances in the civic sector thus lead to biases in policy, biases that electoral politics alone is unable to correct.

A genuinely effective regime is not only adept at promoting cooperation in the execution of complex and nonroutine projects, but is also able to comprehend the consequences of its actions and inactions for a diverse citizenry. The promotion of this broad comprehension is, after all, a major aim of democracy. Even if democratic politics were removed from the complexities of coordination for social production, it still could not be reduced to a set of decision rules. Arrow's theorem shows that majority choices cannot be neutrally aggregated when preference structures are complex,[36] as indeed they are bound to be in modern societies.

Democracy, then, is not simply a decision rule for registering choices; it has to operate with a commitment to inclusiveness. Permanent or excluded minorities are inconsistent with the basic idea of equality that underpins democracy. That is why some notion of social learning is an essential part of the democratic process; all are entitled to have their situations understood. Thus, to the extent that urban regimes safeguard special privileges at the expense of social learning, democracy is weakened.

Those fearful that too much community participation will lead to unproductive policies should widen their own understanding and consider other dangers on the political landscape. Particularly under conditions of an imbalance in civically useful resources, the political challenge is one of preventing government from being harnessed to the protection of special privilege. The social-production model reminds us that only a segment of society's institutions are under the sway of majority rule; hence, actual governance is never simply a matter of registering the preferences of citizens as individuals.

The character of local politics depends greatly on the nature of a community's associational life, which in turn depends greatly on the distribution of resources other than the vote. Of course, the vote is significant, but equality in the right to vote is an inadequate guarantee against the diversion of politics into the protection of privilege. If broad social learning is to occur, then other considerations must enter the picture. "One person, one vote" is not enough.

NOTES

1. James G. March, "The Business Firm as a Political Coalition," *Journal of Politics* 24 (November 1962): 662–678.
2. Chester I. Barnard, *The Functions of the Executive* (Cambridge, Mass.: Harvard University Press, 1968).
3. Oliver E. Williamson, *The Economic Institutions of Capitalism* (New York: Free Press, 1985).
4. Ibid., 10.
5. See Norton E. Long, "The Local Community as an Ecology of Games," *American Journal of Sociology* 64 (November 1958): 251–261.
6. Cf. Graham T. Allison, *Essence of Decision* (Boston: Little, Brown, 1971).
7. See Philip Selznick, *Leadership in Administration* (New York: Harper & Row, 1957).
8. Cf. Bryan D. Jones and Lynn W. Bachelor, *The Sustaining Hand* (Lawrence: University of Kansas Press, 1986).
9. See especially Martin Shefter, "The Emergence of the Political Machine: An Alternative View," in *Theoretical Perspectives on Urban Politics*, by Willis D. Hawley and others (Englewood Cliffs, N.J.: Prentice-Hall, 1976).

10. Clarence N. Stone, Robert K. Whelan, and William J. Murin. *Urban Policy and Politics in a Bureaucratic Age*, 2d ed. (Englewood Cliffs, N.J.: Prentice-Hall, 1986, 104).
11. Stephen L. Elkin, *City and Regime in the American Republic* (Chicago: University of Chicago Press, 1987).
12. Ibid.
13. Cf. Jones and Bachelor, *The Sustaining Hand*, 214–215.
14. But see Elkin, *City and Regime*; Martin Shefter, *Political Crisis/Fiscal Crisis: The Collapse and Revival of New York City* (New York: Basic Books, 1985); and Todd Swanstrom, *The Crisis of Growth Politics* (Philadelphia: Temple University Press, 1985).
15. Robert H. Wiebe, *The Search for Order, 1877–1920* (New York: Hill and Wang, 1967), 10.
16. Russell Hardin, *Collective Action* (Baltimore: Johns Hopkins University Press, 1982); and Michael Taylor, *The Possibility of Cooperation* (Cambridge, Mass.: Cambridge University Press, 1987).
17. Mancur Olson, Jr., *The Logic of Collective Action* (Cambridge, Mass.: Harvard University Press, 1965).
18. Hardin, *Collective Action*.
19. Robert Axelrod, *The Evolution of Cooperation* (New York: Basic Books, 1984).
20. Hardin, *Collective Action*; and David D. Laitin, *Hegemony and Culture* (Chicago: University of Chicago Press, 1986).
21. Taylor, *Possibility of Cooperation*.
22. Charles Tilly, *Big Structures, Large Processes, Huge Comparisons* (New York: Russell Sage Foundation, 1984), 27.
23. Philip Abrams, *Historical Sociology* (Ithaca, N.Y.: Cornell University Press, 1982). For a similar understanding applied to urban politics, see John R. Logan and Harvey L. Molotch, *Urban Fortunes* (Berkeley and Los Angeles: University of California Press, 1987).
24. Cf. Anthony Giddens, *Central Problems in Social Theory* (Berkeley and Los Angeles: University of California Press, 1979).
25. Cf. James G. March and Johan P. Olsen, "The New Institutionalism," *American Political Science Review* 78 (September 1984): 734–749.
26. Abrams, *Historical Sociology*, 331.
27. Ibid.
28. Michael L. Porter, "Black Atlanta: An Interdisciplinary Study of Blacks on the East Side of Atlanta, 1890–1930" (Ph.D. diss., Emory University, 1974); Walter White, *A Man Called White* (New York: Arno Press and the New York Times, 1969); and Dana F. White, "The Black Sides of Atlanta," *Atlanta Historical Journal* 26 (Summer/Fall 1982): 199–225.
29. Kenneth T. Jackson, *The Ku Klux Klan in the City 1915–1930* (New York: Oxford University Press, 1967); and Herbert T. Jenkins, *Forty Years on the Force: 1932–1972* (Atlanta: Center for Research in Social Change, Emory University, 1973).
30. Charles H. Martin, *The Angelo Herndon Case and Southern Justice* (Baton Rouge: Louisiana State University Press, 1976); Kenneth Coleman, ed., *A History of Georgia* (Athens: University of Georgia Press, 1977), 294; and Writer's Program of the Works Progress Administration, *Atlanta: A City of the Modern South* (St. Clairshores, Mich.: Somerset Publishers, 1973), 69.
31. Lorraine N. Spritzer, *The Belle of Ashby Street: Helen Douglas Mankin and Georgia Politics* (Athens: University of Georgia Press, 1982).
32. John Bonner, *Introduction to the Theory of Social Choice* (Baltimore: Johns Hopkins University Press, 1986), 34.
33. Stein Rokkan, "Norway: Numerical Democracy and Corporate Pluralism," in *Political Oppositions in Western Democracies*, ed. Robert A. Dahl (New Haven, Conn.: Yale University Press, 1966), 105; see also [Steven Erie, *Rainbow's End: Irish-Americans and the Dilemmas of Urban Machine Politics, 1840–1985* (Berkeley: University of California Press, 1988)].
34. Matthew A. Crenson, *The Un-Politics of Air Pollution* (Baltimore: Johns Hopkins University Press, 1971); see also Edwin H. Rhyne, "Political Parties and Decision Making in Three Southern Counties," *American Political Science Review* 52 (December 1958): 1091–1107.
35. Clarence N. Stone, "Preemptive Power: Floyd Hunter's 'Community Power Structure' Reconsidered," *American Journal of Political Science* 32 (February 1988): 82–104.
36. Norman Frohlich and Joe A. Oppenheimer, *Modern Political Economy* (Englewood Cliffs, N.J.: Prentice-Hall, 1978), 19–31.

3

The Regime Moment: The Brief but Storied Career of Urban Regimes in American Cities

DENNIS R. JUDD AND DAVID LASLO

THE REGIME MOMENT

Two intertwined themes compose the official story of America's postwar urban experience. The first has assumed the status of a national passion play, its themes rehearsed in a vast popular and scholarly literature: the descent of the inner cities into physical decay and racial turmoil in the years after World War II.[1] The second theme informs a compelling account of the indefatigable efforts of political leaders and civic elites to save inner-city downtown and neighborhoods.[2] By now the recovery of most central cities has become sufficiently secure that both narratives can be read as established history.

To rise to the challenge of urban revitalization in the postwar period, civic elites were forced to solve the defining problem of every political system: find ways to cooperate on behalf of shared objectives.[3] The task of achieving cooperation is difficult to accomplish in American cities because the scope of local governmental authority is extremely limited, public authority is institutionally fragmented, and most resources required for major undertakings are located in the private, not the public sectors. In his landmark book, *Regime Politics*, Clarence Stone describes how civic elites in Atlanta overcame these obstacles to build a foundation for enduring cooperation. Stone traces the history of Atlanta's governance over a 42-year period stretching from 1946 to 1988.[4] For most of this period Atlanta's civic elites were able to sustain an effort to make Atlanta into the leading regional city of the South. It did so by transforming the physical environment of the downtown, providing support for the construction of an airport and a modern rapid transit system, engineering an urban renewal and housing program, desegregating the city's police departments and schools, and solving many other pressing problems.

Stone called Atlanta's civic coalition a "regime," a term meant to suggest that urban power emerged "not from the formal machinery of government, but rather the informal partnership between city hall and the downtown business elite."[5] In Atlanta, the City Hall—business alliance endured for decades because the partners managed to find a means to "promote enough cooperation and coordination for the diverse participants to reach decisions and sustain action in support of those decisions."[6] From Stone's study many scholars assumed that when a consistent pattern of civic cooperation endured over time, a regime was probably in place. Because the "regime" metaphor seemed to be an elegant way to describe the public-private coalitions so common in American cities, it quickly became the dominant paradigm in the scholarly literature on urban power, and it still has not been challenged by any alternative theory of urban power.

From a paper prepared for presentation at the 2010 Annual Conference of the Urban Affairs Association, Honolulu, Hawaii, March 10–12, 2010.

With some trepidation, therefore, we argue here that it is time to regard the concept of the urban regime, as proposed by Stone, as a historically important but now mostly defunct mode of governance in American cities. We were led to this conclusion when we conducted a case study of coalitional power in St. Louis, Missouri, from 1952 to 1996. For more than half a century St. Louis's civic elites were able to mobilize significant resources to address the problems of the downtown. Between 1965 and 2006 almost $1.5 billion of public and private capital was devoted to the task of building an infrastructure to support tourism and entertainment.[7] In less than half a century, public efforts and resources were instrumental in funding four sports facilities, a convention center (twice expanded), a convention hotel, two malls, and a waterfront entertainment district. Looming over all of the downtown is the signature symbol of St. Louis, the Gateway Arch, which was opened in 1967 after thirty years of political maneuvering to secure federal funds.

This cluster of projects helped to preserve the downtown, though just barely, until a critical mass of privately financed development began to appear in the late 1990s. By mid-2006 most of the historic warehouses and garment and shoe factories along Washington Avenue on the north edge of the downtown, where the convention center, convention hotel, and domed stadium are located, were in the process of being converted into housing, retail, and office space. With the opening of a handful of nightclubs and restaurants, on weekends it began to show fitful signs of a street life. A new stadium for the baseball Cardinals, opened in 2006, anchors the southern end of the downtown, and there are plans to construct an "urban village" close by the stadium. Population growth in and near the central business district is an important component of what appears to be an historic turning point. Since the census of 2000, for the first time in decades, the city actually gained population.[8]

In constructing our case study of this half century of activity we attempted to apply Stone's definition of an urban regime to explain the city's ability to mobilize resources, but it was like trying to fit square blocks into round holes. The problem was that in St. Louis a City Hall—business coalition like Atlanta's lasted for only a brief period, from the early 1950s to the mid-1960s,[9] and it fell apart during the troubled decade of the civil rights movement and civil disorders of the 1960s, and it never again emerged. This might have led us to conclude that St. Louis is an unusual case, but our review of the urban literature led us to conclude that its experience follows an historical arc that may be more typical than Atlanta's. We believe that most urban regimes, where they existed, died decades ago. Like the party machines a century ago, urban regimes continue to have historical significance, but few, if any, have managed to survive into the present era.

ST. LOUIS'S REGIME: 1952–1965

Several factors guaranteed that St. Louis would take a long and winding road to recovery, no matter how many resources might be brought to the task. The city's slide began in earnest in the 1930s, prompting *Forum* magazine to publish an article in 1939 commenting on "the desolation and desertion characterizing scores of blocks in the business district."[10] By the 1950s, the wasting disease that infected the downtown seemed to be spreading inexorably into the neighborhoods; "No new office building had been erected downtown in two decades, traffic in the central business district was a nerve-shattering mess, and half the city was blighted."[11] The same rot could be found in all the cities of the industrial belt, but St. Louis's situation seemed to be especially dire.

To combat the decline of the downtown and surrounding areas, a powerful civic coalition composed of an informal but powerful partnership between St. Louis's mayor and civic leaders came together in the years after World War II. In 1950, when St. Louis was selected as the first city in the nation to receive urban renewal funds, Mayor Joseph M. Darst began assembling a coalition to carry the program forward. As recalled by his successor, Raymond Tucker, "About a year ago, a group of distinguished citizens of our community were called into the Mayor's office and there charged by Mayor Darst with the responsibility of giving leadership to a program to take advantage of the Housing Act of 1949. . . many fine business institutions, sixty-nine in number, subscribed to a total in excess of $2,000,000 toward the capital structure of the [redevelopment] corporation."[12] Soon thereafter the Missouri state legislature created the Land Clearance for Redevelopment Authority of St. Louis, the agency charged with administering the urban renewal program.

The massive volume of funds that flowed through the agency altered politics-as-usual by centralizing resources and political authority in the mayor's office and in the broad civic alliance he enlisted to support urban renewal. Its five-member board was appointed by the mayor, and it presided over a program audacious in scope. With $28 million and more to come, it began to clear a 454-acre tract of land just to the west of downtown. The city government continued to operate in its usual fashion, with the aldermen dividing the jobs and the funds made available from the city's own resources, but urban renewal had become the biggest game in town.

Mayor Darst had an even more ambitious remaking of the local power structure in mind when he called together eight of the most powerful businessmen in the city and asked them to form a civic organization to provide more effective leadership in St. Louis. Within a few months the eight civic notables chartered Civic Progress, Inc. Initially, Darst wanted the group to help campaign for a bond issue to finance public improvements and the city's share of urban renewal; he also hoped business leaders would help the city out of its chronic budget woes by supporting a city earnings tax. Over the years Civic Progress worked with Mayor Tucker, who replaced Darst in 1953, by helping to campaign for a $110 billion bond issue, a city earnings tax, a gas tax increase, public school reform, a locally financed downtown redevelopment project, a new downtown sports stadium, and other initiatives. All through this period, the relationship between City Hall and Civic Progress remained close. Soon after assuming office, when Mayor Tucker asked the members of Civic Progress to expand the group by ten members, they agreed to do so. By combining the broad urban renewal alliance with the resources of Civic Progress, Tucker was able to create, in effect, a "mayor's party" that allowed him to bypass the patronage politics that had long defined power in the city.[13]

Throughout the urban renewal era, at a time when two mayors exerted forceful leadership, the collaboration needed to produce the capacity for aggressive action took the form of a stable coalition between two partners, City Hall and the corporate elite. A symmetrical relationship formed around mutual interests made it possible to for the partners to cooperate in defining an agenda of action much more sweeping than the particular undertakings that engaged them. The participants were able to build an impressive capacity to realize their goals because they were able to skillfully use federal urban renewal funds, increase the fiscal resources of city government, and mobilize private contributions on behalf of downtown renewal.

Even when racial turmoil and civil rights protests became the dominant issues in the early 1960s, the alliance held. In 1964, Civic Progress provided financing for an inner-city program called Youth Opportunities Unlimited, to motivate high school dropouts to continue with their education and to learn work skills.[14] A year later, Tucker worked with corporate leaders to establish a race relations committee called the Dialogue Committee, which was comprised of some Civic Progress members and members of the African-American business community.[15] But St. Louis's version of an urban regime turned out to have a fatal weakness because, unlike the alliance in Atlanta, there was no institutional mechanism for keeping the City Hall—business coalition intact through a series of mayoral elections and public controversies. Civic Progress could not act as such an institution because it closely guarded its independence. Mayors did not automatically have a place at the table. Tucker's personality and his long-standing relationship with the members of Civic Progress is the only reason the alliance held together as long as it did. In 1965, when he left office, St. Louis's version of a regime fell apart.

THE ERA OF CORPORATE-CENTERED GOVERNANCE: 1966–1992

When the City Hall-Civic Progress collaboration worked out in the urban renewal era disintegrated, it was replaced by a corporate-centered politics that cast the mayor in a definitively dependent role. Civic Progress remained highly interested in the fate of the downtown, but its relationship with the mayor's office changed fundamentally. By the mid-1960s the city's politics became focused on racial issues, which were generally expressed in a contentious tug of war between white politicians from south-side wards and black politicians from the northern half of the city. Tucker had been a professor at Washington University, but henceforth most mayors would come into office by the route of ward-based politics, a fact that "removed the notion of a separate 'mayor's party' from St. Louis's political lexicon."[16]

Henceforth, the center of gravity moved decisively to the corporate elite, in large part because the centrifugal forces of St. Louis's political system exerted a pull too powerful to resist. St. Louis's mayors could not and did not want to head a "mayor's party" they could use as a counterbalance to the fragmented politics of the municipal government. While the mayor worked in his sphere, Civic Progress pursued its aims on a project-by-project basis; the mayor's support would be recruited as needed. Oppositely, mayors who wished to push their own programs were obliged to enlist Civic Progress's participation, but the relationship was hardly symmetrical. The episodic method of cooperation produced resources for downtown renewal, but on a much diminished scale compared to the past.

A. J. Cervantes, who took office in April 1965, maintained good connections to ward politicians on both the north and south side. He owned an insurance agency and taxicab company, and was perceived by corporate leaders to be "in a very different league."[17] Though he considered neighborhood preservation his highest priority, he undertook a couple of high-profile projects in the downtown. The abject and much-publicized failure of both of them loomed all the larger because they appeared to be pet projects he dreamed up without first securing political support. With the help of a handful of wealthy investors he bought the Spanish Pavilion, designed by Spanish architect Javier Carvajal for the 1965 World's Fair in New York, and had it installed downtown. He thought it was a dramatic way to celebrate the Spanish heritage of the city, "but once it was in place, no one knew what to do with it,"[18] in large part because no one recalled the long vanished Spanish presence. It closed within a year. His other venture came to a less mundane but spectacular end: a few days after his latest purchase, a replica of Columbus's ship the *Santa Maria* arrived at the riverfront and within days sank during a violent storm. Many people in St. Louis interpreted this accident as a tragicomic comment on the state of the downtown and the leadership at the helm of the local state.

In 1973 Cervantes was defeated in his run for a third term by John Poelker, who had served four terms as the city comptroller and was not much connected to ward politics. Some members of Civic Progress gave contributions so that he could unseat Cervantes but this support did not necessarily signal that they would close ranks with City Hall once a new incumbent was installed. Poelker was invited to meetings of Civic Progress regularly and asked for the organization's support on a variety of civic matters, but he was clearly dependent upon their good graces.[19] His successor, James Conway, who came into office in 1977, appeared to be even less bonded with Civic Progress, saying in his run for office in 1977, "these guys aren't exactly my crowd."[20]

When Vincent Schoemehl replaced Conway in 1983, he formed a closer relationship with Civic Progress than any mayor since Tucker. Just thirty-four years old when inaugurated, he aggressively pushed new programs for the downtown and for the neighborhoods. Even so, he was able to forge a less than symmetrical relationship with Civic Progress. Schoemehl was aware that the corporate leaders commanded the resources he needed to pursue his most ambitious plans. He sought the support of Civic Progress one project at a time because they preferred initiatives that could be individually reviewed and that entailed a "relatively brief commitment."[21] This type of relationship caused dismay among some of the aldermen and other public officials, including Comptroller Virvus Jones, who complained, "we're in a position where we don't do anything without their approval."[22]

The impression that Civic Progress controlled the municipal agenda was given some credence when Schoemehl's economic development director, Christopher Grace, observed that Civic Progress "performs essentially a government function."[23] According to evidence gathered by the *St. Louis Post Dispatch*, there had been many instances when the Board of Aldermen began to discuss an issue, only to learn it had already been decided by Civic Progress.[24]

The era of corporate governance became publically obvious in 1992, when a few Civic Progress members became embroiled in a bitter public controversy over a deal they had struck with the city for public subsidies to help support the demolition of the Kiel Auditorium, constructed in 1934, so that a new sports facility for the St. Louis hockey Blues could be built on the site. Much of the passion driving the dispute was energized by widespread resentments directed at the mysterious secret society that seemed to run St. Louis. Stung by criticisms that they were profiting at the public's expense, the corporate executives of Civic Progress withdrew from their high-profile status as the city's powerbrokers, although they have continued to play a pivotal but less public role in St. Louis politics. The vacuum created by the retreat of Civic Progress was filled by a complex and constantly changing ecology of governance composed of many players.

THE NEW ECOLOGY OF GOVERNANCE

The Kiel controversy accelerated a process that was beginning to unfold any-way. In 1997, the roster of Civic Progress members changed substantially due to retirements and corporate mergers and acquisitions that impacted many long-time members of the group.[25] In fact, the group had already been chang-ing; even in the early 1990s over half its members were not native St. Lou-isans.[26] Reflecting the complexion of its new membership, Civic Progress took steps to overcome the impression that it was a secret society. As a symbolic step, it no longer held its breakfast meetings at the members-only Bogey Club.

Until the 1990s it is doubtful that Civic Progress could have redefined its role in community affairs without creating a serious power vacuum. The disorganization of city government would have decisively gridlocked most ini-tiatives. By then, however, other players had come onto the stage, thereby ushering in a new governance arrangement sufficient for overcoming the city's fractured institutional structure. Mid-level and small business owners began to assert themselves. Perhaps of more consequence, independent quasi-public authorities took on an increasing share of responsibility for the financing and administration of downtown projects. In 1984 the Convention and Visitors Commission assumed the task of running the Cervantes Convention Center; in 1989 it handed off administrative tasks to the St. Louis Convention and Sports Authority and shifted its focus primarily to city marketing. The St. Louis Development Corporation was brought into being under state legislation to coordinate the activities of eight authorities involved in economic devel-opment-related activities. The authority strategy had significant advantages because these institutions were able to generate their own resources, develop leadership and professional capabilities, and act with a speed and agility not available to general-purpose governments or to corporate elites.

Flexibility was needed because the mix of participants and the relationships among them had become much more complex than in the past. Depending upon the issue at hand, leadership might come from the mayor, a diverse array of busi-ness leaders, or from professional policy entrepreneurs. Very significant resources could be mobilized for particular projects—sometimes, in fact, on a scale prob-ably larger than in the Civic Progress period. Political support and financing for a domed stadium to host the Rams football team, for example, pooled the resources of many players including, notably, participants from outside the city.

These developments have led to the emergence of a governance triad involv-ing the mayor, the business leadership, and a cadre of professional policy entre-preneurs. Mayoral leadership, or at least acquiescence, continued to be essential for major public initiatives. Although it now operates behind the scenes more than in the past, Civic Progress continues to offer financial support for par-ticular projects, and the other business organizations are closely involved in promotional efforts for the region and the downtown. Special-purpose authori-ties constitute the third leg of the triangle. Major projects can be undertaken without such mechanisms (for example, the new stadium to house the Cardinals baseball team, which opened in 2006, was built by the Cardinals' owners, with indirect financial help from the city). But it is likely that most major undertak-ings will, as time goes by, be financed and administered through specialized institutional mechanisms established specifically for the purpose.

What allows institutions like the Convention and Sports Authority to become partners in governance is that once created they are able to generate ideas, resources, and political presence. The managers of the convention center, for example, work with an array of consultants and industry associations in the meetings industry who supply specialized development, financial, public relations, marketing, and information expertise. Engineering and architectural services are often provided by a handful of national firms. National public relations firms are also often hired to manage promotional campaigns, advise on everything from concept to tax approval campaign to construction. Likewise, national public accounting and public finance consulting firms with specialties in project finance and cost-benefit analysis provide the principal justifications for individual projects, and they justify public subsidies through feasibility and impact analyses. Included in these reports are data and information that is gathered and compiled by industry associations. In turn, accounting and bond-rating firms rely on industry-generated data and reports from consultants. Political support for new initiatives is sought from the mayor and other constituencies on a need-be basis.

By establishing a political presence in these ways, special authorities have become essential components of a complex ecology of local governance that involves City Hall, business, and policy entrepreneurs in a shifting and quite mutable system of power. The center of gravity in this system is in flux, depending upon the particular issue at hand and the relative strength of the participants at any given time. If the issue involves a plan to expand the convention center, the Convention Center Authority generates most of the information and attempts to enlist others in the cause. If City Hall floats an idea dear to the mayor, the center of gravity may shift, on that issue, towards city government. And, finally, if the initiative comes from business, some or all of the other players may need to come on board, but they may hold a veto power, but nothing more.

IS ST. LOUIS TYPICAL, OR EXCEPTIONAL?

There are reasons to believe that the governance strategies in St. Louis have been shaped primarily by a uniquely fragmented governmental structure and divided political culture; if this is so, they may not have necessarily evolved in any other city. This view is entirely logical: every city has a unique history that reflects the composition of its economy, its political structures, and its political traditions and cultures. From this "local autonomy" perspective, the political leaders and civic elites in a city may chart a path shaped mainly by the contours of local politics. However, a review of the literature on urban power leads us to believe that the three power arrangements we found in St. Louis experience have cropped up in other cities. Though the timing may vary, it appears to us that the St. Louis experience may be more typical than exceptional.

The Urban Regimes

It should be noted that the powerful City Hall-business alliance that emerged in St. Louis in the 1950s was a power arrangement that came into being almost everywhere. The passage of the 1949 Housing Act, which funded federally-sponsored urban renewal, catalyzed the formation of executive-centered coalitions in every city that participated in the program.[27] The rise of these tight-knit public-private alliances ushered in a "new convergence of power" that dominated the politics of most large cities.[28] The Allegheny Conference on Community Development, formed in 1943 under the leadership of R.K. Mellon, promoted the revitalization of Pittsburgh's Golden Triangle. It became the template for the New Boston Committee, founded in 1951, the Greater Baltimore Committee, 1955, Civic Progress, 1953, Central Atlanta Progress, 1961, and numerous similar organizations.

By the end of the 1950s, virtually every city in the United States had formed an urban renewal coalition sufficiently powerful that it could remake the urban landscape. Richard J. Daley, first elected mayor of Chicago in 1955, rebuilt the Democratic machine in that city by aggressively launching an effort to revitalize the downtown Loop and lakefront. Richard Lee in New Haven, Connecticut, won the 1952 mayoral election and several terms thereafter by putting together a civic alliance that used urban renewal to wipe out huge areas of the downtown and nearby ethnic neighborhoods.[29] In Atlanta, Mayor William Hartsfield, who was initially lukewarm about big clearance projects, reversed field when he perceived that he could build his political career by cooperating with the desire of downtown businesses to demolish black neighborhoods located close to the central business district.[30] The urban renewal effort built the foundation for Atlanta's regime. In San Francisco, mayors worked with corporate giants and downtown businesses to clear valuable parcels in the market area east and south of the financial district.[31] The aggressive tactics of the civic alliances built to accomplish such purposes were replicated in so many cities that, by the 1960s, the urban renewal program had provoked a national rebellion of civil rights and neighborhood groups.[32] The mobilization of protest against clearance from renewal and highway building eventually destabilized the authority of the mayors who had made their reputations by coordinating the civic coalitions that presided over urban renewal.

Leadership styles changed, but these changes were mediated as much by the contours of local politics as by external pressures: the composition of the local economy, political structures, political traditions, and cultures. Local political leaders and civic elites identified new opportunities and charted their own paths. Mayor John V. Lindsey built his career in New York by taking credit for the flow of new social programs into his city. Mayor Daley in Chicago used the programs to extend his control of jobs and contracts. But in many, perhaps most, cities, mayors lost, at least in relative terms. On the whole the Great Society programs weakened mayoral authority by stimulating new institutions and organizations within the cities. As Frances Fox Piven and Richard A. Cloward have observed, one of the basic aims of the Great Society programs was to establish a direct link between the national government and its inner-city electoral constituency.[33] The main purpose of these programs was fulfilled: black civil rights activists and leaders of organizations were brought into local political systems, and the old political alliances were undercut. The new generation of black mayors that emerged from this process generally found that they had to establish a relationship with the business elite, but the alliance tended to be uneasy on both sides, and it differed from city to city because of the vast gap between the mayor's electoral coalition and the governing coalition.[34]

A Corporate-Centered Politics

In the absence of strong mayoral leadership and in the presence of a contentious electoral politics, corporate elites that wished to carry on the cause of downtown revitalization were forced to find alternatives, just as business leaders had learned to work outside the confines of electoral politics in the heyday of the party machines almost a century before. A study conducted by the Urban Institute indicates that this kind of corporate-centered politics became the norm in many cities. The size of the business groups that presided over downtown agendas varied from fewer than fifty members to as many as two hundred, but even in the larger and more inclusive of them, an executive committee made up of the CEOs of large corporations made the important decisions and operated behind closed doors.[35] For example, in 1982 some "leading business titans" organized Cleveland Tomorrow because they "preferred gatherings among peers in a boardroom, receiving a quick briefing by a colleague or a senior staff officer, and reaching a quick consensus on what to do."[36]

Some of the "messiah mayors" that emerged in the late 1970s and the 1980s were able to reestablish the strong leadership position of City Hall in crafting the municipal agenda. The close cooperation between City Hall and business leadership look a lot like the urban regime in Atlanta that Stone wrote about. With central-city economies in tatters and downtown business districts and neighborhoods in danger of sliding into irreversible decline, these mayors preached a vision of a revitalized city, and managed to assemble an alliance between government officials and business leaders to back the cause. By pursuing policies of fiscal austerity, by giving generous tax breaks and a variety of subsidies, and by forming public-private relationships that privatized urban redevelopment, these mayors stimulated a remarkable period of dramatic urban regeneration not seen since the urban renewal era. Renovated waterfronts, office-tower construction, atrium hotels, festival malls, convention centers, and other facilities defined the essence of a corporate-centered downtown development guided by strong mayoral leadership.[37]

The lesson we draw from this mixed record is that the St. Louis and Atlanta cases are likely to be equally accurate and misleading, depending on the perspective one adopts, and depending upon how far the regime concept is stretched. Regime analysis has suffered from "concept stretching," a process that occurs when the original definition is changed in an attempt to apply it to a variety of contexts.[38] Mossberger and Stoker attribute this problem, in part, to the "softness" of the regime model, but also to the proclivity of scholars to bend the concept to suit their own purposes. They argue that "[B]ecause regime research requires case study methodology, some consistency in conceptualization is needed to be able to compare or to integrate the finding of case studies conducted across a variety of cities."[39] Since the absence of any consistent definition is a defining characteristic of the literature on urban power (we will say more about this later), we doubt that the concept can provide a useful guide for understanding the transitional period after the mid-1960s. It may be enough to conclude that corporate elites remained in charge of the development agenda, whether or not they could find an active partner in the mayor's office.

Globalization and the New Ecology of Governance

In St. Louis, corporate-centered politics came to an end in the 1990s, as did any prospect that even the most activist mayor could forge a collaborative relationship with corporate leaders. The processes that precipitated this sea change in St. Louis were also at work everywhere. Sometime in the 1980s, the globalization of local economies began to reduce the civic engagement of corporate elites. As summarized by Royce Hanson and his collaborators, in several cities,

> . . . waves of mergers and acquisitions transformed local corporate headquarters, converting icons of local industry into mere branches of distant firms. Executive suites were populated with a new generation of managers, many of whom had no local roots and were on career trajectories that involved frequent transfers to branches in other cities. . . . The combination of these forces led to changes in the nature of civic engagement by business leaders,

their commitment to city and region, and the membership and structure of many of their organizations.[40]

These developments ushered in revolutionary changes that have reshaped local politics in the United States. For nearly half a century, efforts to revitalize the central cities required a high level of interest in local affairs not only by mayors and other public officials but also, especially, by corporate elites. By the 1990s, however, civic leadership had become broader, and less focused, than in the past. The fastest-growth sectors of the global economy often are dominated by smaller businesses and high-tech enterprises that work closely with universities, hospitals, and nonprofit organizations. New organizations have come into being to represent these interests; in response, CEO-led organizations inherited from the past have accordingly expanded their membership. It should also be noted that in many cities, non-profit organizations have become important sources of civic leadership.

A second transformation wrought by globalization involves the restructuring of the local state. In the past, municipal government was the primary source of public leadership and public fiscal resources. In recent decades, independent, quasi-public authorities have assumed most of the responsibility for urban development projects, and in the process they have become components of an increasingly complex local state.[41] Within all large urban regions, special authorities have taken responsibility for transportation infrastructure such as highways, roads, bridges, tunnels, mass transit, airports, seaports, and harbors. In addition to the regional activities such as these, special authorities by the dozen finance and manage tourism and entertainment facilities such as convention centers, sports stadiums, museums, and urban entertainment districts. The professional staffs and policy entrepreneurs located in institutions such as these now supply many of the critical entrepreneurial energies and fiscal resources required for major policy initiatives.

In addition, the new generation of special-purpose authorities is not strictly local—they are both local and global. They interact with municipalities and with one another, but also forge linkages with non-local interests, and these linkages are often crucial to their political autonomy and muscle. The politics surrounding convention centers illustrates this point. The staffs of convention centers are closely tied with and identify with the vast meetings industry, and they turn to this industry for information and support when pushing for expanded or new facilities. Consultants' studies are the necessary prelude to bond issuances and tax referenda (where these are necessary). Consulting reports establish an asymmetry of information that gives proponents a monopoly over information, so that opponents appear to be uninformed and biased. More generally, the reports also form the basis of a standard narrative of urban decline and growth that ties the construction or expansion of a convention facility to the future prospects and the image of the city.

The construction of sports stadiums exemplifies this new politics. Special authorities established to promote stadiums have learned to be adept in building political support for new stadiums financed through public subsidies. Because teams sometimes move, or can threaten to, sports cartels and team owners find it easy to persuade cities to meet their demands. Mayors continue to hold a pivotal position, and sometimes may take the lead in public relations campaigns, but they are entirely dependent upon bureaucracies and organizations for even the most basic information. The asymmetry in the relationship is preserved by the sprawling institutional structure that characterizes local politics in the global era.

REGIMES ARE DEAD, LONG LIVE REGIMES

We found the regime concept useful for analyzing decision making in St. Louis for only a brief period of time. Obviously, one might argue that we have used the concept too narrowly. Stone argued that there were probably several regime types, and that the concept is flexible enough to describe a variety of governing arrangements. Stretching the concept in this way would follow in a long tradition established almost as soon as Clarence Stone published *Regime Politics*. As noted by Stoker, "Regime is a label that scholars have used for different purposes."[42] In a similar vein, Davies has observed that regime studies have not employed a consistent conceptual framework.[43] Authors frequently use the word *regimes* merely as a synonym for governance or as a way of referring to political coalitions of all kinds.[44]

In a more perfect world the concept of regimes would have been employed in a consistent manner, but the elasticity of the concept made this more or less impossible. Because urban scholars have yet to discover an alternative metaphor for power in the city, the temptation to stretch regimes to cover almost everything is almost irresistible. Mossberger and Stoker observed that "regimes cannot be assumed to exist in all cities."[45] But if they do not, what does? Nature abhors a vacuum, and theory does as well. Regimes may be dead, but they live on because there have been no other pretenders to the throne.

NOTES

1. The most complete account of this narrative can be found in Robert A. Beauregard, *Voices of Decline: The Postwar Fate of U.S. Cities* (Cambridge, MA: Blackwell, 1993).
2. The outlines of this story can be found in Bernard J. Frieden and Lynn B. Sagalyn, *Downtown Inc.: How America Builds Cities* (Cambridge, MA: MIT Press, 1989), and Jon C. Teaford, *The Rough Road to Renaissance: Urban Revitalization in America, 1940–1985* (Baltimore: Johns Hopkins University Press, 1990).
3. Mancur Olson, Jr. *The Logic of Collective Action* (Cambridge, Mass.; MIT Press, 1965).
4. Clarence Stone, *Regime Politics: Governing Atlanta 1946–1988* (Lawrence: University Press of Kansas, 1989).
5. Stone, *Regime Politics*, p. 3.
6. Stone, *Regime Politics*, p. 6.
7. Infrastructure of Play, p. 80.
8. U. S. Bureau of the Census.
9. David Laslo and Dennis R. Judd, "Building Civic Capacity Through an Elastic Local State: The Case of St. Louis," *Review of Policy Research* (Fall, 2006).
10. Quoted in Jon C. Teaford, *Cities of the Heartland: The Rise and Fall of the Industrial Midwest* (Bloomington: Indiana University Press, 1993), p. 213.
11. James Neal Primm, *Lion of the Valley: St. Louis, Missouri* (Boulder, CO: Pruett Publishing Co., 1981), p. 493.
12. Quoted in Institute of Housing, "Proceedings," (University College, Washington University, St. Louis, March 21–22, 1952, Mimeograph), p. 18.
13. Stein employs the phrase, "the mayor's party," in her book; cf. p. 141.
14. City of St. Louis, files of Mayor Raymond Tucker, meeting notes 10/19/64.
15. City of St. Louis, files of Mayor Raymond Tucker, meeting notes 6/9/65.
16. Stein, p. 141.
17. Ibid., p. 144.
18. Primm, p. 500.
19. Files of Mayor Poelker.
20. Spitzer and Malone, 1979.
21. Stein, p. 198.

22. Hernon, 8/5/91, 5A.
23. Hernon, 8/4/91, 4A.
24. Ibid.
25. p. 5, 1997 Annual Report.
26. Civic Progress Annual Report, 1995: 5.
27. Susan S. Fainstein, Norman I. Fainstein, Richard Child Hill, Dennis Judd, and Michael Peter Smith, *Restructuring the City: The Political Economy of Urban Redevelopment*, rev. ed. (New York: Longman, 1986), pp. 257, 258.
28. Robert H. Salisbury, "The New Convergence of Power in Urban Politics," *Journal of Politics* 26 (November 1964): 775–797.
29. Robert A. Dahl, *Who Governs?: Democracy and Power in an American City* (New Haven, Conn.: Yale University Press, 1961).
30. Clarence N. Stone, *Economic Growth and Neighborhood Discontent: System Bias in the Urban Renewal Program of Atlanta* (Chapel Hill: University of North Carolina Press, 1976).
31. Chester Hartman, *Yerba Buena: Land Grab and Community Resistance in San Francisco* (San Francisco: Glide, 1974).
32. John H. Mollenkopf, "The Post-War Politics of Urban Development," in *Marxism and the Metropolis: New Perspectives in Urban Political Economy*, ed. William Tabb and Larry Sawers (New York: Oxford University Press, 1978).
33. Frances Fox Piven and Richard A. Cloward, *Regulating the Poor: The Functions of Public Welfare* (New York: Pantheon, 1971).
34. Adolph Reed, "The Black Urban Regime: Structural Origins and Constraints," *Comparative Urban and Community Research 1*, No. 1 (1987): 138–139; and "Demobilization in the New Black Political Regime: Ideological Capitulation and Radical Failure in the Post-Segregation Era," in *The Bubbling Cauldron: Race, Ethnicity, and the Urban Crisis*, ed. Michael Peter Smith and Joe R. Feagin (Minneapolis: University of Minnesota Press, 1995), pp. 182–208.
35. Royce Hanson, Hal Wolman, David Connolly, and Katherine Person, "Corporate Citizenship and Urban Problem Solving: The Changing Civic Role of Business Leaders in American Cities," A Report to the Brookings Institution, June 2006 (unpub), p. 12.
36. Hanson et al., p. 11.
37. Bernard J. Frieden and Lynn B. Sagalyn, *Downtown Inc.: How America Builds Cities* (Baltimore: John Hopkins University Press, 1990).
38. Karen Mossberger and Gerry Stoker, "The Evolution of Urban Regime Theory: The Challenge of Conceptualization," *Urban Affairs Review* 36:6 (July 2001), p. 817.
39. Ibid., p. 814. Also see Gerry Stoker, "Regime Theory and Urban Politics," in David Judge, Gerry Stoker & Harold Wolman (eds.) *Theories of Urban Politic* (Thousand Oaks, CA: Sage, 1995), pp. 62–65.
40. Hanson et al., p. 12.
41. Bent Flyvbjerg, Nils Bruzelius, and Werner Rothengatter, *Megaprojects and Risk: An Anatomy of Ambition*. (Cambridge, UK: Cambridge University Press, 2003), Steven Erie, Alan Altshuler, David Luberoff, *Mega-Projects: The Changing Politics of Urban Public Investments* (Washington, DC: Brookings Institution Press, 2003), Jeffrey Sellers, *Governing from Below: Urban Regions and the Global Economy* (Cambridge, UK: Cambridge University Press, 2002).
42. Ibid, p. 63.
43. Davies, op. cit., p. 253.
44. One recent example of concept-stretching occurs in an article by Hamilton, who relies on the notion that "Public private partnership that have longevity are regimes" to conclude that regimes exist at the regional level if nongovernmental actors are involved in decision-making. Similarly, Burns adopts a truncated and incomplete definition of the concept when he attempts to apply regime analysis to educational systems. He complains that "Regime theory does not specifically include governors, state legislatures, state representatives, state departments of education, and other state-level actors as education regime members. . . ." Burns muddies the waters by considering all participants in education decision-making as members of a regime regardless of their actual relationship with one another or the existence of a stable political coalition.
45. Ibid., p. 813. Also see Domhoff on the point that all but one of the regime types (developmental) proposed by Stone may be "largely hypothetical;" see G. William Domhoff, "The Limitations of Regime Theory," *City & Community* 5:1 (March 2006), p. 49.

The New Urban Economy and Local Politics

Three changes in global capitalism have transformed urban economies: service-sector employment has replaced industrial jobs, business activities and populations have deconcentrated within urban areas, and competition among cities has intensified. In Selection 4, H. V. Savitch and Paul Kantor trace these developments. They argue that the radical dispersal of businesses and populations began around the middle of the twentieth century as changes in communication, technology, transportation, and production processes enabled more and more businesses to leave central cities in favor of lower-cost locations in suburbia and the Sunbelt. Where jobs went, people followed. By the end of the century, these movements had transformed the United States into a predominantly suburban nation.

Savitch and Kantor also show that the deindustrialization of urban economies changed how Americans make a living. The United States has become less dependent on industry and hard goods production because business activity has shifted decidedly into services. Where cities once pursued smokestack industries, they now are converting old warehouse, seaport, and industrial districts to tourist destinations, downtown malls, and office centers. In places where armies of blue-collar workers in factories fueled city growth, today it is more likely to be driven by white-collar managers and technicians meeting face-to-face in downtown offices, business parks, and upscale restaurants. Finally, the authors describe how globalization has made cities, suburbs, and even whole regions part of an international marketplace. The latter is characterized by rapid communication, transnational business activities, and a complex linkage among workers, managers, and cultures all over the world.

Savitch and Kantor argue that this "great transformation" is a source of new political challenges for cities of all kinds. Older as well as newer urban centers must compete on a wider playing field as places to work and live. Those who lose in this game of competition struggle to find ways of coping with their diminished fate. Yet the authors do not conclude that local governments are prisoners of the forces of internationalization. Rather, they argue, "there is a variation in the response to globalization." This is not only because cities vary in their resources or capacity. Local responses also reflect the "distribution of power within a city." Globalization has changed the nature of urban politics: the makeup of political coalitions, the relative influence of various interests, and the ability of new groups to mobilize. Cities are not blank slates to be written upon. They are dynamic places, capable of choosing how to respond to the challenges that face them.

Selections 5 and 6 describe how globalization is transforming the political dynamics within cities. In Selection 5 the authors, Royce Hansen, Harold

Wolman, David Connolly, Katherine Pearson, and Robert McManmon demonstrate that the coalitions that govern cities are changing. As in the past, corporate CEOs continue to play a pivotal role in local politics, but power is more widely shared than in the past. In most cities in the postwar era, business leadership came primarily from CEO-led peak organizations. Hometown bankers and corporate elites took the lead in providing capital for redevelopment efforts. But beginning in the 1990s, a wave of mergers and buyouts and the internationalization of finance and corporate management made firms less local and more international; as a result, the participation of civic elites became "shallower, more transient, and less influential." Corporate managers and CEOs still play important roles, but tend to participate in broad-based coalitions that represent a wide variety of interests. At the same time, the urban agenda has become more regional and the influence of mayors has weakened. According to Hansen et al., local business organizations are as apt to work with state and federal officials as with local officials in pursuing urban development projects. These arrangements have made mayors less important; in the past they might have led a powerful downtown coalition, but today they play an important role only when they have something to bring to the table.

This point is reinforced by Selection 6. As previously noted, in the past business elites were hugely influential in promoting economic growth and downtown revitalization, but as Elizabeth Strom points out, in the present era the traditional alliances forged between powerful mayors and downtown business elites are being replaced by looser coalitions dominated by real estate developers, nonprofit institutions, and public sector agencies. Downtown is no longer "the seat of corporate power"; instead, many American downtowns are being transformed into entertainment spaces and locations for upscale residences. The owners and managers of condominium towers, cultural facilities, convention centers, sports venues, and entertainment complexes—working closely with public development agencies—cooperate, as needed, to promote an environment that will be mutually beneficial. In Strom's view, the result is that the ambitious civic agenda once promoted by business elites has given way to a politics guided by a narrower set of issues driven by a variety of interests. Downtown interests remain influential, but they do not necessarily dominate the local political landscape.

4

Cities in the International Marketplace

H. V. Savitch and Paul Kantor

An enormous transformation engulfs the industrial world. The rapidity and consequences are unparalleled. The change is breathtaking. The ancient world lasted for three thousand years, the medieval age for less

From H. V. Savitch and Paul Kantor, Chapter 1, "The Great Transformation and Local Choices" from *Cities in the International Marketplace*, pp. 1–10, 13–17, 19–21, 23, 27–28, 373–374. Copyright © 2002 by Princeton University Press. Reprinted by permission of Princeton University Press.

than a millennium, and the industrial era for about a century. Our postindustrial society has been brought about in roughly three decades, and its pace is quickening. This new revolution has already remade the economic fabric of society, radically altered the behavior of capital, broken down national boundaries, and is remodeling government.

This transformation is particularly profound within liberal democratic states in North America and Western Europe. Since 1970, these states have shed their older industrial capacity and have become societies dominated by the tertiary sector—business, professions, services, high technology, and government. Within these societies capital has changed its configuration. It is more nimble and more multinational.[1] "Flexible production" and "just-in-time inventory" are not only techniques for quick action but they have also changed the operations of capitalism. Corporate ownership is not confined solely to a single nation but can span the globe, putting management in the hands of unlikely collaborators. Archrivals continue their rivalries but also find themselves in partnership with one other; fiercely competing one day and collaborating the next. The giant plane-manufacturer Airbus is a case in point. Its operations are a product of a European high-tech faceoff with America. At the same time, it buys products from its American nemesis, Boeing, and 40 percent of Airbus components are made in the United States.

Migration is another part of the story. Counting refugees alone, one finds that within the last decade 4.3 million have flocked into Germany, France, Italy, and the United Kingdom. Over one million have turned to the United States and Canada.[2] Recent immigrants now make up roughly 10 percent of these last two societies. While North America is regarded as the traditional immigrant haven, the numbers in Western Europe have exploded. During the past decade European officials expected that more than 25 million legal or illegal immigrants would settle on that continent.[3] Meanwhile birth rates of nationals within most Western countries have flattened or declined. The birth rate crisis is most acute in France and Italy, where the newborn cannot keep pace with the rate of mortality. As those birth rates continue to plummet, Europeans will have to rely on even more immigrants to support high living standards and generous pensions.

On the political front transnational pacts have nurtured the transformation by facilitating the movement of goods, people, and common policies across boundaries. The most prominent of these pacts are in the West and include the European Union (EU), which comprises fifteen nations, and the North American Free Trade Association (NAFTA), composed of the United States, Canada, and Mexico.[i] The EU already has a supranational government and bureaucracy that imposes policy on member nations. NAFTA is not that far advanced, but it has begun to affect political life in North America by forcing choices over freer trade, currency supports, and labor policy.

Technology plays a central role in this transformation. Just as previous periods may have been driven by steam locomotion (1780–1840), rail transportation (1840–90), electric power (1890–1930), or petroleum energy (1930–70), so the current era is propelled by the transmission of information. The last quarter of the twentieth century was appropriately called "the information age," and it portended revolutionary technological achievements into this millennium.

By now it may be a commonplace observation that warrants repeating. Ordinary people are communicating faster, they are more directly in touch with events, and they often exchange information person to person. The new world of cyberspace is just one technology that allows this. At the dawn of the postindustrial age, during the mid-1970s, just 50,000 computers existed in the world. That number has now rocketed to 556 million, giving common individuals access to each other across the globe. More than half of Americans and more than a quarter of Western Europeans own computers. In North America and Western Europe, big and small cities are hard-wired for instant communication. Carriers, like BBC or CNN, have established global news networks, allowing the world to witness the same events at the same time. Impressions are created instantly, and reactions occur swiftly. The decreasing cost of telephone service and the spread of fiber optic cables (simultaneously transmitting 1.5 million conversations within the diameter of a human hair) catapulted personal information to new levels. By the year 2000 international telephone calls reached an all-time high of 100 billion minutes.[4] None of these developments can create democracy, but collectively they assure wider dissemination of information, they facilitate freer exchange among people, and they hold potential for greater accountability between rulers and the ruled. Under these conditions, it becomes increasingly difficult to monopolize information, control public opinion, or ignore citizen demands.

The combination of economic, demographic, technological, and political change is cumulative, and will continue to impact the social order. No society encapsulates this transformation more than urban society. Cities are the crucibles through which radical experiments become convention. They are concentrated environments in which people adapt and their resilience is tested. They are the world's incubators of innovation—made possible by critical mass, diversity, and rich interaction. And cities have steadily grown over the centuries to fulfill that role. In the tenth century one of the world's largest cities, Cordoba, held just 300,000 people. Later Constantinople became the leading metropolis and held half a million people. By the eighteenth century London had surpassed every other Western city with one million inhabitants. In the twentieth century New York rose to ascendancy with several million people. Now in the twenty-first century Tokyo, São Paulo, and Mexico City have climbed above ten million inhabitants.

What is more, cities have complemented their role as global innovators with geophysical centrality. Despite enormous changes in technology, cities remain at the juncture of world transportation, as transit points for business, science, and travel of every stripe. This puts cities at the very pivot of transformation. Few statistics demonstrate this better than air traffic. . . .

In just nine short years average passenger traffic jumped by 51 percent while cargo increased by 131 percent. Already a global transit point, Paris more than doubled both its air passengers and cargo, Seoul showed a similar doubling in passengers and cargo, while Amsterdam and London also showed impressive gains. All told, every one of these cities registered gains, and we note that these advance have been made on very substantial bases. Cities are continuing to grow in this global transformation, and indeed are at its very heart. Despite the dip in passenger air traffic after September 11, that transformation is likely to continue and cities will resume their station at the junctures of air travel.

This tells us something not only about the future, but also about the recent past. Cities have been the terrain on which technological, social, and global transformation has taken place. Cities hold the machinery that furnishes each era with a distinct product; they are the progenitors of national culture; and, they are the great mixing cauldrons that supply a unique human hybrid. In providing all of these functions, cities continually remake themselves, reconstruct their productive base, and adapt their physical environment to the necessities of the time.

We examine this transformation . . . along three distinct trajectories: 1) the deindustrialization of urban economies, 2) the deconcentration of older cities, and 3) the globalization process. As we shall see, cities are not necessarily the passive recipients of this change, but have the capacity to guide it and shape its impact. . . .

DEINDUSTRIALIZATION: FOR WHAT?

Just thirty years ago, cities in North America and Europe were bustling with factories, workshops, warehouses, and open air markets. While the great primate cities of New York, London, and Paris had always held financial houses and corporate headquarters, they also were balanced by textile manufacture, light industry, chemical production, and warehousing.[ii]

At the same time, secondary cities took on the heavy lifting. Cleveland, Pittsburgh, Birmingham, Newcastle, Essen, Lille, and Turin were centers for tool and dye making, automobile manufacture, and steel production. These industrial towns were complemented by cities of passage. New Orleans, Liverpool, Marseilles, Hamburg, and Naples were glorious ports, which boasted the world's finest bistros and bawdiest night life.

Secondary cities were the workshops of the industrial world. They also housed large numbers of blue-collar families in a rich social milieu. From London's East End to New Orleans's Garden District, neighborhoods anchored the social life of the city. To be sure, the housing was often substandard and the neighborhoods overcrowded, but they spawned a host of vibrant institutions. Labor unions, shops, schools, churches, and social clubs bound communities together, allowed citizens to connect to public institutions, and gave the city meaning.

The bulk of those factories are now gone and many of the ports are closed. Some workers hold on to remnants of the old economy, some have joined the ranks of the unemployed, and others have found jobs elsewhere. While some working-class neighborhoods are intact, others have been gentrified and enriched with boutiques and expensive specialty shops. Still other inner-city neighborhoods now accommodate immigrants who bring with them a new culture, different foodstuffs, and an altogether distinct way of life (from tea salons to mosques). A substantial number of old neighborhoods, mostly in America and Great Britain, have not been recycled for the gentry or for immigrants. Instead they have fallen into disuse: the houses are abandoned, stores are boarded up, sidewalks are littered, and streets are dangerous. Many social institutions are gone—either they have disappeared or taken new form in the suburbs. . . .

Deindustrialization is generating uneven development and social imbalance. . . . Some cities remain in decay while others have succeeded in remaking themselves. Chicago, Cleveland, Madrid, and Rotterdam saw the collapse of blue-collar employment. Some of these same cities (Madrid and Rotterdam) made up their losses in manufacture through white-collar employment. Other cities like Cleveland, Philadelphia, and St. Louis have not yet recovered from this trauma. The crises of transformation are more widespread in Anglo-American cities than on the European continent. American cities were particularly hard hit, and account for the bulk of those that have yet to recover. In part, this is due to the nineteenth- and early-twentieth-century genesis of American central cities as locations for heavy industry. This is also true for some British cities (Newcastle, Liverpool, Glasgow). Continental cities mostly developed in the trading eras of the seventeenth and eighteenth centuries, and wealth was largely vested in the urban core. Thus, the ecological structure of European cities permitted them to shift more easily to tertiary economies.[iii]

By and large, primate cities did well. London emerged as the banking center where capital could be concentrated, New York as a producer of financial instruments where loans and mergers could be consummated, and Paris as a seat for corporate headquarters and professional services where deals could be struck. Each of these cities carved out niches for themselves as command posts in a larger world economy.[5] In large measure London, New York, and Paris became the forerunners of postindustrialism and established the pace for others.[6] To be sure, these cities already had thriving nests of banks and corporate headquarters, and they were able to build upon economies of agglomeration. Yet primate cities are complex, and during the 1950s high finance made up just a fraction of their economies. Manufacture, ports, and warehousing held the bulk of employment, and losses in these sectors were enormous. After deindustrialization struck, London, New York, and Paris had to refill huge holes in their economies just to stay even.

Secondary cities show greater variation in outcome. Cleveland experienced fiscal collapse in 1978, and nearly 40 percent of its residents are now below the poverty line.[7] Detroit and countless other rustbelt cities in America suffered a similar fate.[8] By contrast, Pittsburgh guided its shrinkage, revived its economy through research and technology, and kept its downtown healthy. In France, grimy, industrial Lille was rebuilt as the crossroads for Northern Europe. Industrial Glasgow has acquired a new downtown, but the rest of the city remains mired in decline.

Port cities have also turned out differently from one another. New Orleans and Liverpool fell into deep decline and have yet to recover. For a while, Hamburg reeled under successive economic blows, but recovered by modernizing its port and diversifying its industry. Today it is one of Europe's success stories and exults in the fact that it has more millionaires per capita than any other city on the continent.[9] Rotterdam, too, managed a partially successful transition by retaining its role as Europe's leading port and by building commercial linkages with Amsterdam and Utrecht.

Deindustrialization has also paved the way for new types of cities. So-called new-age boomtowns or sunbelt cities owe their urban form to late-twentieth-century technology.[10] Their economies usually are based on computers, software, electronics, space technology, or other emerging economic sectors. Their social structure is founded on middle-class outlooks, small families, and private housing. Especially in North America, new-age boomtowns enjoy an abundance of space, and their development spreads out along the corridors of modern freeways.

The United States has a concentration of these cities in its southwest and counts among them Phoenix, Houston, Albuquerque, and San Diego. Canada's boomtowns are found in its westerly open spaces and include Calgary and Vancouver. Boomtowns are not as common in Europe, which is already highly urbanized and lacks much vacant land. Nevertheless, European versions of these cities can be found in Southeast London (Croydon) and Oxford, in Grenoble and Montpellier, in Bavaria (Munich), and in the smaller towns of Italy's Northeast.

In America these boomtowns grew rapidly during the late 1960s and through the 1970s. Upheavals in petroleum and real estate sometimes threw cities like Houston into shock. But Houston recovered and continues to grow. In Canada, Vancouver is fueled by investments from Hong Kong, and it continues to lead that nation. The picture in Europe is hazy, though cities like Oxford and Grenoble have embraced high technology and believe that they are Europe's answer to the Silicon Valley.

In a nutshell, cities in North America and Europe changed substantially during the previous three decades. While the most successful became postindustrial, that status represented a dominant layer of activity, superimposed upon a diminished base of manufacture, shipping, and skilled trades. Less successful cities underwent shrinkage, though many of these managed to secure some postindustrial activity (small downtowns, tourism, stadiums, and exhibition centers). New-age boomtowns thrived on a combination of office employment, services, electronics, and light industry—set in the midst of universities, research centers, and low density development.

This reshuffling of the urban hierarchy has brought old and new cities into a competitive scramble to secure their economic well-being. As old industries decline and new investment patterns emerge, citizens and politicians are drawn into finding a niche for their communities in the new economic order. In the process, cities may be gripped by a certain angst—internal conflicts over means and ends, a belief that if a community does not grow it will surely die, and a rush to move faster.

DECONCENTRATION: THE SPREADING URBAN LANDSCAPE

The great transformation has also influenced human settlement and mobility. Overall, central cities have lost population. This deconcentration of population encompasses a range of different demographic processes, some healthy for cities, others not. Deconcentration entails movement away from places. This includes a movement out of healthy central cities, which allows remaining residents more space and gives departing residents more economical accommodations. We call this *dedensification*. Of course, dedensification also involves movement toward other places. This includes a burgeoning of low-density, metropolitan peripheries, brought about by rising living standards and a desire for single-family housing in the suburbs. It can also mean an entry into newer boomtowns and a search for fresh opportunities and economic betterment (new migration). This kind of movement can facilitate prosperity. On the other hand, deconcentration can also entail an exodus from urban cores because of decaying conditions, leaving these cities as segregated reservations for the poor. We refer to this as *decline*. In this case, population loss usually leaves cities in deeper distress.

Just as population loss does not necessarily mean decline, population growth does not always mean prosperity. Impoverished growth can occur when people move off rural land in search of opportunities elsewhere and fail to find them. We label this *impaction*. Migration into or around cities can also be accompanied by poorer living conditions and unemployment. The upshot has been massive growth without commensurate development. While this experience is uncommon among more mobile North Americans, it does occur in Africa and Latin America. A few European cities have grown while living conditions deteriorated. Whether accompanied by affluence or poverty, new migration and impaction create sprawling urban regions or megalopoli.[11]

In the United States, deconcentration often meant urban decline. As cities lost employment and neighborhoods decayed, some people escaped to the suburbs, while others remained behind in segregated ghettos. Even major cities that managed to remake themselves incurred the ravages of decline because whole neighborhoods fell apart. New York and Chicago did manage population gains during the past decade, but white residents continued to flee and the gains were due to immigration from Latin America or Asia. Population decline was rampant in secondary cities, where immigration was marginal and could not offset losses. Detroit, Cleveland, and St. Louis, once cities with close to or above a million residents, shrunk to less than half that size. Even after devastating losses of the 1970s and 1980s, the past decade was scarcely better, with those cities losing between 5 and 10 percent of their population.[12]

At the same time, urban deconcentration brought enormous prosperity to sunbelt boomtowns and swelled their suburbs. Boomtowns are the paragons of what we think of as urban *growth*. These areas experienced dramatic increases in residential populations, which gave rise to new shopping malls, office complexes, and single-family houses. The transformative years saw a virtual upheaval of inner-city populations, a massive shift of the white middle class into new settlements, and the trek of blacks and Hispanics into what remained of the urban cores.[13]

Some cities in Europe also suffered urban decline and now resemble their American counterparts. For the most part, however, European deconcentration was more genteel, taking the form of urban dedensification. Having begun in the Middle Ages and matured in the industrial era, Europe's cities were already overcrowded. Families often lived in small apartments within congested communities where shopping, recreation, schools, and factories were tightly clustered. Some urban theorists hailed this as the realization of community, but the relatives were less quaint.[14] Space was scarce, private bathrooms often absent, and sanitary conditions dubious. By the 1970s, if people could afford to live in the city, they bought extra space and renovated. If not, they moved out.

A push–pull operated in European cities to shift populations around. The rich, the upwardly mobile, and the single people stayed. Modest income families left because of financial pressures, but were also attracted by the ease of living outside the central city. In contrast to the United States, suburbs were built for those who could not afford to live closer to the center. The best of these were in outlying villages, in "new towns," or further away in new-age boomtowns; and they accommodated middle-class citizens. They were clean, spacious, and featured supermarkets, playgrounds, and schools woven into the residential fabric. The worst, were, low-income projects built in segregated edges or as extensions to impacted cities. They were massive, dingy concrete blocks that accommodated immigrants.

In sum the great transformation produced massive population shifts with different kinds of consequences. . . . Despite differences in geography, size, and population, major cities across the industrial West have undergone economic restructuring, brought on by similar forces. On both continents, populations spread throughout metropolitan areas. Suburbs and boomtowns radically expanded and urbanization proceeded apace. Rural areas shrank and fewer people earned their living through agriculture. Distant towns and rural villages lost population and, in some instances, fell into near vacancy. All told, we see substantial variation among these cities. The ramifications are deeply political. Citizens face a new set of urban challenges, driven by deindustrialization, migration, and a need to adapt.

GLOBAL SWEEP, LOCAL BROOMS

Globalism is an encompassing concept; it covers a broad range of activities, and it has brought both positive and negative results. Foremost among its characteristics is free trade. Open markets rest on a theory of competitive advantage, whereby each locale finds it beneficial to produce goods or services it can most efficiently turn out and to use international markets to acquire products that are best made elsewhere. This has sharpened and refined the division of labor among nation-states. The upshot is an explosive process, in which productivity, consumption, and participation rise at exponential rates. As we have seen and will continue to explore, urban growth has been nothing short of colossal, but it has also been accompanied by deep inequalities and paradoxes.[15,]

Fundamentally, globalism and its attendant free trade are derived from a technological revolution that has shrunk time and distance. We have already mentioned the revolutionary effects of instant communication, and here we amplify how that technology allows nations to achieve deeper levels of economic integration within competitive markets. By now, advanced technology moves $1.5 trillion around the world each day. In the United States international flows of bonds and equities are fifty-four times higher today than in 1970. The comparable figures for Germany and Japan are sixty and fifty times higher. Other research has shown that international trade sustains the global patterning and has brought about changes in economic relationships, social structure, and the significance of geographical place.[16]

A corollary characteristic is standardization. Once goods and information are alike, they become recognizable and interchangeable. Common standards of measurement, universal criteria, interchangeable parts, and identical symbols are essential for globalization. Just as the grid system of streets helped land-development, so too does standardization facilitate globalization. This includes a common currency, established procedures for registering and enforcing patents, and compatible mechanical or electronic equipment. Licenses and professional certification have also become standardized in order to allow human resources to flow across boundaries. Even sports has become standardized. The Olympic Games and Olympic committees legitimate certain sports and sanction rules through which athletic contests are held. Traditionally, American baseball has been capped by the misnomer of a "World Series." Up until recently this was entirely an American affair, but increasingly players and even some teams have been drawn from other nations. The progressive universality of sports today is incontrovertible.

Another wave of global change is heavily political. Globalization has magnified the intercourse between states, localities, and social movements across the world.[17] Signs of this are visible in the rise of multilateral organizations, regional pacts, and talk of a borderless world. States, localities, nongovernmental organizations, and labor increasingly ignore old boundaries and are driven more than before by the seemingly contradictory stimuli of cooperation and competition. For some this has opened new worlds of opportunity, where masses of people can be mobilized for democratic ends. This interaction, both on site and across cyberspace, makes government more accountable and also more replaceable. For others, globalism signifies a concentration of wealth and power, and a threat of lower living standards. This has led to a perilous instability and a thunderous reaction from both left- and right-wing protestors.[iv]

An additional wave of globalization is sociocultural. This involves diffusion of a more open, multipolar, and multicultural society in which migration is a major by-product.[18] What distinguishes current migration from preceding movements is its truncated and temporary patterns of settlement. Commonly, single men live abroad for lengthy periods, while sending remittances to the homeland. When whole families do migrate, they often are treated as long-term aliens, rarely assimilating, and even children born in the host country may not acquire citizenship. Indeed, the telecommunications revolution has given permanency to this temporary status. Cheap, efficient technology compresses space and time, enabling groups to retain homeland ties and preserve indigenous culture. Overseas, ethnic culture is now said to thrive in "transnational space" in which language, habit, and tradition continue regardless of geography.[19]

These aspects of globalization also foster a greater sense of mutual vulnerability. Free trade and competitive advantage have made societies more efficient, but they have also made societies more fragile and susceptible to crisis. In a matter of minutes, turmoil in a single great bank can upset finance at the other end of the world. Currency fluctuations can overturn decades of progress, hitting those at the bottom of the economic scale hardest. As economies become more integrated, localities share more closely both the good and bad times of globalization. Through the 1990s Taipei, Tel Aviv, and Santiago experienced an unprecedented boom. After 2000 the global economy was hit by recession and those cities went bust. The more integrated and the more synchronized the locality with globalization, the greater the upturn and the steeper the downturn.

Vulnerability has many dimensions. Disease travels as swiftly as airline flights and has acquired an international character. The recent exuberance and then depression of stock markets as well as the AIDS epidemic are unfortunate examples of this exposure. Still another dark side of globalism is the spread of terrorism.[20] The ease of travel, instantaneous communication, and quick transfer of money make it possible for terrorists to do their work and attack fragile international linkages.[v] International terror most vividly illustrates the underside of global interdependence. The multinational character of its actors and the slippery content of its operations are especially well suited for porous boundaries. . . . It was at the seams of globalization where international cities and international terror were tragically joined on September 11.

How do cities fit into this overall picture? One might suppose that globalization makes cities less important, as they are swept into a common world of economic competition and social interchange. Presumably, people could be located anywhere, and conduct business via the Internet from a mountaintop retreat.[21] In fact, the opposite is true—at least for some cities. A knowledge-based economy has accelerated face-to-face and informal contact. It has increased an appetite for conferences, seminars, and annual meetings. Additionally, business searches for that extra edge that comes from personal contact.

Globalization also has generated a need for central direction in which financial, legal, and professional services are concentrated within a common locale. Cities have made free trade much easier to accomplish, they have facilitated a new international division of labor, and they have absorbed waves of migration.[22] While not all cities have been blessed with these advantages, many are still efficient and enormously productive work stations for the postindustrial era. Whether one selects a handful of global cities, a larger number of primate cities, or a sampling of regional ones, urban centers lead national productivity, and their total output in goods and services has quickened during the last few decades.[23]

Rising urbanization has occurred concomitantly with globalization and is associated with rising GDP. Metropolitan areas of Europe and North America grew rich during the transformation, though clearly as the process matures the rate of urbanization flattens. . . .

Globalization has not made all urban places alike. Where you live and work matters more than ever in accessing jobs, income, public amenities, schools, and green space. These things are contingent upon "place." Location does make a huge difference. Neat suburban residential enclaves, edge cities, busy commercial downtowns, urban ghettos, vacated industrial areas, and campus-like office parks are all part of a complex urban fabric that differentiates opportunities. Some cities have taken advantage of those opportunities and the enormous wealth that springs from global trade. By the end of the millennium, Foreign Direct Investment (FDI) had reached an all-time high of $865 billion. While it is not possible to trace that investment to every locality, an overwhelming proportion of it went to advanced industrial nations, mostly located in the West. Banks held that money and facilitated investments, and almost all of these institutions were located in major cities. Moreover, along with investment flows, banking assets have gushed over the last few decades. . . .

Even during this short period, most banks substantially increased their holdings. In some cases the aggregation of capital crested by over 300 percent. Place often shapes perspective, and location cannot help influencing decisions. More than ever, cities serve as the command and control centers of those decisions. They have benefited not just from saturated white-collar employment and offshoot industries, but also from their strategic placement in international capital markets. Not all of this has produced salutary results. There are always paradoxes and contradictions connected to change, and the impact of globalization on cities is no exception.

One paradox is that while most metropolitan areas have become wealthier, they also contain rising numbers of the poor. In Western Europe 10 percent of city residents are classified as poor, while the percentage rises in suburbs to roughly 20 percent. The United States reverses these proportions, so that central cities and suburbs respectively hold 21 percent and 9 percent of residents who fall below the poverty line.[24] Quite expectedly, migrants searching for opportunities in cities account for a substantial portion of the poor. More than 50 percent of the populations in New York and Toronto are classified as either ethnic minorities or foreign born. In Paris, the percentage is above 15 percent.

Another paradox is that urban transformation has both expanded the sphere of central cities and shrunk it. In some ways deconcentration has extended central cities by making suburbanites dependent upon them for income, investment, jobs, and culture. One can see this in the huge numbers of commuters pouring into urban cores each day as well as in the many monetary transactions (mortgages, business loans, venture capital) that occur between city financial institutions and the hinterlands. In other ways, deconcentration has also meant an escape from the central city and has created an altogether new urban form. Green cities have sprung up in the more distant countryside and eliminated distinctions between urban and rural life. A newer urban life is built around asphalt, glass, trees, and grass, and it functions apart from traditional central cities.

Still another oddity is that while transformation has made cities into hard-working centers of productivity, it has also made them into sites of gluttonous leisurely consumption. Scholars often write about the dichotomy between investment and consumption whereby different locales tend toward one or the other.[25] Postindustrial cities have united these dichotomies. Complementing an enormous white-collar apparatus of producer services is a burgeoning industry in leisure and consumption. The rise of the office-complex city has been accompanied by the rise of the tourist city. Cities are today in the midst of what Judd and Fainstein describe as a "tourist bubble," whose growth is among the fastest in the world.[26]

Put in historical perspective, these paradoxes are not unusual. Cities have always grown or shrunk alongside technological advance. The introduction of elevators and steel framing allowed for skyscrapers but broke up traditional neighborhoods. Metro lines were a boon for central business districts, but a bust for out-of-the-way small towns. Invention is often a conveyance for what Schumpeter called "creative destruction"[27] and brought about very different results. . . .

"GLOCAL" CHOICES

Deindustrialization, deconcentration, and globalization have put cities on trajectories of change. It is this unusual blend of global challenge and local response that confronts us, and this combination is sometimes denoted by the inelegant terms "glocal" or "glocalization."[28] Like the industrial revolution before it, this revolution can be decisively influenced by government as well as other social institutions.[29] Governments have responded to these challenges in diverse ways. First, leaders and citizens have made strategic decisions about *what kind of community* they want. Some political leaders look to the marketplace for strategic direction, placing a high priority on gaining a competitive advantage for their communities. They ask, how can we find our niche in the regional, national, or world market? What can we do best? Where can we garner capital investment? How can we grow by helping business operate more efficiently? For cities that choose competition, answers to these questions have produced a variety of strategic responses. We see cities remaking waterfronts into tourist attractions, refurbishing downtowns with office towers and convention halls, and trying to attract big bang events such as the World Cup, Expo, or Olympic games, as well as revenue sources such as sports teams, theme parks, or gaming casinos.

Cities then do not just react to the movement of capital but act upon these forces. Although local governments have only limited control over the marketplace, they use public power to engage it. They do so whenever land is recycled, development rights are granted, housing is built, taxes are collected, or capital is borrowed. Moreover cities can profoundly affect factors of production. They can lower overhead costs by building bridges, ports, and airfields. They can tighten up or loosen controls over air pollution. Cities can even affect labor costs by making it easier or more difficult for individuals to access welfare benefits.[30] In making decisions over these issues, cities struggle to resolve an array of problems and influence their own restructuring.

Some leaders try to induce capital investment by reducing risks for business. They may put up bonds that guarantee the building of stadiums or convention halls, they may underwrite loans to potential investors, and they may find themselves forming public–private partnerships in order to assure private investors of unified backing.[31] Cities also aggressively solicit business by lobbying for private capital, bidding for company headquarters, or establishing international offices to stimulate trade.

Cities seeking competitive advantages may also tolerate increased migration, allow informal economies to flourish, and facilitate the supply of cheap goods and services. They may countenance permissive building codes, lax licensing, and an abundance of substandard housing. These newfound resources explain the partial resurgence of textile manufacture in some cities, where old-fashioned sweatshops arise and where illegal immigrants are exploited as low-cost labor. The upscale life-style of postindustrial cities generates a demand for low-paying service jobs. A virtual night shift of unskilled workers commutes into downtowns to clean the office towers, staff the restaurants, and drive the taxicabs. The "reverse commute" of marginal workers into affluent suburbs also helps to maintain an attractive low cost of living.

Alternatively, cities sometimes defy the swells of the marketplace. Local leaders can remain politically sensitive and rely on a logic of populist, antigrowth policies.[32] This logic may well clash with the rationality of the marketplace. Cities may resist the lure of growth and opt for preservationist or caretaker strategies.[33] They may want to protect historic neighborhoods, guard surrounding farmland, or prohibit large discount outlets and suburban malls. Some fear higher taxes and increased congestion. They may want to remain as quiet residential communities.

Large and small cities have resisted economic growth by invoking moratoria on the construction of office towers, using zoning exactions to force concessions from developers, adopting strict architectural codes, requiring underground facilities for automobile parking, and setting aside large tracts for open space.[34] In Western Europe the upsurge of "green parties" has affected urban policies. Green legislators have placed controls on housing costs, limited the price of apartment rentals, and closed off streets to automobiles. Reciprocally, they have used public funds to renovate housing, protected rights of squatters, and reserved sections of the streetscape for bicycles. Populist movements have sometimes arisen to challenge the power of corporate decision makers in places such as Cleveland, Ohio, the Mon Valley in Pennsylvania, and Liverpool, England.

There is variation in the response to globalization. In important ways, world competition has sparked a quest for capital investment and growth. In other ways, the free exchange of ideas and possibilities for collaboration has enabled groups to mobilize. Some scholars have found evidence of a new urban politics based on social issues, increased diversity, and a concern for the environment.[35] They also envision globalized cities as hothouses for the spread of postmaterialist values with its emphasis on citizen activism.[36] The concerns of migrant workers coupled to environmental and populist sentiment could generate counterpressures. Whatever the outcomes, globalization is not a leveling process, and it has created new alternatives.

Who makes decisions over *what* is another question of choice. This ultimately depends upon the existence of assets and the distribution of power within a city. Some scholars argue that urban decision-making is shaped by economics, and they stress growth and competition as the predominant force. From this perspective, cities must give priority to economic growth because they are disciplined by a market that punishes them with loss of jobs and tax revenue.[37] Other scholars argue that political preferences matter more than economic pressures. They see powerful leaders, coalitions, regimes, and growth machines operating to shape economic preferences.[38] There is something to both interpretations. Cities are certainly limited by the assets at their disposal, and they cannot deal with global change unless they have the wherewithal to do so. By the same token, dealing with change requires initiative, and coalitions must be built by political entrepreneurs who mobilize groups and classes.

The important questions deal not only with differences of alternatives taken, but also with the reasons why some cities might be able to choose particular alternatives. Are there structural characteristics that are common to cities choosing similar strategic alternatives? If so, can they be identified and how do they interact? Likewise, do cities that share similar strategic responses to globalism also share similar cultural or political characteristics? If so, what are these and how do they operate? Can we make sense of these varying influences on choice and put them into some logical schema? Finally, what are the lessons learned from this inquiry? Does the international marketplace have a tendency to homogenize cities so that they become alike, or are cities becoming more dissimilar? Given the tension between the global and the local, can one decide which side, if any, prevails? . . .

The classic development conflict occurs between "anti-growth" and "progrowth" coalitions, and includes such debates as whether to adopt building moratoria and preserve historic districts or aggressively recruit private investors and turn downtowns into rows of towering office complexes. This conflict often encompasses a political component where the sides are poised for battle—neighborhood groups, preservationists, and environmentalists on one side versus developers, chambers of commerce, and media boosters on the other. Pro-growth impulses are often driven by a desire to standardize development (trade centers, office towers, tourist attractions) and expand the contributions of multinational firms in the local economy. Anti-growth impulses frequently stem from a desire for citizen participation and local autonomy.[39] These tensions reflect the degree to which local development agendas are influenced by the international market.

Looking at the situation more broadly, we can appreciate that issues of international import are fought on local battlegrounds, and that ultimately these conflicts change the character of cities. Many local challenges and responses have global proportions; decisions flow to and from an international marketplace. This marketplace can either saturate cities with massive investment and political pressure or marginalize them. Either way, cities must respond by accommodating, managing, or resisting these forces.

NOTES

i. Other parts of the world have also formed transnational associations, including the Association of South East Asian Nations (Brunei, Indonesia, Malaysia, Philippines, Singapore, Thailand, and Vietnam) and Mancusor (Argentina, Brazil, Paraguay, and Uruguay).

ii. Primate cities are giant entities, at least twice as large as the next largest city in the nation, and not infrequently they hold 20 percent or more of a nation's population. While primate cities are not always at the nexus of the global economy, they are central to a national economy and generate a substantial portion of its GDP.

iii. There are also cultural, social, and geographical reasons for this. Anglo-American traditions favor country and low-density living, while Continental traditions are more disposed to high-density or clustered environments. In America, the availability of greater space and racial enmity contributed to middle-class white flight.

iv. Instances of both democratic and antidemocratic movements can be traced in some ways to globalization. In 1999 the overthrow of the Indonesian government was made possible by Internet communication in that nation's archipelago. Within the next year, populist, protest movements held large-scale demonstrations in Seattle and Washington, D.C. Populist demonstrations against Iran's repressive theocracy have also been held and gained resonance through telecommunications. On the other side, in the United States neo-Nazi and racist groups have been able to mobilize followers through the Internet. Also, marginal political parties in both America and Europe have capitalized on a reaction against global trade (in the U.S., Patrick Buchanan's Reform Party; in France, Jean-Marie Le Pen's National Front; in Italy Gianfranco Fini's neofascists).

v. Every action has its reaction, and globalism is no different. Vulnerability also has a more fortunate side that can be found in cross-national cooperation and synergy. This kind of complementary interdependence has brought about cooperation in regulating currencies, controlling AIDS and combating terrorism.

1. Knight and Gappert, *Cities in a Global Society*; Judd and Parkinson, *Leadership and Urban Regeneration*.
2. Population Action International, *Global Migration*.
3. Stoltz, "Europe's Back Doors."
4. A.T. Kearney, Inc., "Globalization Index."
5. Sassen, *Cities in World Economy*.
6. Savitch, *Post-industrial Cities*; Sassen, *Global City*.
7. Swanstrom, "Semisovereign Cities"; Hill, "Cleveland Economy."
8. Gappert, *Future of Winter Cities*.
9. Dangschat and Obenbrugge, "Hamburg."
10. Bernard and Rice, *Sunbelt Cities*; Ruble, Tulchin, and Garland, "Globalism and Local Realities."
11. Gotttman, *Megalopolis*.
12. U.S. Bureau of the Census, "Population of the 100 Largest Cities"; State of the Cities Census Data Systems.
13. Sternlieb and Hughes, *Post-industrial America*; Kantor with David, *Dependent City*; Kantor, *Dependent City Revisited*, chap. 6.
14. Mumford, *City in History*; Jacobs, *Death and Life of Great American Cities*; Garls, *Urban Villagers*.
15. Savitch, "Global Challenge."
16. Sassen, *Global City, Cities in a World Economy*; A.T. Kearney, Inc., "Globalization Index."
17. Held, "Democracy."
18. Knight and Gappert, *Cities in Global Society*; United Nations Centre for Human Settlements, *Indicators Newsletter*.
19. Smith, *Transnational Urbanism*.
20. Savitch and Ardashev, "Does Terror Have an Urban Future?"
21. Webber, "Order in Diversity."
22. Kresl, "North American Cities International"; Sassen, *Cities in World Economy*; Glickman, "Cities and International Division of Labor."
23. Prud'homme, "Les sept plus grandes villes du monde"; Savitch, "Cities in a Global Era."
24. European Foundation for the Improvement of Living and Working Conditions, *Living Conditions* (1986); Baugher and Lamison-White, *Poverty*.
25. O'Connor, *Fiscal Crisis of State*; Saunders, "Central Local Relations."

26. Judd and Fainstein, *Tourist City.*
27. Schumpeter, *Capitalism, Socialism and Democracy.*
28. Swyngedouw, "Mammon Quest"; Ascher, *Metapolis ou l'Avenir des Villes.*
29. Polanyi, *Great Transformation.*
30. Logan and Molotch, *Urban Fortunes.*
31. Rubin and Rubin, "Economic Development Incentives."
32. Mollenkopf, *Contested City.*
33. Williams and Adrian, *Four Cities*; Swanstrom, "Semisovereign Cities."
34. Muzzio and Bailey, "Economic Development"; Clavel, *Progressive City.*
35. Clark and Inglehart, "New Political Culture"; Clark, "Structural Realignments."
36. Miranda, Rosdil, and Yeh, "Growth Machines."
37. Peterson, *City Limits.*
38. Stone and Sanders, *Politics of Urban Development*; Stone, *Regime Politics*; Swanstrom, "Semisovereign Cities"; Logan and Molotch, *Urban Fortunes.*
39. Leo, "City Politics"; Clarke and Gaile, *Work of Cities.*

5

Globalization and Leadership in American Cities

ROYCE HANSON, HAROLD WOLMAN, DAVID CONNOLLY, KATHERINE PEARSON, AND ROBERT MCMANMON

Corporate civic elites have played a major role in the building, rebuilding, governance, and functioning of major American cities. In fact, some of the most important policy innovations and development projects in American cities during the 20th century were initiated, supported, or brought to fruition by key business leaders and peak organizations of local chief executive officers (CEOs). Recent urban literature has suggested, however, that there may be increasing disengagement of corporate elites from civic efforts, largely as a result of pervasive economic trends affecting locally owned and based businesses. Ironically, such disengagement comes during a time when federal aid to cities has been curtailed and greater reliance has been placed on the private sector to solve urban problems, leaving many cities with increasing limited means to undertake major initiatives.

Since the end of World War II, CEO-led organizations such as the Allegheny Conference, the Twin Cities Citizen's League, the Greater Baltimore Committee, the Dallas Citizen's Council, and analogous organizations in Atlanta, Cleveland, Detroit, Kansas City, St. Louis, San Francisco, and Milwaukee occupy legendary status as power brokers and agenda setters in their communities. Often founded by executives of local corporations that grew to national or international scale, these organizations were able to mobilize their

From Royce Hanson, Harold Wolman, David Connolly, Katherine Pearson, and Robert McManmon, *Corporate Citizenship and Urban Problem Solving: The Changing Civic Role of Business Leaders in American Cities.* A Report to the Brookings Institution Urban and Metropolitan Policy Program. Washington, DC: George Washington Institute of Public Policy, June 2006, pp. 1, 10–18, 25–27, 29, 34. Reprinted by permission of the Brookings Institution. www.brookings.edu/metro

corporate members' personal devotion to community, their deal-making talent, and their ability to commit corporate financial resources to address redevelopment, environmental quality, transportation, health care, and education issues in their respective cities. In some cases, their initiatives transformed whole sections of cities, both physically and economically. In others, they managed sensitive local issues such as the desegregation of public schools and the integration of restaurants, hotels, theaters, and other places of public accommodation.

The power and influence of these organizations began to wane after the mid-1970s, however, as economic restructuring-deregulation, reorganization, and suburbanization of major industries took hold, and demographic changes produced shifts in political leadership. By this time, professional and business service firms and nonprofit organizations had begun to displace manufacturers as the principal employers of many regions. Successive waves of mergers and acquisitions started to transform many local banks and other businesses from corporate headquarters to branches of larger corporations headquartered in other cities, or even other countries. And new executives, often with tenuous career ties to the locality, gradually began to replace the generation of hometown entrepreneurs and business titans that built their corporations and established CEO-led civic organizations in places where they had deep roots.

Corporate engagement in urban problem solving depends heavily on the heads of major firms located in an area being actively involved in the civic life of their communities—in other words, the extent to which they are willing and able to lend their personal leadership skills, time, ideas, and the slack resources of their firms (executive and professional talent and money) to the arts, education, hospitals, workforce development programs, sports and cultural facilities, and, especially, major economic development projects. The changes in economic structure discussed above have altered the level and nature of this engagement over the past several decades, however.

Substantial changes in an area's manufacturing, services, and FIRE [Finance, Insurance, Real Estate] sectors, and in the number and strength of its largest firms, have had numerous implications for the engagement of corporate CEOs in urban issues. In the case of the FIRE sector, the gain or loss of major banks and other financial institutions has had an effect on both financial contributions to civic causes and, perhaps even more important, the leadership of the corporate community. Declining employment in the traditional manufacturing sector has been accompanied by the demise or relocation of major firms, and with them the loss of prominent CEOs to the region's leadership ranks. And business demands on executives of newer, fast-growing manufacturing firms appear to leave them little time for civic activities.

The universal increase in the services sector presents a more complex situation for civic engagement. It appears to be accompanied almost everywhere by the growth of nonprofit organizations in education and health care, as well as expansion of business services in some areas. In other areas, growth in services may be more oriented to small firms and consumer services. Nonprofit firms tend to have fewer slack resources than large corporations, and their executives may see themselves more as potential beneficiaries of civic engagement by private CEOs than as leaders in the mobilization of private sector economic and civic power. But as they often have a larger stake in the well-being of their city and region, they can be important additions to corporate civic organizations. At the same time, executives of business service firms—such as law, accounting, consulting, and public relations—may replace manufacturers and bankers in the leadership echelons of business, but the organizational culture of the partnerships from which they come may be fundamentally different from those of the corporations they serve.

The presence of Fortune 500 companies provides at least the opportunity to engage those firms and their CEOs in civic life. But with the move of major corporate headquarters to the suburbs, it's not surprising that many executives have shifted their interests away from the city toward more regional issues. And as local Fortune 500 companies are acquired and become branches or divisions of larger corporations with home offices removed to distant places, the managers of those residual branches often have less latitude in their activities and ability to commit financial and other resources to civic projects.

Finally, the culture of business engagement in a metropolitan area and the character of its civic institutions are important factors in determining how corporate executives address urban issues. Some cities have strong traditions of business statesmanship where corporate executives are expected by their peers to take on important civic leadership responsibilities and their firms are expected to make generous contributions to charities and public causes. Where business leaders have created organizations and networks that can mobilize economic resources and talent to influence public policy or economic activity they are more likely to find satisfaction in civic engagement, reinforcing their commitments.

All told, it's clear that economic restructuring has affected CEO engagement in cities and metropolitan areas in myriad and profound ways.

NEW PATTERNS OF CIVIC ENGAGEMENT BY CORPORATE CEOS

Associations composed solely of CEOs were created to bring together in a small, exclusive forum an area's largest employers—those local companies who could make "on the spot" commitments of their firm's resources to support a development project, a change in public policy, a mayoral campaign, a bond referendum, or other major civic initiative. R. L. "Uncle Bob" Thornton, the founder of the Dallas Citizens Council in the late 1930s, famously called its members his city's "Yes and No men." In some cases—as was the case with creation of Cleveland Tomorrow in 1982—the leading business titans of the city regarded the chamber of commerce as slow-moving, ineffective, and primarily designed to provide member services rather than solve big problems. Moreover, they found chamber deliberations tedious and time-consuming. They preferred gatherings among peers in a boardroom, receiving a quick briefing by a colleague or a senior staff officer, and reaching a quick consensus on what to do, how to allocate its costs and responsibilities among the group, and how best to use their influence and money to make it happen.

These organizations typically allowed only CEOs of the largest corporate employers to be members. The banks, utilities, newspapers, department stores, and manufacturers were the mainstays. Professional partnerships and real estate developers often were excluded, and CEOs of nonprofit institutions—universities, hospitals, and foundations—were rarely invited to join. They might have been among a region's largest employers, but their executives rarely had authority to commit unbudgeted resources and they were more likely to be beneficiaries of a civic initiative than instigators of one.

Total membership in some cities was 50 or fewer; in larger urban areas it might include two hundred or more. A small executive committee or board of directors made decisions, usually out of public view. Typically, only CEOs could participate in deliberations or decisions—no substitutes were allowed. In early years, there may have been no staff. Later an executive director or president may have been selected to carry out the decisions of the board and help its officers set the agenda. Additional staffs tended to be small.

Influence flowed from the economic power of the members, the long identification of their firms with the city, and their own deep affection for it. They often regarded their success and that of their companies as bound to the success of the city. Once a course of action had been agreed upon, they used their power to rebuild sections of town, influence the location of public facilities and development projects, make and break mayors, and allocate the resources of foundations they controlled to projects and programs they deemed worthy of support. In Pittsburgh, Atlanta, Cleveland, Baltimore, St. Louis, and Dallas they formed governing coalitions with mayors and managers to undertake major civic improvements. Even in cities where such governing regimes were transitory or unstable they were a force with which public officials had to reckon.

Changes in the role and influence of corporate leadership organizations were beginning to be apparent by the mid-1970s in most metropolitan areas. Many experienced large turnover in membership in the ensuing two decades as waves of mergers and acquisitions transformed local corporate headquarters, converting icons of local industry into mere branches of distant firms. Executive suites were populated with a new generation of managers, many of whom had no local roots and were on career trajectories that involved frequent transfers to branches in other cities. All these institutional changes were accompanied by relocation of many headquarters offices to the suburbs. The combination of these forces led to changes in the nature of civic engagement by business leaders, their commitment to city and region, and the membership and structure of many of their organizations.

The Loss of the Hometown Bankers

Of all the economic sectors, the deregulation and reorganization of banking have had the most pervasive effect on business organizations engaged in urban and regional problem solving. Prior to 1980 most major U.S. cities contained headquarters of one or more major regional banks. National and international banking headquarters were located in only a few of the largest cities. But in the massive reorganization of banking that followed deregulation and the collapse of the real estate and savings and loan industries in the late 1980s, many of the nation's great regional banks were acquired by national and international financial systems headquartered in other cities and were transformed into regional subsidiaries. Bank CEOs with deep roots in and allegiance to their region, some of them reaching back several generations of banking families, were often replaced by managers for whom success was measured by promotion to run a bank in a more important market, and eventually to the bank's central headquarters.

The executive officers of business-civic organizations were virtually unanimous in stressing the importance of bankers to the leadership of their organizations and the financial support of major civic projects. The older generation of hometown bankers had been almost universally engaged in civic affairs, leading peak business organizations and chambers of commerce, and serving as the catalysts in raising funds from their peer executives for civic projects. Many were leaders in the creation of CEO-only organizations in cities such as Pittsburgh, Dallas, Baltimore, Cleveland, and Houston. But while bank executives remain mainstays of corporate civic leadership, in cities where the central headquarters of a bank has been lost through consolidations or mergers, CEO-led civic association executives generally reported a negative effect on civic leadership in general and on their organizations in particular. As one association put it: "Banks used to be the leading civic contributor. Not anymore unless a bank headquarters is in your city." Another said that 20 years ago, "if one wanted to launch a major civic project, you'd go to the CEO of the local bank. You can't do that anymore; the banker doesn't have as much clout, but is probably working harder and devoting more time to the community."

In many cities, CEOs of national or international banking systems continue to play important leadership roles in their headquarters cities. After Wells Fargo Bank moved its headquarters to San Francisco, for example, its executives assumed major leadership positions in area affairs. Its corporate CEO chairs the California Business Roundtable and the COO is treasurer of the Bay Area Council. In Cleveland, National City Corp. and KeyBank CEOs were leaders of Cleveland Tomorrow and played key roles in its merger with the Cleveland Growth Association to form the Greater Cleveland Partnership. Minneapolis–St. Paul remains the headquarters city for three banking systems, and they are among the strongest supporters of the Citizens League. Their executives see a clear business self-interest in helping solve the region's problems. In Pittsburgh, CEOs of PNC Financial Services Group and Mellon Bank are active board members of the Allegheny Conference.

In other areas, the CEOs of major banks headquartered in a city have passed responsibility for representing the bank in urban and regional affairs to a second-in-command, or the head of the regional division. In part this is a function of the demands on the system CEO's time from far-flung branches, investors, and regulators. Although Sun Trust's headquarters remains in Atlanta, for example, it is the regional executive who serves on the board of Central Atlanta Progress.

In cities that have lost bank headquarters, the key to engagement of the new generation of bankers appears to be the autonomy of the regional CEO within the overall system, the corporate culture of the parent corporation, and the length of an executive's tenure in the city. In some cities, the loss of hometown bankers may result in reductions in charitable contributions. In others, it may be that a regional bank CEO lacks authority to commit resources without home office approval. And yet, elsewhere, the regional bank CEO may have had both autonomy and interest in participating in civic life, but is promoted or transferred just as he or she is beginning to know the area well and is ready to take on a major leadership role. In one city, the president of the CEO-based civic association observed that the three major banks changed their role in the community when their leadership changed even though these "local presidents" generally could make commitments to the community without going back to home office.

For example, when Bank of America moved its headquarters from San Francisco to Charlotte, its representation on the Bay Area Council was shifted from the system CEO to the head of the California office, and the strong leadership the bank had provided in the business community was effectively lost. In Milwaukee, the head of the USBank was active in the Greater Milwaukee Committee, but after two years was moved to another city. By contrast, in Houston, where locally-owned banks were acquired by out-of-state systems, the regional executives remain mainstays of the Greater Houston Partnership. Regional executives of J. P. MorganChase, Bank One, Wells Fargo, and Bank of America are typically responsible for branches in a number of states and all play a fairly substantial role in Houston's civic life. For the most part, these banks have been in Texas for some time and they bring in executives that know the market and the city.

General Consequences of Economic Restructuring for CEO Civic Engagement

While the reorganization of banking often produced the most dramatic changes in CEO engagement in urban problem solving, the broader shifts in the economic landscape of urban areas have exacerbated those effects. In addition to banking headquarters, most cities lost locally owned utilities, newspapers, centrally located department stores, and manufacturing companies. Seven of the urban areas in this study lost Fortune 500 companies over the past 20 years, 12 gained them, and in only one—Phoenix—the number stayed constant. But whether they gained or lost big companies, many regions simply now have fewer top executives among whom to spread civic work, and those executives often lack either the interest or experience in civic affairs.

In response, many CEO organizations have expanded their membership to include a broader range of executive talent such as heads of higher education institutions, medical centers, foundations, and business service partnerships in law, accounting, and consulting firms. Several organizations have merged with the regional chambers of commerce and other business-oriented organizations in order to save staffing, time, and financial resources, and to achieve greater solidarity among all sizes and types of business so they can be more effective in achieving common economic and policy goals. Whether retaining a CEO-only membership or becoming part of a merged business partnership, the paid professional executives and staffs of peak business organizations have continued to play a larger and more visible role in civic leadership. And, finally, almost all of the organizations have de-emphasized their engagement in central city affairs and increased their involvement in regional economic development policy.

The Pool of CEO Civic Leaders Is Shallower, More Transient, and Less Influential The pool of executives from which civic leadership can be drawn has become different in its makeup than in prior generations, and it is shallower. Regardless of whether an urban area had an increase or decrease in the number of major corporations, almost all experienced a substantial change in the composition and level of civic leadership by CEOs.

In some urban areas, there are simply fewer corporate headquarters from which talent can be drawn. One CEO, who is a leader in his city's civic life, lamented: "If one turned back 20 years, there were maybe 50 active executives . . . there are now 17. About half of the ones that had been active are gone, there were others that didn't care or were not engaged . . . There are fewer corporate leaders engaged than in the past."

Another pointed out that today's world for CEOs is very different from that of a generation ago. Then, he said, a dozen CEOs knew each other and were always in town. A phone call from their most respected colleague could bring them together within a day, and they could each pledge a million dollars to support a project. "CEOs, whether they want to or not, cannot be gathered effectively anymore," he said. "My travel time has gone up to 50 percent. . . . And, everything is public. I can't invest $2 million dollars of shareholders' money [on a project] that probably won't work, like they did back then. Everything is public now, and you just don't do it."

These comments were mirrored in those of the president of one of the older CEO civic associations: "There is much higher turnover in executive ranks than in past years, as a result of mergers and acquisitions. Globalization has resulted in an incredible increase in the amount of travel for CEOs. The recession only increased their travel requirements. I can no longer have regular meeting schedules for committees, but must poll members to find a 'best' time for meetings. It's tough to get participation. Some are willing to get involved in short term projects." Another said he had such difficulty in scheduling meetings that he now often goes to member firms to make presentations and seek support for projects.

Although the power, cohesion, and engagement of past CEOs are probably exaggerated and even mythic in some cities, there were substantial agreement among the association executives that even where the number of corporate central headquarters has increased, some of the new CEOs are only lightly engaged, if at all, in the civic life of the community or the organization of their peers. In the case of many fast growing firms, such as those in information technology and biomedicine, this may be due to the fact that they have not yet reached plateaus that give their leaders time to devote to civic causes. These executives have not had the opportunity to be mentored for leadership by an older generation of CEOs, and many of their companies have not yet developed an internal culture of civic engagement. For other executives, there may simply be a reluctance to get involved in local civic affairs. Many heads of regional offices of corporations, for example, tend to be more attached to the corporation and their careers than to the cities in which they currently find themselves. Because their assignments tend to be short-term, these CEOs may be especially reluctant to take on projects that require several years to complete or that present hazards to their reputation for effectiveness.

Certainly some new CEOs are deeply engaged in civic life, serving on multiple boards and in a variety of leadership and philanthropic endeavors. But particularly in the case of regional executives, their frequent rotation complicates civic leadership. A number of the association executives tell of grooming an energetic executive for leadership positions, only to have him transferred to another city just as he reaches a key position of influence. This transience deprives an area of a cadre of senior business statesmen, whose long experience in a community can provide valuable counsel and institutional memory for the civic system. And because newly arriving CEOs lack long association with and knowledge of the communities in which they find themselves, they are generally more dependent on their own community affairs staffs and the professional staffs of their civic associations. Their effectiveness in problem solving thus rests on the quality of their briefings, pre-meeting negotiations, and post-event follow through by staff. Their roles, therefore, have shifted from substantive to symbolic engagement, and from fashioning policies and solutions to bestowing legitimacy on or championing decisions formulated by professional staff.

Further exacerbating these issues is the fact that CEOs of regional offices or divisions of corporations headquartered elsewhere, like their counterparts in banking, tend to have less autonomy than the generation of homegrown owner-CEOs that preceded them. Twelve of the 19 organizations for which information was obtained for this study reported a decline in the decision-making autonomy of some of their members whose firms had become regional offices of corporations headquartered elsewhere. Even when a local executive's proposal is approved, the need for central headquarters approval of major commitments of resources can slow launching of projects and can also make executives cautious about tendering support that goes beyond their signature authority.

The Role of Nonprofit Employers and Foundations Has Grown   As the extent and nature of CEO engagement in civic organizations has changed, so too has the composition of their memberships. The nonprofit sector—particularly universities, medical centers, and foundations—has provided a substantial component of the growth in the service employment in most regions, and its engagement in civic affairs has become increasingly important to CEO organizations and the communities they serve.

Universities and medical centers are now the largest employers in many metropolitan areas. They are often incubators of new businesses and supply much of the creative, technical, professional, and management talent that both old and new industries require for success. The chief executives of these institutions have become important members of the peak business organizations in their regions. Community college presidents have increasingly been added, as their institutions are deeply engaged in workforce development, business incubation, and development of minority workers and managers.

Presidents of universities and medical centers tend to have less autonomy to allocate resources and less control of their boards and organizations than top business CEOs. Still, even though they may be supplicants and beneficiaries of the slack resources of corporate donors more often than grantors of resources to others, there are important advantages to including them in the civic organizations of the economic elite. First, most of them cannot move to other locations, and thus tend to have a strong and continuing interest in the quality of life of their areas. Universities are not subject to acquisitions and mergers, although private and some nonprofit medical centers are targets of consolidators. Second, they produce entrepreneurial, professional, and technical talent, and marketable patents to fuel the area's economy. Finally, university and medical center campuses serve as anchors and magnets for growing economic sectors such as information technology, arts, and biomedicine. All the CEO-led civic associations we studied have added higher education and medical institutions to their membership.

A growing number of civic organizations also include local private foundations, although a few exclude foundations as a matter of policy, either feeling that they do not want their agendas to be influenced by foundation priorities, or that their connections with the foundations are sufficiently strong through the overlapping board memberships of CEOs. Private foundation assets have ballooned in many cities, making them important players in establishing the civic agenda, particularly in areas that have lost locally owned banks. A foundation executive pointed out that they differ from the CEOs in that civic issues are the "day job" of the foundation presidents and their staffs.

One of the by-products of industrial reorganizations has been the creation of new private foundations or substantial increases in funding for existing foundations with a substantial focus on local giving. But the foundations are less interested in economic development initiatives—the primary priority for CEO organizations—and instead tend to focus their grants and programs on social, education, health care, and community issues. Although one or more local foundations in most urban areas can be counted on to support projects initiated by the leading business organization, most make relatively few grants for economic development, as such.

A significant exception to foundation reticence in entering the economic development arena has occurred in the Cleveland area. Led by the Cleveland and Gund foundations based in Cleveland, and Akron's GAR Foundation, 70 foundations in northeastern Ohio pooled resources in 2004 to create a three-year $30 million Fund for Our Economic Future. The Fund's objective is to frame a regional economic development agenda designed to produce a long-term economic transformation of the region, track economic progress, and invest in promising initiatives. Initial grants have supported projects and institutions created by the civic organizations of the business elite, but the foundations appear to be staking out new ground, which, while complementary to the business agenda, aims to engage a broader set of stakeholders and issues.

The key to this more aggressive role for foundations in territory once largely occupied by the corporate leadership appears to be a combination of the size of the resources leading foundations can bring to bear on problems and the changing role of foundation executives. Several urban areas have foundations that can easily match levels of corporate largess. Atlanta, Milwaukee, Kansas City, Pittsburgh, Central Indiana, and Philadelphia are home to major foundations with as much flexibility and potential leverage as Cleveland's, should they choose to use it to influence the regional agenda. This can be especially important at a time when corporate leaders tend to have less autonomy in making civic investments, and are less personally attached to the region where they are currently located. Like the universities and medical centers, the foundations are not moving. And although their executives may be mobile, they are increasingly expected by their boards to make strategic investments that can produce improvements in urban conditions, rather than repeatedly fund traditional clients.

Organizational Agendas Have Shifted to the Region   The shift toward a regional agenda has been pervasive among CEO-led civic associations, whether they have merged with other groups or have steadfastly retained their independence of the larger and more inclusive chambers of commerce. The number that have added "Greater," "Regional," "Metro," or "Area" to their names is indicative of the regional emphasis and reflects dispersion into the suburbs of members' corporate headquarters and other major facilities, as well as the growth of metropolitan areas.[1]

With agendas that typically include transportation systems, economic growth, regional workforce development, and business taxes, the leadership and professional staff of these organizations increasingly deal with state officials instead of mayors. Most retain a central city portfolio in large-scale development projects or K-12 education—which also involves a major state policy component—and maintenance of close relationships with mayors and other local elected officials remains important to their effectiveness. Even among these, however, the uneven experience of business leaders in building and maintaining governing coalitions with mayors has led them to work in what are often more hospitable regional arenas.

At the same time, based on their business experience, their members recognize that the economy functions on a regional scale, and therefore have concluded they can be effective in matters of economic development only if they work on a regional, statewide, or multi-state scale. It is also probable that the lack of CEOs with long and deep attachments to the central city, in contrast with the generation that founded many of the organizations, makes the region a more comfortable environment for more transient executives.

Regional issues are more common across the country and more transferable to new venues than central city issues, making them more attractive to executives that rotate through several places in the new corporate environment.

A few organizations, such as the Bay Area Council (BAC) and the Central Indiana Corporate Partnership (CICP), have never considered themselves to be anything but regional organizations and they have no "city" agenda. Both organizations work largely with state and federal officials, and only incidentally with local officials, leaving individual city and county issues to the local chambers of commerce. The Bay Area Council holds a monthly meeting of the major chambers, some of which are members of BAC. The Central Indiana Corporate Partnership has even less connection to individual cities or counties. CICP focuses on macroeconomic strategies to address issues confronting Central Indiana and usually does not pursue a "business" agenda, as such. The MetroHartford Alliance chose the region as the only scale at which they could mount an effective strategy for economic competitiveness in an area that contains a proliferation of small local governments.

Only a few peak business organizations continue to define their mission primarily in central city and "downtown" terms. These include Central Atlanta Progress, the Federal City Council (in Washington, DC), and Detroit Renaissance. Each may be involved in some regional activities, but these are generally supportive of their central city mission. The Federal City Council, for example, is strongly focused on improving schools and libraries in the central city and on major urban development projects such as the Anacostia waterfront and a new baseball facility. Detroit Renaissance and Central Atlanta Progress have focused on CBD and major in-town redevelopment projects.

Governing Alliances with Mayors Have Weakened Regionalism is both a cause and effect of weakened alliances between some business-based civic organizations and central city mayors. These informal alliances in cities such as Pittsburgh, Atlanta, Dallas, Cleveland, and Baltimore produced historic achievements in urban development and public policy. They often endured over many years and different mayoral administrations and were based on the recognition that, as one mayor put it, "I could get elected without the business leaders, but I could not govern without them." On the other hand, only city government could provide much of what business leaders needed—whether it was land, zoning, infrastructure, tax changes, or investments in safety, education, and other services. Mayors realized they needed business support to leverage public investments and to provide legitimacy for important policy initiatives and projects. Their support was also critical in extracting help from state and federal governments.

We found no city where such an alliance was once a defining feature of its governance that currently claimed it had been sustained to the present day. In some places, there does remain a good, even warm relationship between mayors and business leaders and their civic organizations. But even in these cities, it appears to depend heavily on the approach of the incumbent mayor toward business leadership. And because, over time, mayors have varied substantially in their ability to relate to CEOs, whether due to their own political agendas and base, or to lack of understanding of what business leaders can do and how to approach them, there has been growing disenchantment with the mayoralty, despite occasionally rekindled romances with specific mayors. Whether they offered and initiatives were rebuffed, ignored, or scorned, mayoral influence on the agenda of a city's major business organization has declined.

In no city was the relationship with the mayor described as a central feature of the organization, although a number of organizations report that they regularly work in alliance with mayors on major projects. Most acknowledge, however, that the relationship can vary widely from incumbent to incumbent and few seem to have strongly institutionalized relationships—even in cities where public–private regimes once characterized their governance. An association executive summarized his long experience that spanned two cities:

> The relationship differs based on the official. There are two categories of officials: those who are for things and those who are against things. I like working with those who are for things. Some make a career of being opposed to bad things, rather than those who work for the good things. I like those who accept an idea and work for it. The mayor of [the executive's current city] is for things and is enjoyable to work with. In [the executive's former city], the mayor was against new ideas. In cities, it's increasingly important to have a good relationship with the mayor [and the] governor, and . . . it's important to have a relationship with Congress to get your share of federal earmarks. Most cities don't know how to do this, but we have a good delegation and [our organization] works well with them. One of the trends of the future will [be] go after more federal help than ever before.

Another opined that:

> There is an interdependent relationship of the highest order with political leaders. They can't do much without us. The [CEOs] can support or oppose tax issues effectively. There are also many things the [organization] wants— e.g., downtown redevelopment, better state funding of education—that have to have support of political leaders. At times the relationships are difficult. The [organization] will sometimes support things about which it is not enthusiastic to avoid the risk of damage to more important things that are high on its agenda. The quality of the relationship varies with the officeholder. The previous mayor had not been supported by most of the . . . members, but after his election he came to the [organization] and said we needed to work together. A close working relationship was established. He took advice and consulted . . . before undertaking major projects. The current mayor had lots of support from business leaders, but tends to take them for granted. [This mayor] has a very different style and does not have a big circle of advisers. The big change has been that there is no longer an accepted power structure in the city.

These comments were typical of opinions expressed by most other association executives, even those with strong central city and downtown agendas. The change in relationship with mayors appears to be idiosyncratic rather than follow any historical trend. Describing his organization's relationship with four successive mayors, one association executive said it was "poisonous" with one, who feared that asking business for help would be perceived as weakness; "good" with another, "OK" with a third, and "wonderful" with the current incumbent, "who has been able to exist comfortably in both the political and business communities, has brought business into the fold, and [has] taken advantage of services donated to the city."

The reduction in the autonomy of many of a region's CEOs, and in their familiarity with its political system, combined with executive suite turnover and demands on their time produce impediments to swift, bold, and sustained civic action. Dispersion of headquarters across the region, the consolidation of banking, and the loss of dominant home-grown CEOs means that if a city once had a self conscious and cohesive economic "establishment," it probably no longer has one. There simply are fewer "go to" corporate leaders who can mobilize their peers in support of major projects. These conditions induce caution toward taking on "wicked" central city issues, where attempt to ameliorate them can beget new problems that escalate the stakes and widen the conflict. While it may be in their firms' interests to solve such problems, engaging them can be a major drain on time and do little to enhance the career of a branch executive. Buying the naming rights to a sports facility, leading the United Way campaign, or becoming a patron of a museum, university, hospital, or zoo is less hazardous to the reputation of both the firm and its local CEO.

NOTES

1. Examples are the *Greater* Baltimore Committee, Charlotte *Regional* Partnership; *Greater* Cleveland Partnership, *Metro* Hartford Alliance, *Greater* Houston Partnership, Civic Council of *Greater* Kansas City, Council, *Greater* Milwaukee Committee, *Greater* Philadelphia Chamber of Commerce, *Greater* Phoenix Leadership.

6

Rethinking the Politics of Downtown Development

ELIZABETH STROM

Those interested in both the physical and political changes reshaping the downtowns of large American cities can find themselves engaged in two parallel conversations. In the first, found among urbanists from many fields as well as in the popular press, we learn that much of the new (e.g., post-1980) development in American city centers has been focused on activities we might characterize as "consumption"—professional sports, cultural institutions, themed shopping districts, and housing are now taking over areas once dominated by banks, corporate headquarters, and department stores. Downtowns, we learn, are now developed and marketed as mixed districts in which retail, housing, and entertainment may even come to overshadow traditional central business district (CBD) functions.

The second is a conversation mostly among political scientists and political sociologists, who have been interested in the various stakeholders (elected officials and bureaucrats; corporate leaders and peak business associations; neighborhood organizations) who have sought to shape downtown. In this narrative, business elites with a financial and symbolic stake in the economic health of the central business district began mobilizing in many cities during the 1940s and 1950s to protect their investments, which were in many cases thought to be "sunk" and immobile—Richard King Mellon, the Pittsburgh

From Elizabeth Strom, "Rethinking the Politics of Downtown Development," *Journal of Urban Affairs*, Vol. 30, No. 1 (2008), pp. 37–50, 58–61. Copyright © 2008 Urban Affairs Association. Reprinted by permission of Wiley-Blackwell.

financier who mobilized resources behind the redevelopment of downtown Pittsburgh in the 1940s, explained his commitment to his city as an outgrowth of his business interests: "We have a lot of property here. We can't very well move out the banks" (Fitzpatrick, 2000). Business leaders worked with entrepreneurial mayors and development officials, leveraging federal urban renewal funds to shore up downtowns. Although in some cities these downtown-focused coalitions were eventually challenged by neighborhood-based groups seeking a more equitable share of public investment dollars, the basic political science narrative—that downtown development is the project of the city and region's most powerful economic elites—has not been revised.

But if downtown is now less a seat of corporate power and more a "place to play" (Fainstein & Judd, 1999), do these assumptions still hold? If indeed the value and use of downtown land has changed over the past four decades, would not that suggest that the nature and relative strength of downtown development interests would have shifted as well? This article posits that in many U.S. cities, downtowns are no longer the region's economic heart, and they are therefore unlikely to generate the sort of political power assumed in earlier political science studies. I study the players in peak, downtown-focused business organizations as a way to understand who in the business community is most engaged in downtown development issues, and to generate hypotheses about how further research could shed light on the relationship between the geography and the politics of the American downtown.

NARRATIVE ONE: THE NEW DOWNTOWN IS FUN!

Whether for a leisurely walk next to the Reedy River Falls or a night of music and fast-paced entertainment, Downtown Greenville is the place to go for fun just about any day of the week.

—From the Greenville, South Carolina, website[1]

Downtown is a great place to attend family friendly events, dine at one of the 170 plus restaurants, visit over 30 attractions and over 200 retail and service establishments. With over 17 new restaurants and 22 new retail stores that have opened since 2003, you owe it to yourself to come see what all the "fun" is about. Have fun in downtown St. Louis.

—From the Downtown St. Louis Partnership website[2]

Over the past two decades, much of the new development in American downtowns has been the construction of cultural facilities, convention centers, and sports venues. Often these projects have been undertaken with the goal of encouraging tourism, seen by many economic development officials as an important new growth industry (Judd et al., 2003). In addition, city officials and business leaders have better recognized the competitive advantages of central cities for functions like culture and night-time entertainment, as downtowns can offer amenities (access to mass transit, a dense and historically interesting built environment) with which sprawling suburbs cannot easily compete. Downtowns are now marketed as exciting areas in which to be enriched (by museums and concert halls) and entertained (by professional sporting events and themed restaurants). Downtown, we learn from promotion groups, is now officially "fun."

In many downtowns, moreover, market-rate housing has become a major part of the built environment.[3] The growing popularity of market-rate downtown housing is by now even reflected in census data, which show an increase in downtown populations, with more downtown residents who are college educated and who own their homes (Birch, 2005; Perlman, 1998).[4] The trend toward renovating industrial lofts into living space has been underway, at least in some cities, for several decades (Zukin, 1982). Now even office buildings have been repackaged for residential use, as apartments are seen as ways to rescue obsolete, class B office stock in cities like Denver, Tampa, St. Louis (Sharoff, 2001), and Los Angeles (Bergsman, 2004), where a recent study found continued increases in residential population, alongside decline in downtown employment (DiMassa, 2007).

New entertainment spaces and residential districts are often heralded (by city officials and by the local press, if not always by academics—see Fainstein & Judd, 1999; Hannigan, 1998) as signs of a downtown "revival" or "comeback." This narrative of revival, however, overshadows (and indeed, is often intended to overshadow) the key underlying trend found in many American metropolitan areas: downtown is no longer the center of the region's economic life. The traditional CBDs are no longer necessarily their region's largest office markets or their largest employment nodes. In most metropolitan areas, a majority of jobs are found well outside the traditional CBD (Glaeser & Kahn, 2001). And only a few downtowns continue to dominate their metro area office markets. In the cities studied by Lang (2003), traditional downtowns contained about one-third of the area's office space. He and other sources (see, for example, Center City District, 2006) note wide variation between more centralized MSAs (New York, Boston, San Francisco, Pittsburgh, and Chicago are examples) and the most decentralized areas (Las Vegas, Phoenix, Miami, and Houston) where CBDs may contain less than 20% of the region's office space (Center City District, 2006). Both Lang and the Center City District find that the downtown share of the office market is decreasing over time. For example, Philadelphia contained just 27% of its region's office space in 2005, which was down from 41% in 1993—a reflection of the much faster pace of growth in its suburbs (Center City District, 2006).

CBD office space had also, traditionally, been the most expensive in the region (indeed, urban economic theory's "bid-rent curve" assumes that the highest land values will always be at the center (Alonso, 1960). That has also changed. Quite often, newer, peripheral office developments are pricier than the average center city building. The most expensive offices in Atlanta are found in the Buckhead neighborhood (within the city limits, but miles from the downtown); the Philadelphia region's costliest offices are on the suburban Main Line (Center City District, 2006).

And that's why we find office buildings converted into condominiums, banks renovated into theaters, and 50-acre football stadium/parking complexes usurping commercial districts: too few companies are compelled to be downtown, leaving space for more land-intensive and less profitable uses (Ford, 2003). The trend toward big-footprint projects like stadiums and convention centers in downtowns, or of converting office buildings into loft apartments, may be framed by city boosters as signs of an urban resurgence, but in some fundamental way they indicate that a city's downtown has lost its function as the key economic hub and real estate powerhouse of the region.

NARRATIVE TWO: DOWNTOWN AS THE CENTER OF POWER

These changes in land use and economic geography would seem to presage fundamental changes in the urban political economy, but students of urban politics have not yet begun to grapple with their implications. Although there are political scientists who find new ways to write about downtown development (Fainstein, 1994; McGovern, 1998; Turner, 2002), the basic political science downtown development paradigm first developed decades earlier has not been questioned: the redevelopment of the city's center is seen as the project of the most essential regional economic stakeholders who will reap immediate material and longer-term symbolic advantages from a robust urban core. They work in coalition with elected officials and appointed redevelopment directors who gain clear political advantage from their association with the city's dominant economic interests. Much of the urban political science literature on downtown development has been an exploration of these stakeholders and their mutual interests in the physical redevelopment of the city's center (Dahl, 1961; Mollenkopf, 1983; Salisbury, 1964; Stone, 1989; Wolfinger, 1974).

The Peak Business Association: Downtown Development Catalyst

The peak downtown business association has been at the center of downtown development since emerging in the 1940s (Fogelson, 2001), and it has been the focus of much urban development literature. The best known and most successful of these organizations played a dominant role in shaping policies to redevelop their downtowns. Some (e.g., Central Atlanta Progress) did so with an explicitly downtown focus; others (Greater Philadelphia Movement, Allegheny Conference on Community Development) were regional organizations that gave priority to a downtown redevelopment agenda. To ensure their effectiveness, many of these organizations restricted membership to the most prominent businesses (in contrast to Chambers of Commerce that represent all businesses) and required the participation of a company's CEO.

In cities like Boston (Mollenkopf, 1983), San Francisco (McGovern, 1998; Mollenkopf, 1983); Atlanta (Stone, 1989), and Cleveland (Swanstrom, 1985) these groups shaped urban renewal policies and influenced local electoral politics, using these organizations as vehicles with which to "look more broadly, both in time and area," than other local interests were able to do (Stone, 1989, p. 21). The Bay Area Committee, formed in San Francisco in 1946, included the Chief Executives of 23 of the 27 regional Fortune 500 companies, as well as the heads of the four major banks and two newspapers (McGovern, 1998; Mollenkopf, 1983). In Pittsburgh, extensive infrastructure improvement and downtown redevelopment came about when a politically connected mayor, David Lawrence, joined forces with local business leadership, led by financier Richard King Mellon (Ferman, 1996; Sbragia, 1989). Redevelopment in downtown Milwaukee was spearheaded by the Greater Milwaukee Committee, whose membership, according to its 1955 annual report, "owned or managed businesses representing one-fourth of the city's total assessed value of business property" (Norman, 1989, p. 184). Either these business leaders literally invested in downtown, by dint of their ownership of its real estate, or they depended on getting customers/clients to come to downtown locations, or they would derive symbolic benefit from a robust downtown. In all the scholarly work on this topic, there is a stated or implied link between a business firm's concerns with profitability, its presence in or near a city's central business district, and its progrowth activism.

These peak organizations have been identified in the political science literature as central to the project of downtown development, both because they symbolized the collective interests of the most powerful economic actors, and because, by mobilizing this power into an organizational vehicle, they could have real impact on a city's electoral politics and on its redevelopment policies. They would seem, therefore, to be useful institutions to study if one wishes to see whether the private interests guiding downtown development have changed over the years. Are these economic interests still mobilized into peak organizations engaged in downtown development? If not, what do changes in private sector downtown leadership tell us about larger changes in the urban political economy?

TRACKING DOWNTOWN CHANGES THROUGH PEAK ORGANIZATION LEADERSHIP

To understand how urban business leadership has changed, and to suggest the implications of these changes for downtown politics, I have examined the leadership of three such peak organizations in earlier decades. These are the Greater Philadelphia Movement (GPM, formed in 1948), the Greater Baltimore Committee (GBC, formed in 1956), and Central Atlanta Progress (CAP, formed in 1941, when it was called Central Atlanta Improvement Association). I have sought to identify the companies represented on these boards (which I have labeled "leadership companies"), ascertain the sectors in which these companies operated, and discover whether those companies are still in operation (and still in operation in those cities). Although these companies hardly represent any kind of random sample of locally based companies, it is fair to say that these organizations generally have represented the largest, most politically active companies in the area (the Greater Baltimore Committee, for example, specifically sought to engage the heads of the region's largest one hundred businesses). I have used the board of directors or members lists for the years available: 1960 and 1965 for GPM, 1962 for GBC, and 1970 for CAP.

As Table 1 indicates, 26% of these "leadership companies" from the 1960–1970 period were still present in their region or city in 2006; 35% have either gone out of business, been bought out by another corporation headquartered elsewhere, or moved out of the region. It is quite likely that all or most of the 42 (29%) firms for which I could find no information are also

TABLE 1

Percentage of GPM (1960, 1965), GBC (1962), and CAP (1970) Members Still Active in Region in 2006

Peak Org.	No. of Firms in City	No. of Firms in Suburbs	No. of Firms Gone	No. of Whereabouts Unknown
GPM	11 (31%)	4 (11%)	13 (37%)	7 (19%)
GBC	13 (15%)	11 (13%)	28 (31%)	35 (41%)
CAP	14 (56%)	0	11 (44%)	0

Note: Totals for all three groups: 38 (26%); 15 (10%); 52 (35%); 42 (29%).

TABLE 2

Downtown Leadership, 1960–1970

Atlanta, Baltimore, and Philadelphia

	Central Atlanta Progress, 1970 n = 25	Greater Baltimore Committee, 1962 n = 87	Greater Philadelphia Movement, 1960 and 1965 n = 36
Real estate	0	6 (7%)	0
Law	1 (4%)	2 (2%)	8 (22%)
Other professional services	1 (4%)	9 (10%)	2 (6%)
Finance and insurance	10 (40%)	31 (36%)	7 (20%)
Miscellaneous corporate	13 (50%)	37 (43%)	15 (42%)
Nonprofit and education	0	0	2
Public	0	0	0
Other/cannot determine	0	2 (2%)	2 (6%)

defunct, so the percentage of firms represented on these boards that are no longer in the region is likely to be well over 50%. Atlanta has had the highest retention rate, which may reflect the fact that the board list is more recent, but could also speak to the greater economic success of Atlanta, which today has twice as many Fortune 500 headquarters as either Philadelphia or Baltimore, even though it has a smaller population than either of those cities.

The "leadership companies" have been broken down by sector in Table 2. "Other professional service" firms include advertising, accounting, and architecture/engineering. Finance and insurance includes all manner of banks, investment firms, and insurance agencies. The admittedly clumsy "miscellaneous corporate" category includes all those companies not described in any other category (these run the gamut from manufacturers to energy producers to communications and transportation firms to retail establishments).

In Table 3, we see that some sectors have had a more stable presence than others. Law firms seem to be the most likely to have remained intact in their cities, especially in Philadelphia, where eight of the eleven companies from the GPM lists that are still active in Philadelphia are law firms.

In all three cities, the boards of the 1960s and 1970s were dominated by the insurance, banking, financial, and "miscellaneous corporate" sectors (Table 4 gives further breakdown of the dominant corporate sectors found in this category in each city).

On the other hand, the "miscellaneous corporate" category has shown larger decline. First, industrial producers and energy firms had been part of the downtown leadership in earlier decades—both Philadelphia and Baltimore groups had included representatives from major regional subsidiaries of companies like Bethlehem Steel and General Electric, and local companies like Sun Oil. Although a few industrial producers remain in these regions (examples include Black and Decker in Baltimore), the decline in industrial employment since 1970, both nationally and in urban areas, has been documented (Harrison & Bluestone, 1982).

TABLE 3

Stability of 1960–1970 Leadership Firms by Sector (of Firms Whose Sector Could Be Determined), GPM, GBC, and CAP Combined

	In Region (City or Suburb), 2006	Not in Region (Moved, Merged, or Went Out of Business)	Fate Cannot Be Determined
Real estate (n = 6)	2	1	3
Law (n = 12)	12	0	0
Other prof. services (n = 11)	3	2	6
Finance and insurance (n = 47)	14	17	16
Misc corporate (n = 22)	10	9	3
Manufacturing (n = 28)	9	11	8
Retail (n = 13)	1	11	1

But some of the other companies in the "miscellaneous corporate" category represent sectors that, to both scholars and practitioners of an earlier era, seemed particularly place-bound. Local utilities and newspapers had played an important role in downtown growth coalitions (Logan & Molotch, 1987), their deep interest in promoting the local economic base clearly linked to the nature of their business. But even these companies have become less tied to central cities. First, both industries have been able to adjust to the realities of a more dispersed metropolitan region, and have developed their suburban client bases, becoming less dependent on downtown business. Moreover, deregulation, mergers, and acquisitions have changed the nature of both industries. Today, many utilities are part of regional conglomerates with less focus on particular central cities. Newspapers, similarly, are likely to be controlled by one of several national chains such as the McClatchy Company (which owns newspapers in 30 markets) or Gannett. Thus, the conditions in downtown Atlanta, or Philadelphia, or Chicago are simply not as significant a business factor for them as they had once been. Others in this category include transportation and communication companies, which have been affected by industry-wide sea changes since 1970. Local Bell Telephone companies have disappeared, as have regional rail lines such as Philadelphia's Reading or Baltimore's Western Maryland Rail.

TABLE 4

Most Frequently Represented Sectors in the "Miscellaneous Corporate Category," CAP, GBC, and GPM Boards, 1960–1970

	Atlanta	Baltimore	Philadelphia
Retail (department stores)	4	7	2
Energy/Utilities/Communication (local phone companies)	6	4	2
Manufacturing	3	23	10

The most strikingly transformed sector in this "miscellaneous corporate category" is retail, and specifically the once iconic downtown flagship department store. The presidents of these stores were often extremely active in shaping downtown development coalitions (Cohen, 2007), and heavily engaged in civic affairs, sponsoring parades in cities like New York and Detroit, and underwriting the costs of a museum in Newark. Their often large, elaborate downtown buildings were seen as emblematic of the identity of a city's center (Isenberg, 2004). Today, the list of remaining downtown flagship department stores is short indeed. Where a downtown houses a department store it is most likely part of a national chain such as Cincinnati-based Federated Department Stores, which over the years has bought up such downtown fixtures as Macy's, Bloomingdale's, and A&S (New York City), Rich's (Atlanta), Filene's (Boston), Marshall Field (Chicago), Goldsmith's (Memphis), Burdine's (Miami), and Strawbridge's (Philadelphia). As a result of this industry reshuffling, only one of the retailers whose heads had sat on these leadership boards is still in operation (Haverty's Furniture in Atlanta). The decline of the downtown department store is felt in the city's economy, in its downtown power structure, and in its built environment—in some cases flagship stores have simply been demolished (as was Hudson's in downtown Detroit, to the consternation of preservationists—see McGraw, 2002) or reused, as is the case of Muse's seven-story downtown Atlanta store, now loft apartments.

"Leadership companies" in the area of banking and insurance have been similarly depleted in our case study cities. The heads of local banks had been among the most eager participants of urban-renewal era downtown coalitions. These institutions surely seemed to be exceptionally place-bound. Federal regulations made it difficult for banks to operate beyond their local areas, so their fate seemed to be intertwined with the local economy and the value of local real estate. But deregulation has led to a consolidation in the banking industry, as those banks that managed to remain solvent have frequently been bought up by one of five or six national banking giants (Dymski, 1999). Whereas in the 1960s cities like Philadelphia and Baltimore would have been home to some eight or ten substantial, locally controlled banks, today such cities may have no locally controlled banks at all. Richard King Mellon's claim that he cannot "just move our banks," it turns out, was not completely accurate.

The local implications of these industry-wide changes can be found when we look at the fate of leadership companies in this sector. Of the financial institutions represented on the 1960–1970 boards, just 14 of the 47 are still active in their regions. These include a few insurance companies (although some are now part of larger "groups" based in New York or Europe) and a few financial service firms that have remained active. T. Rowe Price and Legg Mason, for example, are two large financial service groups that have remained headquartered in Baltimore. The banks represented on leadership boards, however, have been far less stable. The Greater Philadelphia Movement had six bank presidents on its board in 1960, representing the major local banks of that decade. By 2000 not one of those banks existed. In Baltimore, two of the banks whose presidents served on the Greater Baltimore Committee board in 1962 are still headquartered in Baltimore. The remaining six that could be traced have been bought up by banks in Atlanta, Buffalo, and Charlotte. Atlanta has been the beneficiary of some of this merger activity, as the Atlanta-based Suntrust has emerged as a national leader. Nonetheless, five other local banks have since been absorbed into either Bank of America or Wachovia, and another has been closed. In some cases, too, bank buildings are now put to uses that suggest the new function of the central city built environment: architecturally significant bank buildings in Philadelphia now house the Ritz-Carlton and Loews hotels; San Diego's First National Bank building has been converted to condominiums, and the former Western National and Eutaw Savings Banks in Baltimore now house the France-Merrick Performing Arts Center.

In sum, we see that the most economically dominant companies that had once spearheaded downtown redevelopment in Atlanta, Baltimore, and Philadelphia in the 1960s are largely gone (Hodos, 2002; Holloway & Wheeler, 1991). Apparently, the "place-based" economic interests whose downtown "sunk costs" made them appear as permanent fixtures of the downtown landscape a few decades ago were not as permanent as they had seemed. The literature focused on the urban renewal era could not have anticipated just how many core members of the downtown-based business groups would flee.

Of course, the loss of these particular firms in these particular industries need not suggest the economic decline of the central city—after all, these firms could well have been replaced by other firms in newly dominant industries, in which case the political base of downtown could, despite these changes, remain intact. But there are several reasons to suggest that this has not been the case.

DOWNTOWN LEADERSHIP TODAY

If so many of the firms that had been engaged in downtown development and advocacy have disappeared, is there still a "downtown business interest" articulated in city politics? There is, but I would argue it represents different segments of the business community, and, perhaps related to these sectoral shifts, it organizes itself differently. Today's downtown coalitions are geographically narrower, represented by groups focused only on the downtown (although in some cases their board membership may overlap with the boards of regional groups). At the same time, they have extended their constituency to include nonprofit executives and public officials, very few of which could be found on the boards of 1960–1970.

These contrasts can best be seen by comparing downtown leadership boards of the earlier era with those active today. Ideally, I would have liked to accomplish this by comparing the board figures for GPM, GBC, and CAP from the 1960s–1970s, to those of 2006. I have indeed done this in the case of Atlanta. But in the cases of Philadelphia and Baltimore, a methodological problem emerged, one that is in itself very revealing of the political shifts in downtown leadership. Many of the peak business organizations identified with downtown advocacy in the 1950s and 1960s have either disappeared, or have shifted their focus to broader, regional issues like economic competitiveness, transportation, and education. Meanwhile, downtown-specific organizations have been created in many cities, and these have taken up the downtown-focused agenda first advocated by these earlier business groups. So, for example, the Greater Philadelphia Movement merged, transformed, emerged as Greater Philadelphia First in the 1980s, which in 2003 merged into the regional Chamber of Commerce (ironically, perhaps, as the group had originally formed with the goal of distinguishing the downtown-based corporate and banking concerns from those of regional industrialists—see Adams et al., 1991). By then, it had become largely focused on regional issues, such as encouraging foreign investment and regional cooperation (Hodos, 2002), with no focus on downtown development. But GPM had, in the late 1950s, spun off the Old Philadelphia Development Corporation, intended to help implement the ambitious Society Hill urban renewal plan. The OPDC had ultimately extended its reach to the traditional CBD, renaming itself the Central Philadelphia Development Corporation. The CPDC is thus the real successor to the downtown mission of the Greater Philadelphia Movement.

The Greater Baltimore Committee has remained active, but has dropped its downtown agenda, and today has a purely regional focus. The organization's website notes its historical role in spurring downtown development, but today: "The GBC's mission is to improve the business climate of the Baltimore region by organizing its corporate and civic leadership to develop solutions to the problems that affect the region's competitiveness and viability." Its current priorities are development of biotechnology industries; support for regional transportation; and support for minority business development.[5] Meanwhile, downtown businesses have created the Downtown Partnership of Baltimore to attend to their specific concerns. Although this organization has no "genetic" ties to the Greater Baltimore Committee, it would be the logical place to look for a picture of business leadership in the downtown. In other cities as well, older organizations that had included downtown development as part of a broader agenda have seemed to move in a regional direction while dedicated downtown groups have taken up the central city revitalization banner.[6]

Business leadership concerned with the downtown has thus, at least in some cities, shifted its organizational vehicle from corporate-based, peak business organizations that included citywide and regional interests to organizations more narrowly engaged in the development and maintenance of the CBD. Upon closer observation, it is clear that the business sectors represented by these organizations, and their organizational goals, have changed as well. Table 5 shows the sectoral breakdown of downtown group board members in 2006. Whereas the older organizations were dominated by corporations (including manufacturers and retailers), banks and insurance companies (see Table 2), board membership for the contemporary groups includes scant corporate representation. Atlanta is the exception to this trend; CAP's board still includes such local institutions as Coca-Cola, Delta Airlines, Turner Broadcasting, and BellSouth. Nonetheless, even in Atlanta many of these corporations seem to have lost some of their downtown Atlanta focus, sending vice presidents rather than CEOs to represent them. The local press has frequently commented on the diminished clout of CAP, noting its failure to see its favored projects through, and bemoaning the decline of civic leadership in the downtown (Salter & Scott, 1991; Saporta, 2000; Saporta, 2003). This is consistent with other literature, which suggests that as corporations stretch their geographic presence, they may become less engaged, economically or politically, in their headquarters city. As Kanter notes, "large businesses supplying global customers have weaker ties to specific regions" (2000, p. 166), and most certainly have a reduced interest in the fate of the region's downtown.

In place of banks, corporations, and department stores, we see greater representation of the public and nonprofit sectors. The older boards had no public participation, and the only nonprofit representation was in Philadelphia, where both a construction union and the University of Pennsylvania were part of the leadership coalition. Today, in contrast, most downtown groups include several public representatives *ex officio*, suggesting a more formalized cooperation between private and public interests in downtown development and management.

We also see an increase in nonprofit representation, which includes universities, nonprofit hospitals, and cultural institutions. This suggests the greater

TABLE 5

Downtown Leadership, 2006

	Atlanta, Baltimore, Philadelphia		
	Central Atlanta Progress/Atlanta Downtown Improvement District $n = 72$	Downtown Partnership of Baltimore/ Downtown Management District $n = 64$	Center City District/Central Philadelphia Development Corporation $n = 56$
Real estate	18 (25%)	16 (25%)	15 (27%)
Law	8 (11%)	12 (19%)	9 (16%)
Other professional services	7 (10%)	4 (6%)	9 (16%)
Finance and insurance	4 (6%)	11 (17%)	8 (16%)
Miscellaneous corporate	28 (39%)	4 (6%)	5 (9%)
Nonprofit and education	10 (14%)	9 (14%)	3 (5%)
Public	6 (8%)	8 (13%)	1 (2%)
Other/cannot determine	2 (3%)	0	2 (4%)

importance of large nonprofits as economic actors: Universities and their medical centers are the largest private employers in Philadelphia, New Haven, and the San Francisco Bay Area (Strom, 2005; Wallack, 2005)—and unlike those Mellon-owned banks, they really *cannot* move. Major cultural institutions are increasingly embraced by downtown business leaders as key actors in economic development efforts, and there is now enormous ideological and organizational overlap between downtown booster groups, tourism promoters, and cultural advocates (Strom, 2003).

The dominant business sector on downtown boards today is the real estate industry. On all of today's boards, real estate interests (which include developers and leasing agents) represent approximately a quarter of all representatives. This percentage actually undervalues the importance of real estate to these organizations, however, as many of the law firms and "other professional service" firms (which include a number of architectural firms) are very closely tied to the real estate industry. The combined representation of real estate, nonprofit, and public sectors—three sectors virtually absent from the earlier boards—now comprises about half of the board in Atlanta (47%) and Baltimore (52%), and over a third in Philadelphia (35%). The constituency working for CBD development, at least as represented on peak business association boards, has clearly changed in ways that reflect the changing value and function of the downtown as productive economic space.

Today's downtown groups also rely on organizational and financial structures that were not found among urban renewal-era groups: the self-financed

Business Improvement Districts (BIDs), which are state-enabled special assessment districts in which property owners pay toward the provision of enhanced public services in their district.[7] Today, nearly every downtown development group manages or has a dotted-line relationship to a BID; many downtown BIDS were formed at the urging of downtown organizations and their constituent businesses, no doubt, in some cases as a way to ensure a sufficient income stream to support the organization (Briffault, 1999). These groups, then, function largely as service organizations, collecting fees from local property owners in exchange for providing services, the most common of which include maintenance, façade and street improvements, and marketing (Mitchell, 2001).[8] BIDs and their services have become a key part of the mobilization of downtown interests, because these organizations can then keep a constituency together around the appeal of a service organization; with the special assessment powers they experience limited "free rider" problems (Briffault, 1999; Mitchell, 2001).

One does find variation among downtown groups and BIDs, with better-established organizations led by strong boards and/or experienced and knowledgeable directors playing roles beyond simple service provision.[9] The Center City group in Philadelphia does a great deal of research and planning (see their website, http:/www.centercityphila.org/ for examples of their reports); the Downtown Seattle Association has been active in addressing the problems of affordable housing and homelessness in that city's downtown (Harrell, 2004; Slobodzian, 2005). In Charlotte the Center City Partners board, which unlike many downtown boards still includes many top corporate leaders, functions almost as the downtown planning and marketing arm of both the city and the corporate sectors; plans commissioned by the organization have in several instances been adopted as the official plan of the city. But most downtown groups today are no longer the vehicles of the region's top employers, so they have come to rely more on the skills of their staff (the directors of the downtown groups in both Philadelphia and Seattle have been with their organizations many years, and are well-known and respected figures in political, business, and academic circles), and more generally the professionalization of downtown promotion and management.[10]

THE POLITICAL IMPLICATIONS OF THE NEW DOWNTOWN

How and Why the New Downtown Coalition Is Different

It is clear that the economic base of the downtown leadership has changed, and it is safe to say that downtown is no longer a primary focus of the largest regional economic interests. What is less clear is whether that has an impact on the ability of downtown interests to shape the city's development agenda. Does it matter that the remaining downtown growth interests are developers, brokers, university presidents, and city officials rather than bankers and manufacturers? I would hypothesize that it does, but I admit this hypothesis requires considerably more testing. In theory at least, the significant presence of nonprofit and public officials surely gives these groups a different agenda than their all-private sector predecessors would have had. Although it would be naïve to claim that public officials and nonprofit leaders always engage in urban redevelopment with democratic and eleemosynary goals, it is clear that such leaders are responsible to different constituencies than are their private sector counterparts (Strom, 2005). For public and nonprofit officials, maximizing economic returns is only one of many goals. Nonprofit organizations are responsible to boards of trustees who may place a higher priority on issues like organizational prestige. Public officials need to garner votes from a broad, geographically dispersed constituency, but also care about the reputation of their cities among investors and other political leaders. Certainly, many public officials support the efforts of BIDs to provide enhanced services without dipping into public coffers, although some government leaders may share the concerns of critics who wonder whether this form of privatization has negative consequences for democratic governance (Briffault, 1999). At any rate, the inclusion of public officials on these leadership boards represents a number of trends in the maturation of various "public-private partnership models" (Friedan & Sagalyn, 1989) but it can surely suggest at least some loss of preeminence on the part of the private sector downtown leadership, which can no longer depend on an active cadre of CEOs, and must invite public officials to be part of their decision-making processes in order to gain attention and support.

I would further argue that the replacement of corporate and banking CEOs with real estate developers and managers has altered the position of these downtown associations as well. First, the real estate industry is less central to a region's economic base and its promoters are therefore in a weaker institutional position to operate as insiders in a progrowth regime. Does this mean that real estate developers and owners have no economic significance or political clout? Of course not. Real estate interests can, and in some cities do play a prominent role as campaign funders, and their political largesse can give individual real estate developers excellent access to decision makers. Studies of downtown development have highlighted the centrality of the property development process, which can shape many aspects of a city's center (Fainstein, 1994). At the very least, real estate development has a huge symbolic resonance, for it is the reshaping of the physical built environment—the ribbon cutting ceremonies, the "cranes on the skyline" (Healey & Barrett, 1990) that give political leaders the opportunity to claim credit for positive change. David Harvey notes the importance of the continued construction and destruction of the built environment as part of capitalist reproduction, and points to what he calls the "speculator-developer" as playing a key "coordinating and stabilizing function" in this process (Harvey, 1985, p. 68).

But real estate remains, in Harvey's analysis, a secondary circuit of capital, auxiliary to primary production. Real estate is reactive—its value reflects the eagerness of other sorts of economic actors to locate in a particular place. If city boosters can persuade major corporations to locate in their center, *some* developer will be happy to take advantage of this opportunity.[11] In more concrete terms, real estate is not an export industry;[12] it does not have a large employment base (construction of course is an important part of the job market but construction jobs are largely sub, or sub-sub-contracted, so there is no direct line between a developer and this workforce). Individual developers may use tools such as campaign contributions to open access channels to public decision makers, but cities are not generally in competition for the favors of specific developers the way they are for car makers, pharmaceutical firms, or even football franchises. Indeed, Friedland and Palmer's analysis might suggest that the high level of engagement of real estate interests in activities such as campaign fund-raising indicates their lack of structural power—the most central economic actors, those with the power of exit, need not exert time and energy in these efforts to influence decision makers (Friedland & Palmer, 1984). That real estate now appears to be such a dominant industry in some cities may say more about the dearth of other productive activities than it does about the potential of real estate alone to generate significant economic activity.

My claim here is not that real estate developers—or for that matter, the directors of nonprofit hospitals and universities—wield no influence in the politics of downtown development. Rather, I would maintain that they have influence over a narrower set of issues, with power that is more tactical (e.g., they can draw on it to fight particular, site-specific battles) than structural (e.g., capable of setting a political agenda). Real estate dominated groups, for better or worse, may also have a less ambitious civic agenda. Real estate owners and developers are probably not going to make significant material and symbolic investments of the kind made by companies like GM (in Detroit) or Prudential (in Newark)—it is not in their self-interest or part of their corporate culture to do so. But they also are less likely to play a prominent role trying to shape significant civic or political debates—when real estate is one's primary business, the key question is whether resources will be devoted to block X or block Y, and there may be less of an identification with and commitment to a larger civic agenda.

I further hypothesize that the proliferation of the "business improvement district" model as a way of mobilizing resources around downtown development suggests that this new coalition has different kinds of collective active issues than did earlier groups, which were more reliant on voluntary activities (donations of money and the involvement of corporate CEOs) than on mandated contributions such as those underwriting BID budgets. The creation of BIDs that focus on services and festivals recognizes the survival needs of organizations that cannot count on a base of major employers to sustain them; rather, they rely on material incentives and seek alliances with public and nonprofit officials.

These hypotheses, however, require further testing, as there is surprisingly little research on the local organization of downtown real estate interests.[13] There is also little scholarly research about peak business associations in the post-urban renewal period; a better understanding of the factors behind the shifting missions and leaderships of groups like the Greater Baltimore Committee or the Allegheny Conference for Community Development would provide additional insight into the changing balance of power in downtown governance. Using organizational and newspaper archives and interviews, for example, a researcher could learn when and why such organizations abandoned downtown issues. These methods could also reveal any clear relationships between the sectoral representation on organizational boards and the agendas pursued by these organizations. Additional research could be done on various companies represented on downtown association boards to learn from them first-hand how they view the political roles of their organizations.

IS "DOWNTOWN VERSUS THE NEIGHBORHOODS" STILL A KEY POLITICAL CLEAVAGE?

Urban political scientists, on the one hand, have long been interested in powerful downtown elites; on the other hand, they have shown a great deal of interest in the challenges to these groups, often represented by neighborhood associations adept at utilizing both the electoral arena and other means of protest (DeLeon, 1992; Ferman, 1996; Mollenkopf, 1983). In some cities, would-be mayors successfully attacked downtown development policies, and indeed made their pledges to redirect resources from the central business district to struggling neighborhoods central to their election campaigns. Pete Flaherty, for example, was elected mayor of Pittsburgh in 1969 with the backing of a newly mobilized neighborhood movement (Ferman, 1996); San Francisco voters used the ballot box to challenge downtown interests both by electing sympathetic mayors and councils, and by passing voter initiatives that limited downtown development (DeLeon, 1992; McGovern, 1998). In 1983, Boston voters eliminated mayoral candidates known for their support of downtown development and sent two neighborhood activists, Mel King and Ray Flynn, to compete in a run-off. Flynn, who went on to be elected mayor, reflected, "In 1983, there was a feeling that the downtown interests didn't respect the neighborhoods of Boston. . . . That's how Mel King and I got nominated in 1983. We represented fighters. People knew we were two tough neighborhood guys who were going to stand up to the powerful interests of the city and fight for the neighborhoods" (Nolan, 1993). Some of the political conflicts between populist Dennis Kucinich's supporters and Cleveland's business community reflected this dynamic as well (Swanstrom, 1985).

Is "downtown vs. the neighborhoods" still a key cleavage in U.S. urban politics? I hypothesize that opposition to downtown development is less likely to be the point around which today's urban populist groups mobilize than would have been the case a few decades earlier. To support this hypothesis I have only anecdotal (and admittedly slim anecdotal) evidence. Former Boston Mayor Flynn noted that it was no longer a feature of electoral politics in his city (Nolan, 1993), and interviews with elected officials in Seattle suggested a similar dampening of tensions. In recent elections in Newark, Cleveland, and New York, just to name a few cities, the lines of cleavage did not seem to run between defenders and detractors of downtown development. Of course, there will always be political conflict over the spatial distribution of public resources, but I would argue that in most cities "downtown" is no longer seen as the enemy of those who advocate investment in their own residential neighborhoods.

If indeed this claim is true, there could be many explanations, including the successes of some earlier challengers to downtown who succeeded in implementing growth caps and linkage policies. But I would also argue that downtown simply is not the sort of target it once was. As at least in some cities, downtown has lost corporate headquarters, office space, and symbolic clout, perhaps it has seemed less threatening to neighborhood advocates as well. Moreover, today's downtown groups are busy with activities it is hard to dislike—who is against clean streets, better lighting, and farmers' markets? Indeed, in interviews, some downtown organization leaders explicitly talked about the importance of their food fairs and art walks as effective ways to broaden political support for downtown investment (see endnote 10). New downtown developments are in many cases, as well, championed by a new set of supporters—cultural leaders, university administrators—and are marketed not as buttoned-down business centers but as hip, edgy spaces. Downtown groups are intent on reshaping and marketing downtown as a place to see a ball game, grab a beer, or live in trendy, artist-inspired lofts. As central city areas gain residential population, they themselves become "neighborhoods."

This is an admittedly hard hypothesis to test rigorously. One could choose cities that had manifested downtown versus neighborhood cleavages and study selected elections over time to see if these issues remained salient. Finer-grained case studies of those cities in which electoral politics had once pitted the interests of downtown business against the interests of neighborhood residents could reveal some shifts in electoral rhetoric around development issues, and that such research could help further the goal of better understanding the politics of the new downtown.

In conclusion, American central business districts have undergone dramatic changes in function over the past four decades, and it should be expected that these functional changes would be accompanied by changes in political organization and influence. In an earlier era, the downtown was usually the region's largest employment node and home to its key retailing and financial activities. Regional business leaders saw a healthy downtown as crucial to the success of their enterprises, and they worked, often through peak business organizations, to push for downtown revitalization alongside other business concerns. Today, many of the key business institutions, once at the heart of the downtown coalition, are gone. Downtowns are now less dominant as either economic centers or as the basis of political power. While corporate interests in many cities still work toward downtown improvements, this cause is less central to their mission, and less connected to a broader regional business agenda. Those most concerned with downtown are now real estate interests, who seek allies among nonprofit organizations and forge connections to cultural institutions.

REFERENCES

Adams, C., Bartelt, D., Elesh, D., Goldstein, I., Kleniewski, N., & Yancey, W. (1991). *Philadelphia: Neighborhoods, division, and conflict in a postindustrial city*. Philadelphia: Temple University Press.

Alonso, W. (1960). A theory of urban land markets. *Regional Science Association Journal, 6,* 149–158.

Bergsman, S. (2004). The ground floor: Downtown is up in a revitalized L.A. *Barrons* March 8, pp. 40, 42.

Birch, E. (2005). *Who lives downtown*. Washington, DC: Brookings Institution. Available at www.brookings.edu.

Briffault, R. (1999). A government for our time? Business improvement districts and urban governance. *Columbia Law Review, 99*(2), 365–477.

Center City District (2006). *State of center city 2006*. Philadelphia: Center City District.

Cohen, L. (2007). Buying into downtown revival: The centrality of retail to postwar urban renewal in American cities. *Annals of the American Academy of Political and Social Science, 611*(1), 82–95.

Dahl, R. (1961). *Who governs*. New Haven: Yale University Press.

DeLeon, R. E. (1992). *Left coast city*. Lawrence: University Press of Kansas.

DiMassa, C. M. (2007). Downtown has gained people but lost jobs, report says. *Los Angeles Times*, 21 February, B1.

Dymski, G. (1999). *The bank merger wave*. Armonk, NY: M. E. Sharpe.

Fainstein, S. S. (1994). *The city builders*. Oxford: Blackwell Publishers.

Fainstein, S. S., & Judd, D. (1999). Cities as places to play. In D. Judd & S. Fainstein (Eds.), *The tourist city* (pp. 261–272). New Haven: Yale University Press.

Ferman, B. (1996). *Challenging the growth machine*. Lawrence: University Press of Kansas.

Fitzpatrick, D. (2000). The story of urban renewal. *Pittsburgh Post-Gazette*, May 21.

Fogelson, R. (2001). *Downtown: Its rise and fall*. New Haven, CT: Yale University Press.

Ford, L. (2003). *America's new downtowns: Revitalization or reinvention?* Baltimore: Johns Hopkins University Press.

Friedan, B. J., & Sagalyn, L. B. (1989). *Downtown, Inc.* Cambridge, MA: MIT Press.

Friedland, R., & Palmer, D. (1984). Park place and main street: Business and the urban power structure. *Annual Review of Sociology, 10*, 393–416.

Gendron, R. (2006). Forging collective capacity for urban redevelopment: "Power to," "power over," or both? *City and Community, 5*(1), 5–22.

Gleaser, E., & Kahn, M. (2001). *Job sprawl: Employment location in US metropolitan areas.* Brookings Institution, May. Available at www.brookings.edu.

Gotham, K. (2002). *Race real estate and uneven development: The Kansas City experience, 1900–2000.* Albany: State University of New York Press.

Hannigan, J. (1998). *Fantasy city: Pleasure and profit in the postmodern metropolis.* London and New York: Routledge, 1998.

Harrell, D. C. (2004). Old downtown hotel is on a new mission: Housing the homeless. *Seattle Post-Intelligencer,* 10 November.

Harrison, B., & Bluestone, B. (1982). *The deindustrialization of America.* New York: Basic Books.

Harvey, D. (1985). *The urbanization of capital.* Baltimore: Johns Hopkins University Press.

Healey, P., & Barrett, S. M. (1990). Structure and agency in land and property development processes: Some ideas for research. *Urban Studies, 27*(1), 89–104.

Hodos, J. (2002). Globalization, regionalism, and urban restructuring. *Urban Affairs Review, 37*(3), 358–379.

Holloway, S. R., & Wheeler, J. O. (1991). Corporate relocation and changes in metropolitan corporate dominance, 1980–1987. *Economic Geography, 67*(1), 54–74.

Isenberg, A. (2004). *Downtown America.* Chicago: University of Chicago Press.

Judd, D., Winter, W., Barnes, W. R., & Stem, E. (2003). Tourism and entertainment as local economic development: A national survey. In D. R. Judd (Ed.), *The infrastructure of play* (pp. 50–74). Armonk, NY: M. E. Sharpe.

Kanter, R. M. (2000). Business coalitions as a force for regionalism. In B. Katz (Ed.), *Reflections on regionalism* (pp. 154–181). Washington, DC: Brookings.

Lang, R. E. (2003). *Edgeless cities.* Washington: Brookings Institution Press.

Logan, J., & Molotch, H. (1987). *Urban fortunes.* Berkeley: University of California Press.

McGovern, S. J. (1998). *The politics of downtown development.* Lexington: The University Press of Kentucky.

McGraw, B. (2002). Hudson's name will fade, but family's legacy shines. *Detroit Free Press,* 26 June, B1.

Mitchell, J. (2001). Business improvement districts and the 'new' revitalization of downtown. *Economic Development Quarterly, 15*(2), 115–123.

Mollenkopf, J. H. (1983). *The contested city.* Princeton University Press.

Morçöl, G., & Zimmerman, U. (2006). Metropolitan governance and business improvement districts. *International Journal of Public Administration, 29,* 5–29.

Nolan, M. F. (1993). One inhabitant, able and discrete. *Boston Globe,* 12 September, 16.

Norman, J. (1989). Congenial Milwaukee: A segregated city. In G. Squires (Ed.), *Unequal partnerships: The political economy of urban redevelopment in postwar America* (pp. 178–201). New Brunswick, NJ: Rutgers University Press.

Perlman, E. (1998). Downtown: The live-in solution. *Governing, 11*(9), 28–32.

Salisbury, R. H. (1964). Urban politics: The new convergence of power. *Journal of Politics, 26*(4), 775–797.

Salter, S., & Scott, J. (1991). Problems at CAP top off a bad time for downtown. *Atlanta Journal Constitution,* 3 June, 1.

Saporta, M. (2000). Central Atlanta progress seeks new 'go-to' person. *Atlanta Journal Constitution,* 24 March, 3E.

Saporta, M. (2003). City looks to overcome scarcity of leadership for civic roles. *Atlanta Constitution,* 12 December, 3E.

Sbragia, A. (1989). The Pittsburgh model of economic development: Partnership, responsiveness, and indifference. In G. D. Squires (Ed.), *Unequal partnerships* (pp. 103–120). New Brunswick, NJ: Rutgers University Press.

Sharoff, R. (2001). In St. Louis, office buildings are becoming lofts. *New York Times,* 24 June.

Slobodzian, J. A. (2005). Center city renaissance. *Philadelphia Inquirer,* 27 December.

Stone, C. N. (1989). *Regime politics: Governing Atlanta, 1946–1988.* Lawrence: University Press of Kansas.

Strom, E. (2002). Converting pork into porcelain. *Urban Affairs Review, 38*(1), 3–21.

Strom, E. (2003). Cultural policy as development policy: Evidence from the United States. *International Journal of Cultural Policy, 9*(3).

Strom, E. (2005). The political strategies behind university-based development: The Philadelphia case. In D. Perry & W. Wievel (Eds.), *The university as developer: The university, the city, and real estate development*. Armonk, NY: M.E. Sharpe.

Swanstrom, T. (1985). *The crisis of growth politics*. Philadelphia: Temple University Press.

Turner, R. S. (2002). The politics of design and development in the postmodern downtown. *Journal of Urban Affairs*, 24(5), 533–548.

Wallack, T. (2005). Kaiser top employer on Bay area scene. *San Francisco Chronicle*, 22 February.

Weiss, M. (1987). *The rise of the community builders*. New York: Columbia University Press.

Wolfinger, R. (1974). *The politics of progress*. Englewood Cliffs, NJ: Prentice Hall.

Zukin, S. (1982). *Loft living*. Baltimore: Johns Hopkins University Press.

NOTES

1. http://www.greatergreenville.com/development/dt_fun.asp.
2. http://www.downtownstl.org/.
3. In some cities, downtown housing development benefits from an array of producer subsidies, so "market rate" is not an entirely accurate term. Most new downtown housing is not, however, "assisted" housing, with consumer subsidies and restrictions on residents incomes.
4. The extent of the downtown residential "boom" should not be exaggerated—Birch notes that, in the 45 cities she studies, the net gain in downtown population between 1970 and 2000 has totaled 35,000, while during the same period the suburban parts of these metro areas have gained 13 million residents. But these aggregate numbers obscure the significant downtown residential gains in some cities, where entire new residential districts have been established in downtown areas.
5. From the Greater Baltimore Committee statement of priorities, found on their website (www.gbc.org), accessed March 2006.
6. For example, the Allegheny Conference for Community Development, which had spearheaded the redevelopment of Pittsburgh's "Golden Triangle" through urban renewal programs, is now part of a larger regional alliance with no downtown program focus, while since 1994 a Pittsburgh Downtown Partnership has taken up the task of promoting the downtown.
7. BIDS are not only found in downtowns, but in outlying business areas as well. A 1999 survey found 404 BIDS in 43 states (although some states use other terms for them). Mitchell, 2001; Morçöl & Zimmerman, 2006.
8. Mitchell (2001) also finds many groups reporting involvement in "advocacy," but here advocacy is meant to describe activities working to link public and private sector actors engaged in downtown, rather than a broader involvement in political affairs.
9. Some of these observations are drawn from interviews with heads and board members of downtown organizations in Philadelphia, Seattle, Charlotte, and Detroit between 1999 and 2002 conducted by the author for an earlier research project. Several of those interviewed specifically talked about the decline of CEO board representation, and the strategies they employ to remain effective despite the diminished prominence of their board representation.
10. There is a professional organization, the International Downtown Association, to which most downtown organizations belong. See Gendron (2006) for more on this organization's significance.
11. Although, as Healey and Barrett (1990) note, this process is not unproblematic.
12. A few cities, such as New York or London, have such a concentration of very large real estate interests (developers, architects, financiers) that they do, indeed, export real estate services. In cities that are first-order tourism or second home/retirement magnets, real estate could also be seen as an export industry, as the end users of real estate products spend money earned somewhere else. In these cases, real estate is a more dominant economic sector, and prominent real estate capitalists may also have a more central role in political and civic life.
13. There are some interesting histories of the national real estate industry—see Weiss (1987); as well as local case studies that address the importance of real estate lobby groups in the policymaking process—see Gotham (2002)—but these do not really ask how and why individual property owners and developers organize to effect change in the central business district.

The Politics of Urban Development

L ocal governments struggle to identify effective economic development strategies in a competitive environment that constrains their choices of action. Restructuring on a global scale imposes economic challenges to which cities, suburbs, and metropolitan areas must respond. The selections in this chapter highlight how the imperative for local economic development shapes local politics and decision making. In Selection 7, Edward Glaeser considers the plight of cities struggling to reinvent themselves because economic restructuring has left them behind. Glaeser probes the experience of Detroit, Michigan, in order to examine both the process of urban decline and the politics of regeneration. "Urban reinvention," says Glaeser, "is made possible by the traditional urban virtues that were to be found in nineteenth-century Detroit—educated workers, small entrepreneurs, and a creative interplay among different industries." As he notes, twentieth-century Detroit lost many of these resources. The city became excessively dependent on the auto industry, and worker and entrepreneurial talents became depleted by poverty and suburban flight of people and businesses.

Although Glaeser suggests that Detroit's fall had more to do with economics than politics, he believes the city's political responses to decline have been wanting, and therefore made things even worse. He describes how Detroit was led for decades by a passionate crusader dedicated to challenging racial inequalities while doing little to make the city more attractive to employers and residents. At the same time, Detroit's policies of physical renewal failed to change the city in productive ways and neglected investments in human capital. In contrast, he says, New York and other cities avoided Detroit's fate by pursuing effective development policies. Glaeser concludes that when urban decline leaves few alternatives, as in the case of Detroit, it might be best for them to shrink to a more manageable size that affords opportunities for human creativity.

Glaeser's account raises interesting questions about the importance of local economic and political circumstances in explaining urban decline. Are the kinds of local resources held by cities as critical today when so many business and investment decisions are made at a distance from local communities? Does Glaeser underestimate the role of racial injustice and discrimination in bringing about Detroit's decline and frustrating its reinvention?

Tourism/entertainment, culture, and urban amenities have been extremely important for the revitalization of downtowns and urban economies. Old cities have an advantage in developing these sectors. Jobs are connected to amenities; the affluent residents who live downtown want to commute less but also prefer to live in an environment with exciting street life, nightlife, culture, and entertainment. With their historic architecture, public monuments, redeveloped waterfronts, and older neighborhoods, cities are uniquely positioned to provide an exciting urban culture. Partly for this reason, for the first time in a half century, cities seem to be indispensable to their metropolitan regions. In Selection 8, Elizabeth Strom points out that as the traditional economic base of cities has weakened, culture and the arts have become very important for urban reinvention. Whatever other problems they may face, older cities hold a distinct advantage over suburbs in building a new economy based on culture and arts because of the presence of renovated waterfronts, historic districts, museums, concert halls, opera galleries, and "high culture" assets.

Strom describes how a close collaboration between the private and public sectors has emerged to enhance the presence of culture downtown. Promoters of culture and arts seek public funding for their efforts. At the other end of the bargain, city officials perceive cultural and art institutions as industries that can help drive urban revitalization. Strom believes that this close collaboration raises questions: Does the commercialization of culture exclude artistic endeavors that do not draw big crowds or long lines? Does it bias public support for the arts in favor of events that have quick audience potential, but diminish sustained support for museums and concert halls after they are built? Ultimately, is the quality of life in cities improved or degraded by the new culture–development alliance?

How local communities can use government to shape their economic destinies is the subject of the last two essays. In Selection 9, Paul Kantor and H. V. Savitch argue that local officials can sometimes gain considerable control over their own development even though the pressures to compete are intense. Scholars sometimes depict cities as junior partners to business in the global development game. In theory, business investors have many cities and regions to choose from; cities are often desperate to attract their jobs and dollars. In their comparative analysis of cities in the United States and Western Europe, Kantor and Savitch show that the real world is not always so one-sided. The authors describe how city bargaining advantages relative to business are not uniform; sometimes business actually is the junior partner.

Kantor and Savitch explain that the bargaining advantages of cities are quite dependent on market conditions, local political systems, and national urban policies. For example, some city governments have the advantage of a very favorable market environment for attracting or keeping business; not all are desperate to chase every dollar investors offer. Sometimes this is because there are businesses—entertainment parks, for example—with such large sunk costs that they cannot easily move elsewhere. Alternatively, some global cities, such as London, Tokyo, and New York, serve as global anchors for industries like financial services; this limits the economic competition they face from smaller cities. Still others may have such highly diversified economies that jobs that are lost are easily replaced. In all these circumstances, economic advantages can favor cities, not investors. This, in turn, makes it possible for these city governments to act with greater independence and promote development policies that generate more community benefits than others can.

The authors show that local bargaining advantages are not always economic in nature. Cities that have highly developed democratic political systems are better able to resist business demands. Cities having assistance from national governments that take an active role in urban affairs also are better able to extract concessions from the private sector and limit business power. Kantor and Savitch's comparative research suggests that the role of national governments in supporting their cities may be pivotal. U.S. cities tend to have fewer bargaining advantages than their counterparts in Western

Europe—largely because of the limited role of the federal government in regulating local economic development activity.

Finally, in Selection 10, James M. Smith argues that the nature of governmental intervention in urban development is changing. In his study of Chicago, he points to a number of instances in which state governments and special-purpose authorities have played a central role in urban development politics. Special-purpose authorities are appointed independent agencies created by state governments to help plan, fund, and build large projects, such as sports arenas, convention centers, and other facilities to boost local economies. Smith believes that the increasing reliance upon these governmental agencies in Chicago can be described as an intergovernmental triad: State, local, and private political interests are brought into a close cooperative relationship that is substantially independent of city governments and voters. Decision making is ". . . taking place in state houses, and the corridors of state-created authorities with the necessary powers to bypass local protests and complications."

Smith's observations about the restructuring of politics around city, state, and public authority triads raises many questions about the changing role of private and public interests in urban development. Is one leg of the triad stronger than another? Are state governments, especially the legislatures, causing the power of mayors and other city governmental officials to shrink in favor of state and private sector players? Do private business interests grow stronger, diminish, or stay the same as policymaking shifts to intergovernmental triads? The answers are not obvious. For instance, it remains unclear if triads increase the voice of business in economic development. On the one hand, business representatives dominated the boards of virtually all of the special-purpose authorities in the Chicago cases described by Smith. On the other hand, all were appointed by governors and mayors seeking to protect their own interests in the development game.

The politics of urban development is profoundly influenced by global economic forces enveloping every local community. Yet the selections show local responses to these new economic challenges vary from place to place and over time. The struggle among government and private interests continues to shape the policies that determine the direction of change.

7

Why Do Cities Decline?

EDWARD GLAESER

The corner of Elmhurst Street and Rosa Parks Boulevard in Detroit feels as far from New York's Fifth Avenue as urban space can get in America. Though this intersection lies in the heart of Detroit, much of the nearby land is empty. Grass now grows where apartment buildings and stores once stood. The Bible Community Baptist Church is the only building at the

From Edward Glaeser, *Triumph of the City*, NY: Penguin Press. Excerpts from pp. 41–67, excluding all notes and references.

intersection; its boarded-up windows and nonworking phone number suggest that it doesn't attract many worshippers.

If you walk down Elmhurst, you'll see eleven low-rise homes; four of them are vacant. There are also two apartment buildings—one is less than a third occupied, the other is empty. There are also another ten or so vacant lots and a parking lot, blank spaces that once held homes and apartment buildings. Despite its ruinous condition, the area feels perfectly safe because there isn't enough humanity to create a threat. The open spaces give this neighborhood the feel of a ghost town, where the spirits of Detroit's past bemoan the plight of what was once America's fourth-largest city.

Between 1950 and 2008, Detroit lost over a million people—58 percent of its population. Today one third of its citizens live in poverty. Detroit's median family income is $33,000, about half the U.S. average. In 2009, the city's unemployment rate was 25 percent, which was 9 percentage points more than any other large city and more than 2.5 times the national average. In 2008, Detroit had one of the highest murder rates in America, more than ten times higher than New York City's. Many American cities endured a collapse in housing prices between 2006 and 2008. But Detroit was unique in both missing the boom early in the decade *and* suffering a 25 percent price drop since the bust.

Detroit's decline is extreme, but it's hardly unique. Eight of the ten largest U.S. cities in 1950 have lost at least a sixth of their population since then. Six of the sixteen largest cities in 1950—Buffalo, Cleveland, Detroit, New Orleans, Pittsburgh, and St. Louis—have lost more than half their population since that year. In Europe, cities like Liverpool, Glasgow, Rotterdam, Bremen, and Vilnius are all much smaller than they once were. The age of the industrial city is over, at least in the West, and it will never return. Some erstwhile manufacturing towns have managed to evolve from making goods to making ideas, but most continue their slow, inexorable declines.

But we shouldn't see the exodus from the Rust Belt as an indictment of urban living; the manufacturing cities fell because they had abandoned the most vital features of city life. The old commercial towns, like Birmingham and New York, specialized in skills, small enterprises, and strong connections with the outside world. Those attributes, which also create urban prosperity today, made cities successful long before a single bolt of cloth left a textile mill in Manchester or a single car rolled off an assembly line in Detroit. The industrial town was unlike either those old commercial cities or the modern capitals of the information age. Its vast factories employed hundreds of thousands of relatively unskilled workers. Those factories were self-sufficient and isolated from the world outside, except that they were providing the planet with vast quantities of cheap, identical products.

That model served the West extremely well for about a century. Detroit's car factories provided good wages to hundreds of thousands of people, but over the past fifty years, areas with abundant small firms have grown more quickly than places dominated by enormous enterprises. Skilled cities have been more successful than less educated places, and only 11 percent of Detroit's adults have college degrees. People and firms have moved to warmer areas and away from the chilly Midwest, whose waterways first nurtured the cities that now comprise the Rust Belt. Industrial diversity has been more conducive to growth than manufacturing monocultures, and Detroit practically defined the one-industry town.

While it would be wrong to attribute too much of these places' problems to politics, political mismanagement was often a feature of Rust Belt decline. Perhaps the most common error was thinking that these cities could build their way back to success with housing projects, grandiose office towers, or fanciful high-tech transit systems. Those mistakes came out of the all-too-common error of confusing a city, which is really a mass of connected humanity, with its structures.

Reviving these cities requires shedding the old industrial model completely, like a snake sloughing off its skin. When a city reinvents itself successfully, the metamorphosis is often so complete that we forget that the place was once an industrial powerhouse. As late as the 1950s, New York's garment industry was the nation's largest manufacturing cluster. It employed 50 percent more workers than the auto industry did in Detroit. America's Industrial Revolution practically began in greater Boston, but now nobody associates smokestacks with that city. These places have reinvented themselves by returning to their old, preindustrial roots of commerce, skills, and entrepreneurial innovation.

If Detroit and places like it are ever going to come back, they will do so by embracing the virtues of the great pre- and postindustrial cities: competition, connection, and human capital. The Rust Belt will be reborn only if it can break from its recent past, which has left it with a vast housing stock for which there is little demand, a single major industry that is dominated by a few major players, and problematic local politics. Beneath these cities' recent history lies an instructive older story of connection and creativity, which provide the basis for reinvention. To understand Detroit's predicament and its potential, we must compare the city's great and tragic history with the story of other cities, like New York, that have successfully weathered industrial decline.

HOW THE RUST BELT ROSE

. . . The cities that grew up as nodes along America's nineteenth-century transport network enabled vast numbers of people to access the wealth of the U.S. hinterland. Then, as now, Iowa's rich, dark soil made it a farmer's dream. In 1889, Iowa corn yields were 50 percent higher than the yields in older areas such as Kentucky. Corn may have been easier to grow out west, but its low value per ton made it relatively expensive to ship. Canal boats and railcars played their part in moving calories westward, but so did cities, which helped make produce easier to ship. . . .

. . . Like Chicago, Detroit grew as a node of the great rail and water network long before Henry Ford made his first Model T. Between 1850 and 1890, the city's population increased tenfold, from 21,000 to 206,000 people. Detroit's growth was again intimately tied to its waterway, the Detroit River, which was part of the path from Iowa's farmland to New York's tables. By 1907, 67 million tons of goods were moving along the Detroit River, more than three times as much as the total amount going through the ports of New York or London. . . .

. . . In New York and Chicago and Detroit, entrepreneurs came, eager for access to harbors, other manufacturers, and urban consumers. The money that industries save on transport costs when they locate near each other and their customers is an example of *agglomeration economies*—the benefits that come from clustering in cities. The growing city's large home market and its waterborne access to other customers also enabled industrialists to take advantage of what economists call *returns to scale,* a term for the fact that per unit costs are cheaper in bigger plants that produce more units, like large sugar refineries or car factories. . . .

. . . At the end of the nineteenth century, Detroit looked a lot like Silicon Valley in the 1960s and 1970s. The Motor City thrived as a hotbed of small innovators, many of whom focused on the new new thing, the automobile. The basic science of the automobile had been worked out in Germany in the 1880s, but the German innovators had no patent protection in the United States. As a result, Americans were competing furiously to figure out how to produce good cars on a mass scale. In general, there's strong correlation between the presence of small firms and the later growth of a region. Competition, the "racing men" phenomenon, seems to create economic success. . . .

. . . New York City actually had a larger share of the nation's automobile producers than Detroit in 1900, but there was an explosion in automotive entrepreneurship in Detroit in the early 1900s. Detroit seemed to have had a budding automotive genius on every street corner. Ford, Ransom Olds, the Dodge brothers, David Dunbar Buick, and the Fisher brothers all worked in the Motor City. Some of these men made cars, but Detroit also had plenty of independent suppliers, like the Fisher brothers, who could cater to start-ups. Ford was able to open a new company with backing from the Dodge brothers, who were making engine and chassis components. They supplied Ford with both financing and parts. . . .

. . . The irony and ultimately the tragedy of Detroit is that its small, dynamic firms and independent suppliers gave rise to gigantic, wholly integrated car companies, which then became synonymous with stagnation. Ford figured out that massive scale could make his cars cheap, but supersize, self-contained factories were antithetical to the urban virtues of competition and connection. Ford figured out how to make assembly lines that could use the talents of poorly educated Americans, but making Detroit less skilled hurt it economically in the long run.

Successful car companies bought up their suppliers, like Fisher Body, and their competitors. By the 1930s, only the most foolhardy and well-financed businessman would have dared take on General Motors and Ford. The intellectually fertile world of independent urban entrepreneurs had been replaced by a few big companies that had everything to lose and little to gain from radical experimentation.

HENRY FORD AND INDUSTRIAL DETROIT

As the car companies got out of innovation and into mass production, they no longer saw any advantages to locating in the city. Dense urban centers are ideal places to come up with new ideas, but not ideal places to make millions of Model T's. Ford's desire for massive scale required a factory too large for any city to accommodate. In 1917, he began building his River Rouge plant in suburban Dearborn, southwest of Detroit. At River Rouge, he erected a ninety-three-building complex with 7 million square feet of workspace. River Rouge had its own docks, rail lines, and power plant. Raw materials could be turned into cars within a single facility.

Ford's River Rouge plant began the process of suburbanizing manufacturing that would continue throughout the twentieth century. While the car may have been born in the city, it ended up being a very rebellious child. Automobiles enabled Americans to live in distant suburbs away from streetcars or sidewalks. Trucks enabled factories to locate far away from rail lines. The car and the truck both enabled space-hungry people and firms to leave dense urban areas.

By the 1950s, both New York and Detroit started shrinking as the advantages they once got from their ports and rail yards became far less important because other areas had also acquired easy access to world markets. Between 1890 and today, the real cost of moving a ton a mile by rail dropped from twenty cents to two, so it didn't matter nearly as much whether or not your factory was close to a transport hub. Before World War II, companies put up with high labor costs in Northern cities because the transport network made it so much easier to buy raw materials and ship final products. As transport costs plummeted, it became cost-effective to locate in cheaper places: suburban factories, like River Rouge, Southern right-to-work states, and China. At the same time, the rise of the car made older cities built around trains and elevators seem obsolete. . . .

. . . The industrialization of the Sunbelt was helped—and Northern cities like Detroit and New York were hurt—by the Taft-Hartley Act of 1947, which allowed states to pass right-to-work laws that forbid the formation of closed shops. In right-to-work states, which were often in the South, unions had much less bargaining power because firms could always turn to nonunion workers. Unsurprisingly, manufacturers have steadily drifted to right-to-work states, away from America's older industrial regions. One classic paper compared the effect of right-to-work laws on factory jobs in neighboring counties, on either side of a right-to-work border. It found that manufacturing grew 23.1 percent faster between 1947 and 1992 on the anti-union side of the divide.

High union wages didn't seem like such a drag on Detroit during the first decades after World War II. When the UAW whipsawed the Big Three automakers into raising wages, higher costs were mostly passed along to consumers. The automakers were so profitable that they could withstand some of the most expensive labor costs on the planet. Of course, the car companies weren't above trying to open new plants in states with lower labor costs, which is why Detroit was losing people even before the car industry began to decline.

Industrial decline ultimately hit every older city. Boston's maritime industries, which had grown great on the clipper ships and China trade in the first half of the nineteenth century, became obsolete with the rise of steam-powered ships. New York's garment industry imploded in the late 1960s and 1970s, and the city lost more than three hundred thousand manufacturing jobs between 1967 and 1977. The exodus of urban manufacturing was not inherently a bad thing—making goods in cheap locales made those goods less expensive for ordinary people—but it posed a mortal challenge for the world's industrial cities. . . .

WHY RIOT?

Cities suffer from economic downturns directly, because of the loss of jobs and decline in wages, but negative shocks also have indirect consequences, like social upheaval and falling tax revenues, that can be just as harmful. The collapse of the industrial city was the backdrop for the crime waves and riots of the 1960s, and for an increasingly impotent public sector that was just trying to stay solvent. In the bright, optimistic days of the early 1960s, many American cities turned from old-style machine politicians to young, charismatic leaders. In Detroit and New York, an alliance of liberals and African Americans elected Jerome Cavanagh and John Lindsay respectively. While his predecessors had been seen as abettors of police brutality, Cavanagh promised fairer law enforcement. He launched affirmative-action programs and marched with Martin Luther King Jr. John Lindsay also fought police brutality and supported affirmative action. Lindsay's finest hour may have been in the aftermath of King's shooting, when he walked the streets of Harlem and cooled tempers with warmth and compassion.

But ultimately neither mayor could control the forces that were convulsing his city. Neither can be blamed for failing to halt the manufacturing exodus from his city—the economic headwinds were just too strong. Neither can be blamed for the social unrest that erupted in America's cities during the 1960s, in the wake of economic distress, expanding but unmet expectations, and a breakdown in traditional means of social control. But both mayors made mistakes that contributed to their cities' distress.

Lindsay's besetting sin was his inability to rein in costs, especially when faced with tough municipal unions and transit strikes. Lindsay, initially a Republican, hoped to limit union pay raises, but his background as the congressman from Manhattan's silk-stocking district hardly prepared him to win a brutal street fight with the transit workers. He ended up preferring pay raises to strikes, and the increasing costs of city government were then hidden with increasingly creative bookkeeping, which led straight to New York's near bankruptcy in 1975. Cavanagh's fatal flaw was his penchant for razing slums and building tall structures with the help of federal urban-renewal dollars. Detroit's housing market had peaked in the 1950s and was already depressed when Cavanagh took office. The city was shedding people and had plenty of houses. Why subsidize more building? Successful cities must build in order to accommodate the rising demand for space, but that doesn't mean that building *creates* success.

Urban renewal, in both Detroit and New York, may have replaced unattractive slums with shiny new buildings, but it did little to address urban decline. Those shiny new buildings were really Potemkin villages spread throughout America, built to provide politicians with the appearance of urban success. But Detroit had plenty of buildings; it didn't need more. What Detroit needed was human capital: a new generation of entrepreneurs like Ford and Durant and the Dodge brothers who could create some great new industry, as Shockley and the Fairchildren were doing in Silicon Valley. Investing in buildings instead of people in places where prices were already low may have been the biggest mistake of urban policy over the past sixty years.

Both mayors also failed at fighting crime. New York's murder rate quadrupled between 1960 and 1975, and Detroit experienced a similarly disturbing trend. But racial discrimination and police brutality in both cities led both mayors to emphasize accountability more than enforcement. African Americans were no longer willing to take abuse from white thugs, whether in or out of police uniform. In Detroit, a 93 percent white police force didn't seem all that integrated in a city that was close to 50 percent black. While later mayors, like Rudy Giuliani, would reduce crime with rigorous policing, in the 1960s, it wasn't obvious that aggressive enforcement could keep the peace.

Less than a mile down Rosa Parks Boulevard from the Elmhurst Street corner, a dilapidated park occupies the corner at Clairmount Street. This is the site of an event from which Detroit has still not recovered almost half a century later. In the wee hours of Sunday morning, July 23, 1967, a club on that corner was hosting a party for some returning veterans, when Detroit's police department staged a raid. The vice squad, which had a robust reputation for brutality toward the city's blacks, took a while to cart off the eighty-five partygoers. A jeering crowd of two hundred gathered and began throwing bottles at the cops, who fled. The mob grew and grew, and soon Detroit was ablaze.

Riots are a classic tipping-point phenomenon. Being one of three rioters is dangerous business—the cops are likely to get you—but the chances of arrest are far lower if you're one of three thousand rioters. In Detroit, over a thousand police officers failed to control the thousands of rioters who burned and looted. Cavanagh completely lost control of his city. The riot didn't end until after Tuesday, when thousands of paratroopers from the 82nd and 101st airborne divisions showed up with armed vehicles. By the time this surge quelled the violence, there had been forty-three deaths, 1,400 burned buildings, 1,700 looted stores, and seven thousand arrests.

It's easy to see why Detroit's African-American citizens were moved to riot. They'd been brutalized by a police force full of whites recruited from the South. They'd been systematically excluded from white jobs in the auto industry for decades, and the jobs they did get typically either paid lower wages or offered worse working conditions. Statistics show that Detroit was hardly the only city that had fomented this sort of black anger, and riots were most common in those cities with larger numbers of young, unemployed African Americans.

Cities with more cops actually had smaller riots. Unfortunately, draconian enforcement seems to be the only effective way to stop a riot once it starts. Three of the great experts on civil unrest summarized their research on the link between dictatorship and rioting with the pithy phrase "repression works." Brutal regimes that severely punish rioting have fewer riots, which may explain why democracies see more rioting than dictatorships, and the more progressive cities of the North had far more riots than the Jim Crow South.

Riots are one example of the collective action enabled by cities that may seem to be an unmitigated urban curse, but riots near Steenvoorde began the Dutch Revolt that led to Europe's first modern republic, and unruly mob action in Boston was a critical part of America's road to revolution and republic. Thomas Jefferson wrote that "I view great cities as pestilential to the morals, the health and the liberties of man," but his own liberties owed much to urban agitators like Sam Adams and John Hancock, who succeeded at creating conflict with England precisely because the great port of Boston enabled them to conjure up a mob.

Just like King George III, the leaders of America's cities in the 1960s had two plausible responses to rioting. One was to beef up law enforcement and make the streets safer by locking people up. The other response was to empathize with the rioters and to try to create a more just society. There's much to be said for the second approach, which attracted both Lindsay and Cavanagh. In the 1960s and 1970s, many reform-minded leaders strove to bring greater racial and social equality to their cities. Unfortunately, those leaders only showed how hard it is to right great social wrongs at the city level.

The awful history of American racism helps explain why so many African Americans felt like rioting in the 1960s, but that history doesn't change the fact that those riots did tremendous harm to America's cities, especially to their African-American residents. After all, the rioters weren't burning the homes of prosperous white suburbanites. Those riots and rising crime rates helped create the sense that civilization had fled the city. As a result, many of those who could leave Detroit did.

URBAN REINVENTION: NEW YORK SINCE 1970

As recently as the 1970s, pretty much every older industrial city seemed similarly doomed. Both New York and Detroit were reeling from the decline of their core industries, and if anything, New York seemed worse off because the car industry remained more tightly tied to Motown than the garment sector did to Gotham. In 1977, workers in Wayne County, Michigan, which includes Detroit, were paid more than workers in Manhattan. New York City's government didn't seem any better than Detroit's. In 1975, New York State established the Municipal Assistance Corporation to take over the city's finances and stop it from falling into bankruptcy, despite having some of the nation's highest taxes.

But while Detroit has continued to decline, New York came back.

There's no shortage of explanations for New York's rebirth. Some Yankee fans think that Reggie Jackson's home runs brought back the city's mojo. Hipper urbanists look to Andy Warhol and the arts. Mayor Giuliani credits himself. There is a bit of truth to all of these views, but New York's resurrection was primarily tied to an explosion of entrepreneurship, much of which was in financial services. In 2008, more than $78.6 billion was paid to employees in the sector that the U.S. Census Bureau quaintly calls Securities, Commodity Contracts, and Other Financial Investments and Related Activities. And that doesn't even include all the really big payouts to the people who own financial firms.

Sixty years ago, New York's resilience was already something of a puzzle, and the economist Benjamin Chinitz then argued that the city owed its strength to a tradition of entrepreneurship, which the small firms of the apparel industry had encouraged. Chinitz suggested that the salaried employees of large steel companies in Pittsburgh taught their children to obey their boss and keep their noses clean, but the garment manufacturers of New York taught their kids to take risks. Certainly, financial billionaire Sandy Weill's father, who started as a dressmaker and then switched to importing steel, produced a son who was more comfortable running a company than working for someone else.

Cities have long created intellectual explosions, in which one smart idea generates others. The artistic renaissance in Florence was one such explosion; the industrial revolution in Birmingham and Manchester was another. The growth of finance in late-twentieth-century New York was encouraged by just such an innovation, the ability to quantify the trade-off between risk and return, which made it easier to sell investors riskier assets, from junk bonds to mortgage-backed securities, which in turn enabled riskier, high-return activities, like leveraged buyouts of underperforming companies such as RJR/Nabisco. Today's hedge-fund billionaires are only the latest links in a long chain of connected innovators.

For the millions worldwide who look askance at all of New York's financial innovation, Michael Bloomberg's story, in which a smart trader became an entrepreneur in another sector, might be easier to embrace. In the 1970s, Bloomberg had been riding high at Salomon Brothers, running the firm's trading floor, until he was exiled into the geeky world of systems development before being fired in 1981. Bloomberg then got into information technology, and over the next three decades he grew his company into a behemoth by supplying exactly what increasingly quantitative Wall Street traders wanted—jargon-free keyboards and a vast stream of information that was updated constantly.

But while Bloomberg made his fortune moving information electronically, he knows the value of working face-to-face. He set up his offices in an "open plan," which followed the pattern of Wall Street trading floors like the one he'd run at Salomon, and the unimpeded flow of information within the firm helped his success. In most of the world, rich people surround themselves with big offices and decorated walls, but on trading floors, some of the world's wealthiest people work right on top of each other. Rich traders are forgoing privacy for the knowledge that comes from proximity to other people. In a sense, trading floors are just the city writ small. When Bloomberg switched careers yet again in 2002 to become mayor of New York, he took the open plan with him to City Hall.

While New York was rising as a financial phoenix, Detroit continued its inexorable decline. The Motor City's failure was, in many ways, the legacy of Henry Ford's success. Urban reinvention is made possible by the traditional urban virtues that were to be found in nineteenth-century Detroit: educated workers, small entrepreneurs, and a creative interplay among different industries. Late-twentieth-century Detroit was dominated by a single industry that employed hundreds of thousands of less-skilled workers in three vast vertically integrated firms. What a toxic mixture!

Cities like Detroit with big firms have suffered weaker employment growth than cities with more and smaller employers. In metropolitan areas, a 10 percent increase in the number of firms per worker in 1977 is associated with 9 percent more employment growth between 1977 and 2000. This relationship holds, no matter what types of industries are involved, how old the companies are, or how big the cities are.

Big, vertically integrated firms may be productive in the short run, but they don't create the energetic competition and new ideas that are so necessary for long-term urban success. No small entrepreneur, even with the experience and panache of John DeLorean, could successfully compete with the Big Three. Detroit had stifled the diversity and competition that encourage growth. Moreover, the city of the assembly line had never invested in the educational institutions that enabled more diverse places, like Boston, Milan, and New York, to come back.

Meanwhile, declining transportation costs made it easier for European and Japanese competitors to sell cars in the U.S. market. While Detroit's Big Three had long lost their appetite for radical risk, Soichiro Honda was building fuel-efficient little cars. Detroit's automobile industry stayed afloat with occasional innovations like the minivan and the SUV, but its days of dominance were over. In the 1970s, as high gas prices dampened Americans' appetites for Cadillac Eldorados and Chrysler Imperials, Detroit had nowhere else to go. As the car industry declined, Detroit fell further and further. The age of the industrial city—with its vast factories and powerful unions—was over.

THE RIGHTEOUS RAGE OF COLEMAN YOUNG

Detroit's fall has more to do with economics than politics, but the political response to the city's decline only made things worse. New York responded to the crisis of the 1970s by giving up the dream of ending social injustice at the local level and instead electing centrist, workmanlike mayors—Koch, Dinkins, Giuliani, Bloomberg—who were determined to make the city as attractive as possible to employers and middle-class residents. Detroit was led by a passionate crusader whose anger was understandable but unhelpful.

Coleman Young's family had moved from Alabama to Detroit in the 1920s. He got a job working for Henry Ford but was ultimately blacklisted from the auto industry because of his involvement with labor and civil rights issues. In World War II, Young joined the Tuskegee Airmen as a bombardier. This all-black unit gave African Americans their first opportunity to fly for their country. In 1943, Detroit's simmering racial antipathies exploded in a massive riot, which seems to have started when white youths began attacking blacks in the parks of Belle Isle. White police officers responded by shooting and killing seventeen blacks and no whites. The federal government thought it wise to move Young's all-black bombing outfit, which had been outside Detroit, first to Kentucky and then to Freeman Field in Indiana.

Freeman Field had two officers' clubs, separate but not equal, for the white instructors and the black trainees. Young put his skills as a labor organizer, learned on the streets of Detroit, to work integrating these clubs. En masse, the black officers entered the white club and were arrested. Eventually, after pressure from African-American groups, they were released and transferred back to Kentucky, where the officers' club was open to all but where the white officers could also use another club at Fort Knox.

For eighteen years after the war, Young worked his way up Detroit's political ladder. In 1951 he founded the National Negro Labor Council, whose radicalism attracted the scrutiny of the House Un-American Activities Committee during the McCarthy era. When questioned about his associates, Young refused to answer, explaining that "I am not here as a stool pigeon." Finally in 1963, the times had begun to catch up with his radicalism, and he was elected to the state senate. Three years later, he became the senate minority leader. He pushed through open-housing laws that limited segregation, and he also helped pass Detroit's first income tax.

Local income taxes illustrate the problem of trying to create a just society city by city. The direct effect of Young's income tax was to take money from the rich to fund services that helped the poor. The indirect effect of a local income tax is to encourage richer citizens and businesses to leave. Research by four economists found that in three out of four large cities, higher tax rates barely increase tax revenues because economic activity dissipates so quickly in response to higher tax rates. In a declining place like Detroit, well-meaning attempts at local redistribution can easily backfire by speeding the exodus of wealthier businesses and people, which only further isolates the poor.

After the riot destroyed Jerome Cavanagh's career, he retired, and finally, in 1973, as the black share of Detroit's population continued to rise, Young was elected mayor. His outspoken views gave voice to the long frustrated hopes of Detroit's black community, and he went on to win his next four mayoral elections easily, as Detroit changed from a city that was 55.5 percent white in 1970 to a city that was 11.1 percent white in 2008.

Young's brash style dominated headlines during his twenty years in office. He thought profanity was useful: "You can express yourself much more directly, much more exactly, much more succinctly, with properly used curse words." He argued that whites didn't even know the extent of their racism: "The victim of racism is in a much better position to tell you whether or not you're a racist than you are." Some people thought that Young was urging criminals to suburbanize when he invited them "to leave Detroit" and "hit the eight-mile road," the highway that separates Detroit from its northern suburbs. The mayor certainly had no time for his enemies and was happy to see them leave the city.

Young's bellicosity gave his many supporters the sense that they had a fearless champion fighting for them in City Hall. After years of being treated as second-class citizens, Detroit's African Americans could hold their heads up. Young's bitter experience with racial injustice made him unwilling to whisper sweetly to the city's white population. Moreover, his political interests were only helped by the continuing exodus of Detroit's whites.

THE CURLEY EFFECT

Economists have long argued that the ability of citizens to "vote with their feet" creates competition among local governments that provides some of the same benefits as competition among companies. But there are real limits to that rosy picture. Sometimes, as the story of Coleman Young and Detroit shows, the possible flight of voters can create perverse political incentives that make government worse. I've named this phenomenon the Curley Effect, after Boston's colorful mayor James Michael Curley.

Curley had much in common with Young, and if anything, he was even more argumentative. Curley cast himself as the champion of a poor ethnic minority (the Irish) and rode to victory promising to right old wrongs. Curley frequently made pronouncements that infuriated Boston Brahmins, like calling Anglo-Saxons "a strange and stupid race." He was elected mayor of Boston four times, not quite Young's five terms, but Curley also won a term as governor. Also unlike Young, Curley spent two terms in jail, serving sentences for mail fraud and for taking a Civil Service exam for someone else.

One day in 1916, during Curley's first term as mayor, a British recruiting officer had asked the mayor whether he could invite Bostonians of British extraction to fight on Britain's side during the Great War. Curley replied: "Go ahead, Colonel. Take every damn one of them." After all, Protestant Bostonians of English descent overwhelmingly opposed Curley. The more Boston became a city of poor Irishmen, the more likely it was to reelect James Michael Curley.

The Curley Effect illustrates the danger of ethnic politics, especially in cities where exit is easy. Boston's economy would have benefited if wealthier Yankees had stayed in the city, but Curley did all he could to get rid of them. Likewise, Detroit's economy was hurt by the vast exodus of wealthier whites. Young may never have explicitly told them to leave, but he did little that encouraged them to stay. It's hard not to empathize with the mayor's anger, given the injustices he'd suffered, but righteous anger rarely leads to wise policy.

The mobility of the prosperous limits the ability of any city government to play Robin Hood. The well-off can, with relative ease, walk away from a depressed and declining city. Detroit's middle class escaped Coleman Young by moving to the suburbs.

THE EDIFICE COMPLEX

Young did have an economic strategy for Detroit, but it pursued the wrong objective. Instead of trying to attract smart, wealthy entrepreneurial people, he built structures—making the same error as Jerome Cavanagh, mistaking the built city for the real city. For centuries, leaders have used new buildings to present an image of urban success. The Emperor Vespasian, who ruled Rome in the first century, created an aura of legitimacy with vast construction projects like the Colosseum. Seventeen hundred years later, according to legend, General Grigory Potemkin created a prosperous-looking fake village to impress Empress Catherine the Great. Today urban leaders love to pose at the opening of big buildings that seem to prove that their municipality has either arrived or come back. For decades, the federal government has only exacerbated this tendency by offering billions for structures and transportation and far less for schools or safety.

The tendency to think that a city can build itself out of decline is an example of the edifice error, the tendency to think that abundant new building leads to urban success. Successful cities typically do build, because economic vitality makes people willing to pay for space and builders are happy to accommodate. But building is the result, not the cause, of success. Overbuilding a declining city that already has more structures than it needs is nothing but folly.

In the 1970s, the Detroit Red Wings hockey team threatened to leave for the suburbs. Young responded by building the Joe Louis Arena for $57 million

($205 million in 2010 dollars) and renting it to the Red Wings at bargain rates. The city kept its sports team—but at an enormous cost. In 1987, Detroit opened a monorail system, the People Mover, at a cost of over $200 million (more than $425 million in 2010 dollars). The three-mile system carries about 6,500 people each day and requires about $8.5 million a year in subsidies to operate. It is perhaps the single most absurd public transit project in the country. While it was sold to the public with wildly optimistic ridership projections, it fills only a tiny fraction of its seats. Detroit never needed a new public transit system. The streets below the People Mover are generally empty and could accommodate fleets of buses.

The great hope of the 1970s was the Renaissance Center. The center did receive tax breaks, as well as the enthusiastic support of both Cavanagh and Young, but it was really an example of private rather than public folly. Henry Ford II somehow thought that Detroit could be saved by a vast structure with millions of square feet of new office space. Unfortunately, new space was not what Detroit needed in those years. The Center cost $350 million to build but was sold to General Motors for less than $100 million in 1996. General Motors now occupies Henry Ford II's giant white elephant.

In 1981, Coleman Young and General Motors teamed up for yet another construction project. Young used eminent domain to destroy 1,400 homes in the ethnic neighborhood of Poletown. Activists protested and took the case to the Michigan Supreme Court, but Young still got the land and gave it to General Motors to build a new, high-tech factory inside the city limits. The plant still functions, employing about 1,300 people on its 465 acres, but it's hard to see the benefit of moving more than 4,000 people to create such a land-intensive enterprise within city borders.

Detroit's construction projects certainly changed the look of the city. The Renaissance Center dominates the skyline. Riding on the People Mover feels like a trip to Disney World, if Disney World were in the middle of a desperate city. But as in other declining places, billions were spent on infrastructure that the city didn't need. Unsurprisingly, providing more real estate in a place that was already full of unused real estate was no help at all. The failures of urban renewal reflect a failure at all levels of government to realize that people, not structures, really determine a city's success.

Could an alternative public policy have saved Detroit? By the time Young was elected, Detroit was far gone, and I suspect that even the best policies could only have eased the city's suffering. But it is possible to imagine a different path, if it was taken during earlier decades, when the city was far richer. Perhaps if the city had used its wealth and political muscle, starting in the 1920s, to invest in education at all levels, it could have developed the human capital that has been the source of survival for postindustrial cities.

REMAINING IN THE RUST BELT

That harsh reality of industrial decline and political failures meant that by 2008 Detroit's per capita income was $14,976, only 54.3 percent of the U.S. average. Even before the recession hit, in 2006, Detroit's unemployment rate was 13.7 percent, which was far higher than that of the next largest city. The city's winters are cruel—January temperatures average 24.7 degrees—and Americans do seem to love warm weather. Over the last century, no variable has been a better predictor of urban growth than temperate winters. Given these fundamentals of cold and poverty, perhaps we shouldn't be asking why Detroit declined. Perhaps we should be asking why 777,000 people remain as of 2008.

There are as many different answers to that question as there are people left in Detroit, and each one of them could tell you something that they value about the place. But there is one force that helps explain why most of them stay—cheap, durable housing. Any area's population is linked closely to the number of homes in that area, and homes don't disappear overnight. They are also too valuable to abandon, at least immediately. Their prices drop precipitously, but they remain occupied, often for many decades. According to the Census Bureau, 86 percent of central-city Detroit's housing stock was built before 1960. The average house in the city is valued at $82,000, which is far below the cost of new construction.

When cities are doing well, they can grow very quickly as long as homes can be speedily constructed to house new residents. When cities decline, they decline very slowly, because people are loath to abandon something as valuable as a home. In a sense, the durability of housing is a blessing, because it provides cheap space to people with few resources. The downside of cities kept alive through cheap housing is that they overwhelmingly attract the poor, creating centers of extreme deprivation that cry out for social justice.

SHRINKING TO GREATNESS

Many cities around the world have experienced some version of Detroit's fate, and politicians have implemented many approaches to urban decline. U.S. cities have mainly tried to build their way out of decline. Spain has turned to transportation, spending tens of billions of dollars on high-speed rail, partly as a way to boost economic growth in poorer areas. Other places, like Italy, have used large tax subsidies to encourage enterprise in poorer regions. Many European cities have tried cultural strategies like the Guggenheim Museum in Bilbao. In 2008, Liverpool had a flurry of new construction to celebrate its one-year stint as Europe's capital of culture. Which of these strategies can actually reverse urban decline? Which strategies generate benefits that cover their costs?

In the nineteenth century, when moving goods was enormously expensive, places with good transportation links, like New York or Liverpool, enjoyed a huge edge. Today, moving goods and people is pretty cheap almost everywhere, so further improvements in transportation provide far less of an edge.

Transportation investments are most effective when they radically increase the speed at which a poor area can access a booming, space-starved metropolis. In Spain, a spate of investment in high-speed rail has radically reduced travel times between Madrid and other cities, such as Barcelona and Ciudad Real. The high-speed rail connection shortened the 140-mile trip between Madrid and Ciudad Real to fifty minutes, and presto, people can live in Ciudad Real and work in Spain's largest city. The population of Ciudad Real does seem to have increased since getting the rail connection. In compact England, cities like Birmingham, Manchester, and Liverpool could also grow significantly as a result of extremely fast rail connections to London.

Yet the very things that have helped Ciudad Real benefit from high-speed rail are absent in much of America's Rust Belt. Flying to New York from Buffalo or Cleveland or Detroit will always be faster than taking a train. There's a lot of empty space between New York and these cities, so why would those relatively distant places be natural spots for back-office overflow? Faster links to New York can certainly benefit nearby places like Philadelphia or New Haven, but America's wide-open spaces are just too big for faster ground transportation to revitalize more distant areas.

Another way to bring places back is to give businesses tax cuts when they locate in a disadvantaged area. Research has found that tax breaks significantly increased employment in troubled areas, but it took $100,000 in tax breaks to generate just one job. But regardless of cost, should the national government even be using the tax code to shuffle economic activity around? Would it have made sense to tax nineteenth-century Chicago or Detroit to keep the population of Salem, Massachusetts, growing? Why should national policy encourage firms to locate in unproductive places?

National policy should strive to enrich and empower everybody, not to push people to live in any particular spot. The federal government has no business trying to encourage economic development in the foothills of the Rockies, and it is hard to see the case for spending billions to encourage people to move to politically favored cities. Expensive efforts to renew cities often do more for well-connected businesses than for the poor people living in those declining areas. Even if building a museum in a depressed neighborhood raises property values and brings in a stream of artsy visitors, that won't help the renter who doesn't care for art and now has to pay more for her apartment.

The success of Bilbao's Guggenheim Museum has lent credence to the view that cultural institutions can be successful urban renewal strategies. Frank Gehry's iconic structure has certainly spurred tourism, which rose from 1.4 million visitors in 1994 to 3.8 million in 2005; the museum alone attracts a million visitors annually. There are certainly Bilbao skeptics, however. One study attributed only about nine hundred new jobs to the museum, a project that cost the Basque treasury $240 million. But the bigger problem with drawing lessons from Bilbao is that its experience is far from standard. For every Guggenheim, there are dozens of expensive failures, like the National Centre for Popular Music, built in Sheffield, England, with the hope of four hundred thousand new visitors each year. It attracted a quarter of that number when it opened in 1999 and closed the same year. Leipzig also has a beautiful art museum, with splendid soaring rooms that unfortunately emphasize the museum's paucity of visitors.

Leipzig is worthy of emulation less for its cultural strategy than for its hardheaded policy of accepting decline and reducing the empty housing stock. In 2000, one fifth of the city's homes stock was vacant, a total of 62,500 units. After refusing to accept the reality of decline for decades, the city government finally recognized that those units would never again house anybody and that it made more sense to demolish them and replace them with green space. Bulldozing vacant homes reduces the costs of city services, eliminates safety hazards, and turns decaying eyesores into usable space. Leipzig set a target of destroying 20,000 vacant units.

In the United States, Youngstown, Ohio, which has lost more than half of its 1970 population, has also embraced this vision of shrinking to greatness. In 2005, the city's newly elected mayor immediately earmarked funds for demolishing abandoned homes. Many of these homes are being destroyed. Parks, open space, and large lots will replace once-dense neighborhoods. This strategy won't bring Youngstown's population back, but it will make the city more attractive, less dangerous, and cheaper to maintain. And finally Detroit has itself found a mayor, David Bing, who understands that the people aren't coming back and that empty homes should be replaced with some more reasonable use of space. Mayor Bing is not short on compassion, but he also understands the edifice error. He knows Detroit can be a great city if it cares for its people well even if it has far fewer structures.

Museums and transportation and the arts do have an important role in place-making. Yet planners must be realistic and expect moderate successes, not blockbusters. Realism pushes toward small, sensible projects, not betting a city's future on a vast, expensive roll of the dice. The real payoff of these investments in amenities lies not in tourism but in attracting the skilled residents who can really make a city rebound, especially if those residents can connect with the world economy.

The path back for declining industrial towns is long and hard. Over decades, they must undo the cursed legacy of big factories and heavy industry. They must return to their roots as places of small-scale entrepreneurship and commerce. Apart from investing in education and maintaining core public services with moderate taxes and regulations, governments can do little to speed this process. Not every city will come back, but human creativity is strong, especially when reinforced by urban density.

8

Culture, Art, and Downtown Development

ELIZABETH STROM

American cities have rediscovered their cultural resources. During the past two decades, city officials have learned to value the historic communities that their predecessors have been eager to raze; have dubbed desolate, derelict warehouses "arts districts"; and have committed local tax dollars to their museums and performing arts complexes, many newly built or recently expanded. A survey of 65 U.S. cities (those with populations of 250,000 and above) finds that 71 major performing arts centers and museums have been either built or substantially expanded since 1985.[1] From Charlotte's Blumenthal Hall, to Los Angeles' Getty Museum, to Seattle's Benaroya Hall, a cultural building boom is clearly under way.

Of course, cultural facilities have always concentrated in urban areas. What is new and interesting, first, is that so many new facilities have been built in a relatively short time span, and so many have been built outside traditional cultural centers such as New York, Boston, Chicago, and San Francisco.[2] Second, whereas once the arts were considered a luxury, supported by philanthropy and enjoyed by an elite group of connoisseurs, today's cultural institutions are constructed as an explicit part of a city's economic revitalization program. This shift reflects changes both in the political economy of cities and in the organization and mission of highbrow cultural institutions. This article examines these changes and shows how they have led to an increasingly close and mutually beneficial relationship between urban political, economic, and cultural entrepreneurs.

The urban cultural building boom, this article maintains, represents a confluence of three related trends. First, cities seeking to attract businesses

From Elizabeth Strom, "Converting Pork into Porcelain: Cultural Institutions and Downtown Development," *Urban Affairs Review*, Vol. 38, No. 1, pp. 3–21, copyright © 2002 by SAGE Publications, Inc. Reprinted by permission of SAGE Publications, Inc.

with quality-of-life amenities are eager to support the development of cultural institutions, especially in their once moribund centers. They believe that these institutions will increase the city's symbolic capital and catalyze other, unsubsidized commercial activities. Second, cultural institutions are drawn by their own economic needs and by the imperatives of their funding sources to seek broader audiences and exploit more commercial, income-generating strategies. They are able to achieve these goals without completely sacrificing their aesthetic legitimacy because, third, the boundaries between high culture—once their dominant domain—and popular culture have blurred. Cultural institutions today are thus better positioned than those of 100 years ago to become active stakeholders in urban growth politics.

CULTURE IN THE GROWTH COALITION: WHY BUSINESS AND POLITICAL LEADERS NEED THE ARTS

Business elites have long recognized that the prestige of high arts institutions could bring economic benefit to their hometowns, but policies explicitly drawing on the arts to achieve economic development goals have only recently become common. The urban renewal projects of the 1950s and 1960s occasionally included cultural institutions—landmarks such as New York's Lincoln Center and Washington's Arena Stage were built on sites cleared of tenement housing with the support of city development officials, business elites, and the cultural institutions that would inhabit them (Toffler 1964, 1973). However, during this period, most city planners and business-people still saw investments in culture as incidental to the main city development goals of industrial retention and office and housing development.

By the 1980s, the dominant urban development policy paradigm had shifted away from "smokestack chasing" in which cities competed for investment by offering lower costs (Bailey 1989). Competing for corporate headquarters and producer service firms, economic development practitioners realized, required more than just abating taxes and improving infrastructure. Clark (2000) maintains that today's educated workers are more likely to choose appealing locations, most notably those with attractive natural and cultural resources, and then consider their employment options. In this model, firms that rely on highly skilled labor have greater incentive than ever to either choose amenity-rich locations or to strive to improve the quality of life in their headquarters city. As cities compete for mobile, skilled workers and the firms that employ them, low taxes may be less important than riverfront parks, sports arenas, and historic districts. Moreover, city officials have become ever more aware of the economic importance of tourism and have put a great deal of energy into building and enlarging convention centers (Sanders 1998), subsidizing new hotels, and attracting major retailers (Friedan and Sagalyn 1989; Hannigan 1998; Judd 1999).

Cultural institutions represent an important element of the recreational infrastructure thought to make a city more appealing to tourists and investors (Eisinger 2000; Hannigan 1998). Corporations have come to see the presence of local arts institutions as a business asset, and their support for such organizations represents good business sense as much as philanthropy. Ford Motor's marketing director, who was asked why his company has nearly single-handedly kept Detroit's opera company solvent, noted that the presence of such an institution made it easier to recruit white-collar employees (Bradsher 1999). Donors to the New Jersey Performing Arts Center made this point as well (Strom 1999).

City governments and place-based business elites have become more intent on marketing their cities. Local boosterism, of course, is hardly new, but today professionals with large budgets have replaced the well-intentioned amateurs of an earlier era (Ward 1998; Holcomb 1993). Moreover, as is true throughout the business world, city promoters have moved from a model of *selling,* where one tries to persuade the buyer to purchase what one has, to *marketing,* where one tries to have what the buyer wants (Holcomb 1993). Marketers do not merely come up with a catchy jingle; they seek to remake the city, or at least the most visible part of the city, to conform to the expectations of the affluent consumers they want to attract. Cultural institutions, associated with beauty, good taste, and higher purpose, become singularly important symbolic assets for image-conscious marketers.

At the same time, development practitioners and scholars began to appreciate that the arts comprise a wealth-generating economic sector, one in which urban areas retain a competitive advantage. Since the 1980s, the economic impact of the arts has received considerable attention. In major cultural capitals like New York, the "culture industry," as the production and consumption of the arts is called, comprises an important economic sector (National Endowment for the Arts 1981; The Port Authority of New York and New Jersey 1993). Even in less obvious places, the culture industry plays a measurable economic role (Perryman 2000).

Cultural projects are valued for more than their direct economic impact. They are built in locations well situated to transform waning downtowns, obsolete factory districts, and disregarded waterfronts. New museums and performing arts centers now feature architectural designs that embrace and enhance their surroundings, rather than isolate their audiences from the city around them, as had been the case in an earlier generation (Russell 1999). And the new projects have been seen as a means of bringing life—and economic impulse—to central cities that are too often deserted after business hours. Philadelphia's Kimmel Center for the Performing Arts, it is hoped, will anchor new economic activity in Center City, where until recently check-cashing businesses and nude dance halls were as common as restaurants and theaters. During the past decade, Seattle has built two major arts facilities downtown: a new home for the Seattle Art Museum, opened in 1991, and Benaroya Hall, a performing arts complex built primarily for the Seattle Symphony, which opened in 1998. Seattle business leaders credit these cultural institutions with a downtown revival that includes the development of several major retail complexes and a 40% increase in the number of people living downtown since 1990 (Byrd 1997).

The arts can also lend greater legitimacy to other urban development efforts. One hundred years ago, urban arts patrons were quite clear about their hope that cultural institutions would serve to placate a growing immigrant working class (Horowitz 1976). As Boston entrepreneur Henry Lee Higginson wrote in 1886, "Educate and save ourselves and our families and our money from mobs!" (Quoted in Levine 1988, 205). The social control function of urban arts institutions today is far subtler. To David Harvey (1989), the contemporary urban spectacle—which includes ephemera like street fairs and festivals, as well as more institutionalized cultural facilities and entertainment districts—has become a way of co-opting the oppositional politics of the 1960s. To others, the presence of culture, especially serious, nonprofit culture, can serve to legitimize urban redevelopment among those who would not normally see themselves as its beneficiaries. Large-scale urban renewal projects can be made more palatable to voters and opinion shapers (if not always to those displaced in their wake) when they are packaged as new cultural centers or filled with public art (Miles 1998). In the words of a National Endowment for the Arts official,

> The arts . . . are like Mom and apple pie; they're consensus-makers, common ground. People can easily focus on the arts activities in a new project, instead of dwelling on the complicated costs and benefits public support for private development activity usually entails. (Quoted in Clack 1983, 13)

Arts organizations therefore represent a significant and unique component of the amalgam of downtown consumption palaces Judd (1999) has labeled the "tourist bubble." Urban scholars have analyzed the actors in the urban tourism and entertainment infrastructure, including retail mall developers, convention center operators, and major-league sports franchises, to understand why they are drawn to participate in downtown real estate projects (Friedan and Sagalyn 1989; Rosentraub 1997; Danielson 1997; Sanders 1998). Cultural institutions, however, have not received similar attention from urban political economists, even though their incorporation into urban growth politics begs explanation. Urban scholars have not asked why an elite cultural institution, whose legitimacy has long been based on its ability to showcase the most serious, academically sanctioned art, might join with those seeking to develop and market the city to the widest possible audience. Today's cultural institutions, however, have been affected by some of the same pressures as city governments. Living in a more competitive environment in which entrepreneurship and marketing are held to be the key to their survival, arts organizations have themselves been transformed.

CULTURE, CONSUMPTION, AND REVITALIZATION: WHY ARTS INSTITUTIONS NEED URBAN DEVELOPMENT

Cultural institutions are not just the objects of urban development schemes: They have themselves become active promoters of revitalization and place marketing activities, and they have done so to realize their own institutional goals. Cultural facilities, especially art museums, must expand to remain "competitive" in the art world, and their expansion needs often place them at the center of local development plans. They have at least five important reasons for wanting to be part of the area's revitalization.

First, some of their concerns about the city's economic health may derive from the interests of their trustees (Logan and Molotch 1987). In nearly every city, there is considerable overlap between those who are prominent in the city's highest business circles and those who are active on cultural boards. One study found that 70% of the members of Louisville's most prestigious development organizations also served on the boards of cultural organizations. (In contrast, those active in peak economic development groups were far less likely to be found on human service agency boards, suggesting the unique importance of arts organizations to those most concerned with the city's development) (Whitt and Lammers 1991). It would be a mistake, however, to assume that major cultural organizations are mere extensions of profit-seeking trustees. Cultural board members usually grant the arts professionals a great deal of autonomy in running the institution's operations. Nominations to the most prestigious nonprofit institution boards are coveted; those invited to join are unlikely to jeopardize the hard-earned esteem of their peers by asserting a self-serving agenda (Ostrower 1998).[3] The business interests of board members provide a context for institutional decision making, but they are unlikely to be the primary imperative pushing cultural organizations toward a development agenda.

Second, cultural institutions need to bring their customers—the cultural audiences—to them. People are unlikely to visit a place if the surrounding community is thought to be dangerous. Many cultural consumers are not arts aficionados willing to go anywhere to see, say, a particular Rembrandt, but rather those for whom arts events are part of an entertainment experience. Not only will high crime and extensive physical deterioration put a cultural institution at a disadvantage, but so also will a dearth of amenities like good restaurants.

Third, numerous studies indicate the extent to which cultural institutions depend on tourist visits (the Port Authority of New York and New Jersey 1993; McDowell 1997). New York's Museum of Modern Art estimates that two-thirds of its visits are from out-of-towners, and half of those come from overseas.[4] Of those who visited the Los Angeles County Museum of Art Van Gogh exhibition in 1999, 56% came from outside Los Angeles (Morey and Associates 1999). Cultural institutions therefore have a strong interest in the city's overall appeal to tourists.

Fourth, cultural institutions are heavily dependent on the availability of local volunteers (there are 2.5 volunteers for every paid museum staff member, according to the American Association of Museums). Location in an impoverished city or in a declining neighborhood may make it more difficult to recruit volunteers. Fifth, wealthy individuals and corporations, which provide the program funds for many cultural organizations, usually focus their giving in their hometowns. When a corporation fails or relocates, local arts organizations lose an important source of support.

In sum, arts organizations in thriving areas will have more visitors, more volunteers, and greater fund-raising success than those in depressed areas.

It is clear that arts organizations benefit when their cities are economically healthy. Moreover, cultural groups are learning that they can benefit when they are perceived as one of the sources of that economic health. Today, preparing a study of one's economic impact seems to be a staple of large arts organizations and local arts councils. Such studies are of questionable economic merit (Cwi and Lyall 1977)—as Eisinger (2000, 327) notes, "Consultants hired by project proponents often seem to pull their multipliers out of thin air." But their purpose is not rigorous cost-benefit analysis; rather, they are tools used by arts groups in their efforts to gain funding and political support. The claim that flourishing arts institutions are important to the urban economy has given arts advocates a rationale to appeal for government support even when tight budgets and political controversies might make public arts funding difficult to obtain (Wyszomirski 1995).

By emphasizing their importance to local revitalization, arts administrators have also been able to gain access to new funding sources. The construction of the New Jersey Performing Arts Center (NJPAC) was supported by $106 million in state contributions, mostly from funds earmarked for economic development activities. Such a large sum would not have been made available for a cultural project had it not been able to claim an important regional economic impact—New Jersey's entire annual cultural budget has never been higher than $20 million (Strom 1999). Arts projects in Louisville, Seattle, and Philadelphia all received generous capital grants from state governments, grants that were clearly tied to the economic mission of these institutions. Similarly, major arts institutions are receiving support from private sources that are more interested in urban revitalization than in art. New Jersey financier Ray Chambers, a man who had never shown much interest in cultural activities but who was deeply committed to the future of Newark, spearheaded the development of NJPAC. Clothing manufacturer Sidney Kimmel made clear in remarks broadcast on local radio that his $15 million donation to Philadelphia's new performing arts center was in support of the center's urban revitalization promises. Arts institutions can show funders that their contributions are not mere charity but rather serve as investments in the city's economic future.

NEW AUDIENCES, NEW PATRONS: WHY TODAY'S CULTURAL INSTITUTIONS ARE WELL POSITIONED TO PARTICIPATE IN URBAN DEVELOPMENT

Funding and Organizing High Culture

Cultural institutions may have long had a clear interest in the city's economic health, but only recently have they emerged as ideal partners for the sorts of growth-oriented coalitions described in Mollenkopf (1983), Logan and Molotch (1987), and Stone (1989). The participation of cultural institutions in urban development coalitions has been facilitated by far-reaching changes in arts patronage and arts management ongoing at least since the 1960s. If nineteenth-century institutions looked to wealthy families for financial support, since that time the private collector/patron has been largely eclipsed by more institutionalized forms of funding.[5] Many wealthy families now route their donations through foundations, the largest of which have professional staffs. Since the mid-1960s, the single most important patron of high culture has been the government. The National Endowment of the Arts will have a budget of about $115 million in 2001–2002, and the 50 state governments have allocated $447.5 million for arts and cultural programs in fiscal year 2001 (National Association of State Arts Agencies 2001). During the 1970s, corporate funding became an increasingly significant source of support. According to the Business Committee for the Arts, corporate support for culture increased from $22 million in 1967 to $1.16 billion in 1997,[6] and corporate arts funding tripled during the 1975–1985 period (DiMaggio 1986).

Changes in arts funding affect arts programming in ways that have implications for economic development policies. More so than private patrons, government agencies and corporate donors seek programs with broad audience appeal (Zolberg 1983; Alexander 1996). The National Endowment for the Arts (NEA) and the state arts councils are eager to associate with programs whose popularity can translate into political support for their efforts. For businesses, cultural donations are a "highbrow form of advertising" (Alexander 1996, 2), as corporations seek to attach their names to programs that are highly visible and prestigious. A well-placed, $200,000 cultural donation, according to one corporate foundation official, can have the same impact as $50 million in paid advertising.[7] Government and corporate funding influence the form of cultural offerings as well as the content. Few corporations want to fund a museum's operations; they prefer to attach their name to special, traveling exhibitions that attract large crowds in a number of cities. Alexander (1996) correlates the growth of government and corporate funding with the increasing number of special, "blockbuster" exhibits mounted by museums (and there may well be similar parallels in other kinds of arts institutions). Museum managers see such events as opportunities to attract large, paying audiences (many museums charge for such special exhibits) and generate new members who will continue to support the museum once the special exhibit has moved on.[8]

If such big-ticket events bring benefits for museum managers, they also fit well into the marketing strategies of urban development and tourism officials. Indeed, arts advocates, economic development officials, and the tourism industry have, since the mid-1990s, consciously sought to promote "cultural tourism." An estimated 50 cultural tourism programs have been founded in state, county, and local convention and visitors bureaus, and two national networks, Partners in Tourism (which is sponsored by American Express) and the Cultural Tourism Alliance, hold conferences and publish newsletters on cultural tourism. The Los Angeles County Museum of Art Van Gogh exhibition that drew so many out-of-town visitors had been promoted heavily by the Los Angeles Convention and Visitors Bureau, which advertised "Van Gogh weekend packages" in such upscale publications as *The New Yorker*. The convergence of interests is clear: City marketing officials, arts funders, and ultimately publicity-conscious cultural administrators all find benefit in mounting large, well-publicized exhibits or performances that attract big audiences.[9]

The Shifting Brows

Highbrow arts institutions would have limited value as economic development catalysts, however, if they were catering to a narrow stratum of social elites and art connoisseurs. But a dramatic shift in the way culture is framed and classified has made an expansion of art audiences possible. Boundaries between serious and popular art, and between the audiences who enjoy them, have become increasingly blurred. Of course, even the high—low distinctions that seemed so secure at midcentury were hardly inevitable; rather, scholars have shown them to be largely a product of the mid- to late-nineteenth century (DiMaggio 1982; Levine 1988). In the earlier part of the nineteenth century, concerts might include pieces by Bach or Haydn as well as popular fare; an evening of Shakespeare might be interspersed with acrobatic performances; and fledgling museums displayed works of established, serious artists next to curios (DiMaggio 1982). Even in the late nineteenth century, museums such as Philadelphia's Pennsylvania Museum unapologetically celebrated industrial design alongside European painting (Conn 1998). Such catholic sensibilities soon vanished in favor of more rigid classification schemes that made some cultural artifacts the exclusive terrain of those with education and money. Cultural objects that had once been universally enjoyed, including Shakespearean plays and Italian operas, were reinterpreted so that their more accessible elements were abandoned, and they became the property of the possessors of cultural capital (Levine 1988). That this reclassification took place in the decades surrounding the turn of the century was not accidental: It represented a response on the part of the upper classes to the growing presence and political strength of an increasingly vocal and politically mobilized working class. Defining an elite culture created a safe haven for the upper classes, who could rely on their association with high cultural goods to legitimize their class position (Horowitz 1976; Bourdieu 1984).

High art and popular culture also became institutionally segregated. Earlier in the nineteenth century, high culture had been marketed through the same commercial mechanisms as popular fare. The Swedish opera singer Jenny Lind made a wildly popular American tour in the 1850s under the sponsorship of P. T. Barnum, and European ballerina Fanny Ellsler, who toured the United States from 1840 to 1842, managed to become the darling of economic and cultural elites while still acquiring a mass following and making good profits selling Fanny Ellsler brand garters, stockings, corsets, and shaving soap (Levine 1988).

By the late nineteenth century, however, high and low art forms each had their own institutional home. Profit-driven entrepreneurs disseminated popular culture. The newly created nonprofit corporation, on the other hand, become the vehicle for disseminating high culture. Museums and orchestras so organized had a mix of public and private purposes that suited their patrons. As private corporations, they remained under the control of their appointed trustees. Because they relied on charitable donations, and not on popular political support, they could maintain high standards of elite culture. And because they were nonprofit, they could make claims to have a broader public purpose than a fully private, profit-seeking operation, thus justifying appeals for public support (DiMaggio 1982). Disseminated through the nonprofit corporation, the artifacts of serious culture could maintain their distance from the marketplace.

Today, however, the distinctions so carefully honed in the nineteenth century have become blurred. Rigid classifications fell under attack from several fronts. Gans (1974, 1999) notes a convergence of tastes dating back to the 1920s. The emergence of the middlebrow provided middle classes with more accessible versions of elite art, and today you do not need highbrow credentials to visit a blockbuster event at an art museum or enjoy a foreign film. At the same time, there was a "gentrification" of lowbrow arts, as elite artists and musicians explored jazz and folk art (Peterson 1997). Today, more modern and accessible art forms like jazz, modern dance, film, and photography can be created and consumed in many different venues and at many different levels, challenging the sorts of hierarchies described by Bourdieu (1984). Moreover, theoretical and empirical evidence suggests that the typical upper-class cultural consumer is no longer the snob, whose consumption of elite culture was linked to his or her rejection of other cultural forms, but the "omnivore," who consumes traditional high culture but also partakes of a variety of popular genres (Peterson and Kern 1996). The possibilities for mixing audiences of different classes and art of different genres are far greater today than they were at the turn of the nineteenth century.

The boundaries separating the organization of elite and popular culture have shifted as well. High culture remains the domain of elite, nonprofit institutions, but it is increasingly marketed with reference to the symbols and presentations of popular culture and supported by commercial market mechanisms. Museum shops no longer merely sell postcards and art books. They now feature a whole range of merchandise, some replicas of objects in their collections, some using motifs from objects in their collection (e.g., famous paintings printed on scarves and umbrellas), and some having little to do with their collections but presumably gaining value just by their association with great art. Museums and performing arts centers boast full-scale, four-star restaurants that become part of a city's lure to tourists, and their staffs include people with the business skills needed to help such enterprises run profitably (Alexander 1996).

The obscuring of cultural boundaries has important implications for the value of culture as an element of urban revitalization. Not only can cultural institutions take advantage of the market for arts-associated products. They can also broaden their programmatic offerings without losing their core constituencies. Today's arts organization trustees, apparently mindful of the need to appeal to broader audiences, are able to accept the use of popularizing techniques and commercial marketing without feeling that their elite status is compromised (Ostrower 1998). The Metropolitan Museum features Hollywood costumes; the Guggenheim showcases motorcycles and the work of fashion designer Armani. They do this while displaying their collections of European paintings and Greek sculpture, retaining their base of upscale donors and remaining highly desirable conveyers of status for those fortunate enough to be named to their boards.

Performing arts institutions have exhibited an even greater eclecticism than museums. Because performances are very time limited, a theater's programming can simultaneously appeal to diverse audiences. Indeed, many of today's performing arts centers, built with the goal of having maximum economic impact, contain multiple performance spaces, so that radically different types of performances can take place on the same evening (Rothstein 1998). One need only peruse the calendars of America's leading performing arts centers to find intriguing juxtapositions, as Broadway shows share the theater complex with symphony orchestras, country fiddlers, and travel lectures. In November 2000, just to offer one example, the Tulsa Performing Arts Center's calendar included the Broadway musical Showboat, Brahms Oratorio music, the Moscow String Quartet, the U.S. Marine Band, and a pops concert of Frank Sinatra hits. On one very busy Saturday in February 1998, West Palm Beach's Kravis Center for the Performing Arts hosted singers Steve Lawrence and Eydie Gorme, the Gospel Gala, and the Emerson String Quartet. This is exactly the mix we might expect given the new relationship between the brows. On one hand, distinctions are maintained—these performances all took place in different halls, most likely attracting different audiences who probably conducted themselves according to different codes of behavior. On the other hand, these audiences apparently did not feel that their enjoyment of their brand of art was compromised by their proximity to others enjoying a different kind of performance. A few may have even come back another night to attend one of the other shows.

As long as cultural institutions could not easily cut across genres, their usefulness as vehicles of economic development was limited. They could function as elite establishments, bringing prestige to their city and perhaps attracting a few well-heeled tourists and an occasional amenity-oriented business. However, they would seldom draw large enough crowds or identify with broad enough consumption opportunities to be considered commercial catalysts. On the other hand, organizations offering popular fare might bring in the crowds but would be less likely to earn the support of political and social elites or serve to improve a city's symbolic capital. But this has changed, as we can see when we observe those performing arts center calendars. The Broadway musicals pay the bills. The ethnically diverse programming assures broader political legitimacy. The European art, the symphonic music, the elegant galas affirm an institution's highbrow bona fides to social and economic elites. Institutions of high culture fulfill their unique role within today's urban growth coalitions precisely because they can catalyze profit-generating activities, while bringing their nonprofit, noncommercial credentials with them.

DiMaggio and Powell have theorized that organizations working together in the same "organizational field" come to share structural characteristics to facilitate their relations in a process that is shaped by resource dependencies as well as shared professional norms (DiMaggio and Powell 1983). Peterson has applied this theory to the study of cultural institutions and arts patrons, noting that arts organizations have become more professionalized (there are now

40 graduate programs in arts administration) and specialized as arts funding has shifted from private patronage to bureaucratic support (Peterson 1986). The organizational field of cultural production and consumption can perhaps today be expanded to include not just arts organizations and their funders but also the local officials who are involved in developing and marketing the city's cultural offerings. The marriage of culture and development is thus facilitated by the shared goals and norms of their advocates, and increasingly it is institutionalized through cultural tourism offices, arts district promotional agencies, or national collaboratives like the Institute for Community Development and the Arts, a project uniting the advocacy group Americans for the Arts with the United States Conference of Mayors. All are involved in selling an image of an urbane place of cultural sophistication, in which the museum or performance hall lends its panache to the city around it, which reciprocates by creating an atmosphere that promotes the consumption of culture.

Art and the Economy: A Changing Relationship

The cultural life of American cities has always had a complex relationship to the local political economy. Local cultural landscapes were shaped by social rivalries and boosterist regional competition. Such revered institutions as New York's Metropolitan Opera, for example, were created to display the wealth of newly rich industrialists (Burrows and Wallace 1999); the patrons of Chicago's now renowned art museum and symphony sought to assert their cultural parity with Boston and New York (Horowitz 1976). If late-nineteenth and early-twentieth-century patrons could appreciate the potential benefits that accrued to those who built cultural centers, however, for those founding nineteenth-century museums and concert halls—in contrast to today's cultural entrepreneurs—economic gain remained subtext. Cultural institutions of their era were built to show off wealth, not to generate it. Reporting on the opening of the (at that time very modestly housed) Newark Museum in 1909, the local press proclaimed, "The city is rich! A part of the wealth of its citizens should be invested in paintings, sculpture and other art objects" (Newark Museum 1959, 7). Businessman and arts patron Joseph Choate, speaking at the Metropolitan Museum's opening, stressed the museum's function as an uplifting source of beauty and urged men of wealth to "convert pork into porcelain, grain and produce into priceless pottery, the rude ores of commerce into sculpted marble, and railroad shares and mining stocks . . . into the glorified canvas of the world's masters" (Tomkins 1970, 23). Today, the relationship between the city's economy and its cultural institutions is understood very differently. Kicking off a fund-raising drive for the expansion of the Newark Museum—the same museum celebrated as a symbol of local prosperity in 1909—New Jersey Governor Tom Kean touted the museum and other urban cultural assets as "catalysts of rebirth," "creating the kind of public image needed for growth and new jobs" (Courtney 1984). Countless public officials and donors have similarly proclaimed their support for culture as a means of spurring an economic revival (Byrd 1997; Davies 1998).

The association of economic development and culture has by now become commonplace, and commentary on this new relationship is largely laudatory. There have been a few cautionary voices: Some urban scholars have expressed concern that an urban development strategy whose primary goal is to attract outsiders to privatized entertainment spaces can be undemocratic and exclusionary (Eisinger 2000; Judd 1999), diverting public funds from projects of more direct benefit to most urban residents (Strom 1999). Even those cultural facilities deemed successful will never generate the tax revenue and employment to make them appear to be good investments in a cost-benefit analysis (National Endowment for the Arts 1981),[10] giving rise to the same critiques that have been leveled against subsidized sports and convention venues (Sanders 1998; Rosentraub 1997). Of course, unlike convention center and sport stadium proponents, cultural advocates have never argued that they could justify public subsidy purely through their production of direct economic benefits. Rather, the arts are said to increase the value of other products and deliver noneconomic benefits as well. Many museums and performing arts centers have effective outreach and education programs that make them genuinely accessible. Surely no other "tourist bubble" institution can make such a claim.

Cultural institutions themselves may face conflicts when they adapt their mission to that of the city's economic development strategists. Hoping for the biggest possible impact on their central city areas, economic development proponents are eager to build new museums and concert halls, and less concerned with sustaining these institutions once they are built. Individual and corporate donors also like to contribute to capital campaigns, where their largesse can be rewarded with wall plaques and naming opportunities. As a result, bricks and mortar investments may be favored over support for cultural programs; smaller arts organizations may be overlooked in favor of the larger groups better able to document their economic clout.

The need to prove their economic mettle to political allies and funders becomes yet one more pressure on cultural institutions already hard-pressed to disseminate great art while paying their bills. The fine arts can certainly be "popular," drawing large audiences. There is also art that is unlikely to play to full houses or attract long lines because it is difficult or challenging or cutting-edge. If arts institutions are primarily seen as mechanisms for urban revitalization and are valued for their ability to draw large numbers of people to city hotels and restaurants, they may be less willing or able to realize the scholarly or educational aspects of their work. To be sure, urban development stakeholders are hardly the only ones pushing arts institutions toward a more commercial, less scholarly mission. And museum curators have often been clever at mounting the kinds of shows that will draw the crowds and pay the bills to gain resources to support more esoteric or challenging programs (Alexander 1996). However, too much focus on the arts institutions' economic role may obscure the fact that making money for the city can never be their primary purpose.

REFERENCES

Alexander, V. D. 1996. *Museums and money*. Bloomington: Indiana Univ. Press.

American Association of Museums. 1999. *The official museum directory*. New Providence, NJ: National Register Publishing.

Bailey, J. T. 1989. *Marketing cities in the 1980s and beyond*. Rosemont, IL: American Economic Development Council.

Bourdieu, P. 1984. *Distinction*. Cambridge, MA: Harvard Univ. Press.

Bradsher, K. 1999. A horn of plenty for opera in Detroit. *New York Times*, 28 October, E1, 10.

Burrows, E. G., and M. Wallace. 1999. *Gotham: A history of New York City to 1898*. New York and Oxford, UK: Oxford Univ. Press.

Byrd, J., 1997. Culture at the core. *Seattle Post-Intelligencer*, 9 February, J1.

Clack, G. 1983. Footlight districts. In *The city as stage*, edited by K. W. Green. Washington, DC: Partners for Livable Places.

Clark, T. N. 2000. Old and new paradigms for urban research: Globalization and the Fiscal Austerity and Urban Innovation Project. *Urban Affairs Review* 36 (1): 3–45.

Conn, S. 1998. *Museums and American intellectual life, 1876–1926*. Chicago: Univ. of Chicago Press.

Courtney, M. 1984. Newark museum revives growth plans. *New York Times*, 8 April, B1, 4.

Cwi, D., and K. Lyall. 1977. *Economic impact of arts and cultural institutions: A model for assessment and a case study for Baltimore*. Washington, DC: National Endowment for the Arts.

Danielson, M. N. 1997. *Home team*. Princeton, NJ: Princeton Univ. Press.

Davies, P. 1998. Philadelphia could make big gains from Performing Arts Center visitors. *Philadelphia Daily News*, 17 April.

DiMaggio, P. J. 1982. Cultural entrepreneurship in nineteenth-century Boston: The creation of an organizational base for high culture in America. *Media, Culture and Society* 4:33–50.

———. 1986. Can culture survive the marketplace? In *Nonprofit enterprise in the arts*, edited by P. J. DiMaggio, 65–92. New York and Oxford, UK: Oxford Univ. Press.

DiMaggio, P. J., and W. W. Powell, 1983. The iron cage revisited: Institutional isomorphism and collective rationality in organizational fields. *American Sociological Review* 48:147–60.

Dobrzynski, J. 1998. Blockbuster shows and prices to match. *New York Times*, 10 November, El, 13.

Duncan, C. 1995. *Civilizing rituals: Inside art museums*. London, New York: Routledge.

Eisinger, P. 2000. The politics of bread and circuses. *Urban Affairs Review* 35 (3): 316–33.

Friedan, B. J., and L. B. Sagalyn. 1989. *Downtown Inc*. Cambridge, MA: MIT Press.

Gans, H. J. 1974. *Popular culture and high culture*. New York: Basic Books.

———. 1999. *Popular culture and high culture*. Rev. ed. New York: Basic Books.

Hannigan, J. 1998. *Fantasy city*. London: Routledge.

Harvey, D. 1989. *The condition of postmodernity*. Oxford, UK: Basil Blackwell.

Holcomb, B. 1993. Revisioning place: De- and re-constructing the image of the industrial city. In *Selling places: The city as cultural capital, past and present*, edited by G. Kearns and C. Philo. Oxford, UK: Pergamon.

Horowitz, H. L. 1976. *Culture and the city*. Lexington: Univ. Press of Kentucky.

Janeway, M., D. S. Levy, A. Szanto, and A. Tyndall, 1999. *Reporting the arts: News coverage of arts and culture in America*. New York: Columbia Univ., National Arts Journalism Program.

Judd, D. 1999. Constructing the tourist bubble. In *The tourist city*, edited by D. Judd and S. Fainstein, 35–53. New Haven, CT: Yale Univ. Press.

Levine, L. W. 1988. *Highbrow/lowbrow: The emergence of cultural hierarchy in America*. Cambridge, MA: Harvard Univ. Press.

Logan, J. R., and H. L. Molotch, 1987. *Urban fortunes*. Berkeley: Univ. of California Press.

McDowell, E. 1997. Tourists respond to lure of culture. *New York Times*, 24 April, D1, 4.

Miles, M. 1998. A game of appearance: Public art and urban development—Complicity or sustainability? In *The entrepreneurial city*, edited by T. Hall and P. Hubbard, 203–24. Chichester, UK: Wiley.

Mollenkopf, J. M. 1983. *The contested city*. Princeton, NJ: Princeton Univ. Press.

Morey and Associates, Inc. 1999. Economic impact analysis of the Los Angeles County Museum of Art and the Van Gogh exhibition. Unpublished report.

National Association of State Arts Agencies. 2001. Retrieved 11 April 2001, from www.nasaa -arts.org.

National Endowment for the Arts. 1981. *Economic impact of arts and cultural institutions*. Washington, DC: National Endowment for the Arts.

Newark Museum. 1959. *The Newark Museum: A fifty-year survey*. Newark: Newark Museum.

Ostrower, F. 1998. The arts as cultural capital among elites: Bourdieu's theory reconsidered. *Poetics* 26:43–53.

Perryman, M. R. 2000. The arts, culture, and the Texas economy. Retrieved 15 April 2001, from www.perrymangroup.com.

Peterson, R. A. 1986. From impresario to arts administrator. In *Nonprofit enterprise in the arts*, edited by P. J. DiMaggio, 161–83. New York and Oxford, UK: Oxford Univ. Press.

———. 1997. The rise and fall of highbrow snobbery as a status marker. *Poetics* 25:75–92.

Peterson, R. A., and R. M. Kern. 1996. Changing highbrow taste: From snob to omnivore. *American Sociological Review* 61:900–907.

The Port Authority of New York and New Jersey and the Cultural Assistance Center. 1993. *The arts as industry: Their economic importance to the New York–New Jersey metropolitan region*. New York: The Port Authority of New York and New Jersey.

Rosentraub, M. S. 1997. *Major league losers*. New York: Basic Books.

Rothstein, E. 1998. Arts centers are changing the face of culture. *San Diego Union-Tribune,* 6 December, E10.

Russell, J. S. 1999. Performing arts centers: Using art to revive cities. *Architectural Record,* May, 223–28.

Sanders, H. T. 1998. Convention center follies. *Public Interest* (summer): 58–72.

Stone, C. N. 1989. *Regime politics.* Lawrence: University Press of Kansas.

Strom, E. 1999. Let's put on a show: Performing arts and urban revitalization in Newark, New Jersey. *Journal of Urban Affairs* 21:423–36.

Toffler, A. 1964. *The culture consumers.* New York: Random House.

———. 1973. *The culture consumers.* Rev. ed. New York: Random House.

Tomkins, C. 1970. *Merchants and masterpieces.* New York: E. P. Dutton.

Ward, S. V. 1998. *Selling places.* New York and London: Routledge.

Whitt, J. A. 1987. Mozart in the metropolis: The arts coalition and the urban growth machine. *Urban Affairs Quarterly* 23:15–36.

Whitt, J. A., and J. C. Lammers. 1991. The art of growth. *Urban Affairs Quarterly* 26 (3): 376–93.

Wyszomirski, M. J. 1995. The politics of arts policy: Subgovernment to issue network. In *America's commitment to culture: Government and the arts,* edited by K. Mulcahy and M. J. Wyszomirski. Boulder, CO: Westview.

Zolberg, V. 1983. Changing patterns of patronage in the arts. In *Performers and performances,* edited by J. B. Kamerman and R. Martorella, 251–68. New York: Praeger.

NOTES

1. Major performing arts centers are defined as those with 1,000 seats or more. Major museums are those with annual attendance of 50,000 or more. Because this survey looks only at large cultural facilities, it understates the full extent of cultural building.

2. No doubt cultural institution capital campaigns have been aided by the unusually prosperous 1990s. States and cities had budget surpluses, and wealthy individuals could gain prestige and tax benefits by donating stock market gains to nonprofit arts institutions. Many of these projects, however, originated years before the economic boom.

3. Similar comments were made by cultural trustees of cultural organizations interviewed by the author as part of an ongoing study of Newark- and Philadephia-based organizations.

4. Comments of museum administrator made at the Art of the Deal conference, Rutgers University, New Brunswick, 27 March, 2001.

5. Arts administrators report that individual patrons have gained in importance in the late 1990s; individual giving has been fueled by the strong stock market (comments of museum administrator made at the Art of the Deal conference, 2001).

6. Whitt (1987) has questioned the methods by which the Business Committee for the Arts collects its data; as an advocacy group, it could well be inclined to inflate the importance of business contributions.

7. Comments of corporate foundation executive made at the Art of the Deal conference, 2001.

8. This strategy seems to be successful: Many museums point to big jumps in membership during blockbuster exhibits (Dobrzynski 1998).

9. The media play a role in cementing this convergence of interests. A study of newspaper arts coverage found that visual arts get short shrift in most newspapers, except when blockbuster exhibits come to town. Local media, then, become part of the system making highly visible and popular exhibits useful for arts institutions and local development officials (Janeway et al. 1999).

10. The National Endowment for the Arts studied the arts institutions of six cities and found that only in three did they generate as much or more local revenue than they cost the city in subsidies and services. Had these calculations included the costs of state and federal subsidies, the balance sheet would have even looked less favorable.

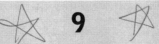

9
Can Politicians Bargain with Business?

PAUL KANTOR AND H. V. SAVITCH

In the summer of 1989, United Air Lines announced it was planning a new maintenance hub that would bring nearly a billion dollars in investment and generate over 7,000 jobs for the region lucky enough to attract it. Within a few short months, officials in over 90 localities were competing for the bonanza and were tripping over one another in an effort to lure United. Denver offered $115 million in incentives and cash, Oklahoma City sought to raise $120 million, and localities in Virginia offered a similar amount. The competition for United was so keen that cities began to bid against one another and asked that their bids be kept secret.

United was so delighted at the level of bidding that it repeatedly delayed its decision in anticipation the offers would get even better. Nearly two years later, city officials in nine finalists were enhancing their incentives, courting United executives, and holding their breaths. Reflecting on the competition, Louisville Mayor Jerry Abramson quipped, "We haven't begun to offer up our firstborn yet, but we're getting close. Right now we are into siblings."[1]

Except for the extremity of the case, there is nothing new about cities questing for private capital. Cities compete with one another for tourism, foreign trade, baseball franchises, and federal grants. Yet, there is another side to this behavior. Although 93 cities competed for the United hub, many others did not, and some cities would have resisted the corporate intrusion (Etzkowitz and Mack 1976; Savitch 1988). When United stalled and raised the ante, Kentucky's governor angrily withdrew, complaining that he would "not continue this auction, this bidding war. There is a point at which you draw the line" ("Governor turns down UAL," *Courier-Journal,* 18 October 1991). In Denver, the legislature's majority leader protested, saying, "United has a ring and is pulling Colorado by the nose." With those remarks and heightening resentment, public opinion began to pull the state away from the lure of United ("UAL bidding goes on," *Courier-Journal,* 22 October 1991).

Such cases do not seem uncommon. Although many cities are willing to build sports stadia, others have turned down the opportunity. For instance, when Fort Wayne, Indiana, declined to go beyond its offer of a short-term low-interest loan to obtain a minor-league baseball team, the franchise was taken elsewhere (Rosentraub and Swindell 1990). Although officials in some cities trip over one another in efforts to attract business by lowering taxes, officials in others raise them. Over the last three years, Los Angeles, New York, and Denver have increased business taxes. Notwithstanding high taxes and locational costs, business continues to seek out such cities as San Francisco, Tokyo, London, Toronto, and Frankfurt.

Nevertheless, the literature on urban politics has not systematically examined such "nondecisional" cases (Bachrach and Baratz 1962) to probe the

From Paul Kantor and H. V. Savitch, "Can Politicians Bargain with Business? A Theoretical and Comparative Perspective on Urban Development," *Urban Affairs Quarterly,* Vol. 29, No. 2, pp. 230–255. Copyright © 1993 by SAGE Publications, Inc. Journals. Reproduced with permission of SAGE Publications, Inc. Journals in the format Textbook via Copyright Clearance Center.

precise circumstances under which local governments can influence the capital investment process. . . .

. . . We propose that questions of how, when, and why local government can influence economic development are best answered by treating political control as something that springs from bargaining advantages that the state has in political and economic exchange relationships with business. Variations in local-government influence are strongly tied to the ways in which the larger political economy distributes particular bargaining resources between the public and private sectors.

Following Lindblom (1977), we find that it is useful to regard this context as a liberal-democratic system in which there is a division of labor between business and government (Kantor 1988; Elkin 1987). The private sector is responsible for the production of wealth in a market system in which choices over production and exchange are determined by price mechanisms. For its part, the public sector is organized along polyarchal lines (Dahl 1971; Dahl and Lindblom 1965) in which public decisions are subject to popular control. Public officials may be viewed as primarily responsible for the management of political support for governmental undertakings; business leaders can be considered essentially managers of market enterprises.

This perspective suggests that even though public and private control systems are theoretically separate, in reality they are highly interdependent. So far as government is concerned, the private sector produces economic resources that are necessary for the well-being of the political community—including jobs, revenues for public programs, and political support that is likely to flow to public authorities from popular satisfaction with economic prosperity and security. For business, the public sector is important because it provides forms of intervention into the market that are necessary for the promotion of economic enterprise but that the private sector cannot provide on its own. Such interventions include inducements that enable private investors to take risks (tax abatements and tax credits), the resolution of private conflicts that threaten social or economic stability (courts, mediation services), and the creation of an infrastructure or other forms of support (highways, workforce training).

Conceptualized in this manner, business and government must engage in exchange relationships (bargaining) to realize common goals. This is done by using bargaining advantages that derive from three dimensions or spheres of interdependence: market conditions, popular-control systems, and public-intervention mechanisms. . . .

Our analysis suggests that there is substantial variation among local governments in their ability to bargain. We also suggest that bargaining advantages tend to be cumulative—that is, the more advantages a city holds, the greater its ability to bargain. Finally, we suggest that because bargaining is a product of political and economic circumstance, so is urban development. Although it may not be possible for a city to manipulate all the variables affecting its bargaining position, most cities can manipulate some and thereby shape its own future. . . .

MARKETS AND PUBLIC CONTROL
OF URBAN DEVELOPMENT

There is little doubt that a businesses' greatest bargaining resource in urban development is its control over private wealth in the capital investment process. It is this dimension of business-government relations that Peterson's (1981) market-centered model of local politics describes. The logic of this model is that cities compete for capital investment by seeking to attract mobile capital to the community; failure to meet the conditions demanded by business for investment leads to the "automatic punishing recoil" (Lindblom 1982) of the marketplace as business disinvests. This notion has been variously interpreted to suggest that business inherently holds a dominant position (Fainstein et al. 1986; Mollenkopf 1983; Logan and Molotch 1987; Jones and Bachelor 1986; Kantor 1988).

Although the market-centered model is a powerful tool for analyzing development politics, it does not fully capture the bargaining relationships that logically derive from it. Specifically, the market perspective tends to highlight only those advantages that accrue to business. Yet, the marketplace works in two directions, not one. If we look at specific market conditions and bargaining demands, it becomes apparent that government also can use the market to obtain leverage over business. Thus we will present a number of common market-centered arguments and show their other side.

The Cities-Lose-If-Business-Wins Argument

In the market model, public and private actors represent institutions that compete to achieve rival goals. Business pursues public objectives only insofar as they serve private needs; if important business needs are not met, local government experiences the discipline of the marketplace as capital and labor seek alternative locations.

Yet, in this description of market dynamics, cases in which local government and business may also share the same goals (as distinct from the same interests) are ignored; in such instances the market model no longer indicates business advantage in the development process. Thus a local government may have an interest in raising public revenue by increasing retail sales while shopkeepers and investors have an interest in maximizing profits. Though their interests are different, they may share the common goal of bringing about higher sales through expanded development. When this happens, bargaining between government and business shifts from rivalry over competing goals to settling differences over how to facilitate what already has been agreed on. This kind of scenario enhances the value of bargaining resources that are mostly owned by the public sector. Development politics focuses on such things as the ability to amass land, grant legal privileges and rights, control zoning, provide appropriate infrastructure, and—not least—enlist public support. Because alternative means of promoting growth are important choices (Logan and Swanstrom 1990), substantial bargaining leverage over development outcomes is placed in the hands of those who manage the governmental process, a point that Mollenkopf (1983) underscored in his study of urban renewal politics.

Yet, this partial escape from the market often is not recognized. Peterson (1981) considered the sharing of interests and goals to be one and the same. Other scholars have often assumed that there is an inherent conflict between private and public goals (Stone and Sanders 1987; Logan and Swanstrom 1990; Swanstrom 1986). However, a strong case can be made that business and government often share common goals. Although they cannot logically share interests, public officials, motivated by different stakes, frequently choose to pursue economic objectives that are also favored by business (Cummings 1988). Although some critics reject progrowth values, these values tend to be supported broadly by local electorates (Logan and Molotch 1987, 50–98; Vaughn 1979; Crenson 1971).

To take a different tack on former head of General Motors Charles Wilson's aphorism, scholars may be too anxious to suggest that if it is good for General Motors, it must be bad for Detroit. Yet, local officials and their publics do not always share this logic. When government and business perceive common goals, such perceptions can have a powerful effect on opportunities for political control over the urban economy. Under these conditions, the ability of political authorities to create political support for specific programs and their willingness to use public authority to assist business can become important bargaining resources for achieving their own interests. At the very least, the extent to which agreement between business and local government is a byproduct of political choice rather than of economic constraint should be a premise for empirical investigation instead of an a priori conclusion.

The Capital Mobility Argument

This argument encompasses an assumption that bargaining advantages accrue to business as it becomes more mobile. Historically, private capital was more dependent on the local state than it is today (Kantor 1988). Technological advances in production, communications, and transportation have enhanced the ability of business to move more easily and rapidly. Changes in the organization of capital, especially the rise of multilocational corporations, have increased business mobility and made urban locations interchangeable. Automation, robotics, and the postindustrial revolution are supposed to enhance capital mobility. Fixed capital has been nudged aside by a new postindustrial technology of flexible capital (Hill 1989; Parkinson, Foley, and Judd 1989).

It would seem to follow that increasing capital mobility must favor business interests. Yet, this conclusion does not always follow, if one considers specific cities and businesses that are caught up in this process of economic globalization. Capital is, in fact, not always very portable. Although cities are frequently viewed as interchangeable by some corporations, many cities retain inherent advantages of location (e.g., Brussels), of agglomeration (e.g., New York), of technological prowess (e.g., Grenoble), or of political access (e.g., Washington, D.C.). The dispersion of capital has triggered a countermovement to create centers that specialize in the communication, coordination, and support of far-flung corporate units. Larger global cities have captured these roles. Much of postindustrial capital has put enormous sunk costs into major cities. One of the more conspicuous examples is the Canadian development firm of Olympia and York, which has invested billions of dollars in New York, London, Ontario, and a host of other cities. As Olympia and York teeters on the edge of collapse, banks, realty interests, and mortgage brokers are also threatened. It is not easy for any of these interests to pull up stakes.

There has been a fairly stable tendency for corporate headquarters operations, together with the ancillary services on which headquarters depend, to gravitate to large cities that have acquired the status of world business centers (Sassen 1988; Noyelle and Stanback 1984). New York's downtown and midtown, London's financial district and its docklands, Paris's La Defense, and Tokyo's Shinjuku are some outstanding examples of postindustrialism that [have] generated billions in fixed investments. Movement by individual enterprises away from such established corporate business centers is unlikely for various reasons, including that this kind of change imposes costs on those owning fixed assets in these locations and disrupts established business networks.

Cities that have experienced ascendant market positions have not been reluctant to cash in on this. When property values and development pressures rose in downtowns, local politicians used the advantage to impose new planning requirements and demand development fees. In San Francisco, a moratorium on high-rise construction regulates the amount and pace of investment (Muzzio and Bailey 1986). In Boston and several other large cities, linkage policies have exacted fees on office development to support moderate-income housing (Dreier 1989). In Paris, differential taxes have been placed on high-rise development and the proceeds used to support city services (Savitch 1988). One should also recognize that market conditions are not immutable.

Local governments may be subject to the blandishments of business at an early stage of development, when there is great eagerness for development and capital has wide investment choices. However, once business has made the investment, it may be bound for the long term. Thus bargaining does not stop after the first deal is struck, and the advantages may shift.

This occurred in Orlando, Florida, where Disney World exacted early concessions from the local governments, only to be faced with new sets of public demands afterward (Foglesong 1989). Prior to building what is now a vast entertainment complex near Orlando, Disney planners capitalized on their impending investment and won huge concessions from government (including political autonomy, tax advantages, and free infrastructure). However, as Disney transformed the region into a sprawling tourist center, local government demanded that the corporation relinquish autonomy and pressured it to pay for physical improvements. Disney struggled to defeat these demands but eventually conceded. With huge sunk investments, Disney executives had little choice but to accommodate the public sector.

So although some industries have grown more mobile, others have not. The issue turns on the relative costs incurred by business and by government when facilities, jobs, and people are moved. How relative costs are assessed and the likelihood that businesses will absorb them influence the respective bargaining postures of business and government.

The City-Cannot-Choose Argument

In the market model, business makes investment choices among stationary cities; because cities cannot move, powerful bargaining advantages accrue to business in the urban development process and supposedly this enables them to exact what they want from local governments. Although this is sometimes the case, it is also true that local communities may have investment choices as well. Some local governments can make choices among alternative types of business investment. In particular, economic diversification enables local political authorities to market the community in a particular economic sector (e.g., as a tourist city, as a research or technical center, or as a sound place in which to retire). Furthur, economic diversification enhances a locality's ability to withstand economic pressure from any particular segment of the business community. This has occurred in cities as far ranging as Seattle, Singapore, and Rome, enabling them to maintain powerful market positions for years, despite profound changes in the world and national economies.

Experience teaches city officials to sense their vulnerabilities and develop defenses against dominance by a single industry. Through diversification, these cities can gain a good deal of strength, not only in weathering economic fluctuations but in dealing with prospective investors. Houston's experience after oil prices crashed moved city leaders to develop high-technology and service industries (Feagin 1988). Pittsburgh's successful effort to clean its air gave that city a new economic complexion. Louisville's deindustrial crisis was followed by a succession of new investments in health services, a revival in the transportation industry, and a booming business in the arts (Vogel 1990). Diversification, which was so instrumental in strengthening the public hand, was actually made possible by government coalitions with business.

The advantages of diversification are most apparent when these cities are compared to localities that are prisoners of relatively monopolistic bargaining relations with business. Officials in single-industry towns are strongly inclined to accommodate business demands on matters of development because they lack alternative sources of capital investment. Crenson (1971) found this pattern in Gary, Indiana, where local officials resisted proposals for pollution control because they feared that U.S. Steel would lay off workers. Similarly, Jones and Bachelor (1986) described how Detroit leaders weakened their market position when they sought to preserve the city's positions as a site for automobile manufacturing. When worldwide changes in the auto industry eroded Detroit's traditional competitive advantages, political leaders fought to subsidize new plants and to demolish an otherwise viable residential neighborhood.

Neither Gary's steel-centered strategy nor Detroit's auto-centered strategy has stemmed their economic decline. The lesson for urban politicians is clear: Instead of vainly hanging on to old industry, go for new, preferably clean business. More than most politicians, big-city mayors have learned well and are fast becoming major economic promoters (Savitch and Thomas 1991).

The City-Maximizes-Growth Argument

Although the market model is built on the supposition that it is in the interest of cities to promote economic growth, not all localities seek to compete in capital markets. To the extent that communities ignore participation in this market, they do not have to bargain with business over demands that they might choose to bring to the bargaining table. Santa Barbara, Vancouver, and Stockholm are cities that have consisted growth and instituted extensive land-use controls. These cities are in enviable positions as they deal with business and developers.

Aside from major cities, there are smaller communities that do not seek to compete for capital investment such as suburban areas and middle-size cities that after years of expansion, now face environmental degradation. Even if these localities have a stake in maintaining competitive advantages as bedroom communities or steady-state mixed commercial/residential locales, their bargaining relationship with business is more independent than in relatively growth-hungry urban communities (Danielson 1976). University towns, in which a self-sustaining and alert population values its traditions, have managed to resist the intrusions of unwanted industry. Coastal cities, which seek to preserve open space, have successfully acquired land or used zoning to curtail development.

Moreover, there are cities in which governmental structures reduce financial pressure and are able to resist indiscriminate development. Regionalism and annexation have enabled cities to widen their tax nets, so that business cannot easily play one municipality off against another. Minneapolis–St. Paul, Miami–Dade, and metro Toronto furnish examples of localities banding together to strengthen their fiscal positions and turn down unwanted growth. In Western European and other non-American nations, cities are heavily financed by central government, thereby reducing and sometimes eliminating the pressure to attract development. For these cities, growth only engenders liabilities.

POPULAR-CONTROL SYSTEMS AND URBAN DEVELOPMENT

Democratic political institutions not only provide means of disciplining public officials, but they constrain all political actors who seek governmental cooperation or public legitimation in the pursuit of their interests. The reality of this is suggested by the fact that business development projects frequently get stopped when they lack a compelling public rationale and generate significant community opposition. This has occurred under varying conditions and in different types of cities. In Paris, neighborhood mobilization successfully averted developers (Body-Gendrot 1987); in London, communities were able to totally redo urban renewal plans (Christensen 1979); in Amsterdam and Berlin, local squatters defied property owners by taking over abandoned buildings; after the recent earthquake in San Francisco, public opinion prevailed against the business community in preventing the reconstruction of a major highway. The existence of open, competitive systems of elections and other polyarchal institutions affords a means by which nonbusiness interests are able to influence, however imperfectly, an urban development process in which business power otherwise looms large.

But do institutions of popular control afford political authorities with a valuable bargaining resource in dealing with business? Are democratic institutions loose cannons that are irrelevant to political bargaining over economic development? From our bargaining perspective, it would appear that these institutions can provide a resource upon which political leaders can draw to impose their own policy preferences when the three conditions described in the following paragraphs are satisfied.

First, public approval of bargaining outcomes between government and business must be connected to the capital-investment process. This is often not the case because most private-sector investment decisions are virtually outside the influence of local government. Even when the characteristics of private projects require substantial public-sector cooperation, many decisions are only indirectly dependent on processes of political approval. Economic-development decisions have increasingly become insulated from the mainstream political processes of city governments as a result of the proliferation of public-benefit corporations (Walsh 1978; Kantor 1993). As power to finance and regulate business development has been ceded to public-benefit corporations, the ability of elected political leaders to build popular coalitions around development issues has shrunk because it makes little sense to appeal to voters on matters that they cannot influence.

On the other hand, the importance of this bargaining resource increases as issues spill over their ordinary institutional boundaries and into public or neighborhood arenas. When this occurs, elected political authorities gain bargaining advantages by putting together coalitions that can play a vital role in the urban development game. Consequently, even the most powerful public and private developers can be checked by politicians representing hostile voter coalitions.

In New York, Robert Mose's slide from power was made possible by mounting public discontent with his later projects and by the intervention of a popular governor who capitalized on this to undercut Moses's position (Caro 1974); Donald Trump's plans for the Upper West Side of Manhattan incurred defeats by a coalition of irate residents, local legislators, and a hostile mayor (Savitch 1988); a major highway (Westway) proposal, sponsored by developers, bankers, and other business interests, was defeated by community activists who skillfully used the courts to question the project's environmental impact.

Second, public authorities must have the managerial capability to organize and deliver political support for programs sought by business. Credible bargaining requires organizing a stable constituency whose consent can be offered to business in a quid pro quo process. However, political authorities clearly differ enormously in their capacity to draw on this resource. In the United States, the decline of machine politics, the weakening of party loyalties and organizations, and the dispersal of political power to interest groups have weakened the capacity of elected political authorities. To some extent, this has been counterbalanced by grassroots and other populist-style movements that have provided a broad base for mayors and other political leaders (Swanstrom 1986; Dreier and Keating 1990; Savitch and Thomas 1991; Capek and Gilderbloom 1992).

In contrast, in Western European cities, the stability and cohesion displayed by urban party systems more frequently strengthen political control of development. In Paris, extensive political control over major development projects is related to stable and well-organized political support enjoyed by officials who dominated the central and local governments (Savitch 1988). In London, ideological divisions between Conservative and Labour parties at the local and national levels limit the ability of business interests to win a powerful role, even in cases involving massive redevelopment such as Covent Garden, the construction of motorways, and the docklands renewal adjacent to the financial city. For example, changes in planning the docklands project were tied to shifts in party control at both the national and local levels. Given the political significance of development issues to both major British parties, it was difficult for nonparty interests to offer inducements that were capable of splitting politicians away from their partisan agendas (Savitch 1988).

Similarly, even highly fragmented but highly ideological political party systems seem capable of providing a powerful bargaining resource to elected governmental authorities. In Italy, many small parties compete for power at the national and local levels. Although this is sometimes a source of political instability, the relatively stable ideological character of party loyalties means that elected politicians are assured of constituency support. Consequently, this base of political power offers substantial bargaining advantages in dealing with business. According to Molotch and Vicari (1988), this enables elected political authorities to undertake major projects relatively free from business pressure. In Milan, officials planned and built a subway line through the downtown commercial district of the city with minimal involvement of local business.

Third, popular-control mechanisms are a valuable bargaining resource when they bind elected leaders to programmatic objectives. If political authorities are not easily disciplined for failure to promote programmatic objectives in development bargaining, business may promote their claims by providing selective incentives (side payments), such as jobs, campaign donations, and other petty favors, to public officials in exchange for their cooperation. When this happens, the bargaining position of city governments is undermined by splitting off public officials from their representational roles—and the process of popular control becomes more of a business resource.

In America, where partisan attachments are weak and where ethnic, neighborhood, and other particularistic loyalties are strong, political leaders are inclined to put a high value on seeking selective benefits to the neglect of programmatic objectives. Although populist mayors have sometimes succeeded in overcoming these obstacles (Swanstrom 1986; Dreier and Keating 1990), the need to maintain unstable political coalitions that are easily undermined by racial and ethnic rivalries limits programmatic political competition.

For example, in Detroit and Atlanta, black mayors have relied heavily on economic development to generate side payments that are used to minimize political opposition; this is facilitated by the symbolic importance that these black mayors enjoy among the heavily black electorates in the two cities. Consequently, they have been able to hold on to power without challenging many business demands (Stone 1989; Hill 1986). In contrast, in Western Europe, where political party systems more frequently discipline public officials to compete on programmatic grounds, bargaining with business is less likely to focus on side payments. As suggested earlier, in France, Italy, and Britain, votes are more often secured by partisan and ideological loyalties and reinforced by progammatic competition than by generating selective incentives for followers.

In sum, city governments vary enormously in their capacity to draw on the popular-control process in bargaining over development. The proximity of electoral competition to development, the capability of officials to organize voter support, and the extent of competition over programmatic objectives are crucial factors that weaken or enhance the resources of city governments.

STATE INTERVENTION AND URBAN DEVELOPMENT

. . . Ironically, integrated national governmental systems appear to enhance local governmental control of urban development, and political structures that decentralize the regulation of market failures afford less local governmental influence. Political systems that accord a powerful urban regulatory role for the national government limit local political authority in urban planning, of course. Yet, these more centralized systems can often work to enhance local governmental bargaining power with the private sector; they do this by making it easier for governments to contain capital movement (overriding private decision making), as well as by permitting localities to draw on the resources, regulatory apparatus, and political support of higher levels of government.

Contrasts between American and some Western European cities illustrate the different bargaining implications of each system. The United States is unique in the degree to which urban public capital investment is highly decentralized. Although the national government provides grants to support highway and other capital projects, this aid is spotty and unconnected to any system of national urban planning. Most important, responsibility for financing most local infrastructure is highly decentralized. Consequently, local and state governments have little choice but to find an administrative means of extracting revenues from the private sector that gives priority to satisfying investor confidence. To market long-term debt, public corporations must contend with investor fears that borrowed funds might be diverted to satisfy political pressures, rather than used for debt repayment. Consequently, major urban infrastructure development is in the hands of public corporations that are only indirectly accountable to urban electorates. These corporations are well known for courting private investors and treating them as constituents rather than as bargaining rivals (Caro 1974; Walsh 1978).

The European experience is quite different. There, most capital expenditures are supported by the central government. In France, upwards of 75% of local budgets are financed by central government; in Holland, the figure is 92%. This relieves some of the pressure on local authorities to compete with one another for capital investment to finance basic services. Local governments in Europe are capable of dealing with business from a position of greater strength.

Beyond this, national government is not as dependent on private capital as local government is and can turn to vast financial and regulatory powers to reinforce public bargaining on the part of national and local governmental authorities.

The case of La Defense, just outside of Paris, is instructive of how state-business relations have been managed in Western Europe. During the 1960s, the national government planned to build another central business district for Paris on the vacant fields of La Defense. Despite skepticism by private investors, funds were allocated by the national government. Just as the project was launched, it was confronted by a fiscal crisis. French business looked on as La Defense reeled from one difficulty to another, and the enterprise was mocked as a "white elephant." The national government responded quickly, infusing the project with funds from the treasury, from nationalized banks, and from pensions. To buttress these efforts, the government clamped down on new office construction within Paris and used other carrots and sticks to persuade corporations that La Defense was the wave of the future. The effort worked, and La Defense became a premier site as an international business headquarters.

La Defense was not built in unique circumstances. To the contrary, it demonstrates the cumulative effect of centralized policy intervention on urban development. It is not unusual for governments throughout Western Europe to pour infrastructure into a particular development area, to freeze the price of surrounding land to prevent speculation, to construct buildings in the same area by relying on public corporations, and to design all the structures in the development site. The last public act is usually to invite private investors to compete for the privilege of obtaining space. Only then does bargaining begin. . . .

Comparison of . . . two antipodal cities [—Amsterdam and Detroit—] permits us to illustrate the cumulative consequences of differences in bargaining resources for political control of business development. To begin with market conditions, Amsterdam has a highly favorable market position because it is at the center of Holland's economic engine—a horseshoe shaped region called the Randstad. The cities of the Randstad (Amsterdam, Utrecht, Rotterdam, and the Hague) form a powerful and diversified conurbation that drives Holland's economy, its politics, and its sociocultural life. Amsterdam itself is the nation's political and financial capital. It also holds light industry, is a tourist and historic center, and is one of northern Europe's transportation hubs. Although Amsterdam has gone through significant deindustrialization (Jobse and Needham 1987) and has lost 21% of its population since 1960, it has transformed its economy to residential and postindustrial uses and is attractively positioned as one of the keystones of a united Europe.

Detroit's market conditions are dramatically less favorable. It is situated in what was once America's industrial heartland and what is now balefully called the Rustbelt. Known as America's Motor City, its economy revolved around automobile manufacture. Deindustrialization and foreign competition have taken a devastating toll. In just three decades, Detroit lost more than half its manufacturing jobs and 38% of its population (Darden et al. 1987). Nearly half the population lives below the poverty line, and one quarter is unemployed (Nethercutt 1987). Detroit has tried to come back to its former prominence by rebuilding its downtown and diversifying its economy for tourism and banking. But those efforts have not changed the city's market posture. Jobs and the middle class continue to move to surrounding suburbs, and any possible conversion of the Rustbelt economy appears slim when viewed against more attractive opportunities elsewhere.

The differences in popular control of these two cities are equally stark. Amsterdam is governed by a 45-member council that is elected by proportional representation (the council also elects a smaller body of aldermen) and is well organized and easily disciplined by the voters. Political parties have cohesive programs geared to conservative, social democratic, centrist, and leftwing orientations. Political accountability is reinforced by a system of elected district councils that represent different neighborhoods of the city. These councils participate in a host of decentralized services including land use, housing, and development.

In contrast, Detroit's government is poorly organized in respect to promoting popular control of economic development. A nine-member city council is elected at large and in nonpartisan balloting. Detroit's mayor [in 1993], Coleman Young, has held power for 16 years and has based his administration on distributing selective benefits, especially city jobs and contracts, while focusing on downtown project development (Hill 1986; Rich 1991). The system affords scant opportunity for neighborhood expression, and the city's singular ethnic composition (Detroit is 75% black) is coupled to a politics of black symbolism that impedes programmatic accountability and pluralist opposition. Indeed, one scholar has described Detroit as ruled by a tight-knit elite (Ewen 1978); two other researchers believed that the city's power was exercised at the peaks of major sectors within the city (Jones and Bachelor 1986).

The two cities also differ dramatically in respect to modes of policy intervention. Like many European cities, Amsterdam is governed within an integrated national planning scheme. The Dutch rely on three-tier government, at the national, regional, and municipal levels. Goals are set at the uppermost levels, master plans are developed at the regional level, and allocation plans are implemented at the grass roots. A municipalities fund allocates financial support based on population, and over 90% of Amsterdam's budget is carried by the national treasury.

By contrast, Detroit stands very much alone. While "golden corridors" (drawn from Detroit's former wealth) have sprung up in affluent outskirts, the suburbs now resist the central city. Attempts at creating metropolitan mechanisms to share tax bases or to undertake planning have failed (Darden et al. 1987). Over the years, federal aid has shrunk and now accounts for less than 6% of the city's budget (Savitch and Thomas 1991). State aid has compensated for some of Detroit's shortfalls, but like most states, Michigan is at a loss to do anything about the internecine struggles for jobs and investment.

Given the cumulative differences along all three dimensions, the bargaining outcomes for each city are dramatically opposite. Under the planning and support of national and regional authorities, Amsterdam has managed its deindustrialization—first by moving heavy industry to specific subregions (called *concentrated deconcentration*) and later by locating housing and light commerce in abandoned wharves and depleted neighborhoods. The Dutch have accomplished this through a combination of infrastructure investment, direct subsidies, and the power to finance and build housing (Levine and Van Weesop 1988; Van Weesop and Wiegersma 1991). Amsterdam's capacity to construct housing is a particularly potent policy instrument and constitutes a countervailing alternative to private development. Between 50% and 80% of housing in Amsterdam is subsidized or publicly built. This puts a considerable squeeze on private developers, who face limitations and availability as well as zoning, density, and architectural controls. As a condition of development, it is not uncommon for commercial investors to agree to devote a portion of their projects toward residential use (Van Weesop and Wiegersma 1991).

Indeed, the bargaining game in Holland is titled toward the public sector in ways that seem unimaginable in the United States. Freestyle commercial development in Amsterdam has been restricted, so that most neighborhoods remain residential. Because of massive housing subsidies, neighborhoods have lacked the extremes of wealth or poverty. Even squatting has been declared legal. Abandoned buildings have been taken over by groups of young, marginal, and working-class populations—thus leading to lower-class gentrification (Mamadouh 1990).

All this compares very differently to the thrust of development outcomes in Detroit. The case of Poletown provides a stark profile of Detroit's response to bargaining with the private sector (Fasenfest 1986). When General Motors announced that it was looking for a new plant site, the city invoked the state's "quick take" law, allowing municipalities to acquire property before actually reaching agreement with individual owners. To attract the plant and an anticipated 6,000 jobs, the city moved more than 3,000 residents and 143 institutions (hospitals, churches, schools, and businesses) and demolished more than 1,000 buildings. To strike this bargain, Detroit committed to at least $200 million in direct expenditures and a dozen years of tax abatements. In the end, the bargaining exchange resulted in one lost neighborhood and a gain of an automobile plant—all under what one judge labeled as the "guiding and sustaining, indeed controlling hand of the General Motors Corporation" (Jones and Bachelor 1986).

In many respects, Poletown reflects a larger pattern of bargaining. The city is now trying to expand its airport. At stake are 3,600 homes, more than 12,000 residents, and scores of businesses. The city and a local bank also have their sights set on a venerable auditorium called Ford Hall. The arrangement calls for razing Ford Hall and granting the developers an $18 million no-interest loan, payable in 28 years. When citizen protests stalled the project, developers threatened to move elsewhere. Since then, Detroit's city council approved the project (Rich 1991).

The polar cases of Amsterdam and Detroit reveal something about the vastly different development prizes and sacrifices that particular cities experience as a result of their accumulated bargaining advantages. Amsterdam is able to use public investment to extract concessions from investors and enforce development standards in a process conducted under public scrutiny. Detroit offers land, money, and tax relief to attract development in a process managed by a tight circle of political and economic elites.

POLITICAL CONTROL OF URBAN DEVELOPMENT

By examining urban development from a state-bargaining perspective, we are able to identify some critical forces that influence local governmental control over this area of policy. From this vantage point, public influence over urban development appears to be tied to differences in market conditions, popular control mechanisms, and public policy systems because these interdependent spheres powerfully affect the ability of politicians to bargain with business. . . .

By using our bargaining perspective, future researchers may be able to overcome the limitations of extant theory and better understand the actual political choices of local communities in economic development.

REFERENCES

Almond, G. 1988. The return to the state. *American Political Science Review* 82:853–874.

Bachrach, P., and M. Baratz. 1962. The two faces of power. *American Political Science Review* 56:947–952.

Body-Gendrot, S. 1987. Grass roots mobilization in the Thirteenth Arrondissment: A cross national view. In *The politics of urban development* edited by C. Stone and H. Sanders, 125–143. Lawrence: University Press of Kansas.

Capek, S., and J. Gilderbloom. 1992 *Community versus commodity* Albany: State University of New York Press.

Caro, R. 1974. *The power broker.* New York: Vintage.

Christensen, T. 1979. *Neighborhood survival.* London: Prism Press.

Crenson, M. 1971. *The un-politics of air pollution.* Baltimore, MD: Johns Hopkins University Press.

Cummings, S., ed. 1988. *Business elites and urban development.* Albany: State University of New York Press.

Dahl, R. 1971. *Polyarchy.* New Haven, CT: Yale University Press.

Dahl, R., and C. E. Lindblom. 1965. *Politics, economics, and welfare.* New Haven, CT: Yale University Press.

Danielson, M. 1976. *The politics of exclusion.* New York: Columbia University Press.

Darden, J., R. C. Hill, J. Thomas, and R. Thomas. 1987. *Race and uneven development.* Philadelphia: Temple University Press.

Dreier, P. 1989. Economic growth and economic justice in Boston. In *Unequal partnerships,* edited by G. Squires, 35–58. New Brunswick, NJ: Rutgers University Press.

Dreier, P., and W. D. Keating. 1990. The limits of localism: Progressive housing policies in Boston, 1984–1989. *Urban Affairs Quarterly* 26:191–216.

Eisinger, P. 1987. *Rise of the entrepreneurial state.* Madison: University of Wisconsin Press.

Elkin, D. 1987. State and market in city politics: Or, the real Dallas. In *The politics of urban development,* edited by C. Stone and H. Sanders, 25–51. Lawrence: University Press of Kansas.

Etzkowitz, H., and R. Mack. 1976. Emperialism in the First World: The corporation and the suburb. Paper presented at the Pacific Sociological Association meetings, San Jose, CA, March.

Ewen, L. 1978. *Corporate power and the urban crisis in Detroit.* Princeton, NJ: Princeton University Press.

Fainstein, S. S., N. I. Fainstein, R. C. Hill, D. Judd, and M. P. Smith. 1986. *Restructuring the city.* 2nd ed. New York: Longman.

Fasenfest, D. 1986. Community politics and urban redevelopment. *Urban Affairs Quarterly* 22:101–123.

Feagin, J. 1988. *Free enterprise city.* New Brunswick, NJ: Rutgers University Press.

Foglesong, R. 1989. Do politics matter in the formulation of local economic development policy: The case of Orlando, Florida. Paper presented at the annual meeting of the American Political Science Association, Atlanta, GA, September.

Governor turns down UAL. 1991. *Courier-Journal,* 18 October, 1.

Hill, R. C. 1986. Crisis in the motor city: The politics of urban development in Detroit. In *Restructuring the city,* 2d ed., by S. S. Fainstein, N. I. Fainstein, R. C. Hill, D. Judd, and M. P. Smith. New York: Longman.

———. Industrial restructuring, state intervention, and uneven development in the United States and Japan. Paper presented at conference: The tiger by the tail: Urban policy and economic restructuring in Comparative perspective. State University of New York, Albany, October.

Jobse, B., and B. Needham. 1987. The economic future of the Randstad, Holland. *Urban Studies* 25: 282–296.

Jones, B., and L. Bachelor. 1986. *The sustaining hand.* Lawrence: University Press of Kansas.

Kantor, P. 1993. The dual city as political choice. *Journal of Urban Affairs* 15 (3): 231–244.

Kantor, P. (with S. David). 1988. *The dependent city.* Boston, MA: Scott, Foresman/Little, Brown.

Levine, M., and J. Van Weesop. 1988. The changing nature of urban planning in the Netherlands. *Journal of the American Planning Association* 54:315–323.

Lindblom, C. 1977. *Politics and markets.* New Haven, CT: Yale University Press.

———. 1982. The market as a prison. *Journal of Politics* 44:324–336.

Logan, J., and H. Molotch. 1987. *Urban fortunes.* Berkeley: University of California Press.

Logan, J., and T. Swanstrom, eds. 1990. *Beyond the city limits.* Philadelphia: Temple University Press.

Mamadouh, V. 1990. Squatting, housing, and urban policy in Amsterdam. Paper presented at the International Research Conference on Housing Debates and Urban Challenges, Paris, July.

Mollenkopf, J. 1983. *The contested city.* Princeton, NJ: Princeton University Press.

Molotch, H., and S. Vicari. 1988. Three ways to build: The development process in the United States, Japan, and Italy. *Urban Affairs Quarterly* 24:188–214.

Muzzio, D., and R. Bailey. 1986. Economic development, housing, and zoning. *Journal of Urban Affairs* 8:1–18.

Nethercutt, M. 1987. *Detroit twenty years after: A statistical profile of the Detroit area since 1967.* Detroit, MI: Center for Urban Studies, Wayne State University.

Noyelle, T., and T. M. Stanback. 1984. *Economic transformation of American cities.* New York: Conservation for Human Resources Columbia University.

Parkinson, M., B. Foley, and D. Judd. 1989. *Regenerating the cities.* Boston, MA: Scott, Foresman.

Peterson, P. 1981. *City limits.* Chicago: University of Chicago Press.

Rich, W. 1991. Detroit: From Motor City to service hub. In *Big city politics in transition,* edited by H. V. Savitch and J. C. Thomas, 64–85. Newbury Park, CA: Sage Publications.

Rosentraub, M., and D. Swindell. 1990. "Just say no"? The economic and political realities of a small city's investment in minor league baseball. Paper presented at the 20th annual meeting of the Urban Affairs Association, Charlotte, NC, April.

Sassen, S. 1988. *The mobility of capital and labor.* Cambridge: Cambridge University Press.

Savitch, H. V. 1988. *Post-industrial cities: Politics and planning in New York, Paris, and London.* Princeton, NJ: Princeton University Press.

Savitch, H. V., and J. C. Thomas, eds. 1991. *Big city politics in transition.* Newbury Park, CA: Sage Publications.

Stone, C. 1989. *Regime politics.* Lawrence: University Press of Kansas.

Stone, C., and H. Sanders, eds. 1987. *The politics of urban development.* Lawrence: University Press of Kansas.

Swanstrom, T. 1986. *The crisis of growth politics* Philadelphia: Temple University Press.

UAL bidding goes on. 1991. *Courier-Journal,* 22 October, 1.

Van Weesop, J., and M. Wiegersma. 1991. Gentrification in the Netherlands. In *Urban housing for the better-off: Gentrification in Europe* edited by J. Van Weesop and S. Musterd, 98–111. Utrecht, Netherlands: Bureau Stedellijke Netwerken.

Vaughn, R. 1979. *State taxation and economic development.* Washington, DC: Council of State Planning Agencies.

Vogel, R. 1990. The local regime and economic development. *Economic Development Quarterly* 4:101–112.

Walsh, A. 1978. *The public's business.* Cambridge: MIT Press.

NOTES

1. Urban Summit Conference, New York City, 12 November 1990.

10

"Re-stating" Theories of Urban Development

JAMES M. SMITH

Among the most influential institutions in urban development, special-purpose authorities and state governments have received the least attention from scholars of urban politics. Though they are often enablers

Direct correspondence to: James M. Smith, Assistant Professor, Department of Political Science, Indiana University South Bend, 2179 Wiekamp Hall, South Bend, IN 46634, E-mail: jms21@iusb.edu.

JOURNAL OF URBAN AFFAIRS, Volume 32, Number 4, pages 425–448.

ISSN: 0735-2166.   DOI: 10.1111/j.1467-9906.2010.00497.x of large development projects, both fiscally and managerially, their influence upon the politics of urban development is rarely a focus of theories or case studies concerning cities in the United States. Extant theories of urban development have focused upon interaction between private-sector elites and local government officials. Group conflict, as well as conflict among individual political actors, has also received significant attention. Resolutions to such conflict, and thus, executable plans for urban development projects, are usually viewed through the lens of compromise among local actors and rarely turn an eye to the extra-local or institutional dynamics of urban development (DiGaetano, 1997). One could include in a list of these approaches many of the major theoretical frames for analyzing urban politics utilized over the past 50 years: elitism/structuralism (Hunter, 1953), pluralism (Dahl, 1961), the growth machine (Logan & Molotch, 1987), and most recently, regime theory (Stone, 1989).

These theoretical frames are losing validity due to changes in development coalitions and partnerships, including the growing importance of special-purpose authorities (Altshuler & Luberoff, 2003; Sbragia, 1996) and the critical role of state governments (Burns & Gamm, 1997; Eisinger, 1998; Pagano, 1990; Turner, 1990). The politics of large-scale urban development are increasingly taking place in state houses and the corridors of state-created authorities with the necessary powers to bypass local protest and complications. In addition to placing the emphasis on local government officials and private-sector elites, theories must begin to consider the institutions political actors create to accomplish development goals and the venues in which political actors make final decisions pertaining to development.

To better capture the character of contemporary development, this article focuses on three governmental venues dictating decision making in Chicago: municipal government (specifically the mayor), state government (particularly the legislature and governor), and state-created special-purpose authorities. Actors from both the public and private sectors operate within these settings to promote an agenda of urban growth. Cases from the 1980s demonstrate that the forging of *formal* partnerships between these institutions, their officials, and private sector elites—not an informal partnership among business elites and local government officials as presented by growth machine and regime theories—has emerged as a key development strategy. I call this state–city arrangement an intergovernmental triad.

In the case of Chicago, intergovernmental triads, once developed, completed and financed significant portions of the city's recent infrastructure aimed at attracting visitors and tourists. Two of the three triads discussed in this article remain intact and play perennial roles in developing Chicago's built environment. Rather than informal coalitions, then, growth interests create and utilize permanent bureaucracies pursuing missions of self-empowerment and development. As such arrangements multiply, concepts such as regimes lose explanatory value. In addition to asserting the importance of this institutional apparatus of urban development in Chicago, the article emphasizes the importance of inserting state governments into the discourse on urban politics generally. The intergovernmental triad highlights the ways in which states have recently become key partners in the process of urban development and suggests that incorporating state governments into studies leads to greater conceptualization of the development process. The creation of special-purpose governments is uncovered as one pivotal outcome of state engagement. The intergovernmental triad, then, represents an approach designed to better capture the changing institutional character of urban development coalitions.

STATE GOVERNMENT IN URBAN RESEARCH

Any urban politics textbook informs readers that state governments in the United States have long exercised significant structural, fiscal, and political power over cities. Discussions of 19th-century state debt restrictions and the legal consensus on Dillon's Rule are common references to state governments' constitutional supremacy over municipal governments. In this vein, Frug (1999) argues that states' dominant legal position relative to their cities has often left municipalities powerless to confront critical issues. Nevertheless, state governments' role in urban development has not been a central focus for most urban scholars (Burns & Gamm, 1997).

Current trends in both public finance and state–city relations suggest that urban scholars should be looking more closely at state governments' role as enablers of local development. Rather than constraining local power, states have cooperated with cities on economic development since the late 1970s (Nice & Fredericksen, 1995; Pagano, 1990). Specifically, local and state actors have formed "intergovernmental partnerships as a means of enhancing the ability of local governments to extract resources, particularly financial ones, from other governments" (Berman, 2003, p. 8). One principal explanation for the emergence of such partnerships has been the decline in federal urban funding, which has forced cities to seek out new fiscal partners and policy venues (Altshuler & Luberoff, 2003; Eisinger, 1998). Thus, intergovernmental partnerships between states and municipalities have been crucial to development in recent decades, with cities taking a more proactive role in courting states to aid their budgets and fund development projects (Berman, 2003). Based on these developments, Berman (2003) takes a position opposite Frug (1999), arguing that U.S. cities have the ability to accomplish more than their predecessors, "although less by themselves" (2003, p. 11).

Reflecting these shifts, certain scholars have redirected attention to interaction between state governments and cities. Sbragia's (1996) account of state governments' involvement in the politics of local finance presents a history of state–local relations in which constraints on local borrowing, and entrepreneurial reactions to them, explain patterns of public investment at the local level. With a similar focus on state-level institutions, Burns and Gamm (1997) study local lobbies' involvement in state legislatures in three states during the late 19th and early 20th centuries and find that "the relationship between states and their creatures was intimate and utterly routine: The ordinary work of state politics was local affairs, and an ordinary branch of local government was the state legislature" (Burns & Gamm, 1997, p. 90).[1]

Studies of regionalism (Gainsborough, 2001; Weir, Wolman, & Swanstrom, 2005), metropolitan governance (Alpert, Gainsborough, & Wallis, 2006; Hamilton, Miller, & Paytas, 2004; Post & Stein, 2000; Sonenshein & Hogen-Esch, 2006; Weir, 1996), and growth management (Anthony, 2004), have also explored the politics of state–city relations. Because regional reform necessitates changes to city charters, state governments should occupy a central space in all such studies. However, according to Hamilton and colleagues, regionalists have not made this connection sufficiently: "All too often, the study of metropolitan areas fails to capture the dynamic relationships that exist between the state and local policies" (Hamilton et al., 2004, p. 150).

In their study of regionalism in New York, Ohio, Michigan, and Illinois, Margaret Weir, Harold Wolman, and Todd Swanstrom develop a typology of state–city coalitions (Weir et al., 2005). The authors identify party-imposed coalitions, interest-based coalitions, and governor-brokered coalitions. The party-imposed coalition was found to be the most prominent of the three and is based on the number of city legislators in the state party caucus; interest-based concerns are temporary and focus on immediate concerns of constituents, not long-term coalition building; and governor-brokered coalitions often cut across party lines and consist of large spending programs that will provide political goods to legislators on both sides of the aisle in the state capitol and city hall (Weir et al., 2005). The authors use this typology to explore avenues for city–suburb cooperation, though such an approach could be utilized in analyzing the coalitions forming to advocate large-scale development in central cities.

Scholars of urban education have also focused on the role of state government in local decision making (Berman, 1995; Burns, 2003; DiLeo, 1998; Henig, Hula, Orr, & Pedescleaux, 1999; Wong & Shen, 2002). Namely, states' role has increased in areas of fiscal management, political accountability, criteria establishment for students with special needs, the allocation of federal grants, and the creation of academic standards (DiLeo, 1998, p. 117). In some instances, state governments have taken complete control over school districts to ensure both accountability and increased educational attainment (Burns, 2003; Wong & Shen, 2002). State governments have also played a central role in mayoral takeovers of urban school districts. These reforms, aimed at increasing accountability, have involved mayoral involvement at the state level in Baltimore (Orr, 2004), Chicago (Shipps, 2004), and Detroit (Mirel, 2004). In the case of Chicago, the Illinois legislature devolved numerous state-level educational powers to Mayor Richard M. Daley (Shipps, 2004, p. 77).

Though existing theories of downtown development do not often include consideration of state government, Burns and Thomas (2004) take a significant step toward incorporating state–city coalitions in such studies. They identify a governor-based coalition in New Orleans operating during the late 1990s and early 2000s. Rather than emphasize the role of the state government in local affairs, however, they argue that urban regime theory should be retooled in order to consider nonlocal actors such as governors or national-level politicians. Elsewhere, Burns (2002, 2003) has argued that state government has the "capacity" to act as a member in the local regime—especially in the case of education policy—while nothing that "regime theory does not include governors, state legislatures, state departments of education, and other state-level actors as education regime members" (Burns, 2003, p. 285).[2] Burns argues that regime theory must be expanded to account for such actors.

The cases from Chicago examined below also reflect a governor-brokered coalition, but suggest that the arguments of Burns (2002, 2003) and Burns and Thomas (2004) need to be taken one step further by leaving the regime framework behind and focusing on a more broadly based, and formal, intergovernmental partnership. In Chicago, these partnerships center on a special-purpose authority and bring together progrowth actors from the state and local levels, and the private sector, with the aim of completing large development projects. In line with the argument that regime theory is not broad enough in its scope (e.g., Burns & Thomas, 2004; DiGaetano, 1997), the Chicago cases reveal that institutional actors must be considered in greater detail—not as members of a regime, but as formal replacements for informal arrangements.

THE INTERGOVERNMENTAL TRIAD AND URBAN DEVELOPMENT IN CHICAGO

In most studies of Chicago's politics of growth, the central figure has been the mayor, and for a long period in the 20th century, the Democratic Party machine.[3] Research presented below emphasizes institution-building and local actors' interaction with the state government where other studies have focused primarily on political interactions at the local level. The era of interest is the time between Richard J. Daley's death in 1976 and the election of his son, Richard M. Daley, in 1989. This period is generally viewed as an era during which Chicago's development politics were adrift. The strong political machine that had guided the city for over 40 years was in disarray, while the City Council was marked by extreme conflict (Grimshaw, 1992; Simpson, 2001). Research presented below offers a different interpretation of the era, one in which the 1980s was a pivotal time for the construction of a governmental infrastructure that continues to play a critical role in producing a postindustrial Chicago able to generate revenue by attracting tourists and middle-class residents back into the city. Though "council wars" have been emphasized in research on this era, the mayors of Chicago between 1980 and 1990 lobbied for large development projects and needed state-level actors' cooperation, especially fiscally, to make such plans a reality.

Bennett and Spirou (2006) discuss this pivotal time in the context of mayoral politics. Their studies of stadium development and neighborhood politics in Chicago (see also Spirou & Bennett, 2003) find that the politics of a reborn downtown, filled with stadiums and other cultural amenities, emerged not during the mayoralty of Richard M. Daley (1989–present), but with one of his predecessors, Harold Washington (1983–1987). Bennett and Spirou (2006) designate this as a "paradox" due to Washington's reputation as a progressive mayor.

Like the sporting infrastructure, plans for the projects discussed below originated under mayors other than Richard M. Daley. Washington held office during the creation of the 1992 World's Fair Authority (WFA) and the Illinois Sports Facilities Authority (ISFA), and he commissioned a Navy Pier Authority before dying in office in 1987.[4] Though he is remembered primarily for his progressive development policies, Washington was critical in laying the foundation for two intergovernmental triads that would pursue large, capital-intensive development projects—projects not out of the ordinary for big-city mayors of this era.

Although Washington played a primary role in constructing the intergovernmental triads discussed below, Illinois governor, Republican James R. Thompson (1977–1991), was the lead figure in their formation. Thompson viewed the creation of authorities as an economic development strategy in itself. After the formation of the ISFA in 1986, Thompson told the *Chicago Tribune:* "I think it's a model of state–city cooperation to achieve a very worthwhile project and I hope it will serve as a model for any further efforts that may be required for the Bears or the Cubs or Disney or Navy Pier or the development of the lakefront or for similar projects in the collar counties, the suburbs and Downstate" (Egler & McCarron, 1986b).[5]

A defining character of special-purpose authorities similar to those Thompson promoted is the way in which they act as mechanisms for concentrating decision-making power by bringing together public and private actors at the state or multistate level. Special-purpose authorities are often praised for their increased fiscal capacity and efficient managerial skills (Doig, 1983) and have been a prominent tool for officials looking to bypass local resistance to development plans (Altshuler & Luberoff, 2003; Sanders, 1992) or restrictions on local borrowing (Sbragia, 1996). Authorities' unelected boards, and often cloaked decision-making processes, have reduced the capacity of voters and residents to influence decision making while increasing private sector influence on the allocation of resources (Burns, 1994; Doig & Mitchell, 1992). Authorities are used for various purposes, and take many forms throughout Illinois and within Chicago;[6] their role in financing and managing large development projects in 1980s Chicago is the focus here.

As opposed to large development projects in which no special-purpose authority is created, the cases below involve institutions where private, state, local, and regional interests have been fused into one political body. Private-sector actors enter the intergovernmental triad directly when members of the local elite are appointed to board positions on authorities.[7] The intergovernmental triad, then, is an institutional arrangement by which the various interests of urban development come together with the institutional capacity, autonomy, and fiscal powers to carry out large development projects (Figure 1). The three nodes of the triad are constituted by the city government (the jurisdiction in which the development is taking place and the interests of which will be represented via board appointments to the authority), the state government (which creates the special-purpose authority, and in most cases finances significant portions of development projects through new and existing revenue streams; the primary source of an authority's fiscal power, however, usually comes from its ability to issue revenue bonds), and the special-purpose authority (depending upon the state, this institution will be known by different names and hold varying amounts of statutory powers—for example, in some cases the authority may have the power to tax—but is characterized by an appointed board made up of private-sector representatives put in place by the other governments involved in the triad. The authority's primary role is implementation and management of urban development). The special-purpose authority, in most cases a product of informal bargaining between state and city actors before its creation, maintains formal relations with the state and city governments through the appointment powers of governor and mayor. Relations between state and local actors may begin informally and in some cases remain that way, as represented by the dashed line between the two in Figure 1; however, the institutional offspring of this bargaining process emerges as its own political entity and pursues its own institutional interests over time.

This intergovernmental arrangement is not unique to Chicago—examples are numerous and are often mentioned briefly in scholarly work on urban development. For example, the Burns and Thomas (2004) piece cited above describes the offloading of gaming policy in New Orleans to "a nine-member quasi-governmental casino corporation" (Burns & Thomas, 2004, p. 798). In Seattle, stadium development shifted to the state level when supporters of a stadium for the Seattle Mariners baseball team failed to win a local referendum—the legislation for the Seattle Seahawks football team was also approved at the state level (Sapotichne, 2007), resulting in the creation of the Washington State Public Stadium Authority, which currently manages the football stadium and an attached event center (WSPSA, 2004). In Denver, the Colorado state government played a critical role in funding a stadium project for the Colorado Rockies MLB baseball team and held appointment powers on the stadium district board (Clarke & Saiz, 2003). This pattern of state involvement and authority creation is common in the politics of convention center expansion

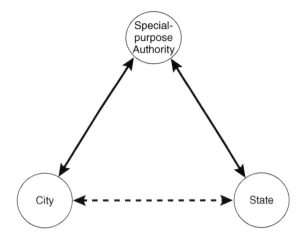

Intergovernmental Triad.

and construction (Sanders, 1992), and other large development projects such as sports stadiums (Altshuler & Luberoff, 2003, p. 34).

Whether or not such patterns directly match the triad found in Chicago, the cases below represent a wider trend in the politics of urban development. The state–city partnership is a prominent model for ambitious urban development in contemporary U.S. cities. Without state government aid and states' willingness to create special-purpose authorities, much of the money used to rebuild America's downtowns would have been unavailable to political actors.

CASE STUDIES: 1992 WORLD'S FAIR, WHITE SOX'S NEW STADIUM, AND NAVY PIER

I now turn to three cases in which the intergovernmental triad operates to varying degrees of effectiveness: Chicago's failed attempt to host the 1992 World's Fair, the construction of a new stadium for the Chicago White Sox, and the redevelopment of Navy Pier into an entertainment district. The state–city coalitions, or intergovernmental triads, Governor Thompson formed in collaboration with Chicago mayors consisted of three institutional actors and four stages. The members of the triad included the Chicago city government (particularly the mayor of Chicago), the state of Illinois (namely the governor and legislative leaders), and the authority created to manage the projects (including the private-sector representatives serving on authority boards). The stages of the projects studied here were: (1) project conception, (2) local/state debate, (3) authority creation, and (4) implementation/project failure.[8] In all cases, key decisions occur at the last possible moment and take place in the Illinois General Assembly, not City Hall.[9] Authority creation follows a similar pattern in the three cases as the state government and Chicago reach power-sharing agreements splitting appointment powers between the mayor and governor (see Tables 1 and 2).

In two of the three cases, authority creation occurs at the debate's culmination and is accompanied by the necessary funding.[10] Additional planning is left to the authority created to manage the project. The process leading up to

TABLE 1

Newspaper Accounts of Authority Creation

Authority	*Chicago Tribune's* Description
1992 World's Fair Authority (WFA)	"A 25-member board to oversee the World's Fair in Chicago in 1992 was approved late Friday night by the Illinois General Assembly. . . . The measure, if certified by the governor, would create a 25-member commission—with 12 members appointed by the governor and 12 appointed by the mayor of Chicago. The chairman would be selected jointly by the two leaders" (*Chicago Tribune,* November 4, 1983).
Illinois Sports Facility Authority (ISFA)	"The 50,000-seat, open-air baseball stadium would be built by a city-state authority with a seven-member governing board. Three members each would be appointed by the governor and the mayor, with a chairman appointed by both. The authority would be empowered to sell up to $120 million in tax-exempt municipal bonds, or enough to cover acquisition of land from the Sox, site improvements, interest and other costs, plus construction of a $60 million ballpark" (*Chicago Tribune,* December 3, 1986).
Metropolitan Pier and Exposition Authority (MPEA)	"Under provisions of the legislation, the new Pier and Exposition Authority will replace the Metropolitan Fair and Exposition Authority, which had run McCormick Place, and will expand its authority to include the renovation of Navy Pier . . . Daley will appoint six of the members of the new panel as well as the chairman. Gov. James Thompson will name the other six members and the executive director of the new authority. The executive director would be a staff officer and not a member of the board" (*Chicago Tribune,* July 3, 1989).

Sources: Chicago Tribune, 1983; Egler & McCarron, 1986a; Recktenwald, 1989.

TABLE 2

Authority Structure and Project Cost

Project	Authority	Number of Board Members	Projected Cost	Project Completed?
1992 World's Fair	1992 World's Fair Authority	25	$1 billion	No
New Sox Stadium	Illinois Sports Facilities Authority	7	$150 million	Yes
Navy Pier	Metropolitan Pier and Exposition Authority	13	$150 million	Yes

Sources: MPEA, ISFA, Chicago Tribune.
Note: Appointment powers shared by Illinois governor and Chicago mayor in all three cases. For WFA, the mayor and governor split appointments evenly with a jointly appointed chair; each official appoints three members to the ISFA board with mayoral approval of a governor-appointed chair; the MPEA board represents six mayoral and gubernatorial appointments with the mayor of Chicago appointing the chairman and the governor appointing the MPEA's chief executive officer.

the creation of the authorities, and the institutional character of the authorities themselves, is closed off from the public and final decisions are not put to the electorate for a vote. Fiscally speaking, authority creation is the enabler of the two projects that reached completion and the primary reason that the World's Fair project survived as long as it did.[11] In all three cases, the necessary funds were viewed as impractical during the debate stages, and yet, when the state enters discussions, projects gain credibility.

The two completed projects, Navy Pier and the new Comiskey Park/U.S. Cellular Field, have been a boon to the local economy—particularly Navy Pier (see Table 3). The Metropolitan Pier and Exposition Authority, which manages Navy Pier, contributed around $169 million in tax revenue in 2006 and reports generating more than $1 billion dollars of total economic activity while attracting 8.5 million visitors per year at Navy Pier alone (MPEA, 2006, 2007). During fiscal year 2006, the ISFA collected $375,936 in ticket revenue at U.S. Cellular Field and $73,000 in special events revenue while posting a regular-season attendance of just under 3 million (Chicago White Sox, 2007; ISFA, 2006). Both sites contribute to the city's tourism infrastructure, which generated $10.9 billion in spending and $616 million in tax revenue during 2006 (Chicago Convention and Tourism Bureau, 2008). Though Chicago did not win the right to host the 1992 World's Fair, the city's attempt to host the 2016 Olympics demonstrates that local boosters did not lose faith in such large events' ability to attract attention to the city. . . .

World's Fair 1992

While hosting the Columbian Exposition World's Fair in 1893, Chicago was toured by hordes of visitors from the United States and across the globe (Cronon, 1991). Civic elites in the early 1980s longed for similar attention, and as they searched for ways to rejuvenate the central area, a World's Fair cropped up as one method of doing so. As one journalist mused, the city was looking for 19th century solutions to its 21st century problems (Longworth, 1985).

▶ TABLE 3

Visitors and Spending in Chicago, 2006

Venue	Visitors	Total Spending	Tax Revenue
U.S. Cellular Field	2,957,414[*]	NA[†]	$448,936[‡]
Navy Pier	8,800,000	$1,200,000,000	$169,000,000[§]
McCormick Place	2,241,324	$3,400,000,000	$169,000,000
Chicago total	*44,170,000*	*$10,900,000,000*	*$616,700,000*

Sources: Chicago Convention and Tourism Bureau (www.choosechicago.com), MPEA Annual Report (2006), MPEA Press Release (2007), ISFA Annual Report (2006), http://chicago .whitesox.mlb.com.
[*]Regular season attendance.
[†]The ISFA does not provide figures relating to total spending in its 2006 annual report. Other research on the venue suggests that spending at U.S. Cellular takes place almost exclusively in the stadium and surrounding parking lots, rather than having a broader economic impact on the city and neighborhood (Baade, Nikolova, & Matheson, 2006; Spirou & Bennett, 2003). The newer facility, however, generates more than one-third more in nonticket revenue than its intracity companion, Wrigley Field (Baade et al., 2006).
[‡]Revenue collected by ISFA on ticket sales and special event sales.
[§]Together with McCormick Place and other MPEA venues.

In this case, the intergovernmental triad approach was adopted after a few years of private-sector lobbying for the Fair. Chicago's business elite formed a tightly knit nonprofit organization, the 1992 Corporation, to advocate the Fair (Shlay & Giloth, 1987). However, rather than work from outside government, some members of the 1992 Corporation would be incorporated into the government (or public-sector) as members on a board of directors for the 1992 WFA. The authority worked closely with the governor of Illinois and the mayor of Chicago, but would ultimately fail due to a lack of fiscal support from the state legislature.

The potential for political rewards associated with a World's Fair-magnitude project would appeal to any mayor (Shlay & Giloth, 1987)—Jane Byrne was no exception. In 1981, she announced that Chicago would officially pursue the 1992 World's Fair (Mier, 1995). The primary local opposition to the Fair arose out of the city's neighborhoods. A group of neighborhood interests calling themselves the Chicago 1992 Committee led the charge against the Fair, producing reports predicting its negative effects and distributing their findings to local political actors (McClory, 1993). On the other side of the debate were the Chicago mayors who held office during the campaign for the Fair—Byrne (1979–1983) and Harold Washington (1983–1987)—and the Governor of Illinois, James R. Thompson. Washington's support was not as forthright as Byrne's or Thompson's; while Washington supported the idea of a Fair in Chicago, he considered it part of his mandate to approach development situations differently than his progrowth predecessors (Mier, 1995).

Thompson played a significant role in promoting the Fair. He pushed legislation through the Illinois General Assembly in 1983 that created the 1992 WFA (*Chicago Tribune,* 1983; Mier, 1995), thus serving as the instigator of the intergovernmental partnership to follow. Many of the local actors leading the push for the Fair took lead roles in the new state-mandated authority. Most significantly, Thomas Ayers, the retired chairman of Chicagoland's energy company, Commonwealth Edison, was named as the WFA's chairman (*Chicago Tribune,* 1983). Ayers was involved in various endeavors tied to downtown redevelopment around this time, including a massive residential redevelopment to the south of the central business district (Wille, 1997).

Political conflict and a cloaked decision-making atmosphere marked the WFA's tenure. The authority closed its doors to the public during meetings and produced reports painting a rosy picture for the Fair's financial impact (Mier, 1995). Political conflicts between the city government and the WFA also arose. Much of this was focused on the assumption that Washington would attempt to slow the WFA's progress. In other cases, conflict involved the tendency of the WFA to negotiate without the consent of the city. For instance, the Authority was at one point in negotiations with the Chicago Park District requesting that the Park District manage Navy Pier and two Lake Michigan harbors during the Fair; however, both of these areas were under city jurisdiction. Washington and his administration were not brought into the discussion immediately, which reportedly angered the mayor (McCarron, 1985). An additional aspect of the lobbying process was convincing state legislators that the Fair was worthy of state funding. Thompson attempted to gain the support of state representatives (Mier, 1995), but legislators were wary of the Fair's nearly $1 billion price tag (Neal, 1985).

In addition to the political rifts between the intergovernmental partners and resistance by neighborhood groups, the finding of a particular feasibility study doomed the Fair's future: even after reducing its projected cost by nearly $200 million, the Fair would lose $50–$350 million (McCarron & Egler, 1985). State legislators were convinced that the money requested was not worth the risk. Just as the WFA was created at the state level and with the support of the governor, it was a state official, House Speaker Michael Madigan, a Democrat from Chicago, who lobbied against the Fair after learning of the projected financial loss. Shortly after Madigan came out against the Fair, Governor Thompson declared Chicago's campaign to host the event dead (McCarron & Egler, 1985).

Shlay and Giloth (1987) attribute the Fair's failure in part to Washington's mixed emotions on the project; McClory (1993) credits a strong coalition of neighborhood interests with weakening the business elite's push for the Fair. The argument presented here places the Fair's downfall more squarely with the inability of the intergovernmental triad and its individual actors to secure state-level funding for the project. In other words, the answer as to why the Fair failed is not entirely a local question. The application of a growth machine or regime framework cannot fully explain this turn of events. Perhaps Washington's support of the Fair was not genuine, but he let the state legislature call his bluff. Despite the insulation from politics that an authority is supposed to provide leaders, the WFA was unable to sway state officials responsible for authorizing the project's funding that it was a responsible investment. This suggests that in certain cases, securing state-level approval may be the most critical aspect of central city development, and certainly one worthy of urban scholars' consideration.

A New Stadium for the White Sox

In the case of building a new stadium for the Chicago White Sox, a great deal of conflict arose over political appointments and power within the intergovernmental triad. The stadium's eventual construction was secured by both the fiscal capacity of the ISFA and Governor Thompson's strong lobbying effort in a late-night legislative session in June 1988. The White Sox's interaction with state and local government can be broken down into four segments: the proposed city-financed, multiteam domed stadium on the near South Side; the Addison, Illinois, option;[12] renewed talks with Chicago and flirtations with St. Petersburg, Florida; and finally, the plan's fruition—a baseball-only stadium sited directly across the street from the team's former home, Comiskey Park. The stadium is currently named U.S. Cellular Field.

By the mid 1980s, White Sox management was earnestly complaining about the outdated structure in which the team played. Comiskey Park, was, at the time, the oldest baseball stadium in Major League Baseball and could not compete with newer structures around the country in terms of revenue and stadium amenities such as luxury boxes (Spirou & Bennett, 2003). This put the franchise in a good position to bargain with the City of Chicago for a new—publicly funded—stadium. The team threatened to relocate if its demands were not met. What complicated the matter in Chicago was the fact that the White Sox were not the only team stadium shopping—the Chicago Bears franchise was in negotiations with its landlord, the Chicago Park District, concerning renovation of Soldier Field, the team's home field, or the building of a new stadium. The solution proposed by the City of Chicago was to build a domed stadium to be used by both teams. Harold Washington and his economic development team suggested that the stadium be located on the near South Side of the city along the Chicago River at Roosevelt Road. The proposed stadium would cost $255 million and require rent payments from both teams. The Sox tentatively agreed to this stadium deal in mid 1986 (McCarron, 1986), but the Bears discontinued talks with the city (Spirou & Bennett, 2003, p. 74).

Just after the failure of the near South proposal, both Mayor Washington and Governor Thompson began discussing the potential creation of a special-purpose authority to finance new stadiums for the respective teams. The first reports of Illinois creating a special-purpose authority to finance and manage a new stadium for the White Sox appeared in June of 1986. The Washington administration drafted legislation to be considered in the Illinois General Assembly that would create an authority with the ability to tax and borrow funds to build a $220 million stadium (Egler, 1986a). The fact that the legislation was generated by the Washington administration demonstrates that city officials viewed authority creation as a development tool rather than a power grab by state officials. Governor Thompson proposed an authority plan shortly after Washington. In his version, rather than appointments to a seven-member board being split between the mayor and governor (as Washington suggested), the governor controlled five spots on a nine-member board with three remaining for mayoral appointment and one for White Sox appointment (Egler, 1986b). Thompson and Washington reached an agreement on a seven-member board for the stadium authority in June of 1986 but the Illinois General Assembly voted against funding the proposal (*Chicago Tribune, 1986*).[13]

Six months later, the Illinois legislature passed a bill creating the ISFA and enabled it to issue $120 million in revenue bonds to pay for a 45,000-seat stadium on 35th Street, just across the street from the old stadium. The bonds would be financed using an increase in the Chicago hotel/motel tax, which would reach 12.1% (Egler & McCarron, 1986c). Even after the state created the ISFA, political conflict threatened the fate of the new stadium.

Just before his death, Washington refused to approve Thompson's nominee for the ISFA chairman position, Thomas Reynolds, Jr., in an attempt to gain concessions from Thompson on a range of issues including a change in the majority needed in ISFA votes (from four to five), an increase in affirmative action minimums (from the state requirement of 10% of contracts to the city's minimum of 25%), and gubernatorial approval of mayoral appointments to the authority that managed the city's convention center at the time (Dold, 1987). The spat between Thompson and Washington concerned Sox management, which entered into talks with the state of Florida regarding the possibility of playing baseball in St. Petersburg in an already under construction domed stadium (Spirou & Bennett, 2003, p. 68).

It was not until June 1988, and after another round of late-night votes in the Illinois General Assembly, that the Sox firmly committed to stay in Chicago. Earlier in the same year, the Sox had state officials in Florida and Illinois working very hard to put together attractive financial packages for the team. The Sox demanded that Illinois come up with a sum greater than the $120 million it had approved at the end of 1986. Legislators in both states passed bills promising either the construction of a new stadium or improvements to existing facilities. It was thought by most that the Sox would move to Florida and that the Illinois legislature would not authorize spending. But a last-minute lobbying effort by Thompson ended in a deal for the Sox better than their first. The new package, still utilizing the ISFA and the triad model, provided $150 million and satisfied White Sox owners Jerry Reinsdorf and Eddie Einhorn (McCarron & Egler, 1988; Pelissero et al., 1991; Spirou & Bennett, 2003). The ISFA completed the stadium on time, but, like the WFA, managed community relations in a way that prompted criticism from displaced residents of the Chicago neighborhood in which the stadium was being built (Spirou & Bennett, 2003).

Previous research on this case focuses on the local conflicts among neighbors of the stadiums, the team, and the city of Chicago (Spirou & Bennett, 2003), and the approach of the "Chicago regime" to stadium development (Pelissero et al., 1991). The analysis offered here points to a different set of relationships between state and local officials that enabled the project to go forward—and at times threatened its success. As in the World's Fair case, any regime or growth machine analysis would have omitted key decision-making elements of the process, which occurred in a venue other than local government. From June 1986 on, the politics of stadium development were primarily state level.

Navy Pier

It is in the third case that the intergovernmental triad model occurs most fluently. The creation of the Metropolitan Pier and Exposition Authority (MPEA) in 1989 built on the lessons learned from the ISFA in that appointments among the governor and mayor were split evenly. Also, each official would be responsible for appointing an executive of the new authority—the mayor would name the chairman of the board of directors and the governor would appoint the agency's chief executive officer. The MPEA's creation was perhaps the most conflict-free of the three cases as a result of its timing—it was created, and thus brought in to manage the redevelopment, after most of the conflict had already played out regarding what should be done with Navy Pier. Perhaps the most crucial aspect of the MPEA's success was the $150 million in state funds targeted for Navy Pier redevelopment that accompanied its creation.

Navy Pier, a part of the Chicago Plan of 1909 (Smith, 2006), was built in 1916 as a multipurpose development that would house industry and serve as a place of leisure for city residents. Today, Navy Pier is Illinois' leading tourist attraction with nearly 9 million visitors per year (MPEA, 2006). The structure itself runs nearly three-fifths of a mile into Lake Michigan and sits to the north of the Chicago River's mouth. The Pier was built to operate as a mixed-use facility for recreation and industry and has since served as a U.S. Naval training base, a campus for the University of Illinois, and as a site for sporadic Chicago events during the 1970s and 1980s—it did not have a primary use from 1965 to 1995 (MPEA, 2008). During these decades many residents and politicians in Chicago saw it as a wasted resource. While other cities around the nation were capitalizing on the revitalization of old industrial structures into profit-making entertainment districts, Chicago was sitting on its hands (and resources).

Three mayors tackled the idea of redeveloping the Pier between 1979 and 1989—all three failed. Jane Byrne proposed a commercial development shaped by James Rouse (Ziemba, 1982) that failed due to a lack of public support for the partial privatization of the Pier. Counter to Byrne's attempted revitalization, Harold Washington's administration envisioned the Pier as an urban park. A report published by the Washington administration, "Window on the Future," set the rhetorical tone for Navy Pier as Chicago's central public space (City of Chicago, 1985). The plan ultimately failed to convince the City Council that it could produce financial benefits for the city. Eugene Sawyer (mayor from 1987 to 1989), created the Navy Pier Development Authority (NPDA), the first step toward utilization of the intergovernmental triad approach (which he was concurrently invested in concerning the new stadium for the White Sox). The primary task of the NPDA was to craft a formal plan for Navy Pier's redevelopment. The NPDA hired the Urban Land Institute to make recommendations on the Pier's redevelopment, taking a significant step toward renewing Navy Pier.[14] There is no way to know with complete certainty, but, based on the fast action of Sawyer's NPDA once it was created, one can assume that it might have been successful had it not run out of time before Richard M. Daley won the 1989 election.

Frustration over this string of mayors' inability to redevelop Navy Pier combined with Thompson's continuing support of large capital projects in Chicago created a policy window for Daley. At this point in the political debates surrounding Navy Pier's future a near-consensus existed among Chicago's political elite that the priority for Navy Pier was to do *anything* rather than let the structure rot in Lake Michigan for another 20 years.[15] Daley collaborated with Thompson to direct state funds to Chicago and Navy Pier that would provide the funding needed to reshape Navy Pier.[16] The culmination of the Daley–Thompson agreement came when the Illinois General Assembly created the MPEA in June of 1989 (McCarron, 1989; Recktenwald, 1989).

With the creation of the MPEA the state authorized the issuance of $150 million in bonds for the redevelopment of the Pier. In addition to providing state funds for Chicago's redevelopment project, the legislation called for the MPEA to manage McCormick Place, the city's convention center (MPEA, 2002; Recktenwald, 1989).[17] The *Chicago Tribune* called the legislative bill a "plum" for Mayor Daley as it gave the city everything it needed to rebuild Navy Pier (Recktenwald, 1989). It also placed many of the important decisions regarding development in the hands of an appointed private elite; the MPEA board of directors was, and is, composed entirely of private-sector representatives. This private representation constitutes one arm of the intergovernmental triad and institutionalizes the private influence and leadership noted as an informal aspect of urban regimes.

At Navy Pier, the MPEA acted efficiently, opening the attraction in 1995 as promised. The development ran the typical course of a public authority-managed project: there was limited interaction with the public (*Chicago Sun-Times*, 1992) and the final product resembled private developments in other cities, which officials in Chicago had been trying to avoid. For example, Benjamin Thompson and Associates, the architectural firm that designed similar tourist areas in Boston and Baltimore (BTA, 1990), led the renovation. The City Council may have turned down the Rouse proposals in the early 1980s, but MPEA decisions ensured a heavy private influence.

Navy Pier's redevelopment caused great stress to a succession of Chicago mayors who worked to change the landmark but could not find the right recipe of public and private action. The city's current mayor, Richard M. Daley, might gladly claim credit for reshaping Navy Pier; without the state aid, however, and particularly without the creation of the MPEA, plans for Navy Pier might have remained idle for some time following his inauguration. The MPEA, and specifically officials' reliance on it for other development projects, has significantly altered the ecology of governance in Chicago. Its presence as a seemingly permanent institution implies that the intergovernmental triad approach, and particularly a system of cooperation between Chicago and Illinois, can become a dominant feature of local politics.

DISCUSSION

The cases presented here reflect a process of urban development in which three elements differ dramatically from previous studies, and specifically the regime approach. Each element reflects the ways in which shifting focus toward institutional actors, and particularly state governments, may help to uncover ways in which current theories of urban development do not accurately characterize contemporary processes. First, and most clearly, the state government, and particularly the state legislative assembly, is the primary decision-making venue for project authorization and the governor a key advocate of the development projects. Second, the resulting governing arrangements include a formal arrangement by which actors from state and local government, and the private sector, manage urban redevelopment. Third, political actors' utilization of special-purpose authorities shapes not only the cases discussed but also the character of growth politics in the city generally. The implications for each of these observations are discussed below.

State government involvement in the three cases is characterized by both gubernatorial lobbying for Chicago development projects and legislative approval for the creation of special-purpose authorities to manage development. In previous efforts to explain state interaction in downtown development (Burns, 2002; Burns & Thomas, 2004), the governor has been characterized as a member of a governing regime. In the Chicago case, the Illinois governor does not fit this characterization. Thompson's level of support for these projects has not been consistent among his successors. His immediate successor, Republican Jim Edgar, did not work as effectively with Mayor Richard M. Daley (see Strahler, 1996; Washburn, 2005),[18] though Republican George Ryan and Daley did agree on many development issues (Spielman, 2002). Thus, Thompson's role in these cases does not match the long-term, stable coalition membership typical of regimes; the cases here suggest that expanding regime theory to include such state-level entry into local development coalitions would reflect what Mossberger and Stoker (2001) identify as parochialism within the regime literature.

In the case that regime theory does not explain governor, or state, involvement in lobbying for local development, other explanations should be explored. The triad approach offered here suggests that creating the permanent development authorities such as ISFA and MPEA may benefit governors and states in two ways. First, special-purpose authorities create distance between elected officials and controversial policy decisions (Foster, 1997, p. 20); once an authority is managing a development, governors may choose to limit their direct interaction with local policy issues. Thus, governors may appease big-city city mayors, constituents, or campaign financiers by helping to fill a funding gap for ambitious urban development projects, but take fewer political risks in doing so. Second, governors may utilize authorities to pursue policies they view as beneficial to the state as a whole, their political party, or their own political interests. In the cases considered above, Thompson's interest in Chicago development can be explained by the fact that governors have a shared interest in their cities' economic health (Eisinger, 1998, p. 104), and particularly in the state's economic capital. Chicago's role as the dominant fiscal engine for the state has certainly played to its favor in state–city relations historically and in these specific cases. And while accounts of Chicago's mayors' ability to significantly influence decision making in the state capitol have at times been overstated (Gove & Preston, 1985), Chicago's influence in state politics should be considered as a feature of this case study that may not apply in other cities.

The intergovernmental triad approach, then, explains the sporadic entry of governors and other state actors onto the scene of urban politics for the purposes of securing cities' economic health or solving large political disputes. This activity does not constitute membership in a regime, which as Stone (1989) instructs, is an informal cooperative arrangement that stays steady over long periods of time. While the state's political influence remains steady because of authorities' formal nature and, in this case, the governor's appointment powers, sustained interest in a broad range of development projects is unlikely.

Formalization of governing coalitions is a second difference in the cases studied here. Rather than "informal arrangements by which public bodies and private interests function together" (Stone, 1989, p. 6), the governing boards of authorities represent a formal joining of public and private for the purposes of decision making.[19] In all three cases, members of Chicago's private sector are invited to take seats on the authority boards. In appointing the WFA board, Governor Thompson and Mayor Washington directly incorporated individuals who had been involved in the private sector's push for the 1992 World's Fair. Also of note is the fact that publishers of the city's two leading newspapers—classic examples of members of a "growth machine" (Logan & Molotch, 1987)—were named to the board. While the private supporters of the White Sox stadium and the Navy Pier redevelopment were not as explicit, mayoral and gubernatorial appointments to the initial boards of directors at the respective authorities reflect a selection of industry representatives that can be viewed as having progrowth interests or acting as members of a regime. Namely, representatives come from fields such as real estate development, construction, labor, and the legal profession. Through this formalization process, authorities and the intergovernmental triad serve as anchors for governance.

This formal mechanism for development raises questions regarding the power-sharing arrangements once the authority is functioning. Is one leg of the triad stronger than another? What are the incentives for each institutional actor in this formal partnership? Does the triad also create drawbacks for states, cities, and authorities? Because of its statutory power over local governments (including the power to create the authorities), the state appears to be the strongest leg in the triad and through the creation of the authority secures an authoritative voice in local development politics. However, in offering fiscal support to Chicago interests, state politicians may be making themselves vulnerable to critics; this may be especially true of governors such as Thompson, who champion big-city interests and may be pressed to find a balance with state-level officials representing constituencies outside of the city in question. Also, though states' fiscal resources are greater than cities they are assisting, they are still finite and becoming overcommitted to urban development may harm states' fiscal health. City government appears to gain in that development projects are being carried out without taking up valuable lines on the city budget—in most cases city officials are increasing capacity without giving up fiscal resources. But Chicago, too, finds itself in a position of vulnerability in that it has given up jurisdiction on areas managed by special-purpose authorities. In terms of its actual input into the triad, the city government appears to be the weakest leg in the arrangement—the city is more concerned with the outcome produced by the two more powerfully vested institutions, the state and special-purpose authority. The special-purpose authorities gain their power through the implementation of the development and the powers they are given to plan future developments; authorities' existence, and thus the existence of triads, is dependent upon their ability to lobby for project authorization and to manage developments efficiently—this makes them both a strong and critical leg in the triad arrangement. Private sector representatives gain a seat at the governing table and do not appear to be giving up any of the influence that they might have had under informal arrangements. By being formally incorporated, private-sector actors may have more power to influence the allocation of resources to networks close to their interests (e.g., voting on the approval of contracts). All actors in the triad, then, have shared interests in the creation and maintenance of this formal mechanism for growth.

State governments' increased role in development and the formalization of the growth coalition are both facilitated by officials' use of special-purpose authorities, the third difference considered here. The intergovernmental triad approach makes authorities a centerpiece for analyses of urban development, rather than a side note, as has been the tendency of many studies focusing on governance and center city development. Authorities are critical to the triad model as they are the institutional mechanism bringing states into the development process and formalizing the private sector's role in decision making. In other words, it is as a result of this institution that the triad, and the resulting formal relationships, exists. Without it, private actors remain as informal actors and the state does not hold a sustained jurisdictional interest.

In addition to acting as the institutional cement for the state–city–private sector relationship, the utilization of special-purpose authorities has two principal effects on the processes of development discussed in the cases above. First, it has further removed decision making from public access points such as referenda (Altshuler & Luberoff, 2003; Sanders, 1992). State and local governments use special-purpose authorities as mechanisms for expediting both the approval of development projects and the decision-making process to follow. Public votes on funding approval were absent in each of the significant development projects considered here. It should not be assumed, however, that policy decisions made within authorities are entirely removed from external checks on power. For instance, in the World's Fair case, the WFA is checked by the state legislature, which votes against authorizing funding for the development. Second, authorities permanently alter the ecology of local government (Judd & Smith, 2007). The creation of special-purpose authorities is not a short-term solution for the challenges associated with large-scale urban development projects; instead, authorities remain as critical elements of urban government long after states create them, likely to pursue their own institutional interests in addition to the initial goals established by their parent governments. For example, in the time since its first project at Navy Pier, the MPEA has expanded the McCormick Place convention center twice, attempted—but failed—to build a domed stadium for the Chicago Bears, planned a second redevelopment at the Pier, and has taken on the task of hotel management in its ownership of the Hyatt McCormick Place. The MPEA was discussed as a fiscal partner in Chicago's failed bid to host the 2016 Olympics (Greising, 2007) and the ISFA had recently negotiated—unsuccessfully— with the Chicago Cubs baseball franchise to purchase Wrigley Field (Bergen, 2008). The intergovernmental triad in Chicago clearly represents more than a temporary political arrangement for short-term political benefit—the institutions affect city politics for decades after their creation.

THEORETICAL IMPLICATIONS

The arguments presented above do not presume that evidence from Chicago is reflective of the politics in all cities or that this approach can constitute a shift in theoretical explanations without further verification in other cities. State government may have a stronger voice in the politics of downtown development in Chicago than in other cities, and triads may be emerging through different bargaining processes, or not at all, in cities other than Chicago. However, the triad approach represents a significant step in both incorporating state government into studies of urban politics and, in doing so, moving toward new theoretical approaches to urban redevelopment.

With these limits in mind, two possible theoretical paths, dependent upon further casework, emerge from this research. If there is sufficient evidence to support the hypothesis that triads exist in other cities in similar form to those documented here, the argument might be made that it represents a manifestation of a new politics of development differing from previous explanations in the three ways detailed above. Conversely, if state governments are involved in large-scale development in other cities in ways different from the triad arrangement, theoretical development should focus more simply on the transitions in urban development related to intergovernmental relations. In either case, the theoretical solution should not be to simply expand regime theory as this takes away from its validity.

Under the first scenario, the emerging theory might argue that, considering recent slow growth tendencies (Purcell, 2000) and transformations in downtown coalitions (Strom, 2008), traditional progrowth interests have utilized state governments' power to create institutions of local government in order to secure their power to influence decision making. Transferring the politics of development to new jurisdictions may ensure that the progrowth interests will remain unaffected by electoral or other shifts at the local level. Recognizing these emergent trends in 1992, Heywood Sanders wrote of a new politics of development, specifically in regard to convention center expansion, in which actors were operating in new institutional spaces such as state halls and special-purpose authorities. According to Sanders (1992), this occurred for two principal reasons; first, it provided access to fiscal resources and second, it reduced the level of conflict surrounding development by limiting the access of opposition groups to debates. The case studies here suggest that the triad may be one of the forms taken by Sanders's new politics of development. By removing the need for electoral compromise, a major pillar of regime theory, actors appear to be finding ways around blockades and clearly securing power over others in pursuit of their own interests.[20] They do so not only through short-term political maneuvering but also through institution building, resulting in the permanent installation of progrowth interests in the local state. If cases in other cities reflect the trends in Chicago uncovered here, the empirics would lead to a theory of institutionalized urban growth politics with closer attention to not only the actors involved, but the nature of the institutions they are engineering and the effects such institutions have on both the built environment of cities and their political character.

The second possibility described would suggest that city officials have replaced the federal government with the state government as a partner in funding large-scale urban development, and, that although the partners are different, redevelopment remains an intergovernmental pursuit in which cities emerge as a dependent institution, lacking the autonomy to accomplish ambitious development independent of external fiscal support. From this perspective, city officials and progrowth interests appear to be pragmatic actors following revenue streams into whichever institutional venue they lead. The involvement of state government, and the creation of special-purpose authorities, serves merely as a method for filling budget gaps. In analyses of such arrangements, individual actors and informal relationships would likely remain as the key variable but alterations in existing theories would be needed to incorporate external and intergovernmental actors. Further research along these theoretical lines would consider the effects of intergovernmental actors on local coalitions and judge whether or not the entrance of such actors significantly reduces the ability of existing theories to explain development outcomes in the same way that I have argued the triad arrangement does. The most significant contribution of these more limited changes would be the recognition of a shift in intergovernmental relations following the period of national urban policy in the mid-to-late 20th century.

The Chicago case cannot provide a conclusive answer as to which theoretical frame fits more closely. But further research in other cities may confirm whether new theory building is necessary or whether slight adjustments can expand existing theories' validity sufficiently. Regime theory, in its current form, does not account for the state-level actors involved in Chicago politics and the institutional mechanisms through which progrowth interests are being pursued. If Chicago turns out to be the exception, the power arrangements and formality of the triad described here may only explain a short period in Chicago's history of development. If the pattern is reflected in other cities, the need for an institutionally based theory of urban growth will be clear, and this research may serve as one of many steps toward building that theory.

Acknowledgments: An earlier version of this article was presented at the 37th Annual Meeting of the Urban Affairs Association, Seattle, April 25–28, 2007. In addition to the editor and three anonymous reviewers, who provided valuable guidance with this final product, the author would like to thank Larry Bennett, Dennis Judd, Nina Martin, Greg Schrock, and Dick Simpson, who commented on earlier versions of the article.

REFERENCES

Alpert, L., Gainsborough, J. F., & Wallis, A. (2006). Building the capacity to act regionally: Formation of the Regional Transportation Authority in South Florida. *Urban Affairs Review, 42*(2), 143–168.

Altshuler, A., & Luberoff, D. (2003). *Mega-projects: The changing politics of urban public investment.* Washington, DC: Brookings Institution Press.

Anthony, J. (2004). Do state growth management regulations reduce sprawl? *Urban Affairs Review, 39*(3), 376–397.

Axelrod, D. (1992). *Shadow government: The hidden world of public authorities—and how they control over $1 trillion of your money.* New York: John Wiley & Sons.

Baade, R. A., Nikolova, M., & Matheson, V. A. (2006). *A tale of two stadiums: Comparing the economic impact of Chicago's Wrigley Field and U.S. Cellular Field.* College of the Holy Cross, Department of Economics Faculty Research Series, Paper No. 06-08. Available at http://www.holycross.edu/departments/economics/RePEc/Matheson_TwoStadiums.pdf, accessed January 23, 2008.

Banfield, E. C. (1961). *Political influence,* New York: Free Press.

Benjamin Thompson & Associates (1990). *Notes, ideas, and images to illustrate a vision for the revitalization of Chicago's Navy Pier: A design and planning scrapbook.* Cambridge, MA: Author.

Bennett, L., & Spirou, C. (2006). Political leadership and stadium development in Chicago: Some cautionary notes on the uses of regime analysis. *International Journal of Urban and Regional Research, 30*(1), 38–53.

Bergen, K. (2008). New Wrigley Field proposal on deck—Thompson says plan uses no tax dollars. *Chicago Tribune,* April 30, Business, 1.

Berman, D. R. (1995). Takeovers of local governments: An overview and evaluation of state policies. *Publius, 25*(3), 55–70.

Berman, D. R. (2003). *Local government and the states: Autonomy, politics, and policy.* Armonk, NY: M.E. Sharpe.

Burns, N. (1994). *The formation of American local governments: Private values and public institutions.* Oxford: Oxford University Press.

Burns, N., & Gamm, G. (1997). Creatures of the state: State politics and local government, 1871–1921. *Urban Affairs Review, 33*(1), 59–96.

Burns, P. F. (2002). The intergovernmental regime and public policy in Hartford, Connecticut. *Journal of Urban Affairs, 24*(1), 55–73.

Burns, P. F. (2003). Regime theory, state government, and a takeover of urban education. *Journal of Urban Affairs, 25*(3), 285–303.

Burns, P. F., & Thomas, M. O. (2004). Governors and the development regime in New Orleans. *Urban Affairs Review, 39*(6), 791–812.

Chicago Convention and Tourism Bureau (2008). *Visitor impact.* Available at http://www.choosechicago .com/media/statistics/visitor_impact/Pages/default.aspx, accessed January 16, 2008.

Chicago Sun-Times (1992). Increase public input in expensive projects. March 22, Editorial, 39.

Chicago Tribune (1983). Ayers heads World's Fair Authority, mayor, governor name 24 others to state board. Nov. 4, News, 4.

Chicago Tribune (1986). . . . And a gift stadium is stalled. July 3, Editorial, 18.

Chicago White Sox (2007). *White Sox individual-game tickets on sale.* Feb. 16, press release. Available at http://chicago.whitesox.mlb.com/news/press_releases, accessed January 12, 2008.

City of Chicago (1985). *Window on the future: The final report of the mayor's Navy Pier task force.* Chicago: Author.

Clarke, S. E., & Saiz, M. (2003). From waterhole to world city: Place-luck and public agendas in Denver. In D. R. Judd (Ed.), *The infrastructure of play: Building the tourist city,* (pp. 168–201). Armonk, NY: M.E. Sharpe.

Cronon, W. (1991). *Nature's metropolis: Chicago and the great west.* New York: W.W. Norton and Company.

Dahl, R. (1961). *Who governs? Democracy and power in an American city.* New Haven, CT: Yale University Press.

DiGaetano, A. (1997). Urban governing alignments and realignments in comparative perspective: Developmental politics in Boston, Massachusetts, and Bristol, England, 1980–1996. *Urban Affairs Review, 32*(6), 844–870.

DiLeo, D. (1998). The state-local partnership in education. In R. L. Hanson (Ed.), *Governing partners* (pp. 109–138). Boulder, CO: Westview Press.

Doig, J. W. (1983). 'If I see a murderous fellow sharpening a knife cleverly. . . ': The Wilsonian dichotomy and the public authority tradition. *Public Administration Review, 43*(4), 292–304.

Doig, J. W., & Mitchell, J. (1992). Expertise, democracy, and the public authority model: Groping toward accommodation. In J. Mitchell (Ed.), *Public authorities and public policy: The business of government* (pp. 17–30). Westport, CT: Greenwood Press.

Dold, B. (1987). Mayor demands more for Sox stadium board. *Chicago Tribune,* August 17, Tempo, 6.

Egler, D. (1986a). Mayor tries new game plan for stadium. *Chicago Tribune,* June 28, News, 4.

Egler, D. (1986b). Legislature may enlist in Sox stadium effort. *Chicago Tribune,* July 1, News, 1.

Egler, D., & McCarron, J. (1986a). Sox, city pitch stadium plan to governor. *Chicago Tribune,* December 3, News, 1.

Egler, D., & McCarron, J. (1986b). Thompson joins stadium team. *Chicago Tribune,* December 4, News, 1.

Egler, D., & McCarron, J. (1986c). Sox stadium is safe at home. *Chicago Tribune,* December 6, News, 1.

Eisinger, P. K. (1998). Partners for growth: State and local relations in economic development. In R. L. Hanson (Ed.), *Governing partners* (pp. 93–108). Boulder, CO: Westview Press.

Foster, K. A. (1997). *The political economy of special-purpose government.* Washington, DC: Georgetown University Press.

Frug, G. E. (1999). *City making: Building communities without building walls.* Princeton, NJ: Princeton University Press.

Fuchs, E. R. (1992). *Mayors and money: Fiscal policy in New York and Chicago.* Chicago: University of Chicago Press.

Gainsborough, J. F. (2001). Bridging the city-suburb divide: States and the politics of regional cooperation. *Journal of Urban Affairs, 23*(5), 497–512.

George, A. L., & Bennett, A. (2005). *Case studies and theory development in the social sciences.* Cambridge, MA: The MIT Press.

Gove, S. K., & Preston, M. B. (1985). State-local (Chicago) relations in Illinois: The Harold Washington era, 1984. *Publius: The Journal of Federalism, 15*(Summer), 143–154.

Greising, D. (2007). McPier to fund 2016 bid. *Chicago Tribune,* March 14, News, 1, 17.

Grimshaw, W. J. (1992). *Bitter fruit: Black politics and the Chicago machine, 1931–1991.* Chicago: The University of Chicago Press.

Hamilton, D. K., Miller, D. Y., & Paytas, J. (2004). Exploring the vertical and horizontal dimensions of metropolitan regions. *Urban Affairs Review, 40*(2), 147–182.

Henig, J. R., Hula, R. C., Orr, M., & Pedescleaux, D. S. (1999). *The color of school reform: Race, politics, and the challenge of urban education.* Princeton, NJ: Princeton University Press.

Hunter, F. (1953). *Community power structure: A study of decision makers.* New York: Anchor Books.

Illinois Sports Facilities Authority (2006). *Annual report 2006.* Available at http://hallpcsupport .com/isfa/AR_2006.pdf, accessed November 5, 2007.

Judd, D. R. (2003). Building the tourist city, Editor's introduction. In D. R. Judd (Ed.), *The infrastructure of play: Building the tourist city* (pp. 3–18). Armonk, NY: M.E. Sharpe.

Judd, D. R., & Smith, J. M. (2007). The new ecology of urban governance: Special purpose authorities and urban development. In R. Hambleton & J. S. Gross (Eds.), *Governing cities in a global era: Urban innovation, competition, and democratic reform* (pp. 151–160). Basingstoke, UK: Palgrave.

Kaplan, J. (1989). Board named to revive pier. *Chicago Tribune,* July 18, Chicagoland, 1.

Lawrence, M. (1987). Sox park measure squeaks by senate. *Chicago Sun-Times,* June 26, News, 21.

Logan, J. R., & Molotch, H. L. (1987). *Urban fortunes: The political economy of place.* Berkeley: University of California Press.

Longworth, R. C. (1985). A postmortem on the fair. *Chicago Tribune,* June 27, Perspective, 27.

McCarron, J. (1985). Rift can be overcome on fair, Kramer says. *Chicago Tribune,* February 15, Chicagoland, 8.

McCarron, J. (1986). Stadium developers win over Sox. *Chicago Tribune,* May 1, Chicagoland, 1.

McCarron, J. (1989). City's development wishes granted. *Chicago Tribune,* July 4, News, 1.

McCarron, J., & Egler, D. (1985). Seeds of fair demise were planted early. *Chicago Tribune,* June 23, News, 1.

McCarron, J., & Egler, D. (1987). Board for Sox park ready to be named. *Chicago Tribune,* April 10, Chicagoland, 3.

McCarron, J., & Egler, D. (1988). Legislators vote to save Sox; bipartisan rally pushes deal through. *Chicago Tribune,* July 1, News, 1.

McClory, R. (1993). The fall of the fair. In D. Simpson (Ed.), *Chicago's future in a time of change* (pp. 388–398). Champaign, IL: Stipes Publishing Company.

Metropolitan Pier and Exposition Authority (2002). *Experience . . . 2002 annual report.* Chicago: Author.

Metropolitan Pier and Exposition Authority (2006). *Keeping pace with success: 2006 annual report.* Chicago: Author.

Metropolitan Pier and Exposition Authority (2007). *Navy Pier selects two by four as new advertising agency.* Press release. Available at http://www.mpea.com/pdf/10_07AdAgency.pdf, accessed January 12, 2008.

Metropolitan Pier and Exposition Authority (2008). *About Navy Pier—History.* Available at http://www.navypier.com/about/history.html, accessed September 17, 2008.

Mier, R. (1995). Economic development and infrastructure: Planning in the context of progressive politics. In D. C. Perry (Ed.), *Building the public city: The politics, governance, and finance of public infrastructure* (pp. 71–102). Thousand Oaks, CA: Sage Publications.

Mirel, J. (2004). Detroit: "There is still a long road to travel, and success is far from assured." In J. R. Henig & W. C. Rich (Eds.), *Mayors in the middle: Politics, race, and mayoral control of urban schools* (pp. 120–158). Princeton, NJ: Princeton University Press.

Mossberger, K., & Stoker, G. (2001). The evolution of urban regime theory: The challenge of conceptualization. *Urban Affairs Review,* 36(6), 810–835.

Neal, S. (1985). Fair's 'Music Man' promises the world. *Chicago Tribune,* June 16, Perspective, 4.

Nice, D. C., & Fredericksen, P. (1995). *The politics of intergovernmental relations* (2nd ed.). Chicago: Nelson-Hall.

Orr, M. (2004). Baltimore: The limits of mayoral control. In J. R. Henig & W. C. Rich (Eds.), *Mayors in the middle: Politics, race, and mayoral control of urban schools* (pp. 27–58). Princeton, NJ: Princeton University Press.

Pagano, M. A. (1990). State-local relations in the 1990s. *Annals of the American Academy of Political and Social Science,* 509, 94–105.

Pelissero, J. P., Heschen, B. M., & Sidlow, E. I. (1991). Urban regimes, sports stadiums, and the politics of economic development agendas in Chicago. *Policy Studies Review,* 10(2/3), 117–129.

Post, S. S., & Stein, R. M. (2000). State economies, metropolitan governance, and urban-suburban economic dependence, *Urban Affairs Review,* 36(1), 46–60.

Purcell, M. (2000). The decline of the political consensus for urban growth: Evidence from Los Angeles. *Journal of Urban Affairs,* 22(1), 85–100.

Recktenwald, W. (1989). The dust clears in legislature's wake, Navy Pier bill a plum for Daley. *Chicago Tribune,* July 3, Chicagoland, 1.

Sanders, H. T. (1992). Building the convention city: Politics, finance, and public investment in urban America. *Journal of Urban Affairs,* 14(2), 135–159.

Sapotichne, J. (2007). Regime capacity and strategic rhetoric: Finding the winning frame in Seattle's sports stadium debates. Paper presented at the annual meeting of the Midwest Political Science Association, Chicago, April 12–15.

Sbragia, A. M. (1996). *Debt wish: Entrepreneurial cities, U.S. federalism, and economic development.* Pittsburgh, PA: University of Pittsburgh Press.

Shipps, D. (2004). Chicago: The national "model" reexamined. In J. R. Henig & W. C. Rich (Eds.), *Mayors in the middle: Politics, race, and mayoral control of urban schools* (pp. 59–95). Princeton, NJ: Princeton University Press.

Shlay, A. B., & Giloth, R. (1987). The social organization of a land-based elite: The case of the failed Chicago 1992 World's Fair. *Journal of Urban Affairs, 9*(4), 305–324.

Simpson, D. (2001). *Rogues, rebels, and rubber stamps: The politics of the Chicago City Council from 1863 to the present.* Boulder, CO: Westview Press.

Smith, C. (2006). *The plan of Chicago: Daniel Burnham and the remaking of the American city.* Chicago: University of Chicago Press.

Sonenshein, R. J., & Hogen-Esch, T. (2006). Bringing the state (government) back in: Home rule and the politics of secession in Los Angeles and New York City. *Urban Affairs Review, 41*(4), 467–491.

Spielman, F. (2002). Dem win good for city, Daley says—casino, O'Hare growth could win with new guv. *Chicago Sun-Times*, November 7, News, 19.

Spirou, C., & Bennett, L. (2003). *It's hardly sportin': Neighborhoods, stadiums, and the new Chicago.* DeKalb, IL: Northern Illinois University Press.

Stone, C. N. (1989). *Regime politics: Governing Atlanta, 1946–1988.* Lawrence, KS: University Press of Kansas.

Stone, C. N. (2005). Looking back to look forward: Reflections on urban regime analysis. *Urban Affairs Review, 40*(3), 309–341.

Stone, C. N. (2008). Urban politics then and now. In M. Orr & V. C. Johnson (Eds.), *Power in the city: Clarence Stone and the politics of inequality* (pp. 267–316). Lawrence, KS: University Press of Kansas.

Strahler, S. R. (1996). What is this? Council wars II? Guv-mayor fight is deeper than Meigs; how biz loses. *Crain's Chicago Business*, September 9, News, 3.

Strom, E. (2008). Rethinking the politics of downtown development. *Journal of Urban Affairs, 30*(1), 37–62.

Turner, R. S. (1990). Intergovernmental growth management: A partnership framework for state-local relations. *Publius: The Journal of Federalism, 20*(Summer), 79–95.

Urban Land Institute (1989). *Navy Pier Chicago* (prepared for the Navy Pier Development Authority). Washington, DC: Urban Land Institute.

U.S. Census Bureau (2002). *Government organization: 2002 census of governments.* Available at http://www.census.gov/prod/2003pubs/gc021x1.pdf, accessed February 4, 2008.

Washburn, G. (2005). Daley feels strongly about Edgar, but it's not just one-sided. *Chicago Tribune*, October 2, Metro, 2.

Washington State Public Stadium Authority (2004). *Meet the PSA.* Available at http://www.stadium.org/meetPSA.asp, accessed October 22, 2007.

Weir, M. (1996). Central cities' loss of power in state politics. *Cityscape: A Journal of Policy Development and Research, 2*(2), 23–40.

Weir, M., Wolman, H., & Swanstrom, T. (2005). The calculus of coalitions: Cities, suburbs, and the metropolitan agenda. *Urban Affairs Review, 40*(6), 730–760.

Wille, L. (1997). *At home in the Loop: How clout and community built Chicago's Dearborn Park.* Carbondale: Southern Illinois University Press.

Wong, K. K., & Shen, F. X. (2002). Politics of state-led reform in education: Market competition and electoral dynamics. *Educational Policy, 16*(1), 161–192.

Ziemba, S. (1982). $277 million plan for rebirth of Navy Pier. *Chicago Tribune*, May 28, News, 1 & 10.

NOTES

1. Though this expansive empirical study identifies the weak link between states and cities in urban scholarship, it focuses on previous eras and does not fill the gap I speak of earlier in this piece.
2. Stone (2005) has argued that regime theory, depending on its context, may indeed involve "intergovernmental channels of communication" (p. 330).
3. Banfield (1961) does treat the state of Illinois as an integral part of the machine era in Chicago, but most negotiations between mayors and governors, alderman and representatives,

come down to winning votes, not building coalitions or generating economic development strategies. Also, Gove and Preston (1985) discuss Richard J. Daley's ability to work with Republican governors, but question the assumption that he could dictate state decisions by mobilizing the Chicago contingent in the Illinois General Assembly. Weir (1996) analyzes the history of governor–mayor relations in Illinois and Chicago, finding that state-level funding has been critical to Chicago's development.

4. Washington's work with state-level actors also complicates the argument that he could not utilize state resources as effectively as previous mayors (see Gove & Preston, 1985).

5. Donald Axelrod (1992) and the Urban Land Institute (1989) have also recognized Thompson's fondness for the creation of authorities as a tool of economic development. Fittingly, he was appointed as chairman of the Illinois Sports Facilities Authority governing board in 2006.

6. Illinois has more special district governments than any other state (U.S. Census Bureau, 2002). The use of such governments for offloading municipal expenses has been a strategy of Chicago mayors in the past (Fuchs, 1992).

7. Private-sector representatives may not be directly involved in development decision-making or lobbying prior to their appointment, but have significant impact on outcomes once appointed to seats on authority boards.

8. In the case of the World's Fair, when the triad approach produced a higher level of conflict, the funding never arrived. The World's Fair Authority was established without fiscal backing and withered as a result.

9. While the World's Fair project was unsuccessful, the final vote of approval for both the White Sox ballpark and Navy Pier's redevelopment occurred during midnight sessions in the Illinois General Assembly. The next morning's newspaper reveals a night of vote trading and lobbying by the governor, or a closed-door session in which the governor of Illinois has made offers to the mayor of Chicago regarding his/her wish list. In both cases, there is no decisive city council vote or referendum.

10. The 1992 World's Fair Authority was created before a funding package had been assembled. The ISFA was created and funded initially in 1986; the funding level was raised to $150 million before the White Sox agreed not to move to Florida.

11. Neighborhood groups protested the Fair and Washington felt pressure to approach it differently than his predecessor, Jane Byrne (McClory, 1993; Mier, 1995); therefore, the placement of the Fair in an authority's jurisdiction likely prolonged the plan's existence. . . .

12. The White Sox purchased land in suburban Chicago before losing a referendum to fund the construction of a new stadium on the site (Spirou & Bennett, 2003, p. 67).

13. This is an excellent example of why state politics and legislative action need to be considered more regularly in narratives and analyses of urban politics. The level of support for projects at the local level may have little meaning if state officials oppose a project.

14. Insight on the NPDA is drawn from a personal interview with a former official. Also, many of the suggestions made in the Urban Land Institute (1989) report the NPDA commissioned were eventually implemented.

15. This line of argument was offered by two former leaders of the MPEA in personal interviews conducted in early 2008.

16. A former MPEA official supported this argument in a personal interview.

17. The Metropolitan Fair and Exposition Authority, which had managed the convention center previously, was dissolved and McCormick Place was placed under the jurisdiction of the MPEA.

18. Daley is quoted in one press report (Washburn, 2005) as saying that "[Edgar] had a political position . . . that it was good to beat up Chicago."

19. Stone (2008) has acknowledged the emergence of formalized growth coalitions but not necessarily their potential intergovernmental nature. He cites the City of Baltimore Development Corporation as an example (p. 306).

20. Whereas regime theory would suggest that dominant members of a regime would be forced to work with the electorate in pursuing the power to accomplish development goals, Sander's description, and indeed the pattern in the research presented here, suggests that progrowth actors are working around such opposition and avoiding the type of compromise described in regime theory. Sanders writes, "What is remarkable in recent years has been the capacity to actually develop [convention centers] in the face of equally persistent voter antipathy and disapproval. What has occurred across a broad range of communities is nothing less than a radical change in structure of local fiscal politics which has, in turn, radically reshaped the character and products of local capital investment" (1992, p. 138).

The Cities: Governing Factional Polities

Ethnic and racial competition, conflict, and accommodation are central to the processes of globalization. New and older groups compete for living space and access to jobs, sharpening rivalries among people of different racial, ethnic, and social class backgrounds. This development has profound consequences for city politics. In order to govern, political leaders must struggle to mobilize new voter coalitions and attempt to satisfy the political claims of voters who have different priorities and life experiences. Thus, city politics increasingly involves rivalry and accommodation as diverse populations assert their presence and identity in local political systems. At the same time, cities struggle to find common ground among competing groups. Competing groups are constrained to put aside rivalries, and seek compromises to enable city governments to achieve common goals. If children are to be educated well, schools must perform effectively. If housekeeping services—such as parks and recreation, street maintenance, police, and fire protection—are to be delivered efficiently, competent administrators must be hired and made accountable. In a factional polity there is considerable tension between democratic impulses and governability. City officials struggle to balance these forces.

The first two selections focus on the political consequences of a changing racial and ethnic politics. Newer immigrants are establishing an uneven but growing political presence in urban politics. A century ago some immigrants— in particular, the Irish—were able to find a voice in the party machines. That avenue is no longer available, but the ballot box still gives recently arrived immigrant groups powerful leverage. In Selection 11, Reuel R. Rogers focuses on coalition building in cities in which newer ethnic and longer established minority groups compete for power. He wonders whether the newcomers will forge coalitions with their native-born counterparts, particularly African Americans. In the past, many believed that race-based alliances between non-white immigrants and African Americans were likely since both have experienced racial discrimination and frequently share other group characteristics, such as lower educational levels and higher rates of poverty, that give them common cause.

Using the case of Caribbean- and American-born blacks in New York City, Rogers notes the absence of alliances between these groups over many years. Common racial interests have not been sufficient to overcome a pattern of inter-minority tensions and political competition. Rogers explains that racial and ethnic awareness does not provide a satisfactory foundation for a broad-based alliance. Indeed, competition for political turf frequently divides Caribbean and African American blacks. Entrenched African American elites have an interest in resisting the mobilization and inclusion of newer Caribbean blacks in order to preserve their hold on jobs and power. For their part, Caribbean minorities seek political recognition and their leaders give priority to constituency building within their own enclave. Rogers also believes that governmental institutions play a part in dividing the two groups. In particular, he says that New York City's decentralized electoral system rewards mobilization of ethnic groups and targeted appeals that become divisive. In addition, the city's one-party politics and lack of rich networks of community-based organizations encourages political faction. The author concludes that race is unlikely to form a stable foundation for governance in big cities like New York for some time, if ever.

The election of racial minorities is of great importance in a nation divided by race. Since the 1970s cities and local governments have led the way in offering electoral opportunities for racial and ethnic minorities. African American and Latino candidates are increasingly successful in winning mayoral and local council elections in cities all over the United States even though their success in gaining national offices has lagged. The contest for the presidency by Barack Obama in 2008 represented a dramatic breakthrough for African American leadership in overcoming the racial divide. Yet the election of African American candidates is an uncertain step with unknown consequences. Does it herald the beginning of a new politics with diminished racial tensions? Or does it trigger greater racial antagonism as white voters resist the political gains of African Americans? Do African American leaders manage to pull voters together as they govern, or does experience with minority government lead to fears and racial favoritism?

Zoltan L. Hajnal surveys mayoral elections during the twentieth century in Selection 12. He reports that over time white voters have generally become more accepting of African American mayoral candidates. Equally important, Hajnal's analysis suggests that black leadership plays an important role in significantly changing the voting behavior of whites and the way white Americans think about African American candidates. He proposes an informational model of voting behavior to explain this. The informational model assumes that when black challengers run for mayoral office, many white residents are uncertain about the consequences of black leadership and fear electing such candidates. Yet after electing African American leaders and experiencing their leadership styles, this new information tends to assure white voters that their fears are not justified. Most whites come to realize the world under African American leadership is not much different than under white leaders, which encourages a deracialized electoral politics. Hajnal believes this model of voting explains white voting behavior in mayoral elections involving black candidates better than electoral theories that predict unchanging racial prejudice or backlash among white voters.

These essentially upbeat findings about the declining role of racial prejudice in urban politics have far-reaching implications for our entire political system. Perhaps most important, they suggest that opportunities for African American leaders in local politics may be a source of profound change in racial attitudes beyond city halls. Whether the positive role of black leadership in changing white attitudes will continue or spread to other governmental levels remains an open question, however. Political competition based on class, racial, and ethnic differences is likely to remain an enduring feature of city politics as long as other sources of social division remain less important. As populations change and age, new urban political coalitions will be forged.

The struggle to find common ground among rival groups is the subject of the last two selections. J. Eric Oliver points out in Selection 13 that integration is a seductive concept: "For most Americans, the image of different races and ethnicities peacefully coming together as a single community is enormously appealing." Although neighborhood racial integration has been fiercely resisted all over the United States and in many urban settings, there are reasons to believe that those who actually experience integrated living will get along and even become more supportive of one other in civic activities. For example, as families of different races share life experiences in integrated neighborhoods, fear and political rivalry among black, white, or Latino populations may dissipate. Integration may bring people of different races together in neighborhood associations and other civic groups formed to solve common problems.

Yet there has been relatively little research on how neighborhood integration works in practice. Do people in racially integrated neighborhoods actually deal with each other and experience community life in positive ways? Does integration enhance or weaken civic engagement in these neighborhoods?

Oliver brings together data from several surveys to conclude that racially integrated neighborhoods do not always bring people closer together in politics. Oliver finds a paradox in the realities of neighborhood integration. Although whites in integrated neighborhoods have more opportunities for interracial contact, they seem to have less sense of community and are less socially connected to people of other races. "The most adverse effects of integration actually may be experienced by whites," he concludes. According to Oliver, integrated living tends to be largely negative for whites in respect to civic life; they are inclined to be less trusting of their neighbors of different races in racially mixed neighborhood settings. African Americans do not share these feelings as much, but they tend to feel more alienated as the number of white neighbors increases. Most minorities score lower in civic participation, such as joining voluntary associations and resident associations, as the percentage of white people in their neighborhood increases. Feelings of alienation are less common among Asians and Latinos in integrated neighborhoods, however. This may be because their participation in civic organizations or in voting is strongly shaped by the process of immigrant incorporation in society (for example, by their immigration status and voting rights), rather than by their neighborhood experiences. Although racial segregation has many harmful effects on people and politics, neighborhood integration does not necessarily foster greater racial harmony or greater civic participation. Integrated neighborhoods present their own obstacles to bringing people together politically.

Changing the distribution of power in city governmental systems is one means of bridging intergroup rivalries and achieving better governmental performance. Mayoral control of the schools is a recent attempt to achieve both goals through governmental reform, especially in cities with large immigrant and interracial populations. In Selection 14, Michael J. Kirst suggests that mayoral control is often precipitated by pressure from business interests seeking better-quality schools in the face of the flight of families to the suburbs. The idea is also supported by many other groups alarmed by signs of failing schools and evidence of poor test performance by students living in minority neighborhoods.

Although mayoral control may be conceived as a simple and direct way of reforming the schools, Kirst describes why it is very complex and takes many forms. Mayoral control involves important tradeoffs among three values: democratic representation, centralized leadership, and efficiency of administration. Shifting power to mayors can incorporate each these three values in different ways. In practice there are a variety of mayoral governance strategies. Kirst relates how mayors in Chicago, Boston, Cleveland, and other cities pursued different reform paths. In some cities the assertion of mayoral control dramatically reduced the participation of parents, teachers, and other groups in favor of efficiency objectives and nonpartisan competence. Indeed, in Chicago mayoral control involved the complete takeover of school boards by board members appointed by the mayor, which virtually made the schools a department of the city government. Elsewhere, however, mayoral control has involved greater attention to participation and professional expertise. It has included such things as the authorization of charter schools, greater transparency and accountability of officials, a partnership among school districts on specific issues, and cooperation among various stakeholders together for school reform.

Kirst notes that there is not much evidence that mayoral control can actually make schools perform better. Nevertheless, this reform is commonly viewed as a necessary "jolt" to shake up a complacent and ossified system. More efforts at mayoral reform seem likely. Failing schools, tight fiscal pressures, and dissatisfied electorates encourage reformers to use governance and organizational changes to enhance the performance of governments, and this includes the schools.

City politics involves political confrontation as diverse racial and ethnic populations assert their presence in local political systems. At the same time, these groups are forced to find common ground in order to make government work. Resolving the tensions arising from democratic accountability, representation of diversity, and governability is a one of the most daunting challenges facing local political systems.

11

Minority Groups and Coalitional Politics

REUEL R. ROGERS

The current wave of non-White immigrants to American cities has prompted a range of important empirical and normative questions for political scientists to ponder. One of the most widely considered is how these newcomers will alter coalition dynamics in demographically diverse cities such as New York and Los Angeles, where alliances are a do-or-die fact of political life. Some researchers have speculated that the non-White racial status of the immigrants and their vulnerability to discrimination will lead them to forge coalitions with native-born minorities, specifically African-Americans (Jennings 1997; Marable 1994; Henry and Munoz 1991). Combating racial discrimination has long been a central political preoccupation for American-born Blacks. Scholars who subscribe to the "minority group" view believe that it will also be a chief concern for the new, non-White immigrants. Their conclusion is that this

From Reuel R. Rogers, "Race-Based Coalitions among Minority Groups: Afro-Caribbean Immigrants and African-Americans in New York City," *Urban Affairs Review*, Vol. 39, No. 3, pp. 283–317, copyright © 2004 by SAGE Publications, Inc. Reprinted by permission of SAGE Publications, Inc.

shared interest will become a powerful basis for interminority alliances, unifying African-Americans and their foreign-born counterparts. In short, this perspective anticipates a grand rainbow coalition among native-born Blacks and recent non-White immigrants from Latin America, Asia, and the Caribbean.[1]

But in cities with significant numbers of African-Americans and non-White newcomers, race-based alliances among these groups generally have proven to be an elusive political goal. Stable coalitions between native-born Blacks and their foreign-born counterparts have not been much in evidence in cities around the country. In New York, for instance, political figures as varied as Al Sharpton and Fernando Ferrer have tried to foster an alliance between African-Americans and Latinos with only the most limited results (Falcon 1988; Mollenkopf 2003). At the other end of the Atlantic seaboard in Miami, African-Americans and Cubans have been at odds for decades (Warren and Moreno 2003). Tensions also have simmered between African-Americans and Asians in Los Angeles (Sonenshein 2003b). In short, political relations between Blacks and recent non-White immigrants have been marked more often by conflict than by cooperation. Although race-based coalitions among native-born Blacks and foreign-born minority groups are widely expected, it turns out that they are actually quite rare.

The rarity of such alliances has led some researchers to speculate that African-Americans are more likely to find themselves in grim political isolation than in any grand rainbow coalition with non-White immigrants (Mollenkopf 2003). A few observers even dismiss the idea of race-based alliances altogether as a misguided and losing electoral strategy in increasingly diverse, multiracial cities, where immigration has scrambled the old Black–White, biracial political calculus (Sleeper 1993). Whatever their future prospects, race-based coalitions between African-Americans and non-White immigrants have not had much success to date.

Why have such race-based alliances been difficult to foster? A number of studies have noted the political conflicts between Blacks and non-White immigrants, to be sure. But very few have provided detailed analyses of why the racial commonalities they share have not been enough to override differences and produce stable alliances between them. . . .

THE CASE STUDY

This article takes up that question with a case study analysis of political relations between African-Americans and Afro-Caribbean immigrants in New York City.[2] These two groups of Black New Yorkers—one native and the other foreign born—together furnish a highly instructive case for exploring why the race-based alliances anticipated by the minority group view have not come to fruition. By the logic of the minority group perspective, rainbow alliances among non-Whites should be most likely when the racial commonalities between them are strong and the racial divisions separating them from Whites are pronounced and politically salient. The strategy for this analysis, then, was to identify a case that fully meets those conditions to give the minority group hypothesis a favorable test.

African-Americans and Afro-Caribbean immigrants living in New York City do just that. As Blacks, the two groups share the same ascriptive racial category, encounter similar forms of discrimination and disadvantage, and have a number of political and economic interests in common. True enough, they also have a history of occasional intergroup tensions, which could undermine any potential for a race-based political alliance between them. Yet the minority group perspective would maintain that racial commonalities, shared interests, and the potential benefits of a race-based coalition should override the intermittent interethnic conflicts.

The analysis reveals, however, that Afro-Caribbeans and African-Americans in New York—like non-White groups elsewhere—have not had much success at fostering a sturdy race-based coalition. I find that relations between Afro-Caribbean and African-American leaders typically have deteriorated in the face of interest conflicts over descriptive representation. The critical role that interest convergence plays in coalition building has been well established by scholars (Sonenshein 2003a). When interests are at odds, alliances crumble, or fail to develop for that matter. But rather than leaving the analysis at that conventional wisdom, the article explores why the racial commonalities the two groups share have not compelled them to settle these differences, as the minority group perspective would predict. It would be simplistic not to expect divisions of some kind among non-White groups. The challenge of any coalition is to overcome the inevitable intergroup differences and emphasize commonalities and compromises. Scholars who subscribe to the minority group view believe that race provides much of the incentive to do so.

I offer evidence from a series of interviews with Afro-Caribbean political leaders, however, that race is not always the unifying category that minority group scholars expect it to be. My analysis of the interview data shows that race, despite its potential as a rallying point, has serious limits as a linchpin for coalitions among non-Whites. In fact, it actually may heighten divisions among racial minority groups by emphasizing some interests over others. The analysis specifies and traces the conditions under which such differences tend to manifest, even in the face of strong racial affinities such as the ones shared by Afro-Caribbean and African-American New Yorkers.

I then turn from the internal dynamics between these two groups to consider whether any external factors may also help to explain why they have been unable to capitalize on their commonalities to forge a stable alliance. I argue that two key New York City political institutions—its parties and elections—have tended to undermine the intraracial commonalities between these two constituencies; these institutions, in fact, often have exacerbated the interethnic conflicts over descriptive representation between them. I also speculate that the lack of an institutional vehicle to bring African-American and Afro-Caribbean elites together to emphasize shared racial interests, address disagreements, and find compromises has also made it difficult for them to sustain a coalition. In sum, the article draws two major conclusions from the case study. First, race has serious limits as a site for coalition building among non-White groups. Second, whatever potential it does hold may be undermined by a city's political institutions. More generally, the article suggests that the literature on coalition building among non-White minorities in cities should be more attentive to how the complexities of race play out in intergroup relations and how institutions shape these dynamics.

THE MINORITY GROUP THEORETICAL PERSPECTIVE

With so few cases of successful race-based alliances between non-White immigrants and African-Americans in the literature, the question is why they are expected to develop at all. Why would scholars who advance the minority group perspective predict such a coalition in light of such limited empirical evidence? First, their expectations rest on the bedrock of dominant historical patterns in American politics. Race has been a long-standing and stubborn dividing line in local, state, and national politics in the United States. "Indeed, throughout American politics, the racial barrier redefined opinions, attitudes, and alignments" (Sonenshein 2003b, 334). In urban politics, race has been a key axis for the ideological divisions and interest conflicts that dominate campaigns, make and break political alliances, and shape voting preferences. For much of that history, Blacks and Whites have been on opposite sides of the dividing line. But even when groups of Blacks and Whites have managed to forge alliances, racial issues often have been the touchstone for interest and ideological convergence between the two (Browning et al. 2003).

Although some observers believe that the new non-White immigrants will blur and diminish the significance of the racial divide in urban politics, minority group scholars predict that it will hold. Only instead of pitting Whites against Blacks, it will divide Whites and non-Whites. Even with limited empirical evidence to date of race-based coalitions between Blacks and the new immigrants, minority group scholars infer from the long history of racial division in this country that such alliances are still likely to develop. They reason that as non-White newcomers meet racial barriers such as the ones African-Americans have encountered, the probability of their making political common cause with their native-born Black counterparts will increase.

Beyond the dominant patterns of racial division in this country, minority group scholars also take their analytic cues from theories of African-American politics. More specifically, the minority group view draws much of its inspiration from the literature on "linked racial fate" in African-American politics (Dawson 1994a; Tate 1993). Scholars have found that African-Americans remain a unified voting bloc in many cities, despite growing class divisions within the population (Stone and Pieranunzi 1997; Reed 1988). Dawson and others contend that the persistence of the racial divide and anti-Black discrimination in American life are what keep middle- and low-income African-Americans in relatively close political step. African-Americans, the argument goes, share a "linked fate" insofar as they all inevitably confront racial disadvantages. Race is, in short, a powerful political common denominator among African-Americans, trumping the divisions between the middle class and the poor. It is essentially the linchpin unifying middle- and low-income Blacks in an intraracial coalition. Similarly, minority group scholars predict that race will override the differences between African-Americans and the new immigrants and encourage them to forge political alliances.

THE PRIMA FACIE CASE FOR AN AFRO-CARIBBEAN AND AFRICAN-AMERICAN ALLIANCE

There are good reasons to expect this prediction to hold for non-White groups in New York City, particularly African-Americans and Afro-Caribbean immigrants. First, racial division and inequality have long been salient features of life in the city. Immigration has increased New York's demographic diversity in recent decades, to be sure: Foreign-born minority groups from Latin America, Asia, and the Caribbean have proliferated, while the numbers of native-born Whites and Blacks have declined. But even in the face of these new patterns of population diversity, familiar racial divisions remain. The city's political and economic sectors are marked by a pronounced racial divide, with well-off Whites often on one side and relatively disadvantaged non-White minorities on the other.

New York's Racial Divisions

New York's racial minorities have made significant advances in the past few decades, to be sure. Blacks, Latinos, and Asians have gone from having virtually no presence on the city council in the 1970s to a level of representation now almost proportionate to their numbers in the population. Racial minorities likewise have elected their own representatives to the state legislature and Congress, as well as to three of the city's five boroughs presidencies (Mollenkopf 2003). There are also signs of minority progress in the economy. Among the more notable trends from the past decade are the increases in Black incomes, Asian educational progress, and Latino business growth (Lewis Mumford Center for Comparative Urban and Regional Research 2002).

But the picture is not altogether sanguine. Even with these advances by racial minorities, Whites continue to enjoy a disproportionate share of the power, influence, and rewards in both the economic and political spheres of New York life. Table 1 indicates that significant disparities remain between the city's White and minority populations on key indicators of economic well-being. White New Yorkers outpace their minority counterparts by a substantial margin in median income. One recent study also uncovered a wide racial gap in neighborhood quality among New York residents (Lewis Mumford Center for Comparative Urban and Regional Research 2002). Whites tend to live in areas of the city with higher incomes, more homeowners, greater numbers of degree holders, and lower poverty rates than their minority counterparts.

Similarly, although New York's minorities have enjoyed considerable political gains in the past two decades, they nonetheless have much less substantive policy influence than Whites do. That is, they have less access to the political levers that actually control policy outcomes. Mollenkopf (2003) noted,

> With the exception of Congressman Charles Rangel . . . none of the city's minority legislators . . . wields great influence within their legislative bodies. . . . The city's minority legislators can and do extract rewards from the White leaders of their bodies, but they do not exert a strong and independent influence on the overall allocation of public benefits. (pp. 121–22)

At the mayoral level, minorities largely have been at the margins or outside of the electoral and governing coalitions assembled by New York's chief executive. Several of the elections for the top office have been racially divisive. What is more, the mayoralty has been occupied by a succession of White politicians. Aside from the short-lived administration headed by African-American David Dinkins, minorities have not played a leading role in the city's mayoral

TABLE 1

Median Income by Groups in New York City

Year	All Groups	Non-Hispanic Blacks	Non-Hispanic Whites	Hispanics	Asians
2000	38,293	50,920	35,629	27,881	41,338
1990	38,706	47,325	31,955	20,402	41,350

Source: Data are from Lewis Mumford Center for Comparative Urban and Regional Research (2002).
Note: Median income for both years adjusted for 2000 dollars.

regimes. Although several have relied on a modicum of minority support, they have been dominated largely by Whites. Blacks, Latinos, and Asians mostly have occupied subordinate positions, if any at all.

Racial Commonalities between Afro-Caribbeans and African-Americans

Although the divisions separating Whites and non-Whites in New York are pronounced and politically salient, there is no reason to believe that they alone would compel a race-based alliance among the city's minority constituencies. The minority group view holds that such divisions are necessary but not sufficient to produce the predicted coalition. According to this perspective, alliances among non-Whites are probable, not only when there is a sharp racial divide in the political system but also when there are strong commonalities among the minority groups. By that logic, minority group scholars perhaps would not be surprised to find that African-Americans have not been able to forge a sustained alliance with the city's Latino or Asian constituencies (Falcon 1988; Mollenkopf 2003).[3]

After all, there are notable cultural, ideological, economic, and even racial differences between native-born Blacks and these immigrant groups. Many Latinos, for instance, do not identify as non-Whites or racial minorities, unlike African-Americans who largely do. In short, the racial commonalities between African-American New Yorkers and their Asian and Latino counterparts are limited; the differences among these groups arguably match or outweigh the similarities.

For African-Americans and Afro-Caribbean immigrants, however, there is a much stronger argument to be made for racial commonalities. The two groups of Black New Yorkers appear to have considerable mutual interests and incentives for forging a race-based alliance. Consider the prima facie case. First, Afro-Caribbeans and African-Americans obviously share the commonality of Black skin color in a country where discrimination against Blacks has a long history. . . .

The two groups experience higher levels of residential segregation than any other population in New York (Lewis Mumford Center for Comparative Urban and Regional Research 2003). Put another way, both Afro-Caribbeans and African-Americans are confined to overwhelmingly Black sections of the city.[4] The neighborhoods where the two groups live tend to be more economically distressed than majority-White areas. Afro-Caribbeans and African-Americans are exposed to the same neighborhood problems, whether they be failing schools, concentrated poverty, or crime. These two groups thus often have overlapping interests in contests over the distribution of public services and resources to city neighborhoods.

Both Afro-Caribbeans and African-Americans also have had their share of neighborhood-level tensions with Whites. Quite a few of New York's most serious cases of interracial conflict from the past two decades have involved either Afro-Caribbeans or African-Americans and White residents. In the late 1980s and early 1990s, the city was convulsed by a series of violent attacks against Blacks by groups of Whites. All but one of these incidents involved an Afro-Caribbean victim (Waters 1996). The two groups also have had turbulent relations with the city's mostly White police force. There is no need to rehearse individual instances of conflict here. But suffice it to say that there have been complaints about police brutality and misconduct from both the African-American and Afro-Caribbean communities.

Finally, Afro-Caribbean immigrants and African-Americans have similar partisan attachments. The two groups are more heavily Democratic than any other constituency—White or non-White—in the New York City electorate. Although first-generation Afro-Caribbean immigrants do not have the same long-standing, historical ties to the party as their native-born counterparts, they nonetheless have favored the Democratic line almost as much as African-Americans in their voting and registration patterns.

This shared party allegiance does not necessarily mean that Afro-Caribbeans and African-Americans have identical ideological outlooks. Indeed, Afro-Caribbean election districts are consistently several points less Democratic than African-American districts. Although both groups tend to be fairly liberal in their political outlooks, there are shades of difference between them on particular policy questions. Afro-Caribbeans, for instance, are supportive of liberal immigration policies, whereas African-Americans are more ambivalent (Fuchs 1990; Rogers 2000). A few case studies also have suggested that Afro-Caribbeans may be a little less supportive than their native-born counterparts of government solutions to social problems (Rogers 2000; Waters 1999). Still, there is no evidence of deep ideological divisions between these two overwhelmingly Democratic constituencies.

Support for the party has led to gains for African-Americans and Afro-Caribbean immigrants at the elite level. African-Americans have secured leadership positions in the Democratic county organizations. The party also has incorporated a handful of Afro-Caribbean elites in recent years. Even with these gains, both groups have less power within the party than Whites do. In Queens and the Bronx, Whites continue to control a disproportionate share of the leadership positions and influence within the Democratic Party; only in Manhattan, and in Brooklyn to a lesser extent, have African-Americans been able to wield a decisive share of power in the party organization. After many decades of unwavering allegiance to the Democratic Party, then, native-born Blacks still do not match their White counterparts in their level of influence over the organization. Afro-Caribbeans, on the other hand, are marginal players, as the party continues to ignore the vast majority of these immigrants.

All in all, the racial commonalities between African-Americans and Afro-Caribbean immigrants are more than skin deep. The two groups have a number of experiences, interests, and partisan viewpoints in common. They also boast a solid cadre of leaders who regularly interact within New York's Democratic Party. All these factors—common interests, shared ideology, and familiar leadership, coupled with the pronounced racial divide in New York City politics—would appear to pave the way for a race-based alliance between Afro-Caribbean immigrants and African-Americans. This is not to say that there are no potential divisions between the two groups. Yet the minority group view would argue that their commonalities and the strategic appeal of a race-based coalition should override such divisions. This perspective recognizes a clear imperative for these two groups of Blacks to "close racial ranks" and forge a stable political alliance (Kasinitz 1992; Carmichael and Hamilton 1967).

Race-based mobilization represents an alternative route into politics for the thousands of Afro-Caribbean immigrants who have been neglected by the Democratic Party. Outnumbered by African-Americans, these newcomers might find it hard to resist the strategic benefits of combining with their native-born counterparts to build a larger Black constituency and thereby achieve incorporation. Likewise, such mobilization could also serve as a potent source of political leverage for African-Americans seeking to enlarge their share of government resources and influence on the direction of public policy. With their combined numbers, the two groups could comprise a powerful minority bloc of voters with the potential to decide election outcomes.

THE EMPIRICAL CASE: A COALITION THAT NEVER CAME

Yet Afro-Caribbean and African-American New Yorkers thus far have been unable to establish a stable coalition. For all their prima facie commonalities, the two groups have been no more successful at fostering a race-based alliance than their non-White counterparts in other cities. There have been instances of political cooperation and common cause between them, to be sure. In 1989, for example, Afro-Caribbean and African-American voters lined up solidly behind Dinkins in his successful first bid for the mayoralty. Together, the two groups were the single largest bloc of voters to support Dinkins in the election (Arian et al. 1991). Since then, these two groups of Black ethnics have also joined together at the voting booth to support high-profile Democratic candidates for state- and citywide office, such as Senator Hillary Clinton and unsuccessful mayoral candidate Mark Green.

Similarly, the episodes of police brutality in Black neighborhoods in the late 1990s galvanized hundreds of Afro-Caribbeans and African-Americans to take to the streets and demand greater police accountability. Both the Dinkins election and the protests against police brutality appealed to the sense of racial solidarity among African-Americans and Afro-Caribbeans. The two instances might well have been viewed as promising precursors to the race-based coalition anticipated by minority group scholars. But these cases of mutual support were episodic and short lived.

Patterns of Conflict

Relations between Afro-Caribbean immigrants and African-Americans over the past two decades more often have been marked by a stubborn undercurrent of tension. My interviews with Afro-Caribbean elites reveal a pattern of friction in the political relationship between the two groups. The conflicts have not extended to rank-and-file Afro-Caribbean and African-American constituents. Nor have they revolved around anything such as competing economic interests, substantive policy differences, or ideological disagreements. Rather, the conflicts typically have been confined to the elite level and have centered mostly on matters of political turf. More specifically, African-American and Afro-Caribbean leaders have clashed over attempts by the latter group to secure descriptive representation and carve out political influence for a distinct Caribbean constituency. African-American leaders have resisted these efforts, whereas their Afro-Caribbean counterparts have complained about the opposition from their fellow Black leaders.

My interview respondents noted that African-American politicians have long been resistant or lukewarm to the prospect of Afro-Caribbean mobilization. One interviewee (November 22, 1996) conjectured that African-American opposition to Caribbean participation was one impediment to greater electoral representation for the immigrant group. As he explained, Afro-Caribbeans have yet to achieve a level of representation proportionate to their numbers, "partially because there has been opposition from African-American leaders." Caribbean Action Lobby (CAL) member and former state senator Waldaba Stewart (interview, May 2, 1997) recalled that many African-American politicians were either slow or unwilling to acknowledge the emergence of an Afro-Caribbean ethnic constituency in the 1980s.

> Ten, fifteen years ago, African-Americans—many of them—took the position that the only relevant issues were African-American issues, and in many respects ignored the growing Caribbean bloc. . . . In the 1980s, they didn't even want us to run for political office.

Indeed, as Kasinitz (1992) has recounted in his study, African-American politicians consistently opposed or refused to support Afro-Caribbean candidates for elective office in the 1980s.

The pattern continued into the 1990s. Consider former city councilwoman Una Clarke's account of her 1991 bid for a legislative seat. Clarke was seeking to represent a heavily Caribbean district in Brooklyn; her victory made her the first Caribbean-born member of the city council. Her account of the campaign underscores her perception that African-American leaders have often resisted Afro-Caribbean mobilization. The Jamaican-born politician (interview, December 13, 20, 1996) recalled,

> I helped to elect almost every African-American in central Brooklyn, and when my time came to run they were far and few in between that supported me. . . . There was not a single African-American that considered themselves "progressive" that did not come to me and did not ask for my support, and for whom I gave it. So when my time came, I thought that everybody was gonna rally around me, that there would not even be a campaign. . . . "Look your time has come." . . . Nothing of the sort happened.

In a 1999 interview, the former city councilwoman lamented, "I never saw bias until I ran in 1991. When I entered office the street talk was 'Why do these West Indians feel they have to be in politics?' " (Dao 1999). To be fair, Clarke did have the support of African-American Congressman Major Owens, who perhaps recognized that backing her would carry important symbolic value in his own increasingly Caribbean district. But staunch opposition to Clarke's campaign came from African-American Clarence Norman, Brooklyn's Democratic county leader. Norman ran his own candidate, fellow African-American Carl Andrews, for the council seat and led an ultimately aborted legal challenge to Clarke's victory in the aftermath of the election. Clarke and Norman have managed to build a cordial, if somewhat delicate, relationship since then (*New York Carib News* 1996a).

The former city councilwoman and other elite respondents also noted that African-American leaders generally have been slow to court Afro-Caribbeans as a distinct constituency. When asked whether African-American politicians reach out to Caribbean-American voters, one campaign organizer (interview, November 24, 1996) replied tersely, "Not enough. And when they do, they reach out half-heartedly." Another respondent (interview, July 5, 1997) offered,

> [Clarence] Norman has enormous political clout because he is the head of the Democratic Party in Brooklyn. From time to time, I've heard Caribbean leaders, including Una Clarke, that he would support other people than them. I'm not sure if that's the case. But I would like to see him in more [Caribbean] events. I would like to see him reach out more to the community.

Clarke rated White politicians slightly higher than African-Americans on outreach to the Caribbean population. She (interview, December 13, 20, 1996) elaborated, "I think White politicians [unlike their Black counterparts] feel compelled to do that kind of outreach. Yes. Marty Markowitz is a well-known example. And I can give other examples too."

More recently, some African-American leaders—Dinkins, Owens, Sharpton, and Rangel—have begun to make their own appeals to the immigrant community. Owens and Sharpton have been particularly vocal about incidents of police brutality involving immigrants from the Caribbean, Latin America, and Africa. Their efforts are clearly intended to acknowledge the growing numbers of foreign-born newcomers to the city and perhaps to prevent conservative interests from pursuing divide-and-conquer tactics among New York's minority constituencies. But some of my respondents still characterize these efforts by African-American leaders as begrudging or lukewarm. One (interview, November 22, 1996) recalled Dinkins's early outreach to Caribbean-Americans. "Oh, we had a rough time getting Dinkins out into the Caribbean community. . . . They say that there were some people in Dinkins's camp who were very anti-Caribbean—African-American people." In sum, many Afro-Caribbean elites remain convinced that some African-American politicians still regard the prospect of Caribbean mobilization with ambivalence or resistance.

Key historical episodes in the relations between Afro-Caribbean and African-American political elites tend to support the views of these respondents. One of the most well known instances of conflict between the two groups came during former mayor Ed Koch's 1985 bid for reelection. A group of approximately 150 politically active Afro-Caribbeans established "Caribbeans for Koch" to back the incumbent mayor's campaign. Support for Koch in the Afro-Caribbean immigrant community was hardly widespread or deep. But the group's aim was largely symbolic. That is, to secure greater access to the mayor and City Hall for Afro-Caribbean immigrants—especially since Koch would likely be reelected. Caribbeans for Koch was thus an early attempt by Afro-Caribbean elites to signal the emergence of their immigrant community as a distinctive ethnic constituency with its own aspirations to political power (Kasinitz 1992, 253).

Whatever the motivation, Caribbeans for Koch was met with a torrent of angry criticism from African-American political leaders. Their outrage was fueled by two major concerns. First, anti-Koch sentiment was pervasive in the African-American community. African-American leaders accused the mayor of fomenting anti-Black racism and exacerbating the city's racial problems with his incendiary rhetoric. In their view, then, Caribbeans for Koch showed complete disregard for the mayor's troubling record on race relations; that insensitivity was perhaps all the more incensing to African-American leaders because it came from a group of Black immigrants, who were expected to be equally as outraged by the mayor's record on race as their native-born counterparts.

Second, Caribbeans for Koch was established at the same time that African-American leaders were attempting to "close ranks" and mount an independent political initiative to replace Koch with a Black mayor. The Coalition for a Just New York brought together scores of Black politicians and activists to identify a candidate and support his campaign. The expectation by organizers was that the group would mobilize Blacks and other minority New Yorkers to help ensure electoral victory. The coalition was riven by internal division, though; their African-American candidate ran a poor campaign and lost. Yet many African-Americans strongly criticized Caribbeans for Koch for working at cross-purposes with the coalition, flouting the goals of African-American political leadership, and undermining the larger struggle for Black empowerment. As one of my elite respondents recalled, the African-American leader of the Coalition for a Just New York, Al Vann, publicly reproached Afro-Caribbean leaders for pursuing divisive strategies. "They were not happy with us [Caribbean American leaders]. Al Vann called our attempts to organize on our own tribalism" (interview, November 22, 1996). The supporters of the Coalition for a Just New York essentially saw this attempt at independent Caribbean mobilization as a strain against the tether of racial solidarity.

There have been more recent political conflicts between the two groups involving issues of racial unity and representation. In fact, the tensions have become more palpable as growing numbers of Caribbean politicians run for elective office in the name of a distinct Afro-Caribbean ethnic constituency. As the numbers of Afro-Caribbean New Yorkers have increased steadily over the past two decades, so too has the political viability and likelihood of such ethnically targeted campaigns by Caribbean politicians. These attempts by Afro-Caribbean political entrepreneurs to organize their fellow immigrants into a distinct voting bloc still engender occasional criticism and resistance from some African-American leaders.

A number of Afro-Caribbean candidates joined the fray in the last round of New York City elections by making direct appeals to their coethnics. The most notable instance was the 2000 race for Brooklyn's Eleventh Congressional District seat between nine-term incumbent Owens and former city councilwoman Clarke. Blacks comprise 55% of the district population; more than two-thirds of them trace their roots to the Caribbean. The large numbers of Afro-Caribbeans in the district is a striking example of how immigration has transformed this stretch of central Brooklyn over the past few decades. Despite these demographic shifts, African-American Congressman Owens had held on to his seat since 1982 without a serious electoral challenge. That is, until he faced a fierce test from Clarke in the 2001 Democratic primary. Although Owens won the primary and went on to retain the seat in a lopsided general election victory, the race was one of the most bitter of the campaign season.

Practically none of the rancor between the two candidates was driven by actual issue disagreements. Rather, it was fueled by two very emotionally charged factors. First, there was the underlying tableau of political betrayal. The two were long-time political allies before Clarke announced her candidacy. Owens described himself as a former mentor to the councilwoman (Hicks 2000b). He thus saw her bid to replace him as an act of political betrayal. Clarke, on the other hand, dismissed the talk of betrayal as a distraction from her true motivation for mounting her campaign: that is, to serve the district's constituents. As she put it, "Too much has been made of friendship. It's about leadership and effectiveness. I don't think he's kept up with the needs of the changing community" (Hicks 2000a). Note that Clarke's mention of the "changing community" might be taken as a thinly veiled reference to the increasing numbers of Caribbean immigrants in the district. Her allusion hints at the other factor that fueled the rancor of the contest between these two candidates.

Even more significant than this personal tableau was the pall of interethnic conflict that hung over the race. Clarke made a point of trumpeting her Caribbean roots, appealing directly to her coethnics, and painting her opponent as anti-immigrant. Her goal clearly was to announce the presence of a distinct Caribbean constituency within the majority Black Eleventh District. Even more critically, she sought to emphasize her affinity with these immigrant voters while at the same time raising doubts about the incumbent's sensitivity to their concerns. Owens, in turn, condemned Clarke for couching her campaign in what he described as a divisive ethnic chauvinism (Hicks 2000a). His complaint was echoed by a number of African-American leaders who sent Clarke a letter urging her to abandon her candidacy. The congressman lamented that Clarke's tactics would split Brooklyn's Black community and undermine the larger cause of Black empowerment. His complaints practically echoed those directed against Caribbeans for Koch by African-American leaders more than 15 years earlier.

CASE STUDY ANALYSIS

The conflicts over descriptive representation between Afro-Caribbean and African-American leaders are striking for how often the question of racial unity is invoked. The fact that racial solidarity has not provided the incentive for the two groups to overcome these differences belies the predictions of the minority group view. The steady recurrence of such conflicts suggests that even racial commonality has its limits as a potential coalition linchpin.

The Limits of Racial Solidarity

The interviews and historical evidence indicate that African-American politicians have had one prevailing criticism against their Afro-Caribbean counterparts in the conflicts over descriptive representation. They complain that the immigrants' efforts to appeal to a separate Afro-Caribbean constituency are divisive and antithetical to the cause of racial solidarity and greater Black empowerment.[5] This lament typically greets electoral campaigns by Caribbean politicians seeking to rally, mobilize, or acknowledge their coethnics as a distinct constituency. The logic behind this line of criticism is straightforward. Appealing separately to Afro-Caribbean immigrants, the complaint goes, is tantamount to splitting apart Black New Yorkers, which in turn undermines Black political power. African-American political leaders have grown increasingly concerned about these potential divisions over the past decade, as the numbers of non-White immigrants in the city have expanded. Their worry is that conservative political interests will look to exploit or even sow divisions between African-Americans and these new immigrant constituencies, thereby dousing any potential for a liberal rainbow coalition led by Blacks. It is the classic divide-and-conquer strategy. Divisions between native- and Caribbean-born Black New Yorkers, they contend, might be put to those very political designs. In short, some African-Americans argue that the mobilization of Afro-Caribbeans as a distinct constituency is ultimately a threat to Black racial solidarity and empowerment.

Afro-Caribbeans, on the other hand, insist that the opposition from African-American leaders is unfair and that appeals to racial unity are beside the point. More precisely, Afro-Caribbean politicians note that the immigrant community is large enough to warrant its own representatives and has distinctive concerns that cannot be taken for granted or glossed over with appeals to

Black racial solidarity. My elite respondents were emphatic on this point. One (interview, December 14, 1996) offered,

> I think because we [Caribbean-Americans] have some separate interests, we have a responsibility to be a distinct bloc, be it around immigration and immigration reform, be it around trade with the Caribbean. I think that we can play a pivotal role. . . . We have that obligation. And I think it's a mistake to use skin color to be the only criterion. To use skin color as the only criterion stifles both African-Americans and Caribbean-Americans.

Another respondent gave a more concise reply to the same question. He (interview, November 23, 1996) explained, "Caribbean-Americans are a distinct bloc. Of course, we share many of the same concerns of African-Americans. But we have our own needs and concerns that you just can't dismiss or take it for granted that they [African-Americans] will understand." A community activist answered the charge that Afro-Caribbean mobilization promotes divisiveness within New York's Black population this way.

> Our comment is that you have different Caucasian or White groups, you have the Irish, the Italian, the this and that. What's wrong with us? Why can't we have that too? Just because we're originally, say from Africa, does that mean we have to think and act the same way? Don't we [Caribbean-Americans] have our own needs and issues? (interview, May 2, 1997)

Furthermore, many resent what they perceive to be African-American leaders' implicit assumption that Afro-Caribbeans will be relegated to junior status in any alliance between the two groups. In a 1996 interview, for example, Clarke bristled when she was asked about African-American county leader Norman's aim to consolidate Black political power in the heavily Caribbean 43rd AD. "There are over 300,000 Caribbean Americans in Central Brooklyn. What consolidation are we talking about here? Nobody will relegate us to second class status" (*New York Carib News* 1996b). It is clear that Clarke's objection is not necessarily to the prospect of a unified Black political bloc; in fact, she and many of the Caribbean-American leaders I interviewed were supportive of the notion of a coalition between the two groups. But her worry is that the political goals and interests of Afro-Caribbean immigrants will be subordinated in any such alliance.

Clarke's concern illuminates an important analytic point about alliances built around the idea of racial solidarity. The former city councilwoman noted that African-American leaders insist on serving as racial agents on behalf of Afro-Caribbean immigrants by appealing to the notion of group unity,[6] but in doing so, they often diminish or ignore the distinctive ethnic interests of their foreign-born counterparts. Appeals to racial group unity or collective racial interests—such as the ones made by Vann, Norman, and Owens more recently—are almost always articulated in an effort to advance very specific agendas, which ultimately favor some interests over others. Vann's Coalition for a Just New York, for instance, invoked the goal of racial group unity to criticize and discourage independent mobilization by Afro-Caribbean politicians. The coalition's expectation was that all Black New Yorkers, native- and foreign-born alike, should fall in line with their hand-picked candidates and issue positions. Their notion of group unity, then, was one in which their agenda took precedence over other interests within New York's Black community, such as Afro-Caribbeans' desire for their own share of political influence.

Of course, racial solidarity in politics does not necessarily prescribe or authorize a particular agenda, set of positions, or slate of candidates. Indeed, calls to racial unity might well be seen as an invitation to discuss and reach negotiated stances on such issues. Yet appeals to racial solidarity often implicitly privilege one set of interests over others without any open debate. Even worse, the resulting bias takes cover beneath the rhetorical gloss of "natural" or "collective" racial interests that benefit the population as a whole. Consequently, interests that ought to be debated or evaluated for how they affect different constituents are instead deemed to be settled and beyond question. The case of African-Americans and Afro-Caribbeans in New York demonstrates that the group that happens to have more influence—whether by virtue of numbers, longer political history, or whatever—has the advantage of framing the agenda in this way. African-American elites in New York thus have often taken the lead in prescribing what is required for a race-based alliance or minority empowerment, even if that agenda is not necessarily conducive to the interests of Afro-Caribbeans or other non-White groups.

Furthermore, the case demonstrates that the notion of racial group unity not only favors specific interests and agendas but also can be used to impose discipline and gatekeeping. Appeals to racial group solidarity are often made in the service of mobilization efforts. But the tensions between African-American and Afro-Caribbean politicians show that racial group unity is a two-edged sword that can also be used to discourage mobilization by particular interests within the Black population, or any minority constituency for that matter. To discipline specific constituencies within the population, dominant elites often stake out certain positions and label them as the ones most in keeping with the aims of racial empowerment and the political preferences of Blacks as a whole.[7] Any interests that appear to deviate from those positions are then conveniently challenged for threatening group unity, the "true" preferences of Blacks, or the cause of empowerment. The criticisms lodged against Caribbeans for Koch by the leaders of the Coalition for a Just New York are an obvious example of this tactic.

Owens employed a similar strategy against Clarke in their 2000 primary battle. The congressman tried to portray the city councilwoman as a supporter of Mayor Rudolph Giuliani, who was notoriously unpopular among Blacks during his tenure in office. He also charged that Clarke had been silent on the issue of police brutality, about which the vast majority of Black New Yorkers were acutely concerned. In contrast, he noted that he had engaged in demonstrations to protest incidents of brutality and had even been arrested (Hicks 2000a). Owens essentially waved his civil rights credentials in support of Blacks, while implying that Clarke had none to show. The strategy served to brand the Caribbean-born candidate as a kind of race traitor, a politician out of step with Black interests and the goal of Black empowerment. Tactics such as these are likely to play a role in the conflicts between Afro-Caribbean and African-American leaders, precisely because questions of racial unity so often come into play.[8]

Why Interest Conflicts Over Descriptive Representation

The analysis demonstrates why race is not the ultimate unifying category that minority group scholars expect it to be, even for two groups of Blacks. Yet the question that remains is why the interest conflicts between Afro-Caribbean and African-American elites have focused on descriptive representation. African-Americans have achieved higher levels of influence in New York City politics than have Afro-Caribbeans and other non-White groups. As the dominant minority group in the Democratic Party, in fact, African-Americans have been able to control a significant share of the material rewards. Mobilization by Afro-Caribbean newcomers, or any other minority group for that matter, could potentially threaten their hold on these political prizes. Entrenched African-American elites thus have a rational interest in maintaining the status quo and resisting Afro-Caribbean mobilization.

Afro-Caribbeans and African-Americans are concentrated in many of the same election districts. The ascension of an Afro-Caribbean to political office could mean the displacement of an African-American incumbent. Several respondents explained this competitive intergroup dynamic.

> There definitely is competition and conflict between the two groups some-times, especially in politics. Part of the problem is, if you want to call it, we are fighting for the same political offices in the same election districts. We're fighting for the same piece of the pie. And African-Americans probably think if Caribbean people get elected they will lose out on their share. (interview, November 28, 1996)

The result is often African-American resistance to Caribbean political initiative and organization. As Clarke (interview, December 13, 20, 1996) put it, "The [African-American] attitude is 'don't try passing me. I've been here.'"

Battles over political turf and representation between the two groups thus devolve into zero-sum struggles. The conflicts are not simply over political office but also access to the government jobs and other prizes that come with it. For some African-American politicians, then, the interest in political self-preservation trumps any vision for race-based mobilization and coalition building between them and their Caribbean-born counterparts. Afro-Caribbean elites, on the other hand, worry that their interest in greater descriptive representation and policy influence will be trumped by African-American political prerogatives.

The competition between African-Americans and Afro-Caribbeans is arguably reminiscent of earlier historical conflicts among White ethnic groups. There were, for example, fierce battles over patronage and positions within the Democratic Party between Jewish and Italian New Yorkers. But there is an important distinction between those earlier interethnic conflicts and the current tensions between African-American and Afro-Caribbeans. The earlier competition for patronage and public jobs among Irish, Italian, and Jewish ethnics was diminished, or at least moderated, as one or the other group moved into private-sector employment and up the socioeconomic ladder. Italian politicians, for instance, had less of a stake in holding on to government jobs when their coethnics began to find success in private-sector professions. They were thus gradually inclined to relinquish patronage positions in government to their Jewish rivals.

Today's African-American political elites, however, are much more reluctant to concede public-sector jobs and positions to their Caribbean-born counterparts. Their determination to hold on to these forms of public patronage is not surprising. Discrimination historically has made it difficult for African-Americans to find jobs and move up the career ladder in the private sector. Government, in contrast, has long furnished them with fair and ample employment opportunities. Indeed, public-sector jobs have helped foster the expansion of a stable African-American middle class in New York and other cities. The incentive to hold on to these public-sector jobs is thus much greater for African-Americans than it was for White ethnics in the past century. To put it more bluntly, the stakes are higher.

African-Americans thus arguably have legitimate reason to worry about Afro-Caribbean political mobilization. Their concern is likely compounded by the widespread perception that Whites often view these foreign-born Blacks more favorably than African-Americans (Waters 1999).[9] Any potential advancement by Afro-Caribbeans essentially raises the specter not only of political displacement but also economic backsliding for African-Americans. By this light, Afro-Caribbeans look less like a racial in-group and potential coalition partner for native-born Blacks and more like a competing out-group that could threaten African-Americans' share of political power and public-sector resources. That threat of competition and displacement calls into question a key assumption of the minority group perspective: that is, that non-White groups are likely to find common cause and grounds for coalition building in their shared racial experiences. For all the galvanizing power that race carries, this has not been the case with African-American and Afro-Caribbean New Yorkers. Clearly, even presumed common racial interests have their limits.

Electoral Institutions

Another weakness of the minority perspective is a failure to consider how institutional factors might influence the way groups perceive and frame their interests. Racial inequalities and divisions in the political system provide considerable impetus for African-Americans, Afro-Caribbeans, and other non-Whites to forge a race-based alliance, to be sure. But whether groups opt to coalesce and capitalize on common interests—racial or otherwise—or go it alone depends to some degree to the incentive structure of the political system. The prospects hinge on how political institutions frame group perceptions about interests, competition, rewards, and so on. In the case of Afro-Caribbeans, the interviews make it clear that the immigrants are inclined to elect their own coethnics to political office rather than having African-Americans serve as their racial agents. The question is how the immigrants came to value ethnic over racial representation.

It turns out that New York's elective institutions may very well dispose them to do so. The city's electoral structure encourages groups to organize and think of themselves primarily as ethnic cohorts, rather than as racial constituents. Electoral jurisdictions in New York City closely follow the outlines of ethnic neighborhoods. The scores of community board, city council, and state assembly seats in New York are based on districts that often track the boundaries of residential enclaves bearing the unmistakable stamp of particular ethnic groups. It is not too much of an exaggeration, then, to conclude that the basic political jurisdiction in the minds of New York politicians and perhaps its voters is the ethnic neighborhood. It is the fundamental unit of the city's political cartography. New York's "city trenches," to borrow Katznelson's (1981) famous phrase, are its ethnic neighborhoods.

Consider the 40th city council district seat, formerly held by Caribbean-born Una Clarke and now occupied by her daughter. The city created this district in 1991 specifically to accommodate the proliferation of Caribbean immigrant enclaves in central Brooklyn. Most of the pressure to establish the seat came from Afro-Caribbean politicians. The new district essentially gave the ethnic group an opportunity to garner its own share of political representation. As Stewart of CAL (interview, May 2, 1997) put it, "We [Caribbean politicians] noticed that other groups had districts to represent their people, we felt we should have some too." His remark suggests that the decision to push for a heavily Caribbean city council district was not merely the result of constituent pressure or elite initiative. Rather, it was encouraged by politicians' perceptions of the institutional logic of the city's electoral districts. Once institutional arrangements are in place, they tend to influence how elites understand their interests, their ties to constituents, and their relations with other groups. Sure enough, the 40th city council seat has come to be held perpetually and predictably by a Caribbean politician, fulfilling the logic of the district's original design.

More generally, the city's electoral battles are waged from these ethnic neighborhood trenches. The most obvious way for an aspiring politician to build a constituent base in New York is to rally and mobilize voters in ethnic neighborhoods. If a politician can put together a sizable, cohesive bloc of ethnic votes at the neighborhood level, he or she essentially can become a serious player in New York's political game. Politicians are thus often encouraged to make ethnic group appeals. Ethnic politics has long been a staple of political life in American cities, to be sure. The ethnic and immigrant enclaves across New York City are a hard-to-miss source of votes. But the close continuity between the design of the city's electoral institutions and the pattern of its ethnic neighborhoods reinforces this ethnically conscious form of political organization and mobilization. Ethnic appeals are practically dictated by the logic of the city's political jurisdictions.

Some researchers have argued convincingly that this neighborhood-based system of representation serves to regulate and perhaps mute interethnic tensions (Skerry 1993; Mollenkopf 1999). On this view, the system channels interethnic conflicts that might otherwise spill over into the streets and translates them to the bargaining table of the political process where they can be managed or resolved. That may explain why cities like New York and San Antonio, which both boast this kind of neighborhood-based system, have been less susceptible to volatile intergroup clashes than Los Angeles, where no such system exists. Nevertheless, this electoral institutional design simply transfers the potential for interethnic tension from the neighborhood to the elite level, where leaders are often encouraged to position themselves and relate to each other as representatives of particular ethnic groups. The interethnic conflicts thus move from the neighborhood level to the party system, the campaign trail, and the legislature.

It is no wonder, then, that relations between Afro-Caribbean and African-American political elites have been plagued by interethnic tensions over descriptive representation. The potential for interethnic conflict between these two groups of Black leaders is fairly telegraphed in the pattern of Black neighborhood settlement across New York City. Recall that African-Americans and Afro-Caribbean immigrants often live in adjoining neighborhoods or even share the same ones. When these areas are carved up into electoral jurisdictions, they easily become arenas for ethnically tinged, intraBlack bickering over descriptive representation. When a district that was predominantly African-American is somehow redrawn to give growing numbers of Afro-Caribbean immigrants a numerical advantage, the strategic incentive for Caribbean political entrepreneurs to make targeted ethnic appeals is hard to resist.

There are a few who avoid playing the ethnic card in campaigns. State Senator John Sampson is a good example. This second-generation Afro-Caribbean New Yorker has largely refrained from making exclusive appeals to his coethnics.[10] He instead campaigns to Blacks generally and scrupulously avoids the interethnic schisms that have erupted among the city's Black leaders. But most other Afro-Caribbean politicians have followed the ethnic strategy. The price of giving in to the temptation is the danger of engendering interethnic conflict with African-American political elites faced with the specter of electoral displacement. The primary battle between Clarke and Owens is just one of the more well-known recent examples. But several cases fit this predicted pattern.

A simple historical comparison helps to demonstrate how the institutional design of New York's electoral districts shapes intergroup dynamics. It is no coincidence that the tensions over descriptive representation between Afro-Caribbean and African-American political elites have emerged only in the past two decades. Prior to 1989, the city council was not composed of the 51 neighborhood-based seats it boasts today. Rather, it consisted of 10 at-large districts, with 2 designated for each of the five boroughs (Macchiarola and Diaz 1993). Council members were elected on a borough-wide basis. Unlike the current neighborhood-based system, the at-large configuration compelled officeholders and candidates to make broad appeals beyond the boundaries of the city's ethnic enclaves.

An Afro-Caribbean politician with aspirations to the city council, for instance, could hardly afford to target only Caribbean voters in select neighborhoods. Minority candidates could win only by making wide cross-ethnic and sometimes cross-racial appeals. Earlier generations of Afro-Caribbean politicians thus refrained from marketing themselves as ethnic representatives of a distinct Caribbean constituency or appealing exclusively to their coethnics. Rather, they attempted to speak for Blacks at large and did not draw a distinction between themselves and their African-American counterparts (Kasinitz 1992; Watkins-Owens 1996). Consequently, there were almost no interethnic tensions over descriptive political representation between the two groups in that earlier era. This is not to say that there were no conflicts at all between Afro-Caribbeans and African-Americans. There were the inevitable cultural clashes and occasional conflicts over jobs when the immigrants first began migrating to New York (Vickerman 1999; Watkins-Owens 1996; Foner 1985; Hellwig 1978; Reid 1939).

Yet the friction between the two groups did not have much of a political dimension.[11] Ethnicity was simply not a major source of division or conflict among Blacks in the electoral sphere. With the shift to neighborhood-based city council seats, however, there is greater electoral incentive for Afro-Caribbean politicians to engage in the kind of ethnically targeted appeals that lead to tensions with African-American leaders. The past two decades have thus seen a marked increase in political conflicts between the two groups. Although this historical shift is not conclusive evidence, it does suggest indirectly that institutional configurations have some casual impact on intergroup racial and ethnic dynamics.

A brief comparison across cities also makes the point. The city of Hartford, like New York, is home to a sizable minority population of American- and Caribbean-born Blacks. Both groups, in fact, comprise roughly similar proportions of the minority population in both cities, although New York fairly dwarfs Hartford in absolute numbers. African-Americans in Hartford, like their counterparts in New York, also have enjoyed greater levels of electoral representation and influence than the city's other minority constituencies. But in the past decade, the other groups have started to make their own serious bids for political power. Afro-Caribbean leaders in Hartford have begun to organize their coethnics to participate in politics, much like their fellow Black immigrants in New York have been doing for the past two to three decades.

Yet these efforts by Hartford's Caribbean-born residents have generated considerably less friction and resistance from African-American leaders there than have the attempts by their counterparts in New York. A number of factors may explain this difference in intergroup dynamics, to be sure. But one important variable may be the design of Hartford's electoral institutions.

Unlike New York's neighborhood-based city council districts, Hartford's legislature is composed of at-large seats. By the logic of the at-large electoral design, ethnically targeted campaigning must be balanced by broader appeals to other constituencies, which ultimately may serve to moderate or minimize interethnic conflict. It bears noting that the Hartford comparison is also not conclusive support for the casual impact of electoral institutions on intergroup dynamics, but it is certainly suggestive.

In the New York case, it should be emphasized that the interethnic tensions between these two groups of Black leaders took shape as Afro-Caribbean ethnic enclaves have developed and expanded to proportions large enough to leave an imprint or have an impact on the pattern of neighborhood-based electoral districts in boroughs such as Brooklyn and Queens. Prior to the 1980s, Caribbean settlements in these areas were too small to have much of an influence on the design of the city's system of elective representation or stand alone as a politically viable ethnic constituency. What is more, African-American and Afro-Caribbean political leaders could talk of representing the city's Blacks without drawing any further ethnic distinctions. Representing Blacks essentially meant African-Americans by and large. With the dramatic growth of the Caribbean immigrant population over the past few decades, however, intra-Black ethnic distinctions have taken on political salience. The potential for intergroup conflict is now reinforced by the city's electoral institutions.

The Absence of an Institutional Mechanism

Still, a final question remains: Why have the two groups been unable to resolve these interethnic differences over descriptive representation to build a coalition around their intraracial common interests and shared policy concerns? If New York's electoral institutions have encouraged or exacerbated the interethnic conflicts between Afro-Caribbean and African-American political leaders, the absence of certain other kinds of institutions have made those differences difficult to bridge. Sonenshein (2003b) was correct that shared interests, ideological compatibility, personal ties, and strong leadership are all essential for forging sturdy intergroup alliances. But his formulation overlooks one other important building block. Institutions are equally as important as interests, ideology, personal relations, and leadership for cultivating and sustaining coalitions. Viable institutions provide a framework for groups to engage in social learning, that is, articulate shared interests, acknowledge distinct ones, reinforce ideological commitments, solidify personal ties, and identify promising leaders.[12]

Race-based alliances among non-White groups do not simply spring from some essential racial viewpoint or presumptive group interest. Rather, such coalitions require an institutional mechanism for expressing and mobilizing substantive, shared racial interests—a point that proponents of the minority group view sometimes miss or overlook. Blacks in Chicago, for instance, developed a network of community organizations in the early 1980s that proved crucial to the election of the city's first Black mayor in 1983 (Grimshaw 1992). This institutional framework allowed Black Chicagoans to negotiate internal divisions, identify a strong mayoral candidate in Harold Washington, and muster the voter mobilization necessary to win the election. Similarly, institutional networks have been critical to successful intergroup coalition building in cities such as Atlanta (Stone 1989). The absence of such an institutional vehicle for New York's Afro-Caribbean and African-American political leaders largely explains their failure to override interethnic tensions and build an enduring race-based alliance.

The Democratic Party may appear, at first blush, to be a potentially viable institutional site for Afro-Caribbean and African-American elites to organize a race-based movement. By virtue of their combined numbers inside the party, the two groups have the makings of a powerful caucus capable of a reform. The overwhelming attachment of African-American and Afro-Caribbean voters to the Democratic Party also gives these leaders the electoral clout necessary for mounting such a challenge. In fact, a Black reform impulse surfaced in the party's Brooklyn organization in the mid-1970s. But it faded as infighting erupted and many of the erstwhile insurgents made peace with the regular Democratic machine. Since then, there has been no major, viable movement for insurgency by Blacks in Brooklyn or the other borough party organizations.

The failure of African-Americans and Afro-Caribbeans to mount an insurgent movement from within the Democratic Party confirms the long-standing common sense of V.O. Key's (1949) 50-year-old observation about one-party systems. Key argued that one-party systems tend to be breeding grounds for factionalism. Factions, he noted, give rise to personality-driven politics that focus on invidious status or group distinctions and drown out substantive policy issues. Hence, one-party systems, such as New York's Democratic organization, are notoriously unsuitable institutions for launching and sustaining reform movements. It is no wonder then that African-American and Afro-Caribbean leaders have been unable to put together an insurgent coalition from within New York's dominant Democratic party. Their relations within the party show all the symptoms of Key's diagnosis: squabbles over turf between individual politicians and disagreements over descriptive representation that deteriorate into interethnic schisms. Congruent with Key's predictions, tensions between Afro-Caribbean and African-American political leaders in the party tend to obscure the substantive issues in which they may share a common racial interest or mutual understanding.

Despite the dominance of the Democratic Party in New York City politics, there is a modest Republican organization that conceivably could serve as a site for establishing a reformist coalition. Mollenkopf (1992, 89) reminds us that the Republican Party played this role in New York politics for many decades, uniting "discontented elements of the city electorate into potent, if short-lived, fusion movements." But it no longer does so today. The Republican Party has lost much of its organizational muscle and has transformed into a more conservative institution. As Mollenkopf (1997, 105) noted, "The Republican party has forsaken its traditional role as the organizational kernel of reform." Even more significantly, the party has made virtually no effort to court African-American and Afro-Caribbean voters. There is thus little chance that African-Americans and Afro-Caribbeans will mount a race-based movement for reform from either the Republican or Democratic Party.

Parties, however, hardly exhaust the list of potential institutional sites from which Afro-Caribbean and African-American New Yorkers could cultivate and sustain a reformist alliance. In fact, minority group scholars note that insurgent movements for greater racial inclusion typically begin from bases outside the conventional party system. Movements for African-American political empowerment and racial reform, for example, historically have begun in churches, civic groups, and neighborhood-based service organizations. These institutions provide a critical site for African-Americans to delineate their interests, clarify ideology, groom leaders, and strike alliances with other groups (Dawson 1994a).[13] In cities such as Chicago and Atlanta, African-Americans used these sites to forge reformist alliances with liberal Whites (Grimshaw 1992; Kleppner 1985; Stone 1989).

In New York, African-Americans attempted to sustain reform movements from a network of community-based organizations in the 1970s and early 1980s. The short-lived insurgent movement led by Al Vann in the 1970s took root in this network (Green and Wilson 1989). Vann's race-based alliance, the Coalition for Community Empowerment (CCE), brought together African-American politicians with ties to Brooklyn's Black churches and the community action programs spawned by President Johnson's War on Poverty and Mayor John Lindsay's liberal neighborhood government policies. The alliance included figures such as Congressman Owens and Assemblyman Norman, who traced their political beginnings to this network of community-based institutions. A handful of Afro-Caribbeans were also involved in the coalition, although none in leadership positions. Most of them had ties to community-based institutions, particularly school and community boards.

In the context of this institutional network, alliance members united around a shared vision for greater Black political empowerment, community control, and racial reform. As members were elected to the state and city legislatures, the alliance became a virtual party within Brooklyn's Democratic Party. The movement collapsed in the early 1980s, however, as its institutional base began to decay. The network of community-based agencies that had furnished an organizational framework for the movement was absorbed by the local city government and lost much of its political independence. Many of these agencies fell into disarray in the face of fiscal retrenchment and federal funding cutbacks. The African-American churches that had also supplied leaders for the movement remained an important part of some Brooklyn neighborhoods, but they struggled to attract younger parishioners. Consequently, they were no longer a leading source of leadership for Black politics in Brooklyn. Bereft of its independent institutional base, the CCE began to lose its way. Internal divisions surfaced, former insurgents were absorbed into the regular party organizations, and the push for reform ebbed.

Just as the movement was deteriorating in the 1980s, the CCE came into conflict with Afro-Caribbean elites who were seeking to win seats on the state assembly. Most of these Afro-Caribbean candidates had no ties to the institutional network that had spawned the African-American-led CCE movement. They were largely entrepreneurial lone wolves, such as Trinidadian-born Anthony Agard, or endorsees of immigrant organizations, such as Panamanian-born Stewart of the CAL. In short, they had no institutional ties to the African-American politicians involved in the CCE. The organization fiercely opposed the Afro-Caribbean candidates in their races for the state legislature. Without a shared institutional framework to build trust and dialogue, African-American politicians in the CCE and Afro-Caribbean elites were unable to resolve their differences in the interest of their shared racial goals.

THE FUTURE OF RACE-BASED COALITIONS

Not much has changed since then. The absence of an institutional mechanism for uniting and building trust between Afro-Caribbean and African-American elites diminishes the prospects of race-based mobilization. Of course, there have been small pockets of mutual cooperation and attempts at shared institution building in parts of Brooklyn and Queens—in political clubs and elsewhere. Recently, for example, native and foreign-born Black New Yorkers established a citywide organization to ensure that their numbers in the population are accurately reflected in the decennial census (John Flateau, personal communication, June 16, 2000). It is too early, however, to tell if the organization will last, especially since it has yet to face the difficult challenges posed by the city's electoral politics; reapportionment, for instance, could easily trigger the usual conflicts over descriptive representation. All in all, then, none of these recent organizational efforts have quite taken firm root; most have been ad hoc and short lived.

One potential institutional network that already has the benefit of longevity is New York's constellation of public unions. Emerging research on labor union activity in cities such as New York and Los Angeles over the past decade suggests that these institutions are beginning to serve a key role in the political adjustment of new immigrants to the United States (Wong 2000). This marks a radical break with a long, notorious history of anti-immigrant activity among American labor unions. Scholars speculate that changing demographic and economic realities have precipitated this shift. The growing numbers of non-White immigrants in American manufacturing and service-sector jobs, coupled with the overall decline in union membership, has compelled labor leaders to recruit these newcomers (Greenhouse 2000).

What is more, the new generation of labor union leaders are drawn largely from the ranks of native-born racial minority groups. African-Americans, for example, are at the helm of several active unions in New York. These native-born Blacks and their Caribbean-born counterparts, in fact, comprise a significant share of the membership in two of the city's most powerful public employee unions, Local 1199 of hospital workers and District Council 37 of city workers. By sharing these institutional vehicles, the two groups can engage in the kind of social learning and mutual search for shared interests that make coalition building easier. It may turn out that these unions prove to be the most promising institutional site for identifying leaders skilled in bridging the intergroup divisions among Afro-Caribbeans, African-Americans, and other racial minority populations. Still, there is an important caution to bear in mind. Much like local party machines, unions historically have been prone to internal wars of ethnic and racial succession (Mink 1986). Whether these union organizations can navigate those potential pitfalls well enough to become a stable site for a race-based alliance remains to be seen.

Some observers speculate that the ideological fervor for race-based mobilization has diminished, with the successes of the civil rights movement and the measurable minority group progress of the past few decades (Sleeper 1993). Simply put, the claim is that race-based movements are politically passé. Post-civil rights concerns, the argument goes, do not generate the same sense of urgency and consensus among minorities that fueled the civil rights movement. The conclusion is that race-based mobilization will be unlikely or difficult to foster in the current ideological climate. Yet Afro-Caribbean and African-American outrage over issues such as police brutality suggests that there are still grounds for race-based mobilization.

This study, however, shows that racial commonalities are not enough to generate an alliance of minority groups; indeed, appeals to racial unity actually may privilege some interests over others and thus heighten divisions among non-White groups. What is more, the institutional design of a city's electoral system may exacerbate these differences. To avoid these perverse effects, political leaders looking to foster race-based alliances must turn to neighborhood and community institutions. Without an institutional framework to identify shared issue concerns, acknowledge distinct interests, and generate dialogue, stable coalitions between African-Americans and Afro-Caribbeans or other racial minority newcomers will be difficult to generate.

REFERENCES

Arian, A., A. Goldberg, J. Mollenkopf, and E. Rogowsky. 1990. *Changing New York City politics*. New York: Routledge.

Browning, R., D. Marshall, and D. Tabb, eds. 2003. *Racial politics in American cities*. 3rd ed. New York: Longman.

Carmichael, S., and C. Hamilton. 1967. *Black power: The politics of liberation in America*. New York: Random House.

Crowder K., and L. Tedrow. 2001. West Indians and the residential landscape of New York. In *Islands in the city: West Indian migration to New York*, edited by Nancy Foner. Berkeley: Univ. of California Press.

Dao, J. 1999. Immigrant diversity slows traditional political climb. *New York Times*. December 28.

Dawson, M. 1994a. *Behind the mule: Race and class in African-American politics*. Princeton, NJ: Princeton Univ. Press.

———. 1994b. A Black counterpublic? Economic earthquakes, racial agenda(s), and Black politics. *Public Culture* 7:195–223.

Falcon, A. 1988. Black and Latino politics in New York City: Race and ethnicity in a changing urban context. In *Latinos and the political system*, edited by F. Chris Garcia. Notre Dame, IN: Nore Dame Univ. Press.

Foner, N. 1985. Race and color: Jamaican immigrants in London and New York. *International Migration Review* 19:284–313.

Fuchs, L. 1990. *The American kaleidoscope: Race, ethnicity, and civic culture*. Hanover, NH: Wesleyan Univ. Press.

Green, C., and B. Wilson. 1989. *The struggle for Black empowerment in New York City: Beyond the politics of pigmentation*. New York: Praeger.

Greenhouse, S. 2000. Despite defeat on China bill, labor is on rise. *New York Times*, April 28.

Grimshaw, W. 1992. *Bitter fruit: Black politics and the Chicago machine*, Chicago: Univ. of Chicago Press.

Hellwig, D. 1978. Black meets Black: Afro-American reactions to West Indian immigrants in the 1920s. *South Atlantic Quarterly* 72:205–25.

Henry, C., and C. Munoz Jr. 1991. Ideological and interest linkages in California rainbow politics. In *Racial and ethnic politics in California*, edited by B. Jackson and M. Preston. Berkeley, CA: IGS Press.

Hicks, J. 2000a. Bitter primary contest hits ethnic nerve among Blacks. *New York Times*, August 31.

———. 2000b. Term limits turn old allies into opponents; protege against mentor, backer against incumbent. *New York Times*, March 22.

Holder, C. 1980. The rise of the West Indian politician in New York City. *Afro-Americans in New York Life and History* 4:45–59.

Jackson, J. 2001. *Harlemworld: Doing race and class in contemporary Black America*. Chicago: Univ. of Chicago Press.

Jennings, J. 1997. *Race and politics: New challenges and responses for Black activism*. London: Verso.

Kasinitz, P. 1992. *Caribbean New York: Black immigrants and the politics of race*. Ithaca, NY: Cornell Univ. Press.

Katznelson, I. 1981. *City trenches: Urban politics and the patterning of class in the United States*. New York: Pantheon.

Key, V. O. 1949. *Southern politics in state and nation*. New York: Vintage.

Kim, C. 1999. The racial triangulation of Asian Americans. *Politics and Society* 27(1): 105–38.

———. 2000. *Bitter fruit: The politics of Black-Korean conflict in New York City*. New Haven, CT: Yale Univ. Press.

Kleppner, P. 1985. *Chicago divided: The making of a Black mayor*. Dekalb: Northern Illinois Press.

Lewis Mumford Center for Comparative Urban and Regional Research. 2002. *Separate and unequal: The neighborhood gap for Blacks and Hispanics in metropolitan America.* Albany, NY: Univ. at Albany Press.

Lewis Mumford Center for Comparative Urban and Regional Research. 2003. *Black diversity in metropolitan America.* Albany, NY: Univ. at Albany Press.

Macchiarola, F., and J. Diaz. 1993. Minority political empowerment in New York City: Beyond the Voting Rights Act. *Political Science Quarterly* 108(1): 37–57.

Marable, M. 1994. Building coalitions among communities of color. In *Blacks, Latinos, and Asians in urban America,* edited by J. Jennings. New York: Praeger.

Mink, G. 1986. *Old labor and new immigrants in American political development.* Ithaca. NY: Cornell Univ. Press.

Mollenkopf, J. 1992. *A phoenix in the ashes: The rise and fall of the Koch coalition in New York City.* Princeton, NJ: Princeton Univ. Press.

———. 1997. New York: The great anomaly. In *Racial politics in American cities,* 2nd ed., edited by R. Browning, D. Marshall, and D. Tabb. New York: Longman.

———. 1999. Urban political conflicts and alliances: New York and Los Angeles compared. In *The handbook of international migration: The American experience,* edited by C. Hirschman, P. Kasinitz, and J. DeWind. New York: Russell Sage Foundation.

———. 2003. New York: The great anomaly. In *Racial politics in American cities,* 3rd ed., edited R. P. Browning, D. R. Marshall, and D. H. Tabb, New York: Longman.

New York Carib News. 1996a. April 23.

New York Carib News. 1996b. October 1.

———. 1988. Black urban regime: Structural origins and constraints. *Comparative Urban and Community Research* 1:138–89.

Reid, I. 1939. *The Negro immigrant: His background characteristics and social adjustments, 1899–1937.* New York: AMS Press.

Rogers, R. 2000. Between race and ethnicity: Afro-Caribbean immigrants, African Americans, and the politics of incorporation, Ph.D. diss., Princeton University.

Skerry, P. 1993. *Mexican Americans: The ambivalent minority.* Cambridge, MA: Harvard Univ. Press.

Sleeper, J. 1993. The end of the rainbow. *New Republic,* November 20–25.

Sonenshein, R. 1993. *Politics in black and white: Race and power in Los Angeles.* Princeton, NJ: Princeton Univ. Press.

———. 2003a. Post-incorporation politics in Los Angeles. In *Racial politics in American cities,* 3rd ed., edited by R. P. Browning, D. R. Marshall, and D. H. Tabb. New York: Longman.

———. 2003b. The prospects for multiracial coalitions: Lessons from America's three largest cities. In *Racial politics in American cities,* 3rd ed., edited by R. P. Browning, D. R. Marshall, and D. H. Tabb. New York: Longman.

Stone, C. 1989. *Regime politics: Governing Atlanta, 1946–1988.* Lawrence: University Press of Kansas.

Stone, C., and C. Pierannunzi. 1997. Atlanta and the limited reach of electoral control. In *Racial politics in American cities,* 2nd ed., edited by R. Browning, D. Marshall, and D. Tabb. New York: Longman.

Tate, K. 1993. *From protest to politics: The new Black voters in American elections.* Cambridge, MA: Harvard Univ. Press.

Vickerman, M. 1999. *Crosscurrents: West Indian immigrants and race.* New York: Oxford Univ. Press.

Warren, C., and D. Moreno. 2003. Power without a program: Hispanic incorporation in Miami. In *Racial politics in American cities,* 3rd ed., edited by R. Browning, D. Marshall, and D. Tabb. New York: Longman.

Waters, M. 1996. Ethnic and racial groups in the USA: Conflict and cooperation. In *Ethnicity and power in the contemporary world,* edited by K. Rupesinghe and V. Tishkov. London: U.N. University.

Waters, M. 1999. *Black identities: West Indian immigrant dreams and American realities.* Cambridge, MA: Harvard Univ. Press.

Watkins-Owens, I. 1996. *Blood relations: Caribbean immigrants and the Harlem community, 1900–1930.* Bloomington: Indiana Univ. Press.

Wong, J. 2000. Institutional context and political mobilization among Mexican and Chinese immigrants. Paper presented at the Immigrant Political Participation in New York City Working Conference, New York, June.

NOTES

1. I use *non-White* and *minority* interchangeably throughout this article to refer to Blacks, Latinos, and Asians. I distinguish these three groups from Whites, who remain the majority racial population in this country. It should be noted that Latinos, unlike the other groups, are not classified as a distinct racial group by the census. In fact, they may identify as Black, White, or other under the census classification scheme. Most opt for White or other. Yet urban scholars typically define Latinos as a minority group by virtue of their numbers and cultural distinctiveness. This article follows that convention.

2. I use *Afro-Caribbean* to refer to Black immigrants from the Anglophone Caribbean region and to distinguish them from their counterparts from the French- and Spanish-speaking Caribbean. Anglophone Caribbean immigrants are the focus of this study. Although I use the term *Afro-Caribbean*, most of these Black newcomers refer to themselves as *Caribbean American* or *West Indian*. New York's Afro-Caribbean immigrants hail from throughout the Caribbean region, but the largest numbers come from Jamaica, Trinidad, and Guyana.

3. Scholars have puzzled over the absence of a strong minority coalition in New York. The city would seem to be fertile soil for this kind of alliance. The fact that one has yet to take root makes New York a "great anomaly" in the urban politics literature (Mollenkopf 2003).

4. Afro-Caribbean immigrants living in these overwhelmingly Black areas have carved out their own distinctive residential niches, often of marginally higher socioeconomic quality than surrounding African-American neighborhoods (Crowder and Tedrow 2001). Yet this modest economic advantage has not won them access to more integrated neighborhoods, a predicament they share with their middle-class African-American counterparts.

5. The obvious irony of this complaint is that African-Americans view attempts by a group of Black immigrants to achieve political influence as a threat to Black empowerment, rather than a step in that direction.

6. I borrow the term *racial agents* from a conversation with Jack Citrin.

7. The essentialist behavioral notions of racial identity that pervade everyday, commonsense thinking in this country follow the same perverse logic. That is, racial groups are deemed to "behave" or "act" in keeping with an identifiable mold. Blacks, say, are expected to be good dancers, or Asians good students. When group members deviate from the behavioral mold, they are labeled racially inauthentic. For a useful discussion of how this essentialist conflation of racial identity and behavior nonetheless allows for an antiessentialist critique of racial categories, see Jackson (2001).

8. Challenging the racial credentials or commitments of a fellow Black politician in electoral competition is a strategy that surfaces even among African-Americans themselves. The famously acrimonious 2002 race between Newark mayoral incumbent Sharpe James and young upstart Cory Booker is a recent example. Although both men are African-American, questions of racial solidarity and authenticity emerged nonetheless. The James camp took the tactic to bizarre extremes when they began circulating rumors that Booker was actually White and passing as Black to win the support of Newark's mostly Black voters. Such strategies likely will become even more common as the Black population becomes more diverse in cities around the country.

9. For a thoughtful discussion on how White perceptions can engender conflict among subordinate minority groups, see Kim (1999, 2000).

10. Sampson's avoidance of the ethnic strategy may be due to his socialization in the United States. Born to Caribbean parents in New York, his ties to African-Americans run deep. His second-generation experiences and how they influence his political choices may be a precursor to the future of Black politics in New York. He is part of a new, expanding population of second-generation Caribbean New Yorkers. These children of Black immigrants likely will have a significant influence on the city's political future, as they become increasingly involved in the electoral process. It remains to be seen whether they will identify mostly as second-generation Caribbean ethnics or as African-Americans. But whatever the case, they may find coalition building with African-Americans easier than their parents have if they interact regularly with their counterparts in institutional settings.

11. African-American leaders at the time accused White party leaders of playing ethnic favorites by doling out the choicest patronage jobs to Afro-Caribbeans, who tended to be better educated than their native-born counterparts (Watkins-Owens 1996; Hellwig 1978; Holder

...more job competition than political conflict, as the party structure was
...ues of social mobility open to Black New Yorkers.
...ers to the process by which potential coalition partners acquire knowledge
...ng of each other's interests (Stone 1989).
...r, these institutions comprise what Dawson (1994b) called the AfricanAmeri-
...public.

12

Black Incumbents and a Declining Racial Divide

ZOLTAN L. HAJNAL

In a nation that has long been divided by race, the election of black leaders is of great historic importance. But it is in many ways an uncertain step with unknown consequences. Black leadership raises both meaningful possibilities and real risks, especially when African Americans are elected in racially mixed areas. After winning elections, black officials must lead communities that are racially diverse and often bitterly divided. How does white America respond to African American leadership? We have anecdotal evidence from various cases, but we know very little about the general pattern and ultimate consequences of black leadership: We don't know whether minority political leadership tends to exacerbate or reduce racial tension, whether black incumbents are more or less successful than their white counterparts in subsequent elections, or under what political, economic, and racial conditions white support can be maintained or increased over time.

THE INFORMATION MODEL

The information model suggests that black leadership should significantly change the voting behavior of whites and the way white Americans think about black candidates because the candidates' terms impart critical information that greatly reduces uncertainty and dispels white fears about blacks and black leadership. The logic is fairly straightforward. When black challengers run for office, many white residents are uncertain about the consequences of black leadership and fear that black leaders will favor the black community over the white community, thereby reversing the racial status quo. To prevent this from happening, large segments of the white community are apt to mobilize to prevent a black electoral victory. But if a black challenger is able to overcome white opposition and win office, most white fears are not borne out. Black leadership may lead to marginal changes to a few aspects of black well-being, but for the vast majority of the white community, the world under

From Zoltan L. Hajnal, *Changing White Attitudes Toward Black Political Leadership*, pp. 14, 15, 41–54, 60–66, 72. © Zoltan L. Hajnal 2007. Reprinted with the permission of Cambridge University Press.

black leaders is strikingly similar to the world under white leaders. Once black officeholders have the opportunity to prove that black leadership generally does not harm white interests, uncertainty should fade, whites' views of blacks and black leadership should improve, and more whites should be willing to consider voting for black candidates. Black leadership therefore serves an important although difficult to observe informational role.

The critical question is not whether whites will vote for blacks but *under what circumstances* they will vote for blacks. And, more specifically, what difference does black incumbency make? Does experience under black incumbents change the way whites think about black candidates, make them more willing to support black incumbents, and reduce the role of race in biracial electoral contests?

DOES INCUMBENCY MATTER?

To begin to answer these questions, I collected data on white voting patterns in a representative sample of mayoral elections involving black candidates. I collected these data with two goals in mind. My first goal was to provide as direct an assessment as possible of the impact of incumbency on the white vote. To do so, I amassed data on white voting patterns in sets of two mayoral elections in cities that have experienced a transition to black leadership. For each case, I contrast the white vote in the first election, in which a black challenger ran successfully against a white incumbent to become the first black mayor of the city, with the white vote in the election immediately following, in which the black mayor ran for reelection against a white opponent.[1] By comparing sets of two elections that involve the same black candidates, I am able to assess the effects of incumbency on the white vote directly. I confine my analysis to general or run-off elections rather than primaries to avoid complications introduced by multiple candidacies and voter disinterest. To analyze other aspects of the electoral outcome, I also collected data on overall turnout and the margin of victory in each election.

My second goal was to be as comprehensive as possible in order to ensure that the results of the data analysis are representative. Since all previous studies had considered only a small number of cases, I decided to create a complete data set that included all relevant cases across the country. To do this, I compiled a set of the entire universe of cases for cities with populations of over 100,000 that fit the criteria just outlined. In total, there were fifty-two elections in twenty-six cities. While this is admittedly a small number, it represents two-thirds of the cases of white–black transition in large American cities. What is happening in this set of cases, then, should be more or less what happens generally when a white mayor is replaced by a black mayor in a large American city.

It is also important to note that my selection criteria do not appear to have created a set of cities with exceptionally liberal or especially racially tolerant white populations. Although some of the cities, such as San Francisco, Minneapolis, and Seattle, are generally seen as liberal, others, including Memphis, Birmingham, and Houston, would be much more likely to be labeled conservative, and still others, Durham and Hartford, for example, fall somewhere in the middle. As we will see, most whites in these cities were not ready for black leadership and not particularly racially tolerant when black candidates were trying to win the mayoralty for the first time. On the contrary, black challengers in many of these cities faced nearly unanimous opposition. And, in many cases, whites turned out in record numbers to try to prevent a black victory. In fact, a comparison of the racial attitudes of white residents in these cities prior to the election of a black mayor with the racial attitudes of white residents in other cities using the survey data from the ANES found no consistent or substantial differences in white views. For these cities, the key to black victory was the black vote, not white support. This comports with existing research that suggests that the size of the black community and the resources of the black community are much more important in determining the success of black candidates than the nature of the white community (Karnig and Welch 1980).

To illustrate how white voters respond to black mayoral leadership, Table 2 presents a comparison of black challenger and black incumbent elections. The numbers tell a fairly clear story: when the same black candidate runs for reelection for the first time as an incumbent, the proportion of white voters who support that candidate grows by an average of 6 percentage points, from 30 to 36 percent of all white voters. A six-point shift in the vote is certainly not unheard of in American elections, and one could argue that this change represents relatively little movement on the part of white voters. Yet this relatively small change is clearly important, for if whites were reacting to incumbent black mayors as they have responded to other forms of black empowerment in the past, we would have seen the opposite: a white backlash characterized by heightened mobilization and resistance. Similarly, if prejudice were the main factor behind white opposition to black candidates, we would most likely see no change at all. The fact that white support grew, even if by a small amount, is very informative.

The growth in white support is more impressive when one considers that whites in these cities had only two or four years (depending on the length of a mayoral term) to experience black leadership. In cities like Los Angeles and Newark, where the same black mayor ran repeatedly for reelection, white support grew with each election. According to Sonenshein (1993), Tom Bradley's white support in Los Angeles grew in each of his first four elections. All told, his white support almost doubled from 32 percent in 1969 to 62 percent in 1985. Thus, the six-point shift may represent only the first step in growing white acceptance of black leadership. In addition, this analysis in some ways understates the exceptional nature of the white support that these black incumbents won. I do not compare the average challenger to the average incumbent but instead focus only on the most successful black challengers. Most black challengers lose their electoral bids. Thus, if I had included a cross-section of all black challengers, the contrast between support for challengers and support for incumbents would be much greater. The limited data that are available attest to this point. In an analysis of a series of city council and mayoral elections in Atlanta, Bullock (1984) found that incumbency more than doubled

TABLE 2

Voting Patterns in Black Challenger and Black Incumbent Elections

	Black Challenger	Black Incumbent
White voters for black candidate (%)	30	36
Margin of victory (%)	12	21
Turnout of registered voters (%)	59	52

white crossover voting. His findings were echoed in an analysis of the vote in mayoral and council elections in New Orleans (Vanderleeuw 1991).

It is worth noting that the black candidates in the sample gained substantial white support as incumbents *despite the fact* that they did not get the boost in electoral resources that most incumbents receive. For most white candidates, incumbency has enormous benefits: it usually means more endorsements, more money, and weaker opponents. This is much less true for the black candidates in my sample. Largely because they needed tremendous resources to be elected in the first place, the majority of these twenty-six black candidates garnered few new electoral resources as incumbents. In 81 percent of the cases, they received no new Democratic Party endorsement when they ran as incumbents. In 62 percent of the cases, they gained no new endorsements from local newspapers. These black incumbents also tended to face strong white challengers. Specifically, 62 percent of the incumbents faced opponents who had the same or a higher level of experience than their opponents in the challenger election. The candidates were able to muster only marginally greater financial resources as incumbents, and one-third actually raised less money than they had as challengers. It would make little sense, then, to attribute the growing white support for these candidates to the conventional resources of incumbency.

The six-point increase in the percentage of white residents who voted black was not the only significant change from the challenger to the incumbent elections. There was an even sharper decline in the absolute number of white voters who opposed the black candidates. Across all twenty-six cities, the number of white votes for the white candidate declined by 19 percent on average between the challenger and the incumbent elections. This result suggests that as many as one-fifth of all white voters who opposed black leadership may have changed their minds sufficiently either to support the black candidate or to choose not to vote at all. As a consequence of both the drop in voter turnout and the higher level of support for the black incumbents, the incumbents' average margin of victory jumped from 12 percent in the challenger elections to 21 percent in the incumbent elections, leading to victory for the black incumbents in all but three cities.

The final factor to consider is voter turnout. Table 2 reveals that turnout decreased substantially in the black incumbent elections. In a little over half of the challenger elections, turnout had reached or exceeded record levels. On average, it exceeded the national average by over 10 percentage points. But this mobilization quickly faded away when blacks ran as incumbents: across the twenty-six cities, turnout dropped from almost 59 percent in challenger elections to 52 percent in incumbent elections, falling in many cases to average or below average levels. In Charlotte, for example, where Harvey Gantt faced well-known white Republican city council members in both of his elections, voter turnout fell by over 15 percentage points from 50 percent in Gantt's challenger run to 34 percent, near the historic norm, in his reelection bid. From this data, it seems that black incumbency at the mayoral level transforms extraordinary black challenger elections into more ordinary contests for reelection.

The opposition that the black challengers faced was by no means totally erased when they ran as incumbents, of course. The data in Table 2 indicate that large numbers of white voters continued to oppose the black incumbents. But in the average case, after a few years of black incumbency, white Americans became more accepting of black leadership. Again, the most remarkable aspect of this shift was not its size but the fact that there was any positive change at all. Peter Eisinger noted, in his study of Atlanta and Detroit, how sharply the elections of black representatives in those cities contrasted with expectations: "What has occurred is particularly noteworthy when it is set against the history of race relations in those two cities themselves, against the habits of racial oppression in American society in general, and indeed against a virtually worldwide tendency to deal with ethno-racial political competition by violent means" (Eisinger 1980: xxi). In many cities, even city residents themselves seemed surprised at their mayoral election's outcome. As one reporter in Birmingham put it, "This city, once branded by the Rev. Martin Luther King Jr. as 'the most thoroughly segregated in America,' accomplished something Tuesday that many of its residents consider remarkable: it reelected its first black mayor with a biracial coalition and the largest victory margin in city history" (Russakoff 1983). The fact that whites' anti-black mobilization declined after only a few years and significantly more whites became willing to support black leadership was not only a positive sign for race relations in these cities—it was a positive change that many did not foresee.

A Broader Phenomenon: All Incumbent Black Mayors

The changes in white voter behavior noted above may be unique to the twenty-six cities in the data set or limited to the first few years of black leadership. To assess black incumbency more broadly, I collected data on the reelection bids that took place in the twentieth century of every black incumbent mayor in every city with a population over 50,000.[2] In each case, in addition to the outcome of the contest, I obtained information on the racial makeup of the city, the race of the opponent, the number of terms the incumbent had been in office, and the number of black mayors who had previously served in the city.

The findings from my analysis of this larger set of cases echo the results for the twenty-six cities. First, black incumbents won in the vast majority of the cases. Since 1965, black mayors have won 78 percent of their reelection bids (98 out of 126 cases). In fact, depending on the exact comparison, black incumbents do almost as well as or even better than white incumbents. Between 1970 and 1985, the only period for which I was able to obtain equivalent data for both black and white mayoral incumbents, black mayors were reelected 89 percent of the time (31 out of 35 cases), a slightly higher rate than white mayors, who were reelected 84 percent of the time (359 out of 429 cases). From these data, it would seem that black and white incumbents are treated almost equally by the American electorate.

Second, there was no sharp decline in black reelection rates over time, and thus little indication that the information provided by black incumbents was losing efficacy over time. Although the first African Americans to serve as mayors of their cities were particularly successful when they ran as incumbents for the first time (winning 83 percent of these reelection bids), they also did well in subsequent electoral bids, winning 74 percent of the time. Equally important, there does not appear to be a major distinction in success rates between the first black mayor of a city and others who follow. The overall reelection rate of cities' first black mayors (80 percent) by no means dwarfs the reelection rate of subsequent black mayors (73 percent).

But does the success of black incumbents have anything to do with white voters? After all, the majority of black mayors represent minority white cities. Given the fact that black voters tend to favor black candidates over white candidates, the success of black incumbents could merely be an artifact of black unity and voting strength and not the result of increasing white support. But this appears not to be the case: if we confine the analysis to minority black cities, where white voters presumably have a good chance of controlling the outcome of the contests, black incumbents still do well. Black mayoral incumbents in minority black cities won reelection over 80 percent of the time, only marginally below the overall white incumbent reelection rate. Moreover, black incumbents did not win these contests simply because white voters were forced to choose between two black candidates. Even in minority black cities in elections in which black incumbents faced a white challenger, black mayoral incumbents won reelection 73 percent of the time (19 of 26 cases). In fact, black incumbents actually did better against white candidates then they did against black candidates.

THE SHIFTING CALCULUS OF THE WHITE VOTE

Across a wide range of cases and on a number of different measures, black mayoral leadership appears to lead to positive changes in white political behavior. These positive changes seem to favor the information model over both the backlash and the prejudice hypotheses, but they do not themselves demonstrate racial learning on the part of white voters. There are a number of possible reasons why black incumbents might be successful and why white voters might change their minds about black leadership. Most officeholders, whether they are white or black, get more support when they run as incumbents. To see if race and racial learning are behind the changes in the white vote observed in the data, more tests are required. In this section, I begin to examine the nature of the white vote more closely to see if the change in the vote can be linked to information. If the information model is accurate, we should see a distinct pattern emerge: in black challenger elections, the white vote should be largely based on racial fears; in black incumbent elections, fear should play a diminished role, and white voters should begin to base their votes on the track record of the incumbent and the specifics of the campaign.

I collected an array of data on the campaigns and candidates for each of the fifty-two elections in the original set of twenty-six cities. To assess the role of race and fear in each contest, I included two different kinds of measures. First, I used a measure of the black population size as a proxy for racial threat. The size of the black population is regularly employed as a measure of racial threat, and in a wide range of cases white political choices have been shown to be shaped by the local racial context (Giles and Hertz 1994; Key 1949). If fears about the consequences of black leadership are in fact driving the white vote in black challenger elections, we should find that white voters' preferences are closely tied to the size of the black community. The larger the black population and the more likely it is that blacks could actually gain control of the local political arena, the more we should see whites fearing black leadership and voting against black candidates.

Second, I included a measure of the racialization of each black candidate's campaign. If fear about racial change is behind white opposition, then what black candidates do or say regarding racial policy should also affect the white vote. The less black candidates talk about serving the black community and the more they run deracialized campaigns that promise a race-neutral administration, the less fear there should be in the minds of white voters and the more likely it should be that white voters will support black candidates. To measure the racialization of a given campaign, I coded the extent to which the black candidates' speeches, policy platforms, and mobilization efforts were targeted at blacks, whites, or both. This is admittedly a subjective measure, but in practice it was fairly easy to divide campaigns into three categories: campaigns that had any sort of explicit, pro-black focus; campaigns that addressed the black community implicitly through a generally pro-black policy agenda or by actively mobilizing black voters and speaking before black audiences; and campaigns that never mentioned black interests and were fairly race neutral. A comparison of the racialization measure employed in this study with a similar measure used in Lublin and Tate (1995) suggests that the coding is valid. If the information model is accurate, this measure should have a bigger effect on the white vote in black challenger elections than in black incumbent elections.

If whites cease to fear the consequences of a black takeover, conventional nonracial factors that are normally important determinants of electoral outcomes should begin to play a more significant role in black incumbent elections. To see if this is the case, I examine the extent to which three basic factors of the electoral context affect the white vote in black challenger and black incumbent elections: candidate quality, political endorsements, and campaign spending. In contests at almost every level of politics, each of these factors has proven to be critical to electoral outcomes. More-qualified candidates—with quality generally measured in terms of political experience—surpass the electoral fortunes of less-experienced candidates at both the congressional and local levels. Similarly, major endorsements have been shown to play a primary role in most local contests. In particular, both political party endorsements and city newspaper endorsements affect voting in local elections. Finally, campaign spending has been closely linked to the electoral fortunes of candidates from presidents all the way down to city council members. Candidates who are able to outspend their opponents by wide margins seem to be much more likely to win at the polls.

The Importance of Race in Black Challenger Elections

In Table 3, I begin to test these propositions by analyzing the aggregate white vote in black challenger elections. Although the number of cases is relatively small and is not necessarily representative of all American cities, the table does reveal a stark, clear pattern. As predicted by the information model, when black candidates challenged for the mayoralty for the first time, the aggregate white vote was tied almost exclusively to racial fears.

The first measure of racial fear indicates that the larger the black population in the cities in the sample—and hence the greater the perceived threat that blacks would gain some measure of control over the local political arena—the less willing whites were to support a black challenger. The size of the black population accounts for the bulk of the variation in aggregate white behavior; by itself, it accounts for 60 percent of the variation in white vote choice. Even considering the selection bias inherent in these cases, it is impressive how closely the white vote was tied to the size of a city's black population. In the five cities with the highest proportion of African Americans, Baltimore, Birmingham, New Orleans, Memphis, and Newark, on average only 16.9 percent of whites supported the black challenger. In contrast, in the five cities where blacks represented the smallest proportion of the population and thus the smallest threat, a slim majority of white voters (on average 50.4 percent) supported the black candidate. Overall, the regression results indicate that a 10 percentage point increase in the proportion of a city's residents who were black led to a 7.2 percentage point drop in white support for the black mayoral candidate.

TABLE 3

Determinants of the White Vote in Black Challenger Elections

	White Support for the Black Candidate
RACIAL FEAR	
Percentage Black of City Population	−0.72 (0.13)***
Racialization of Black Candidate's Campaign	−0.58 (0.26)*
CONVENTIONAL POLITICS	
Candidate Quality	
Quality of White Opponent	0.01 (0.08)
White Incumbent Running	−0.09 (0.07)
Quality of Black Challenger	−0.05 (0.08)
Endorsements	
Democratic Party Endorsement	0.02 (0.05)
Local Newspaper Endorsement	0.01 (0.05)
Constant	0.64 (0.11)***
Adj. R^2	0.67
N	25

Note: OLS regression. Figures in parentheses are standard errors.
***$p < 0.01$
**$p < 0.05$
*$p < 0.10$

The importance of racial threat seems to suggest that these challenger elections were less about the candidates or the specifics of the election than they were about the size of the threat of a black takeover—a conclusion that is echoed over and over again in accounts of the elections. One of the most well-known accounts of Birmingham's election, for example, concluded that "whites worried not so much about Richard Arrington Jr. [the black challenger], but about blacks, the group they believed he represented. Had that day now come when 'the last shall be first, and the first shall be last?'" (J. Franklin 1989: 172). The transition was viewed very similarly in Atlanta, where Peter Eisinger found that "the change was understood not in terms of a turnover in the personnel of city hall but as a loss by one race to the other" (1980: 154). Wilbur Rich's account of Detroit reached the same conclusion: "Many white residents of Detroit responded to the 1973 election of Coleman Young with intense apprehensions and fear. . . . Many whites saw the race as the last stand before the takeover by the onrushing black majority" (1987: 208).

The role played by the black candidate's campaign, and in particular white voters' aversion to racially focused campaigns, also serves to confirm the critical importance of racial fears in these black challenger elections. What black candidates did or did not say about the interests of blacks apparently influenced the white vote in these contests. All else being equal, black challengers who ran essentially race-neutral campaigns garnered almost 60 percent more of the white vote than challengers who ran racially explicit campaigns. Even though all of the twenty-six black challengers tried in some way to assure white residents that they would not be ignored, white voters seemingly keyed in on small differences between campaigns. Thus, a candidate like Harold Washington probably lost substantial white support as a result of telling a black audience "It's our turn," even though most of his campaign was race neutral. And, at the other end of the spectrum, candidates like Thirman Milner, who emphatically told white voters that "there is no such thing as black legislation" and who often repeated his desire to be "mayor of all of Hartford," seem to have been rewarded with additional white votes. Candidate Charles Box recalled that "The key . . . was to take the fear of the unknown out of the equation" (quoted in Colburn and Adler 2003). Box was so concerned about racial fears that he centered his campaign in Rockford on having personal interactions with as many white voters as possible.

In addition to supporting the information model, these findings also contribute evidence toward the resolution of two ongoing debates in the literature on American racial politics. First, the clear negative relationship between white voting behavior and the size of the local black population in these mayoral elections reaffirms the important role that racial context plays in American race relations. Existing studies have reached very different conclusions about how the increasing presence of racial and ethnic minorities affects the white population. Although most studies have found that a larger black population is associated with greater racial antagonism, several recent works have concluded either that there is no relationship at all or that the relationship is positive. The results reported here support the position that a proportionately larger black population *does* represent a racial threat to white voters.

In addition, the relationship between the racial focus of a campaign and the white vote seems to suggest that deracialization can lead to increased white support. Again, there has been considerable debate on this point. Though many have maintained that black candidates can garner white support by deracializing their campaigns, others disagree. In one of the most extensive studies, Wright found that "black [mayoral challengers] in Memphis were unable to garner significant white crossover support regardless of their use of deracialized strategies" (1996: 151). Similarly, Starks contends that "There is no way in which a contemporary American campaign can utilize a deracialization electoral strategy and hope to eliminate race as a factor in that campaign" (1991: 217). But the documented results seem to indicate that whites can be quite sensitive to the kinds of campaigns black candidates run. When black candidates move from a racially explicit campaign to a less racially focused campaign, they are able to attract greater white support. This might lead some to recommend deracializing black campaigns as an effective strategy to increase white support and expand black representation. It is important to consider, however, whether any gains in white support are large enough to offset a possible erosion of black support and black turnout—to say nothing of the restraints on policy changes—that most likely accompany deracialized campaigns.

A Different Calculation in Black Incumbent Elections

But what happens the second time around? Is there, as the information model predicts, a real transformation in the nature of the white vote in black incumbent elections? A comparison of the aggregate vote in challenger and incumbent elections suggests that there is. Table 4 combines the results of the same set of black challenger and black incumbent elections and includes a series of interactions to directly determine if different factors matter more or less in the latter. In the table, each variable that is not interacted with black incumbent elections measures the effect of that variable in black challenger elections. Each interaction directly

TABLE 4

The Transformation of the White Vote between Black Challenger and Black Incumbent Elections

	White Support for the Black Candidate
CONVENTIONAL POLITICS	
Candidate Quality	
Quality of White Opponent	−0.13 (0.07)*
Quality* Black Incumbent Election	−0.23 (0.11)**
Endorsements	
Democratic Party Endorsement	0.02 (0.05)
Party Endorsement* Black Incumbent Election	0.18 (0.08)**
Local Newspaper Endorsement	0.02 (0.04)
Newspaper Endorsement* Black Inc. Election	0.23 (0.12)*
RACIAL FEAR	
Percent Black of City Population	−0.07 (0.00)***
Percent Black* Black Incumbent Election	0.00 (0.00)
Racialization of Black Candidate's Campaign	−0.13 (0.06)**
Racialization* Black Incumbent Election	0.01 (0.09)
Black Incumbent Election	−0.30 (0.17)*
Constant	0.64 (0.11)***
Adj. R^2	0.72
N	48

Note: OLS regression. Figures in parentheses are standard errors.
*** $p < 0.01$
** $p < 0.05$
* $p < 0.10$

assesses how much more or less that variable matters in black incumbent elections. Thus, reading down the table, the significant interactions and the largely insignificant individual variables indicate that it is only after black incumbents have been given a chance to prove themselves that conventional factors begin to play an important role. As experience with black leadership grows and fear about its consequences declines, "politics" begins to play a primary role in voters' choices.

More specifically, Table 4 reveals that conventional factors such as candidate quality and political endorsements matter much more in black incumbent elections than they do in challenger elections. As evidenced by the significant interaction between candidate quality and incumbent elections, the weight that white voters put on the quality of the white opponent grew sharply from the challenger to the incumbent elections. White voters may not have cared who the white candidate was when he or she faced a black challenger; at that point, any white would do. But in black incumbent elections, white voters gave white candidates with experience in citywide office almost 20 percent more votes than candidates with no experience in political office. As one white politician put it, "Race is not as much of a litmus test as it once was. The issue now is who is the best qualified man" (*Sun Reporter* 1993). The reduction in white fears also appears to have increased white voters' attention to newspaper endorsements. These endorsements were essentially meaningless in black challenger elections, but endorsement by the main local newspaper increased white support in the average incumbent election by another 20 percent. As well, party endorsements helped in the black incumbent elections, even though they did not in the challenger elections. The local Democratic Party's endorsement delivered an additional 16 percent of the white vote on average when blacks ran as incumbents.

A second important conclusion to draw from Table 4 is that race still mattered in these elections. The fact that interactions with both of the racial fear variables are insignificant indicates that the size of the black population and the racial focus of the black candidate's campaign remained important to white voters. This is not surprising; even a brief review of these elections reveals that many of them were highly racialized. Chicago, New York, and New Haven, in particular, represent cases where the general trend toward increased white support and diminished racial tension did not apply.

At the same time, there is evidence that race and racial fears were generally less powerful in the incumbent elections. Further analysis indicates that racial fear lost half of its explanatory power: whereas the size of the black population and the racial focus of the black candidate's campaign alone account for 67 percent of the variation in the vote in black challenger elections, these two variables account for only 36 percent of the variation when white residents voted in black incumbent elections. As one reporter put it in Chicago, "Something has changed. The paranoia and ugly racism that ripped the city apart [four years ago] are largely absent this time" (Bosc 1987). Another observer of several black incumbent elections in 1993 simply stated, "Race has faded in many places" (*Sun Reporter* 1993). This conclusion was echoed in a recent study of mayoral voting in Houston (Stein, Ulbig, and Post 2005). Using three different surveys of voters in the city, the study found that racial considerations faded over the course of Lee Brown's tenure in that city. As the authors note: "Racial voting appears to be more influential in minority candidates' first electoral bids. In successive elections, voters come to rely more on their evaluations of the minority incumbent's job performance than their racial-group affiliation" (Stein, Ulbig, and Post 2005: 177). Though the magnitude of the change should not be overstated, it seems that white residents became less likely to base their votes on the race of the candidate and their fear of a black takeover in the incumbent elections. Instead when black incumbents ran for reelection, white residents seemed to more deliberately assess the pluses and minuses of their candidacies. As Sharon Watson put it in her account of mayoral bids in eight cities, "In [reelection] campaigns, while race remains a special factor, it did not seem to overshadow the campaign, as was true of the first elections. Race as an issue appeared neutralized somewhat" (1984: 172).

The Black Incumbent's Record and the White Vote

The analysis to this point has ignored an important aspect of black incumbent elections. If the information model is accurate and white voters change their minds about black leadership largely because experience with black incumbents disproves many of their fears, then a black incumbent's record in office should be an important variable shaping the white vote. The model predicts that black incumbents whose policies take resources from the white community to serve the black community or who preside over cities with faltering economies should do less well than black incumbents who resist pro-black policies and govern under robust local economic conditions. To analyze the influence of black incumbents' records on the white vote, I assess a range of factors related both to overall conditions in each city and to the policies that each black incumbent enacted. Given that the main fears expressed by white residents before the election of a black mayor were a deteriorating economy, falling housing prices, and widespread crime, I included measures of each of these three factors in the model. Since residents might logically also gauge black leadership by local government policy, I assess the impact of local government spending patterns on the white vote by including a measure of how much a city shifted resources from developmental spending toward redistributional functions such as social services, housing, and education during the black mayor's first term. Spending is obviously one of the arenas where black mayors can affect a large number of white residents, and any emphasis on redistributive spending is likely to be perceived by white residents as a strong signal of a black mayor's underlying preferences for serving the black community.

This analysis is displayed in Table 5, which presents the results of a regression explaining the aggregate white vote in black incumbent elections in the same set of twenty-six cities. With a small number of cases and eleven independent variables, the model in Table 5 stretches the limits of what regression analysis can do and should therefore be read with some caution. Nevertheless, the results are suggestive.

The first conclusion is that there are signs of a link between the black incumbent's record and the white vote. The clearest evidence of this is that changes in the local housing market are significantly related to the white vote. If, contrary to white fears, housing prices do not collapse and homeowners do well under black leadership, white residents will tend to reward the black incumbent. This finding parallels emerging research on so-called performance models of mayoral approval (Stein, Ulbig, and Post 2005; Howell and Perry 2004; Howell and McLean 2001). These recent studies have shown that in a small number of cities for which there are survey data white approval of incumbent black mayors is related to white evaluations of local economic conditions and white perceptions of city services.

However, as Table 5 also reveals, for other aspects of the incumbent's record, the existence of any relationship to the white vote is less clear. None of the other factors assessing the incumbent's record significantly predicts the white vote. The most that can be said is that in all three cases the relationship between the incumbent's record and the white vote is in the expected direction.

Thus, another interpretation is that the relationship between a black incumbent's record and the white vote is not nearly as strong as some might have expected. In only the one case—housing prices—is the incumbent's record significantly related to the white vote, and even here the magnitude of the effect is not large. For every one point increase in median housing prices, there is only a one-fifth of a point gain in white support for the black incumbent.

Why doesn't an incumbent's record matter more? Part of the answer may be related to the limitations of the empirical model. Too many variables and too few cases certainly cloud the analysis. The imprecise nature of the measures used in the analysis may also be a contributing factor. Whites, for example, may be more sensitive to housing prices and crime rates in their own neighborhoods than they are to overall changes at the city level. But a third and perhaps more critical answer here is the fact that almost all black incumbents exceed expectations. In the majority of the cities in the data set, per capita incomes grew compared to the national average, and in only two cases were gains in per capita income outpaced by more than 2 percent by gains made at the national level. Median housing prices rarely fell. And although crime rates did rise in the average city, in most cases they did not rise at a rate appreciably

TABLE 5

Determinants of the White Vote in Black Incumbent Elections

	White Support for the Black Candidate
RACIAL FEAR	
Percent Black of City Population	−0.27 (0.16)
Racialization of Black Candidate's Campaign	−1.03 (0.36)**
CONVENTIONAL POLITICS	
Candidate Quality	
Quality of White Opponent	−0.20 (0.08)**
Endorsements	
Democratic Party Endorsement	0.21 (0.08)**
Local Newspaper Endorsement	0.21 (0.12)*
BLACK INCUMBENT'S RECORD	
Local Conditions	
Change in Per Capita Income	0.40 (0.45)
Change in Median Housing Prices	0.21 (0.09)**
Change in Crime Rate	−0.03 (0.08)
Policy	
Change in Redistributive Spending	−0.11 (0.44)
Constant	0.01 (0.20)
Adj. R^2	0.71
N	25

Note: OLS regression. Figures in parentheses are standard errors.
***$p < 0.01$
**$p < 0.05$
*$p < 0.10$

faster than in the nation as a whole. Likewise, local government policy under black incumbents did little to substantiate white fears. The average city did not shift *any* resources from developmental projects to such redistributive programs as welfare, health, and housing, and in only two cases was more than 4 percent of the city budget transferred to redistributive functions. Finally, few of the cities stood out in terms of affirmative action policies. All but one increased black hiring under the black mayor, but only one city increased the proportion of blacks in the public sector by more than 5 percent. The lack of any dramatic change under black incumbents is not surprising, as these results mirror accounts from a range of existing studies. But it is important, because it represents a stark contrast with the expectations and fears of many whites. In essence then, the lesson is the same in almost every city. By maintaining tolerable or even relatively robust economic conditions and by choosing not to shift substantial resources away from the white community, black mayors, in almost all cases, demonstrate that black leadership does not appreciably hurt the white community. The bottom line is that black incumbents can help themselves by introducing policies that benefit the city but in the end all they have to do is not attack the white community. That is often enough to convince some white residents that they are worth supporting.

Changes in the white vote, in the kinds of campaigns white opponents run, and in the success rates of black candidates in minority black locales all hint at a sea change in the views and perceptions of a large segment of the white community. Though it is impossible on the basis of the data presented here to assign this change definitively to the effects of white learning from black leadership, they certainly leave open the possibility that experience with black leaders is fundamentally altering the nature of biracial politics in this country.

REFERENCES

Bosc, Michael. 1987. "Chicago's Mayoral Primary: Racial Lines Are Drawn, But Tempers Are Cooler." *U.S. News & World Report*, February 23:20.

Bullock, Charles S., and Bruce A. Campbell. 1984. "Racist or Racial Voting in the 1981 Atlanta Municipal Elections." *Urban Affairs Quarterly* 20(2): 149–64.

Colburn, David R., and Jeffrey S. Adler, eds. 2003. *African American Mayors: Race, Politics, and the American City.* Urbana, IL: University of Illinois Press.

Eisinger, Peter K. 1980. *Politics and Displacement: Racial and Ethnic Transition in Three American Cities.* Institute for Research on Poverty Monograph Series. New York: Academic Press.

Franklin, Jimmie Lewis. 1989. *Back to Birmingham: Richard Arrington, Jr., and His Times.* Tuscaloosa: University of Alabama Press.

Giles, Michael W., and Kaenan Hertz. 1994. "Racial Threat and Partisan Identification." *American Political Science Review* 88(2): 317–26.

Howell, Susan E., and William P. McLean. 2001. "Performance and Race in Evaluating Minority Mayors." *Public Opinion Quarterly* 65(1) (Feb): 321–43.

Howell, Susan E., and Hugh L. Perry. 2004. "Black Mayors/White Mayors: Explaining Their Approval." *Public Opinion Quarterly* 68(1) (Feb): 32–56.

Karnig, Albert K., and Susan Welch. 1980. *Black Representation and Urban Policy.* Chicago: University of Chicago Press.

Key, V. O. 1949. *Southern Politics in State and Nation.* Knoxville, TN: University of Tennessee Press.

Lublin, David Ian, and Katherine Tate. 1995. "Racial Group Competition in Urban Elections." In *Classifying By Race*, edited by P. E. Peterson. Princeton, NJ: Princeton University Press.

Rich, Wilbur C. 1987. "Coleman Young and Detroit Politics: 1973–1986." In *The New Black Politics: The Search for Political Power*, edited by M. B. Preston, L. J. Henderson, and P. L. Puryear. New York: Longman.

Russakoff, Dale. 1983. "Birmingham Reelects Black: Once-Split City Unites at Polls." *Washington Post*, October 13: A1.

Sonenshein, Raphael J. 1993. *Politics in Black and White: Race and Power in Los Angeles.* Princeton, NJ: Princeton University Press.

Starks, Robert T. 1991. "A Commentary and Response to Exploring the Meaning and Implication of Deracialization in African-American Urban Politics." *Urban Affairs Quarterly* 27(2): 216–22.

Stein, Robert. M., Stacy G. Ulbig, and Stephanie S. Post. 2005. "Voting for Minority Candidates in Multi-Racial/Ethnic Communities." *Urban Affairs Review* 41(2) (Nov): 157–81.

Sun Reporter. 1993. "Black Mayors on the Rise." *Sun Reporter* 56(38): 1.

Vanderleeuw, James M. 1991. "The Influence of Racial Transition on Incumbency Advantage in Local Elections." *Urban Affairs Quarterly* 27(1): 36–50.

Watson, S. M. 1984. "The Second Time Around: A Profile of Black Mayoral Election Campaigns." *Phylon* 45: 165–75.

Wright, Sharon D. 1996. "The Deracialization Strategy and African American Mayoral Candidates in Memphis Mayoral Elections." In *Race, Politics, and Governance in the United States*, edited by H. L. Perry. Gainesville, FL: University of Florida Press.

NOTES

*Editor's note: Readers may wish to consult additional notes, references, and statistical appendices in the original text due to their elimination in this copy.

1. Including cases in which two black candidates run against each other would, obviously, reveal little about white acceptance of black leadership.

2. This data set was compiled using the National Roster of Black Elected Officials, local newspaper reports in each city, and a data set of mayoral names (Wolman, Strate, and Melchior 1996), and it includes the race of the mayor, the challenger, and the winner. As in the first data set, I focus on general or run-off elections rather than primaries, where factors such as multiple candidacies, lack of interest, and limited availability of empirical data complicate empirical analysis.

13

Paradoxes of Integration

J. ERIC OLIVER

Integration is a seductive concept. For most Americans, the image of different races and ethnicities peacefully coming together as a single community is enormously appealing. It epitomizes such classically liberal values as individual respect, justice, and equality before the law; segregation, by contrast, bespeaks of racism, apartheid, and centuries of injustice. But beyond this, integration seems to have some practical benefits, particularly in a multiracial country like the United States. People who live around other races are more tolerant, more likely to have interracial friendships and social contacts, and would seem to be better equipped to live in a larger, multicultural society. Given the high levels of residential segregation and mistrust among America's four major racial groups, integration may seem like a palliative for solving its many racial problems. Indeed, many commentators have suggested that the integration of neighborhoods and civic life is the best way to avoid racial confrontation in the future (Varshnay 2002; Welch et al. 2001). An integrated society, some believe, is not just peaceful, but a civically vibrant community as well.

But before rushing to this conclusion, we need to understand the complexity of integration, particularly in the United States. Since whites remain the largest racial group in the United States, integration inevitably will involve a great deal of minority penetration into predominantly white areas. Integration, under such circumstances, will mean different things for different people: for whites, integration means accepting a larger portion of neighbors as non-white; for most Asians, blacks, and Latinos, integration means leaving their own ethnic enclaves and moving into white neighborhoods.

This type of integration, however, is rarely peaceful or easy. Historically, America's white population has fiercely resisted minority encroachment, and while the cross burnings, lynchings, and other violent measures perpetrated against minorities have declined significantly over the past decades, most whites are still unwilling to accept all but a small number of minorities as neighbors (Meyer 2001). Consequently, for many minorities, moving into a white neighborhood often means facing ostracism, threats, and intimidation (Kryson and Farley 2002; Bobo and Zubrinsky 1996). In the face of such racial animosity, many minorities are quick to abandon white areas and seek same-race neighborhoods that are more welcoming (Clark 1992). In situations in which minorities do not

---

From J. Eric Oliver, *The* Paradoxes of Integration: Race, Neighborhood, and Civic Lite in multiethnic America. Chicago: University of Chicago Press, 2010: PP. 133–151, Appendix A, notes and references.

leave, whites often depart, making neighborhoods "tip" racially from all white to all black or all Latino within a short period of time (Wilson and Taub 2006).

The issue of integration is further complicated by the cultural and linguistic differences among its fast-growing Latino and Asian American populations. Since many Latinos and Asian Americans are immigrants with limited English language skills and different norms of social engagement, their interaction with American society may be quite limited or simply restricted to their own ethnic enclave. For instance, past research on ethnic differences in civic participation finds much lower levels of participation among Asian Americans and Latinos, which is often related to their language skills and familiarity with American cultural norms (Leighley and Vedlitz 1999; Wong 2006). In addition to being stymied by linguistic and cultural barriers, immigrants' community involvement may be reduced by the strong ties to the country of origin among many first-generation immigrants (Jones-Correa 1996). And just as the linguistic and cultural isolation of many immigrants provides incentives to segregate themselves geographically, these same factors may also inhibit their social incorporation even within more integrated settings. Some may even resist a greater social and civic incorporation for fear of losing their own distinct ethnic identity.

In addition, we must consider the larger context of where and how different races in America live. A disproportionately large percentage of blacks and Latinos live below the poverty line, are concentrated in central cities, and have little financial capital. For these groups, housing options are highly limited, and the most likely paths of integration are through economically disadvantaged white neighborhoods or through Latinos migrating into black enclaves. Yet, even more than in middle-class neighborhoods, such migration patterns have been met with either violence, organized resistance, or massive white flight (Rieder 1987; Wilson and Taub 2006). The challenge of integration is further exacerbated by the suburbanization of the metropolitan population, where many predominantly white communities use zoning laws and other restrictions to keep lower income residents out. And, even if minorities are able to penetrate white, suburban neighborhoods, their efforts to find community may be further stymied by the unique social and civic dynamics that affect suburban civic life. Suburban neighborhoods are more likely to be dominated by antisocial architectural forms, be highly segregated by social class, and have relatively lower levels of civic interaction (Oliver 2001). If racial integration means moving to predominantly white areas, it also means the movement into suburban areas, areas that by virtue of their design, economic composition, and political homogeneity may limit the venues for meaningful social interaction and fostering community.

But perhaps the most important problem with our romantic notions about integration is that we have little understanding of how it works in practice, particularly for people's feelings of community and belonging. If our primary concern is building a sense of connection and shared purpose among America's different racial groups, then one of our crucial points of attention should be on how people in integrated settings experience community life. Yet this is a topic for which little research exists. Social scientists have largely overlooked whether civil society is affected by people's racial surroundings. Although a few studies have examined how blacks' feelings of group solidarity and civic involvement change with the racial composition of their environments, researchers have generally not examined whether feelings of community and civic attachment vary for all racial groups (Bledsoe et al. 1995; Cohen and Dawson 1993). As a result, many important questions remain unanswered.

Are people in integrated neighborhoods more or less active in community affairs? Do Latinos and Asians who live in segregated barrios feel less tied to American civil society? Do feelings of community exacerbate or mitigate the higher feelings of racial animosity that exist in segregated neighborhoods?

This [discussion] examines how people's racial environments shape their involvement in community life. As with racial attitudes, feelings of community and civic engagement vary with a person's racial surroundings. But, unlike with racial attitudes, the impact of integration seems largely negative. Whites who live in integrated neighborhoods are less civically active, are less trusting of their neighbors, and feel a weaker sense of community than their counterparts in segregated places. Similarly, African Americans also express greater alienation as the percent of whites in their surroundings increases, although this is less the case for Asian Americans and Latinos, whose civic participation is shaped less by their social surroundings than by their levels of incorporation into American society—citizens and English speakers are far more active in their communities than noncitizens. These findings demonstrate that integration is a complicated process whose implications depend as much on one's individual racial identity as one's incorporation into a predominantly white American culture.

HOW OUR RACIAL ENVIRONMENTS AFFECT OUR FEELINGS OF COMMUNITY AND CIVIC LIFE

Over the past decades, Americans have become preoccupied with their civic life, or at least its putative decline. According to political scientist Robert Putnam's now famous argument, Americans are no longer joining civic organizations as they once did and America's stocks of social capital, the resources that amass from our connections with other people, are beginning to wane (Putnam 2000). With the growth of television, commuting times, and dual-income households, Americans are spending less discretionary time in community activities and more time by themselves. In Putnam's words, Americans are no longer joining bowling leagues but are now "bowling alone." This increasing social isolation putatively brings with it a host of negative consequences such as declining levels of interpersonal trust, social norms of respect for community, and sustained commitments to democratic ideals. This erosion of social capital is seen as a threat to both the health and integrity of American democratic society.

Interestingly, one factor that has gone unnoticed in the hoopla over America's diminishing social capital is its growing racial diversity. America may be a country where people are now bowling alone, and it may be a country made up of a larger number of racial and ethnic groups, but few people have sought to ask whether these phenomena are related. Most published research on the relationship between community heterogeneity and civic participation has come from economists using formal models to generate predictions about the relationships between social environments and individual behavior (e.g., Alesina and La Ferrara 2000). Although such mathematical models offer strong predictions, they provide very little information about the causal mechanisms linking context and behavior. For instance, these models are usually based on the assumption of a social preference for being around people of similar races; in other words, social diversity imposes "costs" because individuals "prefer to interact with others like them because of shared interests, socialization to the same cultural norms, and greater empathy toward individuals who remind them of themselves" (Costa and Kahn 2003, 104). Yet this research provides no detailed evidence to justify these assumptions. The fact that heterogeneity corresponds with less civic engagement is simply taken as proof that the operating mechanisms are at work. This approach is unsatisfactory—not only does it preclude other explanations, but it is not grounded in any theory about civic participation or community life.

To understand how the racial composition of a social environment might affect people's participation in their communities, we must determine why people become involved in local affairs in the first place. In their authoritative study of civic participation in the United States, political scientists Sidney Verba, Kay Schlozman, and Henry Brady identified three factors that determine whether people get involved in local civic activities: resources, interest, and mobilization (Verba, Schlozman, and Brady 1995). People are far more likely to be active in their communities if they have more resources like time and money, if they are interested in a particular set of issues, or if they are asked by others to get involved.

From this perspective, we can see how America's growing racial diversity might affect its civic participation. First, people's feelings about their communities are likely to be shaped by their racial environment. As people live among more people of their own ethnicity or race, particularly in contrast to neighboring different groups, they are likely to have stronger feelings of group affiliation, what scholars commonly refer to as a sense of "ethnic community" (Bobo and Zubrinsky 1996; Dawson 1994). For example, a Latina may have little sense of ethnic community in her home country but feel a strong sense of ethnicity in a barrio of Los Angeles (Jones-Correa and Leal 1996). Researchers find that blacks who feel a greater sense of ethnic community are more likely to be active in volunteer organizations (Guterbock and London 1983). Conversely, people who feel racially ostracized or alienated from their neighbors may withdraw socially and keep to themselves. Feeling less in common with her neighbors, the resident of a heterogeneous community would be less interested in local or community affairs, feel less bound by community norms that encourage civic involvement, and be less motivated to join a local organization (Campbell 2006). Thus one of the first things we would need to consider is whether people in diverse settings have different perceptions of their community than people in homogeneous settings.

Second, racial diversity may constrain the social connections between neighbors and thus limit their opportunities to be mobilized into neighborhood life. Given the high levels of racial mistrust in the United States, people living in diverse settings may have fewer social bonds with their neighbors, which can, in turn, reduce the opportunities to become recruited for a local group. The importance of these social networks cannot be overstated; after all, most people get involved in local voluntary organizations because they are asked at some point to do so (Verba et al. 1995). If people in diverse places are less familiar with their neighbors, the likelihood they will be recruited to join anything from a neighborhood association to the Rotary club will be significantly lower. When looking at the impact of racial surroundings on local organizational involvement, it is essential, therefore, to also look at the informal social ties between residents.

The other factor to consider when thinking about racial environments and community perceptions is the impact of an individual's race. Not all racial and ethnic groups in the United States perceive their communities or involve themselves in civic affairs in the same way. Past research has indicated that Latinos and Asian Americans are typically less engaged in many types of civic activities than whites and blacks (Wong 2006). Few studies, however, have sufficiently explained why such differences exist, whether these differences would translate across all community activities (or if they are simply relegated to political activities), or whether they are differentiated by other factors such as English language ability or citizenship.

Therefore, before going any further, it is important to examine some comparative data on levels of civic and social engagement by individual race and citizenship. Figure 1 displays the average scores by these criteria on four indicators of local social and civic activity in the NPS data. The local activities include an index measure of civic participation, an index score of informal social behavior, the percent of respondents who reported belonging to a neighborhood-based group or association, and the percent who reported working on a neighborhood project during the past year.[1]

Significant racial differences exist in rates of civic and social participation, although these vary significantly by citizenship and the type of activity in question. There are relatively minor differences among racial groups in terms of informally socializing with neighbors. Whites and minority citizens have slightly higher average informal social activity scores than minority noncitizens, but the interethnic differences are not very large. Given that this measure gauges mere informal socializing, we should not expect large differences across racial groups.

However, significant differences occur in more formal civic activity across racial groups. Whites and blacks tend to participate in civic activities at much higher rates than Latinos and Asians, particularly compared with noncitizens. For example, roughly 24 percent of blacks and whites reported participating in a neighborhood group, compared with only 16 percent of Latinos and 14 percent of Asian citizens. Whites and blacks scored over 8 percentage points higher, on average, on the civic participation scale. However, when compared with noncitizens, these differences grow quite substantially. Latino noncitizens score only at one-eighteenth a point and Asian noncitizens score just over one-tenth a point on the civic participation scale compared with the average scores of over a quarter a point for all citizen groups. Latino noncitizens were also far less likely to work on neighborhood projects or belong to neighborhood civic associations.

Similar patterns also exist when looking at different types of civic and social organizations. For example, the MCSUI study has data on the percent of respondents who reported participating in a neighborhood-based civic organization during the past year by race/ethnicity and English language ability. This could include a parent/teacher association or organization (PTA/PTO), a social club, a neighborhood group, a cultural group, or a political

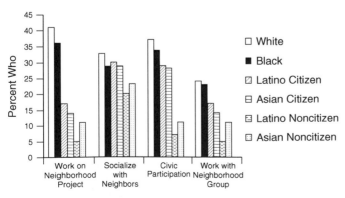

FIGURE 1

Civic participation rates by race and citizenship (2004 NPS).

organization. As with the other findings, there are few consistent racial or ethnic differences in civic activities among incorporated respondents but large differences in civic activity based on English language ability. English-speaking Asians, blacks, Latinos, and whites all participated in organizations at roughly the same level, although whites were more likely to belong to social clubs and political groups and Asian Americans more likely to belong to cultural groups. Among non-English-speaking Asian Americans and Latinos, however, rates of most civic activities were far below the other groups. With the exception of PTAs, under 11 percent of non-English-speaking Latinos and Asian Americans reported belonging to a civic organization, rates of participation that were roughly a third of those with good English skills.

Thus many of the differences in the civic and social activity of Latinos and Asian Americans are clearly related to their lower levels of citizenship and English language ability. Yet even when these factors are considered, some racial differences in the social and civic patterns still remain: whites and blacks are slightly more active in local civic activities and more involved in neighborhood affairs than Latinos and Asian Americans, but they are no more active in informal social activities and sometimes less active in many types of social organizations. Other research suggests that Asian Americans and Latinos are much less civically active because of cultural differences stemming from their countries of origin, a feeling of marginalization in American society, and a lack of group-based mobilization (Wong 2006).

Regardless of its source, Americans' involvement in civic affairs depends, in part, on their own racial identity; the question remains, however, whether this affects the way different groups respond to their racial environments. If Latinos and Asian Americans are already less civically active, then neighborhood effects might even be more of a depressant to their involvement. In other words, if living in an integrated neighborhood makes Latinos less likely to be mobilized or less interested in local civic affairs, then we should expect them to be even less likely to be civically engaged. Yet, among Asians and Latinos, there are no differences (at least among citizens) in informal social activities. Since such informal activities provide opportunities for mobilization and may indicate some level of alienation with a person's community, this would suggest that among incorporated Americans, we may not expect any systematic differences. In other words, the biggest differences may not occur by race or ethnicity but by level of incorporation into American society.

THE EFFECTS OF NEIGHBORHOOD RACIAL SEGREGATION ON CIVIC PARTICIPATION

How much are these differences in civic engagement affected by people's racial environments? To answer this question, let us compare whites and nonwhites. Figure 2 depicts the predicted average number of civic activities for white respondents in the CID data by the percentage white in the neighborhood based on a multivariate regression analysis.[2] Each measure of civic participation is based on questions about membership in seventeen associational groups and additional questions on activities in these groups, such as participation in group activities or doing other voluntary works.[3] As expected, whites in predominantly white neighborhoods are far more likely to engage in the activities of voluntary organizations.[4] The equations predict that a white person living in a predominantly white area (whether it is a metropolis or neighborhood) is

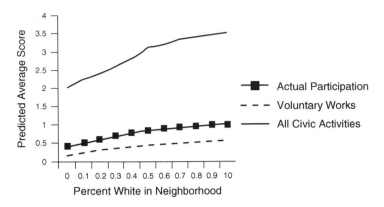

FIGURE 2

Predicted rates of white civic participation by the percent white in neighborhood (2005 CID).

over twice as likely to belong to an organization, participate in organizational activities, or volunteer for an organizational project.

In contrast with whites, living in a predominantly white neighborhood does not bolster minority civic participation; instead, it corresponds with lower levels of civic engagement, although this varies somewhat by race. Among blacks in the CID sample, overall civic participation did not change with the racial composition of their surroundings, but actual participation and volunteering did decline. The equations predict that as the percentage of whites in a black person's neighborhood increases, blacks' average numbers of participatory or voluntary activities drops from 1.5 to zero. Similar declines also occur for Latinos—actual participation and volunteering declines as the percent of whites in the neighborhood increases. Among Latinos in the CID sample, average rates of civic membership also dropped with the percentage of whites in their neighborhood. The equations predict that Latinos who live in neighborhoods that have almost no whites belong to three civic organizations, a rate that drops to zero once the percentage of whites in the neighborhood goes above fifty.

These same trends are also evident in measures of local civic activities. The SCCBS survey asked a series of specific questions about the respondents' neighborhood civic activities.[5] Significant differences occur in the predicted rates of civic and social participation by the racial composition of people's neighborhoods, although these vary considerably by the individual's race. For whites, living in a predominantly white neighborhood coincides with a lower likelihood of belonging to a neighborhood group, but it corresponds with a higher level of informal social activity. The equations predict that a white person living in an all-white community would be 23 percent less likely to belong to a neighborhood group than if he or she lived in a nonwhite neighborhood; yet this same person would also score 8 percent higher on the informal socializing scale. These findings coincide with other research that shows that predominantly white communities have fewer neighborhood groups, largely because such communities are more likely to be suburban locales with fewer social problems (Oliver 2001). Because integrated neighborhoods tend to be in older and more urban areas, they often present neighbors with a wider array of community issues and a more mature civic infrastructure in which to involve residents. But while whites in integrated neighborhoods may be more likely to participate in neighborhood groups they are less socially connected with their neighbors.

Among minorities, a different pattern of neighborhood socializing is evident. For blacks, the racial composition of the community had few distinctive effects on their civic activity above the baseline effects for whites. The biggest difference among blacks is in regards to their informal social ties—unlike whites, blacks' informal social ties do not increase with the percent of whites in their neighborhood. The equations predict that a black person living in a predominantly white community is no more (but also no less) socially active than a black person in a nonwhite community.[6] Latinos and Asian Americans are less likely to be involved in neighborhood groups (a trend consistent with their overall lower levels of civic participation), but they are only slightly less likely to get involved as the percent white in their neighborhoods increases. Latinos also reported lower average scores on the informal socializing scale, although they are more likely to score higher as the percentage of whites in their neighborhood rises. Among Asian Americans, informal socializing declines with the percentage of whites in their neighborhood.

When examining the effects of social contexts on civic behavior, it is important to consider what influences the measures of the social environment may be capturing. The racial composition of a neighborhood is not simply a measure of all its residents' races but also relates to other factors such as its age, urbanity, and political history. Although the regression equations take the economic status of the community into account, it is quite likely that the measure of a community's racial composition also relates to other political factors that could influence people's civic participation. It is quite telling, for instance, that whites are more likely to be civically active as the percent of whites in their community grows, although less likely to belong to neighborhood groups. This disjunction may be due to a lack of compelling problems in the neighborhood. Many predominantly white areas are in suburbs that effectively use municipal powers to reduce the level of social diversity and political problems, hence diminishing the incentive for neighborhood civic action.

It is important, therefore, to keep these factors in mind when examining the effects of neighborhood racial contexts on minority civic participation. Most minorities score lower on the civic participation scale as the percent of whites in their neighborhood rises. This is may be due to a lower level of compelling civic issues in such areas, but it may also relate to a greater level of social ostracism. Blacks in predominantly white areas are not more socially active than those in nonwhite areas, and Asian Americans are less socially involved. As these minorities who live in predominantly white areas are less socially connected than their white neighbors, they may have fewer invitations to be civically involved. They also might be provided with fewer opportunities for interracial contact. Interestingly, in the one exception to this trend, Latinos and Asian Americans are more likely to participate in neighborhood groups when they live in predominantly white areas. Although the exact reason for this trend is unclear, it may be related to a process of immigrant incorporation—Latinos and Asian Americans who move into predominantly white neighborhoods may do so as a part of incorporating themselves fully into American society, and thus they may become more involved in their neighborhood groups. Nevertheless, on the whole, the findings above would indicate that predominantly white neighborhoods are not the most fertile ground for encouraging the civic and social participation of minority groups.

Another way of gauging the social connectedness of minorities in predominantly white areas is to examine their attitudes about their neighbors. If integration contributes to greater social understanding, then presumably people in integrated settings will develop greater bonds with their neighbors. This, however, does not seem to be the case. The SCCBS data queried respondents about their perceptions of their surroundings, asking them how much their neighbors provided them with "a sense of belonging" and how much they trusted their neighbors.[7] Figure 3 depicts the predicted scores on measures of social connection to neighbors by the percent white in the neighborhood from regression equations.

Whites and minorities exhibit sharply different perceptions of their sense of place in their community depending on its racial composition. As the percent of whites in their neighborhoods increases, whites are far more likely to report a sense of trust in their neighbors and a sense of belonging in the community. The OLS equations predict that a white person in an all-white neighborhood would score nearly half a point higher on the neighbor-trust scale than if that same person lived in an entirely nonwhite neighborhood; they would also be 6 percent more likely to report a feeling of belonging in their neighborhood.[8] Whites who live in more segregated surroundings report a greater sense of community and connection with their neighbors than those in less white neighborhoods.

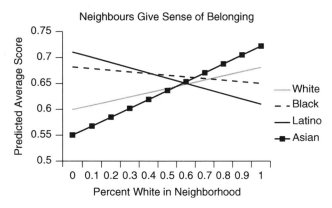

FIGURE 3A
Predicted levels of neighborhood belonging and trust by the percent white in neighborhood (2000 SCCBS).

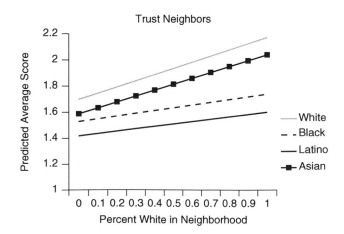

FIGURE 3B
Predicted levels of neighborhood belonging and trust by the percent white in neighborhood, continued (2000 SCCBS).

The opposite trend occurs for blacks and Latinos—as the percentage of whites in their neighborhood increases, they are less likely to report trusting their neighbors or feeling like they belong in their community. When considering the baseline effects plus all the interaction terms, the equations predict that a black person living in an all-white neighborhood will feel far less trusting of their neighbors than a white person in that neighborhood and only slightly more trusting of their neighbors than if they lived in a nonwhite neighborhood. The equations would also predict a similar effect for Latinos—those who live in all-white neighborhoods are much less trusting of their neighbors than whites and only slightly more trusting than Latinos who live in nonwhite locales. Both Latinos and blacks are also less likely to report a sense of belonging with respect to their neighbors as the percent of whites in their surroundings increases. Asians, however, do not appear to be so adversely affected. There were no statistically significant differences between Asian and white respondents in their trust in neighbors or feeling of belonging by virtue of the white percentage in their neighborhood.

The conclusions one draws from these findings depend largely upon which racial group is in question. Minorities have different levels of social and civic involvement and are affected by the racial composition of their surroundings in different ways. African Americans are just as socially and civically active as whites, and, like whites, their civic action declines in predominantly white settings. If there is an encouraging sign from the data it is that blacks in predominantly white neighborhoods are no more civically disengaged than their white neighbors or any more socially alienated than blacks in nonwhite neighborhoods. Integration would not appear to be a major deterrent to black civic engagement or social life.

Latinos and Asian Americans are significantly less civically active than either whites or blacks. However, they are not adversely affected by living in predominantly white areas—Asian Americans and Latinos in predominantly white neighborhoods are just as civically active as those who live in nonwhite neighborhoods and, in some cases, participate more. Latinos, like blacks, are less trusting of their neighbors and are less likely to feel a sense of belonging in their neighborhood as the percent of whites in their surroundings increases, although this is not a factor for Asian Americans. Taken as a whole, it does not appear that integration into white areas is a civically or socially alienating experience for Asian Americans or even many Latinos. The biggest challenge for these groups is in getting them to be more civically and socially active in the first place, which simply may be a function of their unfamiliarity with American society, politics, and culture.

The same cannot be said, however, for whites. Interestingly, the data suggest that the most adverse social effects of integration actually may be experienced by whites. Although whites in predominantly white neighborhoods are less civically active than those in more integrated neighborhoods, this is probably less because of their social connections with neighbors and more because of a lack of compelling issues in predominantly white neighborhoods. Because most predominantly white neighborhoods are located within suburban areas that have fewer social and civic issues drawing citizens into the public realm, it is understandable that neighborhood racial composition would correspond with changing white civic participation. More troubling are the changing social patterns and feelings of community between whites in segregated and integrated communities. Whites in segregated neighborhoods are more socially active with their neighbors and experience greater feelings of neighborly trust and belonging than whites in more integrated neighborhoods. This suggests that as a white neighborhood becomes more integrated, its white residents will become less socially connected with their neighbors. Although whites in integrated neighborhoods may have more opportunities for interracial contact through high levels of civic activity, they may feel less of a sense of community and be less socially connected to people of other races. Paradoxically, it is the social connections of whites that may be most adversely influenced by integration.

CONCLUSION

Since the issuance of the controversial Moynihan report in the late 1960s, a voluminous amount of research has investigated the social consequences of racial segregation in the United States. Most of this research has focused on the social pathologies and inequities that have accompanied the hypersegregation of African Americans. Segregation, particularly of African Americans, has been linked to higher infant mortality, unemployment, and crime rates and numerous other social ills (for example, see Boger and Wegner 1996; Banfield 1970; Orfield 1988; and Pettigrew 1979). Sociologist William Julius Wilson has argued quite extensively that the social isolation of blacks has disconnected them from job networks and other opportunities for economic advancement and has mired them in a permanent underclass status (Wilson 1985). These studies, like most studies of racial residential patterns, focus almost entirely on the experience of minorities in segregated contexts.

But while there is general agreement that segregation has had many harmful by-products, almost no research has been conducted on the experience of people, either white or nonwhite, in integrated neighborhoods. With the exception of research on the performance of black students in integrated schools and recent writings on the Gautreaux desegregation program and the recent Moving to Opportunity housing experiments, relatively little has been written about the lives of minority adults in integrated or predominantly white residential settings. And, as with many aspects of race relations, there is almost no large-scale, quantitative research on how integration affects the lives of Latinos and Asian Americans.[9] We know that segregation has many adverse consequences, but is integration necessarily a more positive experience?

If interracial civic and social connections are the key factors in promoting greater racial tolerance among people in integrated settings, then the findings in this chapter demonstrate that neighborhood racial integration is not guaranteed to bring simple or even desirable consequences. Since any meaningful integration in America will largely be based on the movement of minorities into predominantly white areas, at least over the short run, it is important to focus on how the social and civic experiences of whites and minorities vary between integrated and segregated places. The findings here show different results for different groups. Whites who live in all-white neighborhoods consistently demonstrate greater social connections and more affiliation with their neighbors than those who live in integrated settings. For instance, whites who live in racially mixed neighborhoods on average are 5 percentage points lower in their feelings of neighborhood community and levels of trust than those in all-white neighborhoods. For whites, just as with other minorities, racial homogeneity promotes a feeling of community. Integration, while promoting some types of associational membership, does not enhance feelings of linkage with a place. In fact, it produces just the opposite.

Interestingly, integration may have some of the most important social and civic consequences, not just for minorities, but for America's white population. As the previous chapters showed, neighborhood racial integration may be important for promoting interracial understanding, which would, in theory, enhance the community between whites and other racial groups, particularly African Americans and Latinos. Yet in the short run, this type of community may be difficult to achieve. Whites in integrated neighborhoods may be less racially judgmental, but they do not feel as connected or trusting of their neighbors either. Paradoxically, the very integration that helps whites gain better racial understanding may also undermine a sense of trust and community between their neighbors. If integration is essential for promoting a more racially tolerant view of society at large, it may come at the cost of a sense of community and fellowship among one's immediate neighbors. As long as race continues to be a defining characteristic in American society, the relationship between segregation, white racial attitudes, and the strength of community bonds will remain in tension.

The impact of integration on blacks is related to this point. For hundreds of years, African Americans lived in a society that discriminated against them, banned them from public facilities, and relegated them to the bottom of the social ladder. Accepting a sense of community in the larger society meant accepting a denigrated social position. Consequently, the strongest community ties most blacks formed were within a black society. Since the civil rights era, the state-sanctioned segregation has been undone, but the challenge of community still remains. For blacks, integrating into American society as equal members means facing an enormous residue of past discrimination. Many blacks still feel strong ties and a linked fate with other African Americans and derive a greater sense of community from living in segregated spaces.

Yet if neighborhood integration fosters greater racial harmony through greater civic participation, then one might conclude that the way to promote greater racial understanding between blacks and nonblacks is to encourage greater residential integration. Neighborhood integration is important for blacks not because it increases casual contact (in which blacks may experience prejudice, particularly from whites) but because it fosters an integrated civic and social community. The problem with this argument, however, is that black civic participation is lower in predominantly white neighborhoods. Partly this is because white neighborhoods themselves are less civically active but partly this can be attributed to the difference in the social connectedness of blacks in white neighborhoods. When compared against the black racial percentage in their communities, blacks who live in predominantly black neighborhoods derive a greater sense of community from their surroundings. In the SCCBS data, 78 percent of African Americans in largely black neighborhoods felt community with their neighbors, compared with only 71 percent in neighborhoods with few blacks. Herein lies another paradox of segregation: the neighborhood integration that is so important for creating interracial associational ties also diminishes black social involvement; the solidarity and community provided by segregated black neighborhoods may also sustain racial misperceptions by those who live outside of these areas. But if blacks, like whites, want to overcome the continued barriers of racial difference they see with other races, the conundrum of residential integration must be faced.

Latinos and Asian Americans, as diverse ethnic groups composed largely of immigrants, encounter a much different set of issues with respect to civic and social integration. The biggest challenge for these groups may have less to do with the segregation in their neighborhoods and more to do with their much lower levels of social and civic engagement and the question of identity in a new society. Undoubtedly, this is a function of so many being first- and second-generation immigrants to the United States—many of whom have limited English skills, are noncitizens, have stronger ties to their home countries, or simply feel marginalized by American life. And their incorporation into American civic life will undoubtedly coincide somewhat with their integration into white residential areas. Indeed, the findings show that Latinos and Asian Americans who live in white neighborhoods are actually more civically active. However, for many Latinos and Asians, particularly newly arrived immigrants, residence in a predominantly white neighborhood may not be an optimal option for their social and economic well-being. For many there are also concerns of sustaining their indigenous cultural values and identities, something that may be undermined with further integration into white American society. The challenge for these groups will be in balancing their competing cultural identities—their countries of origin, the United States, and their own ethnic or racial self-perception—all while becoming incorporated into American society. Whether these new identities will serve to act as catalysts to further racial antagonism or blur racial and group distinctions remains to be seen. In the meantime, the cultural and linguistic segregation of many Latinos and Asian Americans may actually be the biggest challenge to promoting better race relations between them and other groups in American society.

For all of these reasons, residential integration itself may be an obstacle to civic and social integration—between the social ostracism of minorities in predominantly white areas, the cultural alienation and low levels of incorporation among many Asians and Latinos, and the prevalence of whites in many civically alienating suburbs, the actual experience of integration may preclude the social and civic engagement that is necessary for promoting racial tolerance. Herein lies another paradox of neighborhood integration and racial animosity: the ameliorative effects of integration are based on the idea that people in such settings are civically and socially engaged with their neighbors. Often, however, this is not the case. Not only are minorities who move into predominantly white areas subject to possible harassment and violence, they may find other barriers to social and civic connections with their neighbors. Integration may also alienate whites who see little in common with or feel different from their nonwhite neighbors. Considering these ideas in light of the previous chapters, one might speculate that a cycle of race, segregation, and community continues to operate in the United States: racial animosity in white areas drives minorities to seek community in minority neighborhoods, which further sustains racial segregation; high levels of racial segregation perpetuate more racial intolerance, which, in turn, bolsters further segregation. Ironically, the very integration that can bridge various social chasms seems to be undercutting the bonding experiences that are so important for fostering racial understanding in the first place.

REFERENCES

Alesina, Albert, and E. La Ferrara. 2000. Participation in Heterogeneous Communities. *Quarterly Journal of Economics* (August): 847–904.

Banfield, Edward. 1970. *The Unheavenly City*. Boston: Little, Brown.

Bledsoe, Timothy, Susan Welch, Lee Sigelman, and Michael Combs. 1995. Residential Context and Racial Solidarity among African Americans. *American Journal of Political Science* 39(2): 434–58.

Bobo, Lawrence, and Camille L. Zubrinsky. 1996. Attitudes on Residential Integration: Perceived Status Differences. Mere In-Group Preference, or Racial Prejudice? *Social Forces* 73(3): 883–909.

Boger, John Charles, and Judith Welch Wegner, 1986. *Race and Poverty in American Cities.* Chapel Hill: University of North Carolina Press.

Campbell, David. 2006. *Why We Vote: How Schools and Communities Shape Our Civic Life.* Princeton, NJ: Princeton University Press.

Clark, William A.V. 1992. Residential Preferences and Residential Choices in a Multi-Ethnic Context. *Demography* 29(3):451–66.

Cohen, Cathy, and Michael Dawson. 1993. Neighborhood Poverty and African American Politics. *American Political Science Review* 87:286–302.

Costa, Dora, and Matthew Kahn. 2003. Civic Engagement and Community Heterogeneity: an Economist's Perspective. *Perspectives on Politics* 1:103–11.

Dawson, Michael C. 1994. *Behind the Mule: Race, Class, and African-American Politics.* Princeton: Princeton University Press.

Guterbock, Thomas, and Bruce London. 1983. Race, Political Orientation, and Participation: An Empirical Test of Four Competing Theories. *American Sociological Review* 48:439–53.

Jones-Correa, Michael, and David Leal. 1996. Becoming Hispanic: Secondary Panethnic Identifications among Latin American-Origin Populations in the United States. *Hispanic Journal of Behavioral Sciences* 18(1):214–54.

Kim, Claire. 2000. *Bitter Fruit: The Politics of Black-Korean Conflict in New York City.* New Haven: Yale University Press.

Krysan, Maria, and Reynolds Farley. 2002. The Residential Preferences of Blacks: Do They Explain Persistent Segregation? *Social Forces* 80:937–80.

Leighley, Jan, and A. Vedlitz. 1999. Race, Ethnicity and Political Participation: Competing Models and Contrasting Explanations. *Journal of Politics* 61:1092–114.

Meyer, Stephen. 2001. *As Long as They Don't Move Next Door: Segregation and Racial Conflict in American Neighborhoods.* New York: Rowman and Littlefield Publishers.

Oliver, J. Eric. 2001. *Democracy in Suburbia.* Princeton: Princeton University Press.

Orfield, Gary. 1988. Separate Societies: Have the Kerner Warnings Come True? In *Quiet Riots: Race and Poverty in the United States*, edited by Fred R. Harris and Roger Wilkins. New York: Pantheon Books, 1988.

Pettigrew, Thomas F. 1979. Racial Change and Social Policy. *Annals of the American Academy of Political and Social Science* 441:114–31.

Portes, Alejandro, and Robert L. Bach. 1985. *Latin Journey: Cuban and Mexican Immigrants in the United States.* Berkeley: University of California Press.

Putnam, Robert. 2000. *Bowling Alone: The Collapse and Revival of American Community.* New York: Simon and Schuster.

Rieder, Jonathan. 1987. *Canarsie: The Jews and Italians of Brooklyn against Liberalism.* Cambridge, MA: Harvard University Press.

Varshney, Ashutosh. 2002. *Ethnic Conflict and Civic Life: Hindus and Muslims in India.* New Haven: Yale University Press.

Verba, Sidney, Kay Schlozman, and Henry Brady. 1995. *Voice and Equality: Civic Voluntarism in American Politics.* Cambridge, MA: Harvard University Press.

Welch, Susan, Lee Sigelman, Timothy Bledsoe, and Michael Combs. 2001. *Race and Place: Race Relations in an American City.* New York: Cambridge University Press.

Wilson, William Julius. 1985. *The Truly Disadvantaged: The Inner City, the Underclass and Public Policy.* Chicago: University of Chicago Press.

Wilson, William Julius, and Richard Taub. 2006. *There Goes the Neighborhood: Racial, Ethnic, and Class Tensions in Four Chicago Neighborhoods and Their Meaning for America.* New York: Alfred A. Knopf.

Wong, Janelle. 2006. *Democracy's Promise: Immigrants and America's Civic Institutions.* Ann Arbor, MI: University of Michigan Press.

NOTES

1. The civic participation scale was a simple count of the number of civic activities the respondent said he or she had engaged in during the past year, including voting, signing a petition, attending a political meeting, working on a community project, and participating in a demonstration. The civic participation index was rescaled to 0 to 1 for this table. The informal social interaction scale was a composite measure of five activities: having friends visit one's home, visiting with relatives, socializing with coworkers outside of work,

hanging out with friends in public places, and playing cards or board games with friends. At least two of the activities had to be engaged in for the scale to be calculated. The index was calculated as the mean of the standardized responses to the five questions. The index was rescaled to 0 to 1.

2. The predicted probability at each point was calculated using CLARIFY software. The full equations are listed in online appendix B, table B18. Together, these items comprise a good battery of indicators of people's civic activities, and the latter three are the best indicators of their participation in local activities. Each of these measures was regressed on a set of predictive variables including the percent white in the metropolitan area and the percent white in the neighborhood as well as a host of individual-level controls for race, income, education, sex, and homeownership.

3. Civic associations are counted as sports clubs, hobby clubs, trade unions, professional associations, consumer organizations, organizations for human rights, environmental associations, religious organizations, political parties, organizations for education, social clubs (for the elderly or the retired or fraternal organizations), neighborhood associations, veterans' organizations, self-help groups, welfare organizations, and any other voluntary civic associations. Questions were asked in order: after seeing the list of civic groups, respondents were asked to report whether they actively participate or do any voluntary works in those associations.

4. Of course, race is not the only contextual determinant of American associational life; the level of affluence is also negatively associated with most civic activities. This finding, which is consistent with that of a prior study (Oliver 2001), suggests that people are highly individualized and socially disconnected particularly in rich and small geographic areas.

5. Online appendix B, table B19, lists the results from multivariate linear regressions that estimate the relationship of individual-level and geographic-level variables to scale, measuring how much they informally socialized with neighbors and whether they participated in a neighborhood group. Once again, the equations control for individual-level factors such as age, education, length of residence, and homeownership and for the level of incorporation into American society using variables for citizenship and political knowledge. The remaining variables estimate the effects of the racial composition of the neighborhood (measured by the percent white) with interaction terms for each of the three minority groups. These interaction terms measure the additional impact of the white percentage of the neighborhood for each minority group and should be viewed in conjunction with the variable measuring the participation rate attributed to that specific group as well as the variable measuring the baseline effect of the white percentage of the neighborhood.

6. Interestingly, black informal social ties do not follow a linear pattern with respect to the black percentage in their neighborhood. Rather, much like their racial views, blacks' informal social activity scores are highest in the middle range of black neighborhoods. Blacks in neighborhoods that are 40–60 percent black score significantly higher on the informal social activity scale than those in neighborhoods that are much less black or predominantly black.

7. For the trust question, respondents were asked, "How much can you trust people in your neighborhood? Can you trust them a lot, trust them some, trust them only a little, or trust them not at all?" The answers to this question were coded on a four-point scale from not trusting to most trusting. For the neighborhood belonging, respondents were asked, "Do people in your community give you a sense of belonging" to which they could answer yes or no. To rate the quality of life in their community, respondents were asked, "On the whole, how would you rate your community as a place to live—poor, only fair, good, or excellent." This was coded into a four-point scale from poor to excellent. These items were then regressed on the same set of predictors used to measure civic and social involvement above. The results are listed in online appendix B, table B20.

8. This last figure was derived from probability estimates from logistic regression equations. Logistic regression was not employed, despite the fact of a dichotomous dependent variable, in order to maintain comparability of coefficients across all equations. There are no substantive differences in the findings between the OLS and logistic regression equations.

9. There are, of course, many individual accounts of Latinos and Asian Americans in American life (e.g., Kim 2000; Portes and Bach 1985), but I could find no systematic research on the civic and social patterns of these groups in relationship to their social surroundings.

APPENDIX A

Data Sources

This book utilizes a combination of census and survey data to analyze the relationship between racial and economic contexts and racial attitudes. It relies primarily on four major surveys and the 2000 U.S. Census. The first is the 1992–94 Multi-City Study of Urban Inequality (MCSUI). The MCSUI data are the product of more than forty researchers at fifteen colleges and universities. A household survey was undertaken of adults over twenty-one years of age, oversampling in census tracts with high proportions of poor and minority residents. Although primarily designed as a study of labor market outcomes, the extensive surveys also had questions regarding racial attitudes and neighborhood choice. The MCSUI is a stratified-area probability household survey from 1994 and 1995 that generated over 8,900 face-to-face interviews with oversamples of blacks, Latinos, and Asian Americans in the metropolitan areas of Atlanta, Boston, and Detroit and in Los Angeles County. Adults twenty-one years and older were interviewed in English, Spanish, Korean, Mandarin, or Cantonese.

The MCSUI oversampled underrepresented minority groups whose small numbers and geographic concentration in the general population often led to lack of sufficient sample sizes in traditional surveys. The Atlanta sample includes 651 whites, 832 blacks, and forty-five persons who identified with neither group. The Boston sample includes 469 whites, 518 blacks, and 833 Latinos. The Los Angeles sample includes 861 whites, 1,119 blacks, 986 Latinos, and 1,055 Asian Americans. Among the 1,055 Asian Americans surveyed, the majority (nearly 80 percent) were of Chinese and Korean origin, and the remainder of the sample was made up of respondents of Japanese and South Asian descent. The majority (88 percent) of the Asian American sample were foreign-born. Over half of the Los Angeles Latino sample (68 percent) were of Mexican origin. Central Americans, primarily from El Salvador and Guatemala, made up the remainder of the sample. Similar to the Asian American sample, the majority of Los Angeles Latinos included in the study (80 percent) were foreign-born. The overwhelming majority of Latinos in the Boston sample were either Puerto Rican or Dominican in descent. To identify the racial context, the census block group of each respondent was identified and matched with appropriate census data. Each block group varies from several hundred to up to two thousand in population size.

The second major survey is the 2000 Social Capital Community Benchmark Survey (SCCBS). Initiated by Professor Robert Putnam and the Saguaro Seminar at the Kennedy School of Government at Harvard University, the SSCBS was designed to measure various indicators of social capital and community involvement. It entailed surveys conducted in forty-one different communities around the United States as well as a national sample. The national sample of over 3,000 respondents contains an oversampling of blacks and Hispanics, totaling at least 500 blacks and 500 Hispanics in all. This required screening to identify households with black or Hispanic residents. This screening was conducted randomly across the continental United States: areas of higher concentration were not targeted in this design. For each respondent, local geography was measured at both the metropolitan and zip code level and once again came from the 2000 U.S. Census.

The third major data set is the Citizen, Information, and Democracy (CID) Survey conducted in 2004. The CID consists of in-person interviews with a nationwide,

(Continued)

> **▶ APPENDIX A (Continued)**
>
> clustered sample of 1,001 Americans who answered an eighty-minute questionnaire. The CID contains extensive questions about civic engagement (both informal social activities and activities in formal clubs or organizations), social capital, democratic values, and diversity. For the CID, the metropolitan area and the census tract of each respondent were identified and supplemented with data from the 2000 census.
>
> The final data set comes from the 2004 National Politics Study initiated by the Program for Research on Black Americans and the Center for Political Studies at the University of Michigan's Institute for Social Research and sponsored by the National Science Foundation, the University of Michigan, and the Carnegie Corporation. From September 2004 to February 2005, 3,339 telephone interviews were conducted in the United States with adults and a large oversample of African American, Latino, and Asian American respondents. The survey queried respondents on their voting preferences, party affiliation, organizational membership, and racial attitudes. The public release of these data included no geographic identifiers and, unlike the other data, was not matched with census data.

14

As Mayors Take Charge: School Politics in the City

MICHAEL W. KIRST

In the early 1990s, after many decades of a limited role in education, mayors in some cities began to take control of their schools. Boston initiated this changed mayoral role in 1991, followed by Chicago in 1995, Cleveland in 1998, Harrisburg, Pennsylvania, in 2000, New York City in 2002, and the District of Columbia in 2007. Baltimore and Philadelphia had considerable mayoral control in the 1990s, but most of it later reverted back to the state. Oakland, California, the District of Columbia, and Detroit initiated partial mayoral control, which failed and was subsequently abandoned. This pattern suggests that the local context is crucial in determining the characteristics and sustenance of mayoral control of schools. Los Angeles, Fresno, and Albuquerque mayors, for example, have all been frustrated in their attempts to take charge of schools, in part because their school districts extend beyond the city boundary.

A basic rationale for mayoral control has been the assumed link between improved schools, city economic development, and retention of middle-class families. An implicit policy assumption is that mayors are better equipped than school boards to highlight school problems and mobilize the personnel and resources needed to solve them. Larry Cuban and Michael Usdan posit a three-pronged

Viteritti, Joseph P. (Editor). *When Mayors Take Charge: School Governance in the City.* Washington, DC: Brookings Institution Press, 2009, p. 46. http://site.ebrary.com/lib/fordham/Doc?id=10338456&ppg=63

theory for why mayoral control might succeed: First, linking urban school governance to existing political structures (including the business community) will produce organizational effectiveness, which will improve teaching and learning as measured by standardized test scores and enhanced coordination with city-provided offerings in recreation, the arts, and medical and social services. Second, better management will make urban school systems more efficient and effective by tightly aligning organizational goals, curriculum, rewards and sanctions, professional development of teachers and principals, and classroom instruction to academic achievement. Third, when noneducators who lead urban districts are connected openly to existing state and local political structures, the chances of improving and sustaining students' academic achievement will increase.[1]

Another theory of action places greater emphasis on enhancement of accountability. Success is partly based on streamlining governance so that fewer people are held accountable by more voters. A single person, the mayor, is accountable rather than several board members elected by subdistricts in staggered elections. In these theories of action, the basic hypothesis is that mayors are better able than school boards to spotlight attention on problems in their districts and increase resources to address those problems.

However, most policy analysts would doubt whether governance changes in and of themselves can directly improve classroom teaching and learning.[2] There is a complex multidirectional flow of influence and resources from government to students. But without new central governance many urban districts cannot adopt major reforms or improvements.[3] Mayors can influence classrooms in many ways by adopting curriculum standards, hiring better teachers, and providing high-quality instructional materials.

TRADE-OFFS AMONG CONFLICTUAL VALUES

Herbert Kaufman has provided an insightful analysis of the evolution of local governance.[4] He demonstrates that historically city governance has been characterized by a search for accommodation among three competing governance objectives: representative democracy, centralized executive leadership, and technical nonpartisan competence. Control by a large subdistrict-elected school board such as that in New York in 1970 would exemplify the first; mayoral control of education, as in New York City, the second; and the third, the civil service system in 1950 that empowered trained and qualified nonpolitical civil servants who made decisions based upon technical and professional considerations.[5] At various stages of New York City's history each of these three governance objectives has been ascendant. The objectives compete and cannot all be maximized simultaneously. The crucial decision at any given time is which one objective should be traded off to make another ascendant. This could depend on the specific conditions and context of the city at a particular time.

The reaction to Tammany Hall spurred the creation of the city's board of education, housed at 110 Livingston Street in Brooklyn, at the beginning of the twentieth century. Nothing exemplifies the goal of professional civil service teacher hiring in the 1950s more than the New York City Board of Examiners, which licensed teachers and principals. The civil rights movement was an important impetus for the decentralized elected boards in 1970. In the 1990s, the shortcomings of the New York City schools' performance and dissatisfaction with the "community-controlled" boards encouraged mayoral takeover. The excessive emphasis on one of the three objectives tends to set in motion demands for redressing the balance. For example, a July 26, 2007, poll conducted by Quinnipiac University indicates that New York public opinion favors more representative democracy with shared control by the next mayor and with a board of education. The same poll, however, concludes that most voters think Mayor Bloomberg's takeover of the public schools has been a success.[6]

Theoretically, one could diminish the need for trade-offs by trying to emphasize all three objectives at once. Mayoral control could be mitigated through decentralized school-site councils like Chicago had in 1992. More decisions could be delegated to professional educators with graduate degrees and selected through civil service examinations. But this fight-power-with-other-power approach would likely lead to stalemates, so choices need to made among the three values and the right balance crafted for a particular local context. This decision can be informed by a review of mayoral control in other cities.

How can one evaluate the arguments favoring redistribution of power from school boards to mayors? One useful concept, called "institutional choice," focuses on the crucial policy decision, of which an alternative institution should be the decisionmaker. For example, courts in the 1960s were reluctant to delegate civil rights protection to local school boards in Alabama. Another type of institutional choice is whether to place various functions in the hands of markets (for example, parental choice of schools) or politics (for example, school board elections). Both of these institutional choices could be problematic. Some parents may not have many good schools to choose from, but turnout for many big-city school elections is less than 15 percent of the district's registered voters. The recent state accountability movement included an institutional choice to enhance the curricular and testing roles of state government by overriding local decisions on what to teach.

Two general characteristics help guide institutional choice in making decisions: agreement on substantive goals and the capacity to achieve them. Substantive goals are crucial because of the need to ensure support for a policy. Courts may be more supportive of civil rights than some school boards, but the courts' substantive goals must be buttressed by a capacity to implement its decisions in the local school context. Courts cannot run school districts very well.

So which institution should be chosen to control the schools? A method for choosing can be called "comparative institutional advantage," that is,

> the distrust directed at one decision-maker [e.g., a school board] must be carefully weighed against the advantages of that decision-maker. Both the advantages and disadvantages of an alternative decision-maker [e.g., the mayor] also must be carefully analyzed. The logic of comparative institutional advantage implies the futility of seeking a perfect or ideal decision-maker or implementation of a policy favored by local citizens. The real world offers a least-worst choice of imperfect institutions to make and implement policy.[7] . . .

LOCAL CONTEXT MATTERS: BOSTON AND CHICAGO ADOPT DIFFERENT STRATEGIES

A closer examination of two cities demonstrates the importance of local context in balancing the three competing values discussed above. Boston put more emphasis on technical expertise under an experienced city superintendent who had a traditional education and professional background. Chicago chose a city administrator with no prior top-level experience in education administration. The two cities' initial change strategies were different. But both cities featured executive centralization under a mayor as its prime value with scant attention to representative democracy. The new powers granted to mayors in Chicago and Boston resulted in fundamental changes in the governance of the large urban education systems in these two cities. These changes could easily be labeled "regime changes."

Chicago has 450,000 students enrolled in six hundred schools with a $6.7 billion budget, while Boston has 58,000 students with a $73.4 million budget. The systems in both cities are now governed by leaders closely affiliated with the mayors and largely answerable to them. Boston now has a school policy committee appointed by the mayor; in Chicago a corporate-style board, also mayor appointed, oversees the city's schools. Out of these governance changes have emerged significant policy changes that have, for the most part, received considerable public support compared with previous governance systems. This analysis encompasses the initial years of mayoral takeover in both cities.

Despite similarities in the changing shape of governance in Boston and Chicago, the mayors and the leaders of the school systems opted for substantially different styles of school reform. School districts in both cities had been fiscally dependent before takeover, but the mayors did not have full control of the school board process. The Chicago superintendent, Thomas Payzant, and Boston's mayor, Thomas Menino, focused on a "professional" model of reform, aligning education standards and building teacher and administrator capacity. In Chicago, on the other hand, the mayor, Richard Daley, and the chief executive officer of the public school system, Paul Vallas, emphasized a top-down model (layered over a previous school-site decentralization reform model) in which the managers create a vision with clear accountability mechanisms and both schools and students receive sanctions if the achievement goals are not met.

Formal governance changes enhancing the role of the mayor were introduced in Boston and Chicago in the late 1980s and the early 1990s. In Boston, a series of decisions between 1989 and 1996, both legislative and electoral, gave the mayor the power to appoint the Boston School Committee. Up until this time, the school committee had been directly elected in some form. This change gave the mayor a much stronger role in the operations of the school system and created a direct line of authority to him.

Boston's mayor Raymond Flynn spearheaded the charge to alter the governance structure of the Boston public schools. He was supported by the state legislature, which was becoming increasingly concerned with the Boston schools, and by the business community. Much of the African American community was skeptical of eliminating an elected school committee, and the Irish of South Boston (who had long held power on the elected committee) also opposed the change.

In Chicago, the governance changes of 1995 granting an enhanced role to the mayor were layered over earlier reforms instituted in 1988. That reform, which was supported by state Democrats and civic activists, shifted power from the district to local school councils. In this legislative change, the mayor's ability to appoint the city's school board was decreased. However, the impetus for this decentralization was not a desire to increase the influence of educators. Rather, Dorothy Shipps argues, it was designed to enhance the influence of parents and community members; she comments that "educators were blamed for the problems and their discretion curtailed."[8] At first there were many candidates for the local-site councils, but over time fewer ran, and competition decreased. Moreover, the system lost considerable central direction, so that over time the value of democratic representation became less urgent, and a stronger executive at the center became a higher priority.

Whereas the 1988 reforms pushed control toward the local schools, the legislation passed in 1995 shifted power up the ladder to the mayor. These changes gave the Chicago mayor more authority than any mayor since before the Progressive Era, effectively turning the education system into a department of city government. Specifically, the 1995 legislation eliminated the school board nominating committee, which had effectively minimized the mayor's ability to select school board members, and replaced the traditional board with an advisory board to the mayor. In this new structure, only one of the five members was to be focused on education (through the chief education officer), and the mayor appointed all members. The legislation also temporarily limited the right of the unions to strike and reduced the number of issues subject to union bargaining.

In both cities, the primary initiators of governance changes granting more power to the mayors were the business community, the mayor (especially in Boston), and state legislators. Local groups, such as community activists and minority group representatives, were not directly involved, and educator organizations including the teacher unions were also peripheral to the debates or opposed the change. Reformers in the two cities had similar reasons for supporting these governance changes. The primary goal in both cases was to establish clearer lines of political authority and responsibility, making the city's mayor ultimately accountable for the progress (or lack thereof) of the public schools.

Although the goals of those who pushed through the governance changes in Boston and Chicago had certain similarities, there were also some important differences. In Chicago, there was a strong emphasis on improving the effectiveness and efficiency of the public schools—particularly the fiscal efficiency of the district. Although improved efficiency was also a factor in Boston, it was not nearly as central to the discussion in that city as was improved classroom instruction.

Another difference between the reforms in these two cities involved the role and purpose of the district's "leader." Reflecting the focus on efficiency, the Chicago Public Schools were to be led by a business-style chief executive officer, rather than a traditional superintendent. In Boston, on the other hand, both Flynn and Menino explicitly wanted a strong educator-leader at the head of the school system. Although Mayor Flynn wanted to be held accountable for the state of the Boston public schools, he claimed he was not interested in being directly involved with the district's operations. Mayor Menino made Tom Payzant a member of his cabinet, but the mayor often spoke for the school system at contentious community meetings. Before coming to Boston, Payzant had been school superintendent in San Diego and Oklahoma City.

Finally, the view of city and state leaders about the capacity of educators to reform education was rather different. In Chicago, there was continual skepticism about the ability (and motivation) of educators to improve schools—both the 1988 reforms, which shifted power toward parents and community members and the 1995 reforms, which granted additional power to the mayor, moved control away from educators. Boston leaders shared some of these concerns, but they were still interested in vesting considerable authority in public education professionals.

BOSTON AND CHICAGO: SIMILAR BUT DIFFERENT

In Chicago, Paul Vallas, a former budget director for the city, moved to the new position of chief executive officer of the Chicago public schools. The selection of Vallas supported the business and other community interests in having someone from outside traditional public education at the helm of the city's schools. In this top-down change model, management creates a vision and defines clear sanctions for individuals and schools that do not make progress toward that vision.

In Boston, Payzant was a much more traditional choice for a district leader, and his selection reflected the mayor's interest in having a professional educator who would stay away (at least to some extent) from the political issues that had consumed much of the time of previous superintendents. Payzant's approach was much more within the framework of traditional education reform, and his primary focus reflected a professional education model involving higher standards and professional educator capacity building through extensive staff development. In short, Boston's local context valued the technical nonpartisan competence of educators much more highly than did Chicago, but both cities moved to trade off representative democracy for more-centralized mayoral leadership.

In 1996 roughly one hundred Chicago City Hall employees came to work in the central office, displacing more traditional education staff. While school-site councils still exist at all the Chicago public schools, their influence has been minimized, and the new central office leaders have increased their role in the functioning of the city's schools. Owing to the combination of no budget crises, no strikes, and a generally positive view among the public of the reforms that Mayor Daly instituted, the legitimacy of the school system improved.

The direct impact of the governance changes on the actual governance structure of the public schools has not been as marked in Boston as in Chicago. The most notable change has been the elimination of the bitter battles within the Boston School Committee and between the committee and the mayor— a logical outcome of the school committee's being appointed rather than elected. As in Chicago, labor relations, particularly with the teachers union, have improved in recent years. Also similar to Chicago, some of the most blatant education budget problems in Boston have disappeared. While the Boston mayor has always influenced the amount of money spent by the public school system, governance changes have allowed him to also influence how those dollars are spent. Unlike Chicago, however, Boston saw no dramatic changes in the structure or staffing of the school district's central office brought about by the installation of city employees in key units.

The style and substance of the education reforms that are taking place in the context of these governance changes are quite different in the two cities. Although accountability measures in Chicago have generally focused on minimal standards and on raising the educational outcomes of the worst-faring students in the city's schools, there have also been changes for those students at the upper end of the performance spectrum. For example, Chicago created alternatives such as magnet schools, accelerated programs such as International Baccalaureate options, and charter schools. Alongside efforts to remove "troublesome or slow-learning students" from regular public schools to other settings such as transition centers and alternative high schools, the push for more "upper-end" options is linked with the goal of bringing middle-class families back into the Chicago public schools.

One hope for increased mayoral control of schools was that mayors would be more able to link together currently fragmented programs designed to support students and families. In Chicago, Mayor Daley has been able to help schools through support from a variety of other city agencies. But there has not been as much integration between schools and children's services as some had wanted.

Overall, two assumptions were part of the initial Chicago strategy. The first is that much of the capacity necessary to improve performance was already available within the public school system and that incentives and sanctions were necessary to draw out this preexisting capacity. Thus there has been less emphasis in Chicago than in Boston on building additional classroom instructional capacity through professional development. The second is that test scores, though perhaps not a perfect measure, are the most logical means of assessing progress in the provision of quality education.

The style of the education reforms being undertaken in Boston, while arising out of a similar governance change, is quite different than in Chicago. Payzant emphasized his long-term commitment to a decade of steady, resolute progress through central district staff training, new materials, and high standards. Chicago left choices about reading curriculum to each school and provided options. Some of the methods Payzant has used include leadership development, whole-school change, diagnostic classroom testing, and creation of a reorganization plan directed at student performance. His focus on teaching and learning issues has included a reliance to some extent on professional educator norms, rather than sanctions, as a means to increase performance. Boston, unlike Chicago, has seen little change in the tenure of administrators or teachers and no talk of radical reconstitution of failing schools.

The different directions taken by leaders in Boston and Chicago were not simply the whims of individual mayors and school district chiefs. Rather, they reflected to some extent the different historical and political contexts of these two cities, especially the desires of powerful constituencies within these cities and states. In particular, the regime changes in both cities reflect the different emphases of the business communities. For example, owing to the role of the business community and Republican legislative leaders in initiating the 1995 reform in Chicago, it is not surprising that a business-style leader like Vallas was initially brought in to direct the school system. Initially, the Boston business community was concerned with fiscal issues, but after mayoral takeover it tended to focus more on issues of curriculum, school quality, and teacher improvement.

In 2005 the Aspen Institute commissioned a team of experienced researchers and educators to evaluate the Boston experience.[9] The study, mostly positive, points out that there is still a long way to go. Boston has a clear theory of instructional improvement and educator capacity building. It has strong central leadership and some noteworthy test score and college transition gains. But graduation rates are low, and the achievement gap by race and ethnicity remains. Stronger central executive leadership has been greatly enhanced, but Boston struggles with how to provide grassroots representation and its impact on school policy.

The Boston Parent Organizing Network, formed by a diverse group of parents, activists, and community members, began to advocate for improvement in the Boston public schools. The parent organization helped create a new position, deputy superintendent for family and community engagement, and a reorganization of the public schools' Family Resource Center. Parents continue to express concerns about the uneven quality of Boston schools and about the quality of instruction for English learners and handicapped students. The Aspen Institute has noted that "from parents and community groups we also heard concerns about inclusiveness. There is a sense that the city's elites— the political leadership, the business community, and the universities—have greater access to decision-making authority than other groups. . . . But many city residents and grassroots groups feel left out. They feel they have opportunities for input but are not at the table when decisions are made."[10]

The Boston school board before mayoral takeover was considered to be fractious and ineffective, so reinstituting that form of democratic representation has been rejected in a voter referendum. However, the newer mayor-appointed seven-member school committee takes two hours for its meetings twice a month. Nonpolicy matters such as contract, personnel, and day-to-day operations are delegated to the superintendent. The mayor handles much of the external politics for the Boston public schools.

THE CLEVELAND CASE

The evolution of Cleveland's education system under mayoral control highlights the difficulties and complexity in assessing the impact of mayoral control.[11] Fifty-five thousand students are enrolled in Cleveland public schools in 2007–08, with a budget of $700 million. The city's mayor, Michael White, appointed Barbara Byrd-Bennett from the New York City school system in 1998, and she stayed through 2006. She was clearly in command of the district, with the school board and the mayor in the background. She assumed leadership of a deeply troubled system, staggering under the weight of a $150 million debt, that recently had been taken over by the state. Observers described the system as being in chaos and despair. Before her arrival in Cleveland, an operating tax increase had been approved by the city's voters in 1996, and Byrd-Bennett was able to gradually pay off the debt and had clean audits from 2001 until she left the post in 2006.

Byrd-Bennett focused on academic improvement using budget increases from state, local, and foundation resources. The elementary school day was increased thirty minutes, with eighty minutes specified for literacy. She recruited a large group of new young teachers along with instructional specialists in math, English, and technology. Teacher training, support services, and computers were added, along with summer schools. She reconfigured the grades into a K–8 structure. Cleveland's expenditures grew by 53 percent from 1998 to 2003, slightly more than the statewide average. There were significant gains in the proficiency pass rates for grades 4 and 6 on reading and math tests. In 2001 Cleveland passed a $335 million school repair bond. The continuation of mayoral control was approved by the voters in 2002 by a significant majority.

But in 2003 Cleveland's budget turned around and fell from $670 million in 2003 to $558 million in 2004. About twelve hundred teachers were cut; nearly all of them were young and had been hired after Byrd-Bennett tried to staff low-performing schools. Class sizes increased substantially, while assistant principals, social workers, and security officers were cut. In 2005 voters turned down a school operating tax by 55 to 45 percent, with white voters highly negative and black voters (who turned out at lower rates) more supportive of the tax increase. The district touted an increase in fourth- and sixth-grade reading scores since 1998 at a rate twice the state average since 1998.

Perhaps Byrd-Bennett stayed too long in the job (she thinks so, as she says in a 2006 newspaper interview).[12] Her compensation and some underpayments to the state created a whiff of scandal. But Cleveland is the poorest city in the nation, and by the time she left, falling property values resulted in a decline in local tax revenue of 17 percent between 1998 and 2006. Ohio's school finance system is not equalized and relies heavily on local property values. Enrollment has declined by 15 percent, and gains in achievement scores turned flat after 2004.

Although there is no groundswell to repeal mayoral control, there is rising criticism that the board is too much a rubber stamp for the administration. In July 2007, the new mayor, Frank Jackson, was criticized by the *Plain Dealer:*

> [The terms of] five of the nine members expired June 30. It was bad enough that City Hall did such an abysmal job of publicizing the openings that only seven candidates initially applied. It is unforgivable that the mayor chose to reappoint four of the members, three of whom could be poster children for the term "ineffectual," and at the same time ousted John Moss. Rather than embrace a board member who is both articulate and engaged in a district business, Jackson instead rewarded members who question little and lead less.[13]

More citizens are turning to the city council for help, but because council members have no direct authority over the school system, they are uncertain about their role. Council members attend community meetings about school closures and reorganizations but cannot do much about citizen concerns. In an exit interview, Byrd-Bennett said that meaningful reform will not take place until community leaders address the deep-seated economic and social problems in city neighborhoods.[14] Early studies of mayoral control, however, have concluded that mayoral integration of children, youth, and family policies with schools has not been impressive.[15]

What can we conclude from this brief Cleveland history? Did mayoral takeover help create the initial student attainment gains? Did more and then less money make a difference in system performance? Is the balance between central executive leadership and democratic representation right? In 2005 an Aspen Institute report praised the Cleveland literacy system and observed that "by every measure, the Cleveland Municipal School District has made steady progress since 1998."[16] The report illustrated how Cleveland had aligned assessment, curriculum, and instruction. Cleveland created an extensive classroom formative assessment to provide early feedback. In order to provide more consistent classroom implementation, Cleveland received funds from the Stupski Foundation and the State of Ohio to integrate human and financial resources into a specific implementation plan. Teachers and principals were provided with pacing charts and standards specific to each grade, along with extensive professional development. Cleveland's instructional approach for standards alignment has significant research support. But other factors intervened, and its future is unclear. Cleveland also demonstrates how different mayors have different views about their role and the risks in basing mayoral control on the attributes of a single mayor. Frank Jackson, the present mayor, has been much less active and assertive than was Mayor White or Mayor Jane Campbell, who succeeded White.

The mayors who have served Cleveland since the institution of mayoral control have never been the public face of the school system. They have worked behind the scenes with a prominent superintendent. A nominating committee screens board candidates, and the mayor appoints them to four-year terms and selects a board president. The mayor and the board appoint the superintendent. This system began in 1998 and voters agreed to keep it in 2002. The board is not especially active in public engagement or public questioning of the superintendent's decisions. The public is allowed to speak at only one of the two board meetings a month. Board committee meetings are private.

THE IMPACT OF MAYORAL CONTROL

One city, Detroit, has retreated from mayoral influence over schools. The Detroit mayor, Dennis Archer, never wanted control, and the Republican legislature's inclusion of a state official on the Detroit board with a partial veto failed to gain much public legitimacy for the Detroit mayor's enhanced role. So it was no surprise that in 2005 the Detroit voters approved an eleven-member school board elected by subdistricts. Even though different city contexts are crucial, a variety of standards can be used to assess overall mayoral impact. A reasonable standard for success is the one used by Ronald Reagan in a 1980 televised debate with President Carter, "Are you better off now than you were four years ago?" Reagan knew the record of inflation, Iran hostages, and other issues inclined the voters to say no—as did Detroit voters in 2005 about mayoral control of the public schools.

Boston and Cleveland voters overwhelmingly reauthorized mayoral control, and the Illinois legislature voted by a large majority to continue the Chicago mayor's role. Partial control by the mayor in Oakland and Washington never worked and was eventually dropped. Jerry Brown, Oakland's mayor, added three members to a seven-person elected school board but decided it was ineffective, so he did not push for renewal. The District of Columbia hybrid model of four mayoral appointees and five elected members was characterized by former mayor Anthony Williams as "trying to drive a car with one pedal." The full control won by the district's mayor, Adrian Fenty, in 2007 has some new features, such as his appointment of an ombudsman for citizen complaints, and might be instructive for other cities.

In sum, none of the present mayor-controlled cities wants the old system back. Boston does not pine for the fractious and ineffective school committee; Cleveland's board was characterized by "nonstop confrontations, intrusions, chaos, and showmanship."[17] Chicago's fifteen-member school board was too large to operate effectively in 1994. New York's central school board, appointed by borough presidents and the mayor, was supplemented by thirty-two decentralized districts with considerable authority. There has been no widespread public support in New York to restore this pre-2002 complex decentralized system.

This does not imply that there is no dissatisfaction with mayoral takeover. One argument heard often is that the mayor cannot fundamentally improve classroom instruction and so ends up facilitating marginal changes in buildings, budgets, labor peace, textbooks, supplies, new teachers, and so on. Moreover, some analysts are disappointed in the mayors' progress in combining education with children and youth policies and services. There are no comprehensive studies of mayoral impact on unions and collective bargaining. Critics contend that mayoral control has been implemented in ways that overstress executive centralization without sufficient attention to representative democracy, citizen participation, or professional technical control.

Boston and Cleveland highlight the uncertain role of city councils in all the mayoral takeover cities. No city has a clear idea of what the council should be doing in terms of public representation and citizen complaints about the schools. The thirteen-member Boston City Council retains its approval of the entire amount of the school budget and holds hearings on school issues. But these council hearings are largely symbolic and theatrical. The council has scant impact on school policy or operations, except a few minor concessions by the mayor on the budget to get the total amount approved. The plan suggested by Los Angeles mayor Antonio Villaraigosa had no formal role for the city council, even though the council has major operational responsibilities for city departments. In sum, if there is no traditional school board, citizens turn to the city council for redress of complaints but with scant impact. The Richmond, Virginia, mayor proposed a role for the city council in nominating school board members and the superintendent in a new mayor-council school takeover plan. These types of divided power arrangements, however, like the partial mayor control structures in Oakland, Washington, and Detroit, raise questions about who is in charge.

GOVERNANCE OPTIONS FOR MAYORS

There are numerous options for mayoral involvement in schools. Complete takeover of school boards, authorization of charter schools, selecting slates of school board candidates, working in partnership with school districts on specific issues, and operating as a convener and facilitator to bring various stakeholders together for school reform. Again, the appearance in some cities of these options, and more, illustrates the importance of distinctive local contexts as an important determinant of the mayor's role.[18]

Governance is not a panacea for all the school systems' problems, and empirical data such as test scores cannot be the only indicator of progress. Choices among governance alternatives must be made, but no alternative will satisfy all demands that confront school systems. Governance choice is a pragmatic process that must set priorities among the three competing objectives outlined earlier: decentralized executive leadership, representative democracy, and technical nonpartisan competence. Chicago went through all of these priorities between 1987 and 1997. In 1987 the city had a powerful general superintendent of schools in charge of a large centralized bureaucracy.

In 1988 Chicago passed a law to devolve considerable decisionmaking discretion to each school site, including selection of the principal by an elected site council. The site council had significant influence over curriculum and some budget categories. The site councils were partially governed by a fifteen-member school board. In 1995, however, the Illinois legislature gave the mayor dominant power, and Mayor Richard M. Daly reasserted his control over many aspects of the school sites' former direction. Chicago's school-site councils lost many of their prerogatives through a complex array of problems such as fiscal deficits, low voter turnout, lack of support from teachers' and principals' organizations, business dissatisfaction, and some poorly performing councils.

One view is that strong centralized leadership by the mayor is needed to "jolt" a complacent and ossified school system. Election of two board members every two years cannot shake up the school system sufficiently. Mayor Fenty assumed control of the District of Columbia schools in summer 2007 and found dilapidated facilities; he saw responses to "urgent requests" being satisfied in 379 days, flags with forty-nine stars, and a backlog of ten thousand work orders.[19] Washington has had seven superintendents in the past ten years. Mayoral control has jolted the system by closing twenty-three schools, firing ninety-eight central office employees, creating an early retirement incentive for teachers, and overhauling twenty-seven underperforming schools.

This suggests a potentially useful longitudinal governance pattern. Centralized mayoral control to jolt the system could be followed by a new balance of mayoral control with democratic representation. The three competing governance objectives could be rebalanced as the city context changes. But the historical lessons of institutional choice also must be kept in mind: what governance array can best help accomplish the objectives of the school system, such as improving classroom instruction and pupil achievement? Moreover, the more divided school governance is, the more difficult it becomes to locate accountability. Some of the key determinants of the preferred governance arrangement depend on which of the three competing objectives (representative democracy, centralized executive leadership, technical nonpartisan competence) is most appropriate for a city at a specific time within a specific historical, political, and educational context.

Whatever its impact, there are political and geographic limits to the spread of mayoral control. Many cities are not contiguous with school districts. For example, San Jose, California, has twenty school districts within its boundary, and southern cities are part of county school districts. The decline in the number of teacher strikes has also removed a crucial trigger for mayoral takeover. But test scores in many cities have not risen sufficiently to offset state and local dissatisfaction. More efforts at mayoral takeover seem likely. And if the mayors do not succeed in cities like Chicago, Boston, and Cleveland, voucher advocates will have a stronger case—at least for the worst-performing big-city schools. Reformers will continue to use governance and organizational changes in an effort to improve the performance of students.

NOTES

1. Larry Cuban and Michael Usdan, eds., *Powerful Reforms with Shallow Roots: Improving America's Urban Schools* (Teachers College Press, 2003).
2. Michael Kirst, *Mayoral Influence, New Regimes, and Public School Governance*, RR-049 (Philadelphia: University of Pennsylvania, Consortium for Policy Research in Education, 2002).
3. Donald McAdams, *What School Boards Can Do* (Teachers College Press, 2006).
4. Herbert Kaufman, *Politics and Policies in State and Local Government* (Englewood Cliffs, N.J.: Prentice-Hall, 1963).
5. David Rogers, *110 Livingston Street* (New York: Random House, 1969).
6. Quinnipiac University Polling Institute, "Congestion Pricing Is Bad, but Fare Hikes Are Worse, New York City Voters Tell Quinnipiac University Poll; Most Say Bring Back Board of Education" (www.quinnipiac.edu/x1302.xml?ReleaseID=1087).
7. William H. Clune, *Institutional Choice as a Theoretical Framework for Research on Education Policy* (Philadelphia: University of Pennsylvania, Consortium for Policy Research in Education, 1987), p. 4.
8. Dorothy Shipps, *School Reform, Corporate Style: Chicago, 1880–2000* (Lawrence: University Press of Kansas, 2006).
9. Aspen Institute, *Strong Foundation, Evolving Challenges: A Case Study to Support Leadership Transition in Boston Public Schools* (Washington, March 2006).
10. Ibid., p. 13.
11. The Cleveland analysis is based on review of interviews and articles in the *Cleveland Plain Dealer* and the *Cleveland Catalyst* and by publications of the Aspen Institute.
12. Lonnie Timmons, "An Exit Interview," *Cleveland Plain Dealer*, February 12, 2006.
13. *Cleveland Plain Dealer*, "A Nice, Compliant School Board," editorial, July 4, 2007.
14. Timmons, "An Exit Interview."
15. Cuban and Usdan, *Powerful Reforms*.
16. Helen W. Williams, "The Cleveland Literacy System: A Comprehensive Approach to Changing Instructional Practice in the Cleveland Municipal Schools," paper prepared for a meeting of the Urban Superintendent Network of the Aspen Institute Program on Education, Washington, June 10–12, 2005.
17. Joseph F. Wagner, "School Board Seats Filled Quietly," *Cleveland Plain Dealer*, June 24, 2007 (www.cleveland.com/clevelandschools/plaindealer/index.ssf?/clevelandschools/more/1182686130140490.html).
18. United States Conference of Mayors, "Mayoral Leadership and Involvement in Education," Research Report (Washington, 2001).
19. Catherine Gewertz, "D.C. Schools Get School Repair Blitz," *Education Week*, September 15, 2007, p. 11.

The Suburbs: Politics in a Changing Political Landscape

The suburbs of the contemporary metropolis reflect the dramatic changes wrought by globalization. In the popular imagination, if not always in reality, the suburban population of the 20th century was made up of white families living in single-family homes on cul-de-sacs with green expanses of lawn. In the 21st century, the suburbs have been transformed. Many of them are now multiracial and multiethnic. Suburban developments now run the gamut from row houses and apartment clusters to McMansions to privatized, gated communities in park-like settings. The dramatic differences between one housing development and subdivision and the next projects an important reality: Some suburbs are becoming more diverse with respect to income, race, and ethnicity but others remain as homogeneous enclaves that sharply separate racial groups and middle- and upper-class suburban residents. The result is a complex, fragmented patchwork. The future of suburbs is uncertain: an enclave politics may persist or there could be a breakdown in historic patterns of segregation of rich from poor, and whites from almost everyone else. For the foreseeable future both trends seem to be at play.

Michael B. Katz and his collaborators argue in Selection 15 that the suburbanization of immigrants is an outcome of the large-scale economic processes associated with globalization. Demographic changes in the Philadelphia metropolitan region show that, like all other social groups, immigrants are stratified and differentiated on the basis of social class, income, and wealth. These differences show up in what the authors call "the region's residential ecology." Because many immigrants have not yet achieved economic success, many of them located in at-risk, inner-ring suburbs and less often in better-off suburbs at the metropolitan periphery. In doing so they locate in suburban jurisdictions already occupied by large numbers of low-income African Americans.

The authors ask some important questions about whether newly arrived immigrants are crowding out or displacing African Americans or native whites from older inner-ring suburbs. They answer in the negative, instead pointing out that the movement of each of these groups can be traced to structural changes in the urban economy. In the 1990s, blacks and foreign-born immigrants who were hurt by economic restructuring tended to settle in suburbs where housing was affordable. Rather than moving, blacks increasingly shared space with the new arrivals. At the same time, however, native-born whites were prompted by these changes to move to newer suburbs located at a greater distance from the urban core. In interpreting these movements, the authors caution that this experience may be different from one metropolitan area to the next, and that even within urban areas the picture is likely to be complex. In either case, though, the spatial mosaic of the suburbs is very unlike the sharp central city–suburban dichotomy of the past.

In Selection 16, Genevieve Carpio, Clara Irazabal, and Laura Pulido examine the political dynamics in two municipal governments that have experienced rapid increases in Latino immigration. Their case studies of Maywood and Costa Mesa, both located in Southern California, is focused on an important concept scholars have called the "Right to the City." In their formulation, the Right to the City is "rooted in urban citizenship as a prerequisite for political participation." They point out that cities and suburbs are sites of political contestation in which this urban citizenship is defined. In the case of Maywood and Costa Mesa, the struggle has involved conflicts over attempts by these municipalities to enact and enforce anti-immigrant policies, on the one hand, and political mobilization among Latinos and others who challenge these practices, on the other. Since it is likely that the political struggles playing out in these two communities are also occurring in many cities across the United States, they serve as a window on the political impact of immigrants in suburban governance in America.

The authors argue that citizenship, political access, and self-governance are becoming linked because of the movement of large numbers of immigrants and minorities into the suburbs. The battles they describe in their cases raise issues about "the right to determine who can and cannot live in the suburb and under what conditions." In Costa Mesa, this issue was joined when the City Council instructed its police department to enforce federal immigration policy. Despite organized opposition to the policy, within the first year 3,000 residents were identified as illegal immigrants and deportation procedures were begun. The authors found that these actions spread fear among Latino residents that they might be subject to racial profiling; in addition, tensions grew between the Costa Mesa police department and the Latino community. In effect, the city had implemented "a discourse of minimal rights" for its Latino residents.

Maywood, though located just a few miles away, took an opposite course. By the turn of the century the city's population was overwhelmingly Hispanic, and a majority of the population spoke Spanish. When the local police department targeted immigrants by an intensified policy of traffic enforcement, a movement to protect immigrant rights was quickly mobilized. The policy of traffic stops was challenged in public forums. Soon activism became focused on local elections. Voter turnout increased, and election victories followed. A majority of the members of the City Council began to challenge police practices. Maywood became known as a Sanctuary City, and its example spread to several other communities that refused to identify, report, or detain illegal immigrants. The lesson from the local battles fought in these communities was that the different definitions of the Right to the City reflected differences in political contest and mobilization.

Selection 17 is drawn from a book that traces the rise of the 54 suburbs listed in the 2000 census having populations of more than 100,000. In *Boomburbs*, Robert E. Lang and Jennifer B. LeFurgy demonstrate that these suburbs were among the fastest-growing jurisdictions in the United States, and were also were among the few rapidly growing large cities when the study was undertaken. Despite their dynamic character, however, they have remained mostly invisible in the public imagination because they lack the historical associations that give older cities their identity. Even so, most of them are more complex and diverse than one might suppose. Defying the suburban stereotype, they have, in Lang and LeFurgy's words,

"grown not because of white flight but because of immigration, influxes of retirees, and business expansion." They have attracted large numbers of Hispanics and
Asian populations, and their black populations have been increasing. The diverse
demography of Boomburbs offers evidence that the urban pattern of the post–
War War II era, when racial minorities were concentrated mostly in older central
cities and a few inner-ring suburbs, is becoming a thing of the past.

In Selection 18, Eric Avila acknowledges that the postwar pattern of "chocolate" cities and "vanilla" suburbs is giving way to a fragmented pattern that
is changing the cultural narratives about suburban life. He finds that the Los
Angeles suburban landscape is truly a mosaic composed of almost every possible
combination of ethnic and racial group, and this picture is made more complex by extreme income and occupational stratification. The "transnational currents" associated with globalization have utterly changed the spatial structure of
the suburbs. There is, on the one hand, the high-tech manufacturing district, or
"technopolis," which employs the highly skilled and highly paid workers who
occupy the top rungs of the global economy. These workers tend to live in exclusive gated communities. At the other end of the occupational spectrum is the
army of low-wage workers, many of them immigrants, who are also products
of globalization; among this group are large numbers of people who work in
sweatshops, do domestic labor, and fill temporary jobs. They live in older, often
deteriorating suburbs. There is, finally, the white middle class, who either move
or take measures to protect their suburbs from rapid racial and social change.

Avila shows that the new spatial pattern challenges the suburban culture based on white identity that was inherited from the old urban pattern.
He points out, for example, that the San Fernando Valley is now home to
ethnic groups from many Latin American and Asian countries. These people
bring their cultural expressions with them: [T]here is the "texture of daily
life in a 'Latino metropolis' such as Los Angeles"—the "symbols and signs
of *Mexicanidad*," which are everywhere on display throughout the region.
The narrative of the postwar suburb now "includes alternative perspectives
and experiences," and what is emerging is "a new definition of urban life."

15

Immigration and the New Metropolitan Geography

MICHAEL B. KATZ, MATHEW J. CREIGHTON,
DANIEL AMSTERDAM, AND MERLIN CHOWKWANYUN

"We are in the midst of a profound remaking of the relationships
between people and place that is both rapid and radical,"
writes geographer Wilbur Zelinsky of recent immigration, "a

JOURNAL OF URBAN AFFAIRS, Volume 32, Number 5, pages 523–547.
Copyright © 2010 Urban Affairs Association.
All rights of reproduction in any form reserved.
DOI: 10.1111/j.1467-9906.2010.00525.x
ISSN: 0735-2166.

reordering of basic perceptions and behavior" (Zelinsky, 2001). With the passage of the Hart-Celler Law in 1965, Congress repealed the infamous nationality-based quotas that had excluded most potential Southern and Eastern European immigrants from the United States.[1] Legislators expected a small increase in immigration. Instead, immigration surged. In both absolute and relative terms, the number of new arrivals nearly matched the size of the massive immigration of the late nineteenth and early twentieth centuries. But they differed in national origins—most no longer arrived from Europe but from Asia and Latin America—and in where they settled. New patterns of immigrant settlement have supplemented existing ethnic enclaves as immigrants have spread out beyond the traditional immigrant gateways in New York, California, Texas, Florida, and Illinois to the Midwest and South, areas from which immigrants had been virtually absent before 1990 (Massey, 2008).

In fact, many immigrants now go directly to suburbs. This new immigrant residential distribution has translated ethnic and racial economic differentiation into spatial form. Aside from those who came to America to farm, most nineteenth and early twentieth century immigrants settled in cities. Urban sociologists described their initial clustering and subsequent dispersion as they gained an economic foothold and acquired the means to move to more desirable neighborhoods farther away from downtowns and across city lines (Park, Burgess, & McKenzie, 1925, p. 239). Today, many immigrants bypass the historic first step by moving first to suburbs. Indeed, a majority of the foreign-born, like a majority of all Americans, now live outside central cities. "Unlike more traditional enclaves of the past that were located downtown," writes immigration expert Audrey Singer, the majority of recent immigrants "are building their new lives in the suburbs, even during their earliest years of settlement in the United States, and they are constructing their communities in different ways" (Frey, 2005; Singer, 2005, 2008). By 2000, roughly 50% of Hispanics and 55% of Asians lived in suburbs (Iceland, 2009, p. 38; see also Odem, 2009, p. 114).

This article examines immigrant suburbanization through a case study of metropolitan Philadelphia between 1970 and 2006 and addresses three issues. First, how are immigrants distributed among central cities and different kinds of suburbs? Are there distinct patterns? Is their distribution similar to or different from that of native whites and African Americans? The second issue is growth: how much did immigrants contribute to overall population growth and to the growth of each type of municipality? The third is interaction. How did the presence of immigrants interact with growth rates among African Americans and native whites?

Using data from metropolitan Philadelphia since 1970, we contend that the diverse class backgrounds of immigrant newcomers, when combined with the spatial inequalities of the contemporary metropolis, have contributed to novel settlement patterns rarely detailed in previous literature, a body of scholarship that is only beginning to take seriously variation in suburban form and to move beyond the intellectual concerns of early twentieth-century sociologists. We find that for economically bifurcated immigrant groups, such as Indians and Koreans, class status strongly influenced place of residence, with rich members living in newer, more affluent and predominantly white suburbs while the comparatively poor remained in older and more ethnically and racially diverse areas. By contrast, poorer immigrant groups, like the Vietnamese, resided in suburbs in significant numbers, but importantly they did so in older suburban areas as well as in the central city. In all of these places, comparatively poor immigrants were joined by African Americans, whose disadvantage, despite talk of their suburbanization, remains inscribed in space. Finally, because they are issues crucial to both policy-makers and scholars, we underscore the importance of immigration to population and economic growth, in this case by comparing these dynamics across the varied topography of an older, struggling American metropolis.

This article is based on the Philadelphia metropolitan area, as defined by the U.S. Census Bureau. We call this area Greater Philadelphia and our project the Philadelphia Migration Project (PMP). The PMP has sponsored the creation of a database that maps the settlement of the foreign-born, native-white, and African-American populations since 1970 (and for some purposes since 1950). The database blends data from two sources: tract-level census files and individual-level data from the Integrated Public Use Microdata Series (IPUMS).[2] The tract data and individual data cover a consistently defined geography, which includes the city of Philadelphia (Philadelphia County) and seven surrounding counties—Bucks, PA; Chester, PA; Delaware, PA; Montgomery, PA; Burlington, NJ; Camden, NJ, and Gloucester, NJ.[3] To differentiate among suburbs, it has borrowed Myron Orfield's typology of municipal settlements (explained further below) and overlaid the population data onto it.[4] We chose Orfield's typology for two reasons: first, it is based on carefully defined criteria applied consistently and with methodological rigor to the selected metropolitan regions throughout the United States. Second, its availability facilitates comparative analysis between metro Philadelphia and other metropolitan areas. Our analysis is constrained by the limits inherent in census data. We are not, for instance, able to analyze patterns below the census tract level and can only obtain attributes about tracts, not groups within tracts. From 1980 on, the census does not include parents' birthplace, which makes it impossible to identify second-generation adults. The generalizability of our results, of course, is limited by the absence of comparable equivalent data. We discuss our reasons for choosing to study Philadelphia below.

IMMIGRANT SUBURBANIZATION AND PREVIOUS SCHOLARSHIP

Suburbs are neither historically fixed nor homogeneous. Rather, they are differently shaped containers, into which people migrate, set up households, find work, worship, and play. They are themselves constructions, built at various points in history from the transportation revolution of the nineteenth century to the communications revolution of the late twentieth century, and reconstructed repeatedly by demographic, economic, social, and political change (Walker, 1978, 1981). Places labeled "suburb" always have in fact varied, as the work of historians has shown (Berger, 1968; Fishman, 1987; Harris, 1996; Hayden, 2004; Jackson, 1985; Nicolaides, 2002; O'Mara, 2005; Self, 2003; Wiese, 2004). Long before World War II, suburbs were industrial as well as residential; they housed working-class as well as middle-class families; and they were home to many African Americans (Kruse & Sugrue, 2006; Nicolaides & Wiese, 2006). But, especially in the post–World War II era, the popular meaning of suburb as a bedroom community populated mainly by families with children retained at least a rough correspondence with reality, reinforced by the massive building of new suburbs like Levittown, highway construction, and by cheap mortgages, especially under the GI Bill. Whatever uniformity existed among them, however, was shattered in the century's last decades. The result, influenced by demographic change, new family configurations, and economic differentiation, was the emergence of new urban forms that called for a redefinition of "suburb" (Katz, 2010).

Immigrant suburbanization is one outcome of the mass migrations associated with economic globalization, a process that has coincided with and shaped the decentralization and reconfiguration of the American metropolis. The human face of economic globalization, immigration, writes sociologist Saskia Sassen, constitutes "one of the constitutive processes of globalization today, even though it is not recognized or represented as such in mainstream accounts of the global economy" (Sassen, 2007). The mobility of labor, as much as that of capital and goods, or the transnational division of labor, marks the internationalization of the world's economy.

Thus, in reality, immigrant suburbanization is a highly differentiated process with origins in the sources of migration outside the United States, the varied composition of immigrant populations, the restructuring of labor markets, and the localization of economic globalization in new and redefined urban forms. "Immigration and ethnicity," argues Sassen, too often are construed as "otherness." Instead, they should be understood "as a set of processes whereby global elements are localized, international labor markets are constituted, and cultures from all over the world are deterritorialized." This view places them "right there at center stage, along with the internationalization of capital, as a fundamental aspect of globalization" (Sassen, 2007). "International migration," write Stephen Castles and Mark J. Miller in their authoritative *The Age of Migration,* "is part of a transnational revolution that is reshaping society and politics around the globe" (Castles & Miller, 2003).

A small literature on immigrant suburbanization has begun to provide an empirically rich portrait of this rapidly growing phenomenon. . . .

Our study incorporates and extends many of the virtues of micro- and macro-analytic approaches. On one hand, it utilizes a robust set of quantitative data while also organizing it in an innovative spatial typology, described later. This typology captures suburban variety much more systematically than previous scholarship on immigrant suburbanization has done. At the same time, it integrates the quantitative findings within the historical literature on Philadelphia, explaining the new patterns as byproducts of the region's development over time—not just as stand-alone variables influencing one another with little indication of regional context. And it links immigrant suburbanization internationally to the impact of economic globalization on initiating migrant streams and restructuring urban space. We want to underscore Douglas Massey's call (1985), made 25 years ago, for examining how "processes of succession and assimilation are affected by structural conditions that determine the relative balance between them." For Massey, some of these conditions included "the state of the housing market (expanding or static)," "the state of the urban economy (growing or shrinking)," "the history and scale of immigration (recent or distant, large or small)," and "the physical stock of the city (pre-industrial, post-industrial)" (Massey, 1985). Though frequently cited because of its thorough appraisal of the "spatial assimilation" concept (which spurred the term's subsequent use), the article's call for a more contextual analysis of the process has been much less frequently heeded. Our study represents an effort to remedy that omission.

PHILADELPHIA AND ITS IMMIGRANTS

At first, Philadelphia might seem an odd case for a study of current-day immigration because it is not one of the major immigrant gateways. In 2006, the foreign-born, excluding Puerto Rican–born, composed 9% of Greater Philadelphia's population. Adding in Puerto Ricans—we will elaborate on this issue below—brings the proportion to 10%. These are small shares compared to 30% for New York, 35% for Los Angeles, and 37% for Miami in 2000, which are major immigrant gateways. However, a few points may be made by way of support for the Philadelphia focus. First, in its share of foreign-born, Philadelphia is like many other American cities—recall that the foreign-born composed little more than 10% of the U.S. population in 2000. These "low-immigrant" cities have received relatively little attention in the scholarly literature. Second, immigration has grown rapidly in Philadelphia—starting from a low of 263,600 in 1970 with a marked acceleration in the 1990s that brought the total in the metropolitan area to 460,891. By 2006, Philadelphia, an important immigrant center in the early twentieth century, was well on its way to becoming what Audrey Singer refers to as a "reemerging immigrant gateway" (Singer, 2008). Between 1995 and 2000, 62% of the foreign-born in Greater Philadelphia had come to the region directly from their home country.[5] And, in all kinds of ways, the importance of immigration to the city and its metropolitan region grows increasingly evident, receiving more attention in the press and from the city government.[6] Third, although not usually rated as a "global city," the Philadelphia region's recent history—overall stagnation, with pockets of success and abysmal decline, industrial sprawl and the unequal rewards of the new service economy—illustrates trends in the national economy that, in turn, result in part from worldwide economic restructuring; its immigrant flows embody the varied reasons individuals leave their home countries and seek residence in the United States; and its spatial characteristics have undergone reshaping and redefinition as a consequence of economic and demographic trends that parallel similar shifts in other American metropolitan regions. In 1910, 84% of the foreign-born living in metro Philadelphia clustered in the central city; by 2006, the number had plummeted to 35%. For these reasons, Greater Philadelphia forms an appropriate site for a case study of immigrant suburbanization.

The foreign-born who have arrived in Philadelphia since the transformation of federal immigration law in 1965 have entered a metropolitan context drastically different from what earlier immigrants faced. In the early twentieth century the concentration of industry in the city center encouraged settlement around Philadelphia's urban core and the formation of a familiar pattern of residency well described by the concentric zone model of the Chicago School. In sharp contrast, Philadelphia is now a regional economy, and, in part for this reason, the descriptive theories of early twentieth-century urban sociologists no longer hold. Where the city proper had once dominated the local economic scene, today industry is radically decentralized, with the once strong central city gravely weakened and the bulk of jobs dispersed throughout nearby suburbs. Meanwhile, the industries that had helped shape earlier immigration to the city are largely defunct. Once one of the country's great manufacturing hubs, Philadelphia and its new regional economy now depend on its service sector. And while members of previous immigration waves entered a relatively robust local economy, recent newcomers have settled in a region struggling with slow rates of economic growth.[7]

Still, despite these bleak aggregate trends, the region enjoyed strength in a variety of sectors, many of them luring immigrants to the area. First, the region is home to over 80 institutions of higher learning, many of them leaders in research, the liberal arts, and technical training. The region became home to a reasonably strong financial and professional service sector, a group of industries capable of offering employment to highly skilled and unskilled immigrants alike. It also has fared well in comparison to the rest of the nation in the fields of legal services, computer services, and consulting. More recently, the Philadelphia region has come to boast a very competitive biotechnology sector and currently compares favorably to the rest of the nation in employment in education, health care, and social services—all areas that attract immigrants (Cortright & Mayer, 2003; Delaware Valley Regional Planning Commission, 2003, 2006; O'Mara, 2001). And while the region overall has not enjoyed a high rate of development, one of the important traits of its industrial decentralization is the existence of pockets enjoying reasonably high rates of growth. It is against this economic backdrop of macro-change that immigrants, African Americans and native-born whites in the Philadelphia region have encountered one another in recent years.

Immigration to Philadelphia has always followed the contours of global economic change and the rhythm of geopolitical upheavals. In the late nineteenth and early twentieth centuries, millions of European immigrants poured into the Philadelphia region in reaction to major economic and political shifts in their homelands—the intensification of commercial capitalism in the European countryside, the weakening of the family farm, or, in the case of Russian Jews, the largest immigrant group in early twentieth century Philadelphia, the spread of the pogrom. Decades later, Eastern European Jews continued to settle in Philadelphia, this time to escape Soviet religious persecution. Meanwhile, changes in U.S. immigration laws, the shift to a new, bifurcated service economy with it heightened demand for both highly educated and unskilled workers, spurred yet another major wave of immigration to the city. To these macro forces was added family reunification, already a potent source of immigration, but given an added boost by the post-1965 preferences in U.S. immigration law. As throughout the United States, the national origins of the region's foreign-born, as well as their numbers, shifted dramatically in the last decades of the twentieth century. The new immigrants inserted not only diversity into the city and region's population but promised to renew its workforce as well. Compared to the native-born resident population, the foreign-born were much younger and much more likely to be of prime working age. Indeed, while the share of 20–30-year-old native-born men and women plummeted, the fraction of the age group composed of immigrants rose sharply, recording a 40% increase in the 1990s. Between 2000 and 2006, immigrants accounted for 75% of metropolitan Philadelphia's labor force growth (Singer, 2008). Philadelphia's future labor force, it is clear, depends on immigration.

In the analysis that follows, Puerto Ricans pose a special problem. Since 1917, they have been United States citizens. As such, they are not counted among the foreign-born by the census. They arrived from a territory with its own culture where the dominant language is not English. They left their homes for many of the same reasons as immigrants from Mexico—forced off the land by the spread of capitalist agriculture and the failure to replace agricultural with other employment. In U.S. cities, they have faced many of the same problems as the foreign-born, disproportionately living in poverty, clustered in run-down areas of old cities, encountering racism, confronting the difficult road to economic and social integration. They compose a massive and distinct migrant stream fully as much as did African Americans moving from the South, and a demographic analysis that ignores their distinctiveness by unreflectively lumping them in with native-born Americans obscures a fundamental aspect of the demography and social ecology of the cities in which they cluster. (On Puerto Ricans in Philadelphia, see Goode & Schneider, 1994; Whalen, 2001.) For these reasons, we include Puerto Ricans as a separate group in our analysis of data based on national origin. Unfortunately, at the tract level the NCDB (Geolytics Inc., 2004) does not allow us to distinguish Philadelphia's Puerto Rican population from the native-born white, native-born black, or foreign-born (Santiago-Valles & Jiménez-Muñoz, 2004).[8]

The hallmark of the new immigration is its diversity, not only in terms of national origins but on other important measures as well, especially education and occupation. In fact, Greater Philadelphia's immigrants embodied the five characteristics that, in Castles and Miller's (2003) analysis, mark current day international migration. They are the *globalization of migration*—the increased numbers of areas both sending and affected by migration; *the acceleration of migration*—the heightened volume of international movements of people; the *differentiation of migration*—the simultaneous inclusion of various types (labor migrants, refugees, permanent settlers) among the migrants to the same destinations with "migratory chains which start with one type of movement often" continuing "with other forms, despite (or often just because of) government efforts to stop or control the movement"; the *feminization of migration*—the increased number of women among migrants in contrast to past male domination; and the *growing politicization of migration*—the imbrication of migration in national and international politics and security arrangements.

The recent history of immigration to Greater Philadelphia reflects these international trends. The increase in numbers, first, shows immigration's *acceleration*. The increased number of countries from which 5,000 or more immigrants arrived in Greater Philadelphia between 1970 and 2006—from 14 to 23—reflected its *globalization*. In 1970, Canada and Europe accounted for all of these countries; by 2005, 16 of the top sending countries were in Asia or Latin America. Taking just individuals age 16 or over, between 1970 and 2006, the numbers among major groups of newcomers rose: Koreans from negligible to 20,099; Vietnamese from negligible to 21,020; Indians from 1,500 to 50,253; Chinese from 1,700 to 24,995; Mexicans from negligible to 26,822 (almost surely an undercount); Filipinos from 2,600 to 14,814; and Puerto Ricans from 17,000 to 50,253.

Within these groups, sex ratios reflected the *feminization* of migration. In two groups, Chinese and Puerto Ricans, they had reached near parity. The remaining groups are notably distinct from each other. Women outnumbered men in the case of Koreans, Vietnamese, and Filipinos. The Filipino sex ratio is particularly pronounced, with nearly two females for every male, recording a female–male sex ratio of 0.55 in 2006. On the opposite end of the spectrum are Indians and Mexicans, both demonstrating a substantial gender skew favoring men. The case of Mexico is particularly pronounced, with slightly over two men per woman in 2006. Clearly, immigration is a deeply gendered story. With only a few exceptions, however, researchers have not systematically analyzed the differences between men and women in reasons for migration, employment, or other measures of economic and social integration.[9] (See Hondagnew-Sotelo, 2003). If immigration's crucial gender story remains obscured, its *politicization* does not. As throughout the nation, immigration became a hot political issue in Greater Philadelphia and, indeed, in the rest of Pennsylvania as well. Local governments, for instance in Riverside and Hazleton, passed anti-immigrant ordinances, while a South Philadelphia owner of a cheese steak stand mounted a sign asking customers to order in English (Maykuth, 2008; Preston, 2007).

In part, the *differentiation* of the region's immigration resulted, as it did elsewhere, from the simultaneous arrival of labor migrants, refugees, and permanent settlers. However, differentiation also reflected the differences among and within immigrant groups in education, occupation, and income. In 2006, Indians, Koreans, Filipinos, and Chinese were the most well-educated and economically successful groups; among males, 59% of Indians, 33% of Koreans, 41% of Filipinos, and 44% of Chinese were in professional, technical, or managerial occupations compared to 27% of native-born whites. (On differentiation among Chinese immigrants, see Li, 2009, pp. 134–137.) Among women, the rank order of professionals, technicians, and managers was roughly the same. Income rankings were similar, too. Median amounts are reported here only for those 25–60 years old in order to avoid school-age respondents; they are given in 1999 dollars. India-born residents of Greater Philadelphia enjoyed one of the highest median per capita household incomes, $69,760, compared to $36,000 for Mexicans (see Table 1). U.S.-born whites recorded a median household income in 2006 of $77,578, notably similar to immigrants from India. More Indians, 66% of men and 57% of women, had at least graduated from college, followed by Filipinos—55% of men and 59% of women—then by the Chinese, 45% for both men and women. For native-born whites the figures were 31% for both sexes.

Vietnamese immigrants were less occupationally successful, affluent, or highly educated than the other Asian groups but still ranked higher on these measures than Mexicans, Puerto Ricans, and native-born blacks. Only 10% of

TABLE 1

Median Household and Individual Income by Select Immigrant Groups—Greater Philadelphia 2000

	Vietnam	Mexico	China	India	Korea
Median HH income (25–60)	$43,000	$36,000	$50,000	$69,670	$50,500
Median individual income (25–60)					
Men	$20,947	$17,472	$29,000	$41,500	$29,550
Women	$15,000	$4,512	$14,000	$18,000	$13,500
Total population	19,556	14,769	17,212	28,290	20,304

Note: These population totals differ slightly from the census derived estimates as these are calculated from the Integrated Public Use Microsample (IPUMS), which is a 5% sample.

black men and 15% of black women held professional, technical, or managerial jobs; for Puerto Ricans the numbers reflect similar disadvantage, 9% of both men and women. Very high numbers of black and Puerto Rican men—51% and 43%, higher than for any other group—fell into the "not listed" occupational category, a measure of their detachment from the labor force. With a median household income of $30,266, Puerto Ricans were among the poorest groups in Greater Philadelphia. Nor had very many men or women from either group—10% of black men and 16% of black women; 6% of Puerto Rican men and 12% of Puerto Rican women—attended higher education for at least four years. These figures point not only to the disadvantage of African Americans and Puerto Ricans but to the widening gender gap among them. In one way, however, all immigrant groups differentiated themselves from African Americans and Puerto Ricans. That was in the percentage of households headed by women: among Mexicans (4%), Chinese (2%), Indians (1%), Vietnamese (13%), and Koreans (6%) compared to 10% among native-born whites, 26% among Puerto Ricans, and 37% among African-Americans.

The diversity that marks immigrants' demographic and social characteristics carries over to where they live, crisscrossing the region with a web of distinctive residential patterns. Immigrants are dispersed unevenly throughout the municipalities of Greater Philadelphia in a pattern that roughly reflects their economic standing.

THE METROPOLITAN CONTEXT: SUBURBAN TYPOLOGY AND EXEMPLARY MUNICIPALITIES

One goal of this article is to show how the distribution and growth of immigrants varied among different kinds of municipalities usually aggregated under the term "suburb." For this purpose, as explained earlier, we borrowed the municipal typology developed by Myron Orfield and his associates and overlaid our own immigration database onto it. The typology divides regions into the following types of municipalities: "urban core" and six varieties of suburbs: "stressed," "at-risk developed," "at-risk developing," "bedroom developing," "suburban job center," and "affluent residential." (Because there were so few affluent suburbs, and they were so small, we omitted them from the analysis.) The median incomes of residents varied among municipal types with incomes highest in the newer suburbs and lowest in the urban core and its older suburbs (see Table 2). Philadelphia County (coterminous with the city) is the urban core (hereafter referred to as the central city) in our study. . . .

Stressed suburbs and at-risk developed suburbs are residential areas with stagnant or declining populations and limited tax capacity. They are largely built out and older than other municipalities. At-risk developing areas also have limited, or unfavorable, financial prospects but are growing. Bedroom developing suburbs combine population growth with an optimistic financial outlook. Suburban job centers and affluent residential areas are marked by their relative wealth, financial solidity, and population growth or stability. In their age of settlement, ethnic diversity, and population growth patterns, these six municipal types may be divided for some purposes into two groups: "old" (central city, stressed suburbs, at-risk developed suburbs) and new (at-risk developing, bedroom developing, and suburban job center.) It is important not to reify this typology, which, itself, is the contingent outcome of a complicated

TABLE 2

Weighted Mean per Capita Income by Municipal Type—2000

	Mean per Capita Income	Number of Tracts
At-risk, developed	$23,891.14	288
At-risk, developing	$26,300.21	211
Bedroom developing	$32,044.45	134
Central city	$16,509.30	369
Stressed suburbs	$14,842.36	86
Suburban job centers	$32,684.45	196
Total		1,284

Source: NHGIS, Census, 2000.
Note: Income estimates are weighted within municipal types by the total tract population.

history and, undoubtedly, will need future revision because the variables on which it is based are in flux. . . .

[There are] complicated patterns of overall population growth among municipal types and the variation in relative percentages of foreign-born, African-American, and native-born residents. Sorting out these patterns requires distinguishing between the three distinct, although related, issues outlined at the start of this [discussion]. First, how are immigrants distributed among municipal types? Are there distinct patterns? Is their distribution similar to or different from that of native whites' and African Americans? The second issue is growth: how much did immigrants contribute to overall population growth and to the growth of each type of municipality? The third is interaction. How did the presence of immigrants interact with growth rates among African Americans and native whites? The analysis that follows examines all three questions.[10]

IMMIGRANT RESIDENTIAL DISTRIBUTION AND SUBURBAN DIFFERENTIATION

The suburbanization of immigration changed the ethnic/racial composition of suburbs. Immigrants did not begin to arrive in Philadelphia in very large numbers until the 1990s. A plurality still settled in the central city and a majority in older types of suburbs, but by 2000 nearly 4 of 10 had either moved or immigrated directly to newer areas, a pattern that revealed the economic differentiation among newcomers. Between 1970 and 2000, the central city went from 62% native-born white to 45% and the stressed suburbs from 70% to 46% (Table 3). Despite increases in their foreign-born populations, other varieties of municipalities remained overwhelmingly native-born white. The shift downward in the native-born white percentage in bedroom developing suburbs between 1970 and 2000 was only about 4 percentage points, from 93% to 89%. Suburban job centers recorded a similarly small decline from 92% to 85%.

Immigrant residential distribution translated ethnic and racial economic differentiation into spatial form. More affluent groups settled predominantly in the newer, more prosperous suburbs; poor groups remained much more often in the central city and older suburbs, while groups bifurcated economically

TABLE 3

Distribution of Population by Nativity and Race within Municipal Types, Metropolitan Philadelphia 1970–2000

Year	1970	1980	1990	2000
1st generation immigrant				
At-risk, developed	21%	20%	18%	17%
At-risk, developing	7%	11%	11%	11%
Bedroom developing	3%	6%	9%	11%
Central city	52%	44%	42%	39%
Stressed suburbs	6%	4%	4%	5%
Suburban job centers	11%	14%	16%	17%
Total	243,473	242,634	251,195	355,801
Native-born—white				
At-risk, developed	27%	26%	24%	23%
At-risk, developing	13%	18%	20%	22%
Bedroom developing	7%	9%	12%	17%
Central city	32%	26%	23%	18%
Stressed suburbs	6%	5%	4%	3%
Suburban job centers	15%	16%	17%	17%
Total	3,950,403	3,665,074	3,661,140	3,552,793
Native-born—black				
At-risk, developed	4%	6%	8%	10%
At-risk, developing	3%	4%	5%	6%
Bedroom developing	1%	2%	2%	3%
Central city	78%	72%	68%	64%
Stressed suburbs	11%	12%	12%	12%
Suburban job centers	3%	4%	4%	5%
Total	843,137	875,227	918,303	1,025,661

Source: Orfield, 2002 (categories); Neighborhood Change Database 1970–2000 (data).

Table 3 shows the distribution of the population by nativity and race within each municipal type at four points in time. For example, in 2000, 64% of the native-born black population lived in the central city and 12% in stressed suburbs.

distributed themselves among both kinds of places. (For a similar grouping of suburbs in metropolitan Washington, DC, see Iceland, 2009, p. 71.) For the purpose of simplifying very intricate patterns, consider, first, the municipalities divided into two groups: (1) the central city and older suburbs (at-risk developed and stressed); and (2) newer suburbs (at-risk developing, bedroom developing, and suburban job centers). In 2006, poorer immigrant groups were found most often in the central city and older suburbs. Such places were home to 55% of Greater Philadelphia's population of immigrants: Cambodians 92%, Vietnamese 81%, Bangladeshi 60%, Pakistani 64% (Table 4).

For this same year, economically bifurcated groups divided more evenly between the older and newer municipal types: 48% of Indians, 51% of Koreans,

---

TABLE 4

Distribution of Selected First Generation Immigrant Groups by Municipal Type—2000

	Cambodia	Vietnam	Bangladesh	Pakistan	India	Korea
At-risk, developed	11%	15%	25%	30%	20%	24%
At-risk, developing	2%	4%	8%	8%	11%	12%
Bedroom developing	3%	4%	6%	9%	17%	13%
Central city	78%	57%	26%	32%	26%	25%
Stressed suburbs	3%	9%	9%	2%	2%	2%
Suburban job centers	3%	11%	26%	19%	24%	25%
Total population	5,783	20,109	2,071	3,534	28,991	21,135

	China	Canada	Germany	Italy	Greece	Mexico
At-risk, developed	14%	19%	19%	20%	31%	12%
At-risk, developing	7%	18%	24%	15%	12%	7%
Bedroom developing	13%	23%	15%	11%	11%	20%
Central city	44%	16%	22%	34%	25%	19%
Stressed suburbs	2%	3%	3%	3%	2%	30%
Suburban job centers	21%	21%	18%	18%	19%	14%
Total population	23,709	7,489	14,315	17,871	4,822	14,349

Source: Census (2000).

---

and 59% of Chinese lived in the older suburbs. The wealthiest immigrant groups, of course, lived most often in the newer areas: 62% of Canadians and 57% of Germans. Of the older immigrants groups, Italians and Greeks remained most residentially divided, with 57% of the former and 58% of the latter living in the older suburbs. Filipinos spread evenly throughout types of municipalities, only slightly favoring the newer. This reflects the location of employment in the medical field, which was widespread across the region. The Filipino population, 18% of which was involved in the health care industry, included 1,452 nurses and 445 hospital attendants as well as many physicians and practical nurses.[11]

Although only 18% of native-born whites remained in the central city, 44% lived in the newer suburbs (Table 3). Sharply divided economically, whites had nearly deserted Philadelphia. The contrast with African Americans could not be sharper. Only a stunningly small 14% of African Americans lived in the newer suburbs while 60% remained in the central city. A surprisingly high 14% of Mexicans lived in bedroom developing suburbs, undoubtedly to be close to jobs in construction, agriculture, and gardening. Some of the poorer immigrant groups lived much less often than others in the central city and more often in the at-risk developed or stressed suburbs. Combined, however, the concentration of poorer groups in the three types of older municipalities stands out. The overall trend—the spatialization of immigrant economic differentiation—remains unmistakable.

IMMIGRATION AND POPULATION GROWTH

Between 1970 and 2000, 51%, and, in the 1990s, 58%, of population growth in Greater Philadelphia resulted from the immigration of the foreign-born.[12] During the 30-year period the population as a whole increased about 5% and the foreign-born population (excluding Puerto Ricans) 46%.[13] Immigration, clearly, was the fuel on which population growth depended.

Population growth differed between older and newer municipalities, with the resulting patterns once again representing the spatial expression of immigrant economic diversity. The analysis that follows uses "foreign-born" as a single category rather than distinct immigrant groups. The reason is that the data in this analysis are from the Neighborhood Change Database, which does not give country of birth. As a result we can look at change over time only by foreign birth. In the newest municipalities the population of native and foreign-born increased consistently. In the at-risk developing tracts, the number of foreign-born rose 40% in the century's last decade. In both of the other newer municipal types—bedroom developing and suburban job centers—both the number and proportion of the foreign-born rose steadily in each decade, particularly in the 1990s. In older suburbs, the foreign-born share of the population went down after 1970 before rebounding late in the century. What accounts for the decline in the older areas after the 1970s? Very likely, it resulted from the death, and perhaps departure, of first generation white ethnics who had immigrated earlier in the century.

Nonetheless, the foreign-born proved more important contributors to population change in the older than in the newer types of municipalities. Between 1970 and 2000, in the three older types, the foreign-born share of the population increased much less than in the newer ones, where it jumped dramatically.[14] In the older areas, central city, and stressed suburbs, immigrants moderated population decline. In newer tracts, both total growth rates and foreign-born rates increased. Overall, by the last decade of the twentieth century, a majority of the population growth in Greater Philadelphia resulted from immigration.

These trends in population growth rearranged the spatial distribution of the foreign-born. The foreign-born, that is, distributed themselves differently in 2000 than in 1970. They were, of course, also completely different types of people, largely European in origin in 1970 and a majority Asian or Latin American in 2000. The total foreign-born population in the central city rose from about 120,000 to 130,000, but this represented a drop from over half (52%) to more than a third (39%) of the foreign-born in Greater Philadelphia (Table 3). Still, there were over twice as many in the central city as in any other type of settlement. Here, too, the shift to residence in newer settlements stands out. The share of the foreign-born in older types of municipalities declined or remained relatively stagnant while big increases occurred in the newer areas: for example, the share of the foreign-born living in bedroom developing suburban tracts increased by a factor of four, from 3% to 11%, and in the suburban job centers it grew by about 50%, rising from 11% to about 17%. These trends likely represent three distinct processes: the death and departure of white ethnics from older municipalities, the social mobility of some recent immigrants who traded residence in the city for newer suburbs, and the movement of some foreign-born, especially in the 1990s, directly to the newer suburbs.[15]

Among the native-born white population, movement out of older and into newer suburban areas resembled trends among the foreign-born. Only the magnitude differed. The native-born white departure from the central city, for instance, was much more dramatic: between 1970 and 2000, the percentage of native-born whites living in the central city dropped from 32% to 18% and in the stressed suburban tracts from 6% to 3% (Table 3). This was a white urban exodus with a vengeance (Gamm, 1999). By contrast, the percentage living in the bedroom developing suburban tracts rose from 7% to 17% (in numbers, from about 275,000 to over 600,000).

In where they lived, as in so much else, African Americans remained distinct from both native-born whites and immigrants. Despite some movement outward, they stayed concentrated in older municipalities. Although the percentage of African Americans in the central city went down, it remained far higher than the percentage among native-born whites or immigrants: 78% in 1970 and 64% in 2000 (Table 3). Taking the three older types of municipalities together highlights the trends: they were home to 93% of blacks in 1970 and 86% in 2000, compared to a decline from 78% to 66% of the foreign-born and of 66% to 44% for native whites (Lacy, 2002, 2004).

Consequently, the African-American share of the central city rose from 32% in 1970 to 45% in 2000 (Table 5). The story was similar in other older types of municipalities while the African-American population grew much less in the newer places, an increase in the bedroom developing suburbs only from 4% to 5% and in suburban job centers from 4% to 7% (Table 5). Clearly, these figures show, African-American suburbanization took its own course, proceeding more slowly than the suburbanization of native-born whites and immigrants and limited for the most part to other older, troubled municipalities near the central city.

THE INTERACTION OF IMMIGRATION, RACE, AND POPULATION CHANGE

The comparative growth rates of immigrants, African Americans, and the native-born raise an important question: were these rates independent, or did they interact with each other and with type of municipality? Did an influx of immigrants crowd out African Americans or native whites? Did the growth of immigrants have different impacts on older and newer municipalities? The answers point to complex and sometimes surprising patterns. Most unexpected was that immigrants generally did not displace African Americans or move into spaces they had vacated. Instead, a rise in the African-American population usually accompanied an increase in immigrants.

TABLE 5				

Distribution of Population across Municipal Types by Nativity and Race, Metropolitan Philadelphia 1970–2000

Year	1970	1980	1990	2000
Central city				
1st generation immigrant	6%	6%	7%	9%
Native-born—black	32%	37%	40%	45%
Native-born—white	62%	57%	53%	45%
Total	2,062,006	1,707,268	1,559,300	1,449,173
Stressed suburb				
1st generation immigrant	4%	4%	4%	7%
Native-born—black	26%	35%	41%	47%
Native-born—white	70%	61%	56%	46%
Total	350,902	289,294	273,263	252,255
At-risk developed suburb				
1st generation immigrant	4%	5%	5%	6%
Native-born—black	3%	5%	7%	11%
Native-born—white	92%	90%	88%	83%
Total	1,148,925	1,041,205	996,037	970,086
At-risk developing suburb				
1st generation immigrant	3%	4%	3%	4%
Native-born—black	4%	5%	6%	7%
Native-born—white	92%	91%	91%	88%
Total	563,707	712,162	815,654	872,541
Bedroom developing suburb				
1st generation immigrant	3%	4%	4%	6%
Native-born—black	4%	5%	5%	5%
Native-born—white	93%	92%	91%	89%
Total	279,479	366,543	492,030	669,511
Suburban job center				
1st generation immigrant	4%	5%	6%	8%
Native-born—black	4%	5%	5%	7%
Native-born—white	92%	90%	89%	85%
Total	631,994	666,463	694,354	720,689

Source: Orfield, 2002 (categories); Neighborhood Change Database 1970–2000 (data).

Table 5 shows the composition of each municipal type by nativity and race at four points in time. For example, in 2000, 45% of the central city population was native-born—white, 45% native-born—black; and 9% immigrant.

At each census, less surprisingly, in older municipalities declining tracts outnumbered growing ones, with the decline greatest in the 1970s. This pattern was reversed in newer suburbs, accelerating in the 1990s. What this shows is the difference immigration made in the last decade of the twentieth century. However, the immigrant population did not track this general growth pattern. The number of immigrants grew in both older and newer areas. The greatest contrast was with the central city. In the central city, the native-born white population declined by over 50% between 1970 and 2000 while the immigrant population steadily increased. Between 1970 and 1980, in the central city 65% of tracts experienced no growth in the immigrant population (Table 6). Between 1990 and 2000, however, these relations reversed, and by the last decade of the century 69% of tracts recorded some growth because of immigration. In the same years, the foreign-born population also grew in 38% of central city tracts where the black population also increased (Table 6).

TABLE 6

Patterns of Population Growth by Nativity and Race with Municipal Types, Metropolitan Philadelphia 1970–1980, 1980–1990, 1990–2000

Years	1970–1980	1980–1990	1990–2000
Central city			
Immigrant only	14%	14%	17%
Immigrant + white	4%	5%	8%
Immigrant + black	11%	16%	38%
Immigrant + white + black	7%	4%	5%
No immigrant growth	65%	63%	31%
Total tracts	367	367	367
Stressed suburb			
Immigrant only	10%	8%	30%
Immigrant + white	2%	8%	1%
Immigrant + black	8%	18%	37%
Immigrant + white + black	10%	7%	6%
No immigrant growth	69%	59%	26%
Total tracts	87	87	87
At-risk developed suburb			
Immigrant only	16%	8%	10%
Immigrant + white	4%	4%	4%
Immigrant + black	21%	21%	45%
Immigrant + white + black	6%	6%	8%
No immigrant growth	53%	61%	34%
Total tracts	289	289	289
Older suburbs[a]			
Immigrant only	14%	8%	14%
Immigrant + white	4%	5%	3%
Immigrant + black	18%	20%	43%
Immigrant + white + black	7%	6%	8%
No immigrant growth	56%	61%	32%
Total tracts	376	376	376

(Continued)

TABLE 6 (Continued)

Years	1970–1980	1980–1990	1990–2000
At-risk developing suburb			
Immigrant only	4%	2%	8%
Immigrant + white	14%	13%	13%
Immigrant + black	10%	4%	18%
Immigrant + white + black	50%	32%	32%
No immigrant growth	22%	48%	28%
Total tracts	211	211	211
Bedroom developing suburb			
Immigrant only	4%	1%	2%
Immigrant + white	21%	14%	18%
Immigrant + black	6%	6%	7%
Immigrant + white + black	53%	55%	61%
No immigrant growth	16%	24%	13%
Total tracts	135	135	135
Suburban job center			
Immigrant only	13%	9%	12%
Immigrant + white	11%	9%	11%
Immigrant + black	14%	16%	32%
Immigrant + white + black	25%	19%	21%
No immigrant growth	36%	46%	24%
Total tracts	195	195	195
Newer suburbs[b]			
Immigrant only	7%	4%	8%
Immigrant + white	15%	12%	14%
Immigrant + black	11%	9%	20%
Immigrant + white + black	42%	33%	35%
No immigrant growth	26%	41%	23%
Total tracts	541	541	541
All tracts			
Immigrant only	11%	8%	13%
Immigrant + white	8%	8%	9%
Immigrant + black	13%	14%	32%
Immigrant + white + black	22%	17%	19%
No immigrant growth	46%	53%	28%
Total tracts	1,284	1,284	1,284

Source: Orfield, 2002 (categories); Neighborhood Change Database 1970–2000 (data).

Table 6 describes combinations of nativity and racial population increase for census tracts within each municipal type during three decades: 1970–1980, 1980–1990, and 1990–2000. It shows, for example, how immigrant and black populations often increased within the same census tracts. Between 1990 and 2000, in at-risk developed suburbs, both immigrant and black populations increased in 45% of 289 tracts.

[a]Older suburbs are comprised of "stressed suburbs" and "at-risk, developed suburbs."

[b]Newer suburbs are comprised of "at-risk, developing" and "bedroom, developing," and "suburban job centers."

By contrast, the foreign-born population increased in only 8% of the tracts where the white population rose (Myers, 1999).

In at-risk developed suburbs, these interconnections between race and nativity stood out even more sharply. Between 1990 and 2000, 45% of the tracts that experienced immigrant growth also recorded an increase in the native-born black population compared to only 4% of the tracts where the number of native-born whites increased. In stressed suburbs, the interactions between the growth of native-born white, black, and immigrant populations mirrored patterns in the central city. For the most part, in older suburbs and the central city immigrants replaced native-born whites but not blacks.

"Replaced" is used deliberately. Native-born whites were not leaving older areas because immigrants were moving in. Their departure, spurred by the loss of jobs occasioned by deindustrialization, animus toward new African-American migrants, and the lure of inexpensive, single-family housing had started much earlier than the immigrant surge in the 1990s. The disparity between the number of growing and declining tracts within older municipalities was, in fact, a good deal larger in the 1970s and 1980s than in the 1990s. Nearly 80% of the tracts in older suburbs and central city recorded native-born white population decline in the 1970s, 1980s, and 1990s. Indeed, the percentage of tracts where the number of native-born whites declined remained remarkably stable during each of the three decades. Thus, potential head-to-head competition for housing and jobs occurred more often between the foreign-born and African Americans than between immigrants and native-born whites. African Americans lacked the resources to move further outward available to most whites. Insofar as proximity bred competition for jobs and housing, immigrants and African Americans confronted each other most directly. However, it is not at all clear how often they competed within the same labor markets for the same jobs and, with vacant housing plentiful, as it was in Philadelphia, they may not have competed for housing very often.

During the 1990s, everyone—blacks, whites, foreign-born—was moving into the rapidly growing at-risk developing and bedroom developing suburbs. Starting with 1970, in bedroom developing suburbs, where immigration was growing, the native-born white population increased as well, rising in nearly 70% of tracts during each decade, starting with 1970. Blacks and the foreign-born also increased in tandem, with both populations increasing in the majority of tracts between 1970 and 2000, the black population increasing in 103 tracts with rising foreign-born populations and decreasing in 28. (Despite its increase, the number of African Americans in these suburbs remained small, never exceeding 5% of the population.)

These trends point to different population histories within older and newer types of municipalities and among native-born whites, African Americans, and immigrants. The populations of older towns and cities became increasingly black and foreign-born. Newer municipalities gained blacks and, even more, immigrants, but they remained overwhelmingly native-born white. Within older places, the decimation of economic opportunity and the arrival of African Americans combined to propel native-born whites to newer suburbs farther from the central city and troubled older suburbs. African Americans, also hurt by economic transformation, lacked the resources to move to newer suburbs in very large numbers (assuming that discriminatory real estate practices would not have excluded them). Even more, their job niche in government and government-related employment meant that they enjoyed more occupational opportunity in the central city and older suburbs, where they faced less residential discrimination. By and large, writing about African Americans' confinement to inner ring suburbs neglects this constraint—the location of public and quasi-public sector jobs—on their geographic mobility. Nationally, in 2000, 43% of African-American women and 19% of African-American men worked in public or publicly supported jobs (Katz & Stern, 2006).

The Philadelphia pattern—increased African-American and immigrant population growth in the same census tracts—was not replicated in all cities. Similar to Philadelphia, in Sacramento low to moderate income suburbs with large immigrant populations gained African Americans, but not whites. In Atlanta, by contrast, the black and immigrant populations generally increased in different places (Datel & Dingemans, 2008; Odem, 2008). What caused this variation remains unclear, but housing stock is a plausible hypothesis. It may be that affordable housing in neighborhoods abandoned by whites attracted both African Americans and immigrants. Their tandem population growth, thus, would be more likely in older than in newer cities and suburbs.

This analysis has opened as many questions as it has answered. Case studies of individual municipalities that look closely at economic mobility, gender differences, poverty, political impacts, interactions with private and public institutions, and inter-group relations rank high on the agenda. So do qualitative studies of individual immigrant groups that investigate why and how they came to settle where they did; where they lived compared to where they worked; and how they experienced life in their new homes. Research also should supplement the economic differentiation model of immigrant settlement explicated in this [discussion] with other models—ethnic enclave, buffer zone, and heterolocality, as described earlier.

Contrary to older sociological frameworks, most immigrants no longer move first to central cities where they initially settle in housing vacated by upwardly mobile white workers and then, as they assimilate, move out of ethnic enclaves to cities' outer rings, where they once again take over the inexpensive housing left behind by white workers moving to the suburbs. To be sure, as we show, although ethnic enclaves still exist in central cities, they have been supplemented, even supplanted, by new patterns. Immigrants now usually go directly to suburbs. But their choice of suburb is not random. It rests on both their own economic circumstances and the opportunities for affordable housing and work in different kinds of municipalities as well as, undoubtedly, on family ties.

Much of the literature on immigrant suburbanization obscures internal economic differentiation—the role of class—within immigrant groups and paints the distinction between city and suburb with a broad brush that misses the internal heterogeneity within metropolitan regions. Settlement patterns, this [discussion] has shown, reflect the interaction between immigrant economic differentiation and the spatial redefinition of the metropolitan area. More well-to-do immigrants often settle in prosperous new suburbs while poorer groups are found most often in older suburbs and the central city. These settlement patterns, in turn, result from the internationalization of labor markets that has accompanied economic globalization, notably the demand for both highly skilled and relatively unskilled workers. The growth and differentiation of suburbs likewise results from the deindustrialization, service and third-sector growth, and spatial redistribution of work that has accompanied the internationalization of manufacturing, trade, finance, and labor markets.

Immigration has become the major source of population and workforce growth in many metropolitan areas. But it has spurred growth most in the central cities and older suburban areas where the majority of immigrants settle. Nonetheless, proportionally, the number of foreign-born residents, and African Americans, has grown most sharply in newer suburbs. Although these affluent suburbs remain overwhelmingly native white, their demographic diversity increased in the 1990s and first years of the twenty-first century, hinting at trends, which, if they continue, will redefine their ethnic composition.

As African Americans began to move into the central city and older suburbs in the 1970s and 1980s, whites decamped in great numbers, fueling suburban growth. Whites left as well because all sorts of work—service, industrial, professional—suburbanized. They left behind inexpensive housing stock, which attracted immigrants. While immigrants replaced native-born whites, they moved in alongside African Americans, with both groups often increasing in the same census tracts. African Americans less often could afford to follow whites to the newer suburbs, where, in any event, they might have received a mixed welcome. They were held in older cities, too, by public and quasi-public jobs, which had become their special occupational niches (Katz & Stern, 2006).

In the late twentieth century, economic globalization reconfigured space as well as work, while immigrant suburbanization reshaped the dynamics of urban growth. Operating through local economic transformation and population flows, economic globalization crystallized in new configurations of place, work, residence, and ethnicity. Immigrant suburbanization in Greater Philadelphia represents one example. The shifting residential patterns of immigrants, native whites, and African Americans resulted from the economic transformations opening up opportunities for inexpensive housing in some sites while creating new kinds of economic opportunities elsewhere and of the population movements unleashed by political upheavals and a new phase in the history of capitalism. In the late nineteenth and early twentieth centuries, during America's first great era of economic globalization, immigration fueled Philadelphia's population growth and mighty industrial engine. It is no less essential today, and for the same reasons. In the earlier era, immigration was tied closely to the emergence of the industrial cities, which housed most of the nation's newcomers. Today it is again linked to a new metropolitan geography, which it is helping to define.

REFERENCES

Berger, B. (1968). *Working-class suburbs: A study of auto workers in suburbia.* Berkeley, CA: University of California Press.

Castles, S., & Miller, M. J. (2003). *The age of migration: International population movements in the modern world.* New York: Palgrave Macmillan.

Cortright, J., & Mayer, H. (2003). Signs of life: The growth of biotechnology centers in the U.S. *Greater Philadelphia Regional Review* (Spring).

Datel, R., & Dingemans, D. (2008). Immigrant space and place in suburban Sacramento. In A. Singer, S. W. Hardwick, & C. B. Brettell (Eds.), *Twenty-first century gateways: Immigrant incorporation in suburban America* (pp. 171–199). Washington, DC: Brookings Institution Press.

Davis, A. F., & Haller, M. H. (1973). *The peoples of Philadelphia: A history of ethnic groups and lower-class life, 1790–1940.* Philadelphia: Temple University Press.

Delaware Valley Regional Planning Commission (2003). *Three decades of job growth and decline in the Delaware Valley: Analyzing the region's economic base by sector.* Delaware Valley Data: Analytical Data Report 10. Philadelphia: Author.

Delaware Valley Regional Planning Commission (2006). Employment base and economic census update. Philadelphia: Author.

Fishman, R. (1987). *Bourgeois utopias: The rise and fall of suburbia.* New York: Basic Books.

Frasure, L. A. (2005). *We won't turn them back: The political economy paradoxes of immigrant and minority settlement in suburban America.* Ph.D. dissertation, University of Maryland, College Park, MD.

Frey, W. H. (1999). New black migration patterns in the United States: Are they affected by recent immigration? In F. Bean & S. Bell-Rose (Eds.), *Immigration and opportunity: Race, ethnicity, and employment in the United States.* New York: Russell Sage Foundation Publications.

Frey, W. H. (2005). Melting pot suburbs: A study of suburban diversity. In A. Berube, B. Katz, & R. E. Lang (Eds.), *Redefining urban and suburban America: Evidence from census 2000* (Vol. 1). Washington, DC: Brookings Institute Press.

Frey, W. H., & Liaw, K. (1998). Immigrant concentration and domestic migrant dispersal: Is movement to nonmetropolitan areas "white flight"? *Professional Geographer, 50,* 215–232.

Gamm, G. H. (1999). *Urban exodus: Why the Jews left Boston and the Catholics stayed.* Cambridge, MA: Harvard University Press.

Geolytics Inc. (2004). *Neighborhood change database 1970–2000 tract data, long form release 1.1.* New Brunswick, NJ: Author.

Golab, C. (1977). *Immigrant destinations.* Philadelphia: Temple University Press.

Goode, J., & Schneider, J. A. (1994). *Reshaping ethnic and racial relations in Philadelphia: Immigrants in a divided city.* Philadelphia: Temple University Press.

Harris, R. (1996). *Unplanned suburbs: Toronto's American tragedy, 1900–1950.* Baltimore, MD: Johns Hopkins University Press.

Hayden, D. (2004). *Building suburbia: Green fields and urban growth, 1820–2000.* New York: Vintage.

Hershberg, T. (1981). A tale of three cities: Blacks, immigrants, and opportunity in Philadelphia, 1850–1880, 1930, 1970. In T. Hershberg (Ed.), *Philadelphia: Work, space, family and group experience in the 19th century.* New York: Oxford University Press.

Hondagnew-Sotelo, P. (Ed.). (2003). *Gender and U.S. immigration: Contemporary trends.* Berkeley and Los Angeles: University of California Press.

Iceland, J. (2009). *Where we live now: Immigration and race in the United States.* Berkeley and Los Angeles. University of California Press.

Jackson, K. T. (1985). *Crabgrass frontier: The suburbanization of the United States.* New York: Oxford University Press.

Jones-Correa, M. (2006). Reshaping the American dream: Immigrants, ethnic minorities, and the politics of the new suburbs. In K. M. Kruse & T. J. Sugrue (Eds.), *The new suburban history.* Chicago, IL: University of Chicago Press.

Katz, M. B. (2010). What is an American city? In M. Chowkwanyun & R. Serhan (Eds.), *American democracy and the pursuit of equality.* Boulder, CO: Paradigm Publishers, forthcoming.

Katz, M. B., & Stern, M. J. (2006). *One nation divisible: What America was and what it is becoming.* New York: Russell Sage Foundation Publications.

Kruse, K. M., & Sugrue, T. J. (2006). *The new suburban history.* Chicago, IL: University of Chicago Press.

Lacy, K. R. (2002). "A part of the neighbourhood?": Negotiating race in American suburbs. *International Journal of Sociology and Social Policy, 22,* 39–74.

Lacy, K. R. (2004). Black spaces, black places: Strategic assimilation and identity construction in middle-class suburbia. *Ethnic and Racial Studies, 27,* 908–930.

Lieberson, S. (1962). Suburbs and ethnic residential patterns. *The American Journal of Sociology, 67,* 673–681.

Massey, D. S. (1985). Ethnic residential segregation: A theoretical synthesis and empirical review. *Sociology and Social Research, 69,* 315–50.

Massey, D. S. (2008). *New faces in new places: The changing geography of American immigration.* New York: Russell Sage Foundation Publications.

Massey, D. S., & Mullan, B. P. (1984). Processes of Hispanic and black spatial assimilation. *American Journal of Sociology, 89,* 836–873.

Maykuth, A. (2008, March 20). Ruling: "Speak English" sign at cheesesteak shop not discriminatory. *The Philadelphia Inquirer*, A1.

Myers, D. (1999). Upward mobility in space and time: Lessons from immigration. In J. Hughes & J. Seneca (Eds.), *America's demographic tapestry: Baseline for the new millennium*. New Brunswick, NJ: Rutgers University Press.

Myers, D., & Cranford, C. J. (1998). Temporal differentiation in the occupational mobility of immigrant and native-born Latina workers. *American Sociological Review*, 63, 68–93.

Nicolaides, B. M. (2002). *My blue heaven: Life and politics in the working-class suburbs of Los Angeles, 1920–1965*. Chicago, IL: University of Chicago Press.

Nicolaides, B. M., & Wiese, A. (2006). *The suburb reader*. New York: Routledge.

Odem, M. E. (2008). Unsettled in the suburbs: Latino immigration and ethnic diversity in metro Atlanta. In A. Singer, S. W. Hardwick, & C. B. Brettell (Eds.), *Twenty-first century gateways: Immigrant incorporation in suburban America*. Washington, DC: Brookings Institution Press.

Odem, M. E. (2009). Latino immigrants and the politics of space in Atlanta. In M. E. Odem & E. Lacey (Eds.), *Latino immigrants and the U.S. South* (pp. 112–125). Athens: University of Georgia Press.

O'Mara, M. P. (2001). *Fight or flight: Philadelphia and its future*. Philadelphia: Metropolitan Policy Cener.

O'Mara, M. P. (2005). *Cities of knowledge: Cold war science and the next Silicon Valley*. Princeton, NJ: Princeton University Press.

Orfield, M. (2002). *American metropolitics: The new suburban reality*. Washington, DC: Brookings Institution Press.

Park, R., Burgess, E. W., & McKenzie, R. D. (1925). *The city*. Chicago: University of Chicago Press.

Preston, J. (2007, July 27). Judge voids ordinance on illegal immigrants. *The New York Times*.

Ruggles, S., Sobek, M., Alexander, T., Fitch, C. A., Goeken, R., Hall, P. K., King, M., & Ronnander, C. (2004). *Integrated public use microdata series: Version 3.0*. Minneapolis, MN: Minnesota Population Center.

Santiago, A. M. (1992). Patterns of Puerto Rican segregation and mobility. *Hispanic Journal of Behavioral Sciences*, 14, 107–133.

Santiago-Valles, K. A., & Jiménez-Muñoz, G. M. (2004). Social polarization and colonized labor: Puerto-Ricans in the United States, 1945–2000. In D. G. Gutiérrez (Ed.), *The Columbia history of Latinos in the United States since 1960* (pp. 87–145). New York: Columbia University Press.

Sassen, S. (2007). *A sociology of globalization*. New York: W. W. Norton.

Self, R. O. (2003). *American Babylon: Race and the struggle for postwar Oakland*. Princeton, NJ: Princeton University Press.

Siembieda, W. J. (1975). Suburbanization of ethnics of color. *The Annals of the American Academy of Political and Social Science*, 422, 118–128.

Singer, A. (2005). The rise of the new immigrant gateways: Historical flows, recent settlement trends. In B. Katz, A. Berube, & R. E. Lang (Eds.), *Redefining urban and suburban America: Evidence from Census 2000* (Vol. 2). Washington, DC: Brookings Institute Press.

Singer, A. (2008). Twenty-first century gateways: An introduction. In A. Singer, S. W. Hardwick, & C. B. Brettell (Eds.), *Twenty-first century gateways: Immigrant incorporation in suburban America* (pp. 11–29). Washington, DC: Brookings Institution Press.

Somekawa, E. (1995). On the edge: Southeast Asians in Philadelphia and the struggle for space. In S.-Y. Chin, J. S. Moy, W. L. Ng, & G. Y. Okihiro (Eds.), *Reviewing Asian America: Locating diversity*. Pullman, WA: Washington State University Press.

South, S. J., Crowder, K., & Chavez, E. (2005a). Exiting and entering high-poverty neighborhoods: Latinos, blacks and Anglos compared. *Social Forces*, 84, 873–900.

South, S. J., Crowder, K., & Chavez, E. (2005b). Geographic mobility and spatial assimilation among U.S. Latino immigrants. *International Migration Review*, 39, 577–607.

South, S. J., Crowder, K., & Chavez, E. (2005c). Migration and spatial assimilation among U.S. Latinos: Classical versus segmented trajectories. *Demography*, 42, 497–521.

Walker, R. A. (1978). The transformation of urban structure in the nineteenth century and the beginnings of suburbanization. In K. R. Cox (Ed.), *Urbanization and conflict in market societies*. Chicago, IL: Maaroufa Press.

Walker, R. A. (1981). A theory of suburbanization: Capitalism and the construction of urban space in the United States. In M. Dear & A. Scott (Eds.), *Urbanization and urban planning in capitalist society* (pp. 383–430). London: Methuen.

Whalen, C. T. (2001). *From Puerto Rico to Philadelphia: Puerto Rican workers and postwar economics*. Philadelphia: Temple University Press.

Wiese, A. (2004). *Places of their own: African-American suburbanization in twentieth century America*. Chicago, IL: University of Chicago Press.

Zelinsky, W. (2001). *The enigma of ethnicity: Another American dilemma*. Iowa City, IA: University of Iowa Press.

NOTES

1. For good discussions of the politics, consequences, and limitations of the 1965 law, see Frasure (2005); Jones-Correa (2006).

2. The IPUMS are a random sample of the long form census (STF-3) up until 2000. For subsequent periods, the data are derived from the American Community Survey (ACS), which is an annual representative sample of the U.S. population. For a complete description of the data see Ruggles et al. (2004).

3. In 2000, Salem County, NJ, was considered part of the Philadelphia metropolitan area by the Office of Management and Budget, which defines the census geography. However, to be consistent over time it was removed from the analysis in the tract and individual data for 2000 and 2006. Although the geography is identical, the estimated population totals can differ slightly due to sampling. These differences will be noted when necessary.

4. Orfield (2002) used municipal boundaries, not census tracts, to categorize suburban areas. To match the tract-level data on the foreign-born, municipalities were assigned to groups of tracts. In cases where the tracts did not match exactly, the municipality within which the majority of the tract resided came to define it. Tracts were selected as the building block to prevent the population counts from becoming disconnected from the geographic boundaries. There were very few cases in which the geography overlapped, as Philadelphia is a slow-growth city, resulting in few tracts being subdivided or changed to accommodate larger populations over time.

5. Authors' analysis; data available on request.

6. For instance, in June 2008, Mayor Michael Nutter issued a broad language access Executive Order covering all city departments.

7. On the settlement patterns of earlier waves of immigrants to Philadelphia, see Hershberg (1981). On earlier waves of immigration to the city more generally, see Davis and Haller (1973) and Golab (1977).

8. Attention to this issue is usually an afterthought or un-addressed entirely in the literature. Here are some articles that give the issue stronger attention than normal: Massey and Mullan (1984); Santiago (1992); South, Crowder, and Chavez (2005a, 2005b, 2005c).

9. An exception is Myers and Cranford (1998).

10. In the interests of space, we have kept tables and figures to a minimum in this article. Data available on request.

11. This is calculated among those with recorded professions.

12. As mentioned previously, the individual and the tract data do not result in identical population estimates. The numbers presented in this section are derived from the tract-level Neighborhood Change database (NCDB; Geolytics Inc., 2004). The estimated number of foreign-born for Greater Philadelphia is generally higher when derived from the individual data, resulting in the percentage of total growth attributable to immigration being higher as well. Therefore, the NCDB tract data are likely to be a conservative estimate of the actual percentage of the total growth attributable to the foreign-born. The distribution described by Table 5 includes only the race/immigrant categories described. The population of greater Philadelphia is somewhat more diverse, and increasingly so, and the total population attributable to the foreign-born is based on change in the total population, including groups not included in Table 5.

13. In this analysis, which necessarily uses the classifications in the NCDB, native-born white unfortunately includes Puerto Ricans. In subsequent analyses, using other sources, we will try to examine the Puerto Rican-born population separately.

14. 8.34%, 54.14%, and 25.35%, respectively, compared to 121.58% in at-risk developing suburbs, 415.94% in bedroom developing suburbs, and 116.96% in suburban job centers.

15. Authors' analysis; data available on request.

16
Right to the Suburb?
GENEVIEVE CARPIO, CLARA IRAZÁBAL, AND LAURA PULIDO

In 2001, the cartoonist of syndicated comic strip *La Cucaracha*, Lalo Alcaraz, created a parody of Grant Wood's famous painting *American Gothic* (Figure 1). In the image, Alcaraz depicts a Latino couple as neighbors to the traditional mid-western couple from Wood's painting. While the Latino couple smiles at the viewer, the white farmer clutches the pitch fork defensively as both he and his companion stare warily at the seemingly out-of-place Latinos. The image by Alcaraz illustrates a dramatic demographic shift in the United States, in which Latino residents, immigrant and non-immigrant alike, are increasingly moving into "non-traditional" areas. These include new regions, as well as a shift from cities to suburbs (Singer, Hardwick, & Brettell, 2008; Singer, 2004). This shift has increasingly generated pro- and anti-immigrant activism in suburbs. We argue these movements for contracted and expanded immigrant rights have been enabled through intersecting city, state, and federal policies, as well as local, regional, and national networks of activists. These dynamics often manifest at the municipal level.

While the urban realm remains the most visible stage for immigrant rights activism, the suburbanization of Latinos has caused unique challenges that call for a reevaluation of approaches and theorizations of immigrant activism. Up until now, the phrase "Right to the City" has been often used as a rallying cry in the struggle for maximizing political access, claiming public space, and expanding spaces of citizenship. Conceived as the right to the urban by Henri Lefebvre (1996 [1968]), the concept has since been expanded by activists and scholars such as the Right to the City Alliance, Mark Purcell (2003), and Don Mitchell (2003) as the right to political participation, public space, and self-governance. By assessing how this right is expanded and constricted for immigrants in two Southern California suburbs, this [discussion] seeks to assess how Lefebvre's concept of Right to the City can be used to better understand pro and anti-immigrant activism and politics in the suburbs of Los Angeles.

Maywood in Los Angeles County and Costa Mesa in neighboring Orange County serve as divergent examples of suburbs struggling over immigration policy (Vázquez-Castillo, 2009; Cienfuegos, 2006). Both cities are residential hubs, historically white, and have experienced large growth in their domestic and international Latino populations over the past 20 years. While the predominantly

Direct correspondence to: Genevieve Carpio, Department of American Studies and Ethnicity, University of Southern California, Los Angeles, CA, USA. E-mail: gcarpio@usc.edu.
JOURNAL OF URBAN AFFAIRS, Volume 33, Number 2, pages 185–208.
ISSN: 0735-2166.
DOI: 10.1111/j.1467-9906.2010.00535.x

FIGURE 1

News Item: Census 2000 Reports Latinos Moving Out of Traditional Areas. From comic strip La Cucaracha. LALO ALCARAZ @2001 Dist. By UNIVERSAL UCLICK. Reprinted with permission. All rights reserved.

Latino city of Maywood has declared itself a "Sanctuary City" in opposition to federal law, predominantly white Costa Mesa was reportedly the first city to partner with Federal Immigration and Customs Enforcement (ICE) to identify and deport unauthorized residents.[1] For each suburb, local activism and electoral activism were gateways for municipal level change. By taking public stances for/ against national immigration enforcement, powerful political and demographic shifts in City Councils, and demonstrations in public spaces, the two cities have come to represent the extremes of the immigration debate in the United States. Using the case studies of these two cities in Southern California, we seek to better understand how the tensions between suburbanites and Latino immigrants are addressed by local governments in the face of shifting ethnoracial geographies in the Los Angeles region. We argue that, in the face of increasing migration by Latinos to suburbs and multi-scalar policies criminalizing immigrants, municipalities and residents are confronting the question, Who has the Right to the Suburb?

RIGHT TO THE CITY AND ITS TRANSFORMATIONS

Since Henri Lefebvre coined the phrase "Right to the City" in 1968, it has sparked a "cry and a demand" for increased access to the urban and a reevaluation of citizenship in the city and beyond (Lefebvre, 1996, p. 168). It serves as a political platform for numerous organizations, including Strategic Action for a Just Economy in downtown Los Angeles, the Miami Worker Center, and the Environmental Health Coalition in San Diego, whose fundamental principles include the right to live in the city and the right to democratic participation and power (TIDES Foundation, 2007). Published shortly before the Parisian student uprisings in May 1968, *The Right to the City* is primarily concerned with "the problems of the city and urban society" (Lefebvre, 1996, p. 177).

Lefebvre sees this as the struggle between industrialization and urbanization, and what he refers to as the tension between exchange value and use value, i.e., the stresses and injustices brought about by the capitalist commodification of things in the urban realm and their concomitant value in monetary terms rather than on their usefulness and contribution to the well-being of residents. Lefebvre describes the Right to the City as "a superior form of rights: rights to freedom, to individualization in socialization, to habitat and to inhabit. The right to the *oeuvre,* to participation and appropriation (clearly distinct from the right to property), are implied in the right to the city" (Lefebvre, 1996, p. 174). At its heart, the Right to the City calls for an economic revolution that prioritizes use value over exchange value, a political revolution that calls for the inhabitants as the agents of social change, and a cultural revolution in which living in the city is in itself a praxis of artistic expression (Lefebvre, 1996).

Since Henri Lefebvre wrote *Right to the City,* the concept has been interpreted and expanded by spatial thinkers including Don Mitchell, Mark Purcell, Peter Marcuse, and Clara Irazábal to conceptualize rights, social struggle, and citizenship claims in a manner that is applicable to the case of non-citizens. For Lefebvre, rights are determined by the inhabitants. Expanding on Lefebvre, Mitchell (2003) asks, who can inhabit the city? Whom should it serve? And by whom should it be governed? Mitchell is primarily concerned with how the "public" is defined and contested. He argues that attacks on public space, through "privatization" and "alienation," are also attacks on the Right to the City. While his work focuses on the homeless, his ideas can also be applied to non-citizens, in the sense that their exclusion from particular spaces through removal is used to constrict who is included in the public and to restrict political participation.

Rather than an individualistic notion of rights based on membership in a nation-state, the Right to the City is divorced from the idea of national citizenship as a prerequisite for political participation. Instead, it is rooted in urban citizenship and the collective use of space. Purcell (2003) questions the usefulness of national scales of citizenship as the basis for rights claims within a global political economy. His concept of the "Right to the Global City" necessarily includes non-citizens in political participation and implies governance by inhabitance. That is, a right earned through everyday life, not necessarily membership in the nation-state. Saskia Sassen (2006) has similarly stated that citizenship and the nation-state are in flux as a result of intensified global economic policies, which require new features of citizenship for emerging postnational and denationalized subjects. Even before this destabilization, U.S. immigration policy had created "impossible subjects" who, according to Mai Ngai (2004), are "a social reality and a legal impossibility" (p. 57). According to Ngai, Mexican and Asian immigrants face divergent citizenship trajectories from white Europeans and Canadians. For non-whites, the designation of a racialized or non-racialized identity, undeserving or deserving citizenship, and social exclusion or inclusion, respectively, all hold implications for whether sovereign rights or constitutional rights are exercised on behalf of each group.

For Latinos, the question of ethnicity serves to legitimize discrimination and exclusion, regardless of actual legal status. This became particularly clear following 9/11 when anti-terrorism and immigration enforcement were packaged together by U.S. ICE (Pulido, 2009). In light of this environment, we suggest a broader notion of citizenship rights and formulate conceptual tools that apply rights, and the Right to the City, to the case of non-citizens. The Right to the City better provides what national citizenship does not guarantee for

Latino immigrant communities: the right to self-governance regardless of citizenship, the right to political participation beyond the electoral, and the right to be agents of political, economic, and cultural change. By expanding claims to the public, residents have the potential to increase public participation. Within the context of Latin American political activism, for example, Clara Irazábal (2008) has argued that "extraordinary events in public spaces have the potential, under certain circumstances, to dramatically expand invented spaces of citizenship" (p. 16). That is, attempts to expand the public through political demonstrations can create new public spaces and citizenship practices that encompass the Right to the City. Irazábal argues that these spaces of citizenship can be distinct from those offered by the nation-state. Taking into account these frameworks, in this article we seek to highlight new forms of citizenship claims and strategies for political participation, as well as efforts to suppress them. The southern California cities of Maywood and Costa Mesa exemplify two such approaches: Maywood's local policies, for the most part, pursue an expansion of rights, while Costa Mesa seeks their contraction.

THE RIGHT TO THE CITY AND LATINO SUBURBS

A reexamination of the suburbs as both sites of contested ethnoracial politics and the Right to the City as an analytical and mobilizing framework is called for in light of suburbs' increasing numbers of immigrant and minoritized residents.[2] First, this requires considering the unique social, economic, and political formation of suburbs; acknowledging the suburb as a site of transgression; and recognizing the suburb as a port of entry for immigrants. Second, it calls for Lefebvre's notions of rights to be applied broadly. The urban realm is privileged as the most visible stage for both claiming Lefebvre's Right to the City and immigrant rights activism today. An overview of news coverage of the immigrant rights marches,[3] for example, reaffirms this presumption. Occurring throughout cities and suburbs, major cities received the most national media attention, reproducing the bias toward the urban realm as the preferred site for immigrant rights activism. Yet suburban spaces have been critical in shaping local political activism and have helped lay the groundwork for residential, educational, labor, and civil rights activism in the larger Los Angeles metropolis. In Los Angeles, where the suburb and city are intimately tied to one another, adopting a Right to the City framework necessarily requires adopting an investment in a regionally oriented vision. Thus, we build on Lefebvre by focusing on the suburb because it is a key part of the metropolitan geography that is both related to and distinct from the city.

While the suburb is a site of contestation, organizing in the suburbs presents a unique set of challenges. Historically, rights in the suburbs have often been expressed as white homeowners' rights. There is abundant literature on this phenomenon. For example, Lisa McGirr in *Suburban Warriors* (2002) and Matthew Lassiter in *The Silent Majority* (2006) discuss how white homeowners were quick to attack outside agitators, threats to individual property rights, and racial integration. Similarly, in her study of a white working-class suburb in Los Angeles, Becky Nicolaides (2002) succinctly summarizes their approach when homogeneity was threatened. She states, "they appropriated the language and logic of the civil rights movement in constructing an opposition argument, which hinged partly on the defense of their status as working, taxpaying white citizens. As white homeowners, they were entitled to their own set of rights" (p. 296)—that is, a set of white homeowner rights based on racial segregation and legitimized through a discourse of individualism. Spatially, the historical processes of suburbanization and decentralization reveal spatial forms of racism in which, for instance, whites have been able to move away from older industrial cores and secure relatively cleaner environments (Pulido, 2000). With suburbs as the epitome of the mythical "American Dream"—rooted in the idea of homeownership, the heteronormative family, and white supremacy—suburbs are becoming a symbolic battleground for who has access to rights (legal or natural) in the United States as the Latino and immigrant population increase.

There is a growing literature on people of color in the suburbs (Saito, 1998; Garcia, 2001; Wiese, 2004; Ochoa, 2004; Kruse & Sugrue, 2006). While Latinos have always settled in suburbs to some degree, there has been a significant intensification occurring as a result of deindustrialization and rising housing costs in the last three decades. This shift has derived from both private land development and the relocation of industry to the suburbs. Within the Southern California Association of Governments (SCAG) region, encompassing the Los Angeles, Orange, San Bernardino, Riverside, Ventura and Imperial Counties, Latino migration has contributed to a net increase in Latino residents from 10% to 40% between 1960 and 2000. Fifteen percent of the nation's total immigrant population and 25% of the nation's unauthorized immigrants live within the SCAG region alone (Chang, 2007). According to a special report by the U.S. Census Bureau on Migration and Geographic Mobility in Metropolitan and Nonmetropolitan America, in 2000 over 324,000 "movers from abroad" migrated to central cities, while over 375,000 migrated to suburbs, in the Los Angeles-Orange-Riverside Metropolitan Area (Schachter, Franklin, & Perry, 2003).[4] That is, more immigrants are migrating to suburbs than to central cities in southern California. Immigrants' new locational choices and the impact of these new settlement patterns on non-traditional receiving communities are being experienced in other metropolitan areas as well, including Phoenix, Atlanta, and Sacramento (Singer, Hardwick, & Brettell, 2008). The large concentration of the nation's immigrant population, the intensification in immigrant suburbanization, and the growth of similar cases throughout the nation make the Los Angeles region a particularly significant site to explore the resulting tension between white homeowners' rights and broader rights claims based on inhabitance.

With suburbs becoming the new immigrant gateway communities (Singer, Hardwick, & Brettell, 2008; Singer, 2004), the exploration of rights in suburbs is crucial to innovative understandings of citizenship, political access, and self-governance. Yet, people of color in suburbs are often treated as apolitical, and suburban struggles are often assumed to be conservative and, as a result, are undertheorized as sites of liberatory struggle. Our case studies illustrate an alternative reading of suburbs, not only as "ethnoburbs" with a high concentration of immigrant and ethnic workers that comprise an "urban mosaic" which promotes economic mobility for residents through social and business networks in a globalized economy (Li, 2006), but also as sites where new identities are formed, racial lines are challenged, and community formation is contested. At the core of the resulting battles, residents are debating who has the right to determine who can and cannot live in the suburb and under what conditions. It is precisely residents' divergent claims to these rights that ignite tension between citizens and non-citizens. The Right to the Suburb allows a way to approach these diverse struggles, while accounting for the unique openings for action allowed in the suburb as a historical, political, and ideological construct. At the same time, claims by immigrants in suburbs offer an exciting way to broaden the application of the Right to the City.

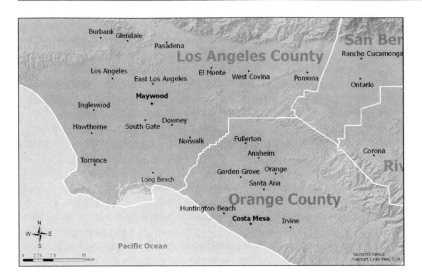

FIGURE 2
Map of Maywood, Costa Mesa, and Surrounding Areas. Courtesy of Laura Harjo, 2009.

By examining the events in Costa Mesa and Maywood, the following sections seek to understand the response of the City Councils, community organizations, and residents to the intensification of Latino migration into these suburbs (Figure 2). We examined City Council minutes, media accounts, demographic data, and archival materials from Costa Mesa and Maywood regarding key events and proposals related to immigrant rights. We asked, how have Costa Mesa and Maywood responded to immigration debates? How have their political and cultural histories affected who is able to live and move freely through the city? And what factors determine how rights are minimized or maximized? Furthermore, how have residents shaped these responses?

COSTA MESA

Best known for upscale shopping, televangelism, and stucco-lined streets, behind the veneer of effortless suburban homogeneity made popular in the TV series *The O.C.* and the *Real Housewives of Orange County* lie some of the most controversial and restrictive approaches to suburban immigration in the nation. Over the past 20 years, Costa Mesa's City Council has passed numerous policies targeting Latino immigrants, from banning soccer in public parks to closing a job center serving day laborers (Caspa, 2008). These attacks were overshadowed when, in one of the most controversial moves made by a municipal government, Costa Mesa's Mayor Allan Mansoor proposed in 2005 a partnership with ICE that would allow local law enforcement agents to identify, process, and detain immigrants. Attempts to reclaim the Right to the Suburb by immigrant advocates through attending City Council meetings and demonstrations proved unsuccessful when countered by conservative council members, influential anti-immigrant organizations, and federal policies extending immigration enforcement to local governments. Claiming to only target immigrants with "aggravated felonies and criminal street gang activity," in its first year of operation over 3,000 people were identified for deportation by a partnership with ICE (City of Costa

Mesa, 2005; Santana & Saavedra, 2007a). Costa Mesa became the program's national leader in deportations and a model for other suburban governments anxious to restrict the growing number of Latino residents. Through a discourse of minimum rights and facilitated by federal policies, Costa Mesa suppressed citizenship claims, restricted political participation, and curtailed the Right to the Suburb for Latino residents and denied it to unauthorized immigrants.

History

Costa Mesa's response to the rise in its immigrant population can at least partially be traced to its political and cultural history. Costa Mesa, described by bestselling satirical author Gustavo Arellano as "condemned to be known as the place where a Mexican-bashing mayor came into office" (2008, p. 146), has a history rooted in exclusion, militarism, and conservatism. Such history made it a fertile ground for the surge of anti-immigrant activism experienced in the 2000s. Located 37 miles southeast of Los Angeles, in central Orange County, Costa Mesa boomed following World War II. Historian Lisa McGirr (2002) has argued that through federal funds granted for defense, Orange County was transformed into a regional power. The construction of the Santa Ana Army Air Base in 1941 brought in soldiers from across the U.S. Many veterans decided to settle in Orange County, and particularly in Costa Mesa, when the Air Base closed at the end of the War in 1946 (Miller, 1981). Despite its closing, many newly located manufacturers were intimately tied to military markets, such as fiberglass, advanced technical ceramic products, and cryogenic pumps. The economic restructuring of industries in inner suburbs such as Maywood, an explosion in suburban tract housing, and white flight from central L.A. following the Watts 1965 rebellion (Pulido, 2000) all contributed to a white population boom in the historically small town. In the 30-year period between 1940 and 1970, Costa Mesa grew from 4,000 residents to 72,000 (Barr, 1981). Even today, the tax income generated from the concentration of manufacturing and high-end retail in the city helps subsidize the affluence of Costa Mesa residents, where the median household income is above $75,000 (City of Costa Mesa Planning Division, 2007). Comparatively, the median household income in all of California was under $60,000 in 2007 (U.S. Census Bureau, 2005–2007). The conservative climate grew in the 1960s during which time, McGirr (2002) argues, there was a growing movement of "suburban warriors" that played a critical role in galvanizing and mobilizing conservatives at the grassroots level in Orange County. The combination of residents with links to the military, a war-based economy, suburban tract housing, and a politically active constituency made Costa Mesa a popular site for conservative homeowners.

The Changing Color of Costa Mesa

While the political-economy and history of Costa Mesa made it a quintessential white suburb for several decades in the twentieth century, it has recently experienced unprecedented growth in its Latino population (Caspa, 2008). From 1970 to 2000, the immigrant population in Orange County grew from 6% to 30%, with the majority of migrants arriving in Orange County between 1990 and 2000 (Center for Demographic Research, 2003).[5] While Costa Mesa remains predominantly white, the population is projected to be predominantly Latino within the next 30 years. According to Chicano activist Nativo Lopez, "Residents here in Costa Mesa see a changing complexion, a racial complexion, and they feel out of place" (Lagorio, 2006). The Costa Mesa City Council has responded to the increasing number of Latinos through recent anti-Latino policies, affecting both immigrants and non-immigrant Latinos, including eliminating the Human Relations Committee, prohibiting adult soccer in public parks, reducing federal funding to organizations that serve minority groups, and closing the Costa Mesa day labor center, an important resource for Latino immigrants seeking employment (Caspa, 2008). In Costa Mesa, a white conservative majority such as that described by Nicolaides (2002), has minimized immigrant rights to retain a certain ideal of the suburb rooted in white homeownership. Costa Mesa's political-economic history compounded with the increasing suburbanization of Latinos in a new scenario laid a strong foundation for activists interested in maintaining their privilege at the cost of minimizing the rights of immigrants and those perceived as immigrants.

Minimizing Rights: Violating Collective Rights, Inhabitance, and Public Space

In 2006, Coyotl Tezcalipoca (Benito Acosta in his non-indigenous name) was forcefully removed from a City Council meeting by the Costa Mesa police department at the order of the Mayor during the public comment section. The Tonantzin Collective, an immigrant rights group in Costa Mesa, began singing "We Shall Overcome"[6] as their representative was removed from the City Council Chambers for speaking against the council's decision to enforce federal immigration policy locally (Figure 3). They were answered by a chorus of opponents singing "God Bless America," ironically, a song written by an immigrant.[7] Immigration enforcement is a federal responsibility, but through the ICE Agreements of Cooperation in Communities to Enhance Safety and Security (ACCESS) program umbrella, ICE is able to partner with state and local law enforcement to provide the training and subsequent authorization to identify, process, and detain immigration offenders they encounter through

FIGURE 3
Detainees Being Screened by Orange County Sheriff's Department for Immigration Status.
Photo by Leonard Ortiz, the Orange County Register.

programs such as 287 (g) and the Criminal Alien Program, also known as CAP (U.S. ICE, 2009b). Whereas Orange County's Sheriff's Department had earlier entered a formal 287 (g) agreement with ICE, Costa Mesa's police department began enforcing federal immigration policy through CAP when residents elected a conservative City Council majority.[8] While the 287 (g) program cross-designated Orange County officers to enforce immigration law, through CAP the Costa Mesa city jail assigned ICE officers to identify and hold deportable legal permanent residents, visa holders, and unauthorized immigrants on an immigration detainer that ensured their removal to ICE custody upon their release (U.S. ICE, 2007). Programs such as these clearly violated immigrants' Right to the Suburb by targeting their inhabitance.

When a partnership with ICE was first discussed in Costa Mesa, the proposal evoked a strong public response. Those in opposition feared it would create ethnic conflict, increase public liability, and foster fear amongst unauthorized workers. Many were concerned it would undermine the relationship between the police and community, lead to racial profiling, and violate the equal protection of all citizens. Others felt it was outside the realm of the local, stating that it diverted the attention of officers to an issue that should be addressed at the federal level and that it turned police officers into immigration agents instead of peace officers. Chief of Police John Hensley, it was later revealed, even privately advised City Council members against enforcing immigration laws out of concern for "community-oriented policing" and the allocation of department resources it required. When asked about his concerns regarding cross-designation of police officers for immigration enforcement in a disposition with the ACLU, Hensley stated "Particularly with Costa Mesa, it was the [Latino] community on the Westside [that worried me]. My belief and opinion at that time was that taking on this program would harm that relationship we worked so hard to create" (Serna, 2008). Those in favor of the motion adhered to a concept of citizenship staunchly rooted in the nation-state, arguing that a person violating national immigration law had no right to be in the city of Costa Mesa. They drew on color-blind anti-terrorism rhetoric that emphasized the intent of the Memorandum of Agreement (MOA) to screen dangerous criminals, arguing it was a public safety issue with reasonable limits. According to City Council minutes, Councilmember Gary Monahan stated "it would target enforcement efforts against those who are involved in aggravated felonies and criminal street gang activity" (City of Costa Mesa, 2005). After the more liberal council member Linda Dixon suggested a study session with community leaders such as the ACLU and LULAC to explore the implications of the contract, she was quickly outvoted by Mayor Allan Manson, Mayor Pro Tem Eric Bever and Councilmember Gary Monahan who "did not feel it necessary to include it in the motion" (City of Costa Mesa, 2005). This was more than an issue of pro- and anti-immigrant binaries. Some residents felt immigrants should be allowed to live in Costa Mesa, regardless of documentation, under certain conditions. The delineation between deserving and undeserving residents was based on an approved set of behaviors—such as temperance, adherence to U.S. laws, industriousness, and a desire to assimilate— which demarcated the boundaries of social exclusion and inclusion. In their own way, residents were disputing who has the Right to the Suburb.

In 2006, newcomer Wendy Leece and incumbent Mansoor were elected to the City Council by running on a joint platform that focused on "improving" Costa Mesa through increasing immigration enforcement (Linder, 2006).

Wendy Leece's campaign echoed the sentiment of Mayor Mansoor. Her campaign website read, "I am concerned three illegal sex offenders were recently found in Costa Mesa and that not all illegal aliens are deported after serving their jail time. I support Mayor Mansoor's proposal to deport major felons and am the only candidate endorsed by the Mayor" (Leece, 2006). In a blog following his election, Mayor Mansoor reflected on his campaign slogan "Improving Costa Mesa." He described his work as part of an "Improver Movement" of residents who suffered from "a general feeling of a low quality of life" and wanted "things fixed" (Mansoor, 2006). For Mansoor, "improving" Costa Mesa meant having "something done about immigration." Perhaps responding to rising tensions between immigrant rights advocates and nativists in suburbs such as Maywood, in a separate blog on illegal immigration he stated, "The American community is standing up and asking its elected officials to uphold the law. We are doing our part in Costa Mesa" (Mansoor, 2007). Another blog entry illustrates his definition of American identity. He stated, "Those that come here should also learn English and have a desire to assimilate." He echoes this sentiment in another blog, "American without a hyphen" (Mansoor, 2006). Mansoor demonstrates that coming from a family of immigrants (according to the blog entry, his father was born in Egypt and his mother in a province of Finland) does not necessarily ensure one will have a more progressive stand on immigration policy. The election of Wendy Leece and Allan Mansoor over more liberal candidates suggests electoral activism can be used to hinder expanded conceptions of citizenship such as the Right to the Suburb. As stated by Dan HoSang, "California's system of direct democracy has proved to be a reliable bulwark against many leading civil rights and anti-discrimination issues" (HoSang, 2007, p. xi). Indeed, this was the case in Costa Mesa.

Within a month of the election, Costa Mesa entered the partnership with ICE despite strong opposition from community organizations and sectors of the public. The agreement gave Costa Mesa's police officers the training, human resources, and legitimation of the nation-state to help them inhibit immigrants' ability to go about everyday acts while in Costa Mesa. This is part of a larger trend in which the federal government is devolving responsibility for immigration-related policies to local governments (Varsanyi, 2008). From Oklahoma to New Hampshire, ICE access cases have arisen in sites far removed from the U.S. borderlands. For instance, there are currently at least 950 ICE-trained officers and 66 active local governments with 287 (g) MOAs (U.S. Immigration and Customs Enforcement [ICE], 2009a). Through stretching the border and its enforcement to new sites, some local governments are contracting rather than expanding spaces of citizenship and belonging for residents.

Whereas other places with CAP MOAs had part-time agents, an ICE officer worked at the Costa Mesa city jail on a full-time basis, thus consuming a great share of federal resources more than a hundred miles from the border and without any apparent national security reasons. This investment allowed Costa Mesa's law enforcement to deport unauthorized residents, legal permanent residents, and visa-holding immigrants at an unprecedented rate (U.S. ICE, 2007). Arrests soared. ICE began training sheriff deputies to conduct checks on 100% of inmates, whether or not they received a conviction, thus violating the City Council's earlier assurance at council meetings that only dangerous criminals would be screened. In its first week of operation, Costa Mesa, now armed with the authority of federal law enforcement, netted 175 immigrants for screening (Robinson, 2007). By the end of the first year, over 3,000 people were identified for deportation (Santana & Saavedra, 2007a). Several of these cases were thrown out by the District Attorney's Office, because the majority were brought in for minor convictions, including jaywalking, driving without a license, and possession of illegal substances (Santana & Saavedra, 2007b). The MOA effectively legitimized the systematic identification, criminalization, and displacement of immigrants living and passing through Costa Mesa. Through enforcing a framework of rights based on membership in the nation-state, and hence criminalizing the inhabitance of unauthorized immigrants, Costa Mesa embraced a minimal discourse of rights that challenged the Right to the Suburb by denying immigrants political access, public space, and collective rights. At the same time, the MOA instilled fear in all Latinos through racial profiling and hurt the relationship between the Costa Mesa police department and the predominantly Latino Westside community (Serna, 2008).

Contestation

Costa Mesa's local approach to immigration enforcement was facilitated by regional networks of anti-immigrant activists and national discourses on immigration policy rooted in exclusion and militarization. Nativist groups, including Save Our State (SOS) and the Minutemen, drew from resources and residents from across Southern California who came to express their support of the MOA at City Council meetings. For those who did not participate in person, online blogs provided updates on the case with articles, photos, and opportunities for public comment. The Minuteman Project reportedly even held a fundraiser for Mayor Mansoor in support of his immigration policy. Justin Akers Chacón and Mike Davis (2006) explain that, behind the Minutemen's color-blind rhetoric that focuses on the illegality of immigrants, rather than their ethnorace lies a racially infused "propaganda of fear." Residents from throughout the county shared their support of the MOA in public comments to the *Daily Pilot,* a local newspaper. In response to an article, "ICE Traces Illegal Immigrants," a striking, though not exceptional, comment stated "Round them all up. In Costa Mesa all you have to do is drive on the West Side of Costa Mesa and you will find hundreds of illegals [*sic*] driving without a license or insurance. Costa Mesa is becoming a Costa Mexico." Similar remarks state, "Get them ICE," "Keep up the great street 'sweeping'," and "I'm glad ICE is doing a fine job cleaning up our fine city," amongst others (Robinson, 2007).

While Costa Mesa's police officers have exercised extreme policing of immigrants, their approach to enforcement has been met by its share of opponents. Some of the most vocal critics of the new policies include the Tonantzin Collective and the Citizens for Constitutional Rights, two local immigration rights groups. Immigrant activists first appealed to the City Council through public comment at City Hall meetings and through an economic boycott. For instance, before Coyotl Tezcalipoca was arrested at a Costa Mesa council meeting, he delivered a heart-felt speech on behalf of the Tonantzin Collective demanding a reversal of the ICE agreement (City of Costa Mesa, 2006a). The Collective equated the efforts of the City Council and ICE towards Latinos to efforts to remove them from Costa Mesa. Tezcalipoca stated, "You Allan Mansoor and Eric Bever this is a task for both of you guys, three of you guys [third council member indicated is unclear], to gentrify Mexicans, Central Americans, and South Americans out of Costa Mesa. We know that you guys want to change the demographics of Costa Mesa. We know your plot and you guys make sure, all of you, make sure that we are going to be here and fight this to the end" (The Watchdog, 2008). During earlier comments, Minutemen leader Jim Gilchrist asked his supporters to stand. When Tezcalipoca asked his supporters to do the same at the same meeting, however, he was arrested for disrupting an assembly and obstructing an arresting officer (Martinez, 2006).

When the attempts of immigrants and their advocates to reclaim the Right to the Suburb were met with constriction of their political participation and their claims for self-governance, they turned to law suits and public demonstrations. Amongst these efforts, the Tonantzin Collective organized a protest at City Council chambers, and Citizens for Constitutional Rights organized a boycott. In April 2006 over a thousand people from Costa Mesa and nearby suburbs marched to the City Hall to protest its anti-immigrant policies and as a response to the federal legislative proposal HR 4437 (Caspa, 2008; Archibold, 2006).[9] By staging protests at the symbolic heart of local anti-immigrant policy, the demonstrations ruptured the authority of the City Council to speak for the people and revealed residents' unrest and their capacity to reclaim decision making authority, albeit temporarily. It is important to note these acts preceded the nation-wide demonstrations protesting HR 4437. Through later joining with regional movements in Downtown Los Angeles, immigrant advocates unified in a common call for expanded rights and a new framework for citizenship.

Mansoor announced his intent to run for the 2010 state legislature, and in November 2009 he was elected. He has promised to continue his commitment to broad enforcement of U.S. immigration policies (Blank, 2009). Concurrently, Coyotl Tezcalipoca partnered with the American Civil Liberties Union to file civil charges against the City of Costa Mesa for violating his freedom of space when he was forcefully removed from the 2006 City Council meeting (Serna, 2008). In December 2009, a federal jury found that his first amendment rights were not violated, a frightening precedent for free speech advocates (Pak, 2009).

MAYWOOD

In Costa Mesa, rising immigration has been met by a discourse of minimal rights exercised through mass displacement, limiting political participation, and restricting immigrants' claims to the suburb. A few miles away, in neighboring Los Angeles County, Maywood's approach to immigration has been transformed into a discourse of maximum rights based on inhabitance. When traffic checkpoints effectively amounted to a "municipal tax" on immigrants, residents of Maywood began to mobilize. They made important strides toward self-governance, including defeating the traffic checkpoints, increasing control over the police through a citizens' commission, and successfully campaigning to elect immigrant advocates to public office. These efforts gained national attention when, in a controversial move, Maywood openly refused to enforce federal immigration law in the wake of HR 4437. Self-appointed a "Sanctuary City," Maywood simultaneously became the target of anti-immigrant activism and a rallying cry for those seeking to extend new understandings of citizenship.

History

Like Costa Mesa, Maywood's response to immigrant rights can at least partially be traced to its political, economic, and cultural history. Located close to the city of Los Angeles, Maywood was the heart of the machinery-metallurgical industries in the Los Angeles region when it was founded in 1924. The availability of factory work, coupled with an abundance of half-acre garden home sites complete with racial deed restrictions, led to a community of white industrial workers (Ahrens & Urbina, 2005). Racial residential restrictions were prevalent and openly advertised in Chamber of Commerce publications. One such advertisement stated, "No property, prior to May 1945, can be sold, conveyed, rented or leased to any person not of the caucasian [*sic*] or white race" (City of Maywood, 1998). This "commonsense" approach to home ownership persisted well beyond the 1950s. For the neighboring city of South Gate, historian Becky Nicolaides (2002) has argued that homeowner rights and white rights were often synonymous. She states, "South Gate residents waged the most forceful arguments against integration by emphasizing the rights and well-being of whites" (p. 301). By the 1980s, however, assembly plants began relocating, businesses closed, and the white majority began moving out of deindustrializing Maywood in Los Angeles County and into neighboring suburbs in Orange County. Whites followed higher-paying jobs in the burgeoning manufacturing sector, while the demand for low-wage labor in Southeast Los Angeles' manufacturing district contributed to the Latinization of its inner suburbs. Despite the privilege Maywood had previously enjoyed as an industrial-residential hub, by 2000 per capita income had fallen to well below that of suburbs in Orange County. Today, manufacturing remains the leading industry employing residents (22%), but many are employed in low-paying production, transportation, and material-moving occupations (42%) (U.S. Census Bureau, 2000). Maywood's downward mobility is similar to other manufacturing suburbs in Southern California, whose residents suffer from compressed wages. The combination of newly vacated housing, proximity to factory work, and the end of racially restrictive housing covenants made Maywood a popular site for new immigrants.

The Latino Majority in Maywood

While Maywood was a white residential-industrial hub throughout the 1900s, by the end of the century it had experienced a major dramatic demographic shift. Between 1970 and 2000, Maywood shifted from 97% White to 96% Hispanic ("Population profile," 1971; U.S. Census Bureau, 2000). The demographic changes were reflected in Latino-oriented publicly sponsored events, printing public documents in Spanish, and electing an all-Latino City Council. Of those who identified as Hispanic on the U.S. Census, almost half identified as non-citizens (42%). It is difficult to assess how many residents are without U.S. authorization. According to a study by the International City/County Management Association (ICMA), about 40% of immigrants nationwide are believed to be unauthorized, which was confirmed by a local council member who estimated that a third to half of the total population in the city of Maywood is unauthorized (ICMA, 2008; Traux, 2006). In Maywood, where Spanish speakers outnumber English speakers, anti-immigrant policies stemmed from tensions between the police department, intraethnic conflict, and discriminatory state and federal policies. However, policies limiting the rights of non-U.S. citizens would be confronted by a movement for maximizing immigrant rights and expanding their Right to the Suburb.

Maximizing Rights: Embracing Collective Rights, Inhabitance, and Public Space

In 2003, Flor Cervantes and her children were left stranded on the sidewalk carrying whatever possessions they could hold as they watched a tow truck drag their car to the impound lot by order of the Maywood traffic division. Unable to afford the charges for a mandatory 30-day hold, which ranged from

$1,000 to $1,600, Cervantes's car was sold at an auction by Maywood's Club Tow (Del Olmo, 2003a). At checkpoints, residents driving down Maywood's main thoroughfare found themselves trapped by blue and red lights as they waited in line for police officers checking sobriety, driver's licenses, and proof of insurance. While the police department claimed the purpose of the checkpoints was to catch intoxicated drivers, residents argued they were intended to criminalize and profit from immigrants.

As a consequence of 1993 Senate Bill 976, applicants without proof of lawful presence in the United States are prohibited from receiving a California driver's license or State ID card. When SB 976 was coupled with a 1987 California Supreme Court decision approving traffic checkpoints to identify drunk drivers, state-sanctioned sobriety checkpoints essentially functioned as local immigrant checkpoints by identifying, criminalizing, and taxing unlicensed Latino immigrants. In 2002, for instance, 1,800 cars were impounded as a result of traffic checkpoints (Del Olmo, 2003a). When compared to the seven drivers that were cited for drunk driving, it becomes clear that checkpoints targeted immigrants and not intoxicated drivers. Maywood began imposing traffic checkpoints after a police officer was killed in a fatal crash with an unlicensed driver, but many believe they remained because of profits gained by the city from towing and impound fees, which are estimated to have been approximately $250,000 a year (Del Olmo, 2003b; Raouf, 1999). Anyone stopped at a traffic checkpoint without a license, e.g., all unauthorized immigrants, had their car impounded, held a mandatory 30-days at a $30-a-day fine, received a citation, and were required to pay a release fee. According to Nativo Lopez, "It amounts to a municipal tax on immigrants" (Anderson, 2007).[10]

The traffic stops became a highly contested issue at City Council meetings, which generated questions about state policies penalizing unauthorized residents and revealed other claims of police abuse including beatings, sexual assault, and racial profiling (Lait & Glover, 2007). These injustices galvanized many Maywood residents. Residents stated that family members without papers avoided visiting them from other cities because they feared their cars would be impounded, teachers reported that the traffic stops were affecting children who were increasingly afraid of the police and whose parents were afraid of driving them to school, and drivers argued that the police were using racial profiling, thus violating the equal treatment of residents (City of Maywood, 2003b). Whereas in Costa Mesa policies were aimed at immigrants and often affected all Latinos, traffic checkpoints more explicitly, though not exclusively, targeted unauthorized immigrants. In Maywood, an all-Latino City Council did not necessarily translate into immigrant-sensitive policy. Instead, it reflected a long-standing tension between native-born and non-native access to rights (Gutierrez, 1995; Ochoa, 2004; Garcia-Bedolla, 2005; Pulido, 2007). The social dynamics in Maywood highlight the extent to which some native-born Latinos have selectively disassociated from immigrants due to fear of stigma and bought in an anti-immigrant sentiment and a law and order mentality that justifies the exclusion of immigrants based on legal status (Garcia-Bedolla, 2005; Pulido, 2007).

Saint Rose of Lima, a local church played a central role as a political and social space for immigrant advocates. After months of public dissent at City Council meetings, the council accepted an invitation from Father David Velasquez to attend a meeting with residents at the church to discuss the effect of checkpoints on locals (City of Maywood, 2003a). This venue shift weakened the hierarchical structure of the council meetings. While never absolving the power structure completely, council members and residents met on closer terms before the priest in a shared social space where they often attend services together. As a result of the meeting, City Council members agreed to waive the 30-day hold for first-time offenders and changed the traffic checkpoints from the early evening, when people were driving home from school and work, to after 10 PM when they were more likely to stop drunk drivers. This was a victory for organizers. Saint Rose of Lima, Comité Pro Uno, a community-based non-profit in Maywood, and One Los Angeles-Industrial Areas Foundation (LA-IAF) led the movement against the traffic stops and were at the forefront of a growing movement for immigrant rights in Southeast Los Angeles (Del Olmo, 2003b). Marcos Hernandez of the LA Metro Project/One LA-IAF, a nonpartisan organizing network that seeks to empower residents to participate in local government, stated, "We have been working with these guys for three months to be able to show them that we have the power to organize" (Cardenas, 2003). Arguing that the police exist to serve the public, Maywood residents and their allies successfully fought for public overview of the police department by a commission composed of members from immigrant rights organizations (City of Maywood, 2006d). Mobilizing to fight the traffic check points gave Maywood activists the networks, training, and experience to help them defeat anti-immigrant policies and fight for the right to inhabit Maywood.

As they continued to gain momentum, activists grew frustrated with City Council members whom they felt did not respect residents. For instance, residents accused members of the council of being corrupt (City of Maywood, 2005b), using "overpowering methods" (City of Maywood, 2005a), and failing to fulfill the responsibilities of their office (City of Maywood, 2005a), and suggested that no one had listened to Latino immigrants (City of Maywood, 2006b). As a result, residents organized to maximize their decision-making authority by seeking to create a new council through voter drives centered at the Saint Rose of Lima Church. In partnership with Los Angeles County–based and nationally organized One LA-IAF, over 100 congregants agreed to recruit 10 registered voters each to discuss their political campaign. Through incorporating Maywood's small size into a grassroots activism model based at the church, their organizing efforts were highly successful. Voter turnout doubled from the previous year with nearly all registered voters casting a ballot (Traux, 2006; Radford 2006). In November 2005, Sergio Calderón and Felipe Aguirre, two immigrant advocates, were elected to the City Council. Representatives from immigrant rights organizations including Padres Unidos de Maywood, League of United Latin American Citizens (LULAC), One LA-IAF, and Union of Neighbors came to greet the new City Council members at their inaugural meeting. The public celebrated what they considered a "historic change" (City of Maywood, 2005a). But it is not the electoral victory that makes this approach consistent with Right to the City. Rather than embracing national citizenship, voter registration and citizenship application workshops were part of a multi-pronged strategy whose overall goal was to increase local political participation and council accountability to all residents, regardless of citizenship status. The discourse adopted by residents was not one of assimilation. Ultimately, they were fighting for the right to be there, to use the suburb freely, and to avoid persecution at work. Their larger goal was to ensure residents could directly affect public policy in the neighborhood, not necessarily to attain U.S. citizenship. Nevertheless, their opposition was intimately tied to issues of national exclusion and federal immigration laws that operate at the local level.

The election of Calderón and Aguirre to the council, which already included immigrant supporter Councilmember Thomas Martin, gave the City Council a liberal majority, leading to the passing of a number of pro-immigrant policies, including declaring a resolution to restore the Dream Act,[11] calling for a moratorium on impounding cars for equipment violations, and requiring the early release of vehicles impounded from unlicensed drivers ineligible for a license. In one meeting, Councilmember Felipe Aguirre specifically asked that the city change state law with regard to more lenient impound policy (City of Maywood, 2006b). By mid-December, the new council reviewed the 30-day holding for impounds and released them to unauthorized immigrants, reducing impounds from 206 cars in December to only 15 in January, a huge victory for organizers (City of Maywood, 2005b, 2006a). Maywood inspired action in other suburbs with traffic checkpoints. For example, on the other side of Los Angeles County, in the city of Pomona, residents and students have protested traffic checkpoints through rallies, attending City Council meetings, and discussing a class action lawsuit (Carpio, personal observation, March 28, 2009; Pomona Checkpoints, 2009). It is a demand for a broader notion of rights, such as those described by Lefebvre, to attain the right to move freely within the city and the right to determine its policies based on their residency in the suburb, regardless of one's citizenship status.

Maywood was a fertile ground to make further claims for rights when in December 2005 the proposed Clear Act amendments to HR 4437 threatened to switch federal citizenship violations from civil to criminal offenses for immigrants and those who helped them, and to rescale the enforcement of immigration laws to state and local law enforcement agencies (GovTrack.us. HR 4437–109th Congress, 2005). In response, on January 24, 2006, Maywood's City Council passed Resolution 5225 opposing the Clear Act and the Sensenbrenner-King Immigration Restriction Bill HR 4437.[12] The Resolution argued that the bill burdened police with enforcement of technical civil immigration status, diverting them from priority tasks of public safety; discouraged immigrants from coming forward to report crimes and suspicious activity making streets less safe; was an unfunded and unsafe mandate imposed on the police department; and violated the police department policy "that officers shall not consider ancestry, race, ethnicity, national origin . . . as sole basis for establishing reasonable suspicion, probable cause, or a basis for requesting consent and search," and "as currently written, is unfairly punitive, and is not reasonably designed to combat terrorism or enhance the security of the United States of America" (City of Maywood, 2006b). Because Maywood was already equipped with a politicized set of residents, activist networks, and a radical City Council opposed to state laws contrary to local interests, it was able to respond to HR 4437 with a resolute defense of immigrants' rights (Figure 4).

By openly opposing the bill, Maywood was soon labeled a Sanctuary City (Cuevas, 2006). Maywood, in addition to other cities, including Berkeley, San Francisco, New Haven, Albuquerque, Seattle, and Durham to name a few, is part of this national movement (ICMA, 2008). The Church of Saint Rose of Lima was at the center of this struggle, part of a larger trend in which immigrants adopt religious spaces and transform them into meaningful spiritual, cultural, and political places (Irazábal & Dyrness, 2010; Kotin, Dyrness, & Irazábal, forthcoming). Similar to the church-based Sanctuary Movement, in

FIGURE 4
Immigrant Rights Demonstration in Maywood. Photo by Leslie Radford

which the church serves as a safe haven from persecution, Sanctuary is a symbolic status taken on by cities who do not allocate funds to enforce federal immigration law, but on the contrary make concerted efforts to make access to education, health, public space, police, and other resources safe for unauthorized immigrants. As described by a survey of local governments' reactions to immigration concerns, "Although the specific provisions of each sanctuary ordinance vary, the common denominators are that they focus on the human rights of the individuals rather than on their legal status, and they generally prohibit local government employees from identifying, reporting, or detaining immigrants or otherwise doing the work of federal immigration officials in the absence of warrants" (ICMA, 2008). For instance, in San Francisco Mayor Newsom launched a Sanctuary City Outreach Campaign, and, in a highly publicized account, in Long Beach, CA, St. Luke's Episcopal Church provided refuge for Liliana Santuario (not her real last name) to prevent the breast-feeding mother from deportation to Mexico. These are part of the New Sanctuary Movement that has emerged as a response to a rescaling of immigrant enforcement to local governments (Bazar, 2007; Office of the Mayor [San Francisco], 2008). In this national movement, immigrants and their allies are demanding the Right to the Country, realized through the Rights to the City/Suburb.

Contestation

But Maywood's stand against anti-immigrant policies did not remain unchallenged. Former City Council member Sam Peña publicly disapproved of the City's opposition to federal law. According to Peña, "They talk about the city of no law and order, and I think Maywood is becoming that" (Becerra & Winton, 2006). Similarly, a minority of residents came to City Council meetings to question Maywood's Sanctuary status (City of Maywood, 2006c). Some had a more extreme approach. After passing Resolution 5225, hate mail and death threats were sent to its main advocates, Councilmen Felipe Aguirre and Thomas Martin (Becerra & Winton, 2006). It is unclear who supported former councilmember Peña or made the threats, but it is evident that at least a portion of Maywood's predominantly Latino residents opposed the progressive stance on immigration in the city. This reaction points to broader trends in which some Mexican Americans and authorized Mexican immigrants adopt anti-unauthorized immigrant positions in an effort to improve their own standing vis-à-vis the pressures they face regarding identity politics, assimilation, and managing interpersonal relationships with new neighbors (Gutierrez, 1995; Ochoa, 2004; Geron, 2005; Pulido, 2009).

Maywood was receiving national attention. As SOS, the Minutemen, and other nativist groups applauded Costa Mesa, even making the Mayor an honorary Minuteman member, anti-immigrant activists from Save Our State crossed county lines to stage a protest at Maywood's City Hall to "punish" the city by disrupting traffic and making the city pay for extra police time, costing Maywood an estimated $20,000 to $30,000 according to Mayor Thomas Martin (Baer, 2006; Rohrlich, 2006). SOS planned similar efforts in other predominantly Latino suburbs in the Los Angeles region, where they met with massive resistance from suburban immigrant supporters (Akers Chacón and Davis, 2006). When news of SOS's protest came out, immigrant activists began organizing a counter-protest already equipped with the networks created when campaigning against the traffic checkpoints. Organizers also used popular media such as MySpace to advertise the counter-rally. One post stated, "The racist group the Minute Men Project is coming this Saturday 26th to the city of Maywood to protest against the city's support for sanctuary to immigrants. Show your opposition to their radical and racist movement" (Black Misfit, 2006). Residents from adjacent suburbs in Southeast Los Angeles including Bell, Bell Gardens, Huntington Park, South Gate, Cudahy, and Lynwood were encouraged to attend. Concurrently, advocates met for mariachi music, lunch, and a citizenship workshop at Saint Rose of Lima Church (Rohrlich, 2006). In Maywood, the city, the region, and the nation intersected.

While some pro- and anti-immigrant activists claimed rights based on a nation-state, best exemplified when a U.S. flag was removed from the post office and replaced with a Mexican flag, many counter-protesters tied the demonstration to larger movements for collective rights divorced from notions of belonging to a nation-state. According to Council Member Sergio Calderón, "I believe that we were exercising our rights and fulfilling our responsibilities as local elected officials in voicing what the majority of our populace held in strong conviction" (Cuevas, 2006). He continued, "Proposed laws, such as HR 4437, are hypocritical in spirit and would accomplish nothing more than creating what would resemble a police state and deny dignity to those who perform our most hazardous and labor-intensive jobs" (Cuevas, 2006). For Councilmember Calderón, the needs of inhabitants, regardless of citizenship, are the main basis of governance. According to counter-protestor María Sauza, "They believe that they can tell people that they are illegals, when it's a human right to look for a better life."[13] Héctor Carreón of *La Voz de Aztlán* echoed this sentiment, "All human beings, regardless of national origin, have the right to 'life, liberty and the pursuit of happiness.' The City of Maywood, CA, should be commended for guaranteeing this fundamental right to its residents of Mexican descent, regardless of their documentation status" (Cuevas, 2006). In Maywood, the dominant basis for rights is not found within the nation-state but instead determined by inhabitance. The movement in Maywood generated proactive measures such as a citizens' committee to oversee the police, the disbanding of the traffic division which ran the checkpoints, and the election of City Council members aligned with the political values of those targeted by the checkpoints. As a result of their efforts, we see increased participation at council meetings, bilingual publications, and a focus on quality of life struggles. These proactive measures suggest that their approach is indeed a Right to the Suburb claim for access to the community (and the ability to move freely within it) as well as a call for self-governance.

CONCLUSION: A TALE OF TWO SUBURBS?

Costa Mesa and Maywood have approached immigrant rights in divergent ways. This is not a simple matter of demographics. Instead, the cases of Costa Mesa and Maywood reveal an alternative vision of rights as the product of historical trajectories, activism, and political leadership. On the one hand, Costa Mesa has partnered with ICE in order to detain, process, and deport immigrants, authorized and unauthorized alike, for minor infractions such as jay walking and riding a bicycle without a helmet. But, while Costa Mesa has criminalized the very act of inhabiting the suburb, Maywood has defied the criminalization of its residents by taking stands against laws that criminalize immigrants, such as HR 4437 and the California Driver's License Bill. Each of these controversial moves depended in part on each suburb's particular sociopolitical histories, the election of City Council members with strong political leanings, and networks of activists who sustained an effective mobilization.

Throughout the United States, most suburbs have adopted an approach that falls between those exemplified by Costa Mesa and Maywood. According to a 2007 survey by International City/County Management Association of 500 local governments, 19% "require local law enforcement officials to obtain federal training on Immigration and Customs Enforcement," and fewer than 5% of respondents have more radical approaches. Amongst these approaches include "designating the city as a sanctuary." The approach each city adopts is in part defined by City Councils but contested and shaped by residents. This contestation is most evident in resident-driven voting drives, public statements in City Council meetings, and demonstrations in symbolic public spaces, such as those in Costa Mesa and Maywood.

When thinking about the larger and lasting social, economic, political, and spatial implications of policies, actions, and cultural trends as related to immigration reform and Lefebvre's Right to the City in Southern California and U.S. society, at least three trends become particularly clear. First, this study suggests immigrant activism is increasingly being generated in suburbs, challenging the assumption that social movements originate in the city. This partnership, at times, draws on resources from the central city but sometimes organizes independently of the city by partnering with or following the example of neighboring suburbs. Second, election-based organizing and local activism can be a highly effective way to enact municipal level change (Vitiello, 2009). In Costa Mesa, approval to enter the partnership with ICE was passed after electing a majority anti-immigrant council, whereas in Maywood the most radical approaches to immigrant rights were passed after residents successfully campaigned for pro-immigrant rights council members. Lastly, seeking to expand or constrict the Right to the City/Suburb necessarily entails multi-scalar efforts. In Maywood and Costa Mesa, discrimination was enabled through intersecting municipal politics, state policies, and federal departments. Similarly, successful organizing efforts called on local organizations, regional networks of activists, and linkages with national discourses on immigration policy.

While divergent, the approaches of Maywood and Costa Mesa are not isolated from one another, but instead reveal a metropolitan level relationship. Each city has used the other to contrast and legitimize its position. For instance, Felipe Aguirre has stated that while immigrants may be attacked in Costa Mesa, they can feel safe in Maywood (Cienfuegos, 2006). In an opposing statement, Costa Mesa Councilmember Eric Bever has criticized Maywood for not enforcing federal laws and asked cities to follow Costa Mesa's example instead, arguing that "freedom does not mean without laws" (City of Costa Mesa, 2006b). While council members have crossed discursive borders, activists have crossed municipal, county, and state borders to participate in public demonstrations for and against immigrant rights. What both anti- and pro-immigrant activist hold in common is that at the center of the debate they are asking, who has a Right to the Suburb; who defines it, enforces it, and enjoys it; and how and to what effects?

This [discussion] suggests a reexamination of the Right to the City as an analytical and mobilizing framework. In practice, this suggests a larger call for regional networks of activists fighting similar battles in a common call for expansion of immigrant rights and the Right to the City/Suburb.[14] This means building networks and coalitions that argue for use value over exchange value, inhabitance as the basis for claims to political participation (rather than membership in the nation-state), and public spaces as contested sites that have the possibility to expand these claims. Furthermore, a Right to the Suburb framework with an emphasis on the new politics of settlement suggests new formations for pro-immigrant and pro-minoritized communities' activism that bridges multiscalar organizing efforts, builds alliances amongst diverse struggles over displacement,[15] and focuses efforts in the suburb for some forms of activism, as a complement to the current model which focuses largely on cities. Through exploring how Lefebvre's concept of Right to the City and the new spatial distribution of immigrants can inform one another, this [discussion] suggests an opening for a new politics of emancipatory change within the terrain of the neoliberalizing United States.

Acknowledgements: Earlier versions of this article were presented at: the Conference "Radical Urbanism: Critical Discourse on the Right to the City," CUNY Graduate Center, City University of New York, December 12th, 2008; and "Diverse Suburbs: History, Politics, and Prospects," National Center for Suburban Studies, Hofstra University, October 22, 2009. The authors thank the anonymous reviewers and the Immigration and Integration Initiative 2007–2008 from the University of Southern California for its support.

REFERENCES

Ahrens, E. W., & Urbina, P. (2005). *Images of America Maywood*. Charleston, SC: Arcadia Publishing.

Akers Chacón, J., & Davis, M. (2006). *No one is illegal: Fighting racism and state violence on the U.S.-Mexico border*. Chicago: Haymarket Books.

Anderson, J. (2007, October 4). Mario's tow truck troubles. *LA City Beat*. Available at http://www.lacitybeat.com/cms/story/detail/?id=6276&IssueNum=226 (accessed March 17, 2008).

Archibold, R. C. (2006, April 2). Latinos protest in California in latest immigration march. *The New York Times*. Available at http://www.nytimes.com/2006/04/02/us/02costamesa.html (accessed December 18, 2007).

Arellano, G. (2008). *Orange County: A personal history, I've been taking notes*. New York: Scribners.

Barr, T. A. (1981). *The story of Costa Mesa*. Costa Mesa, CA: Press of City of Costa Mesa, California.

Baer, D. (2006, March 3). Legal affairs: Costa Mesa's immigration deputies, Part 2. *Day to day*. National Public Radio. Available at http://www.npr.org/templates/story/story.php?storyId=5243884 (accessed December 18, 2007).

Bazar, E. (2007, July 8). Illegal immigrants find refuge in holy places. *USA Today*.

Black Misfit (Username) (2006, August 25). The 'Minute Men' are coming to Maywood, CA! Blog post. Available at Myspace.com (accessed May 4, 2008).

Blank, A. (2009, April 15). Mansoor declares seat bid. *Daily Pilot*. Available at http://www.dailypilot.com/articles/2009/04/15/topstory/dpt-mansoorforassembly04162009.txt (accessed July 8, 2009).

Becerra, H., & Winton, R. (2006, July 13). Hate mail, threats probed in Maywood. *Los Angeles Times*. Available at http://articles.latimes.com/2006/jul/13/local/me-hit13 (accessed March 30, 2008).

Cardenas, J. (2003, August 22). Police checks of cars halted. *Los Angeles Times*. Available at http://articles.latimes.com/2003/aug/22/local/me-maywood22 (accessed March 17, 2008).

Carpio, G. (2009, March 28). Personal observation. *Participation in Demonstration*. Pomona: California on Indian Hill.

Caspa, H. (2008). *Terror in the Latino barrio: The rise of the new right in local government*. Santa Ana, CA: Seven Locks Press.

Cedillo, G. (2004) *A social, public safety, and security: argument for licensing undocumented drivers*. Center for Latin American Studies. CLAS Policy Papers. eScholarship Repository, University of California. Available at http://repositories.cdlib.org/clas/pp/2 (accessed May 14, 2009).

Center for Demographic Research (2003) Orange County immigrants in 2000: An overview. *Orange County Profile*, 8(4).

Chang, P. (2007). *The state of the region 2007: Measuring regional progress*. Los Angeles: Southern California Association of Governments.

Cienfuegos, E. (2006, January 27). Alta California: The tale of two cities. *La Voz de Aztlan*. Available at http://www.aztlan.net/tale_of_two_cities.htm (accessed May 4, 2009).

City of Costa Mesa (2005, December 6). *Minutes of regular meeting of the City Council: City of Costa Mesa*.

City of Costa Mesa (2006a, January 3). *Minutes of regular meeting of the City Council: City of Costa Mesa*.

City of Costa Mesa (2006b, March 21). *Minutes of regular meeting of the City Council: City of Costa Mesa*.

City of Costa Mesa Planning Division (2007). *Community economic profile*. Costa Mesa, CA: Author.

City of Maywood (1998). History of Maywood webpage. Accessed June 12, 2008, from History of Maywood Folder. Cesar Chavez Library. Maywood. CA.

City of Maywood (2003a, August 12). *Minutes of the regular meeting of the Maywood City Council*.

City of Maywood (2003b, August 13). *Minutes of the regular meeting of the Maywood City Council*.

City of Maywood (2005a, November 29). *Minutes of the regular meeting of the Maywood City Council*.

City of Maywood (2005b, December 13). *Minutes of the regular meeting of the Maywood City Council*.

City of Maywood (2006a, January 10). *Minutes of the regular meeting of the Maywood City Council*.

City of Maywood (2006b, January 24). *A resolution of the City Council of the City of Maywood, California, opposing the Clear act and the Sessenbrenner-King immigration restriction bill (H.R. 4437) being considered in Congress, and urging the United States Senate to reject it*. Resolution No. 5225.

City of Maywood (2006c, February 14). *Minutes of the regular meeting of the Maywood City Council*.

City of Maywood (2006d, May 30). *Minutes of the regular meeting of the Maywood City Council*.

Cuevas, H. (Interviewer) (2006, September 7). The safe haven debate. In *Life and Times*. Transcript available at http://kcet.org/lifeandtimes/archives/200609/20060906.php (accessed May 4, 2008). KCET.

Del Olmo, F. (2003a, August 3). Maywood's mean money machine. *Los Angeles Times*. Available at http://articles.latimes.com/2003/aug/03/opinion/oe-delolmo3 (accessed March 17, 2008).

Del Olmo, F. (2003b, August 17). Towing policy is not off the hook. *Los Angeles Times*. Available at http://articles.latimes.com/2003/aug/17/opinion/oe-delolmo17 (accessed March 17, 2008).

Garcia, M. (2001). *A World of its own: Race, labor, and citrus in the making of Greater Los Angeles, 1900–1970*. Chapel Hill: University of North Carolina Press.

Garcia-Bedolla, L. (2005). *Fluid borders: Latino power, identity, and politics in Los Angeles*. Berkeley: University of California Press.

Geron, K. (2005). *Latino political power: Latinos exploring diversity and change*. Boulder, CO: Lynne Rienner Publishers.

GovTrack.us, H.R. 3137–109th Congress (2005). CLEAR Act of 2005, *GovTrack.us (database of federal legislation)* <http://www.govtrack.us/congress/bill.xpd?bill=h109-3137&tab=summary> (accessed May 5, 2009).

GovTrack.us, H.R. 5131–109th Congress (2006). American Dream Act, *GovTrack.us (database of federal legislation)* <http://www.govtrack.us/congress/bill.xpd?bill=h109-5131> (accessed May 5, 2009).

GovTrack.us, H.R. 4437–109th Congress (2005). Border protection, anti-terrorism, and illegal immigration control act of 2005. *GovTrack.us (database of federal legislation)* <http://www.govtrack.us/congress/bill.xpd?bill=h109-4437&tab=summary> (accessed May 5, 2009).

Gutierrez, D. (1995). *Walls and mirrors: Mexican Americans, Mexican immigrants, and the politics of ethnicity*. Berkeley: University of California Press.

HoSang, D. (2007). Racial propositions: *Genteel apartheid in postwar California*. Doctoral dissertation, University of Southern California.

International City/County Management Association (2008). *Immigration reform: An intergovernmental imperative*. Binghamton, NY: Binghamton University.

Irazábal, C. (Ed.). (2008). *Ordinary places, extraordinary events: Citizenship, democracy and public space in Latin America*. New York: Routledge.

Irazábal, C., & Dyrness, G. R. (2010). Promised land? Immigration, religiosity, and space in Southern California. *Space & Culture*, 13(4), 365–375.

Kotin, S., Dyrness, G. R., & Irazábal, C. (forthcoming). Immigration and integration: The religious and political activism of immigrants in Los Angeles. *Progress in Development Studies*.

Kruse, M., & Sugrue, T. (2006). *The new suburban history*. Chicago: University of Chicago Press.

Lagorio, C. (2006, March 28). *Costa Mesa's identity crisis: An O.C. city is getting tough on immigrants—and immigrants are fighting back*. CBS News. Available at http://www.cbsnews.com/stories/2006/03/28/eveningnews/main1447962.shtml (accessed January 8, 2008).

Lait, M., & Glover, S. (2007, April 1). Maywood employs police officers with a history of trouble. *Los Angeles Times*. Available at http://articles.latimes.com/2007/apr/01/local/me-maywood1 (accessed July 9, 2009).

Lassiter, M. D. (2006). *The silent majority: Suburban politics in the Sunbelt South*. Princeton, NJ: Princeton University Press.

Leece, W. (2006). Biography: Wendy Brooks Leece. Available at wendy.leece.com (accessed June 10, 2008).

Lefebvre, H. (1996). *Writings on cities*. E. Kofman & E. Lebas. (Trans.). Oxford: Blackwell.

Li, W. (2006). *From urban enclave to ethnic suburb: New Asian communities in Pacific Rim countries*. Honolulu: University of Hawaii Press.

Library of Congress (2003, April 2). God bless America. *American treasures of the library of congress*. Washington, DC. Available at http://www.loc.gov/exhibits/treasures/trm019.html (accessed May 4, 2008).

Linder, E. (Webmaster) (2006). *Wendy Leece for Costa Mesa City Council homepage*. Available at Wendyleece.com (accessed July 15, 2008).

Mansoor, A. (2006, October 11). *An American without a hyphen*. Available at allanmansoor.com/blog/?p=5 (accessed on April 12, 2008).

Mansoor, A. (2007, November 16). *Illegal immigration*. Available at http://allanmansoor.com/blog/?p=6.

Martinez, B. (2006, January 4). Arrest disrupts Costa Mesa council meeting. *The Orange County Register*. Available at http://www.ocregister.com/ocregister/news/homepage/article929384.php (accessed March 10, 2008).

McGirr, L. (2002). *Suburban warriors: The origins of the new American right*. Princeton, NJ: Princeton University Press.

Miller, E. J. (1981). *The SAAB story: The history of the Santa Ana army air base*. Costa Mesa, CA: The Costa Mesa Historical Society and the SAAB Wing.

Mitchell, D. (2003). *The right to the city: Social justice and the fight for public space.* New York: Guilford Press.

Ngai, M. (2004). *Impossible subjects: Illegal aliens and the making of modern America.* Princeton, NJ: Princeton University Press.

Nicolaides, B. M. (2002). *My blue heaven: Life and politics in the working-class suburbs of Los Angeles, 1920–1965.* Chicago: University of Chicago Press.

Ochoa, G. L. (2004). *Becoming neighbors in a Mexican American community: Power, conflict, and solidarity.* Austin: University of Texas Press.

Office of the Mayor (San Francisco) (2008, April 4). Mayor Newsom launches Sanctuary City outreach campaign. Press release. San Francisco.

Ortega, J. (2006, August 27). Santuario de protestas: Impulsores y detractores de los inmigrantes se encontraron en Maywood. *La Opinión.*

Pak, E. (2009, December 15). Jury: Costa Mesa did not violate latino activist's rights. *Orange County Register.*

Pastor, M., Benner, C., & Matsuoka, M. (Eds.) (2009). *This could be the start of something big: How social movements for regional equity are reshaping metropolitan America.* Ithaca, NY: Cornell University Press.

Pomona checkpoints: Saving lives or ruining lives (2009, May 26). Panel presentation given at California State Polytechnic University, Pomona, hosted by the Multi-Cultural Council.

Pulido, L. (2000). Rethinking environmental racism: White privilege and urban development in Southern California. *Annals of the Association of American Geographers, 90*(1), 12–40.

Pulido, L. (2007). A day without immigrants: The racial and class politics of immigrant exclusion. *Antipode 39*(1), 1–7.

Pulido, L. (2009). Immigration politics and motherhood. *Amerasia Journal, 35*(1), 169–178.

Purcell, M. (2003). Citizenship and the right to the global city: Reimagining the capitalist world order. *International Journal of Urban and Regional Research, 27*(3), 564–590.

Radford, L. (2006, August 27). *Maywood stops the invasion.* Los Angeles Independent Media Center. Available at http://la.indymedia.org/news/2006/08/176057.php (accessed June 3, 2009).

Raouf, N. (1999, July 20). Maywood officer is mourned. *Los Angeles Times.* Available at http://articles.latimes.com/1999/jul/20/local/me-57849 (accessed March 17, 2008).

Robinson, A. (2007, August 24). ICE traces illegal immigrants. Daily Pilot. Available at http://www.dailypilot.com/articles/2007/08/24/publicsafety/dpt-ice24.txt (accessed May 14, 2009).

Rocco, R. (1997). Citizenship, culture, and community: Restructuring in Southeast Los Angeles. In W. Flores & R. Benamayor (Eds.) *Latino cultural citizenship: Claiming identity, space, and rights.* Boston: Beacon Press.

Rohrlich, T. (2006, August 27). Protest targets Maywood's stance. *Los Angeles Times.* Available at http://articles.latimes.com/2006/aug/27/local/me-protest27 (accessed at May 14, 2009).

Saito, L. T. (1998). *Race and politics: Asian Americans, Latinos, and whites in a Los Angeles suburb.* Urbana: University of Illinois Press.

Santana, N., & Saavedra, T. (2007a, December 16). Crime little changed since deportation programs began. *Orange County Register.* Available at http://www.ocregister.com/article/immigrants-ice-immigration-1942524-illegal-year (accessed March 10, 2008).

Santana, N., & Saavedra, T. (2007b, December 17). Felons found in police immigration screening. *Orange County Register.* Available at http://www.ocregister.com/articles/costa-mesa-crime-1942532-immigration-police (accessed March 10, 2008).

Sassen, S. (2006). The repositioning of citizenship: Emergent subjects and spaces for politics. *Berkeley Journal of Sociology, 46,* 4–25.

Schachter, J. P., Franklin, R. S., & Perry, M. J. (2003). Migration and geographic mobility in metropolitan and nonmetropolitan America: 1995 to 2000. *Census 2000 Special Reports.* United States Census 2000. Available at http://www.census.gov/prod/2003pubs/censr-9.pdf.

Serna, J. (2008, September 17). Report: Chief against ICE. *Daily Pilot.* Available at http://www.dailypilot.com/articles/2008/10/27/topstory/dpt-iceopposition091808.txt (accessed July 8, 2009).

Singer, A. (2004, February). *The rise of new immigrant gateways.* Washington, DC: The Brookings Institution Press.

Singer, A., Hardwick, S. W., & Brettell, C. B. (Eds.) (2008). *Twenty-first century gateways: Immigrant incorporation in suburban America.* Washington, DC: Brookings Institution Press.

Southern, E. (1971). *The music of Black Americans: A history* (2nd ed.). New York: W. W. Norton.

TIDES Foundation (2007). *The right to the city: Reclaiming our urban centers, reframing human rights, and redefining citizenship: A conversation between donor activist Connie Cagampang Heller and Gihan Perera of the Miami Workers Center.* San Francisco: Author.

Traux, E. (2006, May 15). Maywood la ciudad santuario. *La Opinión.*

U.S. Census Bureau (2000). *Profile of selected economic characteristics: Maywood, CA.* Available at http://factfinder.census.gov/servlet/SAFFFacts?_event=&geo_id=16000US0646492&_geoC ontext=01000US%7C04000US06%7C16000US0646492&_street=&_county=maywood& _cityTown=maywood&_state=&_zip=&_lang=en&_sse=on&ActiveGeoDiv=&_useEV= &pctxt=fph&pgsl=160&_submenuId=factsheet_1&ds_name=ACS_2007_3YR_SAFF&_ci_ nbr=null&qr_name=null&reg=null%3Anull&_keyword=&_industry=.

U.S. Census Bureau (2005–2007). *Selected economic characteristics: California.* Accessed October 5, 2008, at http://factfinder.census.gov/servlet/ADPTable?_bm=y&-geo_id=04000US06&- qr_name=ACS_2007_3YR_G00_DP3YR3&-context=adp&-ds_name=&-tree_id=3307&-_ lang=cn&-redoLog=false&-format=.

U.S. Immigration and Customs Enforcement, Department of Homeland Security (2007, December 13). *ICE program at Costa Mesa jail nets more than 500 deportable.*

U.S. Immigration and Customs Enforcement, Department of Homeland Security (2009a, May 19). *Delegation of immigration authority section 287(g). Immigration and Nationality Act.*

U.S. Immigration and Customs Enforcement, Department of Homeland Security (2009b, August 28). ICE access.

Varsanyi, M. (2008). Rescaling the 'alien,' Rescaling personhood: Neoliberalism, immigration, and the state. *Annals of the Association of American Geographers, 98:*(4), 877–896.

Vázquez-Castillo, M. T. (2009). Anti-immigrant, sanctuary and repentance cities. *Progressive Planning, 178,* 10–13.

Vitiello, D. (2009). The migrant metropolis and American planning. *Journal of the American Planning Association, 75*(2), 245–255.

Watchdog (Username). Coyotl Tezcatlipoca gets arrested. Costa Mesa, CA. Filmed January 3, 2006. Available at http://www.youtube.com/watch?v=X5ANH_Z0Uzc, accessed May 4, 2008.

Wiese, A. (2004). *Places of their own: African American suburbanization in the twentieth century.* Chicago: University of Chicago Press.

NOTES

1. In this article, we use the adjective "unauthorized" to refer to immigrants that are not legally permitted to be in the United States. We disavow the common adjective "illegal" and "undocumented" to name these immigrants. In the former case, we acknowledge the right of human beings to migrate in search of better living conditions, and thus challenge the designation "illegal." In the latter case, many, if not most, unauthorized immigrants do carry identification documents of their countries of origin and hence are not undocumented.

2. We use the adjective "minoritized" to refer to ethnic groups traditionally considered minorities to signal the common perception and treatment as minorities they are subjected to even when they become majorities in certain areas.

3. The largest urban marches in recent years took place in 2006, protesting a heightened national anti-immigrant climate culminating in the HR 4437 proposal. Hundreds of thousands of immigrants and allies marched in Los Angeles, New York, Chicago, and many other U.S. cities. The events were amply covered by the media (Pulido, 2007).

4. This category includes movers from foreign countries, as well as movers from Puerto Rico, U.S. Island Areas, and U.S. minor outlying islands.

5. Of these immigrants, almost 50% came from Latin American countries, with a large portion also coming from Asia (37%). Latinos as a whole make up a much larger percentage of Costa Mesa residents than Asians and Asian Americans, perhaps further exacerbating concerns over Latino migration (32% and 7%, respectively). (Center for Demographic Research, 2003).

6. A U.S. gospel song that later became a popular protest song during the U.S. civil rights movement. Lyrics include "We shall overcome," "We'll walk hand in hand," and "We shall all be free" (Southern, 1971).

7. Lyrics include "God bless America, my sweet home." It is "America's unofficial national anthem," originally written by Serbian immigrant Irving Berlin in 1918 (Library of Congress, 2003, April 2).

8. The initial intent of the city had been to join the 287(g) program, but the city settled with the Criminal Alien Program because 287(g) proved to be too much of a strain on personnel and finances.

9. This amendment to the Immigration and Nationality Act would strengthen enforcement of immigration law enforcement and intensify securitization of the border between the U.S. and Mexico. The most debatable and opposed part of the Border Protection, Antiterrorism and Illegal Immigration Control Act of 2005 (H.R. 4437) is that it would have made it a felony to reside in the U.S. without authorization and would have penalized those who assisted unauthorized immigrants, including churches and aid workers. It was strongly opposed by immigrant rights advocates, as evident in the wave of rallies in 2006 calling for more progressive immigration reform. H.R. 4437–109th Congress: Border Protection, Antiterrorism, and Illegal Immigration Control Act of 2005 (2005). In GovTrack.us (database of federal legislation). Retrieved December 5, 2010, from http://www.govtrack.us/congress/bill.xpd?bill=h109-4437.

10. For a brief history of traffic checkpoints occurring throughout the Los Angeles region and alternative legislation being proposed, see Cedillo (2004).

11. The Dream Act, or HR 513, would grant permanent resident status to immigrant minors who have (1) lived continuously in the United States, (2) are "of good moral character," and (3) have attained a certain degree of formal education (GovTrack.us. H.R. 5131–109th Congress, 2006).

12. The Clear Act, or HR 3137, was proposed in 2005 to authorize local and state enforcement to "investigate, apprehend, or transfer to federal custody aliens in the United States." Furthermore, it would increase criminal penalties for immigration infractions (GovTrack.us. H.R. 3137–109th Congress, 2005).

13. Original text in Spanish states, "Creen que pueden decirle a la gente que son ilegales, cuando es un derecho de humanos buscar una vida major" (Ortega, 2006). See also Rocco (1997).

14. See Pastor, Benner, & Matsuoka (2009) for more on regional social movements.

15. See TIDES (2007) for more on how the Right to the City Alliance is building national networks to fight displacement.

17

The Ethnic Diversity of Boomburbs

ROBERT E. LANG AND JENNIFER B. LEFURGY

A primary LEGO showpiece, Miniland USA is a celebration of American achievements, a canvas to illustrate the diversification of its peoples and cultures, past and present.

—Legoland Website

The main attraction of Legoland, a theme park just outside of Carlsbad, California, is Miniland USA, which features miniatures of quintessentially American places built from 20 million Legos. Miniland has a replica of Washington, complete with federal museums, monuments, the White House, and the Capitol. It even has a miniature Georgetown and a working model of the Chesapeake & Ohio Canal. Other places in Miniland include the French Quarter of New Orleans, a New England fishing village, and Manhattan. The miniature of California is a hodgepodge of scenes, from an Orange County surfing town to Chinatown in San Francisco.

Adapted from Robert E. Lang and Jennifer B. LeFurgy, *Boomburbs: The Rise of America's Accidental Cities*, pp. 1–62. © 2007, the Brookings Institution. Used with permission.

What's missing from Miniland, however, is the built landscapes so typical of America—the housing subdivision, the retail strip mall, the office park—in short, suburbia. The irony is that Lego building blocks are perfectly suited to make such places, especially the commercial structures. The basic Lego is a small rectangular block. Think of the ease with which the Miniland model makers could depict big-box retail centers or the low-slung, banded-window suburban office building. Just snap a bunch of Legos together and, presto, instant "edge city."[1] It is not as if the Lego folks could have missed knowing about suburban malls and office buildings: Southern California is chock full of them. Such buildings even lie just outside the gates of Legoland, along Interstate 5 as it approaches San Diego. But apparently suburban sprawl does not count as an "American achievement."

Modern suburbia's absence from Miniland USA reflects a national ambivalence about what we have built in the past half century. We made the suburbs, and we increasingly live in the suburbs, but we still often disregard them as real places. Even though one could describe much of modern suburban commercial development as Lego-like, there was little chance that Miniland would include a replica of nearby Costa Mesa, California, which contains the nation's biggest suburban office complex and one of its largest malls.[2]

BOOMBURBS: THE BOOMING SUBURBS

While these booming suburbs may not capture the public imagination, they have consistently been the fastest-growing cities over the past several decades. This growth has not translated into immediate name recognition, except perhaps among demographers, who keep seeing the population growth of these cities exceed that of older cities.

The essence of a boomburb is that people know of them but find them unremarkable and unmemorable. As this book shows, all sorts of high-profile industries and activities occur in boomburbs, but few identify with the city. For example, over a dozen major league sports are centered in boomburbs, but only the Anaheim Mighty Ducks (a hockey team) carries the place name. The fact that the one professional baseball team that had a boomburb identity—the Anaheim Angels—has since become the Los Angeles Angels of Anaheim points to the problem. The city of Anaheim took the trouble to highlight this switch in its entry for Wikipedia.com, an online encyclopedia:

> On January 3, 2005, Angels Baseball, LP, the ownership group for the Anaheim Angels, announced that it would change the name of the club to the Los Angeles Angels of Anaheim. Team spokesmen pointed out that, from its inception, the Angels had been granted territorial rights by Major League Baseball to the counties of Los Angeles, Ventura, Riverside, and San Bernardino in addition to Orange County. New owner Arturo Moreno believed the new name would help him market the team to the entire Southern California region rather than just Orange County. The "of Anaheim" was included in the official name to comply with a provision of the team's lease at Angel Stadium, which requires that "Anaheim be included" in the team's name.

Thus Anaheim, a city with as many residents as Pittsburgh or Cincinnati, is reduced to an addendum on the Angels name—and only then because of a legal technicality.

Scratch most boomburb mayors and you may find that they have a Rodney Dangerfield complex: their cities get no respect. Michael L. Montandon, the mayor of North Las Vegas (one of the nation's fastest-growing boomburbs), tells of an encounter in which the mayor of Salt Lake City dismissed the idea that the two places share common problems, despite the fact that North Las Vegas is both bigger and more ethnically diverse than Salt Lake City.[3]

North Las Vegas is not alone. Few big-city mayors seem to recognize boomburbs as peers, and visa versa. Mayor Keno Hawker of Mesa, Arizona (a boomburb that is now bigger than Atlanta or St. Louis), spent just one year in the U.S. Conference of Mayors before withdrawing his city. His problem (in addition to the stiff dues) was that the other mayors were simply not discussing issues that concerned him.[4] As of 2004 Mesa was the largest city in the nation that does not belong to the U.S. Conference of Mayors.

But boomburbs also have a hard time fitting into the National League of Cities, whose membership is dominated by smaller cities and suburbs. Although most boomburbs do belong to the National League of Cities, their size and growth rates make it difficult for them to share common perspectives and problems with the typical cities in the organization. As one boomburb mayor put it, "How do you relate to cities that are smaller than your city grows in just a year?"

We call boomburbs accidental cities.[5] But they are accidental not because they lack planning, for many are filled with master-planned communities; when one master-planned community runs into another, however, they may not add up to one well-planned city. Too new and different for the U.S. Conference of Mayors and too big and fast growing for the National League of Cities, boomburbs have a hard time fitting into the urban policy discussion. Washington's think tank crowd is simply stumped by them.

It seems that few boomburbs anticipated becoming big cities, or have yet to fully absorb this identity, and thus have accidentally arrived at this status. Part of the confusion may be that in the past the port, the factory, and the rail terminal fueled metropolitan growth. Today booms occur in places with multiple exchanges on new freeways, where subdivisions, shopping strips, and office parks spring up. This is the development zone that Bruce Katz refers to as "the exit-ramp economy."[6] Or as Jane Jacobs would say, boomburbs develop as "micro-destinations" (such as office parks) as opposed to "macro-destinations" (downtowns).[7]

Boomburbs are not traditional cities nor are they bedroom communities for these cities. They are instead a new type of city, a subset of and a new variation of American suburbanization.[8]

Boomburbs are defined as having more than 100,000 residents, as not the core city in their region, and as having maintained double-digit rates of population growth for each census since the beginning year (now 1970). Boomburbs are incorporated and are located in the nation's fifty largest metropolitan statistical areas as of the 2000 census, areas that range from New York City, with over 20 million residents, to Richmond, Virginia, with just under 1 million people.[9] As of the 2000 census, four boomburbs topped 300,000 in population, eight surpassed 200,000, and forty-two exceeded 100,000. The fifty-four boomburbs account for 52 percent of 1990s' growth in cities with 100,000 to 400,000 residents. (The fifty-four boomburbs are listed alphabetically in Table 1.)

Boomburbs now contain over a quarter of all residents of small to midsize cities. There may be just a few dozen boomburbs, but they now dominate growth in the category of places that fall just below the nation's biggest cities.

TABLE 1

Boomburbs, 2000 Census[a]

Anaheim, California	Gilbert, Arizona	Palmdale, California
Arlington, Texas	Glendale, Arizona	Pembroke Pines, Florida
Aurora, Colorado	Grand Prairie, Texas	Peoria, Arizona
Bellevue, Washington	Henderson, Nevada	Plano, Texas
Carrollton, Texas	Hialeah, Florida	Rancho Cucamonga, California
Chandler, Arizona	Irvine, California	Riverside, California
Chesapeake, Virginia	Irving, Texas	Salem, Oregon
Chula Vista, California	Lakewood, Colorado	San Bernardino, California
Clearwater, Florida	Lancaster, California	Santa Ana, California
Coral Springs, Florida	Mesa, Arizona	Santa Clarita, California
Corona City, California	Mesquite, Texas	Santa Rosa, California
Costa Mesa, California	Moreno Valley, California	Scottsdale, Arizona
Daly City, California	Naperville, Illinois	Simi Valley, California
Escondido, California	North Las Vegas, Nevada	Sunnyvale, California
Fontana, California	Oceanside, California	Tempe, Arizona
Fremont, California	Ontario, California	Thousand Oaks, California
Fullerton City, California	Orange, California	West Valley City, Arizona
Garland, Texas	Oxnard, California	Westminster, Colorado

[a]A boomburb is defined as an incorporated suburban city with at least 100,000 in population, as not the core city of their region, and as having double digit population growth in each census since 1970.

Another way to grasp just how big boomburbs have become is by comparing their current populations with those of some better-known traditional cities. Mesa, Arizona, the most populous boomburb at 396,375 residents in 2000, is bigger than such traditional large cities as Minneapolis (population 382,618), Miami (population 362,470), and St. Louis (population 348,189). Arlington, Texas, the third biggest boomburb, with 332,969 people, falls just behind Pittsburgh (with 334,536) and just ahead of Cincinnati (with 331,285). Even such smaller boomburbs as Chandler, Arizona, and Henderson, Nevada (with 176,581 and 175,381 residents, respectively) now surpass older midsize cities such as Knoxville (with 173,890), Providence, Rhode Island (with 173,618), and Worcester, Massachusetts (with 172,648).

By the 2000 census, fifteen of the hundred largest cities in the United States were boomburbs. More significant, from 1990 to 2000, fourteen of the twenty-five fastest-growing cities among these hundred were boomburbs—including five of the top ten. Since the 2000 census, many of the largest boomburbs jumped ahead of their traditional (and much better-known) big-city peers (based on 2002 census estimates). Mesa (with an estimated population of 426,841) edged out Atlanta (estimated at 424,868). Both Arlington, Texas (estimated at 349,944), and Santa Ana, California (estimated at 343,413), passed St. Louis (which lost nearly 10,000 residents by 2002). Anaheim (with an estimated 2002 population of 332,642) is now immediately trailing St. Louis. Aurora, Colorado (286,028), has overtaken St. Paul (284,037). Finally,

Peoria, Arizona (123,239), surged ahead of Peoria, Illinois (112,670), which has actually lost residents in recent years.[10]

To put the boomburb rise in perspective, consider that only about a quarter of the U.S. population lives in municipalities that exceed 100,000 people. The fraction of the population living in cities this size or above peaked in 1930. Boomburbs are among the few large cities that are actually booming. Much of the nation's metropolitan population gains have shifted to their edges.[11]

While some boomburbs are well on their way to becoming major cities, at least as defined by population size, it is not surprising that these places fall below the public radar. But it is interesting how little boomburbs register with urban experts, too. For instance, a recent encyclopedia of urban America that covers both cities and "major suburbs" fails to list even one boomburb exceeding 300,000 people; it does, however, have entries for comparably sized (and often even smaller) traditional cities.[12]

WEBSITES AND WIKIPEDIA

The most comprehensive history available on boomburbs comes from city websites and wikipedia, an online encyclopedia.[13] All fifty-four boomburbs had a city website as of May 2006.[14] Histories appear on thirty of the sites and range from a few perfunctory sentences to lengthy and detailed entries. These histories provide an additional context for examining boomburb origins. They indicate what boomburbs think about their past. Website histories also offer an interesting extension of those found in the WPA Guides. Recall the WPA pre–World War II depiction of a sleepy Sunnyvale, California. The passage below is taken from Sunnyvale's web history and notes the impact of the war.

> Without a doubt, World War II is the single most important event that changed history in Sunnyvale, the San Francisco Bay Area and all of California. Some people date the beginning of the defense era in Sunnyvale with the arrival of Lockheed Missiles & Space Company in 1956. But defense industry roots were planted much earlier because Sunnyvale has a long history of actively recruiting industry by offering land and labor.[15]

The website and wikipedia histories share several common themes. As might be expected, rapid population growth is the biggest topic. In fact, more of the websites mention fast growth (thirty-six) than have full city histories. The forces that sparked this growth are also major themes. The most frequently cited causes for growth are highways, defense industries, water, and annexation. One even lists air conditioning as a factor.

Highways apparently loom large in the Denver area, with both Aurora and Westminster website histories referring to them. Aurora's website says that "the 1970s were prosperous for Aurora with the city benefiting from new highway construction." Westminster's notes that "with a population of 1,686 in 1950, Westminster was still a quiet rural town northwest of Denver. That all changed when the Colorado State Highway Department began construction of the Denver-Boulder Turnpike, a toll-road that operated between the City of Boulder and the Valley Highway (I-25)."[16]

Or consider this entry from wikipedia.org on the role that transportation played in promoting economic development in Olathe, Kansas: "After the construction of the transcontinental railroad, the trails to the west lost importance, and Olathe faded back into obscurity and remained a small, sleepy prairie town until the 1950s. With the construction of the Interstate Highway system and, more directly, I-35, Olathe was directly linked to nearby Kansas City and began an economic boom that accelerated in the 1980s and continues today."

The military turned the San Diego region from an American outpost near Mexico into a strategic metropolis on the Pacific, populating its boomburbs in the process.

The Oceanside website has this to say:

World War II saw Oceanside grow from a sleepy little town to a modern city. With the construction of the nation's largest Marine Corps Base, Camp Pendleton, on her border, the demand for housing and municipal services exceeded supply. The best illustration of the tremendous growth of the city is found in the census figures. The population of Oceanside jumped from the 1940 figure of 4,652 to 12,888 in 1950. In 1952 a special census showed the city's population exceeding 18,000 as the Marine Base grew with the Korean War and more service-connected families moved into the area.[17]

According to Chula Vista's website,

World War II ushered in changes that would affect the city of Chula Vista forever. The principal reason was the relocation of Rohr Aircraft Corporation to Chula Vista in early 1941, just months before the attack on Pearl Harbor. Rohr employed 9,000 workers in the area at the height of its wartime production. With the demand for housing, the land never returned to being orchard groves again. The population of Chula Vista tripled from 5,000 residents in 1940 to more than 16,000 in 1950. After the war, many of the factory workers and thousands of servicemen stayed in the area resulting in the huge growth in population.[18]

The same kind of military-driven growth narratives appear in wikipedia .org. For example, consider the case of Clearwater, Florida:

During World War II, Clearwater became a major training base for U.S. troops destined for Europe and the Pacific. Virtually every hotel in the area, including the historic Belleview Biltmore and Fort Harrison Hotel, became luxury barracks for new recruits. Vehicle traffic regularly stopped for companies of soldiers marching through downtown, and nighttime blackouts to confuse potential enemy bombers were common. The remote and isolated Dan's Island, now Sand Key, was used as a target for U.S. Army Air Corps fighter-bombers for strafing and bombing practice.

Of Fontana, California, wikipedia.org says, "Fontana was radically transformed during World War II by the construction of a steel mill belonging to the Henry J. Kaiser Company." A similar remark is made for the baby boomburb of Renton, Washington: "The town's population boomed during World War II when Boeing built a factory in Renton to produce the B-29 Superfortress. The factory has continued to operate since then, and still produces 737 aircraft. In 2001, 40% of all commercial aircraft were assembled in Renton. Boeing remains the largest employer in Renton."

As one would guess, water fed boomburb growth in the Southwest. This is especially true in the Central Valley of Arizona, where the Phoenix region, like the mythical bird, rose from the ashes of a lost Native American civilization—the Hohokam. The trick Phoenix used was rebuilding the ancient canal system left by the Hohokam. In Mesa, the Mormons got the water flowing early. Its website notes that "water entered the canals in April of 1878."[19] Two early twentieth-century major dam projects greatly enhanced the supply of water to Phoenix—Roosevelt Dam to the northeast and Hoover Dam (originally Boulder Dam) to the northwest. Both of these dams, and the lakes they formed, are often cited in metro Phoenix boomburb website histories. In fact, so many boomburbs around Phoenix mention water and canals one might think the place were Venice, Italy.

As their regions developed, boomburbs gobbled up unincorporated land wherever they could. Gilbert, Arizona, for example, aggressively expanded well beyond its original borders: "Gilbert began to take its current shape during the 1970s when the Town Council approved a strip annexation that encompassed 53 square miles of county land. Although the population was only 1,971 in 1970 the Council realized that Gilbert would eventually grow and develop much like the neighboring communities of Tempe, Mesa, and Chandler."[20] For Gilbert the plan apparently worked, because this boomburb is now the fastest-growing U.S. city above 100,000 residents so far in this decade.

THE BOOMBURBS KEEP BOOMING, 2000 TO 2002

It is worth exploring how boomburbs are doing in the first years of the twenty-first century. Census estimates show that most boomburbs continue to boom.[21] In fact, boomburbs are the fastest-growing U.S. "cities" of over 100,000 people. The nine top growth cities over the period April 1, 2000, to July 1, 2002, were boomburbs.[22] Additionally, boomburbs made up six of the top ten fastest-growing cities from July 1, 2001, to July 1, 2002, including four of the top five of these cities.[23] The five fastest-growing boomburbs (and the five fastest-growing U.S. cities above 100,000 population from 2000 to 2002) are in the Phoenix and Las Vegas metropolitan areas. The next five quick growers are in Southern California—four in the Los Angeles region and one in the San Diego metropolitan area.

Gilbert, Arizona (the fastest-gaining boomburb), grew by nearly a quarter (23 percent) in just over two years.[24] At that pace, Gilbert could easily more than double its population in a decade. The next eight boomburbs following Gilbert all grew by more than 10 percent over the same period. Henderson, Nevada (south of Las Vegas), added 30,722 new residents from 2000 to 2002, leading all boomburbs in number of new people. Henderson was followed by Mesa, Arizona, with a gain of 30,466 people during the period. Almost a third (sixteen) of boomburbs gained over 10,000 residents each.

As a group, boomburbs jumped from 8,915,435 to 9,397,793 in population, or a gain of nearly a half million residents in just over two years. To put that in perspective, consider that that is about how many people lived in all boomburbs in 1950. Together, boomburbs now have a population larger than the Chicago metropolitan area (with 9,286,207 people as of July 1, 2002), the nation's third largest metropolitan area behind New York and Los Angeles.[25]

The "New Brooklyns" Slow Down

The term "new Brooklyns" applies to boomburbs that are now, or are rapidly becoming, immigrant-dominated communities, like the old Brooklyn (the full definition of what constitutes a new Brooklyn is presented later). This particular type of boomburb may also be losing steam. New Brooklyns such as Hialeah in Florida and Santa Ana and Anaheim in California have foreign-born populations that either match or exceed that of Brooklyn, N.Y. (which has a 38 percent foreign-born population). Other examples of new Brooklyns include Pembroke Pines, Florida, Irving, Texas, and Aurora, Colorado, all of which have a foreign-born population that greatly exceeds the national average of 11 percent.

New Brooklyns tend to be old, dense, and built-out suburbs, which dampens their population growth. As Rick Hampson observes, "Although the New Brooklyns were once new settlements on the suburban frontier, they're getting old. Their housing, accordingly, is more attractive to immigrants looking for bargains and is less attractive to longtime [mostly native-born] Americans, who can afford to move up."[26] Some new Brooklyns can continue to gain population (if not quite boom) provided that their foreign-born population maintains a high rate of natural increase. These places have also seen a turnover, as young immigrant families replace older empty-nest couples, which also adds to population growth. In time, the foreign-born population will age and assimilate, which should slow down the new Brooklyns even further.

THE FUTURE OF BOOMBURBS

For now, most boomburbs seem to be humming right along. But many will experience relative decline in perhaps the not too distant future. One problem could be that the West (where most boomburbs are found) is running out of water. Almost all of the West's current water sources—from Denver to Southern California—have been overallocated.[27] Unless more water is diverted from agriculture or new supplies are tapped, the West will face a crisis that could significantly dampen the growth rates of its boomburbs.

Even assuming that the problem of water supply for new growth is resolved, the current group of boomburbs will ultimately experience much slower population gains. The fact is that no place can (or should) boom forever. Today's boomburbs are tomorrow's mature cities. But a whole new batch of boomburbs and baby boomburbs is already emerging. Look at the Central Valley of Arizona; as Tempe stalls and Mesa slows down, places such as Goodyear and Buckeye are just getting started. The future of boomburbs is discussed more fully in the final chapter of the book.

Finally, the economic drivers of urban growth are ever shifting. As noted, many boomburbs and baby boomburbs got a big lift initially from World War II and were sustained by cold war defense industries. Defense helped ratchet up boomburb growth just as suburbanization swept the metropolis. The general patterns that tilted U.S. growth to the suburbs in the post–World War II years as highlighted above—new highways, cheap mortgages—helped further develop boomburbs.

Recent boomburb expansion is due in part to a continued urban shift to the Sunbelt. Most boomburbs and baby boomburbs possess two qualities in particular that the urban economist Edward Glaeser argues drive growth: sun and sprawl.[28] Glaeser developed the idea that growth derives from a combination of sun, sprawl, and skills (or human capital). The Glaeser "three S" concept provides an alternative to Richard Florida's "three Ts," or talent, tolerance, and technology.[29] As a *New York Times Magazine* article on Glaeser's work notes:

> Glaeser likes to point out the close correlation between a city's average January temperature and its urban growth; he also notes that cars per capita in

1990 is among the best indicators of how well a city has fared over the past 15 years. The more cars, the better—a conclusion that seems perfectly logical to Glaeser. Car-based cities enable residents to buy cheaper, bigger houses. And commuters in car-based cities tend to get to work faster than commuters in cities that rely on public transit.[30]

Boomburbs, as mostly warm, auto-friendly environments, fit this description. As a result, boomburbs and baby boomburbs should continue to grow until these drivers lose their steam and a new development model emerges.

WHO LIVES IN THE BOOMBURBS?

As much of the research based on the 2000 census reveals, the 1990s witnessed a radical departure from standard demographic trends. Hispanics passed African Americans as the nation's largest racial or ethnic group, while the Asian American population strengthened its presence by more than 50 percent.[31] The proportion of foreign-born persons reached 11.1 percent, the highest level since 1930. This surge of immigration is changing how communities plan and develop, especially since slightly more than half of all of immigrants who arrived in metropolitan areas in the 1990s chose to live outside central cities.

The country's median age is 35.3 years—the oldest it has ever been. Aging baby boomers are becoming empty nesters and fueling the development of "active adult" communities. Suburbs now contain more nonfamily households (largely young singles and elderly people living alone) than married couples with children.[32] In 2000 less than 25 percent of all households nationwide were nuclear families. This is a significant change from 1970, when the figure stood at around 40 percent. The nuclear family is a shrinking phenomenon, as acceptance of nontraditional approaches to marriage, divorce, childbearing, and cohabitation grows.

Overall, the share of racial and ethnic minorities living in the suburbs increased substantially in the 1990s—moving from less than one-fifth to more than one-quarter of all suburbanites. This trend is most evident in metropolitan areas that had a strong immigrant base. A study by the demographer William Frey finds that the growth of racial and ethnic groups fueled the 1990s population growth.[33] According to this study, in the largest 102 metropolitan areas, more than half of the Asian population and nearly half of the Hispanic population lived in the suburbs. Blacks showed the greatest increase in suburban living—in 1990 less than 33 percent of blacks lived in the suburbs studied; in 2000, almost 40 percent did.

During the past ten years suburban growth outpaced city growth irrespective of whether a city's population was falling, staying stable, or rising.[34] Minorities have driven most of this growth, and this is reflected in the boomburbs. Most but not all are ethnically and racially diverse. The majority of boomburbs have Hispanic populations above the national average, and Hispanics make up over half the population in six boomburbs and five baby boomburbs. Over three-quarters of boomburbs have Asian populations above the national average, and 85 percent of boomburbs had foreign-born populations above the national average of 11 percent.

Not only are boomburbs ethnically diverse, they also contain different strata of income. While most boomburbs are affluent, few are exclusive. Boomburb percentages, compared to the top fifty metropolitan areas, rank higher in categories such as race, foreign-born population, and median income. However, the percentages of families in poverty, postgraduate education, home owner-ship, and white non-Hispanic populations are lower. This chapter examines the demographics within boomburbs (using primarily census data); discusses their ethnic, educational, and economic diversities; and identifies two subcategories that emerge from the data: "new Brooklyns" and "cosmoburbs."

RACE AND IMMIGRATION

Some boomburbs defy the suburban stereotype put forth over the last four decades by cultural critics. They have grown not because of white flight but because of immigration, influxes of retirees, and business expansion. These suburbs have developed their own economies and diverse populations in boom-burbs and baby boomburbs since 1980. Although baby boomburbs started off and remain more white, Hispanic immigration has grown as a greater share of their population over the last twenty years.

Boomburbs are surprisingly diverse in their Hispanic and Asian popula-tions. For example, forty-five of the fifty-four boomburbs have Hispanic pop-ulations larger than the national percentage, which is about 12 percent. Five boomburbs are over 50 percent Hispanic. Hialeah, Florida, with 90 percent Hispanic population, tops the list; the other nine of the top ten are in Califor-nia. Similarly, forty-two of the fifty-four boomburbs have a higher percentage of Asians than the U.S. percentage of 4 percent.

As of 2000, blacks were 12.3 percent of the U.S. population. The big-gest gains were in Florida's baby boomburbs of Lauderhill, Miramar, and North Miami. Ten boomburbs lost black population during the 1990s (Irvine, Oceanside, Fremont, Thousand Oaks, Simi Valley, Oxnard, Sunnyvale, Daly City, Santa Ana, Hialeah), but the remaining forty-four boomburbs increased their black population. The black population of Gilbert, Arizona, rose from only forty-one persons in 1980 to well over 2,000 in the year 2000.

Boomburbs also contain a high percentage of foreign-born residents. Although only 11 percent of the U.S. population is foreign-born, a typical boomburb is 21 percent foreign-born. Forty-six of the fifty-four boomburbs have foreign-born populations higher than the national average. Further, there is a high correlation between share of Hispanic population and share of foreign-born population.[35]

New Brooklyns

Certain boomburbs with large foreign-born, working-class populations can be classified as "new Brooklyns." Much like Brooklyn New York, of a century ago, working immigrant families who speak English as their second language densely populate these cities. Although they have relatively large populations, as in the old Brooklyn, they play a secondary role in their region. Manhattan was home to the cosmopolitan tastemakers, while Brooklyn was Manhattan's bedroom community, where immigrants lived in tightly clustered neighbor-hoods and strived for middle-class existences.[36]

New Brooklyn boomburbs are characterized by a significant percentage of working-class, foreign-born citizens who speak another language besides English at home. They also contain populations claiming to have had no schooling at all, a higher than the national average of renters, and a relatively high population of families in poverty. Median household incomes are either slightly above or close to the national median. Baby boomburbs that meet similar criteria are Lynwood, California; South Gate, California; North Miami, Florida; and Rialto, California.

New Brooklyn suburbs are more ethnically diverse than their core cities, meaning they have a higher percentage of Hispanics and Asians than their core cities.

New Brooklyns tend to have larger than average family sizes. Most new Brooklyns rank above the national average family size of 3.1 members. Santa Ana has the highest (4.6), followed by Oxnard (3.9) and Ontario (3.6). The highest baby boomburbs are Lynwood (4.9), South Gate, California (4.2) and Chino, California (3.9). According to the 2000 census, three new Brooklyns—Santa Ana, Oxnard, and Hialeah—are among the top ten boomburbs with the highest incidence of crowded units. The incidence of overcrowding is now at record levels in California.[37]

NOTES

1. The term *edge city* was coined by Joel Garreau, *Edge City: Life on the New Frontier* (New York: Doubleday, 1991); also see Robert E. Lang, *Edgeless Cities: Exploring the Elusive Metropolis* (Brookings, 2003).
2. Observers began to note the trend in the late 1990s. See Haya El Nasser and Paul Overberg, "Suburban Communities Spurt to Big-City Status," *USA Today*, November 19, 1997, p. A4; David Brooks, *On Paradise Drive: How We Live Now (And Always Have) In the Future Tense* (New York: Simon and Schuster, 2004); David Brooks, "Patio Man and the Sprawl People," *Weekly Standard* 7, no. 46 (2002): 19–29.
3. Michael L. Montandon, personal conversation with Robert Lang, March 12, 2004. Interestingly, a referee for this book asserted that North Las Vegas is not comparable with Salt Lake City in part because it "does not confront an array of urban problems" and that Salt Lake City has a "more diverse population." The fact is that North Las Vegas has plenty of urban problems, including a high poverty rate. In addition, North Las Vegas's population is a quarter foreign-born and half minority. In other words, North Las Vegas is considerably *more* diverse than Salt Lake City (which is 70 percent non-Hispanic white) and even than Las Vegas itself. The misread of North Las Vegas by the referee shows that North Las Vegas's mayor was on to something. Apparently no one, not even urban experts who review books, think his city is diverse and has urban problems.
4. Keno Hawker, personal conversation with Robert Lang, March 10, 2004.
5. Jonathon Barnett first used the term *accidental cities*, but he was referring specifically to zoning. Jonathon Barnett, "Accidental Cities: The Deadly Grip of Outmoded Zoning," *Architectural Record* 180, no. 2 (1992): 94–101.
6. Bruce Katz, "Welcome to the 'Exit Ramp' Economy," *Boston Globe*, May 13, 2001, p. A19. Freeway exits as an economic development tool came up in several interviews with boomburb mayors.
7. Jane Jacobs, "The Greening of the City," *New York Times Magazine*, May 16, 2004.
8. The 2000 census marks the first time that a critical mass of suburban cities passed the 100,000-population threshold, and this study is the first-ever book-length treatment of those cities. But see Robert Fishman, *Bourgeois Utopias: The Rise and Fall of Suburbia* (New York: Basic Books, 1987); Garreau, *Edge City*; Carl Abbott, "'Beautiful Downtown Burbank': Changing Metropolitan Geography in the Modern West," *Journal of the West* (July 1995): 8–18; Carl Abbott, *The Metropolitan Frontier: Cities in the Modern American West* (University of Arizona Press, 1993); Carl Abbott, "Southwestern Cityscapes: Approaches to an American Urban Environment," in *Essays on Sunbelt Cities and Recent Urban America*, edited by Raymond A. Mohl and others (Texas A&M University Press, 1990).
9. This was done so that almost all boomburbs had full data for their starting point. Many boomburbs were unincorporated places before 1970, making it impossible to track their population changes before that date.
10. Lang and Simmons, in "Tale of the Two Peorias," note that Peoria, Arizona, passing Peoria, Illinois, reflects the shift in population to the South and West.
11. Robert E. Lang and Dawn Dhavale, *Reluctant Cities: Exploring Big Unincorporated Census Designated Places*, Census Note 03:01 (Alexandria, Va.: Metropolitan Institute at Virginia Tech, 2003).
12. Neil Larry Shumsky, ed., *Encyclopedia of Urban America: The Cities and Suburbs* (Santa Barbara, Calif.: ABC-CLIO, 1997).

13. Wikipedia (www.wikipedia.org) is an open-source, web-based encyclopedia and as such it is subject to error. The information obtained from this site was crosschecked against other sources, including conversations with local officials.

14. Besides histories, many other interesting facts about boomburbs appear on their websites. For example, fourteen websites include detailed demographic profiles of the city.

15. See Sunnyvale.ca.gov/local/SVC%20CHRONOLOGY1.htm.

16. See www.auroragov.org/Visitors%20Guide/Pages/ Our%20History.cfm; www.ci.westminster .co.us/city/history/default.htm.

17. See www.ci.oceanside.ca.us/community/history_ print.asp.

18. See www.chulavistaca.gov/About/History.asp.

19. See www.mesalibrary.org/about_mesa/pdfs/MesaHistory-0703.pdf.

20. See www.wikipedia.org.

21. The U.S. census produces yearly estimates for population change at the subcounty level, based on the distributive housing unit method. This method uses building permits, mobile home shipments, and estimates of housing unit loss to update housing unit change since the last estimate. The census developed a household population estimate by applying the occupancy rate and the average person per household from the latest census to an estimate of the housing units. The estimates obtained from this method are controlled for by comparing to the final county population estimate. "U.S. Bureau of the Census' Estimates and Projections Area Documentation Subcounty Total Population Estimates," 2003 (eire.census.gov/popest/topics/methodology/citymeth.php).

22. Ibid. The tenth-ranked city was Joliet, Illinois, which nearly qualified as a boomburb but failed to sustain double-digit growth for all five decades since 1950.

23. Quoted in Lori Weisberg, "Chula Vista No 7 in the Nation in Galloping Growth," *San Diego Union Tribune,* July 10, 2003, p. A1.

24. According to a *New York Times* story, Gilbert "issues building permits only to developers who build within an [homeowners] association." Quoted in Motoko Rich, "Homeowner Boards Blur Line of Who Rules the Roost," *New York Times,* July 27, 2003, p. 14.

25. Office of Management and Budget, *Metropolitan Statistical Area Definitions,* June 6, 2003.

26. Rick Hampson, "'New Brooklyns' Replace White Suburbs," *USA Today,* May 18, 2003, p. A1.

27. Shaun McKinnon, "Water: Growing Demand, Dwindling Supply," *Arizona Republic,* July 6, 2003, p. A1.

28. Edward L. Gleaser, "The New Economics of Urban and Regional Growth," in *The Oxford Handbook of Economic Geography,* edited by G. L. Clark, M. P. Feldman, and M. S. Gertler (Oxford University Press, 2000). Also see Richard Florida, "The Great Creative Class Debate: The Revenge of the Squelchers," *The Next American City 5* (2004): 18–24.

29. Richard Florida, *The Rise of the Creative Class: And How It's Transforming Work, Leisure, Community, and Everyday Life* (New York: Perseus, 2002).

30. Jon Gertner, "Home Economics," *New York Times Magazine,* March 5, 2006, pp. 20–31.

31. The 2000 census considered race and Hispanic origin to be distinct. This book uses the Office of Management and Budget definition of Asian, which is a person having origins in the Far East, Southeast Asia, or the Indian subcontinent. See also William H. Frey and Alan Berube, "City Families and Suburban Singles: An Emerging Household Story," in *Redefining Urban and Suburban America: Evidence from Census 2000,* edited by Bruce Katz and Robert E. Lang (Brookings, 2003).

32. Ibid.

33. William Frey, "Melting Pot Suburbs: A Study of Suburban Diversity," in *Redefining Urban and Suburban America: Evidence from Census 2000,* edited by Bruce Katz and Robert E. Lang (Brookings, 2003).

34. Robert E. Lang, *Edgeless Cities: Exploring the Elusive Metropolis* (Brookings, 2003).

35. Robert Suro and Audrey Singer, "Changing Patterns of Latino Growth in Metropolitan America," in *Redefining Urban and Suburban America: Evidence from Census 2000,* edited by Bruce Katz and Robert E. Lang (Brookings, 2003).

36. The Brooklyn of today is experiencing a renaissance and is becoming home to cultural institutions and young, urbane, middle-class refugees from the Manhattan housing market. A *New York Times Magazine* article featured Brooklyn's emerging hipness and a bohemian culture that eclipses Manhattan's. James Traub, "The (Not Easy) Building of (Not Exactly) Lincoln Center for (Not) Manhattan," *New York Times Magazine,* April 25, 2004, p. 28.

37. Patrick A. Simmons, *Patterns and Trends in Overcrowded Housing: Early Results from Census 2000,* Census Note 09 (Washington: Fannie Mae Foundation, 2002).

18
Fear and Fantasy in Suburban Los Angeles
ERIC AVILA

In our present age of accelerated globalization, Los Angeles is under-going yet another round of economic restructuring and demographic upheaval . . . another new Los Angeles has taken shape, and the cultural matrix of chocolate cities and vanilla suburbs is giving way to new social interactions that mirror the striking changes that have transformed the region since the postwar period. The city's capacity for rapid change and incessant innovation has perforated the physical and cultural boundaries that distin-guished white space from black space, and although the noir city and its heterosocial interactions have made a certain comeback in recent decades, race continues to shape the cultural geography of the contemporary urban landscape in more powerful and less subtle ways. Once more, the cultural landscape of Southern California's everexpanding urban region holds clues to the countervailing forces of twenty-first-century urbanism.

Furthering the extremes between white wealth and nonwhite poverty, the demographic transformation of Los Angeles and its environs poses a powerful challenge to the regional hegemony of suburban whiteness. Since 1970, the vast influx of immigrant populations into Southern California has transformed the region from a bastion of middle-class whiteness into a Third World citadel. In 1970, 71 percent of Los Angeles County's population was non-Hispanic white or Anglo, and the remaining 29 percent of the population was divided among Latinos (15 percent), African Americans (11 percent), and Asian/Pacific Island-ers (3 percent). By 1980, the non-Hispanic white population had dropped to 53 percent, and ten years later it had fallen further to 41 percent. Throughout the 1970s, large-scale immigration from Latin America and Asia, coupled with a moderate growth in the African American population, inflated the region's non-white population. Immigration to the region continued to expand throughout the following decade as the population of Asians and Latinos swelled. By 1990, Latinos comprised 36 percent of the city's population; African Americans and Asians constituted 11 percent respectively. Today's Los Angeles ranks among the most diverse urban regions in the world and the city once heralded as the "nation's white spot" now mirrors the polyglot diversity that defines the city and even its past.[1]

Fueling and fueled by demographic growth, economic restructuring in Southern California simultaneously enforces and enervates existing patterns of racial and ethnic inequality. Since the 1970s, the increasingly transnational currents of economic exchange have positioned the Los Angeles urban region to emerge as a "nodal point" within a new global economy. The manifestations of economic globalization in Southern California have furthered the sociospatial extremes of progress and poverty that have been manifest throughout every stage of capitalist urbanization. On the one hand, the region shelters a growing number of high-tech manufacturing districts, or "technopoles," which extend to the furthest corners of the urban region. In the southernmost portions of Orange County and the western fringes of the San Fernando Valley, where gated communities and high-end subdivisions guard the latest incarnation of suburban whiteness, high-tech manufacturers such as Hughes Aircraft Missile Systems Group, Micropolis, and Rocketdyne further the industrial and residential sprawl that began in earnest during the early 1940s. The region's high-tech economy, which has penetrated the entertainment industry to a certain extent, sustains the class standing of a highly skilled group of managers, business executives, scientists, engineers, designers, and celebrities who continue to reap the rewards of the region's economic prosperity.[2]

At the other end of the economic spectrum and concentrated within the region's multiple urban centers, a low-skill, low-wage, nonunionized workforce, comprising mostly women and undocumented Latino and Asian immigrants, has been taking shape alongside the growth of the manufacturing sector since the 1970s. In contrast to the high unemployment and economic decline that befell other major American cities through the phase of deindustrialization during the 1970s and 1980s, Los Angeles' manufacturing economy grew steadily throughout the 1970s and intensified during the following decade, when the infusion of Asian capital into the regional economy bolstered the production of manufactured goods such as apparel, furniture, jewelry, and machinery. Such growth, however, entails mixed consequences for Southern California's expanding immigrant populations, who are drawn by the prospects of job availability but face new depths of exploitation. The sweatshop has made a comeback within Southern California's industrial landscape in recent decades, providing an often overlooked reminder that the "new" Los Angeles runs on the sweat of immigrant labor.[3]

Between these extremes, the great white middle class, which dominated the image and reality of the postwar urban region, is making its departure. Throughout the Reagan era, the flight of major manufacturing firms from the region's industrial geography dislodged whites from their suburban neighborhoods, creating space for new concentrations of racialized poverty. This transformation was most visible in the communities of Southeast Los Angeles, which nurtured the suburban white identity explored in previous chapters: South Gate, Huntington Park, Maywood, Bell, Bell Gardens, Vernon, and Cudahy. The departure of industrial giants such as General Motors, Firestone Tires, Weiser Lock, Bethlehem Steel, Dial, and Oscar Meyer from this area during the 1980s entailed a set of profound social consequences that undermined the cultural order of the postwar urban region. White workers and their families, who enjoyed full benefits and union representation, have taken flight, and, in their stead, recent arrivals from Mexico and Central America find work in the expanding low-wage, non-union sector and take shelter in cities crippled by shrinking tax bases and reduced services.[4]

While the brand of suburban whiteness that took shape within the cultural transition from the centralized, industrial city to the postwar urban region becomes a relic of the past, its legacy continues to shape California politics. The politics of white home ownership remains a powerful force in the state and its triumphs in recent decades have profound implications for the quality of race relations in the United States. In 1978, the passage of Proposition 13 marked a major victory for white homeowners and their brand of "identity politics" in California, much like the two-term presidency of Ronald Reagan. In the 1990s, California voters passed a series of measures that targeted immigrant groups and racial minorities. Looking back to the buoyant expressions of suburban whiteness that highlighted the cultural landscape of the postwar urban region, the current strategies to preserve white hegemony reflect a brazen attempt to maintain some semblance of the precarious social order that enjoyed a brief life span between the midcentury manifestation of the noir city and the current denouement of a Third World urbanism.

Film noir underscored the imperatives of suburban home ownership as a bulwark against the crisis of the public city; Proposition 13 surfaced in 1978 as a measure to secure that imperative for millions of California homeowners. The unbridled growth that swept across the region entailed a mixed set of consequences for suburban homeowners. On the one hand, the unceasing demand for homes generated higher property values, but, on the other hand, higher home prices brought higher property taxes, which basically doubled every few years. At the same time, the recession of the mid-'70s heralded a stagnation of real income and frustrated consumer efforts to live the suburban good life that California symbolized. Proposition 13, a measure that would lower property taxes by 60 percent, won by an overwhelming majority in California and inspired a similar set of homeowners' revolts in other states. In Los Angeles, Proposition 13 won by overwhelming majorities in white council districts, while it failed by a similar majority in the city's only black district.

Proposition 13 cannot be understood in isolation from the larger cultural context that dawned on Southern California during the postwar period. When Yvonne de Carlo warns Burt Lancaster in the climactic scene of the film *Criss Cross,* "You have to watch out for yourself; I can't help it if people don't know how to take care of themselves," she recites the creed that suburban homeowners adopted in their insular political outlook that disavowed any connection to other urban constituencies. Instead, the supporters of Proposition 13 campaigned with slogans such as "Vote for yourself! Vote for Proposition 13!" Proposition 13 upheld what Clarence Lo describes as a consumer model of citizenship, which is predicated upon the relentless pursuit of commodities that sustained popular idealizations of suburban domesticity. Such idealizations informed the dominant cultural narratives of Southern California's postwar urban region and guided the ascendance of tax-cutting conservatism that disavowed the interdependency of social groups and instead promoted self-interest as a primary goal of political struggle. Proposition 13 drastically reduced property taxes at the expense of public services such as schools, libraries, and police and fire protection, services that racial minorities have been increasingly forced to rely on. In this capacity, Proposition 13 continued the privatization of social life that began during the postwar period and widened the spatial and racial divide between chocolate cities and vanilla suburbs.[5]

Many proponents of Proposition 13 also endorsed the concurrent antibusing movement, in which white suburban parents sought to preserve the postwar racial order by resisting state efforts to send their children to schools in black and Latino neighborhoods. In suburban communities of both the San Fernando Valley and Orange County, where Proposition 13 won overwhelming support, local organizations such as the PTA marshaled opposition to busing programs, sponsoring constitutional amendments to limit busing, challenging busing in court, and seeking to elect public officials who opposed busing. The racist underpinnings of the antibusing campaign during the mid-'70s were not self-evident, but against the official effort to elide the racial geography of the postwar urban region through school desegregation, white suburban families defended their distance from the racialized city and, with it, the right to maintain school policies that sent white middle-class children to white schools in white neighborhoods.[6]

The political culture that sustained both Proposition 13 and the antibusing movement is essentially the same as that which bestowed two consecutive presidential terms on Ronald Reagan, who championed the rights of homeowners and consumers in their pursuit of privatized self-interest. Reagan's victory in the White House confirmed Southern California's prominence within the national political culture, not unlike the proliferation of homeowners' revolts throughout the nation following the success of Proposition 13 in 1978. The triumph of the New Right by the late 1970s was made possible by the support of various regional constituencies, but the course of political events in Southern California—beginning with the 1950 defeat of Helen Gahagan Douglas, bolstered by the simultaneous victory against public housing, and gaining further momentum with the 1964 cancellation of the Rumford Fair Housing Act—prefigured the subsequent victories of a new brand of Republican conservatism predicated upon the values enshrined in places like Disneyland. By the mid-1980s, at the height of the Reagan era, the brand of suburban whiteness that first took shape within Southern California's cultural landscape had entered the symbol iconography of the American Way and remained under the stewardship of a countersubversive coalition that targeted civil rights crusaders, feminists, antiwar demonstrators, and gay activists as culpable for the social ills and economic malaise wrought by economic restructuring, deindustrialization, and the dismantling of the welfare state.[7]

Reagan's legacy endured through the 1990s and found powerful expressions in the culture and politics of California. One year after the end of the Reagan-Bush-era and on the heels of the Rodney King uprising of 1992, the film *Falling Down* engendered controversy among national audiences for its neonoir portrayal of the white man's identity crisis in contemporary Los Angeles. "D-Fens," an unemployed engineer suffering a nervous breakdown, begins a killing spree as he walks from downtown Los Angeles to the beach. In the tradition of noir's white male antihero, D-Fens trudges through the racialized milieu of the city, attacking a Korean market, a fast-food outlet, a Chicano gang, and a neo-Nazi. The city that once resonated with compelling expressions of suburban whiteness is now alien territory for D-Fens, an inhospitable nonAnglo landscape that renders white male identity obsolete.

That filmmakers could market the fin de siècle crisis of white male identity as entertainment points to the very real challenge to whiteness posed by the demographic transformation of California and Los Angeles at the end of the twentieth century. In this context, California voters approved a series of measures that extended a note of nativist hostility to people of color. In 1994, Proposition 187 triumphed at the polls, denying public services to undocumented workers and their families. Although the measure's implementation has been indefinitely delayed by the courts, it targets California's immigrant population as a scapegoat for the economic woes that befell the state during the recession of the early 1990s. The specter of white identity politics surfaced twice again in the remainder of the decade. In 1996, as if the racial wrongs of the past had been righted, Proposition 209 brought a decisive end to affirmative action in both public service contracts and higher education, and in 1998, Proposition 227 terminated bilingual education programs in public schools to advocate "English only" as state law. The causes and consequences of these measures have been explored elsewhere; suffice it to say here that they signal last-ditch attempts to preserve what vestiges of suburban whiteness remain at the outset of the twenty-first century.[8]

Popular culture in the age of white flight thus maintains a powerful legacy, and although the future of that legacy is uncertain, the current phase of demographic upheaval in Southern California annihilates the racial identities imposed on the spaces of the postwar urban region. Watts, for example, no longer symbolizes the geographic core of black Los Angeles, as a massive in-migration of Latino immigrants dissolves the postwar boundary between white and black Los Angeles. South Gate and Huntington Park, where Southern California's Dust Bowl migrants reinvented themselves in the image of middle-class whiteness after World War II, are the current epicenter of *México de afuera,* as Mexican immigrants reestablish communal ties in the wake of deindustrialization and white flight. A large and expanding Koreatown lies just west of downtown Los Angeles, a new suburban Chinatown centered on Monterey Park has taken shape to the east, and a band of Cambodian and Vietnamese communities has grown to the south, extending from the older Japanese community of Gardena to Long Beach and into Orange County, where the city of Westminster is now known as Little Saigon.[9]

Perhaps even more striking, the San Fernando Valley now shelters a heterogeneous mix of Mexicans, Salvadorans, Guatemalans, Armenians, and African Americans. For a generation of white Americans in search of suburban domesticity, the Valley offered affordable housing and homogeneous neighborhoods, and its location on the northern side of the Santa Monica Mountains promised a comfortable distance from a Los Angeles mired in the mythology of film noir. The landscape of today's Valley, however, reveals a striking record of the demographic changes that have ensued over the past thirty years. On Van Nuys Boulevard, once the heart of white suburbia, Spanish has displaced English as the unofficial language of public signage. All around the Van Nuys business district, travel agents advertise discount tickets for international travel carriers such as Avianca and Aeroméxico. The native fare of El Salvador, Peru, India, Armenia, and a dozen other nations is served in the boulevard's myriad storefront diners. Most institutions that catered to the Valley's original white constituency are now gone: department stores have been replaced by *pupuserias* and *mueblerias,* the First Presbyterian Church closed after its English-speaking constituency plummeted, and the *San Fernando Daily News,* founded as the *Van Nuys Call* in 1911, left for tonier quarters in Woodland Hills. The "New Valley" harbors scant traces of the suburban good life that dominated the cultural imagery of postwar Los Angeles, and its public settings now echo the cultural dissonance of the polyglot noir city.

Amid the browning of the San Fernando Valley, homeowners there are mobilizing a campaign to authorize the secession of the Valley from the city of Los Angeles, in what would be the largest municipal divorce in national history. Valley VOTE (Voters Organized toward Empowerment), a grassroots organization established in 1998, has gathered sufficient signatures on petitions to push the secession drive to its most advanced stage ever. Whether or not the proponents of secession will have their way, the current move to secede from the city of Los Angeles inherits a tradition of municipal discord in Southern California and reflects a long-standing antipathy to the urban behemoth on the southern side of the Santa Monica Mountains.

The social, economic, political, and spatial transformations that engulf today's Los Angeles entail a set of cultural expressions that reflect both the extension and the extinction of popular culture in the age of the white flight. On the one hand, recent scholarship illuminates the cultural manifestations of contemporary urbanism by looking to Los Angeles as a window onto the "theming" of American culture and society. Through the disparate points of Southern California's urban expanse, scholars cite the most spectacular examples of the privatization of public life: From the self-contained citadel that has become downtown Los Angeles—including the cylindrical glass towers of John Portman's Bonaventure Hotel—to the gated communities of Orange County's "exopolis," to the ersatz urbanism of City Walk, Los Angeles and its environs support the many "variations on a theme park" that condition the experience of urban life at the outset of the twenty-first century. While generally eschewing the broader historical context that sanctions such cultural formations and often ignoring their immense popularity among white and nonwhite consumers alike, such observations generally deplore the corporate sponsors of contemporary public culture, emphasizing the manipulative and coercive strategies built into the design of contemporary public space.[10]

On the other hand, by looking "way, way below" the glass and neon facades of the contemporary metropolis, one can identify competing cultural expressions that emanate from the city's diverse neighborhoods. During the 1980s, amid the deindustrialization of South Central Los Angeles, black youth forged a cultural style that centered upon the distinctively West Coast sounds of hip-hop music. Gangsta Rap made its debut on the streets of Los Angeles through the innovative sounds of Ice-T, Eazy-E and NWA, Ice Cube, Snoop Doggy Dogg, and Dr. Dre, who drew upon African American cultural traditions such as descriptive storytelling and funk music, while utilizing samplers, drum machines, engineering boards, and other components of the latest in digital technology. Gangsta Rap of the late 1980s and early 1990s, as Robin Kelley and Tricia Rose point out, spoke to the realities of ghetto life for young black heterosexual men in postindustrial America, and proffered a genre of black popular culture that proved overwhelmingly popular not only in chocolate cities, but also, if not especially, in vanilla suburbs.[11]

Although the cultural palimpsest of contemporary urbanism supports the musical expressions of young black men, it also reflects the cultural stylings of the city's Mexican and Latino populations. A striking preference for big cities among Latinos brings a transformative energy to the texture of daily life in a "Latino metropolis" such as Los Angeles. As the old barrio of East Los Angeles gives way to the exponential growth of Spanish-speaking neighborhoods and subdivisions, the symbols and signs of *Mexicanidad* are visible throughout the urban region. Immigrant homeowners from Mexico and Central America are investing "sweat equity" in their homes, using paint and inexpensive landscaping materials to reverse the deterioration of urban neighborhoods crippled by deindustrialization and white flight. Bohemian enclaves of Chicano communities in East Los Angeles and the San Gabriel Valley support the proliferation of bilingual cafés and bookstores. Accustomed to the convivial spaces of *plazas* and *mercados* in Latin American cities, Latino immigrants and their children make vital use of playgrounds, parks, squares, libraries, and other endangered public spaces that their more affluent counterparts in the city tend to ignore. Amid the current re-Mexicanization of Los Angeles, with the addition of other Latino populations, we are witnessing an ethnic transformation of the urban landscape on a scale unparalleled in history.[12]

So what's left of popular culture in the age of white flight? What remains of the cultural institutions explored in this book, and how have they fared in light of recent social transformations? Hollywood continues to fixate upon Los Angeles in its dystopian spectacles of urban decadence, and film noir and science fiction maintain their popularity at the box office. In the early 1970s, at the outset of an economic recession and in the wake of the turbulent 1960s, Los Angeles occupied a starring role in a brief noir revival, climaxing with *Chinatown* by Roman Polanski, whose tragic and bizarre encounter with the Manson family in 1969 inspired his dark and morbid vision of Los Angeles and its past. Disaster films such as *Earthquake* and *The Towering Inferno* also kept the spotlight on Southern California, portraying Los Angeles as an epicenter of the moral catastrophe that dawned in the era of Watergate. The following decade witnessed *Blade Runner,* rendering its futuristic nightmare of a Los Angeles dominated by global capital and teeming with Third World populations, while a spate of neonoir films of the late 1980s and early 1990s, most notably *The Grifters, The Player, Reservoir Dogs, Pulp Fiction, Short Cuts,* and *L.A. Confidential,* keeps a tight focus on the darkness lurking behind the sunny façade of the Los Angeles landscape.

More striking, however, is the recent arrival of new voices that add their own distinct inflection to the canons of film noir and science fiction. With a nod to Chester Himes, Walter Mosley established his presence in American literature with the 1990 success of *Devil in a Blue Dress,* which portrays the investigations of Easy Rawlins, a black private detective in 1940s Los Angeles who unravels the depths of white racism at the core of Southern California's black city. In a similar vein, Octavia Butler brings a black feminist perspective to her futuristic vision of Los Angeles in *Parable of the Sower,* which renders a bleak portrait of a city overcome with violence and fear in the year 2027. Like all durable genres of American popular culture, film noir and science fiction have incorporated new perspectives that extend and broaden their appeal over time; while Los Angeles, ravaged by successive episodes of racial violence throughout the second half of the twentieth century, remains a favorite site for collective fantasies of urban despair.

Meanwhile, Hollywood finds new ways to recycle its former glory as a means to urban redevelopment. Responding to a cycle of decline throughout the 1980s and 1990s, Hollywood developers have enlisted the support of Los Angeles' Community Redevelopment Agency to bring consumers and tourists back to Tinsel Town. Their most recent *coup de main* has been the Hollywood and Highland Redevelopment Project, built by the Canadian developer Trizec Hahn, the nation's largest owner of downtown office space. At a price of 615 million dollars, the Hollywood and Highland complex occupies one and a half city blocks of downtown Hollywood, containing a mazelike 425,000-square-foot retail mall, a two-thousand-seat multiplex cinema, and an auditorium designed as a permanent home for future Academy Awards ceremonies. With architectural references to the glories of old Hollywood, including a partial reconstruction of the extravagant movie set from D.W. Griffith's 1916 film, *Intolerance,* Hollywood is now reclaiming its former glamour as a means of reversing decades of urban decline.[13]

Disneyland is alive and well, though its constant renovation and ongoing expansion illustrate the extent to which today's audiences have outgrown the thematic imagery and cultural stereotypes that dominated the park's landscape in its postwar heyday. Racial difference no longer supplies a central theme of Disneyland. Aunt Jemima's Pancake House is now the River Belle Terrace and the grinning mammy has been retired from the kitchen. Audio Animatronic animals singing country music have replaced the Indians who once performed at Frontierland. And though Disneyland remains a cornerstone of "family entertainment," this did not preclude park officials from ignoring the vehement protests of the Christian Right and extending domestic-partner benefits to employees in 1995. Moreover, the recent successes of Disney films such as *Mulan* and *Pocahontas* indicate an openness to new stories and images that include the perspectives of racial minorities and women.[14] Would Walt Disney have approved of these changes? That question is impossible to answer, but the business acumen and sensitivity to the changing moral climate that Disney exhibited throughout his career would seem to imply his willingness to make such modifications in the midst of a rapidly changing world.

The Walt Disney Company's more sensitive portrait of racial and ethnic diversity, however, parallels the ongoing Disneyfication of public and private space. Today, Disneyland rests alongside Downtown Disney, a shopping and entertainment complex that presents Southern Californians with a neon-lit simulacrum of the noir city that Orange County residents shunned a generation earlier. While Disney executives repackage the noir city as their latest "attraction," American cities and suburbs today increasingly weave the themed experiences of Disneyland into the fabric of daily life. The brand of suburbanism that took shape in locales such as Orange County during the 1950s now extends its reach into the archetypal noir metropolis. In New York City, under the patronage of Mayor Rudolph Giuliani, the Walt Disney Company spearheaded an effort to revitalize Times Square, investing thirty-two million dollars in the renovation of the New Amsterdam Theater on Forty-second Street. Enticed by a slew of tax breaks and zoning incentives, Disney and other entertainment conglomerates—Nike, Warner Brothers, Virgin—are struggling against the presence of homeless vagrants and porn dealers to rescue Times Square from its previous noir incarnation.[15]

An even more portentous example of how Disney continues to blur urban fantasy and reality, Celebration, U.S.A., reflects the Disney Company's latest effort to establish its definition of community. Celebration, U.S.A., south of Orlando, Florida, extends across five thousand acres, complete with its own school, post office, downtown, pool, and parks. There is also a "town hall" designed by the noted architect Philip Johnson, though it serves no political function since the Disney Company retains the powers of planning and governance for Celebration's first twenty years. Not unlike the planners of Lakewood and countless other suburban housing developments, Disney and Osceola County arranged a mutually beneficial deal to keep low-income housing out of Celebration, U.S.A. Such an arrangement allows for larger profits on the sale of homes and higher property tax revenues, but, in the suburban tradition, minimizes racial diversity and severely limits civic experience.[16] If Celebration, U.S.A., maintains some remnants of suburban whiteness in Florida, Southern California harbors other reminders of Disney's cultural roots. Recently, the Ronald Reagan Presidential Library in Simi Valley, California, featured the exhibit "Walt Disney: The Man and His Magic."

The Dodgers retain their popularity among diverse Southern California baseball fans, and Dodger Stadium endures in the Chavez Ravine. Whatever ill will lingered between the Dodgers and local Chicanos over the Arechiga evictions, the arrival of a rookie pitcher from Etchohuaquila, Sonora, in 1981 sparked an intense passion for Dodger baseball among Chicanos and Mexican baseball fans alike. In his first year of pitching for the Dodgers, Fernando

Valenzuela led his team to its fifth World Series victory, and with that, "Fernandomania" descended upon the Spanish-speaking world. Valenzuela's overwhelming popularity demonstrated the new cultural flavor of major-league baseball and illustrated how popular cultural institutions can reinforce distinct cultural identities, even as they appeal to broader audiences. The particular appeal of Dodgers baseball for the city's diverse constituencies continues, as Asian Americans also enjoy a special claim to the Dodgers in recent years. Representing the recent advances by Korean players in the major leagues, Chan Ho Park signed a ten-million-dollar contract with the Dodgers in 2001. Park follows in the footsteps of Hideo Nomo, who pitched for the Dodgers between 1995 and 2000, arousing the loyalties of Southern California's Japanese American community, which maintains an enduring enthusiasm for the game of baseball, dating as far back as the war years, when baseball games provided a momentary distraction from the indignities of internment. Today, as during the postwar period, the Dodgers continue to model interracial cooperation on the field before the city's diverse constituencies in the stands.[17]

Meanwhile, civic officials elsewhere look to Dodger Stadium as an example of how not to build a ballpark. On April 11, 2000, San Franciscans celebrated Opening Day for Pacific Bell Park (now known as SBC Park), a throwback to Boston's Fenway Park and its generation of urban ballparks. In contrast to the sprawling, 250-acre site of Dodger Stadium, SBC Park sits upon a mere 13 acres in the city's South of Market neighborhood, a newly gentrified area adjacent to downtown. Designed by Joe Spear of HOK Sport, the architect of Baltimore's Camden Yards and Cleveland's Jacobs Field, SBC Park offers a more modest—albeit more nostalgic—alternative to the monumentality of Dodger Stadium. Garbed in ivy, brick, and limestone, SBC Park rejects the solemn gray concrete that clothes Dodger Stadium, and its expansive view of the San Francisco Bay delivers a scenic connection to the surrounding region. Most unlike Dodger Stadium, however, SBC Park maintains a mere five thousand parking spaces, one fifth of which are usually empty during any given home game. The park's accessibility to public transportation and its close proximity to the city's many neighborhoods diminish the necessity for the automobile. While it might be unfair to compare SBC Park to a stadium built four decades ago, its success suggests that the designers of Ebbets Field, Fenway Park, and Wrigley Field just may have had it right all along.

Finally, although Southern Californians continue to exercise their preference for the private automobile, the freeway's benefit to urban life is more suspect than ever. Traffic congestion remains an enduring civic nightmare, and with recent population gains and a growing number of commuters willing to drive longer distances to work, today's freeways now more than ever fail to provide rapid access to the disparate points of the urban region. Freeway construction continues, though the master plan for freeways established by the Division of Highways in 1958 remains only half completed. Local residents are far more vocal in their opposition to highway construction, as the recent controversy surrounding the extension of the 710 Long Beach Freeway through South Pasadena illustrates. In the 2001 mayoral campaign, candidate Antonio Villaraigosa won the support of that community by announcing his opposition to the completion of the 710 project, denouncing that freeway as "a throwback to another era."

Growing frustration with the freeway and the automobile has intensified the search for alternative forms of public transportation. Today, the Metropolitan Transit Authority maintains its effort to build an extensive rail transit system throughout the urban region. The Blue Line from Los Angeles to Long Beach opened in 1990, and parts of the Green Line (from Norwalk to Hawthorne) and the Red Line (from downtown to the San Fernando Valley) have followed suit. Whether the vast majority of Southern Californian commuters will relinquish their automobiles in favor of rail transit remains uncertain, but hundreds of millions of dollars continue to pour into a transit system that may or may not alleviate traffic congestion on the region's freeways. Meanwhile, working-class communities of color continue to depend on the city's overcrowded and inadequate bus system. The Bus Riders' Union, a grass-roots organization dedicated to improving bus service, continues its fight against fare increases and route cancellations. During the age of the freeway, Los Angeles has sustained a kind of "transit apartheid" in which the experience of moving through urban space remains contingent upon class and color.[18]

The age of the freeway may be passing, but the street is making a comeback within the city's diverse communities. Los Angeles' emergence as the nation's preeminent Latino metropolis brings the street-oriented culture of Chicanos and Mexican immigrants to the very center of a new civic life. The city streets support the informal economy that relies upon the public display of goods and services. Day laborers congregate on sidewalks or parking lots, looking for a day's work in the vicinity of paint and hardware stores. *Vendedores* and *vendedoras* sell produce and flowers at freeway off-ramps and along median islands. Although such public interactions are commonplace within Latino neighborhoods, they are new to more affluent neighborhoods. Westside communities are taking their cue from their Eastside counterparts and learning to enjoy the pleasures of street life. Farmers' markets draw large crowds throughout the city's diverse neighborhoods, offering a weekly festival for adults and children. In the posh quarters of West Hollywood, planners have recently completed a massive redevelopment project to enhance street life along Santa Monica Boulevard. Sunset Strip and its more modest imitations throughout the Southern California metropolis continue to attract increasingly diverse crowds in search of the city's nightlife. Contrary to popular stereotypes about the freeway metropolis, the street is reclaiming its place at the center of a changing public life.

The cultural forms that nurtured a suburban white identity during the postwar period now include alternative perspectives and experiences. Since the postwar period, whiteness and white flight no longer have been the master narratives that shape the texture of American cultural life, at least in cities on the cutting edge of social transformations. Other narratives have been inserted into the built environment since the postwar period, and their vitality points to a new definition of urban life at the outset of the twenty-first century. Whether or not the recent appreciation of multiculturalism and diversity will empower marginal social groups, however, is an open question. If cultural expressions of suburban whiteness inaugurated a greater disparity between white suburban affluence and nonwhite urban poverty during the postwar period, can we expect the current incarnation of Los Angeles as a "world city" to bring about a more equitable reconfiguration of urban social relations? As whites have become a demographic minority in the Los Angeles urban region, new forms of urban popular culture model new configurations of race and space and encompass even more diverse cultural expressions. As the urban landscape mirrors the city's great diversity in more equitable ways, whiteness will lose its saliency as a defining principle of urban culture and identity. Once again, Los Angeles, a city often recognized as a cultural trendsetter, may be the first to model this development. Though the city once supported powerful expressions of suburban whiteness, it may be, in the not too distant future, that to imagine a white identity in a region teeming with nonwhite peoples will be to conjure a historical fiction from the city's past.

NOTES

1. William A. V. Clark, "Residential Patterns: Avoidance, Assimilation and Succession," in *Ethnic Los Angeles*, ed. Roger Waldinger and Mehdi Bozorgmehr (New York: Russell Sage Foundation, 1996), 115.
2. Allen J. Scott, "High-Technology Industrial Development in the San Fernando Valley and Ventura County: Observations on Economic Growth and the Evolution of Urban Form," in *The City: Los Angeles and Urban Theory at the End of the Twentieth Century*, ed. Allen J. Scott and Edward W. Soja (Berkeley: University of California Press, 1996), 293.
3. Janet Abu-Lughod, *New York, Chicago, Los Angeles: America's Global Cities* (Minneapolis: University of Minnesota Press, 1999), 364–65.
4. Raymond A. Rocco, "Latino Los Angeles: Reframing Boundaries/Borders," in *The City: Los Angeles and Urban Theory at the End of the Twentieth Century*, ed. Allen J. Scott and Edward W. Soja (Berkeley: University of California Press, 1996), 374–75.
5. Clarence Y. H. Lo, *Small Property versus Big Government: Social Origins of the Property Tax Revolt* (Berkeley: University of California Press, 1990).
6. Ibid., 57–60; Abu-Lughod, *New York, Chicago, Los Angeles*, 379–82.
7. Michael Paul Rogin and John L. Shover, *Political Change in California: Critical Elections and Social Movements, 1890–1966* (Westport, Conn.: Greenwood Publishing Corporation, 1970), 173–78; George Lipsitz, *The Possessive Investment in Whiteness: How White People Profit from Identity Politics* (Philadelphia: Temple University Press, 1998), 136–38.
8. Abu-Lughod, *New York, Chicago, Los Angeles*, 383–85.
9. Edward W. Soja, "Los Angeles, 1965–1992: From Crisis-Generated Restructuring to Restructuring-Generated Crisis," in *The City: Los Angeles and Urban Theory at the End of the Twentieth Century*, ed. Allen J. Scott and Edward W. Soja (Berkeley: University of California Press, 1996), 443.
10. Michael Sorkin, ed., *Variations on a Theme Park: The New American City and the End of Public Space* (New York: Hill and Wang, 1992); Edward W. Soja, *Postmetropolis: Critical Studies of Cities and Regions* (Oxford: Blackwell Publishing, 2000), 233–63.
11. Robin D. G. Kelley, *Race Rebels: Culture, Politics and the Black Working Class* (New York: Free Press, 1996), 183–227. See also Tricia Rose, *Black Noise: Rap Music and Black Culture in Contemporary America* (Hanover, N.H.: University Press of New England, 1994).
12. Mike Davis, *Magical Urbanism: Latinos Reinvent the U.S. City* (London: Verso, 2000). See also Victor M. Valle and Rodolfo D. Torres, *Latino Metropolis* (Minneapolis: University of Minnesota Press, 2000); Gustavo Leclerc, Raul Villa, and Michael J. Dear, *Urban Latino Cultures* (Thousand Oaks, Calif.: Sage Publications, 1999); and Marta López-Garza and David R. Diaz, *Asian and Latino Immigrants in a Restructuring Economy: The Metamorphosis of Southern California* (Stanford, Calif.: Stanford University Press, 2001).
13. "Can Hollywood Get Its Glitz Back?" 12 November 2001, www.businessweek.com/magazine/content/01_46/b3757018.htm.
14. Jim Rawitsch, "Moving Right Along," *Los Angeles Times Magazine*, 13 July 1986, 1.
15. Samuel R. Delany, *Times Square Red, Times Square Blue* (New York: New York University Press, 1999); Ada Louise Huxtable, "Reinventing Times Square: 1990," in *Inventing Times Square: Commerce and Culture at the Crossroads of the World*, ed. William R. Taylor (Baltimore: Johns Hopkins University Press, 1991), 356–70.
16. Dana Cuff, *The Provisional City: Los Angeles Stories of Architecture and Urbanism* (Cambridge, Mass.: MIT Press, 2000), 334–35; Andrew Ross, *The Celebration Chronicles* (New York: Ballantine Books, 1999); Douglas Frantz and Catherine Collins, *Celebration, U.S.A.: Living in Disney's Brave New Town* (New York: Henry Holt, 2000).
17. Samuel O. Regalado, *Viva Baseball! Latin Major Leaguers and Their Special Hunger* (Urbana: University of Illinois Press, 1988), 122–28.
18. Roger Keil, *Los Angeles: Globalization, Urbanization, and Social Struggles* (New York: John Wiley and Sons, 1998) xxxi–xxxii; Kelley, *Race Rebels*, 232–33.

Fiscal Strain and Reform in a Federal System

The Great Recession of 2008 and 2009 hit urban areas all over the country very hard. In cities and suburbs officials have found it difficult to cope with the social dimensions of the continuing economic downturn; indeed, in many places they have had to reconsider even their most fundamental responsibilities. With only a few exceptions cities were forced to cut expenditures and services, sometimes drastically. The impact of service cutbacks was magnified by budget reductions being imposed by state governments, which were feeling similar pressures; indeed, many states were cutting a wide range of social services. Such measures seemed especially painful because they came when social problems were becoming visibly worse. Many commentators compared the problems within urban and rural areas alike with those of the Great Depression.

The American federal system is being tested as local, state, and federal officials grapple with the fallout from the troubled economy. Following President George W. Bush, President Barack Obama acted swiftly to enlarge the scale of federal governmental intervention in the economy. By raising taxes and cutting services, states and cities were making the recession worse and, in effect, canceling out much of the economic stimulus undertaken by the federal government. This is part of the reason why aid to state and local governments was included in the $787 billion stimulus package passed by Congress on February 13, 2009. The American Recovery and Reinvestment Act sent $79 billion of fiscal assistance directly to the states. Of immediate relevance to the cities, it also authorized $144 billion for infrastructure projects undertaken by state and local governments and $41 billion for school districts. The stimulus package provided a greater influx of federal money than at any time since the 1930s, but it did not restructure the intergovernmental system, and it did not spare local governments from making deep cuts in their budgets, a circumstance that is made unavoidable by the U.S. intergovernmental system, which requires cities to rely heavily upon their own sources to generate the revenues necessary to carry out their responsibilities.

In Selection 19, Paul Kantor asks if this and other efforts to change governmental policy and to stimulate markets is likely to bring the problems of American cities and suburbs more within the national orbit of power. A fundamental question must be raised: How will America's decentralized and market-driven model of urban development respond to federal efforts? Is the decentralized American model becoming outdated? Kantor argues that the economic crisis is unlikely to precipitate big changes in governmental responsibilities within the federal system by shifting power and authority upward. He demonstrates that even though the economic crisis has modestly increased federal governmental attention to urban affairs, the three major pillars that sustain the decentralized American model are not being challenged by President Obama's electoral coalition.

One pillar is the devolutionary impulse extending back to the Founding Fathers that discourages concentration of governmental power even in the face of big sacrifices to social equality. Another pillar is the economic competition among cities and states in which people and businesses "vote with their feet" in choosing places to live or invest. In the radically decentralized federal system local governments have little choice but to react to changing market pressures or be left behind in the competitive struggle for economic growth. The third pillar is the massive public investment by localities and states in promoting their economies. Local and state governments routinely subsidize business activities with a plethora of tax, loan, regulatory, and other incentives in hopes of capturing investment. Voters and public officials have a stake in making the system work for their own jurisdiction. Thus, political division and economic rivalry among states and communities discourages national political coalitions favoring policies that might change the way the system works.

Kantor concludes that President Obama's urban initiatives may eventually enhance the federal role in assisting urban areas, but they are unlikely to alter the American model in major ways. Although Obama is committed to helping cities, he must work within the contours of a system that is profoundly shaped by government fragmentation, economic competition, and localism in public policies. The resilience of the American model highlights how deeply suspicious many Americans are about concentrating power even during times of crisis. In effect, the U.S. model can be regarded as a political choice, not a result of overpowering economic forces brought about by global capitalism. Changes in urban policy can arise only if new political coalitions gather enough force to challenge old assumptions. So far the economic crisis has not achieved this, and it is not likely to do so soon.

Selection 20, which is taken from a policy brief issued in December 2010 by the Congressional Budget Office (CBO), documents in some detail the close connection between the economic downturn and the budgetary capacity of local governments. According to the report, local governments are the last in line of several dominoes to fall since 2008. Housing prices declined by 27% beginning in June 2006, which impacts the ability of local governments to generate revenues from property taxes. Revenues for state governments have fallen sharply and, as a result, the states have reduced the funds available for local governments. The squeeze on local budgets comes from the other direction, too: higher unemployment levels translate into an increased need for social and other services. As the CBO report points out, this fiscal situation is structural; there is not a lot that local governments can do about it except to adjust.

Local governments have tried to do this in a variety of ways. They have reduced spending, reduced contributions to pension funds, postponed capital investments in infrastructure, increased taxes and fees, delayed payments and pay dates to contractors and employees, and increased their short-term and long-term debt. In some cases states have helped cities exercise these options, but just as often they have made things worse. In the extreme case of a municipal default, several states have legal provisions that would allow them to assert direct oversight of a city, but so far these powers have rarely been implemented.

In dire cases local officials may decide that their only option is to declare bankruptcy, although in nearly half the states the legislature would need to pass a specific law allowing such a move. Bankruptcy would allow a municipality to restructure its debts and negotiate with creditors, but the political and economic consequences that would flow from such a drastic remedy acts as a significant deterrent. In the end, cities will cope with the Great Recession by doing what they do best: finding creative ways to solve their own problems.

Selection 21 is based on a survey conducted annually by the National League of Cities on the state of city finances. This report, which was issued in September 2011, adds significant information about the serious budgetary problems now facing cities: "Revenue and spending shifts in 2010 and 2011 portray a worsening fiscal picture for America's cities. The projected decline in 2011 revenues represents the fifth straight year-to-year decline going back to 2007." The authors of the report, Christopher Hoene and Michael Pagano, observe that the Great Recession and the continuing economic downturn have created structural conditions that will make it difficult to turn things around any time in the foreseeable future. In reporting the survey results, they point out that, "Cities ended fiscal year 2010 with the largest year-to-year reductions in general fund revenues and expenditures in the 25-year history of the survey." In their estimation, the continuing housing crisis and falling tax revenues from property, sales, and other sources have made fiscal stringency the "new normal" for city finances.

Despite declining fiscal capacity, it is not easy for cities to reduce expenditures for many public services. In particular, the authors point to rising costs of health benefits, pension costs, infrastructure, and public safety. The latter three are especially difficult to cut in the short term, if at all, because cities are legally committed to maintaining prior pension obligations; are obliged to maintain existing infrastructure such as roads, water, and sewer systems; and are expected to provide police services and other services that preserve the safety and security of their citizens. Accordingly, cities have made deep cuts in workforces, public works, libraries, parks and recreation programs, and many have reduced the health care benefits for municipal employees. Many cities maintain reserve balances that they can use to avoid more drastic remedies, but as the authors observe, these are sure to decline.

In light of the current mood in Washington, D.C., to slash federal spending it is very unlikely that cities will be able to count on an increase in federal assistance. As Hoene and Pagano show, the states, too, have made reductions that affect the fiscal capacity of local governments. In some ways the scope of the problem facing cities is unprecedented, and it will be interesting to see how they respond. However, local public officials have always been resilient and resourceful, and presumably they will be in this circumstance, too.

19

City Futures: Economic Crisis and the American Model of Urban Development

PAUL KANTOR

Assessing the future of Western industrial cities invariably humbles the craft of social science.[1] Looking forward from where we are forces us to evaluate a staggering number of developments that have lasting impact on the contemporary urban world, but have yet to be well understood. This surely includes the globalization of finance, immigration flows, deindustrialization, creation of new information technologies, internationalization of economic and social exchange, and many other influences. The scope and complexity of these forces render predictions of specific urban futures speculative at best. This essay takes a more modest step in probing the urban future: examining the American model of development in light of its contemporary challenges. Although the American model has enjoyed remarkable ascendancy during recent decades, world economic crisis and political change in the USA compel us to question its sustainability. Does it have a future? Can it survive today's economic crisis? What can the American experience teach about the future that is valuable for other cities in the West? These giant questions cannot be definitively answered, but I believe the United States' present encounter with changing capitalism offers important lessons.

THE AMERICAN MODEL

First, let us look at the essence of the American urban model. On the surface, it truly seems to be driven by the power and logic of capitalism. American cities, states and regions scramble for jobs and dollars in relentless competition or they face the consequences of falling behind as businesses and people choose to invest or relocate elsewhere (Peterson 1981, Logan and Molotch 1987, Fainstein 1994, Kantor 1995). In contrast to most European cities, American local governments remain highly dependent upon their own source revenues, making local government pursuit of tax revenues a high priority in governance. It is also one of the most fragmented and pluralistic urban systems in the world, with major metropolitan areas divided into hundreds or even, as in the case of New York, more than 2000 separate governmental jurisdictions, including counties, school boards, municipalities, special utility districts, towns, villages and other entities. Despite its haphazard appearance, this system often appeals to economic conservatives who like the way its competitive features impose a discipline on what local governments can and cannot do, tying the economic fortunes of local communities to the winds of economic change (Tiebout 1962). Yet to others, this system is a social monstrosity. Critics fault it for tolerating glaring social inequalities, as the least competitive communities are abandoned, and deep divisions based on race and income often result across whole metropolitan areas (Oliver 2001, Swanstrom *et al.* 2006, Kantor and Judd 2009).

This American model has global reach, despite its social warts and flaws. European cities that once rejected devolution in urban policy now freely experiment with it. Although Western European governments usually have resisted much of the fiscal or governmental decentralization of an American scale, EU countries, including the more 'statist' ones such as France and the Netherlands, have spent decades undertaking devolutionary fiscal and administrative measures in the American spirit (Jouve and Lefèvre 2002, Savitch and Kantor 2002; Brenner 2004). Further, efforts to build US-style networks that involve lateral cooperation and coordination within city regions have grown throughout Western and Central Europe as governments seek new venues and 'partnerships' for managing urban economic and social problems without the hand of central governmental decision-makers at the centre of action (Salet *et al.* 2003). Although there remain important differences in the ways European and American cities compete for capital investment, there is little doubt that American-style decentralist approaches and public–private partnership ideals have inspired a host of local government reforms throughout the industrial West for more than three decades. Market-oriented politics, public entrepreneurship, and the marriage of privatism and efficiency now dominate public discourse in running cities well beyond North America (Brenner and Theodore 2002).

Trouble in the Heartland

Despite such influence beyond its borders, is the American model now troubled in its own heartland? An economic crisis arising from free market excesses and the rebirth of the power of the liberal left in the USA now converge. Presently there is widespread questioning of many economic and political fundamentals within the private sector, among leading economists, and within both of the major parties (Jacobs and King 2009). Beginning with the waning days of the Bush administration, big government is back. It has happened with a speed and on a scale few anticipated. What does this mean for America's cities?

The economic crisis has clearly loosened traditional ideological moorings in American politics, precipitating major departures in the role and scope of government. Economic restructuring happening now in the USA is precipitating an unprecedented expansion of federal governmental responsibilities. For months, the Obama administration has rolled out initiatives of awesome scale to respond to new fears of economic crisis, often with reluctant backing by Wall Street and corporate decision-makers. These involve vast sums of public expenditure and debt that Americans have not seen before.

Even though massive budget deficits had accumulated during the Bush administration, federal economic intervention to address the financial crisis dramatically increased much further before this president left office. It then grew even faster during the first half of 2009 as President Obama, Treasury officials and Congress overcame traditional sources of rivalry to spend, loan and guarantee massive heaps of dollars in order to stave off collapse of the nation's banks, investment houses and troubled homeowners. In the months since, we have witnessed unprecedented expansion of federal power—reaching into entire industries, the banking system, the financial markets, foreign trade, consumer affairs, and in virtually all local communities affected by the crisis. The national government became a major investor-owner in some of the nation's major auto companies, insurance companies, financial conglomerates, and mortgage lenders. Congress passed an economic stimulus measure in excess of three quarters of a trillion dollars that, among other things, averts financial collapse of some state governments and funds wide-ranging new infrastructure projects all over the country. The Obama administration also launched legislation to reform the entire federal economic regulatory structure, including provisions to consolidate federal regulatory responsibilities, enhance the power of the Federal Reserve and create a new systemic risk overseer for the marketplace as a whole. The breadth of the federal governmental response presently rivals and probably will eventually overshadow the assertion of power during the New Deal.

This rapid shift to expansionary government may have begun under economic crisis, but is also propelled by the rebirth of a powerful new Democratic political majority. President Obama's electoral victory and the Democratic sweep of both houses of Congress in 2008 parallels a shrinking Republican political base following one of the least popular Presidents in modern history. Although the longer-term meaning of the 2008 election and the political changes within the electorate remain uncertain, the new political majority has already dramatically altered the governmental agenda in Washington, DC (Bartels 2008, Nelson 2009). Despite escalating federal expenditures and debt burdens, the Obama administration quickly moved to restore several social programs marginalized during the Bush years and has embarked on major reforms in healthcare, transportation and social assistance. Although the strength of this lurch to the centre-left in American politics will surely gather greater opposition from within and without as specific programs evolve in the legislative process and the plight-of-the-economy changes, it seems clear that many dominant political assumptions that limited debate over the reach of government during the past quarter century no longer prevail. In particular, the decades-old politics based on relying on markets as solutions to public problems while reducing what government does is losing hegemony (Brown and Jacobs 2008).

A New American Model?

Will such a massive recasting of government and market bypass America's cities? Or will economic reconstruction forge a new national urban policy, bringing American cities more within the national governmental orbit of power—perhaps even making urban America in the future look more like Europe, where prevailing urban policies have long engaged most national governments?

Despite the scope and depth of these changes, the ongoing convergence of economic crisis and new politics is unlikely to alter the American model very much, at least for the foreseeable future. The main reason for this admittedly counterintuitive conclusion: US urban development policy will remain anchored in local politics, despite the crisis of modern post-industrial capitalism. Although contemporary economic upheaval is unleashing huge political changes at the national level, powerful local political interests remain as pillars supporting the American model. These political interests are so resilient and deeply embedded that even a capitalist crisis of world proportions is unlikely to undermine them very much.

Let us examine this thesis of stability amidst upheaval. To begin, the market-like features of the American urban system are actually more myth than reality. The role of the state in promoting entrepreneurial style development is huge, as described below. Most important, the economic competition among governments at the core of the American model is not a byproduct of post-industrial capitalism. Rather, the model springs from deliberate political choices made by local, state and national governments over many years to permit private-sector impulses to play a key role in city-building. Most of these choices were not made to accommodate post-industrial capitalist developments, because they usually preceded them (Kantor 2007, p. 1995).

It is true that the post-industrial economy of the past 50 years or so unleashed fundamentally new forces influencing the shape of the urban system in the United States, as it did elsewhere. Land, labour and capital all underwent radical reorganization and dispersal. In the USA, as in other nations, many businesses that once were strongly tethered to the factories, downtowns and railway terminals of major cities were liberated from these central places and became freer to relocate to other areas, well outside the big cities, where they could reap new cost advantages. Computer technologies, telecom services, and the availability of lightweight and other man-made materials such as plastics, enabled manufacturing businesses to move away from sources of raw materials. The growth of services rapidly replaced manufacturing production as the major sector of the economy. Transformation to a predominantly office-based economy permitted businesses to shift these operations more easily to sites in suburbia, the Sunbelt and abroad. The organization of capital also changed fundamentally, typically decentralizing divisional operations in scattered locations while only concentrating corporate headquarters functions in traditional urban centres.

Dispersal of jobs was accompanied by the scattering of urban populations. The post war years were coloured by a trek to suburbia of historic proportions and on a scale that has not been duplicated in other Western industrial nations. In the USA, suburbanization was strongly influenced by race, as more than 5 million African Americans moved to Northern cities. This new presence accelerated the flight of white families from inner-city areas to the suburbs, creating highly segregated metropolitan areas all over the Midwest and Northern sections of the USA by the 1970s.

This process of deconcentration and deindustrialization has relentlessly continued, creating a situation where many cities have become more interchangeable as business sites while corporate investors are better able to pick and choose among cities, suburbs and even rural areas competing for their investments. It is a phenomenon experienced by virtually all Western industrial nations in recent decades, posing essentially similar problems for their political systems.

THE PILLARS OF THE AMERICAN MODEL

Political counter-movements invariably accompany economic revolutions for reasons of social protection (Polanyi 1944). Thus urban policies to confront the forces unleashed by economic restructuring were fashioned throughout the West. What distinguishes the USA, however, is that the political order for managing and channelling these new social forces stands apart from the political systems in Europe and other industrial nations. In the USA, the dominant political response has been to maintain and even extend an urban system that radically decentralizes governmental power and authority and discourages shifting problem-solving to higher levels of government (Kantor 1995). It is based on three pillars: devolution, intergovernmental competition, and public entrepreneurship.

The Devolutionary Impulse

The ideal of small-scale politics and the notion that local people know best how to solve their own problems has a long history in America, extending back to the Founding Fathers. Thomas Jefferson especially celebrated the local community he found in rural areas, towns and villages, while casting suspicion on central governmental power (Wood 1992). This outlook inspired the forging of a decentralist urban policy throughout the nineteenth and twentieth centuries. Once constructed, this formed a political edifice strongly directing America's response to post-industrial change.

Initially, state governments played the crucial role. As families and jobs left central cities, state governments enabled suburbanites to incorporate into autonomous local governments that could assert control over land use and keep out unwanted people, industries and other 'intrusions', including people of colour, public housing and the poor. People leaving the cities and their problems were permitted to fragment entire metropolitan areas into hundreds or, as in New York, even more than a thousand local governments, each competing to minimize service burdens and keep taxes low. Bringing in the tax revenues and keeping out the 'undesirables' became the suburban governmental mantra. At the same time, state governments supported this by refusing to permit central cities to expand their territorial boundaries as wealth exited into unincorporated areas; they passed laws enabling suburbanites to create special district governments to provide services beyond their local government's reach, such as commuter transportation, water, sewers and other services that could only be financed by large scale governments. The result is the divided metropolis we know today (Danielson 1976, Judd and Swanstrom 2008). Despite their increasing social diversity in recent years (Teaford 2008), the suburbs as a whole remain a bastion of white upper-income groups while the central cities house those left behind (Orfield 2002, Berube *et al.* 2006).

The federal government's policies reinforced building of this decentralist order, and in doing so stimulated the creation of a more market-driven urban society. During the initial post-war decades, federal urban programs dramatically expanded to play a dual role. With one hand, the federal government subsidized urban economic competition among cities, suburbs, and regions through a bevy of programs that stimulated flight of people from extant urban centres. For example, federal mortgage guarantee programs for veterans and mid-income families were biased in favour of new suburban locations, rather than older inner city areas. The interstate highway program, begun in the 1950s, subsidized the use of the automobile to commute to distant suburban locations while denying even the modest use of federal funds for mass transit until the 1970s. National defence programs that expanded rapidly during the Cold War favoured governmental spending in military-related projects in newer locations in the Sunbelt, rather than older metropolitan areas (Mollenkopf 1983).

With the other hand, federal policymakers also attempted to address some of the harsh social consequences of these policies. During this period, central cities still played a major role in national electoral coalitions of the Democratic Party. Housing and urban renewal programs were launched to assist downtown renewal, while later programs of the 1960s Great Society agenda focused on addressing urban poverty. Most forms of federal intervention were geared to helping central cities to become more competitive in attracting private investment, not seeking ways of containing the scramble among cities, states and regions for competitive advantages (Kantor 1995).

By the 1970s, however, the population movement to the suburbs and Sunbelt, together with national partisan electoral realignments, diminished the importance of central city electorates in national party coalitions. This triggered almost continuous political marginalization of the cities during succeeding years. Fuelled by a powerful conservative tide and a new Republican political majority, the last decades of the century witnessed almost continuous withdrawal of the federal government from the cities and the diminution of national urban programs (Conlan 1998). Beginning with the last two years of the Carter administration, Democratic as well as Republican administrations undertook major cuts in federal aid to cities, as well as the housing and economic development initiatives of earlier years. Direct federal aid to cities per capital peaked at 17.5% of city own-source revenues in 1977 and fell to 5.4% in 2000 (Wallin 2005). It has since remained relatively flat. In 2008 federal outlays to state and local governments comprised almost the same proportion of federal outlays as in 1999 (US Office of Management and Budget 2009). These changes in federal policy to shift more governmental responsibilities downwards reflects the power of electorates in the suburbs and Sunbelt.[2] They believe they benefit from permitting neoliberal forces to guide changes in urban development; it has little to do with having to accommodate global capitalism (Caraley 1992, Weir 1996).

Intergovernmental Competition

These changes in the policies of higher-level governments reconstituted the rules under which urban economic development took place in the post-industrial USA. That is, an implicit national urban policy was forged that essentially mandated a radical devolution of decision-making to the lowest governmental levels, forcing cities, suburbs and towns to compete for their survival and economic well-being by attracting jobs and dollars from increasingly footloose business investment markets. The rules of this game are simple: people and businesses are free to 'vote with their feet' in choosing places to live and invest. National urban policy is a means of enforcing this by encouraging industrial dispersal and limiting higher governmental intervention in assisting cities that become losers in intergovernmental warfare for economic growth. Cities have little choice but to lean close to the market if they are to survive. In effect, the federal system of government is designed to permit market pressures to play a larger role than they might otherwise play in guiding urban economic restructuring. It is not a result of markets, but of politics, that markets have the power to set urban agendas (Kantor 2007).

Public Entrepreneurship

Today, American voters do not challenge the matter of decentralization very much. Whole communities have acquired compelling political interests in making the system work for themselves. Indeed, a new regulatory state has emerged in which local and state governments dominate the scene. This political response has very little to do with liberalism or conservatism, Republicans or Democrats or other ideological divisions because virtually every city, county, town and state has supported forms of new public intervention (Eisinger 1988, Kantor 1995, Savitch and Kantor 2002, pp. 101–148). There is broad support in local communities to avoid letting market pressures alone determine their destiny, a common response to economic upheaval on the part of urban communities (Polanyi 1944). Businesses, electorates, homeowners, taxpayers, civil servants, elected officials, and almost every other vulnerable local interest resist allowing economic competition to drive what happens to them in their communities (Logan and Molotch 1987). When national government proves unresponsive to their demands, historically they have turned to local government and the states (Sbragia 1999). Therefore, in a political system where localities must raise most of their tax revenues by themselves and can expect little compensatory national or state financial assistance, pressure to seek business growth and minimize social service burdens is irresistible.

Consequently, local and state governments now routinely subsidize urban business investment with a plethora of tax, loan, regulatory and other business incentive programs in an effort to bend the pressures of the marketplace to their favour. These programs usually seek to control the supply side of the development process. They have dramatically proliferated over the past several decades (Kantor 1995, Anderson and Wassmer 2000). State governments have created new economic development agencies, and legislatures have passed laws providing authority of local and state agencies to provide bounties of nearly all descriptions in order to promote the expansion of existing businesses or to lure new ones into their jurisdictions. In nearly every large city in the USA there is hardly a major investment project—such as a shopping mall, office building, skyscraper, industrial park, new factory or other development—that gets built without very large subsidies of some kind from the governmental jurisdictions where these projects occur. Sometimes termed the new 'Entrepreneurial State', it signifies closer engagement between government and business (Eisinger 1988). Even though abundant evidence shows this kind of intervention often has limited effect on business relocation and investment (Anderson and Wassmer 2000), few city councils or state legislatures are willing to entrust economic outcomes to whatever the private sector may bring.[3] In 2005, the US Supreme Court acknowledged this vital engagement of public and private sectors in the landmark case of *Kelo vs. City of New London* by deciding that local officials could seize private property to sell to another private party for the sole purpose of increasing the property's economic value to the community (Kantor 2007).

THE POLITICS OF WINNERS AND LOSERS

These are deeply entrenched interests. The various winners in the American system discourage tinkering with the urban economic landscape from Washington, DC. Proliferating urban centres in the newer parts of the USA, especially in the Sunbelt, almost uniformly resist national efforts to level the playing field or doing much to save older cities that are no longer very competitive. By 2000, the 15 Sunbelt states held 222 electoral college votes compared with only 180 for 14 Frostbelt states (Judd and Swanstrom 2008, p. 214). Sunbelt suburban development with pro-growth electorates has continued to expand in recent years due to the proliferation of so-called 'boomburbs' scattered throughout the region (Lang and LeFurgy 2007).

Older urban areas also are often unsupportive of governmental efforts to even out urban economic competition. Large income gaps between lagging central city populations and more prosperous suburban enclaves undercuts metropolitan-wide coalitions on a broad range of urban issues, both regional and national (Weir 1996, Rusk 1999). Although city–suburban income gaps fell in the 1990s, differences have remained large due to big variations in city–suburban income among regions, especially in the Midwest and North East (Swanstrom *et al.* 2006, p. 150). Simple city and suburban growth patterns do not capture the increasingly complex patterns of uneven economic development in American suburbia. The mostly suburban 'growth counties' which represent more than 38% of US population growth during the last 50 years are not very concentrated. They are found in 27 states and 41 metropolitan areas, leaving only 7 out of 50 of the largest metropolitan areas without at least one growth county (Lang and Gough 2006, p. 64).

The economic resurgence of many older central cities, such as New York City, Chicago, Boston, and Los Angeles, further undercuts the possibility of regional consensus on urban policy despite the clamour of big city mayors for more federal aid. Since the 1990s, there has been an upsurge in downtown living after decades of decline. From 1990 to 2000, downtown populations increased in 18 of major 24 cities studied by Fannie Mae and the Brookings Institution (Sohmer and Lang 2006, pp. 1–4). The increasing importance of many older big cities as business centres, the expansion of tourism and culture as urban industries, and migration from abroad have separated an entire stable of prosperous central cities from their declining Rustbelt cousins (Card 2009). As a result of these substantial variations in growth and decline, the US urban scene is more socially and economically fragmented than ever, making regional, metropolitan or even central city political cooperation very difficult. The dominant interest constellation in urban America spurs nearly all localities and states to seek ways of using their own assets to grow and become wealthier, rather than spending much political capital on team-playing in national politics in hopes of evening out development opportunities in some distant future.

The Obama Urban Policy: Limited Experimentation

The Obama political coalition that is bringing about major changes in the domestic political agenda is unlikely to significantly challenge the traditional urban model. Once deeply entrenched, the highly fragmented system of so many governments seeking competitive advantages discourages even ardent reformers from quickly seeking national solutions to its fundamental shortcomings. There is greater political payoff in funnelling massive government aid to save General Motors, but to leave struggling Detroit and other places like it more to their own devices. When cities fail, it is their fault; but when giant businesses fail, it is everybody's problem—because the losses cannot be contained within municipal borders. Thus, we witness starkly contrasting national responses as the Obama administration undertakes bold new intervention in struggles with the economic crisis, while casting about cautiously for a new urban policy. By May, 2009 two of the nation's leading auto makers, General Motors and Chrysler, cost the federal government $50 billion and $15.5 billion, respectively, and the US Treasury estimated that General Motors, which was essentially taken over by the federal government, would eventually need as much as $30 billion more (Maynard and de la Merced 2009). In contrast, Detroit, the nation's 11th largest city whose population has fallen to 850,000 from a peak of 1.9 million and has the highest poverty and foreclosure rates in the country, was left struggling with a deficit of more than $200 million (McKee and Ortolani 2008). As federal bailout of the automakers poured forth, Standard and Poor downgraded Detroit's bonds to junk status (only a handful of US cities are rated as low) (Reuters 2009). Although Detroit was to share in some $3 billion in federal stimulus money being funnelled to the state of Michigan, and would surely share in an auto-maker recovery, the radically different federal responses to the failure of a business and the failure of a city says much about power and interests in America.

Current urban policy that is taking shape surely will shift more in favour of assisting urban areas than anything in recent decades under Republican rule. Yet it remains rooted in localism and competition, making only tentative steps in other directions in a process of cautious experimentation. During his presidential campaign, Barack Obama developed a blueprint for urban initiatives that promised restoration of urban aid, especially in housing and transportation. But most of this document (Obama 2008) and subsequent addresses about economic development are devoted to redefining 'urban' to mean metropolitan regions and avoid inner-city connotations (Schulman 2009a). Although this redefinition may eventually expand the political coalition supporting greater federal urban intervention, it limits redistributive activism.

President Obama paints a new vision of the nation's urban policy, but it is one that remains profoundly anchored in intergovernmental competition and localism. Indeed, its centrepiece is encouraging greater public entrepreneurship and cooperation by governmental clusters in order to support innovation in next-generation industries. Localism dominates organizing these endeavors. President Obama's newly established Office of Urban Policy is headed by a very respectable Bronx politician with no national political experience at all; this is hardly a firm start in the direction of asserting a federal presence as a counterweight to local impulses. Finally, the economic crisis has not been used as much of an opportunity to rebuild a stronger federal role in managing the urban economy. The massive economic stimulus program Congress enacted in 2009 provides for little coordination, even though it could reshape the entire urban landscape.

In effect, President Obama's dedicated urban initiatives work within the contours of the existing system of intergovernmental politics, rather than providing building blocks for a new one having greater national oversight or seeking ways of limiting wasteful competition among localities for development. For example, because Washington allowed the states to decide how transportation stimulus money is allocated, the 100 largest metropolitan areas received less than half of the $26 billion for highways, bridges and other projects (Schulman 2009b). Absent are any proposals to use federal power to even the urban economic playing field or to contain bidding wars among localities and states that has led to waste of public resources attempting to bribe business offering to move jobs into town. For instance, there appears to be no interest in restoring some form of revenue sharing or otherwise shifting federal aid to make localities less dependent on their own source revenues in the long run. Even though state and local tax competition in bidding for business could be limited by the use of federal grant-in-aid penalties, these alternatives are not yet subjects of serious debate. Radical decentralization, intergovernmental competition and public entrepreneurship to boost private sector investment remain the pillars of US urban policy.

That a fresh national urban policy does not spring even from a city-friendly and liberal president elected on a tide of public unhappiness with the old order is suggestive of the political barriers to change. Fragmented government and the competing interests of local public sectors are deeply entrenched in the USA, limiting the scope of what debate over national urban policy is about even during economic crisis. This reality led Thomas P. 'Tip' O'Neill, who served 34 years in Congress and was speaker the House, to famously observe that in America, 'all politics is local'. And he could well have extended this to say, 'all economics is politics'.

THE TRIUMPH OF POLITICAL CHOICE

The resilience of the American model highlights how deeply suspicious many Americans are about concentrating power even in the face of big sacrifices to social equality and threat of economic crisis. But there is also a more positive lesson in the American urban experience that should not be overlooked, particularly because it speaks to the urban future beyond the USA. Ironically, the US model shows how global capitalism does not drive urban change, even in the capital of capitalism. American post-industrial cities have long promoted a competitive urban development style as a matter of public policy, not because of overpowering economic forces leaving little alternative. Despite its flaws as social policy, its resilience also empowers American citizens to slowly experiment with new directions in urban policy even in the midst of economic crisis. In time, the new political coalition now leading America may gather greater force and reconsider deeply rooted assumptions about the nation's urban development.

Although American commitment to localism may be unique, the American experience suggests how much the building and organization of democratic political institutions matters everywhere. Whether decentralized or highly nationalized, the ways in which cities and regions develop strongly reflect a nation's political choices in sustaining some kinds of governance practices, but avoiding others. From this perspective, predicting the future of cities is strongly tied to people's willingness to invest political capital to sustain forms of governance that promote the kind of urban development they want. Whether the American model is copied or rejected elsewhere in the future is essentially a matter of political choice.

REFERENCES

Anderson, J.E. and Wassmer, R.W., 2000. *Bidding for business.* Kalamazoo, MI: Upjohn Institute.

Bartels, L., 2008. *Unequal democracy.* Princeton, NJ: Princeton University Press.

Berube, A., Katz, B., and Lang, R.E., eds., 2006. *Redefining urban and suburban America.* Washington, DC: Brookings Institution.

Blair, J. and Reese, L., eds., 1999. *Approaches to local economic development.* Thousand Oaks, CA: Sage.

Brenner, N. and Theodore, N., eds., 2002. *Spaces of neoliberalism.* London: Blackwell.

Brenner, N., 2004. *New state spaces.* New York: Oxford University Press.

Brown, L.D. and Jacobs, L.R., 2008. *The political abuse of the public interest.* Chicago, IL: University of Chicago Press.

Caraley, D., 1992. Washington abandons the cities. *Political Science Quarterly*, 107 (1), 20–34.

Card, D., 2009. Immigration: how immigration affects U.S. cities. *In:* R.P. Inman, ed., *Making cities work.* Princeton, NJ: Princeton University Press, 158–200.

Conlan, T., 1998. *From new federalism to devolution.* Washington, DC: Brookings Institution.

Danielson, M., 1976. *The politics of exclusion.* New York: Columbia University Press.

Eisinger, P., 1988. *The rise of the entrepreneurial state: state and local economic development policy in the United States.* Madison, WI: University of Wisconsin Press.

Fainstein, S., 1994. *The city builders: property, politics, and planning in London and New York.* Cambridge: Blackwell.

Jacobs, L. and King, D., 2009. America's political crisis: the unsustainable state in a time of unraveling. *Political Science*, 42 (2), 277–286.

Jouve, B. and Lefèvre, C., 2002. *Local power, territory and institutions in European metropolitan areas.* London: Frank Cass.

Judd, D. and Swanstrom, T., 2008. *City politics.* New York: Pearson Longman.

Kantor, P., 1995. *The dependent city revisited: the political economy of urban development and social policy.* Boulder, CO: Westview Press.

Kantor, P., 2007. Globalization and the American model of urban development: making the market. *Metropoles* 1, 31–68. Available from: http://metropoles.revues.org

Kantor, P. and Judd, D., eds., 2009. *American urban politics in a global age*. New York: Pearson Longman.

Lang, R.E. and LeFurgy, J.B., 2007. *Boomburbs*. Washington, DC: Brookings.

Lang, R.E. and Gough, M.Z., 2006. Growth counties: home to America's new suburban metropolis. *In:* Berube, A., Katz, B., and Lang, R.E., eds. *Redefining urban and suburban America*. Washington, DC: Brookings Institution, 61–82.

Logan, J. and Molotch, H., 1987. *Urban fortunes*. Berkeley, CA: University of California Press.

Maynard, M. and de la Merced, M.J., 2009. Will G.M.'s story have a hero? *New York Times*, Sunday Business, 26 July, 1, 9.

McKee, M. and Ortolani, A., 2008. *G.M.'s bust turns Detroit into urban prairie of vacant-lot farms* [online]. Available from: http://Bloomberg.com/apps/news?pid=20601087?refer=home&sid=aMV8_J49diks

Mollenkopf, J., 1983. *The contested city*. Princeton, NJ: Princeton University Press.

Nelson, M., ed., 2009. *The election of 2008*. Washington, DC: CQ Press.

Obama, B., 2008. *Organizing for America: urban policy* [online]. Available from: http://origin.barachobama.com/issues/urban_policy

Oliver, J.E., 2001. *Democracy in suburbia*. Princeton, NJ: Princeton University Press.

Orfield, M., 2002. *American metropolitics*. Washington, DC: Brookings.

Peterson, P., 1981. *City limits*. Chicago, IL: University of Chicago Press.

Polanyi, K., 1944. *The great transformation*. Boston, MA: Beacon.

Reuters, 2009. *S&P downgrades Detroit bonds to junk status* [online], 6 Jan. Available from: http://reuters.com/articlePrint?articleID=USTRE50608720090107 [Accessed 15 Dec 2009].

Rusk, D., 1999. *Inside game, outside game*. Washington, DC: Brookings Institution.

Salet, W., Thornley, A., and Kreukels, A., eds., 2003. *Metropolitan governance and spatial planning*. London: Spon Press.

Savitch, H.V. and Kantor, P., 2002. *Cities in the international marketplace: the political economy of urban development in North America and Western Europe*. Princeton, NJ: Princeton University Press.

Sbragia, A., 1999. *Debt wish*. Pittsburgh, PA: University of Pittsburgh Press.

Schulman, R., 2009a. *Obama paints a new vision for nation's urban policy* [online]. Available from: http://voices.Washingtonpost.com/44/2009/07/14

Schulman, R., 2009b. Big city leaders call stimulus a fine start; but advocates hope funding measure is just a down payment on broader plan. *Washington Post*, 17 Feb, p. A03.

Sohmer, R.R. and Lang, R.E., 2006. *Downtown rebound*. Washington, DC: Fannie Mae Foundation and Urban Institute.

Swanstrom, T., *et al.*, 2006. Pulling apart: economic segregation in suburbs and central cities in major metropolitan areas, 1980–2000. *In:* A. Berube, B. Katz, and R.E. Lang, eds. *Redefining urban and suburban America*. Washington, DC: Brookings Institution, 143–166.

Teaford, J.C., 2008. *The American suburb*. New York: Routledge.

Tiebout, C., 1962. A pure theory of local expenditures. *Journal of Political Economy*, 64 (5), 416–426.

US Office of Management and Budget, 2009. *Budget of the United States Government*, historical tables, annual, table 414. Washington, DC: US Government Printing Office.

Wallin, B.A., 2005. *Budgeting for basics: the changing landscape of city finances*. Discussion paper. Washington, DC: Brookings Institution.

Washington Post, 2009. Rethinking the cities (editorial). 15 Jul, p. A18.

Weir, M., 1996. Central cities loss of power in state politics. *Citiscape*, 2 (2), 23–40.

Wood, G., 1992. *The radicalism of the American Revolution*. New York: Knopf.

NOTES

1. This essay is based on a plenary address to the *City Futures '09* conference sponsored by the European Urban Research Association and the Urban Affairs Association, 4–6 June 2009 in Madrid, Spain. I am grateful to the reviewers of *Urban Research and Practice* for their helpful suggestions and to Anna Kantor for valuable editorial assistance.

2. The voters in central cities of the 32 largest metropolitan areas constituted only 12% of the electorate in 2000, but represented 27% in 1944 (Judd and Swanstrom 2008, p. 201).

3. There is considerable evidence that most business incentive programs simply move jobs from one locality to another, rather than yielding much increase in new wealth that otherwise would not happen. (See Kantor 1995, Blair and Reese 1999, and Anderson and Wassmer 2000.)

20

Fiscal Stress Faced by Local Governments

CONGRESSIONAL BUDGET OFFICE

CAUSES OF FISCAL STRESS FOR LOCAL GOVERNMENTS

Fiscal stress—a gap between projected revenues and expenditures—can be short term, in the case of transitory economic shocks, or long term, in the case of structural budget imbalance. Such structural imbalance may arise from persistent economic shocks or from other factors.

Transitory Economic Shocks

Weak economic conditions lead to fiscal stress for local governments by reducing their tax revenues, lessening the state aid they receive, increasing the demand for some services, and triggering investment losses. Primarily because of their reliance on property taxes—a relatively stable source of funds that makes up just over a quarter of revenues—local governments have experienced less fiscal stress during the recent economic downturn than have state governments. That relative stability may change, however. Nationally, house prices fell by 27 percent from the year ending in June 2006 to the year ending in June 2010 (see Figure 1).[1] Although property tax collections increased 31 percent over that same period, the decline in house prices implies that collections will probably fall in the coming years as local governments gradually update property tax assessments to reflect lower market values. On average, collections of property tax revenues lag behind changes in house prices by three years.[2] Even small declines in collections could cause fiscal stress when the cost of providing public services is growing.

State governments provided 30 percent of revenues for local governments in 2008. However, state revenues—primarily from income and sales taxes—have plummeted during the weak economic conditions of the past two years (see Figure 2). States have consequently reduced spending, in part by cutting the amounts provided to local governments. Because periods of local and state fiscal stress tend to occur concurrently, aid to local governments often falls when it is needed most. Following the 2001 recession, total transfers to cities declined by 9 percent from 2002 to 2004.[3] Although data on changes in local aid during the recent recession and slow recovery are not yet available, a recent survey indicates that 22 states reduced aid to local governments in fiscal year 2010, and 20 states have proposed additional cuts in 2011.[4] According to another survey, almost 40 states cut spending for K–12 education in fiscal year 2010, and 31 governors proposed to cut such funding in their budgets for 2011.[5] (States have different options available to them when responding to fiscal stress. For a brief description of those options, see Box 1.)

A series of issue summaries from the Congressional Budget Office, December 2010.

This brief was prepared by Elizabeth Cove Delisle. It and other CBO publications are available at the agency's Web site (www.cbo.gov).

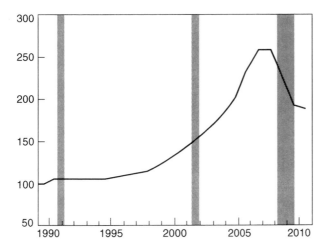

FIGURE 1

Prices for Single-Family Homes, July 1988 to June 2010.
(Index, July 1988–June 1989 period = 100)

Notes: The S&P/Case-Shiller index tracks repeat sales of existing single-family homes financed by all types of mortgages. The data plotted are annual, showing the average value in periods running from July through June. The shaded vertical bars indicate periods of recession.
Source: Congressional Budget Office based on the S&P/Case-Shiller Home Price Index.

Economic contractions also often result in increased demand for a host of public services. The unemployed or those facing a reduced work schedule may lose access to health insurance, increasing demands on public hospitals or clinics. Crime generally increases during economic downturns, increasing the need for police protection.[6] People who lose income often opt for less-expensive modes of transportation, such as public transit. As the number of people unemployed increases, so does the demand for job training programs and services provided by public libraries or social welfare offices.

Local governments also may experience fiscal difficulties that result from investment losses; when large, such losses can be extremely disruptive (see Box 2).

Structural Budget Imbalance

Long-term imbalances in local budgets arise from a variety of sources that can be difficult to disentangle. Political dynamics frequently play an important role. When a council or other legislative body and the executive fail to agree on a budget—often when the two bodies are dominated by different political parties—deficits may occur. Arrangements with local groups such as public-employee unions may also be a factor. For example, according to a bankruptcy filing of Vallejo, California, the inability of the council and the mayor to control labor costs was the main reason for the filing.

In addition, demographic shifts, particularly occasions when high- or moderate-income households move out of a local jurisdiction, may contribute to long-term budget imbalance. Such shifts are often closely related to the relocation of businesses out of the inner cities and into the surrounding suburbs.[7] As businesses move away, the jurisdiction's tax collections drop. Over time, the need for public services also increases as personal incomes fall and unemployment increases.

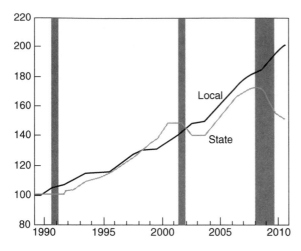

FIGURE 2

State and Local Governments' Tax Collections, July 1988 to June 2010.
(Index, July 1988–June 1989 period = 100)

Notes: The data plotted are annual, showing the average value in periods running from July through June.
Values have been adjusted for inflation.
The shaded vertical bars indicate periods of recession.
Source: Congressional Budget Office based on data from the Department of Commerce, Bureau of Economic
Analysis.

Budget imbalance also may result or be exacerbated when a locality lacks adequate budgetary or financial controls. For example, questionable accounting procedures and loose fiscal management allowed New York City officials to mask growing deficits over a period of several years, eventually resulting in deficits so large that the financial markets would no longer finance them.[8] Budgetary controls—including balanced budget requirements, debt limits, and tax and expenditure limits—restrict elected officials' ability to spend more on operating expenses than they raise in revenues. The extent to which states require local governments to comply with budgetary controls varies from state to state. Financial controls, including audit practices and financial oversight bodies, help to ensure that resources are allocated to the purpose for which they were intended. Such controls also improve the transparency and accuracy of information that the locality provides to the public about its operations.

Borrowing by local governments may be both a response to and a cause of fiscal stress. If an operating deficit is caused by temporarily poor economic conditions, issuing short-term debt may help to alleviate those pressures. However, local governments that spend more than they collect in revenues for a number of years usually reach a limit on their ability to postpone reconciling that difference, at which point they face even more difficult decisions.

LOCAL GOVERNMENTS' RESPONSES TO FISCAL STRESS

Local governments can decrease spending and increase taxes and fees in response to fiscal stress, although the extent of those adjustments can be limited

◤ BOX 1

States' Options for Addressing Fiscal Stress

States collectively have experienced more fiscal stress during the recent economic downturn than have their local counterparts, in part because of their greater dependence on more-volatile sources of revenues such as income and sales taxes. For local governments, collections of tax revenues grew in real (inflation-adjusted) terms every year for the past 20 years, and grew 9 percent from the year ending June 2008 to the year ending June 2010 (see Figure 2).[1] In contrast, collections of tax revenues by state governments fell in real terms during a few years in the past two decades and dropped 13 percent from the year ending June 2008 to the year ending June 2010.

When considering how to adjust their spending and revenues in response to fiscal stress, state governments can face a number of constraints. Eleven states restrict lawmakers' ability to increase taxes by requiring more than a simple majority vote for any legislation that would do so beyond some statutory or constitutional limit.[2] Most states also have laws that require the legislature to pass and/or the governor to enact a balanced budget. States' ability to raise revenues (like local governments') is also constrained by their need to retain and attract residents and by political considerations. In addition, state spending is sometimes required by federal laws that impose mandates and by conditions of federal assistance—such as matching requirements for funding for education and Medicaid.[3]

States can issue short-term debt to fund operating deficits and long-term debt to fund capital investments and contributions to pension or health care funds. However, the amount of debt that can be issued is limited in most states by state law or the state constitution.

States often turn to the federal government for assistance during periods of fiscal stress. In the past, such assistance has included grants, tax credits, loans, and guarantees on debt. From state fiscal year 2008 to state fiscal year 2009, federal aid as a share of total state spending increased from 26 percent to 30 percent.[4] The American Recovery and Reinvestment Act (ARRA) provided assistance to states. In particular, as of September 2010, the federal government had sent $71 billion to states in additional Medicaid grants and $36 billion through the State Fiscal Stabilization Fund, established by ARRA. Excluding the additional assistance provided under ARRA, federal payments to states for Medicaid from early 2009 to September 2010 were $453 billion. Also, in an effort to restart loan purchases by state housing finance authorities (HFAs) that faced high interest costs on their debt because of market turmoil and the failure of several debt insurers, the Treasury provided $24 billion to states in 2010. That support, which consisted of purchases of new debt and credit support to increase the liquidity of outstanding debt, significantly reduced debt-service costs for HFAs, allowing them to purchase new mortgages and to support lending to first-time and low-income home buyers.

If a state was under great fiscal stress, it could default on its debt, but the last state to do so was Arkansas in 1933. The federal government could not take control of a state's fiscal operations, primarily because the U.S. Constitution protects the states from federal infringement on their sovereignty. Furthermore, under federal law, states cannot file for bankruptcy.

(Continued)

BOX 1 (CONTINUED)

Notes

1. Many but not all local governments have fiscal years that begin in July and end in June.
2. National Association of State Budget Officers, *Budget Processes in the States* (Washington, D.C.: NASBO, 2008).
3. For a detailed description of federal mandates, see Congressional Budget Office, *Intergovernmental Mandates in Federal Legislation,* Issue Brief (July 2009).
4. National Association of State Budget Officers, *State Expenditure Report* (Washington, D.C.: NASBO, 2009). Many states' fiscal years end in June.

BOX 2

Examples of Investment Losses That Were Disruptive for Local Governments

In the rare instances in which investment losses are extremely large, they can cause severe fiscal distress for local governments. The losses of Alabama's Jefferson County are one example. Beginning in 2003, Jefferson County attempted to lower the cost of its debt for its sewer system by replacing its fixed-rate debt with variable-rate debt. Because interest rates fluctuate, the county simultaneously entered into an agreement with an investment bank whereby the county would provide fixed payments to the bank in exchange for variable-rate payments that the county could use to pay bondholders. That arrangement was flawed, however, because the two variable rates were tied to different indexes. Eventually, those indexes and the payments based on them diverged, causing the county to default in 2008.

Another example is the Orange County Investment Pool's losses in 1994 of $1.7 billion (which were about 22 percent of its assets). The losses of the pool, which was created to manage the revenues of about 200 local governments, occurred primarily because its manager invested heavily in assets whose value would fall if short-term interest rates rose. Beginning in early 1994, the Federal Reserve Board increased short-term rates, causing the value of the pool's investments to drop, triggering withdrawals by local governments and calls by private banks for the collateral held by the pool to back loans.

by state and federal requirements as well as other factors. Local governments can also shift payments and receipts or borrow funds to bridge a gap between spending and revenues.

Decreasing Spending

Local governments reduced spending in real terms by 0.6 percent in 2008 and by 1.9 percent in 2009. Although comprehensive data on local spending are not yet available for fiscal year 2010, according to the National League of Cities, more than 90 percent of the cities that responded to its annual survey expected to cut expenditures in fiscal year 2010 relative to the amount needed to maintain services at the fiscal year 2009 level.[9] Since 1970, local governments have rarely reduced their workforces, but they did so by 241,000 employees, or 1.7 percent, between December 2007, when the recession began, and November 2010.[10]

Contributions to pension funds or health care funds for retirees are particularly vulnerable to delay during times of fiscal stress. State or federal laws generally do not require local governments to make annual contributions to those funds (unless the state fund covers local employees), and political pressures often lead to delays in those payments as a way of avoiding cuts in services or increases in taxes. Local governments also often postpone capital investments during times of fiscal stress.[11] The effects of postponing those investments are often not immediate, but particularly for single-purpose entities such as water or sewer districts, continually doing so may ultimately result in the failure of a system or, alternatively, the need to make a large investment down the line when the funds to do so may not be readily available.

The ability of some local governments to decrease spending is sometimes limited by federal and state requirements, particularly laws that require local governments to pay for a portion of the costs of certain services. For example, more than half of the states require local governments to contribute a share of the costs of the state's Medicaid program. Many states also restrict the way local governments deliver services—regardless of the local government's fiscal situation. For example, many states cover some local employees under their pension plans and restrict the extent to which local governments can reduce their contributions to the plans when revenues fall.

At some point, reducing spending may entail much larger future costs. Deferring maintenance can shorten the service lifetime of equipment or increase future repair costs. Missed pension contributions can lead to large budget shortfalls when benefits come due. Eventually, residents of a locality may decide to move out of the area if service levels are cut (or taxes increased) too much, causing the local government to collect less in revenues than it did before.

Increasing Taxes and Fees

Local governments also can raise taxes and fees in response to fiscal stress. Despite the decline in property values over the past four years, for example, some combination of tax rate increases, lagged updates of the assessed values to which local property tax rates are applied, and expansion of the tax base through new construction has led to increased property tax collections over that period. However, such collections will probably fall in the next few years as the drop in property values is reflected in assessed values; local governments might then decide to increase taxes and fees to make up for the losses. Some states limit the extent to which local governments can increase tax rates or collections in a given year. Those limits most often apply to property tax rates but also extend to sales tax rates, assessments, and fees in some states.

Shifting the Timing of Payments

When spending exceeds revenues, local governments can delay scheduled payments or undertake other temporary measures that balance their budgets in one year by pushing costs into subsequent years. Examples of such measures include selling and leasing back public property, delaying payments to contractors, and shifting pay dates for employees. Local governments that repeatedly use such practices are likely to face higher prices from suppliers, and their payments on leased-back property may exceed the cost of owning those assets.

Postponing contributions to pension or health care funds may also represent a short-term shift in payments.

Borrowing

Local governments can borrow to cope with fiscal stress. Like delaying payments, borrowing postpones rather than resolves the need to pay for expenses, and it may increase those expenses because of debt-service costs. The most common forms of borrowing include the use of short-term debt to fund operating deficits and the use of long-term debt to fund capital expenses or contributions to pension or health care funds. Local governments also may borrow against future streams of revenues, such as the payments from settlements of tobacco cases that some are receiving. Short-term borrowing usually must be paid off within a year to 18 months, depending on state law. Some states allow municipalities to refinance short-term debt with new debt, but in most cases, states limit the number of times that such debt may be refinanced. Prevailing interest rates in the market for municipal debt also limit how localities use debt to finance current expenditures.

Municipalities that accumulate a large debt burden and that are perceived as having a significant risk of default tend to pay considerably higher interest rates than those that borrow more conservatively. Those differences in borrowing costs widen during economic downturns. Toward the end of 2008, the spread relative to the yield on Treasury bonds spiked to more than 5.5 percentage points for municipal issuers of 30-year bonds rated BBB but was less than 1 percentage point for issuers of AAA-rated bonds. Since then, rate spreads for all but the safest issuers have narrowed but remain elevated over historical levels, particularly for bonds of longer maturity. Another factor leading to some municipal governments' higher borrowing costs has been a sharp reduction in the availability of municipal bond insurance. A countervailing effect on borrowing costs, however, has been the generally low level of interest rates.

STATES' RESPONSES TO LOCAL GOVERNMENTS' FISCAL STRESS

States may assist a local government that faces fiscal stress by providing more aid or by allowing the local government to collect additional tax revenues. If a local government experiences a high level of fiscal stress, the state may increase its oversight or even take over the fiscal operations of the locality.

Increasing State Aid or Allowing Additional Tax Collections

Before decreasing spending or increasing taxes or fees, most local governments seek additional aid from state governments. State aid takes many forms, including increased revenue sharing, additional grants, and the provision of debt guarantees. States can help alleviate changes in revenues caused by local shifts in population by redistributing revenues from one jurisdiction to another. Alternatively, states can adjust taxes that cross jurisdictions, such as commuter or nonresident income taxes, to reduce the incentives for people to move to new areas. States also may expand the types of taxes that a local government can impose in times of fiscal stress—such as allowing a locality to impose a new sales tax—or they may increase the maximum tax rate a locality may impose. For example, Massachusetts, in its fiscal year 2010 budget, allowed localities to impose a tax of 0.75 percent on sales of restaurant meals.[12]

Providing Oversight or Assuming Control

In the event of severe fiscal stress, a state may opt to directly oversee a municipality using a financial control board or other management mechanism. At least 15 states have passed laws establishing a method of detecting and managing fiscal stress at the local level. The laws generally set criteria for determining when a local government is experiencing stress, what must be done to resolve the problem, who has the power to implement a recovery plan, and when the local government no longer is subject to the state oversight procedures.[13] Among those 15 states, 7 can assume fiscal management of a local government using a financial control board or other manager.[14] States other than those 15 have sometimes established oversight authorities for ailing governments on an ad hoc basis, by enacting legislation to address the fiscal problems of a single entity. For example, when New York City neared default in 1975, the state of New York established three oversight bodies whose duties included overseeing the city's accounting practices; managing its borrowing and outstanding debt; approving its budgets; approving contracts with employees; and, when necessary, seizing its bank accounts and directing its operations.[15]

FEDERAL RESPONSES TO LOCAL GOVERNMENTS' FISCAL STRESS

The federal government assists local governments through grants, loans, debt guarantees, and certain provisions of the tax code. Because local governments derive their authority from states, federal control of local governments would probably violate the U.S. Constitution, which protects the states from federal infringement on their sovereignty. Therefore, the federal government cannot establish an oversight program for a local government or force it to take action to address fiscal stress; it can only encourage the actions it seeks by attaching conditions to the aid it provides.

Federal assistance reaches local governments either directly, when a federal agency provides funds or other assistance to a local government itself, or indirectly, when a state passes federal assistance through to a local entity. Direct federal aid to local governments makes up a small portion of local revenues: only 4 percent in 2008. Data regarding the amount of federal assistance that reaches local governments indirectly are unavailable; Census data track state assistance to local governments, some of which includes funds that pass from the federal government to states and then to local governments.

Federal aid is rarely provided to local governments specifically because they are experiencing fiscal stress, but aid has been provided recently for local governments in areas that were affected by the economic and housing down-turns and by natural disasters. For example, in August 2010, the Congress provided $10 billion for aid to the states, almost all of which was required to be conveyed to local school districts to fund jobs in education. The Congress also provided a total of $6 billion in 2008 and 2009 for state and local governments to purchase, rehabilitate, and sell foreclosed properties through the Neighborhood Stabilization Program. That grant program required states to allocate funds to local areas experiencing the greatest percentage of foreclosures. Earlier, the federal government created the Gulf Opportunity Zone Tax Credit and Community Disaster Loans programs, which were targeted to localities in Gulf states affected by Hurricanes Katrina and Rita. Several decades ago, in 1975, the federal government helped New York City by providing up to $2.3 billion in short-term loans to the city.

Local governments also benefit from the federal tax code. The largest amount of support has come from provisions that allow taxpayers to deduct local property taxes and either local income taxes or sales taxes (but not both) from their federal tax liability.[16] Substantial support has also come from a provision that allows taxpayers to exclude from federal income tax the interest earned on municipal bonds.

LOCAL GOVERNMENTS' DEFAULT OR BANKRUPTCY

Local governments that experience significant fiscal stress may default on their debt or file for bankruptcy. Default occurs when a municipal government fails to make an interest or principal payment to bondholders or when it violates a term of a bond agreement. Municipal bankruptcy is a process established in federal law that allows a local government to restructure its debt and other obligations under the supervision of a federal court. Both default and bankruptcy are extremely rare.

Default

Of the 18,400 municipal bond issuers rated by Moody's Investors Service from 1970 to 2009, only 54 defaulted during that period. The vast majority of the entities that defaulted were special districts that issued debt to support housing or health care facilities; only six were counties, cities, or towns.[17] In most cases, investors eventually recovered most or all of what they were owed. But defaults on municipal debt have risen in the past few years; this year defaults have exceeded $4 billion.

Municipalities that encounter a large, sudden loss of revenues or an increase in the cost of debt service sometimes default. Both Jefferson County, Alabama, and Orange County, California, defaulted on debt when interest rates moved in an unexpected direction, requiring the municipalities to make large payments (see Box 2). A default may also lead a municipality to file for bankruptcy, in part to protect itself from lawsuits or court orders related to the default.

BANKRUPTCY

In the past 70 years, about 600 governmental entities have declared bankruptcy—with about 170 of those occurring between 1988 and 2005.[18]

As specified in Chapter 9 of the Bankruptcy Code, a governmental entity must meet four main criteria before filing for bankruptcy:

- The entity must be a political subdivision, public agency, or instrumentality of a state (a state itself may not file);
- State law must authorize its governmental entities to use Chapter 9;
- The entity must be insolvent; and
- The entity must negotiate in good faith with its creditors to restructure its debt outside of the bankruptcy, to the extent practical.

Laws in 26 states authorize local governments to file for bankruptcy under Chapter 9. Among those states, 12 impose no restrictions on the ability of municipalities to file, while 14 require local entities to seek approval from a state authority, such as the governor, the attorney general, or a bond commission, before filing. In Georgia, state law prohibits municipalities from filing at all. The other 23 states have not passed laws to address Chapter 9. Local governments in those states would not be allowed to file for bankruptcy unless the state passed a law explicitly permitting them to do so.[19]

To establish insolvency, a judge must determine that the municipality cannot use its reserves, reduce expenditures, raise taxes, borrow, or postpone debt payments to pay its obligations to creditors. In a Chapter 9 case, a bankruptcy court is prohibited from interfering with the municipality's property, revenues, or political or governmental powers. Consequently, the court may not require the municipality to sell property, raise taxes, or remove officials from office. However, a municipality's unreasonable failure to exercise its taxing powers could violate its duty to act in good faith—disqualifying the municipality from bankruptcy protection.[20]

Benefits of Bankruptcy. One key advantage of bankruptcy is the "automatic stay," which is issued by a court and prevents creditors from taking action against the municipality and its officials without approval from the court. Outside of bankruptcy, a local government may incur legal costs and spend time addressing legal claims as they arise, making the task of forming and implementing a solution to its fiscal problems difficult. In addition, paying claims as they arise may cause a government's problems to snowball by diverting funds from municipal services or debt service. The stay prevents such a scenario. Moreover, while a stay is in place, bondholders cannot force municipal officials to raise taxes in order to make debt-service payments.

Another important advantage of bankruptcy is that courts can implement a restructuring plan without the consent of every creditor. To gain the approval of the court, the plan must have the approval of two-thirds of each class of creditors whose interests would be impaired by the plan. Outside of bankruptcy, creditors that did not agree to a restructuring would maintain the rights provided to them in law and in their bond covenants. For example, Orange County's restructuring agreement gave participants in the investment pool 77 cents on the dollar, an amount some creditors would have been unlikely to accept outside of bankruptcy.

The bankruptcy process may also allow a municipal government to reduce its labor costs by facilitating the consent of employee unions to changes in labor contracts. For example, Vallejo, California—which filed for bankruptcy in May 2008—restructured its labor agreements with three out of four unions, reducing its health care obligations to retirees by 75 percent, from $135 million to $34 million.[21] The city also was able to cut its personnel costs for police protection by 18 percent from the level specified in the contract in place before the bankruptcy, saving a total of about $6 million in fiscal years 2009 and 2010.[22]

Limitations of Bankruptcy. Because a restructuring plan requires the consent of two-thirds of each class of creditors whose interests would be impaired by the plan, a municipality may emerge from bankruptcy in an only slightly better fiscal position than it had when it entered bankruptcy. If new debt is part of the plan to alleviate a municipal government's cash flow problems, the government's obligations may be stretched out over time rather than eliminated. Consequently, the restructuring may constrain government operations for years after the restructuring plan is approved by the court. Orange County, for example, is still paying debt service on a portion of the $1.2 billion of bonds it issued in 1995 and 1996 to exit bankruptcy; the need to pay debt service limits the county's ability to cut taxes, cover increased costs of existing services, and pay for new services. In all cases, some of the fiscal gains from restructuring will be offset by the legal costs the municipality incurs during the process.

In addition, bankruptcy does not necessarily eliminate the political dynamics and state laws that may make recovery difficult. For example, in an attempt to emerge from bankruptcy, Orange County put an increase in its sales tax on the ballot, but the measure was rejected by the voters. State laws that, for example, limit property tax rates or require local governments to contribute a certain percentage of their employees' pension costs each year also continue to limit the ability of municipalities to address their fiscal problems.

NOTES

1. Standard & Poor's, S&P/Case-Shiller Home Price Indices, U.S. National Index, 2nd quarter, 2010.
2. Byron Lutz, "The Connection Between House Price Appreciation and Property Tax Revenues," *National Tax Journal*, vol. 61, no.3 (September 2008), pp. 555–572.
3. Christopher W. Hoene and Michael A. Pagano, "Fend-for-Yourself Federalism: The Effect of Federal and State Deficits on America's Cities," *Government Finance Review* (October 2003).
4. National Governors Association and the National Association of State Budget Officers, *The Fiscal Survey of States* (Washington, D.C.: NASBO, June 2010).
5. National Conference of State Legislatures, *State Measures to Balance FY 2010 Budgets* (May 2010) and *State Measures to Balance FY 2011 Budgets* (September 2010).
6. Eric D. Gould, Bruce A. Weinberg, and David B. Mustard, "Crime Rates and Local Labor Market Opportunities in the United States: 1979–1997," *Review of Economics and Statistics*, vol. 84, no. 1 (February 2002), pp. 45–61.
7. Congressional Budget Office, *New York City's Fiscal Problem: Its Origins, Potential Repercussions, and Some Alternative Policy Responses*, Background Paper (October 1975).
8. Ibid.
9. Christopher W. Hoene, *City Budget Shortfalls and Responses: Projections for 2010–2012* (Washington, D.C.: National League of Cities, December 2009), p. 2.
10. CBO's calculation based on Department of Labor, Bureau of Labor Statistics, Current Employment Statistics, Table B-1, October 8, 2010. Since its peak in August 2008, employment by local governments has fallen by 360,000.
11. See Rebecca Hendrick, "The Role of Slack in Local Government Finances," *Public Budgeting and Finance*, vol. 26, no. 1 (2006), pp. 14–46; and David R. Morgan and William J. Pammer Jr., "Coping with Fiscal Stress: Predicting the Use of Financial Management Practices Among U.S. Cities," *Urban Affairs Quarterly*, vol. 24, no. 1 (1988), pp. 69–86.
12. Massachusetts Department of Revenue, "Bulletin: Local Option Excises," July 2009; www.mass.gov/Ador/docs/dls/publ/bull/2009/2009_15B.pdf.
13. Anthony G. Cahill and others, "State Government Responses to Fiscal Distress: A Brave New World for State-Local Intergovernmental Relations," *Public Productivity and Management Review*, vol. 17, no. 3 (Spring 1994), p. 255.
14. Charles Coe, "Preventing Local Government Fiscal Crises: Emerging Best Practices. *Public Administration Review*, vol. 68, no. 4 (July/August 2008), p. 762.
15. Martin Shefter, *Political Crisis, Fiscal Crisis: The Collapse and Revival of New York City* (New York: Columbia University Press, 1992), pp. 132–134.
16. The law allowing taxpayers to deduct local income or sales taxes expired at the end of 2009.
17. Jennifer Tennant and Kenneth Emery, *U.S. Municipal Bond Defaults and Recoveries, 1970–2009* (New York: Moody's Investors Service, February 2010).
18. Andrew Ward, "GASB Issues Exposure Draft on Bankrupt Municipalities," *The Bond Buyer*, vol. 368, no. 33140 (June 30, 2009), p. 21.
19. Chad Farrington, "Municipal Bankruptcies Imminent? Not So Fast," *Columbia Management Midyear Perspectives* (August 2010), p. 2.
20. See, for example, Sullivan County Refuse Disposal Dist. 165 B.R. 60 (Bankr. D.N.H. 1994).
21. Nicholas Gelinas, "Beware the Muni-Bond Bubble; Where State and Local Finances Are Untenable, Investors Should Stop Throwing Good Money After Bad," *Wall Street Journal*, May 22, 2010.
22. City of Vallejo, "City of Vallejo and Police Officers Association Reach Agreement on Labor Contract" (press release, Vallejo, California, January 27, 2009).

21

City Fiscal Conditions in 2011[1]

CHRISTOPHER W. HOENE AND MICHAEL A. PAGANO[2]

The nation's city finance officers report that the fiscal condition of cities continues to weaken in 2011 as cities confront the persistent effects of the economic downturn.[3] Local and regional economies characterized by struggling housing markets, slow consumer spending and high levels of unemployment are driving declines in city revenues. In response, cities are continuing to cut personnel, infrastructure investments and key services. Findings from the National League of Cities' latest annual survey of city finance officers include:

- As finance officers look to the close of 2011, they project declining revenues, with corresponding spending cutbacks in response to the economic downturn;
- The pace of decline in property tax revenues quickened in 2011, reflecting the inevitable and lagged impact of real estate market declines in recent years;
- Ending balances, or "reserves," while still at high levels, decreased for the third year in a row as cities used these balances to weather the effects of the downturn;
- Fiscal pressures on cities include declining local economic health, infrastructure costs, employee-related costs for health care, pensions, and wages and cuts in state aid; and,
- Confronted with these pressures and conditions, cities are making personnel cuts, delaying or cancelling infrastructure projects and cutting local services—cuts that have implications for jobs and national economic recovery.

MEETING FISCAL NEEDS—THE "NEW NORMAL"

Since 2008, nearly all reflections on the economy and on government fiscal position mention the Great Depression of the 1930s that began with the stock market crash on Black Tuesday, 29 October 1929. "Not since the Great Depression . . ." is an oft-used prelude to many descriptions of the current period. A similar refrain is heard when policy analysts and citizens discuss cities. In reality, however, the Great Recession that began with the bursting of the housing bubble in 2007 and the sharp drop in stock markets in 2008, did not begin to wreak havoc on cities' revenue profiles until a few years later.

For cities, the collective impact of property values continuing at levels far below their 2007 peaks, consumer spending slowing as the household savings rate increases, consumer confidence eroding and markets possibly entering a double-dip recession is the worst since the Great Depression. Yet, America's cities are not looking to the past as a guidepost for the future. Indeed, lower property values and declining sales may portend something entirely new, a 'new normal.'

In 2011, 57 percent of city finance officers report that their cities are less able to meet fiscal needs than in 2010 (See Figure 1). City finance officers' comparative assessment of their cities' fiscal conditions from year to year in 2011

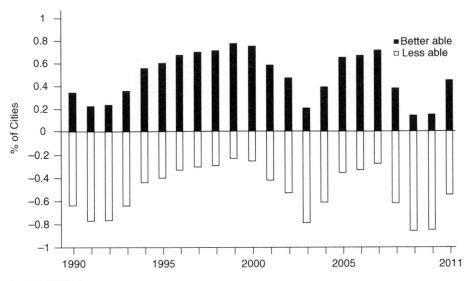

FIGURE 1
% of Cities "Better Able/Less Able" to Meet Financial Needs in FY 2011.

improved from their 2010 assessment, when 87 percent of city finance officers said their cities were less able to meet fiscal needs than in 2009, the highest level in the history of NLC's 25-year survey. The 2011 findings suggest that city finance officers' perceptions are still mostly negative, but they are not necessarily worsening and may reflect a "new normal" in terms of their assessment and expectations of meeting nearer-term financial needs. Finance officers in cities that rely more upon property taxes (73%)—the most common local tax source—are more likely to say that their cities are less able to meet fiscal needs in 2011 than those in cities reliant upon sales taxes (50%) or income taxes (47%).

REVENUE AND SPENDING TRENDS

Cities ended fiscal year 2010 with the largest year-to-year reductions in general fund revenues and expenditures in the 25-year history of the survey.[4] In constant dollars (adjusted to account for inflationary factors in the state-local sector), general fund revenues in 2010 declined –3.8% from 2009 revenues, while expenditures declined by –4.4%.[5] Looking to the close of 2011, city finance officers project that general fund revenues will decline by –2.3% and expenditures will decline by 1.9%.

Revenue and spending shifts in 2010 and 2011 portray a worsening fiscal picture for America's cities. The projected decline in 2011 revenues represents the fifth straight year-to-year decline going back to 2007. Over the same period, year-to-year expenditures have declined in three of the last four years. In comparison to previous periods, the most recent decade, with recessions in 2001 and 2007–09, continues to be characterized by volatility in city fiscal conditions. With a national economic recovery that has been weak or stalled, and taking into account a lag between economic shifts and the effects for city budgets, it seems very likely that cities will confront further revenue declines and cuts in city spending in 2012. (For more on the lag between economic changes and city revenues, see Appendix A).

Tax Revenues

The fiscal condition of individual cities varies greatly depending on differences in local tax structure and reliance. While an overwhelming majority of cities have access to a local property tax, many are also reliant upon local sales taxes, and some cities (fewer than 10% nationally) are reliant upon local income or wage taxes. Understanding the differing performance of these tax sources and the connections to broader economic conditions helps explain the forces behind declining city revenues.[6]

Property Taxes. Local property tax revenues are driven primarily by the value of residential and commercial property, with property tax bills determined by local governments' assessment of the value of property. Property tax collections lag the real estate market, because local assessment practices take time to catch up with changes. As a result, current property tax bills and property tax collections typically reflect values of property from anywhere from 18 months to several years prior.

The effects of the well-publicized downturn in the real estate market in recent years are increasingly evident in city property tax revenues in 2011. Property tax revenues in 2010 dropped by –2.0% compared with 2009 levels, in constant dollars, the first year-to-year decline in city property tax revenues in fifteen years. Property tax collections for 2011 point to worsening effects from the downturn in real estate values, projected to decline by –3.7%. The full weight of the decline in housing values is now evident in city budgets, and property tax revenues will likely decline further in 2012 and 2013 as city property tax assessments and collections catch up with the market.

Sales Taxes. Changes in economic conditions are also evident in terms of changes in city sales tax collections. When consumer confidence is high, people spend more on goods and services, and city governments with sales-tax authority reap the benefits through increases in sales tax collections. For much of this decade, consumer spending was also fueled by a strong real estate market that provided additional wealth to homeowners. The struggling economy and the declining real estate market have reduced consumer confidence, resulting in less consumer spending and declining sales tax revenues. City sales tax receipts declined in 2010 over previous year receipts by –8.4% in constant dollars, the largest year-to-year decline in fifteen years. However, city sales tax revenues appear to have stabilized in 2011. They are projected to essentially remain flat (increase of 0.3%) over 2010 levels.

Income Taxes. City income tax receipts have been fairly flat, or have declined, for most of the past decade in constant dollars. Local income tax revenues are driven primarily by income and wages, not capital gains. The lack of growth in these revenues suggests that economic recovery following the 2001 recession was, as many economists have noted, a recovery characterized by a lack of growth in jobs, salaries and wages. Projections for 2011 are for a decrease of –1.6% in constant dollars, as wages and salaries continue to reflect local job losses and a national unemployment rate hovering around 9%.

City finance officers are therefore predicting decline or little growth in all three major sources of tax revenue for cities in 2011. With national economic indicators pointing to continued struggles and the lag between changing economic conditions and local revenue collections, all indications point to continuing challenges for city budgets in the coming years.

FACTORS INFLUENCING CITY BUDGETS

A number of factors combine to determine the revenue performance, spending levels and overall fiscal condition of cities. Each year, NLC's survey presents city finance directors with a list of factors that affect city budgets.[7] Respondents are asked whether each of the factors increased or decreased from the previous year and whether the change is having a positive or negative influence on the city's overall fiscal picture. Leading the list of factors that finance officers say have increased over the previous year are employee health benefit costs (86%) and pension costs (84%). Infrastructure (79%) and public safety (63%) demands were most often noted as increasing among specific service arenas. Increases in prices, in general, were also oft-mentioned (84%). Leading factors that city finance officers report to have decreased are levels of state aid to cities (60%), the local tax base (53%) and the health of the local economy (42%). When asked about the positive or negative impact of each factor on city finances in 2011, at least seven in ten city finance officers cited employee health benefit costs (82%), pension costs (80%), prices (78%) and infrastructure demands (70%) as negatively effecting city budgets. A majority of city finance officers also cited the level of state aid (58%), employee wage costs (56%) and public safety costs (54%) as having a negative effect.

REVENUE ACTIONS AND SPENDING CUTS

City finance officers were also asked about specific revenue and spending actions taken in 2011. As has been the case for much of the past two decades, regardless of the state of the economy, the most common action taken to boost city revenues has been to increase the levels of fees for services. Two in five (41%) city finance officers reported that their city has taken this step. One in four cities also increased the number of fees that are applied to city services (23%). Twenty percent of cities increased the local property tax in 2011. Since the mid-1990's, irrespective of economic conditions, the percentage of city finance officers reporting increases in property taxes in any given year has been at about this same level. Increases in sales, income or other tax rates have been far less common, as continued to be the case in 2011 (See Figure 2).

When asked about the most common responses to prospective shortfalls this fiscal year, by a wide margin the most common responses were instituting some kind of personnel-related cut (72%) and delaying or cancelling capital infrastructure projects (60%). Two in five (42%) reported that their city is making cuts in services other than public safety and human-social services (services that tend to be higher in demand during economic downturns), such as public works, libraries, parks and recreation programs. One in three finance officers (36%) reported modifying health care benefits for employees (See Figure 3).

The 2011 survey also asked about specific types of personnel-related cuts made in 2011. The most common cut was a hiring freeze (68%). Half (50%) of cities reported salary or wage reductions or freezes and nearly one in three (31%) cities reported employee layoffs or reducing employee health care benefits (30%). Other personnel actions included early retirements (25%) and furloughs (19%). Many cities have used some combination of these types of actions in an effort to reduce personnel costs. The combination of these personnel-related cuts is resulting in a significant reduction in the size of local government workforces. In 2010, a separate NLC survey on local jobs projected a total reduction in city and county employment of nearly 500,000 positions from 2009 to 2011.[8] More recently, the U.S. Bureau of Labor Statistics' latest national unemployment numbers, as of

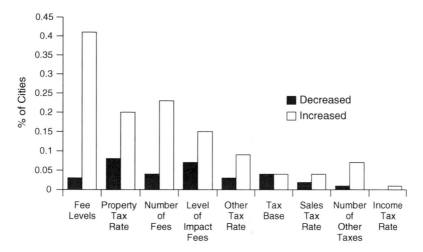

FIGURE 2
City Revenue Actions in 2011.

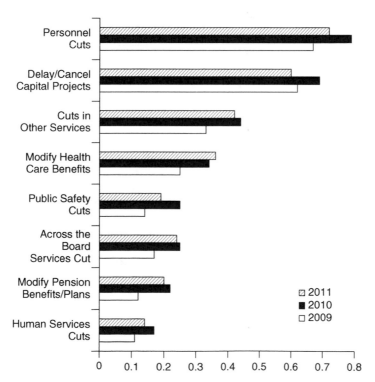

FIGURE 3
City Spending Cuts in 2009–2011.

August 2011, revealed that total local government employment in the U.S. had decreased by 550,000 jobs from peak levels in 2008.[9]

State budgets have also been confronted with several years of shortfalls and constraints. The Center on Budget and Policy Priorities reports that states are facing their fourth year in a row of budget-cutting, with the 2012 cuts being deeper than in previous years.[10] In many cases, the cuts that states are making reduce aid and transfers to city governments. NLC's 2011 survey asked city finance officers about the types of state actions they've encountered since 2009, including cuts in general aid (50%), cuts in state-shared and/ or state-collected revenues (49%), revocation or reduction of reimbursement programs or other transfers (32%), cuts in funding for services that cities and other local governments deliver on behalf of state governments (22%) and transfer of state program responsibility (17%). Amid the politics of state budget-balancing, sometimes state actions are also taken that reduce or limit local authority (13%).

This mix of state actions, taken by state leaders to balance state budgets, adds to the cyclical economic pressures and constraints that cities and other local governments are confronting. Looking across state and local actions in response to fiscal stress reveals the pro-cyclical nature of state-local fiscal actions—that during economic downturns, the decisions that state and local leaders make to balance budgets often exacerbate the effects of the downturn for other levels of government, for jobs and for the quality of life and well-being of individuals and communities.

ENDING BALANCES

One way that cities prepare for future fiscal challenges is to maintain adequate levels of general fund ending balances. Ending balances are similar to reserves, or what might be thought of as cities' equivalents to "rainy day funds," in that they provide a financial cushion for cities in the event of a fiscal downturn or the need for an unforeseen outlay. Unlike states' "rainy day funds," there is no trigger mechanism—such as an increase in unemployment—to force release of reserves; instead, reserves are available for spending at any time or for saving for a specific purpose. Ending balances, which are transferred forward to the next fiscal year in most cases, are maintained for many reasons. For example, cities build up healthy balances in anticipation of unpredictable events such as natural disasters and economic downturns. But ending balances are also built up deliberately, much like a personal savings account, to set aside funds for planned events such as construction of water treatment facilities or other capital projects. Bond underwriters also look at reserves as an indicator of fiscal responsibility, which can increase credit ratings and decrease the costs of city debt, thereby saving the city money. Finally, as federal and state aid to cities has become a smaller proportion of city revenues, cities have become more self-reliant and are much more likely to set aside funds for emergency or other purposes.

Prior to the recession, as city finances experienced sustained growth, city ending balances as a percentage of general fund expenditures reached an historical high for the NLC survey of 25 percent. However, as economic conditions have made balancing city budgets more difficult in recent years, ending balances have been increasingly utilized to help fill the gap. In 2010, cities reduced their ending balances to 17.4 percent of expenditures. And, in 2011, city finance officers projected ending balances at 15.4 percent of expenditures. If this projection holds, since the high point in 2008, cities will have drawn down total ending balances by nearly 40 percent (from the high of 25.2% to 2011's 15.4%).

Beyond 2011

2011 reveals a number of continuing trends for city fiscal conditions. The impacts of the economic downturn are clear in city projections for final 2011 revenues and expenditures and in the actions taken in response to changing conditions. The local sector of the economy is now fully in the midst of realizing the effects of the recession from 2007–2009 and the, to date, anemic economic recovery. The effects of depressed real estate markets, low levels of consumer confidence and high levels of unemployment will continue to play out in cities through 2011, 2012 and beyond. The fiscal realities confronting cities include a number of persistent concerns:

- Real estate markets continue to struggle and tend to be slow to recover from downturns; projections indicate a very slow recovery of real estate values, meaning that cities will be confronted with declines or slow growth in future property tax collections not just in 2011 but most likely through 2012 and 2013;
- Other economic conditions—consumer spending, unemployment and wages—are also struggling and will weigh heavily on future city sales and income tax revenues;
- Large state government budget shortfalls in 2011 and 2012 will likely be resolved through cuts in aid and transfers to many local governments;
- Two of the factors that city finance officers report as having the largest negative impact on their ability to meet needs are employee-related costs for health care coverage and pensions. Underfunded pension and health care liabilities will persist as a challenge to city budgets for years to come; and
- Facing revenue and spending pressures, cities are likely to continue to make cuts in personnel and services, and to draw down ending balances in order to balance budgets.

NOTES

1. This selection is based upon the City Fiscal Conditions Survey, a national mail and online survey of finance officers in U.S. cities conducted by the National League of Cities in the spring-summer of each year. This is the 26th edition of the survey, which began in 1986. The full report was issued by the National League of Cities on September 27, 2011.
2. Christopher W. Hoene is Director of the Center for Research and Innovation at the National League of Cities. Michael A. Pagano is Dean of the College of Urban Planning and Public Affairs at the University of Illinois at Chicago. The authors would like to acknowledge the 272 respondents to this year's fiscal survey. The commitment of these cities' finance officers to the project is greatly appreciated.
3. All references to specific years are for fiscal years as defined by the individual cities. The use of "cities" or "city" in this report refers to municipal corporations.
4. The General Fund is the largest and most common fund of all cities, accounting for approximately 55% of city revenues across the municipal sector.
5. "Constant dollars" refers to inflation-adjusted dollars. "Current dollars" refers to non-adjusted dollars. To calculate constant dollars, we adjust current dollars using the U.S. Bureau of Economic Analysis (BEA) National Income and Product Account (NIPA) estimate for inflation in the state and local government sector. Constant dollars are a more accurate source of comparison over time because the dollars are adjusted to account for differences in the costs of state and local government.
6. For more information on variation in local and state tax structures, see "Cities and State Fiscal Structure," (NLC, 2008) at http://www.nlc.org/FileLibrary/FindCitySolutions/Research Innovation/Finance/cities-state-fiscal-structure-2008-rpt.pdf.

7. The factors include: infrastructure needs, public safety needs, human service needs, education needs, employee wages, employee pension costs, employee health benefit costs, prices and inflation, amount of federal aid, amount of state aid, federal non-environmental mandates, federal environmental mandates, state non-environmental mandates, state environmental mandates, state tax and expenditure limitations, population, city tax base and the health of the local economy.
8. See "Local Governments Cutting Jobs and Services" (NLC, 2010) at http://www.nlc.org/File Library/FindCitySolutions/ResearchInnovation/Finance/local-governments-cutting-jobs-services-rpt-jul10.pdf.
9. See http://www.bls.gov/news.release/empsit.nr0.htm.
10. See http://www.cbpp.org/cms/index.cfm?fa=view&id=3526.
11. For more information on differences in state and local fiscal structure, see "Cities and State Fiscal Structure," (NLC, 2008) at http://www.nlc.org/FileLibrary/FindCitySolutions/Research Innovation/Finance/cities-state-fiscal-structure-2008-rpt.pdf.

APPENDIX A

The Lag Between Economic and City Fiscal Conditions

We often refer to the lag between changes in the economic cycle and the impact on city fiscal conditions. What does this mean? The lag refers to the gap between when economic conditions change and when those conditions have an impact on reported city revenue collections. In fact, cities likely feel the impacts of changing economic conditions sooner. However, because reporting of city fiscal conditions occurs, in most cases, on an annual basis, whether through annual budget reporting or NLC's annual survey, those impacts tend to not become evident until some point after the changes have started to occur.

How long is the lag? The lag is typically anywhere from 18 months to several years, and it is related in large part to the timing of property tax collections. Property tax bills represent the value of the property in some previous year, when the last assessment of the value of the property was conducted. A downturn in real estate prices may not be noticed for one to several years after the downturn began, because property tax assessment cycles vary across jurisdictions: some reassess property annually, while others reassess every few years. Consequently, property tax collections, as reflected in property tax assessments, lag economic changes (both positive and negative) by some period of time. Sales and income tax collections also exhibit lags due to collection and administration issues, but typically no more than a few months.

Figure 2 shows year-to-year change in city general fund revenues and expenditures. It also includes markers for the official U.S. recessions from 1991, 2001 and 2007–2009, with low points, or "troughs," occurring in March 1991, November 2001 and June 2009, respectively, according to the National Bureau of Economic Research (NBER). Comparing the dates of the recessions to the low point of city revenue and expenditures as reported in NLC's annual survey (typically conducted between April and June of every year), we see that the low point for city revenues and expenditures after the 1991 recession occurred in 1993, approximately two years after the trough of the U.S. economic recession (March 1991 to March 1993). After the 2001 recession, the low point for city revenues and expenditures occurred in 2003, approximately 18 months after the trough of the U.S. economic recession (November 2001-April 2003). Our reporting on this lag is dependent upon when the annual NLC survey is conducted, meaning that there is some degree of error in the length of the lag—for instance, had the survey been conducted in November of 1992, rather than April of 1993, we might have seen the effects of changing economic conditions earlier. Nevertheless, the evidence suggests that the effects of changing economic conditions tend to take 18–24 months to be reflected in city budgets.

APPENDIX B

About the National League of Cities Survey

The City Fiscal Conditions Survey is a national mail and email survey of finance officers in U.S. cities. Surveys were mailed and emailed to a sample of 1,055 cities, including all cities with populations greater than 50,000 and, using established sampling techniques, to a randomly generated sample of cities with populations between 10,000 and 50,000. The survey was conducted from April to June 2011. The 2011 survey data are drawn from 272 responding cities, for a response rate of 26 percent. The responses received allow us to generalize about all cities with populations of 10,000 or more.

Throughout the report, the data are occasionally compared for cities with different tax structures and population sizes. Also, the number and scope of governmental functions influence both revenues and expenditures. For example, many Northeastern cities are responsible not only for general government functions but also for public education. Some cities are required by their states to assume more social welfare responsibilities than other cities. Some assume traditional county functions. Cities also vary according to their revenue-generating authority. Some states, notably Kentucky, Michigan, Ohio and Pennsylvania, allow their cities to tax earnings and income. Other cities, notably those in Colorado, Louisiana, New Mexico and Oklahoma, depend heavily on sales tax revenues. Moreover, state laws may require cities to account for funds in a manner that varies from state to state. Therefore, much of the statistical data presented here must also be understood within the context of cross-state variation in tax authority, functional responsibility and state laws. City taxing authority, functional responsibility and accounting systems vary across the states.[11]

When we report on fiscal data such as general fund revenues and expenditures, we are referring to all responding cities' aggregated fiscal data included in the survey. As a consequence, the data are influenced by the relatively larger cities that have larger budgets and that deliver services to a preponderance of the nation's cities' residents. When asking for fiscal data, we ask city finance officers to provide information about the fiscal year for which they have most recently closed the books (and therefore have verified the final numbers), which we generally refer to as FY 2010, the year prior (FY 2009) and the budgeted (estimated) amounts for the current fiscal year (FY 2011).

When we report on non-fiscal data (such as finance officers' assessment of their ability to meet fiscal needs, fiscal actions taken or factors affecting their budgets), we are referring to percentages of responses to a particular question on a one-response-per-city basis. Thus, the contribution of each city's response to these questions is weighted equally.

Sprawl and Regional Solutions

For well more than a century cities and urban regions in the United States have been growing ever outward. During the twentieth century the central cities became ringed by independent suburban jurisdictions; by 2000, the U.S. Census counted 87,849 local governments in the United States. For a long time scholars have noted that the extreme fragmentation of urban regions makes it difficult to find solutions to problems that are truly regional in scope. The sprawled metropolis has also spawned a set of chronic problems; urban sprawl is blamed for everything from traffic congestion and gridlock to air pollution, the loss of open space and farmland, polluted water, and even obesity. And yet it is hard to envision a solution because the old urban form, which found a central city surrounded by spreading suburbs, is giving way to a metropolitan pattern characterized by many nodes of activity. A lively debate is being waged about how to solve the problems of today's urban regions. Some people call for governmental reform, but at the other end of the spectrum some question whether sprawl is a problem at all.

Since at least the 1920s, urban reformers have said that the answer to the worst problems of the metropolis is to reduce the number of governments within metropolitan regions. Advocates for comprehensive reform argue that the fragmentation of metropolitan areas into hundreds of jurisdictions makes it extremely difficult to address issues that exist at a regional level. Despite repeated campaigns calling for consolidating local governments, however, few have succeeded because suburban governments have fought threats to their powers and citizens loyal to the ideal of small government have resisted reform.

The essays that follow provide a profile of a movement with more modest aims called the New Regionalism. Rather than reducing the number of governments, the new regionalists have emphasized the importance of reducing inequalities among suburban jurisdictions in tax burdens and the provision of services and curbing the competition for economic growth among local governments. One of the most heralded victories for the advocates of these goals occurred in Minneapolis–St. Paul, Minnesota, in 1971, when the state legislature approved a plan to partially equalize local revenues by requiring cities and towns in some parts of the state to participate in tax-sharing plans. Local governments surrounding Minneapolis participated in a regional tax-sharing arrangement that required each city to place the taxes gained from an increase in the value of commercial industrial growth into a common pool. The purpose of this tax-sharing scheme was to curb the use of tax abatements and direct subsidies designed to lure shopping centers and other businesses to particular municipalities.

In Selection 22, Myron Orfield describes how the attempt to achieve a measure of regional coordination was accomplished in Minneapolis–St. Paul. Orfield acknowledges that metropolitan reform is difficult and controversial, but he claims it is possible if political movements representing diverse interests are mobilized. In the past, attempts to build regional political coalitions in Minneapolis–St. Paul were built on weak foundations—notably leaders dedicated to abstract "good government" ideals of metropolitan consolidation. Their attempts to build support for reform fell short because they failed to convince voters and powerful interests that their goals were practical and achievable. By contrast, the leaders of the New Regionalism focused on the task of persuading central-cities to join forces with older suburbs, which shared similar problems of decaying neighborhoods, sagging tax bases, and a retrenching local economy. The Twin Cities success in building some measure of regional tax sharing was enabled by this new political coalition—a coalition that, Orfield claims, potentially exists in other metropolitan areas around the country.

The case for challenging sprawl through more comprehensive forms of regional governmental intervention is made in Selection 23 by David Rusk. He believes that the core regional issue is growth management. His discussion shows that the way local government is organized is closely linked with the problems of social division and the quality of life in metropolitan areas. Rusk argues that sprawl has enveloped urban communities all over the United States, but that the problems it causes are worst in so-called "inelastic" cities where central cities have been unable to annex surrounding suburban communities. In these areas, social problems are concentrated in the inner cities while suburban governments capture a disproportionate share of regional wealth. By contrast, "elastic cities," mostly located in the western and southwestern rim of the United States, have been permitted to extend their governmental boundaries more easily. According to Rusk, this allowed them to mitigate some of the consequences of sprawl, resulting in less segregated and socially healthier cities and suburbs. Yet Rusk warns that even elastic cities are no longer able to keep up with the continued sprawl of people and jobs. He concludes that the answer is to create "big-box" regional governments that can contain unplanned growth.

Like Orfield and Rusk, most scholars believe that urban sprawl is a problem worth treating, even if they may differ on how far to go in finding a solution. It is, therefore, important to acknowledge an alternative perspective. In Selection 24, Fred Siegel argues that sprawl ". . . is not some malignancy to be summarily excised, but, rather, part and parcel of prosperity." Siegel claims that fragmented government offers abundant advantages. It enables people who live in badly governed central cities to escape to other jurisdictions that provide an array of alternative places to live, shop, and conduct business. Most of all, he believes that fragmented government avoids the dead hand of a single, powerful regional government that may restrict change. Although Siegel concedes that there may be cases of successful regional governments, as in Portland, Oregon, time will tell if such examples can be copied elsewhere. In the meantime, he prefers to address common regional issues through one-off measures like tax sharing and the prohibition of public policies that favor suburban growth over central-city development.

Taken together, these selections show why an energetic debate continues about how to manage the problems of urban regions in the twenty-first century. Local controversies over metropolitan governance will continue to be lively because despite the obvious problems associated with urban sprawl and governmental fragmentation, people are deeply attached to their local communities and many of them are not comfortable with ambitious proposals to change the way they govern themselves.

22

Building Consensus

MYRON ORFIELD

FORTY YEARS OF MINNESOTA METROPOLITAN POLITICS

Skeptics tell me that regional equity reform will never happen in America's metropolitan regions because the suburbs are now in charge of American politics. It may be true that the suburbs are in charge of American politics. But the politics of metropolitan reform is not about cities versus suburbs or, for that matter, about Democrats versus Republicans.

The suburbs are not a monolith, economically, racially, or politically. Surrounding America's central cities, with their high social needs and low per capita tax wealth, are three types of suburbs. First are the older suburbs, which comprise about a quarter of the population of U.S. metropolitan regions. These communities are often declining socially faster than the central cities and often have even less per household property, income, or sales tax wealth. Second are the low tax-base developing suburbs, which make up about 10–15 percent of U.S. metropolitan regions. They are growing rapidly in population, especially among school-age children, but without an adequate tax base to support that growth and its accompanying overcrowded schools, highway congestion, and ground water pollution. Both the central city and these two types of suburbs have small tax bases, comparatively high tax rates, and comparatively low spending. Median household incomes are also comparatively low: $25,000–30,000 in central cities in 1990, $25,000–40,000 in older suburbs, and $35,000–50,000 in low tax-base developing suburbs. Families in these communities are thus extremely sensitive to property tax increases. A third type of suburb is the high tax-base developing community. These affluent communities, with the region's highest median incomes, never amount to more than 30 percent of a region's population. They have all the benefits of a regional economy—access to labor and product markets, regionally built freeways and often airports—but are able to externalize the costs of social and economic need on the older suburbs and the central city.

From Myron Orfield, "Conflict or Consensus? Forty Years of Minnesota Metropolitan Politics," *The Brookings Review*, Fall 1998, pp. 31–35. Copyright © 1998 The Brookings Institution. Reprinted with permission.

Suburbs and cities can also be surprisingly diverse in their electoral results. Not all suburbs are Republican—or all cities Democratic. In Philadelphia, Republicans control almost all the suburbs and even the white working-class parts of the city. In Pittsburgh, Democrats control virtually all suburban seats except the highest property-wealth areas. In San Francisco, almost all suburbs are represented by Democrats, while in Los Angeles and Southern California, most of the white suburbs are represented by Republicans. In general, Democrats build their base in central cities, move to the older and low tax-base suburbs, and, if they are very effective, capture a few of the high tax-base suburbs. Republicans do just the opposite. In many states the balance of power rests on electoral contests in a few older suburbs or low tax-capacity developing suburbs.

Minnesota has been engaged in the politics of metropolitan regional reform for almost 40 years. Over the decades, three types of metropolitan coalitions have sought to move policy reforms through the state legislature. The first, a Republican-led bipartisan coalition, engaged in some bitter legislative fights; the second, a consensualist-led coalition, eschewed controversy; the third, a Democratic-driven bipartisan group, revived the real-world reform political style of their Republican predecessors. The following short history of metropolitanism in Minnesota suggests the complexity of coalition politics— and my own conviction that, while compromise and accommodation is the necessary essence of politics, regional reform, like all other real reform movements in U.S. history, necessarily involves some degree of controversy.

THE PROGRESSIVE REPUBLICAN VANGUARD

In the 1960s and 1970s, metropolitan reform efforts in Minnesota's legislature were led by "good government" Rockefeller Republicans and reform Democrats—in a sense the progressives that Richard Hofstader wrote of in his *Age of Reform*. Joined by leaders of local corporations, they took aim at waste in government and set out to plan and shape a more cohesive, cost-effective, efficient, and equitable region. Though they sought rough metropolitan-wide equity in Minnesota's Twin Cities, they were not typical practitioners of class warfare. They valued equity because they knew from hard-headed calculation the costs of inequity and of destructive competition for development among municipalities in a single metropolitan region.

In some ways progressive Republican regionalism was an elegant, direct, limited-government response to growing sprawl and interlocal disparity. Joining Minnesota's Governor LeVander were Oregon's Tom McCall, Michigan's Miliken and Romney, and the great Republican mayor of Indianapolis, Richard Lugar. Had the country heeded their far-sighted strategy, the 1980s and 1990s might have been much different for the central cities and older suburbs.

In Minnesota the progressive Republicans and reform Democrats created regional sewer, transit, and airport authorities for the Twin Cities, as well as a Metropolitan Council of the Twin Cities with weak supervisory powers over these authorities. (Making the Met Council an elected body was a top goal, but it failed in a tie vote in 1967.) They also created a metropolitan land use planning framework and enacted Minnesota's famous tax-base sharing, or fiscal disparities, law, which, since 1971, has shared 40 percent of the growth of our commercial and industrial property tax base among the 187 cities, 49 school districts, and 7 counties in our region of some 2.5 million people.

The battle to pass the fiscal disparities act was brutal. Though the legislation, introduced in 1969, had its origins in the ethereal world of good government progressivism, its political managers were shrewd vote counters who made sure that two-thirds of the Twin City region's lawmakers understood that the bill would both lower their constituents' taxes and improve their schools and public services. Some of the progressives' key allies were populists who did not hesitate to play the class card with blue-collar voters in the low property-value suburbs. Probably not coincidentally, the populists collected most of the votes. The progressives pragmatically swallowed their compunctions.

The fiscal disparities bill that passed in 1971 was supported by a coalition of Democratic central-city legislators and Republicans from less wealthy suburbs—essentially the two-thirds of the region that received new tax base from the act. A few more rural Republicans who had a strong personal relationship with the bill's Republican sponsor went along. The opposition was also bipartisan—Democrats and Republicans representing areas in the one-third of the region that would lose some of their tax base. Debate over the bill was ugly. Republican Charlie Weaver, Sr., the bill's sponsor, was accused of fomenting "communism" and "community socialism" and of being a "Karl Marx" out to take from "the progressive communities to give to the backward ones." One opponent warned that "the fiscal disparities law will destroy the state." "Why should those who wish to work be forced to share with those who won't or can't help themselves?" demanded a representative of the high property-wealth areas. Amid growing controversy, after two divisive failed sessions, the bill would pass the Minnesota Senate by a single vote.

Not until 1975—after court challenges that went all the way to the U.S. Supreme Court (which refused to hear the case)—did the fiscal disparities law finally go into effect. The last legal challenge to the law came in 1981, a decade after passage. High property-wealth southern Twin Cities suburbs were finally rebuffed in the Minnesota Tax Court. But representatives and state senators from high property-wealth Twin Cities suburbs have tried to repeal the statute in virtually every legislative session for the past 25 years.

A NEW APPROACH

The tough progressive reformers were followed by consensus-based regionalists whose preferred approach, it has often been joked, was to convene leaders from across metropolitan Twin Cities in the boardroom of a local bank to hum together the word "regionalism." Highly polished professional policy wonks, the new generation of leaders leaned more to touring the country extolling the virtues of regional reform, which many had no part in accomplishing, than to gritty work in city halls and the legislature to make it happen. To make matters worse, business support for regionalism began to erode. The rise of national and multinational companies created a cadre of rotating, frequently moving executives who, facing a more competitive business environment, eschewed controversy in favor of political action that would boost the bottom line.

By the 1980s, proponents of the regional perspective in Minnesota had dwindled to the chairman of the Citizens League, a local policy group financially supported by the region's big businesses; a half-dozen legislators; two or three executives of declining power; and the editorial board of the Minneapolis paper.

Meanwhile, some suburbs, particularly the high property-wealth developing ones that saw no gain but plenty of loss coming from metropolitan action, rebelled. Over the course of the 1980s, as the Twin Cities region rapidly became more like the rest of the nation—more racially and socially segregated—and as fundamental divisions hardened, those suburbs hired high-priced lobbyists and prepared for a fight to dismantle "regional socialism." Metropolitanism's opponents, tough and organized, began to control the regional debate.

During 1980–90, state lawmakers gradually dismantled the metropolitan authority that had been put in place in the 1960s and 1970s. They stripped the Met Council of its authority over major development projects: the downtown domed stadium, a new regional race track, and even the Mall of America—a local landmark that by its sheer size had a thunderous effect on the retail market in central Minneapolis and St. Paul and the southern suburbs. They severely weakened the land use planning statute by giving supercedence to local zoning. They also overturned the Met Council system of infrastructure pricing, abandoned a regional affordable housing system, and shelved well-conceived regional density guidelines. And they took a hard, well-financed run at the fiscal disparities system.

Sometimes the consensus-based regionalists would oppose the changes, but more often they seemed unable to stomach controversy. Their general response to the newly assertive high property-wealth suburbs was to seek accommodation. Meanwhile, developers in the high property-wealth suburbs and their lawyers obtained coveted seats on the Met Council itself.

The first generation of regionalists had fought bloody fights for land use planning, the consolidation of regional services, and tax equity. A decade later, the consensus-based regionalists were reduced to building regional citizenship through a proposal for a bus that looked like a trolley car to connect the state capital to downtown St. Paul. Times, and tactics, had clearly changed.

The proud legacy of the first-generation regionalists was in shambles. In 1967, the Twin Cities had created a regional transit system with a tax base that encompassed seven regional counties and 187 cities. By 1998, what had been one of the most financially broad-based transit systems in the nation was struggling with below-average funding per capita. The Met Council, now in thrall to developers, allocated virtually all federal resources to its large highway building program. Finally, the Citizens League and the consensus-based regionalists, perhaps to curry favor with the rebellious high property-wealth suburbs, used their influence both to defeat the development of a fixed-rail transit service and to fragment and privatize the transit system. By the early 1980s, the southwestern developing suburbs, the most prosperous parts of the region and those that benefited most from the development of a regional sewer and highway system, were allowed to "opt out" of funding the transit system that served the region's struggling core.

In 1991, the Met Council was on the verge of being abolished. A measure to eliminate the Council passed on the House floor, and the governor opined that the Council should either do something or disappear. The consensus-based regionalists, frustrated after a decade of difficulty, were not even grousing about legislative roadblocks. They had moved on to champion school choice and had joined the business community in an effort to cut comparatively high Minnesota business property taxes.

THE THIRD GENERATION

Out of this state of affairs emerged a new type of regionalist, of which I count myself one. Most of us were new to politics in the 1990s, and we were spurred to action by worrisome conditions in the Twin Cities, where concentrated poverty was growing—at the fourth fastest rate in the nation.

To address the growing concentration of poverty in the central cities, we began to investigate reforms, particularly in fair housing, at a metropolitan level. We began to wonder, in particular, whether the sprawl at the edge of the Twin Cities area was undermining the stability at the core and whether the older suburbs, adjacent to the city, were having equally serious problems. As we learned more about the region's problems, we came to appreciate the metropolitan structure that had been put in place 20 years before—a structure severely out of fashion and irrelevant in liberal circles. "What does land use planning in the suburbs have to do with us?" asked our central-city politicos. "We need more of a neighborhood-based strategy," they said. We were also received as fish out of water when we went to the Met Council and the Citizens League to discuss our regional concerns. "This is not what the Met Council is about," they said. "It is about land use planning and infrastructure, not about urban issues or poverty."

In addition to the concentration of poverty at the core, we grew interested in the subsidies and governmental actions supporting sprawl. We were inspired by the land use reforms in Oregon and the work of Governor Tom McCall, Henry Richmond, and 1,000 Friends of Oregon. We read the infrastructure work of Robert Burchell at Rutgers. We became aesthetically attached to New Urbanism and Peter Calthorpe, its proponent of metropolitan social equity and transit-oriented development.

Our third-wave regionalism gradually became broader based. We added environmentalism and the strength of the environmental movement to what had heretofore been a sterile discussion of planning and efficiency. We also brought issues of concentrated poverty and regional fair housing into an equity discussion that had previously been limited to interlocal fiscal equity. The dormant strength of the civil rights movement and social gospel also readied itself for metropolitan action and activism. In only a few years, hundreds of churches joined the movement for regional reform.

We also mobilized the rapidly declining, blue-collar suburbs—angry places unattached to either political party—to advance regional reform. Blue-collar mayors, a few with decidedly hostile views toward social and racial changes in their communities, united with African-American political leaders, environmentalists, and bishops of the major regional churches to advance a regional agenda for fair housing, land use planning, tax equity, and an accountable elected regional governance structure.

In fact, probably the most important element of the new regional coalition was the older, struggling, fully developed suburbs—the biggest prospective winners in regional reform. To them, tax-base sharing means lower property taxes and better services, particularly better-funded schools. Regional housing policy means, over time, fewer units of affordable housing crowding their doorstep. As one older-suburban mayor put it, "If those guys in the new suburbs don't start to build affordable housing, we'll be swimming in this stuff."

Winning over these suburbs was not easy. We had to overcome long-term, powerful resentments and distrust, based on class and race and fueled by every national political campaign since Hubert Humphrey lost the White House in 1968. But after two years of constant cajoling and courting and steady reminders of the growing inequities among the suburbs, the middle-income, working-class, blue-collar suburbs joined the central cities and created a coalition of great political clout in the legislature.

In 1994 this coalition of central-city and suburban legislators passed the Metropolitan Reorganization Act, which placed all regional sewer, transit, and land use planning under the operational authority of the Metropolitan

Council of the Twin Cities. In doing so, it transformed the Met Council from a $40 million-a-year planning agency to a $600-million-a-year regional government operating regional sewers and transit, with supervisory authority over the major decisions of another $300-million-a-year agency that runs the regional airport. That same year, in the Metropolitan Land Use Reform Act, our coalition insulated metro-area farmers from public assessments that would have forced them to subdivide farm land for development.

In both 1993 and 1994 the legislature passed sweeping fair housing bills (both vetoed); in 1995 a weakened version was finally signed. In 1995 the legislature passed a measure that would have added a significant part of the residential property tax base to the fiscal disparities pool. While the measure passed strongly, it too was vetoed. In 1996 a statewide land use planning framework was adopted, and a regional brownfields fund created. Throughout the process, we restored to the Council many of the powers and prerogatives that had been removed from it during the 1980s in the areas of land use planning and infrastructure pricing. In each area of reform—land use planning, tax equity, and regional structural reform—we were initially opposed by the consensus-based regionalists as "too controversial," only to have our ideas adopted by them a few years later as the political center of gravity began to change.

WORTH FIGHTING FOR

Like all real reform, regional reform is a struggle. From the fight against municipal corruption and the fight against the trusts to the women's movement, the consumer movement, the environmental movement, and the civil rights movement, reform has involved difficult contests against entrenched interests who operated against the general welfare. Today, we are told that the Age of Reform is over. We are in an age of consensus politics, when calmer words—"collaboration," "boundary crossing," "win-win" strategies—carry more promise than "assertive" ones.

In every region of this nation, [roughly] 20–40 percent of the people live in central cities, 25–30 percent in older declining suburbs, and 10–15 percent in low tax-base developing suburbs. These communities, representing a clear majority of regional population, are being directly harmed by an inefficient, wasteful, unfair system. Studies indicate that the regions in the nation that have the least economic disparity have the strongest economic growth and those with most disparity are the weakest economically. The social polarization and wasteful sprawl that are common in our nation take opportunity from people and businesses, destroy cities and older suburbs, waste our economic bounty, and threaten our future.

Those who care about these problems must "assert" themselves to reverse these trends. We must engage in a politics that is free of personal attacks and sensationalism, that is conducted with a smile and good manners—like the progressives. At each roadblock, we must seek a compromise that moves equity forward, before we entrench unproductively. We must achieve the broadest possible level of good feeling, gather for our cause as many allies as we can from all walks of life and from all points of the compass. We must educate and persuade. However, if there are those who stand in our path utterly—who will permit no forward movement—we must fight. We must fight for the future of individuals, for the future of communities, and for the future of our country.

In the end, the goal is regional reform, not regional consensus.

23

Growth Management

DAVID RUSK

THE CORE REGIONAL ISSUE

Urban sprawl is consuming land at almost three times the rate of population growth. On the threshold of the twenty-first century, the rate of outward expansion of low-density development is outstripping the ability of even the most annexation-minded central cities to keep pace. The leadership of almost all central cities (whether locked in like Cleveland or expansionist like Charlotte) faces a common challenge: defending their city's viability by controlling sprawl through regional growth management.

Regional growth management must also be a key target of the social justice movement in America. While barriers based purely on race are slowly coming down, barriers based on income are steadily rising in most metropolitan areas. Sprawling regional development patterns are closing off avenues of advancement for low-income minorities. Sprawl is leading to (1) greater dispersion of jobs, placing low-skilled jobs beyond the reach of many low-skilled potential workers; (2) growing fiscal disparities, which impair the quality of services in inner cities and older suburbs; and (3) greater concentrations of poverty, which have devastating impacts on the education of inner-city children.

Strong regional growth management practices, by themselves, will not be instant solutions for all these problems. Growth management is the essential framework within which access to low-skilled jobs can improve, fiscal equity can be achieved, and greater economic integration can be promoted. The political coalitions necessary to secure, through state legislatures, effective regional growth management will also be the source of support for other policies (such as regional tax-base sharing or fair-share affordable housing) that can achieve greater social equity.

HIGHWAYS AND SPRAWL

Suburbanization has been a constant phenomenon in America, beginning with the first national census in 1790 that reported on the "suburbs" of Philadelphia.[1] America's urban experience has been a history of changes in transportation modes that constantly extended urban development outward from the core settlement. However, though suburbanization as we know it began in earnest with mass automobile ownership in the 1920s, it accelerated from the mid-1950s onward. Indeed, America's most influential urban planner may well have been President Dwight David Eisenhower.

In 1956 the Republican president convinced a Democratic Congress to launch the federal interstate highway system. In the midst of the cold war, the new law was styled the National Interstate and Defense Highway Act. In political myth, it was born out of young Major Eisenhower's experience in leading an army convoy coast to coast shortly after World War I—a journey of fifty-nine days!

From a vantage point four decades later, the interstate highway system has been militarily insignificant in our overcoming the Soviet Union. However, the interstate highway system has had a fateful impact on America's cities.

In order to build new interstate highways, federal highway appropriations were ratcheted up dramatically. In one decade, total federal highway outlays rose fivefold from $729 million (fiscal year 1956) to $4 billion (fiscal year 1966). By fiscal year 1996, the federal highway program had expended $652 billion (in 1996 dollars), compared to just $85 billion in federal mass transit aid (which was initiated in 1965).[2]

The great bulk of the 43,000-mile interstate system may be interurban—connecting different urban regions—but its primary impact has been *intra*urban—promoting low-density, sprawling development around core cities. With federal highway grants typically covering 90 percent of project cost, building sprawl-supporting highways was virtually cost-free for state governments. Other inducements to highway construction and sprawl were cheap gasoline (based on low federal and state taxes); easy, interest-deductible automobile loans; other federal infrastructure grants (such as $130 billion in wastewater treatment grants); and housing finance and tax systems that greatly favored homeowners over apartment dwellers.[3]

What picture emerges from calculating the growth of America's "urbanized areas" (as contrasted with the growth of county-defined metropolitan areas)? The 1950 census reported that 69 million people resided in 157 urbanized areas covering almost 13,000 square miles. By 1990 the population of these same 157 areas had grown to over 130 million people occupying almost 46,000 square miles. While urbanized population grew 88 percent, urbanized land expanded 255 percent (almost three times the rate of population growth). By 1990 the average resident of these 157 communities was consuming 90 percent more land area than just 40 years before.[4]

CENTRAL CITIES AS QUASI-REGIONAL GOVERNMENTS

Many political commentators and scholars may decry the absence of metropolitan government in America. However, at midcentury there was still an implicit system of quasi-regional governance in place in the great majority of America's metropolitan areas: the dominance of the central city that spread a de facto unity over its region. Almost 60 percent of the nation's metropolitan population lived in 193 central cities. Most area children attended the city school system. Most area residents used city parks and libraries. Most area workers rode city buses, streetcars, and subways to blue- and white-collar jobs within the city or occasionally, to nearby factories just outside the city limits. Most of the region's voters cast their ballots for the same set of local offices. Although there were often fierce rivalries among ethnic and racial groups, city-based public institutions were unifying forces (except in the legally segregated South with its sets of parallel institutions).

Annexation and merger, of course, were the tools of municipal expansion, and they had been used by even the oldest American cities in their youth. In the nineteenth century, Boston grew from the compact, colonial port town that was besieged by General Washington's rebel forces from Dorchester Heights to a metropolis of 48 square miles. In the process Boston not only absorbed Dorchester Heights itself but the city of Roxbury (1867) and, leaping Boston Harbor in 1874, the city of Charlestown as well.[5]

In one afternoon in 1854, by act of the Pennsylvania General Assembly, the city of Philadelphia grew twentyfold in territory, filling all of Philadelphia County. In the process five of the nation's most populous cities disappeared: Spring Garden (ninth), Northern Liberties (eleventh), Kensington (twelfth), Southwark (twentieth), and Moyamensing (twenty-eighth).

In 1897 the New York General Assembly enacted the most ambitious restructuring of regional governance yet. The state legislature abolished the cities of New York and Brooklyn (the nation's first and seventh most populous cities), combined them with three largely rural counties (Queens, Richmond, and Bronx), and created the 315-square-mile New York City, the nation's first metropolitan government.

By the mid-twentieth century, of course, the territorial expansions of Boston, Philadelphia, and New York were history (and largely forgotten history, at that). In fact, throughout New England, New York, New Jersey, and Pennsylvania, the political boundaries of 6,236 cities, boroughs, villages, towns, and townships were set in concrete. On the threshold of accelerated urban sprawl, the Northeast had become a region of "inelastic" cities.[6]

Growing territorial inflexibility was also settling in over much of the Middle West, which through the Continental Congress's enactment of the Land Act of 1785 had inherited New England's pattern of township government. State laws might provide for municipal annexation, but cordons sanitaires of incorporated suburbs already surrounded many cities, such as Detroit and Cleveland. Throughout the Middle West, townships hastened to incorporate as independent municipalities as to avoid annexation. After 1950 Chicago would succeed only in annexing twenty square miles for the new O'Hare Airport.

ANNEXATION VERSUS HIGHWAYS

At midcentury, central-city officials in regions other than the Northeast or Middle West could reasonably anticipate that annexation and mergers would continue to maintain their "elastic" city status as near-regional governments. They often had other tools available to shape development patterns. Many cities owned and operated regional water and sewage treatment systems; some exercised extraterritorial planning jurisdiction. With such powers, most southern and western cities expected to successfully maintain their "market share" of regional development.

By the 1990s, they had been proven wrong. The highway system decentralized America's metropolitan areas so rapidly and relentlessly that almost no city's annexation or merger efforts were able to keep pace.

Table 1 charts the territorial growth of the country's fifty most annexation-minded central cities from 1960 to 1990. Each added at least forty-six square miles to its municipal jurisdiction—an area equal to the city of Boston or the city of San Francisco. City-county consolidation was the mechanism for most of the largest expansions: Nashville-Davidson (1964), Jacksonville-Duval (1968), Indianapolis-Marion (1970), Lexington-Fayette (1973), and Columbus (Georgia)-Muskogee (1977). The champion of territorial imperialists was Anchorage, which by merging with Anchorage Borough in the mid-1960s ballooned from

TABLE 1

Territorial Growth of the USA's 50 Most Elastic Cities, 1960–90
Square miles unless otherwise specified

City[a]	Area 1960	1990	Increase	Percent Increase
Albuquerque	56	132	76	135
Anchorage-Anchorage	13	1,698	1,685	13,482
Austin	50	218	168	339
Bakersfield	16	92	76	474
Birmingham	75	149	74	99
Charlotte	65	174	110	169
Chattanooga	37	118	82	223
Colorado Springs	17	183	167	997
Columbus	89	191	102	114
Columbus-Muskogee	26	216	190	719
Corpus Christi	38	135	97	257
Dallas	280	342	63	22
Denver	71	153	82	116
Durham	22	69	47	215
Fort Worth	141	281	141	100
Fresno	29	99	71	247
Houston	328	540	212	65
Huntsville	51	164	114	224
Indianapolis-Marion	71	362	291	408
Jackson	47	109	63	134
Jacksonville-Duval	30	759	729	2,412
Kansas City	130	312	182	140
Knoxville	25	77	52	204
Las Vegas	25	83	59	237
Lexington-Fayette	13	285	272	2,088
Little Rock	28	103	75	264
Memphis	128	256	128	100
Montgomery	32	135	103	325
Nashville-Davidson	29	473	444	1,532
Oklahoma City	322	608	287	89
Omaha	51	101	50	97
Orlando	21	67	46	219
Phoenix	187	420	233	124
Portland	67	125	58	86
Raleigh	34	88	55	163
Reno	12	58	46	387

(Continued)

TABLE 1 (CONTINUED)

City[a]	Area 1960	1990	Increase	Percent Increase
Sacramento	45	96	51	114
Salt Lake City	56	109	53	94
San Antonio	161	333	173	107
San Diego	192	324	132	68
San Jose	55	171	117	214
Shreveport	36	99	63	174
Tallahassee	15	63	48	316
Tucson	71	156	85	120
Tulsa	48	184	136	284
Wichita	52	115	63	122
Total	3,383	11,025	7,642	226

[a]Hyphenation indicates city-county consolidation.
Sources: Author's calculations based on census reports.

13 square miles to 1,698 square miles.[7] Oklahoma City, Phoenix, and Houston annexed the most territory by conventional means. Collectively, the fifty cities more than tripled their municipal territory in three decades.

RUNNING HARD BUT FALLING BEHIND

Most of these fifty cities still lost market share of regional growth. . . . As a group, despite tripling their municipal territory, the percentage of the regions' urbanized populations that were city residents dropped from 65 percent in 1960 to 51 percent in 1990. The cities' share of metropolitan population declined more precipitously, from 60 percent in 1960 to 43 percent in 1990.

Over the three decades, only nine cities—Anchorage, Jacksonville, Nashville, Lexington, Columbus (Georgia), Colorado Springs, San Jose, Bakersfield, and Fresno—increased their market shares of both urbanized and metropolitan populations. However, the high-water mark for the consolidated jurisdictions' market shares typically occurred at the moment of the city-county mergers. During the 1980s, for example, Jacksonville, Nashville, Lexington, and Columbus experienced slower population growth than surrounding counties.

Even though these fifty most annexation-oriented cities are slowly losing ground in the face of accelerating urban sprawl, there is still strong justification for continued annexation. As suburban subdivisions are built around central cities, elastic cities are able to absorb some of that growth within their expanding municipal boundaries. By capturing shares of new, middle-class subdivisions, elastic cities maintain greater socioeconomic balance. Average incomes of residents in elastic cities are typically equal to or even higher than average incomes of suburban residents. Tapping broad, growing tax bases, elastic-city governments are better financed and more able to rely on local resources to address local problems. Although no community is free of racial inequities, minorities are more evenly spread out within the "big boxes" of elastic cities. Segregation by race and income class is reduced.

By contrast, "inelastic" central cities are frozen within fixed city limits and surrounded by growing, independent suburbs. By the 1990s, the downtown business districts of many inelastic cities may have revived as regional employment and entertainment centers, but most inelastic-city neighborhoods are increasingly catch basins for poor blacks and Hispanics. With the flight of middle-class families, inelastic cities' populations have dropped steadily (typically by one-quarter to one-half). The income gap between city residents and suburbanites steadily widens. Governments of inelastic cities are squeezed between rising service needs and eroding tax bases. Unable to tap areas of greater economic growth (their independent suburbs), inelastic-city governments rely increasingly on federal and state aid. Suburban areas around inelastic cities are typically fragmented into many "little boxes"—multiple smaller cities and towns and "mini" school systems. With, at best, a heritage of exclusionary practices or, at worst, continuing practice of such policies, the fragmented governmental structure of these little-box regions reinforces racial and economic segregation.

BIG BOXES VERSUS LITTLE BOXES

A comparison of the very elastic cities with twenty-three "zero-elastic" cities illustrates these characterizations (Table 2). As a group, in four decades (1950–90), these twenty-three zero-elastic cities expanded their municipal areas by an average of only 3 percent—in sharp contrast to the very elastic cities' record of more than tripling their municipal areas in just three decades (1960–90).

By the 1990 census, the average income of zero-elastic city residents had fallen to 66 percent of suburban levels, while the average income of residents in very elastic cities was 91 percent of suburban levels. Zero-elastic cities averaged lower bond ratings (A) than highly elastic cities (AA).

In 1990, by a common demographic measure, African Americans were much more segregated within the metropolitan housing markets in zero-elastic

---

TABLE 2

Comparing Socioeconomic and Fiscal Health of 23 Zero-Elastic Cities and 50 Very Elastic Cities and Their Respective Metropolitan Areas

Criteria	Zero-Elastic Cities/ Metro Areas[a]	Highly Elastic Cities/Metro Areas
Income of city residents as a percentage of suburban income (1989)	66	91
City bond rating (1993)[b]	A	AA
Metropolitan Segregation Index[c]		
Housing (1990)	74	53
Schools (1990)	74	46
Poor households (1989)	42	31

[a]Zero-elastic cities are New York, Newark, Paterson, Boston, St. Louis, Providence, Detroit, Washington, D.C., Pittsburgh, Cleveland, Baltimore, Hartford, Minneapolis, Rochester, Syracuse, Jersey City, New Haven, Chicago, San Francisco, Philadelphia, Buffalo, Bridgeport, and Cincinnati.
[b]Bond ratings are those assigned by Moody's Investor Services in their 1991 Municipal Data Book.
[c]For segregation indexes, 100 = total segregation.

Sources: Author's calculations based on census reports.

core cities (an index of 74) than within metropolitan housing markets in highly elastic core cities (an index of 53).[8] For the 1989–1990 school year, the school segregation index matched segregated housing patterns in the zero-elastic regions (74 for both indexes), whereas schools were significantly less segregated (an index of 46) than neighborhoods (an index of 53) in the highly elastic regions. Finally, poor households living in zero-elastic regions were more likely to be segregated away from middle-class households (an index of 42) than those residing in highly elastic regions (an index of 31).[9]

GOVERNANCE STRUCTURE COUNTS

A clear regional trend appears when the two groups of metropolitan areas are compared. Of the fifty very elastic cities, all but Indianapolis and Columbus (Ohio) are located in the South and West, while all twenty-three of the zero-elastic cities are in the Northeast and Middle West, except Baltimore, Washington, D.C., St. Louis, and San Francisco.[10]

However, the preceding discussion on racial and economic segregation is not just a disguised way of describing Rust Belt versus Sun Belt sectional differences. Within an urban region, how local governance is organized has an impact on issues of social mobility.

The clearest impact is on school segregation. In the decades after the U.S. Supreme Court declared segregated schools unconstitutional, school desegregation suits were brought in both southern and northern courts. Southern states (such as Florida, North Carolina, and Tennessee) tend to have big-box school districts that often are countywide. Court-ordered school desegregation plans integrated schools not just within elastic central cities but across city boundaries into the central county's suburban areas.

In the North, however, little-box school districts mirror little-box city, village, and town governments. In its 1974 decision *Milliken v. Bradley,* the U.S. Supreme Court ruled that suburban school districts would not be required to participate with central-city districts in school desegregation plans unless it could be shown that state action had brought about such segregation. With white, middle-class anxiety about local schools intensifying the lure of new suburban homes, central-city school districts like Cleveland, Rochester, and Minneapolis were left to integrate systems that rapidly became heavily minority enrollment districts.

For example, with 115 independent suburban systems, metropolitan Detroit has the nation's most racially segregated public school systems. It is the unspoken mission of many little school boards to "keep our schools just the way they are for children just like ours"—whoever "our children" happen to be. That mission is more readily achieved with 115 separate school districts empowered to erect walls around themselves—a pattern repeated over and over again in little-box regions.

"Keeping our town just the way it is for people just like us"—whoever "us" happens to be—has also been the mantra of suburban town councils and planning commissions in little-box regions. Exclusionary zoning policies reign. By contrast, because planning commissions and city councils of big-box governments are accountable to more diverse constituencies, they are less likely to implement policies that divide residents as rigorously by income, with the attendant consequences for racial and ethnic segregation.

In the 1990s, southern metropolitan areas are less racially segregated than northern metropolitan areas, but not primarily because "black and white

Southerners always lived closer together than Northerners did." That conventional wisdom doesn't stand up very well to historical analysis. In 1970 the average residential segregation index for eighteen major northern metropolitan areas (including San Francisco-Oakland and Los Angeles) was 85 compared to an average index of 79 for fourteen major southern metropolitan areas—hardly a major difference. By 1990 the northern average had edged down 7 points to 78, but the southern average had dropped 15 points to 64.[11] It is the dynamics of housing markets within big-box central cities, reinforced by public school integration policies (and generally growing regional economies), that largely account for the greater pace of residential desegregation in the South.

Maintaining central-city elasticity is important both for the city's economic and fiscal health and for the region's social health. Wherever cities still have annexation powers, they should use them prudently. Whenever state legislatures or local voters can be persuaded to approve city-county consolidations, the effort should be made.[12]

However, even the most elastic central cities cannot hope to maintain their traditional role as quasi-regional governments that largely control regional development. Annexation strategies have been overwhelmed by the sprawl-inducing effect of the federal interestate highway system and the networks of state highways supporting it.

For example, Charlotte, North Carolina, has carried out successfully one of the most sustained annexation programs. From 1950 to 1996, Charlotte expanded from 30 square miles to 225 square miles. In the process Charlotte captured 83 percent of all population growth within Mecklenburg County, the boundary of its 1950 metropolitan area. However, in those same decades, Charlotte's actual metropolitan area expanded beyond Mecklenburg County to embrace seven counties and fifty municipalities covering 3,700 square miles in two states. Charlotte can no longer call the regional development tune. The Queen City must negotiate transportation and land-use issues with other local (and independent) governments.

If Charlotte could not annex new development fast enough to maintain regional hegemony, no elastic city can. Elastic cities of the South and West now face the same phenomenon of sprawling development beyond their grasp that in earlier decades victimized inelastic cities of the Northeast and Middle West.

THE REGIONAL AGENDA

Don Hutchinson, president of the Greater Baltimore Committee, the area's regional business leadership organization, laid out the regional challenge most succinctly. "If regionalism isn't dealing with land-use, fiscal disparities, housing, and education," the former Baltimore County executive stated, "then regionalism isn't dealing with the issues that count."

In pursuit of that philosophy, in July 1997 the Greater Baltimore Committee issued a policy statement, *One Region, One Future,* that urged adoption of three major initiatives:

- Regional growth management policies that lead to redevelopment and reinvestment in older neighborhoods and reduce the infrastructure costs to the governments and taxpayers of the region.
- Policies that result in a system of tax-base sharing in the region. Any system should focus on the growth in the tax base and could draw upon a number of different models that have been adopted across the country.

- A policy for developing affordable housing throughout the metropolitan area. A key goal of this policy should be to avoid creating concentrations of people living in poverty.[13]

Baltimore's *One Region, One Future* is a policy statement that should serve as a model for business leadership in all metropolitan areas.

LAND USE: THE KEY ISSUE

Land-use planning is the pivotal issue. Fiscal disparities, lack of affordable housing, and poor public schools all reflect uneven regional development patterns.

Fiscal disparities arise as new subdivisions, commercial areas, and office parks lead to devaluation and abandonment of older property. Wide fiscal disparities typically emerge most virulently in little-box regions where central cities and suburban jurisdictions alike have fixed jurisdictional boundaries. Elastic cities do not suffer from fiscal disparities. Indeed, elastic cities act as an internal revenue-sharing mechanism, taxing wealthier city neighborhoods to maintain adequate service levels in poorer city neighborhoods. (Highly elastic cities such as Charlotte, Lexington, and Albuquerque annex so much high-end new development that they are wealthier than their suburban neighbors.)

Growing economic segregation in most metropolitan housing markets is a reflection of postwar development patterns. Cities always have had richer and poorer neighborhoods. However, many older city neighborhoods contain a greater variety of housing types than typical postwar suburban subdivisions. As a result, many city neighborhoods contain households that range widely in income.

The greater economic homogeneity of suburban subdivisions partly reflects the fact that homebuilding has changed from a retail industry to a wholesale industry. Postwar homebuilders have learned to apply factory-like production techniques to building sites. Specialized crews (foundation layers, framers, plumbing and electrical installers, sheetrock hangers, roofers) move from site to site with factory-like precision. The result is that, within a given subdivision, a builder will erect large numbers of similar homes priced for a relatively narrow band of potential homebuyers.

Suburban planning and zoning policies often magnify the effect of such industry practices. By setting large minimum lot sizes, limiting the location of (or banning outright) townhouse complexes, apartments, and mobile home parks, local governments encourage economic segregation.

In too many urban regions, where a child lives largely determines the quality of the child's school experience. The problem is not primarily fiscal disparities among different local school districts—the target of many education reformers. The core issue is that a child's school performance is heavily influenced by the socioeconomic status of the child's family and classmates. For example, in communities across the country, 65 to 85 percent of the school-by-school variation in standardized test scores is explained by variations in the school-by-school percentage of low-income students.[14] The most effective education reform for improving poor children's school performance would actually be housing reform: mixed-income housing policies that integrate poor children into middle-class neighborhoods and middle-class neighborhood schools.

TARGET: NEW STATE GROWTH MANAGEMENT LAWS

Growth management is rapidly emerging as the top regional issue of the next decade. There are two key targets: state legislatures, which control land-use rules, and federally required metropolitan planning organizations, which shape the allocation of federal transportation grants.

There are only twelve states that have enacted statewide growth management laws. They vary in effectiveness from strong (Oregon) to almost purely exhortatory (Georgia). In 1999, however, the Georgia legislature created a powerful Georgia Regional Transportation Agency to take charge of transportation and land-use decisions in sprawl-choked metropolitan Atlanta.

The two most recent state land-use reform laws have been adopted in Maryland (1977) and Tennessee (1998). Maryland governor Parris Glendening's Smart Growth Act strengthens a weak state planning law adopted in 1993. The Smart Growth Act ostensibly does not place new mandates on local planning, which is controlled almost entirely by county governments in Maryland. However, it restricts state highway, sewage treatment, and other infrastructure grants (and the federal grants they match) to established urban areas.

Tennessee's new state planning law popped forth virtually unnoticed by growth management advocates nationally. It had an unconventional origin—an obscure amendment to another Tennessee law that was adopted by voice vote in the waning minutes of the 1997 legislative session. To the Tennessee Municipal League's consternation, the stealth amendment suspended Tennessee's annexation laws for one year, wiping out existing cities' powers to veto the incorporation of new municipalities within five miles of their city limits. To ensure against annexation, proposals to incorporate mini-municipalities (dubbed "toy towns" by opponents) sprang up like weeds. By the time the Tennessee Supreme Court declared that the amendment was unconstitutionally adopted by the legislature, residents of unincorporated areas had initiated proceedings to create forty-four toy towns (including one that was simply a condominium apartment building near Knoxville).

During the heated controversy, Tennessee's speaker of the house and the lieutenant governor (the presiding officer of the state senate who had created the stealth amendment) appointed a broad-based commission to review the state's annexation laws. Under the urging of the Tennessee Advisory Commission on Intergovernmental Relations, the commission expanded its mission to consider the broader need for regional land-use planning.

The result was enactment of the Annexation Reform Act of 1998—a title that reflects the law's origins but not its broad scope. Through a complex process, the new law requires counties to adopt comprehensive land-use plans. The plans must designate urban growth boundaries for existing municipalities (which will also be their twenty-year annexation reserve areas), rural preservation areas, and "planned growth areas" (which may allow some "new town" development).

Though undoubtedly not as rigorous a growth management directive as Oregon's law, the new Tennessee law has real teeth. Counties that fail to adopt a comprehensive land-use plan by July 2001 will no longer be eligible for a long list of state infrastructure funds, including participation in federal highway grants.

NEW ALLIES

Tennessee's new growth management law may have been born under unique circumstances, but there is growing public pressure for antisprawl legislation developing in many states, particularly in the Middle West, where no state has yet adopted a statewide growth management law. New recruits to the legislative struggle—business leaders, church coalitions, and inner-suburb mayors—are joining forces with environmentalists and farmland preservationists, growth management's more traditional advocates. Some key examples:

- A new association of business leadership groups in Pennsylvania, the Coalition of Mid-Sized Cities, has targeted enactment of a smart-growth, antisprawl law as its top priority.
- In Missouri a coalition of eighty churches—Protestant and Catholic, black and white, city and inner suburb—is lobbying for a new state growth management law for Greater St. Louis.
- In Ohio the recently established First Suburbs Consortium, initially formed by ten suburban mayors from communities around Cleveland, told the Governor's Task Force on Agricultural Preservation in 1997 that a strong state land-use law might be desirable to save farmland, but it was essential for the survival of older suburban communities.

"Since the late 1940's, policies have consistently encouraged the abandonment of boroughs and cities in Pennsylvania, and discouraged the redevelopment of existing neighborhoods and established commercial and industrial sites," explains Tom Wolf, president of Better York, owner of a multistate chain of builders' supply yards, and a leader of the Coalition of Mid-Sized Cities.[15] In addition to Better York, the coalition includes a dozen business groups such as the Lehigh Valley Partnership, Lancaster Alliance, and Erie Conference on Community Development.

"In the end, no one wins in a system that makes prosperity a temporary and fleeting phenomenon," Wolf continues. "No one wins in a system that has already condemned our cities and older boroughs to economic stagnation and decline. And no one wins in a system that ultimately threatens to do the same thing to our townships. The point is that public policies that encourage sprawl are neither smart nor right.

"We need to change the rules of the game," Wolf concludes. "Most of all we need to change the rules governing land-use planning.". . .

LAND-USE PLANNING: THE PORTLAND MODEL

Across the continent, business and civic delegations, state and local politicians, and professional planners are flocking to Portland to see the practical results of nearly twenty-five years of operating under different rules of the game. In 1973 the Oregon legislature enacted the Statewide Land Use Law. It required that urban growth boundaries be drawn around cities throughout the state. Portland Metro, the nation's only directly elected regional government, is responsible for land-use and transportation planning in the 1.5-million-person metropolitan area. Anticipating a 50 percent growth of population over the next forty-five years, in November 1997 the Portland Metro Council voted 5–2 to add less than 8 square miles to Portland's existing 342-square-mile urban growth boundary. (The two dissenting votes felt the expansion was too little.)

Opposition to greater expansion was led by many local officials, like Mayor Gussie McRobert of suburban Gresham, as well as by many environmentally concerned citizens. Portland's urban growth boundary has succeeded in protecting farmland in Oregon's rich Willamette Valley. If the Metro Council sticks to its plans, over the next forty-five years, only about four square miles of current farmland will be urbanized—as much farmland as is subdivided in the state of Michigan every ten days.[16]

A big bonus is that shutting down suburban sprawl has turned new private investment back inward into existing neighborhoods and retail areas.

Mayor McRobert's Gresham as well as Milwaukie, Oregon City, and other older suburbs are booming. Property values in Albina, Portland's poorest neighborhood, doubled in just five years. As Metro councilor Ed Washington, whose District 6 includes Albina, explained his vote for the small boundary expansion, "We are having redevelopment in my district for the first time in forty years; we don't want to lose it."

By the mid-1990s, Portland's economy had become superheated by a high-tech investment boom. With $13 billion in new, high-tech construction underway, workers flocked to the Portland area. From 1990 to 1996, the Portland area's population grew 16 percent, putting extreme pressure on the housing supply. Housing prices shot up 60 percent, and many area homebuilders and other allies launched a campaign against the region's tight land-use controls.[17]

In the midst of an affordable-housing crisis, the Metro Council adopted a wide-ranging package of regulatory actions and incentives to increase the production of affordable housing. A tough, mandatory inclusionary zoning ordinance (patterned on the successful program in Montgomery County, Maryland)[18] was deferred after several legal challenges before the state Land Conservation and Development Commission that regulates local growth management.

CITIZEN ACCOUNTABILITY: THE PORTLAND MODEL

Portland Metro is the joint creation of both the Oregon legislature (1979) and local citizens (through three separate referenda, including adoption of a home rule charter for Portland Metro in 1992). Covering three counties and twenty-four municipalities, Portland Metro is responsible for regional solid waste disposal, regional air and water quality, the regional zoo, and the Oregon Convention Center. In the new home rule charter, the area's citizens affirmed that long-range planning is Metro's "primary" function. Metro's long-range planning function includes responsibility for both land-use and transportation planning.

Portland area citizens know where the crucial decisions affecting the future of their region are made: Metro. They know when and how such decisions will be made: in well-advertised public meetings after extensive public hearings. (In revising the Portland 2040 plan, Metro held 182 public hearings and presentations.) And citizens know who will make the decisions: the seven Metro councilors and Metro chief executive who are directly elected by the region's citizens. Land-use and transportation decisions are the issues that dominate political campaigns for Metro's elected offices. The result is that there is a much higher level of knowledgeable citizen engagement in regional planning issues in the Portland area than in any other regional community in the United States.

TRANSFORMING METROPOLITAN PLANNING ORGANIZATIONS

A Republican-controlled Congress dominated by self-anointed "conservatives" enacted in 1998 a $217 billion Transportation Efficiency Act (TEA-21). The country is poised for another massive round of federal transportation spending. Over the next six years, the federal government will spend almost one-third as much for highway and transit construction as was spent in the previous four decades. How this new generation of transportation investments will affect the growth and shape of America's urban areas will be determined largely by metropolitan planning organizations (MPOs).

For decades, deciding how federal transportation funds would be used was primarily the province of the Federal Highway Administration and state highway departments. That changed with the Intermodal Service Transportation Efficiency Act of 1991 (ISTEA). In the judgment of the National Association of Regional Councils, ISTEA "marked a radical and visionary transformation of the nation's transportation policy."[19]

Prior to ISTEA, local planning input was largely limited to prioritizing laundry lists of projects within narrow, federally prescribed program allocations. Under ISTEA, MPOs for all urbanized areas with at least 200,000 residents acquired broad discretion to allocate lump-sum federal funds among road, bridge, and transit projects.

About half of all MPOs are "regional councils," voluntary consortia of local governments with a variety of interests beyond transportation planning. Other MPOs are regional economic development organizations, transportation planning agencies, and arms of state highway departments.

In the years since ISTEA was enacted, most MPOs have not had as "radical" and "transforming" an impact as the National Association of Regional Councils originally anticipated. However, transportation planning certainly has acquired a much more local flavor. Had the MPO structure been eliminated (as several key congressional powers proposed), TEA-21 would have dealt a massive blow to the cause of regional planning; instead, TEA-21 will provide continued impetus to the evolution of regional land-use planning.

There has been a uniquely American asymmetry about the relationship between land-use planning and transportation planning. It is inconceivable that a land-use plan could largely ignore an area's network of roads and highways, yet transportation plans often have been developed as if they dealt only with transportation problems.

However, transportation decisions *are* land-development decisions. Who can doubt today that the primary impact of interstate beltways was not to route interstate traffic swiftly and conveniently around major cities (as originally justified) but was rather to generate major suburban commercial, industrial, and residential development? In urban areas the great majority of interstate highway users are local-origin cars and trucks.

Metropolitan planning organizations are federated bodies. Their boards are composed of individuals appointed by member governments and agencies. This raises two problems for organizations faced with increasingly tough, important decisions.

First, the primary loyalty of most board members is to their home jurisdictions. This is particularly true of local elected officials serving on MPO boards (who usually constitute all or a majority of board members). This makes it difficult to achieve an overall regional perspective. Second, federated boards can rarely survive judicial scrutiny when challenged under the "one person, one vote" standard.

PRECEDENTS FOR ELECTED REGIONAL ORGANIZATIONS

Very limited precedents suggest that voluntary regional structures like MPOs will evolve into limited-purpose regional governments directly elected by the region's citizens. Portland Metro began as the Metropolitan Services District, with a seven-member federated board of local elected officials—one each from the city of Portland and Clackamas, Multnomah, and Washington counties and three representing other cities in each of the three counties. A parallel organization, the Columbia Region Association of Governments (CRAG), started as a federated board of representatives from four counties and fourteen cities and grew to represent five counties and thirty-one cities. As one observer noted, "The difficulty in building consensus around a [comprehensive regional land-use plan] reflected a fundamental tension in using the council of governments model to develop regional policies. . . . [CRAG board members] were often torn between the imperatives of regional issues and the need to protect their own community from unwanted costs, programs, or development initiatives."[20]

In 1977 the Oregon legislature abolished CRAG, assigned its regional planning responsibilities to the Metropolitan Services District, and authorized replacing the federated, appointed board with a directly elected twelve-member council and elected chief executive. In 1978 the Portland area electorate approved the changes. (The voters reduced council membership from twelve to seven and renamed the organization "Portland Metro" when the home rule charter was adopted in 1992.)

During the postwar years, another regional organization had evolved in the Seattle metropolitan area. Seattle Metro was a well-respected regional wastewater and transit authority governed by a federated board. By 1992, however, with the growth of the region's population, the Metro Council had grown from its original sixteen members to forty-five.

Controversy increasingly revolved around the makeup and power of the federated Metro Council. After a dozen abortive efforts by the state legislature to reorganize Metro, the debate took a decisive turn in 1990 when a federal district judge ruled that the Metro Council's federated structure violated the constitutional one-person, one-vote guarantee. After further local controversy, legislative debate, and missed court deadlines, Metro Council members proposed merging Metro into King County government. Under the merger proposal approved by voters in November 1992, a single legislative body—the Metropolitan County Council—replaced the King County and Metro Councils, in effect expanding the King County Council from nine to thirteen members elected by district.

To give cities "a voice and a vote" in developing countywide comprehensive planning policies, three new bodies were mandated in a charter amendment to the King County charter: the Regional Transit Committee, Regional Water Quality Committee, and Regional Policy Committee. Each committee has twelve voting members: six Metro County Council members and six members divided between Seattle and suburban cities. The Metro County Council is the only body that is legally empowered to enact plans and policies. However, the County Council can override a regional committee recommendation only if at least eight of the thirteen council members agree. Otherwise, a regional committee's recommendations automatically become law.

A third nationally recognized regional body—the Twin Cities Metropolitan Council—is on the brink of passing from appointed to elected status. Since its legislative creation in 1967, the "Met Council" has been governed by a seventeen-member board appointed by Minnesota's governor. Although members are residents of sixteen districts into which its seven-county jurisdiction is divided, they and their full-time chairman are, in practice, accountable to the governor that appointed them, not to their neighbors. The Met Council functions like another state agency.

For three decades the Met Council carried out land-use planning functions and exercised loose oversight over three regional wastewater and transit agencies. The regional agencies, however, pursued increasingly independent directions. In 1994, seeking greater regional unity, the Minnesota legislature abolished the three agencies and placed their functions directly under the Met Council. The Metropolitan Reorganization Act transformed the Met Council from a planning body with loose supervisory control into an operational agency with a budget of more than $400 million and supervisory control over the $300 million Metropolitan Airports Commission. "After Hennepin County," noted state representative Myron Orfield, leader of the legislature's regional reform bloc, "the Met Council was Minnesota's second largest unit of government in terms of budget, and perhaps its most significant in terms of authority."[21]

A regional public agency with so much authority and spending so many tax dollars, Orfield and other colleagues argued, ought to be directly accountable to the citizens of the region. A bill to convert membership on the Met Council from gubernatorial appointment to direct election was defeated narrowly in the 1996 legislative session but passed in 1997, only to be vetoed by the governor. There are strong prospects that a similar bill will pass and become law in the near future.

DEALING WITH THE REGIONAL ISSUES THAT COUNT

The growing political support for state land-use planning laws and the increasing level of federal transportation grants are leading in the same direction: the evolution of stronger regional planning organizations. In some states existing regional planning organizations are likely to have their planning authority extended into housing policy, regional revenue sharing, and economic development policy. Some may also become vehicles for management of regionwide infrastructure programs formerly carried out by independent authorities.

I would like to offer some crystal ball gazing. Though there is little pragmatic evidence to date, I believe that as regional organizations become more operationally significant and the impact of their planning decisions becomes better understood, public demand may convert some of them into directly elected rather than appointed bodies.

Thus in coming decades, directly elected metropolitan governments are likely to evolve in a growing number of regions. They will not be unitary governments. (Anchorage is the country's only such example covering an entire metropolitan area.) They will not replace the mosaic of local governments as primary providers of local services. Their powers will appear limited but will be vitally important, since they will affect regional land-use and transportation planning, affordable housing, fiscal disparities, and major regional infrastructure investments—the "outside game." These evolving metropolitan governments will deal with the issues that count for the wealth and health of regions and the future of their central cities.

NOTES

1. Unless otherwise noted, all data in this article are drawn from the author's calculations based on various decennial census reports; Department of Commerce, *Statistical Abstract of the United States*, various editions; and Department of Commerce, *Historical Statistics of the United States: Colonial Times to 1970 (1975)*.
2. Executive Office of the President, *Budget of the United States Government, Historical Tables for Fiscal Year 1996*, table 8.7.
3. The outstanding value of all federally aided home mortgages (including Fannie Mae and Freddie Mac's portfolios) was $2.5 trillion in 1995. By contrast, the annual direct federal appropriation for rental housing assistance for low-income households was $26 billion. In 1996 the federal tax code provided $94 billion in tax incentives for homeowners compared to less than $9 billion in tax incentives for investors in rental properties.

4. Over the next three decades, the census recognized another 239 urbanized areas. By 1990, 396 urbanized areas contained 61,000 square miles of urbanized land—about 2 percent of our land mass.

5. By the centennial of the American Revolution, the site of the Battle of Bunker Hill (that is, Breed's Hill) and all other major landmarks of the siege of Boston lay well with Boston's city limits.

6. "Elastic cities" expand their boundaries through annexation or, more rarely, city-county consolidation to absorb many new suburban areas. "Inelastic cities" are trapped within fixed city limits by either bad state annexation laws or being surrounded by incorporated suburbs. For a full discussion of the consequences of city elasticity and inelasticity, see David Rusk, *Cities Without Suburbs*, 2d ed. (Johns Hopkins University Press, 1995).

7. As of 1990, less than one-tenth of the land within Anchorage's city limits was classified as "urbanized" by the Census Bureau.

8. The segregation indexes are "dissimilarity indexes" that describe the relative unevenness of the distribution of target populations. On a scale of 0–100, a score of 0 indicates an absolutely even distribution, or complete integration; a score of 100 indicates an absolutely uneven distribution, or complete segregation. The measurements are made on a census tract by census tract basis (that is, largely without regard to political boundaries). Dissimilarity indexes cited are drawn from a report by Roderick J. Harrison and Daniel H. Weinberg, *Racial and Ethnic Segregation in 1990* (Bureau of the Census, Department of Commerce, 1992).

9. With the assistance of the Urban Institute in Washington, D.C., I calculated dissimilarity indexes for attendance zones of all public high schools in 320 metropolitan areas, based on computer tapes provided by the National Center for Education Statistics, for the 1989–1990 school year.

10. The term *South* refers to the seventeen states and the District of Columbia that maintained legally segregated school systems until the U.S. Supreme Court's epochal *Brown v. Board of Education* decision in 1954.

11. See David Rusk, *Inside Game/Outside Game: Winning Strategies for Saving Urban America* (Century Fund and Brookings, 1999), p. 73.

12. In the 1990s, voters have approved three new city-county consolidations: Athens–Clarke County and Augusta–Richmond County, both in Georgia, and Kansas City–Wyandotte County, Kansas.

13. Greater Baltimore Committee, *One Region, One Future* (1997).

14. See David Rusk, *Abell Report: To Improve Poor Children's Test Scores, Move Poor Families* (Baltimore: Abell Foundation, July 1998).

15. David Rusk, "Renewing Our Community: The Rusk Report on the Future of Greater York," *York Daily Record* (November 20, 1997), p. 2.

16. The Michigan Society of Planning Officials estimates that Michigan is subdividing farmland at the rate of ten acres an hour.

17. Housing prices escalated rapidly in other regions of the booming Pacific Northwest and Rocky Mountain states. Without any urban growth boundary in effect, Albuquerque, for instance, experienced a similar increase in housing prices and for much the same reason. In both Albuquerque and Portland, Intel was building $4 billion chip factories.

18. In 1973 the Montgomery County Council adopted the Moderately Priced Dwelling Unit (MPDU) ordinance. It requires that in any new housing development of fifty or more units builders must make at least 15 percent of the units affordable for households in the lowest third of the county's income range. To compensate builders for lost profits from developing 15 percent of their property at less than market potential, the MPDU ordinance provides up to a 22 percent density bonus. In the twenty-five years under the policy, home-builders have built over 10,000 affordable units in compliance with the MPDU policy. The county's Housing Opportunities Commission, which, by ordinance, has right of first purchase for one-third of the MPDU units, has purchased over 1,500 units as rental properties for very low-income tenants. While economic segregation has increased in most urban areas, Montgomery County's dissimilarity index for poor households has been stable at a low 27 rating—a direct consequence of the county's MPDU policy and other mixed-income housing initiatives.

19. National Association of Regional Councils, *Regional Reporter 3* (January 1992), p. 1.

20. Carl Abbott and Margery Post Abbott, "Historical Development of the Metropolitan Service District," prepared for the Metro Home Rule Charter Committee.

21. Myron Orfield, *Metropolitics* (Cambridge, Mass., and Washington, D.C.: Lincoln Institute of Land Policy and Brookings, 1997), p. 133.

24

Is Urban Sprawl a Problem?

FRED SIEGEL

Suburban sprawl, the spread of low-density housing over an ever-expanding landscape, has attracted a growing list of enemies. Environmentalists have long decried the effects of sprawl on the ecosystem; aesthetes have long derided what they saw as "the ugliness and banality of suburbia"; and liberals have intermittently insisted that suburban prosperity has been purchased at the price of inner-city decline and poverty. But only recently has sprawl become the next great issue in American public life. That's because suburbanites themselves are now calling for limits to seemingly inexorable and frenetic development.

Slow-growth movements are a response to both the cyclical swings of the economy and the secular trend of dispersal. Each of the great postwar booms have, at their cyclical peak, produced calls for restraint. These sentiments have gained a wider hearing as each new upturn of the economy has produced an ever widening wave of exurban growth. A record 96 months of peacetime economic expansion has produced the strongest slow-growth movement to date. In 1998, antisprawl environmentalists and "not-in-my-backyard" slow-growth suburbanites joined forces across the nation to pass ballot measures restricting exurban growth.

Undoubtedly, the loss of land and the environmental degradation produced by sprawl are serious problems that demand public attention. But sprawl also brings enormous benefits as well as considerable costs. It is, in part, an expression of the new high-tech economy whose campus-like office parks on the periphery of urban areas have driven the economic boom of the 1990s. And it's sprawl that has sustained the record rise in home ownership. Sprawl is not some malignancy to be summarily excised but, rather, part and parcel of prosperity. Dealing with its ill effects requires both an understanding of the new landscape of the American economy and a willingness to make subtle trade-offs. We must learn to curb its worst effects without reducing the wealth and freedom that permit sprawl to develop.

Rising incomes and employment, combined with declining interest rates, have allowed a record number of people, including minority and immigrant families, to purchase homes for the first time. Home ownership among blacks, which is increasingly suburban, has risen at more than three times the white rate; a record 45 percent of African Americans owned their own homes in 1998. Nationally, an unprecedented 67 percent of Americans are homeowners.

Sprawl is part of the price we're paying for something novel in human history—the creation of a mass upper middle class. Net household worth has been increasing at the unparalleled annual rate of 10 percent since 1994, so that while in 1970, only 3.2 percent of households had an annual income of $100,000 (in today's dollars), by 1996, 8.2 percent of American households could boast a six-figure annual income. The new prosperity is reflected in the size of new homes, many of whose owners no doubt decry the arrival of still more "McMansions" and new residents, clogging the roads and schools of the

From Fred Siegel, "Is Regional Government the Answer?" Reprinted with permission from *The Public Interest*, No. 137 (Fall 1999), pp. 85–98. © 1999 by National Affairs, Inc.

latest subdivisions. In the midst of the 1980's boom, homebuilders didn't have a category for mass-produced houses of more than 3,000 square feet: By 1996, one out of every seven new homes built was larger than 3,000 square feet.

TODAY'S TENEMENT TRAIL

Sprawl also reflects upward mobility for the aspiring lower-middle class. Nearly a half-century ago, Samuel Lubell dedicated *The Future of American Politics* to the memory of his mother, "who pioneered on the urban frontier." Lubell described a process parallel to the settling of the West, in which families on "the Old Tenement Trail" were continually on the move in search of a better life. In the cities, they abandoned crowded tenements on New York's Lower East Side for better housing in the South Bronx, and from there, went to the "West Bronx, crossing that Great Social Divide—the Grand Concourse—beyond which rolled true middle-class country where janitors were called superintendents."

Today's "tenement trail" takes aspiring working- and lower-middle class Americans to quite different areas. Kendall, Florida, 20 miles southeast of Miami, is every environmentalist's nightmare image of sprawl, a giant grid carved out of the muck of swamp land that encroaches on the Everglades. Stripmalls and mega-stores abound for mile after mile, as do the area's signature giant auto lots. Yet Kendall also represents a late-twentieth-century version of the Old Tenement Trail. Kendall, notes the *New Republic's* Charles Lane, is "the Queens of the late twentieth century," a place where immigrants are buying into America. Carved out of the palmetto wilderness, its population exploded from roughly 20,000 in 1970 to 300,000 today. Agricultural in the 1960s, and a hip place for young whites in the 1970s, Kendall grew increasingly Hispanic in the 1980s, as Cubans, Nicaraguans, and others who arrived with very little worked their way up. Today, it's half Hispanic and a remarkable example of integration. In most of Kendall, notes University of Miami geographer Peter Muller, "You can't point to a white or Latino block because the populations are so intermixed."

Virginia Postrel, the editor of *Reason*, argues that the slow-growth movement is animated by left-wing planners' hostility to suburbia. Others mock slow-growthers as elitists, as in the following quip:

Q: What's the difference between an environmentalist and a developer?
A: The environmentalist already has his house in the mountains.

But, in the 1990s, slow-growth sentiment has been taking hold in middle- and working-class suburbs like Kendall, as development turns into overdevelopment and traffic congestion becomes a daily problem.

REGIONAL GOVERNMENT

One oft-proposed answer to sprawl has been larger regional governments that will exercise a monopoly on land-use decisions. Underlying this solution is the theory—no doubt correct—that sprawl is produced when individuals and townships seek to maximize their own advantage without regard for the good of the whole community. Regionalism, however, is stronger in logic than in practice. For example, the people of Kendall, rather than embracing regionalism, are looking to slow down growth by *seceding* from their regional government. Upon examination, we begin to see some of the problems with regional government.

Kendall is part of Metro-Dade, the oldest major regional government, created in 1957. The largest of its 29 municipalities, Miami, the fourth poorest city in the United States, has 350,000 people; the total population of Metro-Dade is 2 million, 1.1 million of whom live in unincorporated areas. In Metro-Dade, antisprawl and antiregional government sentiments merge. Despite county-imposed growth boundaries, residents have complained bitterly of overdevelopment. The county commissioners—many of whom have been convicted of, or charged with, corruption—have been highly receptive to the developers who are among their largest campaign contributors. As one south Florida resident said of the developers, "It's a lot cheaper to be able to buy just one government." The south Florida secessionists want to return zoning to local control where developers' clout is less likely to overwhelm neighborhood interests.

When Jane Jacobs wrote, in *The Death and Life of Great American Cities,* that "the voters sensibly decline to federate into a system where bigness means local helplessness, ruthless oversimplified planning and administrative chaos," she could have been writing about south Florida. What's striking about Metro-Dade is that it has delivered neither efficiency nor equity nor effective planning while squelching local self-determination.

The fight over Metro-Dade echoes the conflicts of an earlier era. Historically, the fight over regional versus local government was an important, if intermittent, issue for many cities from 1910 to 1970. From about 1850 to 1910, according to urban historian Jon Teaford, suburbanites were eager to be absorbed by cities whose wealth enabled them to build the water, sewage, and road systems they couldn't construct on their own. "The central city," he explains, "provided superior service at a lower cost." But, in the 1920s, well before race became a central issue, suburbanites, who had increasingly sorted themselves out by ethnicity and class, began to use special-service districts and innovative financial methods to provide their own infrastructure and turned away from unification. Suburbanites also denounced consolidation as an invitation to big-city, and often Catholic, "boss rule" and as a threat to "self-government."

In the 1960s, as black politicians began to win influence over big-city governments, they also joined the anticonsolidation chorus. At the same time, county government, once a sleepy extension of rural rule, was modernized, and county executives essentially became the mayors of full-service governments administering what were, in effect, dispersed cities. But they were mayors with a difference. Their constituents often wanted a balance between commercial development, which constrained the rise of taxes, and the suburban ideal of family-friendly semirural living. When development seemed too intrusive, suburban voters in the 1980s, and again in the 1990s, have pushed a slow-growth agenda.

THE NEW REGIONALISM

In the 1990s, regionalism has been revived as an effort to link the problem of sprawl with the problem of inner-city poverty. Assuming that "flight creates blight," regionalists propose to recapture the revenue of those who have fled the cities and force growth back into older areas by creating regional or metropolitan-area governments with control over land use and taxation.

The new regionalism owes a great deal to a group of circuit-riding reformers. Inspired by the arguments of scholars like Anthony Downs, one of the authors of the Kerner Commission report, and sociologist William Julius Wilson of Harvard, as well as the example of Portland, Oregon's metro-wide government, these itinerant preachers have traveled to hundreds of cities to spread the gospel of regional cooperation. The three most prominent new regionalists—columnist Neil Peirce, former Albuquerque mayor David Rusk, and Minnesota state representative Myron Orfield—have developed a series of distinct, but overlapping, arguments for why cities can't help themselves, and why regional solutions are necessary.

Peirce, in his book *Citistates,* plausibly insists that regions are the real units of competition in the global economy, so that there is a metro-wide imperative to revive the central city, lest the entire area be undermined. Less plausibly, Orfield in *Metropolitics* argues that what he calls "the favored quarter" of fast-growing suburbs on the periphery of the metro area have prospered at the expense of both the central city and the inner-ring suburbs. In order both to revive the central city and save the inner suburbs from decline, Orfield proposes that these two areas join forces, redistributing money from the "favored quarter" to the older areas. Rusk argues, in *Baltimore Unbound,* that older cities, unable to annex the fast growing suburbs, are doomed to further decline. He insists that only "flexible cities"—that is, cities capable of expanding geographically and capturing the wealth of the suburbs—can truly deal with inner-city black poverty. Regionalism, writes Rusk, is "the new civil rights movement."

There are differences among them. Orfield and, to a lesser degree, Rusk operate on a zero-sum model in which gain for the suburbs comes directly at the expense of the central city. Peirce is less radical, proposing regional cooperation as the means to a win-win situation for both city and the surrounding region. But they all share a desire to disperse poverty across the region and, more importantly, recentralize economic growth in the already built-up areas. The latter goal is consistent with both the environmental thrust of the antisprawl movement and the push for regional government. In a speech to a Kansas City civic organization, Rusk laid out the central assumption of the new regionalism. "The greater the fragmentation of governments," he asserted, "the greater the fragmentation of society by race and economic class." Fewer governments, argue the new regionalists, will yield a number of benefits, including better opportunities for regional cooperation, more money for cash-strapped central cities, less racial inequality, less sprawl, and greater economic growth. However, all of these propositions are questionable.

BETTER POLICIES, NOT FEWER GOVERNMENTS

Consider Baltimore and Philadelphia, cities that the regionalists have studied thoroughly. According to the 1998 *Greater Baltimore State of the Region* report, Philadelphia has 877 units of local government (including school boards)—or 17.8 per 100,000 people. Baltimore has only six government units of any consequence in Baltimore City and the five surrounding counties—or 2.8 per 100,000 people. Greater Baltimore has fewer government units than any other major metro area in the United States. As a political analyst told me: "Get six people in a room, and you have the government of 2,200 square miles, because the county execs have very strong powers." We might expect considerable regional cooperation in Baltimore, but not in Philadelphia. Regionalism has made no headway in either city, however. The failure has little to do with the number of governments and a great deal to do with failed policy choices in both cities.

Rusk does not mention the many failings of Baltimore's city government. He refers to the current mayor, Kurt Schmoke, just once and only to say that Baltimore has had "excellent political leadership." In Rusk's view, Baltimore is "programmed to fail" because of factors entirely beyond its control, namely, the inability to annex its successful suburbs. In the ahistorical world of the regionalist (and here, Peirce is a partial exception), people are always pulled from the city by structural forces but never pushed from the city by bad policies.

Baltimore is not as well financed as the District of Columbia, which ruined itself despite a surfeit of money. But Baltimore, a favorite political son of both Annapolis and Washington, has been blessed with abundant financial support. Over the past decade, Schmoke has increased spending on education and health by over a half-billion dollars. He has also added 200 police officers and spent $60 million more for police over the last four years. "His greatest skill," notes the *Baltimore Sun*, "has been his ability to attract more federal and state aid while subsidies diminished elsewhere." But, notwithstanding these expenditures, middle-class families continue to flee the city at the rate of 1,000 per month, helping to produce the sprawl environmentalists decry.

Little in Baltimore works well. The schools have been taken over by the state, while the Housing Authority is mired in perpetual scandal and corruption. Baltimore is one of the few cities where crime hasn't gone down. That's because Schmoke has insisted, contrary to the experiences of New York and other cities, that drug-related crime could not be reduced until drug use was controlled through treatment. The upshot is that New York, with eight times more people than Baltimore, has only twice as many murders. Baltimore also leads the country in sexually transmitted diseases. These diseases have flourished among the city's drug users partly owing to Schmoke's de facto decriminalization of drugs. According to the Centers for Disease Control and Prevention (CDC), Baltimore has a syphilis rate 18 times the national average, 3 or 4 times as high as areas where the STD epidemic is most concentrated.

FLEXIBLE CITIES

Rusk attributes extraordinary qualities to flexible cities. He says that they are able to both reduce inequality, curb sprawl, and maintain vital downtowns. Rusk was the mayor of Albuquerque, a flexible city that annexed a vast area, even as its downtown essentially died. The reduced inequality he speaks of is largely a statistical artifact. If New York were to annex Scarsdale, East New York's average income would rise without having any effect on the lives of the people who live there. As for sprawl, flexible cities like Phoenix and Houston are hardly models.

A recent article for *Urban Affairs Review,* by Subhrajit Guhathakurta and Michele Wichert, showed that within the elastic city of Phoenix, inner-city residents poorer than their outer-ring neighbors are subsidizing the building of new developments on the fringes of the metropolis. While sprawl is correlated with downtown decline in Albuquerque, in Phoenix it's connected with what *Fortune* described as "the remarkable rebound of downtown Phoenix, which has become a chic after-dark destination as well as a residential hot spot." There seems to be no automatic connection between regionalism and downtown revival.

Orfield's *Metropolitics* provides another version of an over-determined structuralist argument. According to him, the favored quarter is sucking the inner-city dry, and, as a result, central-city blight will inevitably engulf the older first-ring suburbs as well. He is right to see strong pressures on the inner-ring suburbs, stemming from an aging housing stock and population as well as an influx of inner-city poor. But it is how the inner-ring suburbs respond to these pressures that will affect their fate.

When Coleman Young was mayor of Detroit, large sections of the city returned to prairie. But the inner-ring suburbs have done fairly well precisely by not imitating Detroit's practice of providing poor services at premium prices. "Much like the new edge suburbs," explains the *Detroit News,* "older suburbs that follow the proven formula of promoting good schools, public safety and well-kept housing attract new investment." Suburban Mayor Michael Guido sees his city's well developed infrastructure as an asset, which has already been bought and paid for. "Now," says Mayor Guido, "it's a matter of maintenance . . . and we offer a sense of history and a sense of community. That's really important to people, to have a sense of belonging to a whole community rather than a subdivision."

SUBURB POWER

City-suburban relations are not fixed; they are various depending on the policies both follow. Some suburbs compete with the central city for business. In south Florida, Coral Gables more than holds its own with Miami as a site for business headquarters. Southfield, just outside Detroit, and Clayton, just outside St. Louis, blossomed in the wake of the 1960s' urban riots and now compete with their downtowns. Aurora, with a population of more than 160,000 and to the east of Denver, sees itself as a competitor, and it sees regional efforts at growth management as a means by which the downtown Denver elite can ward off competition.

Suburban growth can also help the central city. In the Philadelphia area, economic growth and new work come largely from the Route 202 high-tech corridor in Chester County, west of the city. While the city has lost 57,000 jobs, even in the midst of national economic prosperity, the fast growing Route 202 companies have been an important source of downtown legal and accounting jobs. At the same time, the suburbs are creating jobs for residents that the central city cannot produce, so that 20 percent of city residents commute to the suburbs while 15 percent of people who live in the suburbs commute to Philadelphia.

The "new regionalists" assume that the prosperity of the edge cities is a function of inner-city decline. But, in many cities, it is more nearly the case that suburban booms are part of what's keeping the central-city economy alive. It is the edge cities that have taken up the time-honored urban task of creating new work.

According to *INC* magazine, the 500 fastest growing small companies are all located in suburbs and exurbs. This is because local governments there are very responsive to the needs of start-up companies. These high-tech hotbeds, dubbed "nerdistans" by Joel Kotkin, are composed of networks of companies that are sometimes partners, sometimes competitors. They provide a pool of seasoned talent for start-ups, where engineers and techies who prefer the orderly, outdoor life of suburbia to the crowds and disorder of the city can move from project to project. Henry Nicholas, CEO of Broadcom, a communications-chip and cable-modem maker, explained why he reluctantly moved to Irvine: "It's hard to relocate techies to L.A. It's the congestion, the expensive housing—and there's a certain stigma to it."

Imagine what the United States would be like if the Bay Area had followed the New York model. In 1898, New York created the first regional government when it consolidated all the areas of the New York harbor—Manhattan, Brooklyn, Queens, the Bronx, and Staten Island—into the then-largest city in the world. The consolidation has worked splendidly for Manhattan, which thrives as a capital of high-end financial and legal services. But over time, the Manhattan-centric economy based on high taxes, heavy social spending, and extensive economic regulation destroyed Brooklyn's once vital shipping and manufacturing economy.

In 1912, San Francisco, the Manhattan of Northern California, proposed to create a unified regional government by incorporating Oakland in the East Bay and San Jose in the South. The plan for a Greater San Francisco was modeled on Greater New York and called for the creation of self-governing boroughs within an enlarged city and county of San Francisco. East Bay opposition defeated the San Francisco expansion in the legislature, and later attempts at consolidation in 1917, 1923, and 1928 also failed. But had San Francisco with its traditions of high taxation and heavy regulation succeeded, Silicon Valley might never have become one of the engines of the American economy. Similarly, it's no accident that the Massachusetts Route 128 high-tech corridor is located outside of the boundaries of Boston, even as it enriches the central city.

THE PORTLAND MODEL

The complex and often ironic history of existing regional governments has been obscured by the bright light of hope emanating from Portland. It seems that in every generation one city is said to have perfected the magic elixir for revival. In the 1950s, it was Philadelphia; today, it's Portland. In recent years, hundreds of city officials have traveled to Portland to study its metropolitan government, comprehensive environmental planning, and the urban-growth boundary that has been credited with Portland's revival and success.

While there are important lessons to be learned from Portland, very little of its success to date can be directly attributed to the growth boundary, which was introduced too recently and with boundaries so capacious as not yet to have had much effect. Thirty-five percent of the land within the boundary was vacant when it was imposed in 1979. And, at the same time, fast growing Clark County, just north of Portland but not part of the urban-growth boundary, has provided an escape valve for potential housing pressures. The upshot, notes demographer Wendell Cox, is that even with the growth boundary, Portland still remains a relatively low-density area with fewer people per square mile than San Diego, San Jose, or Sacramento.

Portland has also been run with honesty and efficiency, unlike Metro-Dade. Blessed with great natural resources, Portland—sometimes dubbed "Silicon forest," because chipmakers are drawn to its vast quantities of cheap clean water—has conserved its man-made as well as natural resources. A city with more cast-iron buildings than any place outside of Manhattan, it has been a leader in historic preservation. Time and again, Portland's leadership has made the right choices. It was one of the first cities to reconnect its downtown with the riverfront. Portland never built a circumferential freeway. And, in the 1970s, under the leadership of Mayor Neil Goldschmidt, the city vetoed a number of proposed highway projects that would have threatened the downtown.

In 1978, Portland voters, in conjunction with the state government, created the first directly elected metropolitan government with the power to manage growth over three counties. Portland metro government has banned big-box retailers, like Walmart and Price Club, on the grounds that they demand too much space and encourage too much driving. This is certainly an interesting experiment well worth watching, but should other cities emulate Portland's land-management model? It's too soon to say.

Good government is always important. But aside from that, it's hard to draw any general lessons from the Portland experience. The growth boundaries may or may not work, and there's certainly no reason to think that playing with political boundaries will bring good government to Baltimore.

LIVING WITH SPRAWL

What then is to be done? First, we can accept the consensus that has developed around preserving open space, despite some contradictory effects. The greenbelts around London, Portland, and Baltimore County pushed some development back toward the city and encouraged further sprawl as growth leapfrogged the open space. The push to preserve open space is only likely to grow stronger as continued growth generates both more congestion and more wealth, which can be used to buy up open land.

Secondly, we can create what Peter Salins, writing in *The Public Interest*[1] described as a "level playing field" between the central cities and the suburbs. This can be done by ending exurban growth subsidies for both transportation as well as new water and sewer lines. These measures might further encourage the revival of interest in old fashioned Main Street living, which is already attracting a new niche of home buyers. State and local governments can also repeal the land-use and zoning regulations that discourage mixed-use development of the sort that produces a clustering of housing around Main Street and unsubsidized low-cost housing in the apartments above the streets' shops.

Because of our strong traditions of local self-government, regionalism has been described as an unnatural act among consenting jurisdictions. But regional cooperation needn't mean the heavy hand of all-encompassing regional government. There are some modest, but promising, experiments already under way in regional revenue sharing whose effects should be carefully evaluated. Allegheny County, which includes Pittsburgh, has created a Regional Asset District that uses a 1 percent sales tax increase to support cultural institutions and reduce other taxes. The Twin Cities have put money derived from the increase in assessed value of commercial and industrial properties into a pot to aid fiscally weaker municipalities. Kansas and Missouri created a cultural district that levies a small increase in the sales tax across the region. The money is being used to rehabilitate the area's most treasured architectural landmark, Kansas City's Union Station.

Cities and suburbs do have some shared interests, as in the growing practice of reverse commuting which links inner-city residents looking to get off welfare with fast growing suburban areas hampered by a shortage of labor. Regionalism can curb sprawl and integrate and sustain central-city populations if it reforms the misguided policies and politics that have sent the black and white middle class streaming out of cities like Baltimore, Washington, and Philadelphia. Regional cooperation between the sprawling high-tech suburbs and the central cities could modernize cities that are in danger of being left further behind by the digital economy. In that vein, the District of Columbia's Mayor Anthony Williams seized on the importance of connecting his welfare population with the fast growing areas of Fairfax County in Northern Virginia. The aim of focused regional policies, argues former HUD Undersecretary Marc Weiss, should be economic, not political, integration.

Sprawl isn't some malignancy that can be surgically removed. It's been part and parcel of healthy growth, and curbing it involves difficult tradeoffs best worked out locally. Sprawl and the movement against sprawl are now a permanent part of the landscape. The future is summed up in a quip attributed to former Oregon Governor Tom McCall, who was instrumental in creating Portland's growth boundary. "Oregonians," he said, "are against two things, sprawl and density."

NOTES

1. "Cities, Suburbs, and the Urban Crisis," *The Public Interest*, No. 113 (Fall 1993).

The Politics of Urban Resilience

"**R**esilient" cities and urban regions are adaptable enough to cope with the challenges posed both by sudden disasters and longer-term trends that threaten the health, welfare, and well-being of their citizens. Globalization has brought some new threats. The relationship of citizens to American cities has been challenged by the rise of international terrorism. In the aftermath of terrorist strikes here and abroad, scholars and citizens are debating the strategies that might be used to reduce the possibilities that terrorism events may occur, and how to make the cities resilient when they do. Some believe that security threats may fundamentally change urban life. Physical changes include the "hardening" of buildings, dispersing economic activities, and undertaking an enlarged and intrusive police presence. Some observers have even suggested that terrorism challenges the viability of all densely settled communities. Catastrophic natural disasters raise similar issues.

The terrorist attacks on New York City on September 11, 2001, showed that cities and urban regions that are able to respond to major disasters can recover quite rapidly. In contrast, when New Orleans was overwhelmed by Hurricane Katrina on August 29, 2005, it became apparent that urban infrastructure, urban resources, and governmental capacity were not sufficient to respond immediately to the disaster or to deal adequately with its long-term consequences. The Great Recession that began in 2008 and the accompanying mortgage meltdown shows that shocks to urban systems may come in many forms, and that cities and urban regions will be confronting different kinds of stresses in coming decades. These stresses have many causes: air, water and soil pollution; the local impacts of global climate change; large-scale demographic movements; uneven economic growth; poverty, unemployment, crime, and social conflict; and increasing demands for mobility, energy, and water.

Politics and governance are central factors in determining urban resilience. To respond to natural and man-made disasters and gradual environmental changes, cities must possess the ability to design, finance, and manage complex urban infrastructures needed for a secure social and physical environment. They must be able to do something else as well: maintain strong social and political systems capable of change. In the wake of the events of 9/11, Hurricane Katrina, and more recent disasters such as tornadoes, flooding, and fires, a debate has broken out concerning the question of how local, state, and federal governments should prepare for, respond to, and recover from such disasters.

In Selection 25, H.V. Savitch expresses the view that cities are resourceful even when faced with calamity. He describes how even cities that have suffered the most terrorist attacks—such as New York, London, and Jerusalem—have demonstrated great resilience. He believes these cities recovered quite rapidly because of their intrinsic value as centers of economic activity and social life, as well as because of their political capacity to address the consequences of terrorism. For example, business activities sprang back to life in New York City within a short period after 9/11 and have flourished since. The author suggests the "natural dynamism" of large cities provides enormous capacity for recovery and revival, particularly when it is aided by national programs to further enhance it. He recommends coordination among all levels of government to improve their security over a sustained period of time.

Stephen D. Stehr suggests in Selection 26 that much is known about how to make cities and regions safer, but that political and economic calculations often make effective responses difficult. An inherent problem is that the mitigation of disasters is likely to be the responsibility of local governments, while the economic costs of recovery and reconstruction are borne by higher-level governments, especially the federal government. He asserts that local governments have few incentives to make preparedness for disasters or their mitigation high priorities because federal governmental programs and private insurance will provide assistance if and when the disaster occurs.

Stehr also believes that political pressures at all levels of government confound rational planning for disasters. The competition for local development encourages cities to give greater attention to economic growth, rather than to public safety and disaster recovery. Federal governmental attention to homeland security in an age of terrorism often diminishes interest of federal officials in planning for natural disasters even though they may be more likely to happen than terrorist events. Stehr concludes that the vulnerability of cities to disasters is essentially a political matter determined by the dominant narrative or interpretation of how such events should be managed.

Stehr's conclusion resonates in Selection 27. Since the devastation of New Orleans by Hurricane Katrina in August 2005, the beleaguered city still struggles to rebuild and recover. Peter F. Burns and Matthew O. Thomas describe how the impact of the disaster has not pulled the various political players at the state and local levels closer together in support of recovery efforts. This continues despite the suffering and losses to the city.

Burns and Thomas describe how the emergency brought opportunities for state and local political leaders as well as citizens to cooperate to change the dysfunctional aspects of local politics. This sometimes led to successful policy innovations, especially in education. Nevertheless, lack of cooperation between the state and the city has generally prevailed in coping with the aftermath of the disaster. Friction between state and local officials persists over big policy priorities, as well as on issues of political corruption. This has happened because the hurricane did not change enduring sources of state–local political rivalry. Burns and Thomas describe a long history of deep intergovernmental distrust and tension over money, control, and policy priorities. State and city electorates also voice important differences about how New Orleans should be treated, with Louisiana residents less interested than city residents in restoring the historic city's economic role. The authors underscore how city governmental agencies make political conflict inevitable. Indeed, at one time four different commissions representing city and state power brokers simultaneously claimed to lead the planning of the city's recovery.

State–local relations have not always obstructed emergency responses to other disasters. There may be some singular features of the New Orleans experience that increase distrust between city and state governments there, but those are not likely to explain the many problems of coordination and cooperation. Indeed, when tropical storms Katia and Lee struck the East Coast in August 2011, causing massive flooding and damage to basic infrastructure such as roads and bridges, bickering immediately broke out about how to respond at all levels of government. In Congress Republicans adamantly demanded any money spent by the federal government for disaster relief had to be offset by budget cuts elsewhere. Republican governors sparred with federal administrators. Such a response does not bode well for the ability of cities to respond to and recover from natural disasters or acts of terrorism.

What is the proper relationship between the federal government and the cities? Do cities possess the capacity to respond to all problems that may face them? Making cities face the burdens once shouldered by the federal government does not help them to generate the resources necessary for responding to such events as Hurricane Katrina and the terrorist attacks; clearly, much of New Orleans' problem can be traced to the chronically dire straits of the city budget. Sometimes local governments demonstrate the capacity to respond, sometimes they clearly do not. There are problems that can overwhelm any local government, no matter how competently it may be run. Although there are many advantages to the American system of urban governance, the extreme decentralization in our federal system has some drawbacks, too.

25

Cities in a Time of Terror

H. V. SAVITCH

9/11 DYSTOPIA

September 11 will best be remembered because it came to symbolize a new consciousness and brought about a new era. For all the rightful recognition that day brought, it also drew an extremely dismal picture of the urban future—or, as it is called here, 9/11 dystopia. The elements of 9/11 dystopia were manifested in different responses to the attack. One was an emotional response reflecting a deep pessimism that saw cities falling into stifling fear and dark repression. Another had more to do with a strategic response, and saw the path to national survival in movement away from cities and toward a "defensive dispersal" of people, housing, and industry. The last was burrowed in a belief that cities had gone astray because of their infatuation with "tall buildings." According to this creed, skyscrapers not only compromised the values of sound planning but made cities vulnerable to attack. Each of these responses is taken up.

The most emotional responses were drawn in the days immediately following 9/11 and denoted a new world of darkness. Often heard were predictions

From H. V. Savitch, *Cities in a Time of Terror: Space, Territory, and Local Resilience*, (Armonk, NY: M.E. Sharpe, 2008), pp. 148–154, 156–161, 162–167, 220–224. Copyright © 2008 by M.E. Sharpe, Inc. Reprinted with permission.

about growing repression by armed police, bounty hunters, and authoritarian rulers. Image makers produced a frightful picture. Brought into vogue again were films like Fritz Lang's *Metropolis,* an expressionist work made in 1920s Germany, and Ridley Scott's *Blade Runner,* an American cult classic released during the 1980s. While separated by more than half a century, both films show the city at its worst—lorded over by technology gone mad, ridden by social divisions, and headed for self-destruction.

At a scholarly level, Harold Lasswell's 1941 classic, "The Garrison State," was brought back to life to show the political temper of 9/11 dystopia. The article presaged an equally bleak urban future.[1] Lasswell wanted to "consider the possibility" that we would face a world where "specialists in violence" would become the most powerful group. He went on to write that "internal violence would be directed principally against unskilled manual workers and counter-elite elements, who have come under suspicion."[2] As he saw it, society was there to be ruled by those who could manipulate appealing symbols and dominate mass opinion through public relations. Lasswell's "garrison state" went far beyond Madison Avenue manipulation and took the coercive form of military control coupled with modern technology. Its cardinal rule was obedience, service, and work. In many ways, the idea of a "garrison state" was influenced by the rising fascism of the 1930s, but to some it seemed applicable to the days following 9/11 when the FBI launched large-scale searches and police swarmed downtown streets.

This was dystopia's emotional mindset, and it was filled by the speculation of newspaper columnists, popular writers, and academics. Little more than a month after 9/11, Mike Davis referred to "military and security firms rushing to exploit the nation's nervous breakdown." They would "grow rich," he wrote, "amidst the general famine." Davis predicted that "Americans will be expected to express gratitude as they are scanned, frisked, imaged, tapped and interrogated. . . . Security will become a full-fledged urban utility like water and power."[3] Davis was no less ominous about the economy as he declared that the coming days

> may likely be the worst recession since 1938 and will produce major mutations in the American city. There is little doubt, for instance, that bin Laden et al. have put a silver stake in the heart of the "downtown revival" in New York and elsewhere. The traditional city where buildings and land values soar toward the sky is not yet dead but the pulse is weakening.[4]

While Davis was at an extreme end of dystopia, others in the planning profession joined him. One professional voiced concern that "the war against terrorism threatens to become a war against the livability of American cities."[5] At about the same time, Columbia University planner Peter Marcuse flatly predicted of 9/11 that "the results are likely to be a further downgrading of the quality of life in cities, visible changes in urban form, the loss of public use of public space, restrictions on free movement within and to cities, particularly for members of darker skinned groups, and the decline of open popular participation in the governmental planning and decision-making process."[6] These were not isolated commentaries, and similar diagnoses were published along with Marcuse's article in the *International Journal of Urban and Regional Research.*[7]

In the midst of this, another group of writers took a different tack, arguing instead for a change in urban strategy. Their watchword was "defensive dispersal," and the idea was to find a path that would ensure safety. "Defensive dispersal" dates back to the 1950s, when interstate highways were lauded because they produced low-density suburbs that would elude a single devastating bomb. The Housing Act of 1954 had reinforced defensive dispersal by promoting low-density peripheral development. Other advocates of dispersal laid out a scheme to build "a dispersed pattern of small, efficient cities" with radiating expressways in order to thwart an enemy attack.[8] Once 9/11 hit, the idea of defensive dispersal was revised and linked to the digital age and a broader movement toward decentralization. As the theory went, compact cities had out-lived their usefulness and were not as efficient as planners might have thought. Building density by vertically storing people and industry was outmoded, and modern industry would operate far more efficiently on an expanded horizontal scale. Even air pollution would be better controlled by dispersing population across wide-open spaces rather than confining people to compact cities. The digital age had rendered compact cities unnecessary by permitting people to communicate across vast distances.[9] Besides, since we were already a suburban nation, why not push this trend further and gain a defensive edge?

The theory of defensive dispersal was promoted by editorialists from the *Wall Street Journal,* who saw an advantage in sprawled cities, and by journal-ists at the *Detroit News,* who noted that in the wake of September 11, "the constituency for density had probably thinned out."[10] Other writers began to think aloud about the dangers of density and saw a trend in the making. In an article titled, "The De-Clustering of America," Joel Kotkin wrote, "the disper-sion of talent and technology to various parts of the country and the world has altered the once fixed geographies of talent."[11] By this thinking, countering terror also coincided with low-density and unstructured patterns of settlement where anything could be done anywhere. As Kotkin saw it:

> This dispersion trend has been further accelerated by the fallout from Sep-tember 11. Already, many major securities companies have moved operations out of Manhattan. . . . Many of them have signed long-term leases and aren't coming back. Financial and other business service firms are migrating to the Hudson Valley, New Jersey, and Connecticut.[12]

Finally, 9/11 dystopia was reinforced by a belief about the declining quality of urban life. This was a testimony about values that needed to be restored and it was based on an aversion to tall buildings. Far from being an effort to abandon the city, these writers wanted to reinstate a more traditional European-styled city, whose human scale would facilitate closer identity within a meaningful community. For these value-oriented theoreticians, tall buildings had not only robbed the city of its humanity, but brought suffocating congestion to its streets and overloaded its fragile infrastructure. Packing people into floor upon floor of skyscraper was intolerable, and it created an abysmal condition, which they labeled "urban hypertrophy."[13] Having discredited tall buildings because of their seeming threat to humanity, it was not a far step to point up the risks of inhabiting them and predicting their demise. Two urban writers mounted the campaign against tall buildings, writing shortly after 9/11 that "We are con-vinced that the age of skyscrapers is at an end. It must now be considered an experimental building typology that has failed. We predict that no new mega-towers will be built, and existing ones are destined to be dismantled."[14]

To say the least, 9/11 dystopia was stark. It either saw little future for cities or argued for their complete reconception. It was predicated on some narrow possibilities. Either society had rotted from the inside and the attacks were to be expected, or cities had left themselves exposed to September 11 by misplaced development and they should be abandoned or revamped. Taken as a whole, the 9/11 disillusion was a reaction to recent decades of urban devel-opment and its remedies left little room for leeway.

THE RESILIENT CITY

Understanding Resilience

At best, 9/11 dystopia missed the mark and at worst it ignored a city's capacity for resilience. Before exploring this proposition, we might ask how people who had observed and studied the city for so long could have been so mistaken. Any number of explanations is plausible. Among the more apparent reasons for the miscalculation was that lower Manhattan's devastation was so extensive that it distorted individual perspectives. A single stroke of so great a magnitude had so stunned the public, and created so dark a cloud, that it was to difficult to spot a silver lining much less see sunlight. Amid the gloom one could only portend additional gloom. Another explanation for the distortions of 9/11 dystopia is less generous. This rests on the ideology of its analysts—from both the political left and the political right. As this explanation goes, some commentators were so convinced about the righteousness of their belief that they saw its vindication in any act or circumstance. Their predictions were couched in a polemic that sought to justify its premises. A final explanation would deny that 9/11 dystopia was entirely wrong. It might go on to argue that most of the analyses and predictions were basically correct. Dystopia's defenders might cite the growth of surveillance and the shrinkage of urban space to convince an audience that their prognosis was correct. Those who held a dim view of the city might also point to the continuing flight to the suburbs. While this has some plausibility, the facts about what happened to New York (and other cities) after being attacked do not quite fit.

Any assessment of resilience works best when guided by the historic or empirical record, most particularly by other cities that underwent warfare, terror, or endemic violence.[15] While this is a complicated matter, the majority of findings point in a similar direction. The salient conclusion is that most cities have a remarkable capacity for resilience. Cities may well experience short-term negative effects from an attack, but under varying conditions and over varying periods of time they do recover. Moreover, recoveries are not accompanied by a period that gives to a rise a "garrison state" or repressive politics.[16] To the contrary, cities in free societies retain the fundamentals of local democracy, and while citizens may feel pangs of anxiety, their day-to-day habits are unchanged.[17]

To get a better idea of how resilience works, we can think of cities as large agglomerations of human settlement, social relations, and factors of production—held together and made dynamic by an extensive infrastructure. What makes cities dynamic is circular causation, where fortuitous circumstances trigger positive effects, which in turn feed those circumstances again to produce still more positive effects. Lying at the heart of this repetitive process is the magnitude of the city and its dynamic agglomeration. Generally speaking, the larger and more dynamic the city, the more difficult to set it in reverse. Any attack would have to be massive in order to permanently halt these self-generating processes. Even when subject to enormous shocks, cities seem to regenerate and spring back to life.

The most complete picture on the effects of violent shock to urban society can be found in studies of conventional warfare. Research on select cities examines their experience with intense periods of incessant bombing, firestorms, or even atomic warfare, and shows them to be remarkably resilient. In the United Kingdom and France, London and Paris experienced years of air bombing, close combat, or military occupation. In Germany, cities like Cologne, Hamburg, Berlin, and Dresden were subject to heavy aerial bombardment. In

Japan, the devastation in Tokyo and especially Hiroshima and Nagasaki was much greater. Large sections of Japanese cities were destroyed and hundreds of thousands of people killed. Yet all of these cities in Europe and Asia recovered, and most went on to a period of unprecedented prosperity.[18]

A somewhat more complicated picture emerges from cities under terrorist attack. As we know, urban terror is a different type of warfare that emphasizes longer assaults on civilians, persistent attacks geared toward the decontrol of territory, and sustained efforts to paralyze normal life. Rather than extensive and abrupt shock, most terror consists of low-intensity warfare that is supposed to wear the enemy down through protracted friction.[19] It stands to reason that urban terror might affect cities in different ways than conventional military action. In these cases, the evidence points to varying degrees of recovery over varying periods of time. While the findings are qualified, they still are reasonably optimistic. Studies of American cities indicate that they are "highly unlikely to decline in the face of even a sustained terrorist campaign."[20] Other research on Italian cities demonstrates short-lived economic effects lasting for about a year after attack.[21] Another line of work on Israeli and Basque cities shows longer-term effects from terrorism, though in the absence of continued attacks these effects do wear off.[22]

We should understand that resilience is not an absolute or a matter of either being resilient or not. Cities are resilient to different extents, in different ways, and have different periods of recovery. Much depends on the size of the city, the strength of its economy, and its social coherence. These factors can then be coupled to the frequency and severity of attack to obtain a more nuanced picture of recovery. From all indications, the resilience of New York and London are different from that of Jerusalem.

How might we know whether resilience has been achieved? While it is normally difficult to precisely sort out the effects of one variable upon another, assessing resilience involves the simpler task of determining the extent to which a previous condition has been reinstated.[23] Simply put, the threshold for resilience can be satisfied by establishing whether a city has bounced back after sustaining an attack or wave of terror. For example, after a city experienced mega terror we would want to know whether the population has returned, or after a city incurred smart terror whether an infrastructure has been rebuilt. Measurable results should then tell us whether an area has recovered, the extent of that recovery, or whether any recovery took place. Resilience might also be achieved if an attack had not changed fundamental conditions or had no significant effect on normal life. This would mean a city had seen no adverse change and withstood an intended shock. A city meeting these criteria could be seen as resilient.

Different Cities/Different Resilience

As we know, New York's terrorism has been sporadic and marked by one enormous blow. With over 3.5 million jobs and a gross product of $400 billion, New York possesses one of the largest local economies in the world.[24] Almost 64 percent of the city's agglomeration is located in Manhattan, and most of that is concentrated in its midtown or downtown business districts.[25] High finance undergirds this great financial edifice, and its geographic concentration makes it vulnerable to attack. September 11 showed just how smart terror could pinpoint critical assets.

London's terrorism has been less murderous, though more frequent, and has occurred in cyclical patterns since the 1970s. Its economy is similar in size to New York's, with an employment base of close to 4 million jobs and a gross product of over $250 billion.[26] London's central business district is concentrated in The City and in the central boroughs of Westminster and Kensington, lying to the west. Much like New York's business cores, these areas are driven by high finance.[27] While the cycle of attacks in the 1990s targeted The City, the attack of 7/7 was somewhat more dispersed, occurring in Westminster and The City, but also just astride these boroughs.

By comparison with its two giant counterparts, Jerusalem's socioeconomic profile is quite modest and its pattern of continued terror differs. Jerusalem's 180,000 jobs and its gross product of $14 billion are a fraction of its giant counterparts.[28] Also, unlike the other two cities, Jerusalem is not an economic capital but a political and religious one. Its central business district consists of moderately priced retail shops, restaurants, and a few important banks. Government buildings and cultural institutions are scattered throughout the city.

One asset that all three cities have in common is an important tourist industry, though this too greatly varies in size. London is one of the foremost tourist destinations of the world, and its tourism reached a zenith in 2005 with 14.9 million foreign visitors. New York's tourism is less than half that much, having reached its height in 2005 with 6.8 million international tourists. Tourism is one of Jerusalem's major industries, and its tourism reached a pinnacle in 2000 with 953,000 visitors. Unlike more stable industries, the elasticity of tourism relative to terror is a useful a barometer of local resilience.

Under the circumstances, we would expect the resilience of these cities to be markedly different from one another, and it is. Among the factors used to assess recovery in New York, London, and Jerusalem are employment, tourism, and office markets.

Resilience in New York, London, and Jerusalem

In the immediate period after 9/11, New York employment fell sharply and the city lost more than 100,000 jobs.[29] The drop was precipitous, linked directly to the collapse in lower Manhattan, and it occurred in the few months after September. The bulk of the lost employment occurred in the area around the World Trade Center, though it also spread to other parts of Manhattan and the rest of the city. For a time, the job situation was bleak, but by 2004 the city's employment began to move upward; by the end of 2005 the city's job base had reached 3.6 million.[30]

London's cyclical violence burst out again between 1990 and 1993, when financial institutions were targeted by the IRA. By comparison to New York, these attacks were pinpricks, though they engendered a huge psychological response, which eventually led to the "ring of steel." While it is not possible to attribute the subsequent drop in London's employment to these attacks, the falloff was significant. Once the cycle of terror had ceased, London was down by about 450,000 jobs from the previous period.[31] As in New York, the number crept up in subsequent years, and by the turn of the century employment reached a high that hovered around the 4 million mark.

For Jerusalem, the key period of terror occurred in the fall of 2000 through 2002. Here, too, the City Center was targeted, though neighborhoods within a short distance were also struck. Unlike London, the targets were people, rather than financial institutions. While businesses were severely affected and many closed, others waited out the storm. The Israeli government also stepped in to bolster the local economy.[32] Apparently, government programs made up for private business failures and through these years jobs remained at about 180,000. By 2003, terrorism subsided and employment rose to 183,000; it has since modestly continued on that trajectory.[33]

There are instances when employment falls after an attack and gradually rises as terrorism subsides. There is also variability in each city and instances where an attack had no discernible effect on employment. The first attack on New York's World Trade Center (1993) left no imprint. To the contrary, employment continued to rise through the 1990s. The second, much bigger attack (2001) left a deep imprint, but by 2004 the city showed signs of recovery. London fell into a trough just as the IRA struck in the early 1990s, but its employment dramatically accelerated through time. Jerusalem fared somewhat worse and also somewhat better. Its drop-off was not as steep, but its recovery was slower and more modest.

Might all this be coincidence and tied to other factors? No doubt exogenous factors played a role, though we can see the same fall and rise in other sectors of the local economy, particularly tourism. Foreign tourism is a useful gauge of resilience because of its sensitivity to large-scale, highly publicized violence. If a city were resilient, we would expect foreign visitors to return within a reasonable period of time. Indeed, in the immediate years after 9/11, New York's tourist traffic plummeted. A year after the attack, tourism had dropped by 25 percent compared to its pre-attack level, and by the second year it had fallen by more than 29 percent from its pre-attack level.[34] For a while it appeared the tourist industry would fade, but by 2004 it was back up and by 2005 the industry had fully recovered to its pre-disaster level of 6.8 million foreign visitors annually.

London's tourism was hardly touched by the attacks of 1990–93 and tourism actually increased. By 1995, London's tourism had grown to more than 13 million foreign visitors each year. Following some erratic years, London tourism continued to rise until the attacks of July 7, 2005.[35] The attacks of that summer changed everything, wreaking also a short-term effect on tourism. During the month after 7/7, tourism fell by 18 percent from the previous year and the decline persisted into August.[36] Not until September did tourism begin to revive, and it has now climbed to an all-time high. A possible explanation for the difference between the pre– and post–7/7 tourist reaction was the human toll of the latest attacks. London demonstrated again that mega terror aimed at people is more damaging to the tourist industry than smart terror aimed at things.

Jerusalem, where attacks have been especially aimed at people, [also] bears out this generalization. During the 1990s, low terror corresponded to high tourist visits and the number of foreign visitors surpassed 950,000 at the turn of the century. By the end of 2000, Jerusalem was in the throes of al Aqsa violence. Terrorism shot up and we can see tourism plummeting during this period. As casualties from terror continued to rise through the years 2001 and 2002, tourism continued to fall. By the end of 2003, terrorism had taken a sharp decline and tourism rose once again. The trend toward lower terrorism and higher tourism continues through 2004. With the decline of terrorism, Jerusalem began to bounce back, though it is still a distance from record levels.

Office markets also reflect a city's capacity for resilience. They indicate willingness to invest in a city, use clustered environments, and take a chance on tall buildings. Jerusalem has relatively little of this kind of investment and almost no tall buildings, and we put that case in abeyance. But New York and London are the world's corporate office capitals and exemplify the dynamics of urban agglomeration.

New York's rebound is instructive. After the loss and injury to lives, the most devastating effect of 9/11 was the loss of buildings and office space. The city's estimated property and attendant losses reach as high as $83 billion. The figure includes the loss of six buildings of the World Trade Center and the complete destruction of 13.4 million square feet of office space. Putting this in perspective, the destroyed space equaled the entire office stock in the city of Detroit.[37]

Under clouds of distrust for tall buildings, one might have expected the disaster that befell New York to have eliminated its market demand. Indeed, for a while the office market continued to soften, even in the wake of space shortages created by 9/11. In the two years after 9/11, office vacancies rose in Manhattan and elsewhere around the nation. By 2005, however, office markets had turned around. Mid-Manhattan vacancies shrunk to below 8 percent while lower Manhattan fell below 11 percent. Manhattan's office markets were not back to the halcyon days of the late 1990s, but they had considerably improved from the devastation of 9/11 and by 2005 they were the envy of much of the world.

The news was good on other fronts as well. Surveys showed that more than half the displaced tenants had returned to lower Manhattan and many other firms had chosen New York locations.[38] Most encouraging, the bulk of those who sought new locations chose tall buildings of twenty stories or higher.[39] Elsewhere in the country, tall buildings were doing quite well. From Boston to Dallas, developers continued to put up skyscrapers and fill them. Among the first to ride the tide was developer Donald Trump, who tried to build Chicago's tallest skyscraper. Trump has also set his sights for a tall hotel and tower in Toronto.

Office markets have been even stronger in London. Vacancy rates in the central boroughs have halved in just two recent years. By 2006, empty office space had fallen to under 5 percent. The largest development firms push hard to obtain construction permits for skyscrapers, albeit with great public controversy about their aesthetic desirability. The most fervid rush and the sharpest controversies transpire over who had already built or was about to build the tallest building. As of this writing, permission was granted to build London Bridge Tower, which will rise 1,000 feet (305 meters) above street level and will become Europe's tallest building. London also behaved in an untraditional manner when its plan explicitly endorsed tall buildings, cheered on by the effusive support of its socialist mayor.[40]

As Igal Charney points out, tall buildings have continued to appeal to cities.[41] Sometimes called "trophy" or "designer" buildings, they are now a source of prestige. Moscow and Seoul have already approved buildings that are twice the height of those planned for Chicago, Toronto, and London. Dubai has already granted permission to construct the world's tallest building. These new buildings exceed the height of the former Twin Towers.[42]

Finally, as if to defy the admonition against tall buildings (and possible attackers), skyscrapers are once again springing up at ground zero. The Freedom Tower is now under construction and so, too, is a 2 million square foot office tower not far away. As of this writing banks and financial houses are planning other skyscrapers in the area. While lower Manhattan's central business district had slipped after 9/11, it is now rising again as one of the nation's foremost financial centers.

Tall buildings have persisted against the wishes of dystopian value writers as well as the laws of economics. As commercial ventures, tall buildings are inefficient. Skyscrapers forever fight against their own weight because so much capacity is consumed supporting their upper height. Numerous airshafts, elevators, pillars, and other supports take up 30 percent of potentially rentable space. In the aftermath of 9/11, the idea of constructing still more vulnerable targets seemed inconceivable. One economist expressed his fear that "for at least a decade, the primary real estate issue regarding terrorist attacks will not be 60 versus 100 story buildings . . . but whether any unsubsidized buildings will be built by the private sector at all."[43] On this issue, modern economists have been outpredicted by architectural philosophers of another era. The "tall office building," wrote Louis Sullivan in 1896, "is one of the most stupendous, one of the most magnificent opportunities that the Lord of Nature in His beneficence has ever offered to the proud spirit of man."[44]

Resilience and Other Considerations

A fair assessment of these cities would conclude that they rebounded from disaster because of the strength of their social fabric, the dynamism of their economies, and the optimism of their citizenry. In his review of post–9/11 American cities, Peter Eisinger remarks, "If the texture and pace of city life are clouded somewhat by public anxiety about terror, the actual changes urban dwellers encounter in their daily lives in most places in the country and at most times are small and relatively unobtrusive."[45] With some qualification about *time of recovery,* much the same could be said for other cities around the world. For most other cities struck by terror, *time* is a key element in judging recovery because those cities lack the magnitude of New York or London.

Jerusalem presents the alternative view of a major, mid-sized city. In the midst of wave after wave of attack, the city looked as if it would never recover. This author was in Jerusalem observing the situation during one such wave and wrote in a later article:

> At least for the moment parts of downtown Jerusalem have begun to resemble older American urban cores that were shattered by de-industrialization. [Their] worn look creates a "broken windows" atmosphere that can only discourage business. . . . Once thriving retailers have now left and rental signs hang everywhere. Some rents have dropped by as much as 90 percent. Those properties that have been rented sell cheap, fast-turnover merchandise. Once upscale jewelry shops now offer inexpensive souvenirs for sale. Former clothing shops have been converted into storage facilities. Accessories and trinkets hang in store windows or lie on makeshift stands. The upper floors of some buildings have been turned into gambling rooms, exotic dancing studios and sex clubs. Downtown appears to be struck by the effects of a crime wave (bleak and downgraded) rather than war (complete devastation and rubble).[46]

The passages continue in this article, emphasizing that any pessimism about the city's future should be tempered by a number of caveats about drawing hasty conclusions. Among these was that "Jerusalemites are resilient, and even after a bloody attack they persevere."[47] Since then, the city has continued to recover. Foreign tourists have returned to its hotels, downtown streets are refilled, and restaurants have reopened. Tourism has not yet returned to its peak year of 2000, but it has come close and for a single recent year has now exceeded 850,000 foreign visitors. The city is also experiencing a real estate boom. Housing, retail, and office markets are robust and in many places prices have gone above pre-terrorism levels. While not all sectors have fully recovered, most have made substantial progress. Clearly, if Jerusalem's 700,000 residents show this capacity for resilience, we can say it is not the sole preserve of mega or global cities.

We should also acknowledge that while resilience entails recovery, it does not erase a disaster. Critical events, like terrorism, do leave a mark of one kind or another. Sometimes that mark can germinate into a movement that had been hardly discernible before terror struck; at other times it can accelerate recognized trends. Jerusalem's experience with attacks catalyzed an existing exodus of households from the center into the peripheries. The attack on New York catalyzed an existing movement of business from lower Manhattan to mid Manhattan. London's bout with terrorism took a society that was heavily ridden with surveillance and made it even more so. The final word on urban resilience may never be written, but Tom Wolfe's maxim that "you can't go home again" rings ever so true.[48] The challenge is to make that very different future a more secure one.

SUSTAINING A BETTER FUTURE
The National Approach to Sustaining Resilience

Much of a city's resilience stems from its agglomerative nature and what might be called its natural dynamism. But this is hardly the end of the story, because a city's capacity for resilience is neither automatic nor is it unassisted. Rather, local resilience is helped and sustained by government. Government at all levels makes recovery possible and plays a critical role, whether that takes place by building infrastructure, educating the citizenry, stabilizing the social order, protecting society, or taking responsibility for a host of functions. For some, the laissez-faire state might have appeal, but it does not exist. Even private insurance is publicly regulated, publicly assisted, and often publicly subsidized. When great calamities strike, government is the foremost actor in rescue and reconstruction. Usually government at upper and mid levels takes the lead. At mid levels, states or provinces can play a role in staunching a crisis, but their geographic limitations and their resource constraints are insufficient to the task. Operating from the top down, national government is best able to cast the widest nets and most capable of coordinating local efforts. National government is also best able to enlist private enterprise or nonprofit organizations to work with authorities at all levels. Generally, the greater the breakdown the more it requires national attention.

This was certainly the case in the post–9/11 era, when free markets failed and most insurance companies refused coverage to high-risk clients. In the United States, the biggest and most vulnerable cities found themselves in a dire situation. Terrorism insurance was especially difficult to obtain in New York, Chicago, Los Angeles, and San Francisco. This put property developers in a quandary because lenders required insurance before a project could be financed. The absence of available underwriters went beyond new building construction and affected city debt ratings as well those of other public agencies. Since then, insurance premiums have risen dramatically, increasing the costs for both public and private sectors. On the public side, premiums for New York's transit system rose by 300 percent, and in the private sector, the owners of the Empire State Building paid 900 percent more for a lesser policy.[49]

Some insurance companies began to write "sunset clauses" into their policies that were designed to relieve them of future obligations. Other insurance companies have either refused to underwrite large-scale projects or charged enormous premiums to do so. Shortly after 9/11, more than $15.5 billion in real estate projects were suspended or canceled because developers could not obtain insurance.[50] In San Francisco, insurance for the Golden Gate Bridge doubled. In Baltimore, insurance companies refused to issue coverage for its International Airport and sporting events in Camden Yards. Under pressure from the state government of Maryland, the companies later relented.

America's federal government sought ways to fill the void and hastily strung together a broad safety net. The foremost means of doing this was the

Terrorism Risk Insurance Act of 2002, or TRIA. The act was extended in 2005 through the end of 2007, presumably allowing the insurance market to stabilize and resume normal pricing. Only commercial establishments are eligible and only foreign attacks are insured. In the event of an attack, TRIA covers 90 percent of losses, after deductible payments are met. Losses above $100 billion are not covered by the act. TRIA also limits liability by precluding payments for property damages due to a CBRN (chemical, biological, radiological, or nuclear) attack. Overall, the restrictions are intended to spread the risk between the federal government, private insurers, and the insured.

Elsewhere in the world, the part played by national government in providing terrorism insurance varies quite a bit. France, Spain, and Australia make coverage mandatory, and national government has a direct role in making sure that coverage is complete and equitable. France has established common insurance pools with higher premiums for developers who undertake new construction. The United Kingdom allows insurance to be optional. This has posed problems for British theatergoers and other mass audiences. As prospects of a mega attack increased over recent years, so too did insurance premiums, and public events have borne the brunt of the pain. Insurance rates increased by 200 percent or more for highly publicized events. In tangible terms, this meant that the cost for a concert at the National Theater jumped by 250,000 pounds; the cost of an event at the royal Opera House rose by 500,000 pounds. Given the circumstances, the public would have to forego some events or pay more for a ticket. Because many cities depend upon culture and entertainment to drive their economies, the increased prices for a time dampened the revenue capacity of these sectors. Troubled by this turn of events, Londoners referred to the change as the "Bin Laden effect."[51]

The most positive view of terrorism insurance would acknowledge that it establishes a net below which victims should not fall. More tenuously, the net can be broken by excessive damages (above $100 billion) or by attacks that are not covered. Terrorism insurance is a retroactive way of ensuring a degree of economic security. While post-disaster relief is important, proactive measures are just as important. These, however, are not quite as clear cut; they involve an amorphous array of actions and are conducted by governments and private actors at multiple levels.

Multi-Governance Approaches to Sustaining Resilience

Grand policies can be proclaimed from high political posts and ambitious goals can be announced by presidents, prime ministers, and cabinet members. When all is said and done, however, the action is accomplished at the local level. City politics is the politics of the trenches, where mayors and local officials take matters in hand, do the actual implementation, and face constituents. This is particularly true of the United States, where local police are responsible for public safety and exercise considerable autonomy over policy choices.

Referring to the American situation, Susan Clarke points out that the greater the national security threat, the more important the local role.[52] Clarke is correct, and it could be added that threats do not rest at a single level but in a skein of multiple governments at all levels. There is something about imminent crises that creates a need to pull together different levels of government, even when the immediate challenge is to clarify results in an incomprehensible tangle of relationships. Lyndon Johnson's War on Poverty invigorated intergovernmental relations just as George W. Bush's War on Terror has given intergovernmental relations a new twist. Sloganeering aside, the agenda of each "war" has been considerably different. Johnson's war converted cities into centers of development and income redistribution, while Bush's war has brought to cities an agenda of security and watchfulness.

The attention paid to terrorism at a local level is far reaching. A recent poll of Americans showed that terrorism was at the very top of the agenda. Fully 79 percent of the American public believed terrorism was "very important" (compared to 66 percent for Europeans).[53] At the local level, nearly three-quarters of American municipalities have invested in some type of emergency preparedness (technology, security, disaster preparedness). Cities have conducted mock drills, closed off buildings, rerouted traffic, and added police and have begun to reorient their emergency medical services.[54] While homeland security no longer tops the list of local priorities, it does appear within the top thirty-eight issues that public officials consider most important to address.[55]

The jumble of intergovernmental cooperation is bound together by federal funding. The major distributor of this largesse is the U.S. Department of Homeland Security (DHS). Since 9/11, that department had dispensed over $18 billion in assistance to states and localities.[56] Because the Patriot Act requires a minimum distribution of assistance, all fifty states plus Washington, DC, and U.S. territories received some amount. Within the DHS money pot, the largest program pertaining to cities is the Urban Areas Security Initiative, or UASI, whose total funding in 2006 was approximately $711 million. UASI funding is based on a formula that assesses three basic risk factors—namely, *threat, vulnerability,* and *consequences.* In theory, this should gear funding toward cities facing the greatest probability of attack and potential damages. Realities are different, though, and UASI funding has now been distributed to over 50 localities; central cities ranging in size from New York's 8 million to Sacramento's 445,000 are included.

UASI funding for 2006 [shows] variation in amounts from a high of 124 million for America's largest city to the lesser amount of 7 million for smaller cities. The per capita amounts are revealing. Taking two high-risk examples, New York City and Washington, DC, were among the highest recipients in both absolute and per capita expenditures. Each city also received a handsome proportion of the total budget. New York City garnered 18 percent while Washington, DC, received 7 percent. Relative to the previous year, however, both of these high-risk cities were down by 40 percent. New York's mayor, Michael Bloomberg, and Washington's mayor, Anthony Williams, protested the cuts. As their reasoning went, each city had already incurred much higher expenses than other localities and each would continue to be an exceptionally sought-after target.[57] Homeland Security was not persuaded and instead awarded increases to smaller cities. Sacramento's allocation increased by 17 percent while Jacksonville's funding rose by 26 percent.[58]

For New York and Washington, DC, as well as other cities, police protection and its costs are critical. In addition to heightened protection in densely packed built-up areas, the new War on Terror mandates that airports and other forms of interstate transportation be covered with additional local police. Yet legislation pertaining to homeland security often prevents federal support for police overtime or hiring new personnel.[59]

While the costs for protection flow to cities, not all the reimbursements follow. More often than not, states receive funding and pass it down to cities with instructions for the application of that funding. There are times when state priorities differ from those of their cities, widening the gap between response and need. Judgments about priorities are very subjective, and invariably political consideration will enter the mix, thereby shifting the emphasis from protecting targets to distributing rewards.

The conversion from a pinpointed policy measure to a more amorphous monetary benefit is hardly new to Washington.[60] Beneath the surface, a political pageant has been played out. In this pageant, allocations are spread to cities that can offer the rosiest presentation and summon the best rationales. What was once an initiative to concentrate funding in seven high-risk urban areas has been turned into pork-barrel legislation that distributes funding to a larger list of low-risk recipients. The allocations may very well be put to public use, but they are not well connected to the likelihood of attack. Policy analysts might say that a measure to ensure security has been turned into a distributive policy to reward friends and placate opponents.[61]

Inefficient spending may be the least of the obstacles confronting homeland security. The real problem lies in how to sustain the capacity for resilience over a lengthy period of time. At bottom, the objectives of homeland security are riddled by questions of how cooperation can be mustered across diverse metropolitan boundaries and how any momentum can be kept up. Individual metropolitan areas differ by size, number of jurisdictions, socioeconomic composition, political demands, and local culture. Ensuring security within any single area requires working with a great many parties—mayors, legislators, bureaucrats, and private contractors—where motivations differ, problems vary, and rewards are asymmetrical.[62] It is difficult enough to concert collective action among like-minded actors, but how to sustain a common objective amid this political cacophony is a challenge.

The challenge is magnified by the inherent inertia of public protection. Both *time* and *place* are critical but unknown elements. Given the perspective of time, we know that even the most frequently struck cities experience long periods of calm. Typically, assaults occur at the end of extended intervals and those periods can stretch into months or years. This is true even for one of the most incessantly struck cities—Jerusalem. That city experienced intermittent peace in the 1990s and has enjoyed another period of calm during the last three years. Taking New York as another example, more than seven years elapsed between the first and second attacks in lower Manhattan. Since 9/11, more than five years have gone by without an attack, and there is no telling when or if another such event will occur in New York. From the perspective of place, attacks could occur almost anywhere. Big, global cities have seemingly limitless targets. Is a transit system that stretches for miles most likely to be hit? Or is any one of the sixty-plus skyscrapers that fill Manhattan at greater risk? Or is a mass-attended concert most susceptible to attack?

It is by now commonplace in security circles to remind people that terrorists can choose both time and place, while defenders must always be on alert. Attackers require just one success, while protectors require a success rate of 100 percent. It is hardly surprising that over a period of time and at varying places, cities fall prey to what can be called asymmetrical reactions that swing between lethargy and hyperactivity. As used here, asymmetrical reactions are either not commensurate with the problem at hand or out of synchrony with the time trajectory of terrorism or not fully cognizant of realities.

The pattern is familiar to airline passengers during heightened periods of alert. It was particularly vivid for those who found themselves in the midst of an alert in August 2006 because of a threat to blow up aircraft flying out of London.

The general scenario is something like this: During the first blush of training, security is ready and alert. In the absence of an emergency, alertness gradually fades. As readiness reaches a low point, an attack or threat catches personnel off guard. Having realized they were unprepared, security officials enter a period of hyperactivity or overvigilance. Picayune rules replace common sense, ordinary actions are viewed with unwarranted suspicion, and authority becomes overbearing. This behavior continues for a while, only to lapse again until the next real emergency.

Asymmetric reaction occurs in most cities around the world. Soon after terror struck Moscow, the militia closed roads, put public transport under intense surveillance, and began implementing strict rules concerning the possession of identification papers. Within a few months the alerts wore off and security forces fell into a state of indifference.

There are no easy answers to the problem of asymmetrical reaction. Any remedy must achieve a steadiness of response that is based on competence and practiced teamwork. The machinery of counterterrorism can be oiled by plans, drills, simulations, and "table-top" exercises. This might not be a substitute for the real thing, but it does enable first responders to be ready for the unexpected. Another remedy is to develop flexible responses that can be raised or lowered in measured steps. The key to achieving this lies in synchronized intergovernmental coordination. Governments can begin that process by clarifying and respecting mutual responsibilities. At the local level, officials should be able to comply with higher-level regulations, while avoiding the trap of goal displacement or becoming lost in mounds of rules. At national and state levels, authorities should exercise oversight while also delegating discretion to local actors, so they can exercise judgment and retain a sense of purpose. The balance between accountability and freedom of action is difficult to achieve, much less maintain over time. Terrorists depend upon surprise, and even modest reductions in uncertainty can mitigate the shock of attack.

CONCLUSIONS

The fears arising from 9/11 dystopia underestimated the city's capacity for resilience in the face of war or terrorism. That capacity not only varies by frequency and severity of attack, but also by the size of a city and the dynamics of its agglomeration. The ability of cities to bounce back from violent shock can be seen in the experiences of New York, London, and Jerusalem. In those cities, employment, investment in tall buildings, and tourism often suffered varying degrees of decline. However, over time, these sectors recovered and some went on to do exceedingly well. Tourism is particularly sensitive to outbreaks of large-scale violence, but this industry too sprang back to life once terrorism abated.

For all the natural resilience attributed to cities, government plays a critical role in their recovery. In Europe, national governments helped establish a better equilibrium between insurance carriers and consumers. In the United States, national policies were instrumental in restoring insurance coverage in high-risk cities. The U.S. federal government also provided a system of aid to localities in order to deal with threats from urban terror. This aid has a tendency to be spread and watered down because of political pressures. Terrorism is still an important concern in North America and Western Europe, and still occupies an important place on the local government agenda. In many instances, local government is responsible for training and furnishing a cadre of first responders. While this has been a positive step, it is not without its problems. The challenges besetting government at all levels lie in bringing about collective action and sustaining long-term commitments. Governments also face problems in maintaining stable levels of performance. High performance is compromised by common patterns of asymmetrical reaction to terrorism, defined as a situation where behavior is not commensurate to an event. This is difficult to remedy, though a beginning can be made by synchronizing intergovernmental coordination and simulating critical events.

NOTES

1. See Harold Lasswell, "The Garrison State," *American Journal of Urban Sociology* 46 (January 1941): 455–468.
2. Ibid., p. 455.
3. See Mike Davis, "The Flames of New York," *New Left Review* 12 (November–December 2001): 45.
4. Ibid., p. 44.
5. David Dixon, "Is Density Dangerous? The Architects' Obligations after the Towers Fell," in *Perspective on Preparedness*, Belfare Center for International Affairs and Taubman Center for State and Local Government, Harvard University (October 12, 2002): 1.
6. See Peter Marcuse, "Urban Form and Globalization after September 11: The View from New York," *International Journal of Urban and Regional Research* 23, 3 (September 2002): 596–606. For Marcuse's quote, see p. 596. Marcuse held much the same opinion in an earlier article. See Peter Marcuse, "Alternate Visions for New York City: By Whom, for Whom," *MetroPlanner* (January–February 2002), p. 3.
7. There appeared to be a uniformity of opinion in most of the published articles. See the *International Journal of Urban and Regional Research* 26 (September 2002): 589–590, and 27, 3 (2003): 649–698.
8. Michael Dudley, "Sprawl as Strategy: City Planners Face the Bomb," *Journal of Planning Education and Research* (Fall 2001): 52–63.
9. The idea actually began in the 1960s and was elaborated during the 1990s. See Melvin Weber, "Order in Diversity: Community without Propinquity," in *Cities and Space: The Future*, ed. Lowdon Wingo, Jr. (Baltimore, MD: Johns Hopkins University Press, 1963). For later and cruder versions, see Harry Richardson and Peter Gordon, "Market Planning: Oxymoron or Common Sense?" *Journal of the American Planning Association* 59 (Summer 1993): 59–77; and Peter Gordon and Harry Richardson, "Are compact Cities a Desirable Planning Goal?" *Journal of the American Planning Association* 63 (Winter 1997): 95–107.
10. Quoted in Keith Schneider, "Sprawl Not an Antidote to Terror," *Elm Street Writers Group* (Michigan Land Institute, December 2001).
11. See Joel Kotkin, "The Declustering of America," *Wall Street Journal*, August 12, 2002, p. A12. For extended discussion, see Joel Kotkin, *The New Geography: How the Digital Landscape Is Reshaping the American Landscape* (New York: Random House, 2000).
12. Ibid.
13. James Kunstler and Nikos Slingaros attribute the term "urban hypertrophy" to Leon Krier. See Leon Krier, *Leon Krier: Houses, Palaces, Cities* (New York: St. Martin's Press, 1984). See James Kunstler and Nikos Slingaros, "The End of Tall Buildings," *Planetizen* (September 17, 2001), available at www.panetizen.com/oped/item.php.
14. Ibid.
15. See Edward Glaeser and Jesse Shapiro, "Cities and Warfare: The Impact of Terrorism on Urban Form," *Journal of Urban Economics* 51 (March 2002): 205–224; and Ronald R. Davis and Weinstein E. David, "Bones, Bombs and Breakpoint: The Geography of Economic Activity," *American Economic Review* 92 (December 2002): 1269–1289. See also Steven Brackman, Harry Garretsen, and Mark Schramm, "The Strategic Bombing of German Cities during World War II and Its Impact on City Growth" *Journal of Economic Geography* 42, 2 (2004): 201–208.
16. For varying interpretations of the war on terror, including the garrison state, see Kathe Callahan, Melvin Dubnick, and Dorothy Olshfski, "War Narratives: Framing Our Understanding of the War on Terror," *Public Administration Review* 66, 4 (July–August 2006): 554–568.
17. See Peter Eisinger, "The American City in an Age of Terror: A Preliminary Assessment of the Effects of September 11," *Urban Affairs Review* 40, 1 (2004): 115–130.

18. Ibid. Brackman, Garretsen, and Schramm, *Strategy Bombing*, do point out that cities in West Germany (FRG) incurred a temporary impact but fully recovered, while those in East Germany (GDR) did not and the Allied bombing had a permanent impact. While the authors do not venture into why the FRG cities would show a different recovery than GDR cities, a plausible reason might be that FRG cities were located in more dynamic, aggressive, and productive national economies. Those economies acted differently on their respective cities.

19. In distinguishing between conventional warfare and terrorism, we can talk about the unbounded friction of urban terror. This friction is akin to the experience of the Middle Ages, where plunder and siege lasted for 20, 30, or 100 years. In these instances, constant invasions and centuries of pillage caused many cities to wither or disappear (see Pirenne, *Medieval Cities*). The Thirty Years' War resulted in a radical depopulation of German cities in which Marburg and Augsburg lost more than half their inhabitants, never to regain their predominant status (C.V. Wedgewood, *The Thirty Years War* [Garden City, NY: Doubleday, 1961]). Another way of understanding how the friction of terror might affect cities is to examine the relationship between crime and urban settlement. Like terrorism, crime creates chronic apprehension and paralyzes normal life. Much as guards, gates, and surveillance are used to thwart terror, so too are they employed to prevent criminal aggression.

20. James Harrigan and Philippe Martin, "Terrorism and the Resilience of Cities," *Economic Policy Review* (November 2002): 97–116.

21. Robert Greenbaum and Andy Hultquist, "The Impact of Terrorism on Italian Employment and Business Activity" (unpublished manuscript, 2006).

22. For the Israeli case, see Zvi Eckstein and Daniel Tsiddon, "Macroeconomic Consequences of Terror: Theory and the Case of Israel" (paper presented at the conference on "Public Policy," Carnegie-Rochester, November 21–22, 2003); and Daniel Felsenstein and Shlomie Hazam, "The Effect of Terror on Behavior in the Jerusalem Housing Market" (unpublished manuscript, Institute of Urban and Regional Studies, Hebrew University of Jerusalem, 2005). For the Basque case, see Alberto Abadie and Javier Gardeazabai, "The Economic Costs of Conflict: A Case Control Study for the Basque Country," National Bureau of Economic Research (Cambridge, MA, September 2001).

23. Resilience can also be complex, and Vale and Campanella adumbrate its processes beginning with the onset of disaster to rebuilding. The purpose here is simpler and involves narrowing down a condition to see whether the disruption endures, for how long, and whether there has been a restoration. See Lawrence Vale and Thomas Campanella, eds., *The Resilient City: How Modern Cities Recover from Disaster* (New York: Oxford University Press, 2005).

24. For an account of New York's economy after 9/11, see Edward Hill and Iryna Lendell, "Did 9/11 Change Manhattan and the New York Region as Places to Conduct Business?" in *Resilient City: The Economic Impact of 9/11*, ed. Howard Chernick (New York: Russell Sage, 2005), pp. 23–61.

25. Ibid., p. 35.

26. Gross city product is calculated differently from one country to another, and this may account for the London's lower figure. See Corporation of London, *London/New York: The Economies of Two Cities at the Millennium*, Executive Summary (London: Corporation of London, June 2000), p. 16.

27. Ibid., sec: 2, "Driving Forces of Change in London and New York Economies."

28. Jerusalem Institute for Israel Studies, 1999–2000, *The Jerusalem Yearbook*, available at www.jiis.org.il/shnaton.

29. U.S. Department of Labor, Bureau of Labor Statistics, *Current Employment Survey*, 2006. See also Eisinger, "The American City in an Age of Terror," *Urban Affairs Review* 40, 1: 115–130; and Hill and Lendell, "Did 9/11 Change Manhattan and the New York Region as Places to Conduct Business?" in Chernick, ed., *Resilient City*.

30. See Chernick, ed., *Resilient City*, for the period up through 2004, and James Parrot, *New York City's Labor Market Outlook with a Special Emphasis on Immigrant Workers*, New York: Fiscal Policy Institute, December 2005.

31. The year taken for the previous period is 1989 and the year taken for the cessation of terror is 1994. As of this writing, data on London were not available to assess the employment effects due to the attacks of July 2005. See City of London Corporation, *City Research Focus*, available at http://www.cityoflondon.gov.uk/Corporation/business_city/research_statistics/Research+periodicals.htm#focus, and *Annual Business Inquiry*.

32. See H. V. Savitch and Garb Yaacov, "Terror, Barriers and the Re-topography of Jerusalem," as well as Hank V. Savitch, "An Anatomy of Urban Terror."

33. Jerusalem Institute for Israel Studies, "Statistical Yearbook of Jerusalem 2001–2004."

34. The comparisons made are between the pre-attack year of 2000 and the post-attack years of 2002 and 2003. The tourist figures cited in this section deal with tourism from other nations, or "foreign tourists." New York statistics are obtainable on the New York City Official Tourism Website at http://www.nycvisit.com/content/index.cfm?pagePkey=57.

35. Visit London Corporate, *London Monthly Trends, Monthly Visitor Index* (London: Visit London, July–September 2005).

36. Ibid.

37. Franz Fuerst, "The Impact of 9/11 on the Manhattan Office Market," in *Resilient City*, ed. Howard Chernick (New York: Russell Sage, 2005) pp. 62–98.

38. Ibid. About 20 percent of firms chose to move out of the city.

39. Ibid., p. 81.

40. See Igal Charney, "Reflections on the Post-WTC Skyline: Manhattan and Elsewhere," *International Journal of Urban and Regional Research* 29 (March 2005): 172–179.

41. Ibid.

42. Ibid. The skyscraper in Dubai will rise to over 2,300 feet (705 meters). The antenna/spire of the World Trade Center was 1,731.9 feet (527.9 meters) and its roofline was 1,368 feet (417 meters).

43. Quoted in Edwin Mills, "Terrorism and U.S. Real Estate," *Journal of Urban Economics* 51 (2002): 198–204.

44. Quoted in "Special Report: The Skyscraper Boom," *Economist*, June 3, 2006, pp. 65–67.

45. Eisinger, "The American City in an Age of Terror," p. 126.

46. Savitch, "An Anatomy of Urban Terror," p. 388.

47. Ibid., p. 389.

48. Thomas Wolfe, *You Can't Go Home Again*, 2d ed. (New York: Harper Perennial Classic, 1998).

49. Jonathan Schwabish and Joshua Chang, "New York City and Terrorism Insurance in a Post 9/11 World," *Issue Brief* (Partnership for New York City, September 2004).

50. National Underwriter Company, *Property and Casualty/Risks and Benefits* (National Underwriter Company, November 2002).

51. Editorial, *London Times*, December 14, 2002. p. 1.

52. Susan Clarke and Erica Chenoweth, "The Politics of Vulnerability: Constructing Local Performance Regimes for Homeland Security," *Review of Policy Research* 23, 1 (January 2006): 95–114.

53. German Marshal Fund, *Transatlantic Trends: Key Findings*, p. 7.

54. National League of Cities, "Cities Report Change in Financial Conditions," *State of American Cities Survey*. (Washington, DC: National League of Cities, 2001).

55. Ibid.

56. U.S. Senate, Undersecretary of Preparedness George Foresman, Department of Homeland Security, speaking "For the Record" to the Committee on Homeland Security (June 21, 2006), p. 3. This does not take account of other sources, and some have pegged the total amount at $28.9 billion. See Clarke and Chenoweth, "Politics of Vulnerability."

57. U.S. House Committee, Mayor Michael R. Bloomberg of New York City and Mayor Anthony Williams of Washington, DC, speaking on "DHS Terrorism Preparedness Grants: Risk-Based or Guess Work?" to the Committee on Homeland Security (June 21, 2006).

58. Department of Homeland Security, *FY 2006 Urban Area Security Initiative (UASI) by Urban Areas* sec. 2 (Washington, DC, 2006).

59. For a discussion of this see Peter Eisinger, "Imperfect Federalism: The Intergovernmental Partnership for Homeland Security," *Public Administration Review*, (July/August 2006): 537–545.

60. This is a political logic that decades ago marked efforts to create full employment and model cities. See, for example, Charles Haar, *Between the Idea and the Reality* (Boston: Little, Brown, 1975).

61. See Theodore Lowi, "American Business, Public Policy, and Case Studies and Political Theory," *World Politics* 16: (1964): 677–715; and Paul Peterson, *City Limits* (Chicago: University of Chicago Press, 1981).

62. See Clarke and Chenoweth, "Politics of Vulnerability."

26
The Political Economy of Disaster Assistance
STEPHEN D. STEHR

T he devastation wrought in the cities of the Gulf coast by Hurricanes
Katrina and Rita has once again cast a spotlight on disaster policy and
administration in the United States. Although presidential disaster declarations over the past decade have averaged approximately one per week, many
go unnoticed except by those directly affected. But so-called "megadisasters,"
characterized by significant loss of life, widespread physical and economic damage, and extensive media attention act as a catalyst for a reexamination of current policies and procedures. As the economic costs associated with disasters
have grown (Cutter and Emrich 2005), these debates have increasingly focused
on disaster relief and assistance programs and how urbanized regions might
mitigate damages before they occur (Mileti 1999; Platt 1999). This is not an
issue that is likely to go away anytime soon. Many of the nation's most populous urban areas are situated in coastal areas that are at high risk from naturally
occurring events such as earthquakes or hurricanes. According to the Census
Bureau, more than half of the nation's 297 million people live in coastal areas—
most in major cities—and seven of the top 10 fastest-growing states are coastal.
Cities nationwide are subject to an array of natural hazards such as riverine
flooding, wildfires, ice storms, tornados, drought, and volcanic eruptions. In
the post–September 11 environment, all cities are considered to be at some level
of risk to terrorist attacks that have the potential of causing many of the same
types of problems (e.g., large-scale evacuation of citizens; urban search and rescue; public health and environmental concerns; mass casualty management and
victim identification; victim compensation; reconstruction of public infrastructure; business continuity) that are also associated with natural events.

Despite the increasing vulnerability of urban areas to catastrophic events,
relatively little attention has been explicitly paid to issues that would inform
both the literatures concerning urban studies and those that focus on the social
science aspects of disaster.[1] This article represents a modest attempt to begin
a dialogue between those who study more traditional topics in urban governance and those who study how communities prepare for, respond to, and
recover from disasters. My primary focus is on two related questions: First, is it
possible to reconcile the competing forces of economic development decisions
and political calculations with hazard mitigation policies? Under the current
structure, local officials have very few incentives to mitigate hazards secure in

Author's Note: Portions of the research reported here were supported by a grant from the National
Science Foundation (CMS 0234100). The opinions presented in this article are the author's and do
not necessarily reflect those of the National Science Foundation. The author would like to thank
the anonymous reviewers who provided useful comments on an earlier draft.

the knowledge that federal aid will be forthcoming following an event. Recovery from large-scale urban disasters also lays bare local political dynamics that may have been obscured prior to the event (Kantor 2002). But they also expose longer-term national political trends and priorities as they relate to disaster preparedness and response capabilities. A second question relates to the possibility of incorporating the idea of community resilience into discussions of sustainable development. As Savitch points out, our collective understanding of the life of cities goes through recognizable paradigmatic shifts (Savitch 2003). It remains to be seen if some of the forces discussed in this article have reached a critical mass and will launch a new paradigm focused on safe cities.

The history of disaster relief and assistance policy in the United States can be characterized as having brief periods of intense political activity typically following a major disaster or a series of disasters, followed by longer periods where interest in the subject wanes (May 1985). This has resulted in a fragmented set of policies that, over time, have significantly increased the financial exposure of the federal government (Platt 1999). There are four primary means through which postdisaster assistance is administered: (1) government programs (primarily implemented through the federal government); (2) charities and philanthropic organizations; (3) private insurance; and, (4) the court system chiefly through tort claims and bankruptcy filings.[2] Federal disaster assistance is provided through approximately 30 separate programs that offer aid to individuals and families, businesses, states and municipalities, special districts, and not-for-profit organizations (Jordan 2005). A wide range of financial strategies is utilized including direct grants to stricken communities and individuals, low interest disaster loans, federal public works programs to remove debris and rebuild public infrastructures, disaster unemployment benefits, mental health and legal services, environmental cleanup, and federal income tax deductions for uninsured casualty losses.

Federal aid is intended to be supplemental to funds dedicated by state and local governments. The Federal Disaster Assistance Act of 1988 (the Stafford Act)—the primary federal law governing disasters—specifies a 75/25 ratio of federal/nonfederal cost sharing of disaster assistance with state and local governments. However, recent presidents of both parties have raised the federal share or waived nonfederal contributions entirely (Platt 1999, p. 17). Although these waivers are no doubt motivated in part by compassion, presidents (and members of Congress) are also under intense political pressure to act quickly and generously, particularly in election years. Several recent studies have documented a connection between presidential elections, congressional politics, and level of disaster relief allocated to specific areas (Garrett and Sobel 2003; Reeves 2005).

Postdisaster response and recovery assistance has historically made up the vast majority of federal spending on disasters. According to a report issued by the Bipartisan Task Force on Funding Disaster Relief, approximately three-quarters of all federal spending on disasters between 1977 and 1994 was expended to pay for postdisaster recovery (U.S. Senate 1995). This same report charged that the federal government discourages state, local, and individual self-reliance by offering federal disaster assistance too readily. It seems reasonable to conclude that in some instances disaster assistance has become a form of political "pork barrel," particularly in cases where genuine need seems to be absent.[3]

The implementation of disaster assistance in New York City following the terrorist attacks of September 11 illustrates the basic structure of relief policies. According to a report completed by researchers at RAND, the total amount of direct disaster assistance delivered to victims, businesses, and government entities was $38.1 billion (Dixon and Stern 2004). Of this amount, slightly more than half ($19.6 billion, or 51%) was paid out by insurance companies. Through 2004, government programs accounted for $15.8 billion (42%) of total relief payments but this figure will grow as monies allocated but not yet expended are spent. Despite an unprecedented mobilization charitable distributions accounted for only 7% of total assistance.[4]

Soon after the attacks, President George W. Bush promised $20 billion in federal money to help the New York City area recover from 9/11. Although some may have interpreted this pledge to mean that New York City would receive a lump sum payment, in reality the aid package was structured to provide for both immediate needs as well as long-term assistance. The flow of federal aid to New York City and its inhabitants is being tracked by the New York City Independent Budget Office (IBO). By its accounting, approximately 30% ($6.3 billion) of the money was expended on emergency response activities. The majority of this money (approximately 70%) was provided to New York City to pay for debris removal and overtime costs for the police and fire departments and to establish an insurance pool to protect the city and its contract workers against lawsuits resulting from work at the World Trade Center site (IBO 2004). Only a small portion of the response funds (about 10%) were provided as direct aid to individuals or as low interest loans to property owners. About 20% ($4.4 billion) of $20 billion appropriated by Congress was designed to spur economic recovery in Lower Manhattan and to help alleviate the budget crisis the city faced in the wake of the attack. Most of these funds were provided directly to New York City government (38% or $1.7 billion) or for business assistance grants (26% or $1.2 billion). The remaining $9.7 billion (most of which have not yet been spent) will go for long-term rebuilding projects primarily in the area of transportation improvements.

Although care should be taken in generalizing from this admittedly unprecedented case, several lessons emerge nonetheless. First, insurance companies provided about 50% of the total compensation provided. These monies went to individuals (mostly through life insurance policies) and affected businesses. As it turns out, there is empirical evidence to suggest that the 50% figure is a reasonable assumption in many natural disasters as well (Pielke 2005). Second, most of the assistance provided through federal programs was administered to New York City with a smaller portion going to businesses that were damaged, destroyed, or disrupted. In fact, aside from the approximately $7 billion that was expended through the VCF, a relatively small amount of direct assistance was provided to individuals. Finally, disaster recovery and reconstruction—even when the physical damage is relatively concentrated as it was in New York City—does not take place overnight. It is estimated that it will take approximately 10 years to fully expend the entire $20 billion authorized by Congress (IBO 2004).

Although disaster assistance is commonly thought to include only those activities that occur following an extreme event, a more comprehensive approach also includes pre-event mitigation and preparedness activities designed to eliminate or reduce event impacts. As Lindell and Prater (2003) point out, there are strong and important linkages between hazard mitigation and preparedness practices, and community recovery and reconstruction outcomes. An inherent problem in the structure of disaster assistance is the fact that the mitigation and preparedness are largely the responsibility of local governments while the economic costs of recovery and reconstruction are borne elsewhere. Subnational governments and individuals owning property in hazardous areas to a large extent control decisions that determine the ultimate effectiveness of mitigation and preparedness measures adopted at the local level; in most cases, these parties have few incentives to make these policies a high priority because federal programs will provide assistance should a disaster occur (May 1985; Stehr 1999). Adding to the problem is that well-intentioned government programs sometimes undermine each other. Rutherford Platt argues that a vast array of federal spending and economic development programs such as highway construction, housing, urban renewal, shoreline stabilization, water pollution abatement, and river control projects may undercut the goals of hazard mitigation by indirectly sponsoring development and redevelopment in areas of recurrent hazard (Platt 1999). It remains to be seen if a "paradigm shift" from a political-economic logic of urban development to one based in public security and protection will inform decisions regarding the rebuilding of New Orleans (Savitch 2003).

Going beyond the pressures associated with local economic development decisions and the problems it creates in creating workable response and assistance policies, disaster policy is also a by-product of other, seemingly unconnected policy decisions. For instance, decisions made in the arenas of national security policy, urban policy, and social policy have traceable impacts on current disaster policy. Following September 11, planning to detect and prevent terrorist attacks all but eliminated federal interest in preparedness and response activities and funding for natural disaster mitigation projects (Holdeman 2005; Tierney 2005). Significantly, the Federal Emergency Management Agency (FEMA), the agency established to coordinate hazard mitigation, and disaster response and recovery policies, was stripped of its cabinet-level status when it was placed within the newly created Department of Homeland Security. Project Impact, a hazard mitigation program started during the Clinton administration to provide grants to cities, was eliminated in 2001 although it was costing only about $20 million per year. This devolution of responsibility can be seen as merely one part of a "new" urban policy whereby cities are expected to take on additional responsibilities for protecting their citizens (Eisinger 2004). This is also part of a larger trend. As William Barnes recently reported, federal funds as a percentage of municipal revenues reached a high in 1978 at about 17% and have declined steadily since then to less than 5% (Barnes 2005). Some observers have interpreted the events in New Orleans as resulting from decades of federal urban disinvestment, exurbanization, and "white flight," which have left the central cores of many cities "abandoned" (Graham 2005), or as "exposing the unacknowledged inequalities" that are the result of years of failed social policies (Frymer, Strolovitch, and Warren 2005).

CAN WE CREATE RESILIENT CITIES?

For at least the past decade, community resilience has been a prominent topic among academic urban planners and natural disaster researchers. Dennis Mileti defines the concept this way: "Local resiliency with regard to disasters means that a locale is able to withstand an extreme natural event without suffering devastating losses, damage, diminished productivity, or quality of life and without a large amount of assistance from outside the community" (Mileti 1999, pp. 32–33). One aspect of community resilience focuses on hazard mitigation—that is, activities designed to reduce or eliminate long-term risk to people and property and break the cycle of damage, reconstruction, and repeated damage from disasters. These efforts include such actions as stricter building codes, engineering retrofits, land use planning, and property acquisition (Hardenbrook 2005; Godschalk et al. 1999; Burby 1998). How successful are these efforts likely to be? Certainly there will be localized success stories. However, as this article points out, there are strong political and economic forces at work that will make widespread urban hazard mitigation difficult to achieve. One promising avenue to pursue is the concept of "comprehensive emergency management." This idea is rooted in the notion that loss-reduction efforts should be oriented toward integrating mitigation, preparedness, response, and recovery activities suitable for a variety of localized hazards whether natural, technological, or human caused. But implementing this concept costs time and money and requires local political and administrative leadership. In the absence of national incentives to create resilient communities, the provision of public protection will continue to fall largely on urban governance structures.

In their recent book, *The Resilient City,* Vale and Campanella raise a number of important questions that could help inform a more robust dialogue between urbanists and those who study the social science aspects of disaster (Vale and Campanella 2005, pp. 12–13). For example, they pose the question: what does it mean for a "city" to "recover"? As regional hubs of economic, social, and cultural activities, cities recover to the extent that they return to some semblance of predisaster normalcy in human and economic relationships. But large-scale disasters also raise value-laden questions such as who will set the priorities for recovering communities? How will short-term recovery forces be balanced with long-range planning? Will predisaster inequities be replicated as part of the recovery process? Who will be displaced (and at what cost) as neighborhoods are rebuilt? What are the proper roles of local, state, and federal officials in an intergovernmental disaster assistance system? What dominant narratives will emerge to help us interpret what transpired and inform future hazard policies? By addressing these and many other important questions, a richer and more complete understanding of the vulnerability of cities to hazards could emerge that would serve to inform research from a variety of professional perspectives.

REFERENCES

Barnes, W. 2005. Beyond federal urban policy. *Urban Affairs Review* 40(5): 575–89.

Burby, R., ed. 1998. *Cooperating with nature: Confronting natural hazards with land-use planning for sustainable communities.* Washington, D.C.: Joseph Henry Press.

Cutter, S., and C. Emrich. 2005. Are natural disaster losses in the U.S. increasing? *EOS: Transactions, American Geophysical Union* 86(41): 381–96.

Dixon, L., and R. Stern. 2004. *Compensation for losses from the 9/11 attacks.* Santa Monica, CA: RAND.

Eisinger, P. 2004. The American city in the age of terror: A preliminary assessment of the effects of September 11. *Urban Affairs Review* 40(1): 115–29.

Frymer, P., D. Strolovitch, and D. Warren. 2005. Katrina's political roots and divisions: Race, class, and federalism in American politics. Understanding Katrina: Perspectives from the social sciences. Web site created by the Social Science Research Centre. University of Maryland, http://www.understandingkatrina.ssrc.org (accessed September 19, 2005).

Garrett, T., and R. Sobel. 2003. The Political Economy of FEMA Disaster Payments. *Economic Inquiry* 41(3): 496–509.

Gerber, B., D. Cohen, B. Cannon, D. Patterson, and K. Stewart. 2005. On the front line: American cities and the challenge of homeland security preparedness. *Urban Affairs Review* 41(2): 182–210.

Godschalk, D., T. Beatley, P. Berke, D. Brower, and E. Kaiser. 1999. *Natural hazard mitigation: Recasting disaster policy and planning.* Washington, D.C.: Island.

Graham, S. 2005. Cities under siege: Katrina and the politics of metropolitan America. Understanding Katrina: Perspectives from the social sciences. Web site created by the Social Science Research Center, University of Maryland, http://www.understandingkatrina.ssrc.org (accessed September 19, 2005).

Hardenbrook, B. 2005. The need for a policy framework to develop disaster resilient regions. *Journal of Homeland Security and Emergency Management* 2(3): Article 2.

Holdeman, E. 2005. Destroying FEMA. *Washington Post,* August 30, 2005.

Jordan, M. 2005. Federal disaster recovery programs: Brief summaries. CRS Report for Congress, Congressional Research Service. August 29, 2005.

Kantor, P. 2002. Terrorism and governability in New York City: Old problem, new dilemma. *Urban Affairs Review* 38(1): 120–27.

Kestin, S. 2005. FEMA battered by waste, fraud. South Florida *Sun-Sentinel,* September 18, A1.

Lindell, M. K. and C. Prater. 2003. Assessing community impacts of natural disasters. *Natural Hazards Review* 3(2): 176–85.

May, P. 1985. *Recovering from catastrophes: Federal disaster relief policy and politics.* Westport, CT: Greenwood.

Mileti, D. 1999. *Disasters by design: A reassessment of natural hazards in the United States.* Washington, D.C.: Joseph Henry.

New York City Independent Budget Office. 2004. Three years after: Where is the $20 billion in federal WTC aid? Inside the budget. August 11, 2004.

Pielke, R. 2005. Historical economic losses from hurricanes: Where does Katrina fit in? Center For Science and Technology Policy Research, University of Colorado, http://www.sciencepolicy.colorado.edu (accessed September 19, 2005).

Platt, R. 1999. *Disasters and democracy: The politics of extreme natural events.* Washington. D.C.: Island.

Reeves, A. 2005. Political disaster? Presidential disaster declarations and electoral politics. Department of Government, Harvard University (unpublished manuscript).

Savitch, H. 2003. Does 9–11 portend a new paradigm for cities? *Urban Affairs Review* 38(1): 120–27.

Stehr, S. 1999. Community recovery and reconstruction following disasters. In *The handbook of crisis and emergency management,* edited by A. Farazmand, 345–57. New York: Marcel Dekker.

Tierney, K. 2005. The red pill. Understanding Katrina: Perspectives from the social sciences. Social Science Research Center, University of Maryland, http://www.understandingkatrina.ssrc.org (accessed September 19, 2005).

U.S. Congress. Senate. Bipartisan Task Force on Funding Disaster Relief. Report of Senate task force on funding disaster relief. 104th Congress. Document No. 104–4.

Vale, L., and T. Campanella, eds. 2005. *The resilient city: How modern cities recover from disaster.* Oxford: Univ. Press.

NOTES

1. In the aftermath of the attacks of September 11, some urban scholars have turned their attention to issues related to homeland security (Gerber et al. 2005) and urban terrorism (Eisinger 2004; Kantor 2002).
2. This article will focus primarily on the governmental component of disaster assistance.
3. Reporters at the South Florida *Sun-Sentinel* examined 20 of the 313 disasters declared by the Federal Emergency Management Agency from 1999 to 2004. They concluded that 27% of the $1.2 billion paid out went to areas where official reports showed minor damage or none at all (Kestin 2005).
4. In exchange for establishing the September 11th Victim Compensation Fund (VCF) to provide compensation to families of those who were killed and to the seriously injured, Congress limited the role of the tort system in part to protect the airlines involved in the attacks and the owners of the World Trade Center.

27

Politics, Federalism, and the Recovery Process in New Orleans

PETER F. BURNS AND MATTHEW O. THOMAS

A new New Orleans. That's what many thought, and even more hoped, would emerge after Hurricane Katrina attacked New Orleans. Local, state, and national figures thought that Katrina provided an opportunity for the city to start anew. In public, they advocated a new city, one that kept the New Orleans' charm, attractions, and culture but lost the area's negative aspects. In reality, much, but not all, of the new New Orleans resembled the old New Orleans. In particular, schisms between the public and private sector, whites and African Americans, and state and city government persisted in post-Katrina New Orleans. By contrast, a newer New Orleans appeared, particularly in the realm of governance.

Why, given such huge trauma, physical damage, and social disruptions, was there a reversion to some old patterns? Most stories on the friction between the state of Louisiana and the city of New Orleans attribute at least some of the tension to Mayor C. Ray Nagin's endorsement of two other gubernatorial candidates, one of whom was a Republican, instead of Kathleen Blanco, a fellow Democrat, in the 2003 gubernatorial primary and runoff. Certainly, personal animosity and political differences between the mayor and the governor complicated the relationship between Louisiana and New Orleans, but factors beyond personal politics also explain the endurance of state–local tensions.

Why did governance change while other policy areas remained stagnant? In this article, we examine how deeply rooted historical patterns of state–local conflict reasserted themselves even after the terrible destruction of Katrina and the redemptive promise of a new beginning. We also explain how state government, some city leaders, and some New Orleanians took advantage of the opportunities presented by Hurricane Katrina to change certain aspects of governance in New Orleans.

To better understand how and why state government affects urban affairs, this article specifies those dimensions of the state–local relationship that influence how New Orleans rebuilds. It uses an historical analysis to identify the most important ways in which pre-catastrophe relations affect the recovery process. This article's broader implications illustrate the effect of state government on urban affairs and the influence of aspects of history on present conditions.

From Peter F. Burns and Matthew O. Thomas, "A New New Orleans? Understanding the Role of History and the State-Local Relationship in the Recovery Process," *Journal of Urban Affairs*, Vol. 30, No. 3, 2008, pp. 259–271. Copyright © 2008 Urban Affairs Association. Reprinted by permission of Wiley-Blackwell.

NEW ORLEANS: THEN AND NOW

In July of 2005, the population of New Orleans stood at 452,170.[1] One month later, after the Katrina-breached levees flooded the city, the population all but disappeared. Essential city services, such as police and fire, barely operated, and all other governmental services halted. In essence, the city shut down.

Prior to Katrina, tourists flocked to New Orleans, feasting on its food, architecture, nightlife, and especially its music. The city's port, although diminished from its heyday, remained an important hub. A number of universities, including Tulane, Loyola, the University of New Orleans, Xavier, and Dillard, as well as the LSU Medical School, provided significant intellectual capital. These assets offered some promise for improvement after Katrina but New Orleans also needed to face the negative aspects of its past. Prior to Hurricane Katrina, the city struggled with issues of corruption; and city services, especially public schools, lagged far behind other jurisdictions. In the wake of Katrina, the city faced unfathomable challenges to recovery.

By July of 2006, a year after Katrina, the population of New Orleans had rebounded to 223,388, making the population about half of the pre-Katrina population. But other critical measures of capacity illustrate the challenges faced by the city. In that same month, only 22% of the child care centers, only 39% of the city's hospitals (9 of 23), and only 45% of the public transportation routes were open or operational. By August of 2006, only 41% of the city's public schools welcomed students.

Two years after Katrina, the population continued to increase, rising to almost 70% of the pre-Katrina population. Estimates in November 2007 indicate that blacks made up 58% of the city (*The Associated Press*, 2007). Prior to Hurricane Katrina, African Americans constituted slightly more than 66% of the city's population. Approximately 80% of New Orleans flooded as a result of the breached levees. The Uptown section of New Orleans, buffered by the city's natural levee, received the least amount of damage.

Whites in Uptown New Orleans lost some power and many elected positions, as the city's racial demographics changes over time, but they continued to exert considerable influence over public policy. They use campaign contributions, a good-government agency called the Bureau of Governmental Research (BGR), and access to the media, especially *The Times-Picayune*, to exercise power. One example of this influence occurred in 2004 when whites formed coalitions with some African Americans to stop the school board from firing Superintendent of Schools Anthony Amato. Of the five members who opposed Amato, three lost their seats and two did not seek reelection in the school board election of 2004.

The city's demographic shifts affected election results in post-Katrina New Orleans (Krupa, 2007b). In 2007, the New Orleans City Council became majority-white for the first time in 22 years. Throughout New Orleans, elected positions, including judges, city council members, and state legislators, which were held by blacks for years, have switched to white-officeholders in the post-Katrina period. At the time of the November 17, 2007, special election to fill a vacant, citywide council seat, black registered voters outnumbered white registered voters by more than 92,000, but turnout in majority-white districts was higher than turnout in majority-black districts (Krupa, 2007b).

Because of increases in the population, tax revenues, which plummeted in the immediate aftermath of the storm, continue to grow, reaching 94% of the pre-Katrina revenues. This positive sign is tempered by the city's continuing infrastructure dilemma. After two years, only 57% of hospitals, 62% of schools, and 38% of day care centers were in operation. When those within and outside New Orleans look at these figures and others like them, they characterize the rebuilding as slow.

Many displaced New Orleanians face the choice of returning to a city that cannot provide adequate healthcare, and those former residents with children must wrestle with the decreased capacity of the child care system and the limited number of public schools. Adding to those concerns, the city still struggles to adopt a comprehensive rebuilding plan, and the Road Home Program has a poor track record at issuing payments (see below). These two New Orleans, pre-and poststorm, are very different, but may in fact be influenced by similar trends. One of these historical patterns that continues to influence politics in the city is the character of state–local relations.

THE IMPORTANCE OF STATE–CITY RELATIONS

An investigation of the state–local dimension of the recovery is important because cities are creatures of the state (Burns & Gamm, 1997). Cities look increasingly toward state government for financial assistance in this era of devolution. Absent private leadership in cities, governors and state legislators have the potential to champion certain projects and policies in cities (Burns & Thomas, 2004). An analysis of the effect of state–local relations on rebuilding New Orleans also provides insight into other areas—race, culture, income, and class—that may affect how the city recovers from this disaster.

The Louisiana governor and legislature play important roles in the rebuilding of New Orleans. Because of devolution, the Louisiana governor maintains the authority to disperse federal recovery funds to New Orleans. The governor and state legislature propose and pass policies on how the city will not only govern itself but also execute police powers—including the education of New Orleans school children—in the aftermath of Katrina.

The focus on how state–city relations influence New Orleans' recovery does not indicate that this relationship is the only aspect of the recovery process. Clearly, other relationships, including those between races, public and private leaders, and community groups and government, also affect the manner in which New Orleans rebuilds after Hurricane Katrina. In addition to the aforementioned effects that state government exerts on city politics and policy, we also focus upon the role of state government because many critics argue that the study of urban affairs pays too little attention to extra-local actors, namely governors, state legislatures, and state bureaucracies (for example, see Burns, 2002; Burns & Thomas, 2004; Harding, 1995; Kantor, Savitch, & Haddock, 1997; Lauria, 1996; Sites, 1997).

HISTORICAL TENSIONS BETWEEN CITIES AND STATES

Historically, states and large cities have had an antagonistic relationship (Berman, 2003). As Berman (2003) notes, "One of the most persistent themes in state–local relations has been the conflict between state legislatures and the largest cities in the states" (p. 53). Louisiana versus New Orleans, New York State versus New York City, Illinois versus Chicago, Michigan versus Detroit, Missouri versus Kansas City and St. Louis, Maryland versus Baltimore, among many other places, typify the conflict between state-level actors and big cities (for example, see Stonecash, 1989). But what are the sources of tensions between these levels of government?

Money

An overview of the history of state–city relations in the United States in general, and the interactions between the state of Louisiana and New Orleans in particular, suggests several potential explanations for prolonged conflict between these levels of government (Berman, 2003). Money, control, and differences between urban and rural areas constitute deeply rooted historical patterns that influence city–state relations (Berman, 2003). Historically, cities and state government fight over money. The battle over finances intensified in the 1980s when state government's involvement in urban and local affairs increased mainly because of three factors: A large federal deficit, President Ronald Reagan's view that the federal government failed to achieve victories in the war on poverty and other social problems, and the federal government's decision to devolve policy responsibilities to the states (Liner, 1989; Pagano, 1990; Stonecash, 1998). In this devolution period, cities wanted more money from the state government with fewer strings while states sought greater control and oversight over the dollars they allocated to urban governments.

Finances traditionally divide the state of Louisiana and the city of New Orleans. The rest of Louisiana argues that New Orleans receives a greater share of the state's resources than it contributes to Louisiana's coffers. Among other things, legislators from outside New Orleans opposed special state subsidies for the New Orleans Saints NFL team, the Superdome, a downtown arena in the city, an amusement park, and the state's only land-based casino.

In lobbying for mandatory crossing arms at all railroad crossings in the vicinity of schools, for example, a state senator from the northwestern corner of Louisiana argued, "There's a lot of people for giving millions and millions to the Superdome. But to save a child's life . . . we say it costs too much" (McGill, 2001). This kind of rhetoric has characterized state politics and relations between Louisiana and New Orleans for decades.

Editorials by *The Advocate,* a major newspaper in the state that is based in Baton Rouge, echoed what many outside New Orleans felt (and continue to feel) about state assistance to the city. After the state's bond commission approved millions for special projects in New Orleans in 1997, *The Advocate* concluded, "It's become an unfortunate and unpleasant fact of life: The New Orleans area grabs off the bulk of the state capital outlay money, and the rest of the state is left holding the bag" (*The Advocate*, 1997).

More than seven years later and in the midst of debates about state funding for a new football stadium in New Orleans, *The Advocate* (2004) argued, "We are delighted that the governor [Kathleen Blanco] explained the political reality to the New Orleans community: The rest of the state is not interested in paying $400 million-plus for a football stadium. And the existing state subsidy to the New Orleans Saints is widely resented" (*The Advocate*, 2004, p. 6).

A longstanding conflict exists over whether the state can trust New Orleanians to spend the aid it allocates to the city. Corruption and mismanagement afflict New Orleans' public bureaucracy, especially its school system. In 2003, for example, an audit revealed that the school system paid more than $31 million to former and even deceased workers (McGill, 2003). Less than a year later, a federal court indicted eleven people for this fraud and theft (Simpson, 2004).

The federal government also charged two insurance brokers for receiving money in exchange for favorable treatment on school contracts (Simpson, 2004). In 2004, the federal government blocked the New Orleans' school board's attempt to fire Superintendent Anthony Amato, who by most accounts was succeeding in improving city schools. Most recently, Ellenese Brooks-Simms, the former president of the New Orleans School Board, pled guilty to federal bribery charges, further tainting the legacy of the school system (Maloney, 2007).

Control

Control over urban affairs traditionally divides state government and cities. State governments have attempted to control city politics and policy for several reasons. Some try to dictate urban politics for political and personal gains. In the mid 19th century, state legislators and political parties used patronage in the cities to gain electoral support in urban areas (Berman, 2003). State intervention into urban affairs has increased when governors and legislators either believed that cities could not handle the problems that confronted them or attempted to address corruption in city government. To say the least, urban actors, especially those in control, resent the assertiveness of state government.

In 2003, the state legislature and voters across Louisiana proposed and ratified a constitutional amendment to allow the state to take over failing schools. This amendment applied mainly to New Orleans. Proponents of the takeover amendment argued that the continual failure to improve the quality of education in some districts in general, and in New Orleans in particular, led them to support this policy reform. The president of the Louisiana Senate, a Republican who represented part of New Orleans, referred to the low quality of education in the city as tantamount to "intellectual slavery" (McGill, 2003).

In the vote on the amendment, three-fifths of the Louisiana electorate ratified the takeover amendment. New Orleans supported the takeover measure with 56% of the vote. The amendment received high support, 60–70%, among parishes in the New Orleans Metropolitan Statistical Area (MSA).

Part of the reason for the support for the amendment in New Orleans was the city's dismal view of the Orleans Parish School District. At the time, New Orleans' residents held negative views of the city's public schools. In a 2000 survey, half of the New Orleans' residents who were surveyed characterized the city's elementary schools as poor whereas 61% held this view four years later (University of New Orleans Survey Research Center, 2000). Only 1% of respondents characterized these schools as excellent in 2004. In that year, New Orleans' residents regarded education as the city's second biggest problem behind crime. Despite these perceptions, 44% of the New Orleans electorate opposed the move to allow the state to assume direct control over schools that performed miserably.

The vote on the takeover amendment split along racial lines within the city of New Orleans. Voters in predominantly white districts overwhelmingly supported the amendment. Majority African-American districts strongly opposed state takeovers of failing schools.

In the pre-Katrina period, governors and state legislators were hesitant to provide exorbitant sums to the city because of New Orleans' reputation for corruption and patronage. They wanted a way to control the outcomes, and avoid sending good money after bad. In 2001, Louisiana Senator John Hainkel, who represented part of New Orleans, advocated the dissolution of the New Orleans Board of Education. He cited corruption, poor test scores, and overall mismanagement for his position; in response, a white member of the

New Orleans school board regarded Hainkel's position as one dominated by a "plantation mentality," in which the senator assumed that the people of New Orleans could not govern themselves adequately (Gray, 2001).

New Orleans versus the Rest of the State

Cultural and racial divides between central cities and other areas throughout the state also heighten tensions between urban areas and state government (Gimpel & Schuknecht, 2002). Over time, a clear division existed between rural areas and cities. One source of this conflict involves which entities will control city politics. Another concerns stark differences in policy preferences. People outside of the cities, especially those in rural areas, were anti-immigrant, anti-Catholic, and anti-alcohol, among other things (Berman, 2003). By contrast, cities had high percentages of immigrants and Catholics and tolerant views on alcohol consumption. State legislatures translated these views into an anti-urban bias.

Stark differences between New Orleans and the rest of Louisiana, especially, but not exclusively, the northern part of the state, explain some of the tensions between the city and the state. Louisiana is a rural state; New Orleans is urban. Catholicism dominated New Orleans; Protestantism was the prominent religion in north Louisiana.

Over time, various governors, legislators, mayors, and other actors played out the animosity and even hatred that Louisianans in general, and those in the northern portion of the state in particular, felt toward New Orleans. Huey Long (governor from 1928–1932) and Earl Long (governor from 1939–1940; 1948–1952; 1956–1960 and lieutenant governor from 1937–1939) typified north Louisiana's disdain for all things New Orleans, namely its religion, racial composition, and culture.

Debates over control of the city and race continued to divide Louisiana governors and state legislatures against New Orleans after the Longs left office. Along with the Louisiana legislature, Governor Jimmie Davis (1944–1948; 1956–1960) opposed the *Brown v. Board of Education* decision and the integration of New Orleans public schools. In a special session of the legislature, the governor and state legislature passed a series of segregationist laws to circumvent the *Brown* decision (Garvey & Widmer, 2001). Governor Davis went so far as to take over the New Orleans schools to prevent desegregation. When that failed, he worked with the legislature to pass rigorous anti-integration laws (Crain, 1968; Parent, 2004, pp. 108–109).

Davis and the state legislature "abolished the Orleans Parish School Board, forbade all transfers, ordered the closing of any school under a desegregation order, and revoked the accreditation of integrated schools and the certification of any teachers at those schools" (Parent, 2004, p. 108). These actions to oppose racial integration illustrate the lengths state leaders went to in order to exert power over New Orleans. They also highlight the differences between the state and the city.

Edwin Edwards' (1972–1980; 1984–1988; 1992–1996) fourth and final gubernatorial election highlighted the enduring racial and religious tensions between the rest of Louisiana and New Orleans. David Duke, Edwards' opponent in the 1992 gubernatorial election and former Grand Wizard of the Knights of the Ku Klux Klan, received his strongest support from white Protestants and those in the rural parishes in north Louisiana (Robertson, 1991). In campaign speeches for the U.S. Senate in 1990, Duke "preached that the poor and minorities received too much assistance from the government and that the middle class did not get enough, instead being forced to pay for programs to assist the poor" (Renwick, Parent, & Wardlaw, 1999, p. 288).

New Orleans and Louisiana traditionally battle over the importance of the city to the rest of the state. Most actors in New Orleans claim that as New Orleans goes economically, so goes the rest of the state. Consequently, they argue that the state should provide financial resources to New Orleans because of the city's ability to generate revenue to state coffers.

Prior to his inauguration in 2002, Mayor-elect Ray Nagin told reporters, "Around the state, people understand that if New Orleans really gets going, it's good for the rest of the state" (Gyan, 2002). A year later, Nagin told the legislature, "We thank you for not hurting us yet" (*The Times-Picayune,* 2003). This statement clearly indicated that Nagin understood that legislators from around the state did not understand that what is good for New Orleans is good for the rest of the state.

In 2003, Governor Mike Foster's (1996–2004) former chief of staff, who served as president of the New Orleans Metropolitan Convention and Visitors Bureau at the time, argued, "The reality is that wherever you're from and whatever political bias you have, cultural orientation or background, if the city of New Orleans fails as an enterprise, so does the state. If New Orleans prospers, the state prospers" (Sayre, 2003).

LOUISIANA–NEW ORLEANS RELATIONS IN THE POST-KATRINA ERA

How have these dimensions of the Louisiana–New Orleans historical-conflict played out in post-Katrina New Orleans? Which elements of the predisaster relationship affected the interactions between these levels of government and the manner in which New Orleans recovered after Katrina, and why? Which dimensions didn't have much of an impact at all, perhaps even when they were thought to possibly have such potential, and why?

An historical overview suggests that financial assistance, control over urban policies, programs, and bureaucracies, and cultural, socioeconomic, and racial differences will be the greatest sources of conflict between New Orleans and Louisiana in the post-Katrina period. We trace the interactions between Louisiana state government and New Orleans city government in the aftermath of Hurricane Katrina in order to determine which dimensions of the state–city relationship set the stage for what transpired after Katrina. Specifically, we examine the extent to which financial aid and funding are correlated with enduring state and local tensions. Then, we address whether attempts by Louisiana's state government to control governance and policy in post-Katrina New Orleans continued the conflict between the state and the city. Finally, we examine how residents from New Orleans and the rest of the state prioritize policy options in the post-Katrina period in order to determine if significant differences continue to exist between these parts of the state.

Money

Typically, urban politics involves struggles over scarce resources, including funding. Ironically, in some instances of post-Katrina New Orleans, it appears that available funding remains unspent. Nearly a year to the day after Hurricane Katrina hit New Orleans, Mayor Nagin complained, "No real resources to help us stand up have gotten down to our level. Zero" (Krupa, 2006, p. 1). The object of Nagin's criticisms was Governor Blanco, who responded that the state allocated $225 million from the Federal Emergency Management Agency (FEMA) to the city (Krupa, 2006). In response to the governor, the mayor's assistant chief administrative officer noted that Blanco included aid in her $225 million total that FEMA, and not the state, gave directly to city agencies (Krupa, 2006).

As Blanco and Nagin fought over funding levels for the city, members of Blanco's Administration insisted that Nagin need only request funds and he would receive them, but the state seemed unwilling or unable to detail the process for these requests (New Orleans CityBusiness, 2007). In a related example, FEMA recently indicated that New Orleans was eligible for hundreds of millions of dollars in road and infrastructure repairs through Public Assistance grants, but that the city's Department of Public Works had not yet produced a necessary list of storm-damaged streets. The city responded that it was unaware of the grant program, and that it did not want to waste time cataloguing damage when other pressing issues remained (Warner, 2007).

In his 2007 State of the City address Nagin touted the city's success, but he made it clear that the state could be doing much more to help New Orleans. He blamed the state for its repeated failures to issue Road Home monies in a timely manner, and criticized the federal government for not properly compensating the city (Krupa, 2007a). The inability of the state and local governments to work together continued to affect the recovery.

Control to Improve Governance

The city of New Orleans supported most attempts by the state to control or change governance in post-Katrina New Orleans. Local leaders and citizens tended to either support or not outwardly oppose efforts by the state to improve public institutions and eliminate patronage, mismanagement, and corruption in the city. Hurricane Katrina provided an opportunity for the governor, the state legislature, and New Orleans citizens to attack the city's corruption and mismanagement. They took advantage of this opportunity by proposing, passing, and ratifying measures to make New Orleans government more efficient and leaner.

In the name of relief for New Orleans, the governor and the state legislature altered the structure of New Orleans public schools. According to Governor Blanco, Hurricane Katrina represented "a golden opportunity for rebirth" of New Orleans (Robelen, 2005, p. 1). The state seized the moment and reconfigured the Orleans Parish School system. This moment was met by some resistance but many others in the city either supported the transformation or held a neutral view.

In the first special session devoted to rebuilding New Orleans, the Louisiana legislature authorized the state to take over 107 of the 128 schools in the Orleans Parish School District (Ritea, 2006). At the beginning of the first full school year after Katrina, the School Recovery District (RSD), which is the entity created by the state in the takeover amendment in 2003, controlled nearly 90% of the schools in New Orleans (Gewertz, 2006). By August of 2007, the city had three school systems: the Recovery School District, which is operated directly by the state, charter schools, which were authorized by the state, and the old Orleans Parish School District (Simon, 2007). "The

[RSD] system serves slightly more than a third of all city public school students, while close to 20,000 students attend the city's 40 charter schools and five traditional schools are still managed by the Orleans Parish School Board" (Simon, 2007, p. 1).

In the second special session, the governor and the state legislature proposed a constitutional amendment to eliminate the New Orleans levee board. More than 80% of voters in the state and 90% of voters in New Orleans ratified this amendment. Another constitutional amendment consolidated the number of assessors in New Orleans from seven to one. In the vote to ratify the assessors amendment in November of 2006, 78% of the voters throughout Louisiana supported this measure and 68% of the New Orleans electorate favored the consolidation. The state legislature also streamlined other offices in New Orleans, including the sheriffs and the clerks of court (Russell, 2006).

Control of Rebuilding

In the post-Katrina period, issues about how to rebuild, which entities should lead the recovery, and the allocation of federal relief funds deeply divided the state of Louisiana and the city of New Orleans. One of Nagin's initial attempts to provide a revenue stream for the city involved a plan to allow as many as seven new land-based casinos in New Orleans (Mowbray, 2005). Notwithstanding the monopoly state government previously granted to the downtown Harrah's Casino, Nagin's plan drew other criticism. Almost immediately, Blanco "urged caution" for the plan (*The Times-Picayune,* 2005). The idea would have required significant legislation, including the creation of a casino-zone in the city, as well as willing investment from the business community. Blanco's lack of support, as well as skepticism on the part of the state legislature, caused Nagin to eventually withdraw the plan (*Wall Street Journal,* 2005).

Louisiana and New Orleans created multiple commissions to deal with the city's recovery. Federal funding requires disbursement agencies, and a recovery commission is an appropriate mechanism to allocate these funds. Both Nagin and Blanco created separate recovery commissions to deal with the aftermath of Katrina. Not to be outdone, New Orleans' City Council created a third commission, and Lt. Governor Mitch Landrieu (the eventual run-off candidate in the 2006 mayoral race in New Orleans) instituted yet another. Of the four, Nagin's Bring New Orleans Back Commission and Blanco's Louisiana Recovery Authority (LRA) proved most consequential. The City Council and Landrieu commissions faded from the start, and while the Bring New Orleans Back Commission provoked significant debate about the character of the reconstruction of the city, its proposed blueprints were marred by the now infamous "green-dot" map, which covered formerly occupied neighborhoods with potential green space. The uproar from the plans of the Bring New Orleans Back Commission forced Nagin to distance himself from his own commission, and left the LRA as the only effective recovery commission in the state.

The creation and implementation of the state's Road Home Program illustrate the ongoing battle over control of programs. Governor Blanco designed this program to award housing funding for those affected by Hurricanes Katrina and Rita. She created the Road Home to disburse federal block grants when the federal government decided against creating a national-level bureaucracy. In a move that appeared politically motivated, the program was initially named Governor Blanco's Road Home Program. Blanco's public identification with the program served to promote a possible reelection campaign, and to lessen credit to Nagin, but, as time passed, Blanco decided to drop her name from the program as its performance dwindled.

Almost immediately, the Road Home Program faced a variety of difficulties. The LRA put together the proposal for the program without knowing the extent of federal funding for the program, leaving open questions about award sizes, and once the legislation to create the program was finalized, critics questioned the ethics of hiring the same consulting firm that helped draft the plan, to also administer the program (Maggi, 2006). The consulting firm, ICF International, started slowly, processing just a fraction of the applications received in the 2006 calendar year (Grace, 2006).

ICF continued to receive blame over the handling of Road Home claims. The firm, awarded a contract worth an estimated $756 million, infuriated the claimants with their plodding pace (Hammer, 2007). ICF blamed Parish offices for the lengthy closing process, and the mammoth tasks facing the LRA led Lt. Governor Landrieu to call for the establishment of a federal oversight committee, modeled after the Tennessee Valley Authority (Hammer, 2007). It turned out that parish government offices were not the only ones to blame for the delays. ICF, based in Virginia, failed to hire local appraisers to determine pre-Katrina home values, and when it recognized this flaw it turned to a subcontractor in California, which hired a subcontractor in Florida to procure a list of local appraisers in Louisiana, diluting the funding for the program while paying the subcontractors' fees (Gill, 2007).

Reacting to the failures of the LRA and the Road Home program, Nagin called for local control of the Road Home within the city limits. While highlighting the accomplishments of his administration in reviving city government, and the fact that his administration remained free of the historical corruption of the city, Nagin testified to a congressional subcommittee visiting New Orleans that he should be allowed to administer the funds to local awardees (Filosa, 2007). The state ignored Nagin's pleas, but the mayor's desire to control the funding for the rebuilding indicates a continuance of the tension-filled relationship between the state and New Orleans.

The state and the city never saw eye-to-eye on how to lead the recovery process. They disagreed about the creation of the recovery commissions, Nagin's casino plan, and the Road Home program. Recovery from such devastation is never easy, but other states affected by Katrina, such as Mississippi and Alabama, presented more streamlined processes. In previous disasters, states such as Florida proved able to unite to recover from past hurricanes, but New Orleans and Louisiana could not unify to pursue common goals.

Differences between New Orleans and the Rest of the State

Public opinion polls illustrate the continuing schisms between New Orleans and the rest of Louisiana. New Orleans residents and people throughout the state hold contrasting views of state government's spending priorities, the most important issues to the state, and the emphasis on rebuilding New Orleans (The Public Policy Research Lab, 2007).

In the spring of 2007, 46% of New Orleans residents regarded rebuilding as one of the state's three most important problems. By contrast, 30% of the people in the New Orleans metropolitan area excluding New Orleans, 29% of those in Baton Rouge, 20% of citizens in Southwest Louisiana, and just 13%

of the residents in north Louisiana held this view (The Public Policy Research Lab, 2007).

In the spring of 2007, nearly 70% of New Orleanians agreed that Louisiana should continue to focus on rebuilding New Orleans, even if that effort meant paying less attention to the rest of the state (The Public Policy Research Lab, 2007). By contrast, 47% of residents in Baton Rouge, 36% of those in north Louisiana, 35% of citizens in the New Orleans metropolitan area excluding New Orleans, and 32% in Southwest Louisiana held this opinion. Overall, 51% of Louisiana residents believed that the state paid too much attention to rebuilding New Orleans and that it needed to think about other issues and other areas of Louisiana (The Public Policy Research Lab, 2007).

ENDURING TENSIONS AND OPPORTUNITIES FOR COLLABORATION

Clearly, battles over finances and which entity allocates those resources constitute one of the most important ways that the pre-catastrophe relations influenced the recovery process. The state of Louisiana hesitated to provide funds directly to New Orleans in the pre-Katrina period and this tendency became amplified in the post-Katrina era. New Orleans and the state also battled over which entity would dictate how the city rebuilds. Residents in the city of New Orleans and those throughout the rest of the state continued to maintain contrasting views about the importance of New Orleans to the rest of the state. By contrast, the city of New Orleans collaborated with the rest of the state in approving the elimination of the levee board and the reduction in the number of assessors in Orleans Parish. Many even accepted major changes to the city's school system without much resistance.

Why did certain state–local tensions continue while others tended to subside? Distrust of public officials in New Orleans explains why friction persisted in some areas but waned in others. Hurricane Katrina did not alter the governor and state legislature's distrust of the city of New Orleans. Money drives the rebuilding of New Orleans and therefore, it sits at the center of the tensions between the city and state government. The state of Louisiana did not want the city to control hundreds of millions of federal recovery dollars. The city's continuing problems with corruption and mismanagement led the state to want to account for, oversee, and dictate the terms of the spending of federal funds.

Hurricane Katrina did not change how the city felt about not receiving aid. The city leaders complained about not getting the money in a timely fashion and the delay frustrated them. In the post-Katrina period, the pattern of state–local battles over money intensified.

The state's motivation for changing the number of assessors and eliminating the levee board also stemmed from a lack of trust in the ways that New Orleans managed its public policies. Hurricane Katrina gave an opportunity to the state and others to attack mismanagement. Many residents in New Orleans supported changes in the number of assessors and the elimination of the levee board because they too wanted an elimination of corruption and mismanagement in the public sector.

Hurricane Katrina resulted in key demographic changes in the city. Studies of the 2006 mayoral election indicate key shifts in the New Orleans electorate, with blacks losing 10% of their share of the electorate, while whites gained a 10% share. As noted above, these changes, including a higher percentage of white voters, as well as an upward shift in the income of voters, strongly influenced post-Katrina elections. The constitutional change to the levee boards illustrates this shift. In this instance, the business community also joined in the call for the levee board consolidation (*New Orleans CityBusiness*, 2006). The change in the racial composition of the electorate, and perhaps more importantly, the shift in class levels of the electorate, lead to the possibility that when the interests of the remaining electorate coincide with the interests of the state—in this example, the desire for increased accountability and a reduction in the possibility of corruption and malfeasance—the city and state can cooperate.

Several factors explain the favorable or neutral reactions to the state's control over so many schools in Orleans Parish. First, as a result of Hurricane Katrina, many residents of predominantly white districts, which strongly supported the takeover measure in 2003, remained in the city after the storm. By contrast, many residents of majority-African American, which opposed the takeover measure in 2003, had yet to return to the city by the start of the 2006 school year.

Next, the status of the school system was so awful that proponents of the reform saw the hurricane as an opportunity to improve the beleaguered district. Third, the RSD put the state in control of one-third of the schools, but other reforms increased local control. The creation of charter schools promised to increase local input in the functioning of New Orleans public schools, and many residents supported this change.

In areas other than education, elected officials and citizens in New Orleans wanted the city, not the state, to control the rebuilding of the city. Hurricane Katrina did not change how those who remained in New Orleans felt about local autonomy. Throughout time, localities have feared losing autonomy to higher levels of government, and certainly, the state's efforts to control the rebuilding enflamed New Orleanians' attitudes that the city was losing autonomy.

Hurricane Katrina did not change how the rest of the state felt toward New Orleans. In fact, it intensified the debate over the value of New Orleans to the rest of the state. State legislators from areas outside New Orleans will have to approve funding, policies, and other laws geared toward the recovery of the city. Decisions about how much to spend on New Orleans and whether to facilitate the rebuilding over issue-areas depends upon how these legislators regard the centrality of New Orleans to the state. Survey data indicate that people outside the New Orleans metropolitan area are much less enthusiastic about rebuilding the city than are those within this area. These opinions, which are often filtered through elected representatives, continue to heighten the tension between the city and the state. They influence the recovery because the state legislature will pursue spending and policy priorities that are not linked to the rebuilding of New Orleans. The tendency of those from north Louisiana and other parts of the state to want to focus on areas other than rebuilding New Orleans is a carryover from the pre-Katrina period.

The aftermath of Hurricane Katrina illustrates the significant role state government plays in urban affairs. The city's governance structure changed after Katrina and state government led this effort. The governor and legislature championed efforts to eliminate the levee board in New Orleans and to cut the number of city assessors to one. The sluggish speed of the recovery, especially in the area of housing rebuilding and payments, is attributable in part to the state's hesitancy to allocate federal funds to the city.